T0190050

IFIP Advances in Information and Communication Technology 591

Editor-in-Chief

Kai Rannenberg, *Goethe University Frankfurt, Germany*

Editorial Board Members

TC 1 – Foundations of Computer Science
  Luís Soares Barbosa, University of Minho, Braga, Portugal

TC 2 – Software: Theory and Practice
  Michael Goedicke, University of Duisburg-Essen, Germany

TC 3 – Education
  Arthur Tatnall, Victoria University, Melbourne, Australia

TC 5 – Information Technology Applications
  Erich J. Neuhold, University of Vienna, Austria

TC 6 – Communication Systems
  Burkhard Stiller, University of Zurich, Zürich, Switzerland

TC 7 – System Modeling and Optimization
  Fredi Tröltzsch, TU Berlin, Germany

TC 8 – Information Systems
  Jan Pries-Heje, Roskilde University, Denmark

TC 9 – ICT and Society
  David Kreps, University of Salford, Greater Manchester, UK

TC 10 – Computer Systems Technology
  Ricardo Reis, Federal University of Rio Grande do Sul, Porto Alegre, Brazil

TC 11 – Security and Privacy Protection in Information Processing Systems
  Steven Furnell, Plymouth University, UK

TC 12 – Artificial Intelligence
  Eunika Mercier-Laurent, University of Reims Champagne-Ardenne, Reims, France

TC 13 – Human-Computer Interaction
  Marco Winckler, University of Nice Sophia Antipolis, France

TC 14 – Entertainment Computing
  Rainer Malaka, University of Bremen, Germany

IFIP – The International Federation for Information Processing

IFIP was founded in 1960 under the auspices of UNESCO, following the first World Computer Congress held in Paris the previous year. A federation for societies working in information processing, IFIP's aim is two-fold: to support information processing in the countries of its members and to encourage technology transfer to developing nations. As its mission statement clearly states:

> IFIP is the global non-profit federation of societies of ICT professionals that aims at achieving a worldwide professional and socially responsible development and application of information and communication technologies.

IFIP is a non-profit-making organization, run almost solely by 2500 volunteers. It operates through a number of technical committees and working groups, which organize events and publications. IFIP's events range from large international open conferences to working conferences and local seminars.

The flagship event is the IFIP World Computer Congress, at which both invited and contributed papers are presented. Contributed papers are rigorously refereed and the rejection rate is high.

As with the Congress, participation in the open conferences is open to all and papers may be invited or submitted. Again, submitted papers are stringently refereed.

The working conferences are structured differently. They are usually run by a working group and attendance is generally smaller and occasionally by invitation only. Their purpose is to create an atmosphere conducive to innovation and development. Refereeing is also rigorous and papers are subjected to extensive group discussion.

Publications arising from IFIP events vary. The papers presented at the IFIP World Computer Congress and at open conferences are published as conference proceedings, while the results of the working conferences are often published as collections of selected and edited papers.

IFIP distinguishes three types of institutional membership: Country Representative Members, Members at Large, and Associate Members. The type of organization that can apply for membership is a wide variety and includes national or international societies of individual computer scientists/ICT professionals, associations or federations of such societies, government institutions/government related organizations, national or international research institutes or consortia, universities, academies of sciences, companies, national or international associations or federations of companies.

More information about this series at http://www.springer.com/series/6102

Bojan Lalic · Vidosav Majstorovic ·
Ugljesa Marjanovic · Gregor von Cieminski ·
David Romero (Eds.)

Advances in Production Management Systems

The Path to Digital Transformation and Innovation of Production Management Systems

IFIP WG 5.7 International Conference, APMS 2020
Novi Sad, Serbia, August 30 – September 3, 2020
Proceedings, Part I

 Springer

Editors
Bojan Lalic (iD)
University of Novi Sad
Novi Sad, Serbia

Ugljesa Marjanovic (iD)
University of Novi Sad
Novi Sad, Serbia

David Romero (iD)
Tecnológico de Monterrey
Mexico City, Mexico

Vidosav Majstorovic (iD)
University of Belgrade
Belgrade, Serbia

Gregor von Cieminski (iD)
ZF Hungária Kft.
Eger, Hungary

ISSN 1868-4238 ISSN 1868-422X (electronic)
IFIP Advances in Information and Communication Technology
ISBN 978-3-030-57995-1 ISBN 978-3-030-57993-7 (eBook)
https://doi.org/10.1007/978-3-030-57993-7

This Springer imprint is published by the registered company Springer Nature Switzerland AG
The registered company address is: Gewerbestrasse 11, 6330 Cham, Switzerland

Preface

We live in a time where just one factor (i.e., COVID-19) could change the game plan for the global manufacturing economy. Digital transformation has been going on in the last decade, and it seems that not all the countries and companies are utilizing all the opportunities that it could provide to build new digital capabilities such as 'digital resilience.' A digital transformation path towards Industry 4.0 in manufacturing is more important than ever. Yet, how to approach the development and scaling of digital technology is a question that keeps executives awake at night and academics in a constant quest. The current digital transformation of manufacturing has so far mostly been studied from the perspective of the cyber-physical production system as drivers of change. However, there are several other enablers, including artificial intelligence; additive and hybrid manufacturing; 5G-enabled manufacturing; digital assistance systems based on augmented, virtual, and mixed reality; industrial, collaborative, mobile, and software robots; advanced simulations; cloud and edge technologies; and data-driven product-service systems. These are the key components of a digital transformation and the main research thrusts in the production management systems research community. Thus, the question of how to find the path to the digital transformation and innovation of production management systems is of eminent importance.

The International Conference on Advances in Production Management Systems (APMS 2020) in Novi Sad, Serbia, brought together leading international experts from academia, industry, and government in the area of digital transformation and innovation to discuss globally pressing issues in smart manufacturing, operations management, and supply chain management in the Industry 4.0 era. Under influence of COVID-19, the event was also digitally transformed: For the first time in its history the APMS conference was organized in a 'hybrid mode,' meaning face-to-face as well as online conference sessions. A large international panel of experts reviewed all the papers and selected the best ones to be included in these international conference proceedings. The topics of interest in APMS 2020 included Digital Supply Networks, Data-Driven Production Management, Sustainable Production Management, Cloud and Collaborative Technologies, Smart Manufacturing and Industry 4.0, Data-Driven Services, Digital Lean Manufacturing, and Digital Transformation Approaches in Production Management.

The proceedings are organized into two parts:

- The Path to Digital Transformation and Innovation of Production Management Systems (Volume 1)
- Towards Smart and Digital Manufacturing (Volume 2)

The conference was supported by the International Federation of Information Processing (IFIP) and was organized by the IFIP Working Group 5.7 on Advances in Production Management Systems and University of Novi Sad, Faculty of Technical Sciences, Department of Industrial Engineering and Management. We would like to thank all contributors for their high-quality work and for their willingness to share their innovative ideas and findings. We are also indebted to the members of the IFIP Working Group 5.7, the Program Committee members, and the Scientific Committee members for their support in the review process of the papers. Finally, we appreciate the generous support from both the Ministry of Education, Science and Technological Development and Provincial Secretariat for Higher Education and Scientific Research of the Republic of Serbia.

August 2020   Bojan Lalic
                                                 Vidosav Majstorovic
                                                 Ugljesa Marjanovic
                                              Gregor von Cieminski
                                                    David Romero

Organization

Conference Chair

Bojan Lalic   University of Novi Sad, Serbia

Conference Co-chair

Gregor Von Cieminski   ZF Hungária Kft., Hungary

Program Chair

Vidosav Majstorovic   University of Belgrade, Serbia

Program Co-chair

David Romero   Tecnológico de Monterrey, Mexico

Program Committee

Thorsten Wuest   West Virginia University, USA
Paolo Gaiardelli   University of Bergamo, Italy
Ilkyeong Moon   Seoul National University, South Korea

Organizing Committee Chair

Ugljesa Marjanovic   University of Novi Sad, Serbia

Doctoral Workshop Chair

Milan Delic   University of Novi Sad, Serbia

International Advisory Committee

Farhad Ameri   Texas State University, USA
Ilkyeong Moon   Seoul National University, South Korea
Hermann Lödding   TUHH, Germany

Organizing Committee

Danijela Gračanin   University of Novi Sad, Serbia
Nemanja Tasić   University of Novi Sad, Serbia
Nenad Medić   University of Novi Sad, Serbia

Tanja Todorović	University of Novi Sad, Serbia
Slavko Rakić	University of Novi Sad, Serbia
Marko Pavlović	University of Novi Sad, Serbia
Jelena Ćurčić	University of Novi Sad, Serbia
Dragana Gojić	University of Novi Sad, Serbia
Nemanja Majstorović	University of Belgrade, Serbia

Scientific Committee

Erry Yulian Triblas Adesta	International Islamic University Malaysia, Malaysia
Erlend Alfnes	Norwegian University of Science and Technology, Norway
Thecle Alix	IUT Bordeaux Montesquieu France
Susanne Altendorfer-Kaiser	Montanuniversitaet Leoben, Austria
Farhad Ameri	Texas State University, USA
Bjørn Andersen	Norwegian University of Science and Technology, Norway
Eiji Arai	Osaka University, Japan
Frédérique Biennier	INSA Lyon, France
Umit S. Bititci	Heriot Watt University, UK
Magali Bosch-Mauchand	Université de Technologie de Compiègne, France
Abdelaziz Bouras	Qatar University, Qatar
Jim Browne	University College Dublin, Ireland
Luis Camarinha-Matos	Universidade Nova de Lisboa, Portugal
Sergio Cavalieri	University of Bergamo, Italy
Stephen Childe	Plymouth University, UK
Hyunbo Cho	Pohang University of Science and Technology, South Korea
Gregor von Cieminski	ZF Friedrichshafen AG, Hungary
Adolfo Crespo Marquez	University of Seville, Spain
Catherine Da Cunha	École Centrale de Nantes, France
Frédéric Demoly	Université de Technologie de Belfort-Montbéliard, France
Shengchun Deng	Harbin Institute of Technology, China
Melanie Despeisse	Chalmers University of Technology, Sweden
Alexandre Dolgui	IMT Atlantique, France
Slavko Dolinšek	University of Ljubljana, Slovenia
Sang Do Noh	Sungkyunkwan University, South Korea
Heidi Carin Dreyer	Norwegian University of Science and Technology, Norway
Eero Eloranta	Helsinki University of Technology, Finland
Soumaya El Kadiri	Texelia AG, Switzerland
Christos Emmanouilidis	Cranfield University, UK
Åsa Fasth-Berglund	Chalmers University of Technology, Sweden

Manuel Fradinho Duarte de Oliveira	SINTEF, Norway
Jan Frick	University of Stavanger, Norway
Paolo Gaiardelli	University of Bergamo, Italy
Adriana Giret Boggino	Universidad Politécnica de Valencia, Spain
Samuel Gomes	Belfort-Montbéliard University of Technology, France
Bernard Grabot	INP-ENIT (National Engineering School of Tarbes), France
Gerhard Gudergan	FIR Research Institute for Operations Management at RWTH Aachen University, Germany
Thomas R. Gulledge Jr.	George Mason University, USA
Hironori Hibino	Tokyo University of Science, Japan
Hans-Henrik Hvolby	Aalborg University, Denmark
Dmitry Ivanov	Berlin School of Economics and Law, Germany
Harinder Jagdev	National University of Ireland at Galway, Ireland
John Johansen	Aalborg University, Denmark
Hong-Bae Jun	Hongik University, South Korea
Toshiya Kaihara	Kobe University, Japan
Duck-Young Kim	Ulsan National Institute of Science and Technology (UNIST), South Korea
Dimitris Kiritsis	École Polytechnique Fédérale de Lausanne, Switzerland
Tomasz Koch	Wroclaw University of Science and Technology, Poland
Pisut Koomsap	Asian Institute of Technology, Thailand
Gül Kremer	Iowa State University, USA
Boonserm Kulvatunyou	National Institute of Standards and Technology, USA
Thomas R. Kurfess	Georgia Institute of Technology, USA
Andrew Kusiak	University of Iowa, USA
Lenka Landryova	Technical University of Ostrava, Czech Republic
Jan-Peter Lechner	First Global Liaison, Germany
Gyu M. Lee	Pusan National University, South Korea
Ming K. Lim	Chongqing University, China
Hermann Lödding	Hamburg University of Technology, Germany
Marco Macchi	Politecnico di Milano, Italy
Gökan May	École Polytechnique Fédérale de Lausanne, Switzerland
Jörn Mehnen	University of Strathclyde, UK
Joao Gilberto Mendes dos Reis	UNIP Paulista University, Brazil
Vidosav D. Majstorovich	University of Belgrade, Serbia
Hajime Mizuyama	Aoyama Gakuin University, Japan
Ilkyeong Moon	Seoul National University, South Korea
Dimitris Mourtzis	University of Patras, Greece
Irenilza de Alencar Naas	UNIP Paulista University, Brazil
Masaru Nakano	Keio University, Japan

Gündüz Ulusoy	Sabancı University, Turkey
Bruno Vallespir	University of Bordeaux, France
Agostino Villa	Politecnico di Torino, Italy
Hans-Hermann Wiendahl	University of Stuttgart, Germany
Joakim Wikner	Jönköping University, Sweden
Hans Wortmann	University of Groningen, The Netherlands
Thorsten Wuest	West Virginia University, USA
Iveta Zolotová	Technical University of Kosice, Slovakia
Bojan Lalić	University of Novi Sad, Serbia
Uglješa Marjanović	University of Novi Sad, Serbia
Byung Do Chung	Yonsei University, South Korea
Gengzhong Feng	Xi'an Jiaotong University, China

Contents – Part I

Advanced Modelling, Simulation and Data Analytics in Production and Supply Networks

A Robust Multi-commodity Rebalancing Process
in Humanitarian Logistics 3
    Xuehong Gao and Xuefeng Jin

Towards a Unified Reliability-Centered Information Logistics Model
for Production Assets 11
    Florian Defèr, Günther Schuh, and Volker Stich

Characterization of Energy Consumers in Production Systems
with Renewable On-Site Power Generation 19
    Julia Schulz, Felix Rosenberg, Valerie M. Scharmer,
    and Michael F. Zaeh

A Simulation Model Supporting the Production Optimization
for High-Precision Machines Assembly 28
    Andrea Monti, Donatella Corti, and Dario Pietraroia

Agent-Based Modeling and Analysis of Dynamic Slab Yard Management
in a Steel Factory 37
    Hajime Mizuyama

A Simulation Analysis of Part Feeding to Assembly Stations with Vertical
Robotic Storage and Retrieval Systems 45
    Elena Tappia, Emilio Moretti, and Marco Melacini

Process Mining in Manufacturing: Goals, Techniques and Applications 54
    Darko Stefanovic, Dusanka Dakic, Branislav Stevanov,
    and Teodora Lolic

Bayesian Modelling for Product Testing and Release 63
    John G. Wilson

Advanced, Digital and Smart Manufacturing

The Use of Organizational Innovation Concepts
in Manufacturing Companies 73
    Iztok Palčič, Simon Klančnik, Robert Ojsteršek, Tone Lerher,
    Borut Buchmeister, and Mirko Ficko

Systems Engineering Approach to Identify Requirements for Digital
Twins Development.   82
  Ali Gharaei, Jinzhi Lu, Oliver Stoll, Xiaochen Zheng, Shaun West,
  and Dimitris Kiritsis

Manufacturing Operations Management for Smart Manufacturing –
A Case Study.   91
  Michael Meyer-Hentschel, Oliver Lohse, Subba Rao,
  and Raffaello Lepratti

Industry 4.0 on Demand: A Value Driven Methodology to Implement
Industry 4.0   99
  Deborah Leone and Andrea Barni

Gamification of Operational Tasks in Manufacturing   107
  Makenzie Keepers, David Romero, Jannicke Baalsrud Hauge,
  and Thorsten Wuest

Technology Adoption in the Industry 4.0 Era: Empirical Evidence
from Manufacturing Companies   115
  Nenad Medic, Zoran Anisic, Nemanja Tasic, Nikola Zivlak,
  and Bojan Lalic

Towards the Definition of an Impact Level Factor of SME Features Over
Digital Transformation.   123
  Melissa Liborio Zapata, Lamia Berrah, and Laurent Tabourot

Industry 4.0: Maturity of Automotive Companies in Brazil
for the Digitization of Processes   131
  Sergio Miele Ruggero, Nilza Aparecida dos Santos,
  José Benedito Sacomano, Antonio Carlos Estender,
  and Marcia Terra da Silva

General Readiness Assessment of Industry 4.0: Evidence from Serbian
Manufacturing Industry   139
  Tanja Todorovic, Bojan Lalic, Vidosav Majstorovic,
  Ugljesa Marjanovic, and Nemanja Tasic

Digital and Virtual Quality Management Systems

Assembly Issue Resolution System Using Machine Learning
in Aero Engine Manufacturing   149
  Jörg Brünnhäußer, Sonika Gogineni, Jonas Nickel, Heiko Witte,
  and Rainer Stark

Introduction to Material Feeding 4.0: Strategic, Tactical,
and Operational Impact   158
    Marco Simonetto and Fabio Sgarbossa

Cloud-Manufacturing

Cycle Time Estimation Model for Hybrid Assembly Stations
Based on Digital Twin.   169
    Dimitris Mourtzis, John Angelopoulos, and Vasileios Siatras

Cyber-Physical Production Systems and Digital Twins

Digital Shadows as an Enabler for the Internet of Production   179
    Günther Schuh, Andreas Gützlaff, Frederick Sauermann,
    and Judith Maibaum

The Transformation Towards Smart(er) Factories: Integration Requirements
of the Digital Twin   187
    S. Waschull, J. C. Wortmann, and J. A. C. Bokhorst

IIOT Interoperability

Towards Inter-Operable Enterprise Systems – Graph-Based Validation
of a Context-Driven Approach for Message Profiling.   197
    Elena Jelisic, Nenad Ivezic, Boonserm Kulvatunyou, Scott Nieman,
    Hakju Oh, Sladjan Babarogic, and Zoran Marjanovic

Supply Chain Planning and Optimization

Software-Based Assistance System for Decision Support
on Supply Chain Level   209
    Maria Linnartz and Volker Stich

Integration of Triple Sustainable Management by Considering
the Multi-period Supply Chain for Next-Generation Fuel   217
    Waqas Ahmed, Biswajit Sarkar, and Mujtaba Hassan Agha

Potential Benefits of Reverse Blending in the Fertilizer Industry   227
    Latifa Benhamou, Pierres Fenies, and Vincent Giard

Effectiveness of Vendor Managed Inventory - VMI: A Study Applied
in a Mining Company   237
    Alexandre Formigoni, João Gilberto Mendes dos Reis,
    Roberto Padilha Moia, Caio Flávio Stettiner,
    and João Roberto Maiellaro

Value Chain Integration – A Framework for Assessment   243
  Inger Gamme, Bjørn Andersen, Håkon Raabe, and Daryl Powell

A Dynamic Hybrid Berth Allocation Problem with Routing
Constraints in Bulk Ports   250
  Hamza Bouzekri, Gülgün Alpan, and Vincent Giard

Blockchain-Based Secured Collaborative Model for Supply Chain Resource
Sharing and Visibility   259
  Tarun Kumar Agrawal, Ravi Kalaiarasan, and Magnus Wiktorsson

Gripper Types and Components in Robotic Bin Picking.   267
  Patrik Fager, Stefano Rossi, Robin Hanson, Lars Medbo,
  Omkar Salunkhe, Mats I. Johansson, and Åsa Fast-Berglund

A Stochastic Model for a Two-Level Disassembly Lot-Sizing Problem
Under Random Lead Time.   275
  Ilhem Slama, Oussama Ben-Ammar, Alexandre Dolgui,
  and Faouzi Masmoudi

Digital and Smart Supply Chain Management

ERP in Industry 4.0 Context.   287
  Vidosav Majstorovic, Slavenko Stojadinovic, Bojan Lalic,
  and Ugljesa Marjanovic

Identifying the Opportunities for Enhancing the Digital Readiness Level
of the Supply Chain   295
  Chiara Cimini, Fabiana Pirola, and Sergio Cavalieri

Intelligent Logistics Networks Management

The Role of Last-Mile Delivery in the Future of E-Commerce   307
  Fernanda Alves de Araújo, João Gilberto Mendes dos Reis,
  and Paula Ferreira da Cruz Correia

Production-Storage and Transport Integrated Planning for a Multi-site
Mining Industry   315
  Asma Rakiz and Pierre Fenies

Artificial Intelligence and Blockchain Technologies in Logistics and DSN

Evaluating a Blockchain-Based Supply Chain Purchasing Process
Through Simulation.   325
  Geraldo Jose Dolce Uzum Martins, Jacqueline Zonichenn Reis,
  Benedito Cristiano A. Petroni, Rodrigo Franco Gonçalves,
  and Berislav Andrlić

Questionnaire Model for Paraconsistent Quality Assessment of Software
Developed in SalesForce   333
   Luiz Roberto Forçan, Jair Minoro Abe, Luiz Antônio de Lima,
   and Samira Sestari Nascimento

Novel Production Planning and Control Approaches

Supporting the Decision of the Order Processing Strategy by Using Logistic
Models: A Case Study.   343
   Janine Tatjana Maier, Tammo Heuer, Peter Nyhuis,
   and Matthias Schmidt

Order Acceptance and Scheduling with a Throughput Diagram.   351
   Christopher Mundt and Hermann Lödding

Machine Learning and Artificial Intelligence

Machine Learning-Supported Planning of Lead Times in Job
Shop Manufacturing   363
   Kathrin Julia Kramer, Carsten Wagner, and Matthias Schmidt

Connected, Smart Factories of the Future

Identifying Key Business Processes that Can Benefit from Industry
4.0 in the Gas Sector.   373
   Nikolaos A. Panayiotou, Vasileios P. Stavrou,
   and Konstantinos E. Stergiou

The Impact of Industry 4.0 Connectivity on the Collaboration Along
Brazilian Automotive Supply Chain.   381
   Nilza Aparecida dos Santos, Sergio Miele Ruggero,
   José Benedito Sacomano, Antonio Carlos Estender,
   and Marcia Terra da Silva

Manufacturing Systems Engineering: Agile, Flexible, Reconfigurable

Towards a Reference Model for Configuration of Reconfigurable
Manufacturing System (RMS).   391
   Erica Capawa Fotsoh, Nasser Mebarki, Pierre Castagna,
   Pascal Berruet, and Francisco Gamboa

Automatic Design of Dispatching Rules with Genetic Programming
for Dynamic Job Shop Scheduling   399
   Salama Shady, Toshiya Kaihara, Nobutada Fujii, and Daisuke Kokuryo

A Literature Review on the Level of Automation and New
Approach Proposal   408
   Hasnaa Ait Malek, Alain Etienne, Ali Siadat, and Thierry Allavena

De-risking Investments in Industrial Systems Using Real Options Analysis:
Case of Phosphates Fertilizer Firm   418
   Imane Essaadi and Richard de Neufville

Data-Driven Replenishment Method Choice in a Picking System   427
   Simon Hummelshøj Sloth, Magnus Abildsten Bøgh,
   Christian Møller Nielsen, Konstantinos Panagiotis Konstantinidis,
   and Inkyung Sung

Business Process Management for MES Deployment: Some Lessons
from a Bearings Manufacturer Experience   433
   Hervé Verjus, Vincent Clivillé, Lamia Berrah, Romain Gandia,
   and Claude Chapel

An Application of a DSML in Industry 4.0 Production Processes   441
   Marko Vještica, Vladimir Dimitrieski, Milan Pisarić, Slavica Kordić,
   Sonja Ristić, and Ivan Luković

Towards an Industry-Applicable Design Methodology for Developing
Reconfigurable Manufacturing   449
   Alessia Napoleone, Ann-Louise Andersen, Thomas Ditlev Brunoe,
   Kjeld Nielsen, Simon Boldt, Carin Rösiö, and David Grube Hansen

Reconfigurable Manufacturing: Lesson Learnt from
the COVID-19 Outbreak   457
   Alessia Napoleone and Lorenzo Bruno Prataviera

Digital Assistance Systems: Augmented Reality and Virtual Reality

Virtual and Augmented Reality as a Digital Support to HR Systems
in Production Management.   469
   Danijela Lalić, Dunja Bošković, Bojana Milić, Sara Havzi,
   and Jelena Spajić

Application of Virtual Reality Technologies for Achieving Energy Efficient
Manufacturing: Literature Analysis and Findings.   479
   E. G. Nabati, M. T. Alvela Nieto, A. Decker, and K.-D. Thoben

Smart Products in Smart Manufacturing Systems: An Opportunity
to Utilize AR?   487
   Joshua Gross and Thorsten Wuest

Evaluation of Augmented Reality in Industry   495
   Tone Lise Dahl, Manuel Oliveira, and Emrah Arica

Circular Products Design and Engineering

Finding and Capturing Value in e-Waste for Refrigerators Manufacturers
and Recyclers   505
  Clarissa A. González Chávez, Mélanie Despeisse, Björn Johansson,
  and David Romero

Circular, Green, Sustainable Manufacturing

Sustainable Business Model Innovation in the Furniture Supply Chain:
A Case Study   515
  Mikhail Shlopak, Bella B. Nujen, and Jon Halfdanarson

A Basic Study on Scheduling Method for Electric Power Saving
of Production Machine   524
  Masayuki Yabuuchi, Toshiya Kaihara, Nobutada Fujii,
  Daisuke Kokuryo, Satoko Sakajo, and Yoshito Nishita

Sustainability in Fabric Chains and Garments for a Circular Economy   531
  Solimar Garcia, Irenilza de Alencar Nääs,
  Pedro Luiz de Oliveira Costa Neto, João Gilberto Mendes dos Reis,
  Valdice Neves Pólvora, Luiz Antonio de Lima,
  Angel Antonio Gonzalez Martinez, and Vanessa Santos Lessa

Planning Environments of Hospital Laboratories: An Exploratory Study   538
  Aili Biriita Bertnum, Marco Semini, and Jan Ola Strandhagen

Knowledge and Practices Towards Sustainability and Circular Economy
Transitions: A Norwegian Manufacturing Perspective   546
  Jon Halfdanarson and Nina Pereira Kvadsheim

A Methodology to Integrate Sustainability Evaluations into Vendor Rating . . .   554
  Alessandro Fontana, Silvia Menato, and Andrea Barni

Environmental and Social Lifecycle Assessments

Travel-Times Analysis and Passenger Transport Disutilities in Congested
American Cities: Los Angeles, New York, Atlanta, Austin, and Chicago   565
  Helcio Raymundo and João Gilberto M. dos Reis

Socio-Cultural Aspects in Production Systems

The Interdependencies of Quality Management, Knowledge Management
and Innovation Performance. A Literature Review   575
  Marina Zizakov, Stana Vasic, Milan Delic, Marko Orosnjak,
  and Srdjan Vulanovic

Insights from a Top-Down Lean Subprogram Deployment in a Production
Group: A Tactical Perspective 583
   Sara Linderson, Monica Bellgran, and Seyoum Eshetu Birkie

Tools for Evaluating Human Factor Aspects in Production
and Logistics System. 591
   Vivek Vijayakumar and Fabio Sgarbossa

Economy and Its Symbiosis with Circularity. 599
   Abelino Reis Guimarães Neto, Rodrigo Rodrigues,
   Jacqueline Zonichenn Reis, Julio Cesar Raymundo,
   and Rodrigo Franco Gonçalves

Data-Driven Manufacturing and Services Operations Management

First Steps to the Digital Shadow of Maintenance Services' Value
Contribution. 609
   Frederick Birtel, Achim Kampker, and Volker Stich

Reshoring of Service Operations: Evidence from a Delphi Study. 617
   Paolo Gaiardelli, Albachiara Boffelli, Matteo Kalchschmidt,
   Daniel Bellazzi, and Simone Orom Samorani

Digital and Physical Testbed for Production Logistics Operations 625
   Jannicke Baalsrud Hauge, Masoud Zafarzadeh, Yongkuk Jeong, Yi Li,
   Wajid Ali Khilji, and Magnus Wiktorsson

Principles and Research Agenda for Sustainable, Data-Driven Food
Production Planning and Control. 634
   Maggie Bresler, Anita Romsdal, Jan Ola Strandhagen,
   and Olumide E. Oluyisola

Product-Service Systems in DSN

Agile Guideline for Development of Smart Services in Manufacturing
Enterprises with Support of Artificial Intelligence 645
   Mike Freitag and Oliver Hämmerle

Collaborative Design and Engineering

Framework for Identifying Gripper Requirements for Collaborative Robot
Applications in Manufacturing 655
   Omkar Salunkhe, Patrik Fager, and Åsa Fast-Berglund

A Novel Value Driven Co-creation Framework. 663
   Geir Ringen, Halvor Holtskog, and Torgeir Welo

Autonomous Mobile Robots in Hospital Logistics..................... 672
    Giuseppe Fragapane, Hans-Henrik Hvolby, Fabio Sgarbossa,
    and Jan Ola Strandhagen

Interorganizational Learning in Manufacturing Networks 680
    Geir Ringen, Frode Paalsrud, and Eirin Lodgaard

Author Index 687

Contents – Part II

The Operator 4.0: New Physical and Cognitive Evolutionary Paths

Facilitating Operator Participation in Continuous Improvement:
An Investigation of Organizational Factors   3
  Eirin Lodgaard, Silje Helene Aschehoug, and Daryl Powell

Improving the Safety of Using Didactic Setups by Applying
Augmented Reality   11
  Srdjan Tegeltija, Vule Reljić, Ivana Šenk, Laslo Tarjan,
  and Branislav Tejić

Production Management as-a-Service: A Softbot Approach   19
  Brunno Abner, Ricardo J. Rabelo, Saulo P. Zambiasi,
  and David Romero

Knowledge Strategies for Organization 4.0 – A Workforce
Centric Approach   31
  Magnus Bjerkne Gerdin, Åsa Fast-Berglund, Dan Li,
  and Adam Palmquist

Challenges for the Operator 3.0 Addressed Through the Enabling
Technologies of the Operator 4.0   37
  Malin Tarrar, Peter Thorvald, Åsa Fast-Berglund, and David Romero

Agent- and Skill-Based Process Interoperability for Socio-Technical
Production Systems-of-Systems   46
  Åsa Fast-Berglund, David Romero, Magnus Åkerman, Björn Hodig,
  and Andreas Pichler

Digital Transformation Approaches in Production Management

Challenges in Data Life Cycle Management for Sustainable Cyber-Physical
Production Systems   57
  Mélanie Despeisse and Ebru Turanoglu Bekar

Explainable AI in Manufacturing: A Predictive Maintenance Case Study   66
  Bahrudin Hrnjica and Selver Softic

Retrofit Concept for Textile Production   74
  Felix Franke, Susanne Franke, and Ralph Riedel

Organizational Enablers for Digitalization in Norwegian Industry   83
    Lars Harald Lied, Maria Flavia Mogos, and Daryl John Powell

Concept of PLM Application Integration with VR and AR Techniques   91
    Jan Duda and Sylwester Oleszek

The Big Potential of Big Data in Manufacturing: Evidence
from Emerging Economies   100
    *Marko Pavlović, Uglješa Marjanović, Slavko Rakić, Nemanja Tasić,
    and Bojan Lalić*

A Conceptual Model for Deploying Digitalization in SMEs Through
Capability Building   108
    Zuhara Chavez, Jannicke Baalsrud Hauge, and Monica Bellgran

The Potential of Game Development Platforms for Digital Twins
and Virtual Labs: Case Study of an Energy Analytics and Solution Lab   117
    Ali Abdallah, Matthias Primas, Ioan Turcin, and Udo Traussnigg

The Application of ICT Solutions in Manufacturing Companies in Serbia . . .   122
    *Danijela Ciric, Teodora Lolic, Danijela Gracanin, Darko Stefanovic,
    and Bojan Lalic*

Achieving Business Model Innovation with the Personalized Product
Business Model Radar Template   130
    Egon Lüftenegger

Integrating Electronic Components into 3D Printed Parts to Develop
a Digital Manufacturing Approach   138
    *Ioan Turcin, Ali Abdallah, Manfred Pauritsch, Cosmin Cosma,
    and Nicolae Balc*

Digital Transformation and Its Potential Effects on Future Management:
Insights from an ETO Context   146
    Antoni Vike Danielsen

Applying Contextualization for Data-Driven Transformation
in Manufacturing   154
    Sonika Gogineni, Kai Lindow, Jonas Nickel, and Rainer Stark

Digital Transformation for more Sustainable Supply Chains

Smart Contract-Based Blockchain Solution to Reduce Supply Chain Risks . . .   165
    Fabian Dietrich, Ali Turgut, Daniel Palm, and Louis Louw

Towards Sustainability: The Manufacturers' Perspective   174
    Olena Klymenko, Lise Lillebrygfjeld Halse, and Bjørn Jæger

Data-Driven Applications in Smart Manufacturing and Logistics Systems

Smart Factory Competitiveness Based on Real Time Monitoring
and Quality Predictive Model Applied to Multi-stages Production Lines.   185
    Nicola Gramegna, Fabrizio Greggio, and Franco Bonollo

A New Application of Coordination Contracts for Supplier Selection
in a Cloud Environment.   197
    Reza Tavakkoli-Moghaddam, Mohammad Alipour-Vaezi,
    and Zahra Mohammad-Nazari

Workforce Assignment with a Different Skill Level for Automotive Parts
Assembly Lines   206
    Hyungjoon Yang, Je-Hun Lee, and Hyun-Jung Kim

A Framework of Data-Driven Dynamic Optimisation for Smart
Production Logistics   213
    Sichao Liu, Lihui Wang, Xi Vincent Wang, and Magnus Wiktorsson

Decentralized Industrial IoT Data Management Based on Blockchain
and IPFS   222
    Xiaochen Zheng, Jinzhi Lu, Shengjing Sun, and Dimitris Kiritsis

Integrated Platform and Digital Twin Application for Global Automotive
Part Suppliers.   230
    Jinho Yang, Sangho Lee, Yong-Shin Kang, Sang Do Noh,
    Sung Soo Choi, Bo Ra Jung, Sang Hyun Lee, Jeong Tae Kang,
    Dae Yub Lee, and Hyung Sun Kim

Analyzing the Characteristics of Digital Twin and Discrete Event
Simulation in Cyber Physical Systems.   238
    Erik Flores-García, Goo-Young Kim, Jinho Yang, Magnus Wiktorsson,
    and Sang Do Noh

Streaming Analytics in Edge-Cloud Environment for Logistics Processes. . . .   245
    Moritz von Stietencron, Marco Lewandowski, Katerina Lepenioti,
    Alexandros Bousdekis, Karl Hribernik, Dimitris Apostolou,
    and Gregoris Mentzas

An Improvement in Master Surgical Scheduling Using Artificial Neural
Network and Fuzzy Programming Approach.   254
    Ahmad Ghasemkhani, Reza Tavakkoli-Moghaddam, Mahdi Hamid,
    and Mehdi Mahmoodjanloo

SKOS Tool: A Tool for Creating Knowledge Graphs to Support Semantic
Text Classification.   263
    Farhad Ameri, Reid Yoder, and Kimia Zandbiglari

Data-Driven Services: Characteristics, Trends and Applications

The Successful Commercialization of a Digital Twin in an Industrial
Product Service System   275
   Oliver Stoll, Shaun West, Paolo Gaiardelli, David Harrison,
   and Fintan J. Corcoran

Using Service Dominant Logic to Assess the Value Co-creation
of Smart Services   283
   Oliver Stoll, Shuan West, and Cosimo Barbieri

Engineering of Data-Driven Service Systems for Smart Living: Application
and Challenges   291
   Henrik Kortum, Laura Sophie Gravemeier, Novica Zarvic, Thomas Feld,
   and Oliver Thomas

The Role of Service Business Models in the Manufacturing
of Transition Economies   299
   Slavko Rakic, Nenad Simeunovic, Nenad Medic, Marko Pavlovic,
   and Ugljesa Marjanovic

System Architecture Analysis with Network Index in MBSE Approach -
Application to Smart Interactive Service with Digital Health Modeling-   307
   Toshiya Kaihara, Nobutada Fujii, Daisuke Kokuryo, and Mizuki Harada

The Data-Driven Product-Service Systems Design and Delivery
(4DPSS) Methodology   314
   Roberto Sala, Alessandro Bertoni, Fabiana Pirola,
   and Giuditta Pezzotta

Data-Driven Maintenance Delivery Framework: Test
in an Italian Company   322
   Roberto Sala, Fabiana Pirola, and Giuditta Pezzotta

Towards a Comparative Data Value Assessment Framework for Smart
Product Service Systems   330
   Lennard Holst, Volker Stich, Günther Schuh, and Jana Frank

Impact of Platform Openness on Ecosystems and Value Streams
in Platform-Based PSS Exemplified Using RAMI 4.0   338
   Michela Zambetti, Till Blüher, Giuditta Pezzotta, Konrad Exner,
   Roberto Pinto, and Rainer Stark

Industry 4.0 Data-Related Technologies and Servitization:
A Systematic Literature Review   347
   Michela Zambetti, Roberto Pinto, and Giuditta Pezzotta

A Framework to Support Value Co-creation in PSS Development   361
    Martha Orellano, Xavier Boucher, Gilles Neubert, and Anne Coulon

The Future of Lean Thinking and Practice

Utilizing Lean Thinking as a Means to Digital Transformation
in Service Organizations   371
    F. P. Santhiapillai and R. M. Chandima Ratnayake

On the Need of Functional Priority and Failure Risk Assessment to
Optimize Human Resource Allocation in Public Service Organizations   379
    F. P. Santhiapillai and R. M. Chandima Ratnayake

Assessing the Value of Process Improvement Suggestions   387
    Torbjørn H. Netland, Hajime Mizuyama, and Rafael Lorenz

On the Necessity for Identifying Waste in Knowledge Work
Dominated Projects: A Case Study from Oil & Gas-Related
Product Development Projects   396
    F. P. Santhiapillai and R. M. Chandima Ratnayake

Lean Thinking: From the Shop Floor to an Organizational Culture   406
    Paulo Amaro, Anabela C. Alves, and Rui M. Sousa

Digital Lean Manufacturing and Its Emerging Practices

A Learning Roadmap for Digital Lean Manufacturing   417
    Anja Bottinga Solheim and Daryl John Powell

Investigating the Challenges and Opportunities for Production Planning
and Control in Digital Lean Manufacturing   425
    Daryl Powell, Eirin Lodgaard, and Heidi Dreyer

New Forms of Gemba Walks and Their Digital Tools in the Digital Lean
Manufacturing World   432
    *David Romero, Paolo Gaiardelli, Thorsten Wuest, Daryl Powell,
    and Matthias Thürer*

New Reconfigurable, Flexible or Agile Production Systems in the Era of Industry 4.0

A Computational Method for Identifying the Optimum Buffer Size
in the Era of Zero Defect Manufacturing   443
    Foivos Psarommatis, Ali Boujemaoui, and Dimitris Kiritsis

A Bi-objective Scheduling Model for Additive Manufacturing
with Multiple Materials and Sequence-Dependent Setup Time   451
    Reza Tavakkoli-Moghaddam, Shadi Shirazian, and Behdin Vahedi-Nouri

Dynamic Distributed Job-Shop Scheduling Problem Consisting
of Reconfigurable Machine Tools   460
    Mehdi Mahmoodjanloo, Reza Tavakkoli-Moghaddam, Armand Baboli,
    and Ali Bozorgi-Amiri

Towards a Non-disruptive System for Dynamic Orchestration
of the Shop Floor   469
    Milan Pisarić, Vladimir Dimitrieski, Marko Vještica,
    and Goran Krajoski

Assembly Process Design: Performance Evaluation Under Ergonomics
Consideration Using Several Robot Collaboration Modes   477
    Anthony Quenehen, Stephane Thiery, Nathalie Klement,
    Lionel Roucoules, and Olivier Gibaru

A Method of Distributed Production Management for Highly-Distributed
Flexible Job Shops   485
    Daiki Yasuda, Eiji Morinaga, and Hidefumi Wakamatsu

A Digital Twin Modular Framework for Reconfigurable
Manufacturing Systems   493
    Hichem Haddou Benderbal, Abdelkrim R. Yelles-Chaouche,
    and Alexandre Dolgui

Reconfigurable Digitalized and Servitized Production Systems:
Requirements and Challenges   501
    Magdalena Paul, Audrey Cerqueus, Daniel Schneider,
    Hichem Haddou Benderbal, Xavier Boucher, Damien Lamy,
    and Gunther Reinhart

The Impact of Dynamic Tasks Assignment in Paced Mixed-Model
Assembly Line with Moving Workers   509
    S. Ehsan Hashemi-Petroodi, Simon Thevenin, Sergey Kovalev,
    and Alexandre Dolgui

Balancing and Configuration Planning of RMS to Minimize Energy Cost . . .   518
    Audrey Cerqueus, Paolo Gianessi, Damien Lamy, and Xavier Delorme

Operations Management in Engineer-to-Order Manufacturing

Factors Affecting Shipyard Operations and Logistics: A Framework
and Comparison of Shipbuilding Approaches   529
    Jo Wessel Strandhagen, Yongkuk Jeong, Jong Hun Woo, Marco Semini,
    Magnus Wiktorsson, Jan Ola Strandhagen, and Erlend Alfnes

Using the Smartphone as an Augmented Reality Device in ETO Industry   538
Niklas Jahn, Axel Friedewald, and Hermann Lödding

Exploring the Path Towards Construction 4.0: Collaborative Networks
and Enterprise Architecture Views.   547
Ovidiu Noran, David Romero, and Sorin Burchiu

The Potential for Purchasing Function to Enhance Circular Economy
Business Models for ETO Production   557
Deodat Mwesiumo, Nina Pereira Kvadsheim,
and Bella Belerivana Nujen

Planning Procurement Activities in ETO Projects   565
Kristina Kjersem and Marte Giskeødegård

Maturity Model for Successful Cost Transformation in ETO Companies   573
Johann Gregori and Ralph Riedel

Backlog Oriented Bottleneck Management – Practical Guide
for Production Managers   581
Roman Ungern-Sternberg, Christian Fries,
and Hans-Hermann Wiendahl

Cross-Functional Coordination Before and After the CODP:
An Empirical Study in the Machinery Industry   590
Margherita Pero and Violetta G. Cannas

Production Management in Food Supply Chains

Short Agri-Food Supply Chains: A Proposal in a Food Bank   601
Aguinaldo Eduardo de Souza, João Gilberto Mendes dos Reis,
Antonio Carlos Estender, Jorge Luiz Dias Agia, Oduvaldo Vendrametto,
Luciana Melo Costa, and Paula Ferreira da Cruz Correia

Analysis of the New Frontier of Soybean Production in Brazil   609
José Alberto de Alencar Luz, João Gilberto Mendes dos Reis,
and Alexandre Formigoni

Prediction of Cold Chain Transport Conditions Using Data Mining   616
Clayton Gerber Mangini, Nilsa Duarte da Silva Lima,
and Irenilza de Alencar Nääs

Environmental Impact Classification of Perishable Cargo Transport
Using Data Mining   624
Manoel Eulálio Neto, Irenilza de Alencar Nääs,
and Nilsa Duarte da Silva Lima

Economic and Environmental Perfomance in Coffee Supply Chains:
A Brazilian Case Study   631
   Paula Ferreira da Cruz Correia, João Gilberto Mendes dos Reis,
   Rodrigo Carlo Toloi, Fernanda Alves de Araújo, Silvia Helena Bonilla,
   Jonatas Santos de Souza, Alexandre Formigoni,
   and Aguinaldo Eduardo de Souza

Managing Perishable Multi-product Inventory with Supplier Fill-Rate,
Price Reduction and Substitution.   640
   Flemming Max Møller Christensen, Kenn Steger-Jensen,
   and Iskra Dukovska-Popovska

Digital Technology Enablers for Resilient and Customer Driven Food
Value Chains   649
   Christos Emmanouilidis and Serafim Bakalis

Gastronomic Service System Design

Human–Robot Hybrid Service System Introduction for Enhancing Labor
and Robot Productivity   661
   Takeshi Shimmura, Ryosuke Ichikari, and Takashi Okuma

Forecasting Customers Visiting Using Machine Learning and
Characteristics Analysis with Low Forecasting Accuracy Days   670
   Takashi Tanizaki, Yuta Hanayama, and Takeshi Shimmura

A Study on Menu Planning Method for Managed Meal -Consideration
of the Cost of Ordering Ingredients-   679
   Kyohei Irie, Nobutada Fujii, Daisuke Kokuryo, and Toshiya Kaihara

Service System Design Considering Employee Satisfaction Through
Introducing Service Robots   686
   Tomomi Nonaka, Takeshi Shimmura, and Nobutada Fujii

Product and Asset Life Cycle Management in the Circular Economy

Exploring Synergies Between Circular Economy and Asset Management   695
   Federica Acerbi, Adalberto Polenghi, Irene Roda, Marco Macchi,
   and Marco Taisch

Information Flows Supporting Circular Economy Adoption
in the Manufacturing Sector   703
   Federica Acerbi and Marco Taisch

A Conceptual Model of the IT Ecosystem for Asset Management
in the Global Manufacturing Context.   711
   Adalberto Polenghi, Irene Roda, Marco Macchi,
   and Alessandro Pozzetti

Production Ramp-Up Strategies for Product

Part Selection for Freeform Injection Molding: Framework
for Development of a Unique Methodology   723
    Elham Sharifi, Atanu Chaudhuri, Brian Vejrum Wæhrens,
    Lasse G. Staal, and Saeed D. Farahani

A Model for Cost-Benefit Analysis of Production Ramp-up Strategies   731
    Khaled Medini, Antoine Pierné, John Ahmet Erkoyuncu,
    and Christian Cornet

Key Factors on Utilizing the Production System Design Phase
for Increasing Operational Performance   740
    Md Hasibul Islam, Zuhara Chavez, Seyoum Eshetu Birkie,
    and Monica Bellgran

Business Model Development for a Dynamic Production
Network Platform   749
    Stefan Wiesner, Larissa Behrens, and Jannicke Baalsrud Hauge

Changeable Closed-Loop Manufacturing Systems: A Case Study
of Challenges in Product Take-Back   758
    Markus Thomas Bockholt, Ann-Louise Andersen, Thomas Ditlev Brunoe,
    Jesper Hemdrup Kristensen, Michele Colli, Peter Meulengracht Jensen,
    and Brian Vejrum Wæhrens

Author Index   767

Advanced Modelling, Simulation and Data Analytics in Production and Supply Networks

A Robust Multi-commodity Rebalancing Process in Humanitarian Logistics

Xuehong Gao[1,2(✉)] and Xuefeng Jin[3]

[1] Department of Safety Science and Engineering, University of Science and Technology Beijing, Beijing, China
gao2016@pnu.edu
[2] Department of Industrial Engineering, Pusan National University, Busan, Republic of Korea
[3] Alibaba (China) Co., Ltd., Alibaba Supply Chain Platform, Hangzhou, China

Abstract. After disasters occurred, many refugees have to suffer a lot. To relieve this detrimental situation, various commodities are distributed to the pre-determined warehouses. However, the initial multi-commodity distribution may be imperfect, which results in some warehouses having surplus commodities compared to other unmet warehouses. Hence, it is necessary to rebalance commodities among those warehouses. Because of the uncertain environment after a disaster, the demand is usually uncertain. To plan this multi-commodity rebalancing process appropriately, it is usually assumed that the collected data are uncontaminated. However, this assumption can be easily violated due to the uncertain environment or human error, which results in the biased estimation of the solution. In this study, we propose a strategy for remedying the difficulties associated with data contamination so that a set of robust decisions are obtained. Through a case study, we show that the proposed strategy facilitates effective decision-making in the multi-commodity rebalancing when the data contamination is involved.

Keywords: Robust optimization · Nonlinear · Mathematical programming · Humanitarian logistics

1 Introduction

Based on the Emergency Event Database (EM-DAT, www.emdat.be), large-scale natural or man-made disasters had occurred frequently since the 1900s. Recently, large-scale disasters such as the 2008 Wenchuan Earthquake in China, 2011 Earthquake and Tsunami in Japan, 2018 Earthquake and Tsunami in Indonesia, 2019 Forest Fire in Australia, 2019 COVID in the world, and 2019 Plague of Locusts from Kenya result in a great number of refugees. To relieve this detrimental situation, medical and living commodities should be distributed to and stocked at the pre-determined warehouses.

As the initial multi-commodity distribution happened before the disasters, it is impossible to match with the practical situation, which results in some warehouses having surplus commodities compared to other unmet warehouses. The undersupply of commodities worsens human suffering and results in an increased mortality rate.

© IFIP International Federation for Information Processing 2020
Published by Springer Nature Switzerland AG 2020
B. Lalic et al. (Eds.): APMS 2020, IFIP AICT 591, pp. 3–10, 2020.
https://doi.org/10.1007/978-3-030-57993-7_1

In contrast, the oversupply of commodities may also occur in some other affected areas. To make full use of any surplus commodities, it is necessary to conduct a multi-commodity rebalancing process to rebalance the commodities among the warehouses. However, the collected information about the demand may be inaccurate during the critical hours right after disasters [1]. Also, the collected data may be contaminated due to human error. The above two factors result in a biased rebalancing strategy. Neither strategic approaches nor quantitative models to handle this multi-commodity rebalancing under data contamination. Thus, we investigate the multi-commodity rebalancing problem with data contamination and propose a robust optimization model for remedying the data contamination so that a set of robust decisions can be obtained.

The remainder of this paper is organized as follows. Section 2 reviews previous studies about commodity rebalancing (also referred to as redistribution) in humanitarian logistics, highlighting the novelty of this study. In Sect. 3, we present the problem description and propose a strategy for remedying the problem with data contamination. Then a mixed-integer nonlinear programming (MINP) model is formulated for the problem. Next, a linearization approach is applied to linearize the model. In Sect. 4, we compare different methods in a case study. Finally, Sect. 5 concludes this study with contributions and further directions.

2 Literature Review

The logistics related problem in disaster response has been extensively studied by many researchers [2–6]. However, the commodity rebalancing is also an important part in relief supply chain planning [7, 8]. However, this commodity rebalancing has been received insufficient attention in the past. In what follows, we review the studies about commodity rebalancing in disaster response. Then the research gap is discussed and the novelty of this study is summarized.

To the best of our knowledge, the commodity redistribution was firstly proposed by Lubashevskiy [9, 10] who implemented the required redistribution of vital resources between the affected and neighboring cities in the disaster area. However, they did not consider any uncertainty. Then Gao and Lee [11] considered a multi-commodity redistribution problem under demand uncertainty. Based on the above study, Gao and Lee [12] considered the multi-commodity redistribution process happens in a multi-modal transportation system when multiple disaster areas are involved. Sarma, Das [13] and Sarma, Das [14] also introduced different mathematical models for humanitarian logistic applying the fact of redistribution of resources. After that, Gao [8] and Gao [15] modified the terminology from "multi-commodity redistribution" to "multi-commodity rebalancing" as its appropriate and suitable description to the problem. Later Gao [7] defined the multi-commodity rebalancing in disaster response, which is given by *"The multi-commodity rebalancing process in disaster response is to rebalance the commodities from the oversupplied nodes to unmet nodes over the transportation network to satisfy the potential demand at all nodes (relief centers)"*. And the relief centers were divided into three groups, namely (i) complete supply relief centers, (ii) complete demand relief centers, and (iii) potential demand or supply relief centers, where the multi-commodity rebalancing process was conducted among these three groups of relief centers.

As the collected data is easily contaminated due to human error and inaccurate information right after disasters, it results in a biased rebalancing strategy. For more details on the data contamination and its effect, one should refer to Park [16]. However, neither strategic approaches nor quantitative models to handle this multi-commodity rebalancing under data contamination. To address this challenge and fill this research gap, a robust approach that is less sensitive to the outliers or noises is warranted. As a consequence, we investigate the multi-commodity rebalancing problem under data contamination and propose a strategy for remedying the difficulties associated with data contamination so that a set of robust decisions can be obtained.

3 Robust Optimization Model

3.1 Problem Description

Suppose that a large-scale disaster strikes an area where a set of warehouses have been pre-identified to stock the commodities. These stocked commodities are used to support basic lives. Inevitably, some warehouses end up having surplus commodities, whereas others end up having insufficient commodities. To reduce human suffering and make full use of any surplus commodities, it is necessary to plan a multi-commodity rebalancing strategy to rebalance the commodities among the warehouses.

The complex and dynamic nature of a large-scale disaster creates a highly uncertain environment. It is difficult to determine how much of a particular commodity a warehouse will require in the future, which makes the demand uncertain. Here, the demand is classified into several independent scenarios. The uncertain demand is represented as a set of discrete stochastic quantities, and a specific realization is considered as a scenario. For each commodity type, there is a set of scenarios Ξ. For a particular scenario $\xi \in \Xi$, there is a probability of occurrence $p(\xi)$ such that $p(\xi) \geq 0$ and $\sum_{\xi \in \Xi} p(\xi) = 1$. As the inaccurate information usually exists, the demand quantity is considered as the outlier in this study. What we need to is identifying these warehouses and determine the outgoing and incoming shipments at the warehouses. Before the model is proposed, an assumption is stated in advance. Each of the warehouses is a separate unit and the weighted values of the warehouses are given.

3.2 Notations

The parameters and decision variables used in this model are shown as follows:

Sets

$\mathcal{R}$ Set of warehouses, indexed by $r \in \mathcal{R}$, $(r \neq c)$.
$\mathcal{E}$ Set of commodity types, indexed by $t \in \mathcal{T}$.
Ξ Set of scenarios, indexed by $\xi \in \Xi$.

Parameters

W_r Weight of warehouse r.
S_{rt} Stock level of commodity-type t at warehouse r.
D_{rt}^{ξ} Demand of commodity-type t at warehouse r in scenario ξ.
P_{rt}^{ξ} Probability of occurrence for D_{rt}^{ξ}.
O_{rt}^{ξ} Outlier demand for commodity-type t at warehouse r in scenario ξ.
N Number of scenarios in Ξ.

Decision variables

qo_{rt} Quantity of outgoing commodity-type t at warehouse r.
qi_{rt} Quantity of incoming commodity-type t at warehouse r.

3.3   Robust Strategy

To copy with the uncertain demand, many researchers use expected demand [7, 17, 18]. Given a set of discrete demand quantities $D_{rt}^1, D_{rt}^2, \ldots, D_{rt}^N$ with corresponding probabilities $P_{rt}^1, P_{rt}^2, \ldots, P_{rt}^N$, such that $\sum_{\xi \in \Xi} P_{rt}^{\xi} = 1$, the expected demand is given by

$$\mathbb{E}(D_{rt}^{\xi}, \xi) = \sum_{\xi \in \Xi} D_{rt}^{\xi} P_{rt}^{\xi} \tag{1}$$

The above-expected demand can be considered as the weighted mean. However, the weighted mean is not a robust outlier-resistant location estimator. As the median is a robust outlier-resistant location estimator [19], instead of using weighted mean, we use the median to represent the demand at warehouse r, which is denoted by $\mathbb{M}\left(D_{rt}^{\xi}, P_{rt}^{\xi}, \xi\right)$ and given by

$$\mathbb{M}(D_{rt}^{\xi}, \xi) = \text{Median}\left(D_{rt}^1, D_{rt}^2, \ldots, D_{rt}^N\right) \tag{2}$$

3.4   Robust Optimization Model

The problem is formulated as the following MINP model.

$$\text{Min } \Psi_1 = \sum_{t \in \mathcal{T}} \sum_{r \in \mathcal{R}} W_r \left[\text{Median}\left(D_{rt}^1, D_{rt}^2, \ldots, D_{rt}^N\right) - (S_{rt} + qi_{rt} - qo_{rt})\right] \tag{3}$$

s.t.

$$\sum_{r \in \mathcal{R}} qi_{rt} = \sum_{r \in \mathcal{R}} qo_{rt} \quad \forall t \in \mathcal{T}. \tag{4}$$

$$qo_{rt} \leq S_{tr} \quad \forall r \in \mathcal{R}, t \in \mathcal{T}. \tag{5}$$

$$qi_{rt} \cdot qo_{rt} = 0 \quad \forall r \in \mathcal{R}, t \in \mathcal{T}. \tag{6}$$

$$S_{rt} + qi_{rt} - qo_{rt} \leq \text{Median}\left(D_{rt}^1, D_{rt}^2, \ldots, D_{rt}^N\right) \quad \forall r \in \mathcal{R}, t \in \mathcal{T}. \tag{7}$$

$$qi_{rt} \text{ and } qo_{rt} \text{ are nonnegative variables} \quad \forall r \in \mathcal{R}, t \in \mathcal{T}. \tag{8}$$

The objective function (3) aims to minimize the total weighted unmet demand at warehouses. Constraint (4) ensures the balance between incoming and outgoing shipments. Constraint (5) restricts that the outgoing shipment is not greater than the stock level. Constraint (6) ensures that either outgoing or incoming shipments could happen. Constraint (7) restricts that the commodity after rebalancing is not greater than the demand. Constraint (8) defines the decision variables.

3.5 Linearization Method

The above model is nonlinear due to Constraint (6). It is significant to propose a linearization strategy for the above MINP model so that it can be solved by using CPLEX. Consequently, we introduce a big positive value M and two auxiliary binary variables into the model. These two auxiliary binary variables are given by

$$i_{rt} = \begin{cases} 1 \text{ if } qi_{rt} > 0 \\ 0 \text{ otherwise} \end{cases} \quad \forall r \in \mathcal{R}, t \in \mathcal{T}. \tag{9}$$

$$j_{rt} = \begin{cases} 1 \text{ if } qo_{rt} > 0 \\ 0 \text{ otherwise} \end{cases} \quad \forall r \in \mathcal{R}, t \in \mathcal{T}. \tag{10}$$

Then the MINP model can be reformulated as the following mathematical model.

$$\text{Min } \Psi_1$$

s.t.

Constraints (4), (5), (7) and (8)

$$i_{rt} + j_{rt} \leq 1 \quad \forall r \in \mathcal{R}, t \in \mathcal{T}. \tag{11}$$

$$qi_{rt} \leq i_{rt}M \quad \forall r \in \mathcal{R}, t \in \mathcal{T}. \tag{12}$$

$$qo_{rt} \leq j_{rt}M \quad \forall r \in \mathcal{R}, t \in \mathcal{T}. \tag{13}$$

Constraint (11) guarantees that either an outgoing or incoming shipment could happen. Constraints (12) and (13) restrict the quantities of incoming and outgoing shipments, respectively.

4 Numerical Example

This study considers a numerical example that includes eleven warehouses and two commodity types based on the study of Gao [7]. Let the outlier value be 10000, which exists in warehouses 1, 5, and 9. The proposed mathematical model is implemented in the CPLEX (Version: 12.6). All the experiments are run on a computer with an Intel(R) Core(TM) i7-7700 CPU@3.6 GHz under the Windows 10 Pro system.

To evaluate the robustness of the proposed robust optimization model against the outliers, we compare the results for the numerical example using different models. We first present the optimal solution in Fig. 1 without considering data contamination and then compare different methods and present the results in Table 1 when the data contamination is involved.

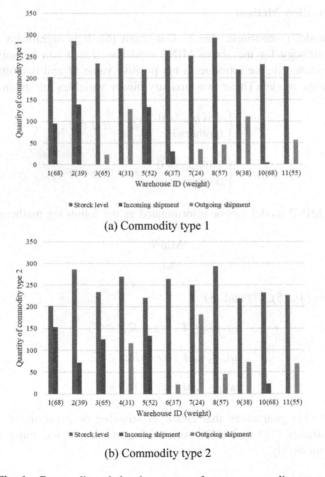

(a) Commodity type 1

(b) Commodity type 2

Fig. 1. Commodity rebalancing strategy for two commodity types

As shown in Table 1, it provides an outlier resistance behavior for commodity type 1 in different models. The solution obtained using the robust optimization model is quite close to the solution through the method in Gao [7]. After considering the outlier, the method in Gao [7] is strongly sensitive to the outlier, whereas the proposed model is quite stable to obtain the solution that is still quite close to the true optimal solution.

Table 1. Comparison of commodity rebalancing strategies.

ID	Without outlier				With outlier in warehouses 1, 5, and 9							
	Gao [7]		Robust model		Gao [7] $O_{11}^N = 10^4$		Gao [7] $O_{51}^N = 10^4$		Gao [7] $O_{91}^N = 10^4$		Robust model	
	qo_{r1}	qi_{r1}	qo_{r1}	qi_{r1}	qo_{r1}	qi_{r1}	qo_{r1}	qi_{r1}	qo_{r1}	qi_{r1}	qo_{r1}	qi_{r1}
$r = 1$	0	89.8	0	95	0	1051.3	0	89.8	0	89.8	0	95
$r = 2$	0	134	0	139	0	95.9	0	96.1	0	75.5	0	139
$r = 3$	10.6	0	23	0	282	0	282	0	282	0	23	0
$r = 4$	123.7	0	129	0	274	0	274	0	274	0	129	0
$r = 5$	0	137.3	0	133	0	137.3	0	1098.6	0	137.3	0	133
$r = 6$	0	34.6	0	30	0	34.6	0	34.6	0	34.6	0	30
$r = 7$	33.5	0	35	0	285	0	285	0	285	0	35	0
$r = 8$	49.8	0	46	0	300	0	300	0	300	0	46	0
$r = 9$	115	0	111	0	115	0	115	0	0	866.9	111	0
$r = 10$	0.5	0	0	4	0.5	0	0.5	0	0.5	0	0	4
$r = 11$	62.6	0	57	0	62.6	0	62.6	0	62.6	0	57	0

5 Conclusion and Future Study

This study focused on the multi-commodity rebalancing problem under data contamination in disaster response. We proposed a robust optimization model to formulate the problem. Then we applied a linearization method for the model so that it could be solved in CPLEX. Next, the solutions were obtained to illustrate the effectiveness of the proposed method. Finally, we compared the results of different methods in a case study to verify the outperformance of the proposed method in overcoming the outlier in the multi-commodity rebalancing problem. The limitation of this study is that the data contamination only exists in the demand for commodities.

In future work, some directions are meaningful that could be explored deeply from the following two perspectives. This study only focuses on the multi-commodity rebalancing process. However, it would be interesting to consider how to transport these commodities among the warehouses. Another future consideration is to develop a more reliable multi-commodity rebalancing by considering a multi-period process.

Acknowledgment. This research was partially supported by the National Research Foundation of Korea (NRF) grant funded by the Korea government (NRF-2017R1A2B4004169), the China-Korea cooperation program managed by the National Natural Science Foundation of China and the NRF (NRF-2018K2A9A2A06019662), and National Natural Science Foundation of China (71861167002, 5183000192).

References

1. Kirac, E., Milburn, A.B., Wardell III, C.: The traveling salesman problem with imperfect information with application in disaster relief tour planning. IIE Trans. **47**(8), 783–799 (2015)
2. Pérez-Rodríguez, N., Holguín-Veras, J.: Inventory-allocation distribution models for postdisaster humanitarian logistics with explicit consideration of deprivation costs. Transp. Sci. **50**(4), 1261–1285 (2015)
3. Chen, Y., et al.: The regional cooperation-based warehouse location problem for relief supplies. Comput. Ind. Eng. **102**, 259–267 (2016)
4. Gao, X., et al.: A hybrid genetic algorithm for multi-emergency medical service center location-allocation problem in disaster response. Int. J. Ind. Eng. **24**(6), 663–679 (2017)
5. Gao, X., Nayeem, M.K., Hezam, I.M.: A robust two-stage transit-based evacuation model for large-scale disaster response. Measurement **145**, 713–723 (2019)
6. Besiou, M., Van Wassenhove, L.N.: Humanitarian operations: a world of opportunity for relevant and impactful research. Manuf. Serv. Oper. Manag. **22**(1), 135–145 (2020)
7. Gao, X., A bi-level stochastic optimization model for multi-commodity rebalancing under uncertainty in disaster response. Ann. Oper. Res. 1–34 (2020)
8. Gao, X.: A stochastic optimization model for commodity rebalancing under traffic congestion in disaster response. In: Ameri, F., Stecke, K.E., von Cieminski, G., Kiritsis, D. (eds.) APMS 2019. IAICT, vol. 567, pp. 91–99. Springer, Cham (2019). https://doi.org/10.1007/978-3-030-29996-5_11
9. Lubashevskiy, V., Kanno, T., Furuta, K.: Resource redistribution method for short-term recovery of society after large-scale disasters. Adv. Complex Syst. **17**(05), 1450026 (2014)
10. Lubashevskiy, V., Kanno, T., Furuta, K.: Resource redistribution under lack of information: short-term recovery after large scale disasters. J. Adv. Simul. Sci. Eng. **3**(1), 1–16 (2016)
11. Gao, X., Lee, G.M.: A stochastic programming model for multi-commodity redistribution planning in disaster response. In: Moon, I., Lee, G.M., Park, J., Kiritsis, D., von Cieminski, G. (eds.) APMS 2018. IAICT, vol. 535, pp. 67–78. Springer, Cham (2018). https://doi.org/10.1007/978-3-319-99704-9_9
12. Gao, X., Lee, G.M.: A two-stage stochastic programming model for commodity redistribution under uncertainty in disaster response. In: 48th Proceedings of International Conference on Computers and Industrial Engineering, Auckland, New Zealand (2018)
13. Sarma, D., et al.: Redistribution for cost minimization in disaster management under uncertainty with trapezoidal neutrosophic number. Comput. Ind. **109**, 226–238 (2019)
14. Sarma, D., Das, A., Bera, U.K.: An optimal redistribution plan considering aftermath disruption in disaster management. Soft. Comput. **24**(1), 65–82 (2019). https://doi.org/10.1007/s00500-019-04287-7
15. Gao, X. A bi-level stochastic optimization model for commodity rebalancing in humanitarian operations. In: 49th Proceedings of International Conference on Computers and Industrial Engineering, Beijing, China (2019)
16. Park, C.: Determination of the joint confidence region of the optimal operating conditions in robust design by the bootstrap technique. Int. J. Prod. Res. **51**(15), 4695–4703 (2013)
17. Laporte, G., Louveaux, F.V., Van Hamme, L.: An integer L-shaped algorithm for the capacitated vehicle routing problem with stochastic demands. Oper. Res. **50**(3), 415–423 (2002)
18. Liao, Z., Rittscher, J.: A multi-objective supplier selection model under stochastic demand conditions. Int. J. Prod. Econ. **105**(1), 150–159 (2007)
19. Hampel, F.R., et al.: Robust statistics: the approach based on influence functions, vol. 196. Wiley, Hoboken (2011)

Towards a Unified Reliability-Centered Information Logistics Model for Production Assets

Florian Defèr[✉], Günther Schuh, and Volker Stich

Research Institute for Industrial Management (FIR) at RWTH Aachen,
Campus-Boulevard 55, 52074 Aachen, Germany
Florian.Defer@FIR.RWTH-Aachen.de

Abstract. Reliability-centered maintenance for production assets is a well-established concept for the most effective and efficient disposition of maintenance resources. Unfortunately, the approach takes a lot of effort and relies heavily on the knowledge of individuals. Reliability data in Computerized Maintenance Management System (CMMS) is scarce and almost never used well. An automated risk assessment system would have the potential to contribute to the dissemination and effective use of risk information and analysis. The individuality of production setting, however, prevents current systems from being practically relevant for most industries. The presented approach combines ontologies to store and link knowledge, an information logistics model displaying the various information streams, and the Internet of production to take the different user systems and infrastructure layers into account. The provided model of a reference digital shadow for risk information and a detailed information logistics model will help software companies to improve reliability software, standardize and enable assets owners to establish a customized digital shadow for their production networks.

Keywords: Risk analysis system · Asset management · Criticality analysis · Intelligent support system · Risk management · Information logistics model · Internet of production · Digital shadow

1 Introduction

The percentage of productive maintenance work is stated by *WIREMAN* at 25 to 35% [1], which corresponds to about 9 h of productive maintenance work in a continuous shift system per day per full time equivalent (FTE). Reliability-centered approaches in maintenance provide a powerful tool to identify the right maintenance strategy for each asset, choosing the most effective improvement projects and giving comprehensive guidance for operational disposition. The approach was introduced in the 1960s aircraft industry and published by *NOWLAN and HEAP* in 1978 [2]. *BLOOM* states that only 40% of the introduced reliability concepts in production plants are successful. In addition, a high percentage of these implementation attempts are very superficial and therefore the real success rate is much lower [3]. Within the following paragraphs, five main reasons are given why the implementation of a more than 40 year old concept is

© IFIP International Federation for Information Processing 2020
Published by Springer Nature Switzerland AG 2020
B. Lalic et al. (Eds.): APMS 2020, IFIP AICT 591, pp. 11–18, 2020.
https://doi.org/10.1007/978-3-030-57993-7_2

still a big challenge. First, however, the next paragraph provides a brief introduction to reliability and risk for production assets.

1.1   Reliability and Risk in Production and Maintenance

There is currently no generally valid definition of risk in the literature, as the broad range of the term allows for a wide variety of perspectives [4]. In terms of asset reliability, risk is closely linked with the performance of the assets. For example, POLLANZ defines risk as "negative influence on the achievement of objectives" [5]. Consequently, risk in maintenance management can be described as the product of the probability of occurrence and the impact on the effectiveness of the plant or asset [6].

$$Risk = \text{probability of occurrence} \times \text{impact on the effectiveness} \qquad (1)$$

The task of maintenance is to identify the reasons for these deviations and to take countermeasures [7].

1.2   Holdbacks for the Implementation of Reliability Concepts

The holdbacks for the implementation of reliability-based approaches can be clustered into five groups: Increasing system complexity, complex failure modes, subjective risk identification, complex risk aggregation, and insufficient data. In the following sections, these clusters are briefly explained.

Increasing System Complexity: The concept of the value chain defined by Porter in 1985 [8] no longer holds true for today's companies and is transforming more and more into complex value-added networks [9]. This means that companies can have many different value-added chains within the same production plant, which, in addition to generating various potentials, leads to different, interconnected and more complex risks [10]. The increasingly close networking of different systems and production areas resulting from Industry 4.0 also adds new and complex risks for manufacturing companies [11].

Complex Failure Modes: Reliability concepts deal with the individual error causes of each component and can therefore define the ideal action to be taken instead of just having to replace the component regularly [2]. Limitations exist if the error mechanism or the overall system is not properly understood [2], which is more and more difficult given the increasing complexity of assets. These patterns cannot be predicted for a single asset, but can only be predicted by looking at reference plants [12].

Subjective and Dynamic Risk Identification: In many cases, a risk determination is only possible post ex, since the multitude of risks cannot be estimated and data for easily comparable investments do not exist. This not only means that in most cases only a risk diagnosis is possible, as risks cannot be predicted. But also that risks that have already occurred are heavily over or underestimated (recall bias, illusory correlation etc.) [13]. Since vulnerability is not static, it is even more difficult to measure risk

[14]. For example, age and quality of maintenance have an enormous influence on how susceptible a production asset is to failure [12].

Complex Risk Aggregation and Interdependencies: The difficulty lies in the coupling of effects, since individual events can represent an acceptable risk, but are extremely intensified by a coupling effect [15]. It is not possible to estimate overall risks, thus procedures for risk aggregation are necessary [16].

Insufficient Data: However, many risks cannot be predicted for the individual asset and can only be predicted by looking at reference plants [12]. This makes applying failure data from one system to another difficult even for identical standard systems [17]. Hence, it is necessary to have a huge amount of data and find an adequate way to take variations in the environment, process and so on into account. The assessment of risks is usually expressed in language, which makes it even harder to analyze [18].

1.3 Derivation of Research Needs

Production risks are mostly determined in a manual, workshop-like process, which takes place a few times in the life cycle of the assets. The gathered information of these workshops are subjective, scattered across information silos and difficult to compare. Modern information systems offer the possibility to make generalizations based on large data sets and to derive recommendations for action. The possibility of learning from data represents a great potential not only within the own organization, but also beyond. This potential is not used in current organizations and information systems. The various internal and external data silos must be linked and in order to do so, use cases have to be derived from actual business needs. Risk assessment is one of the most crucial concepts for maintenance management. An automated risk modelling could further dissemination and enable a more efficient and effective maintenance organization. For the establishment of a comprehensive risk modeling, there needs to be a data logistics model to fuse the different data types and needs together.

2 Risk Modelling and Knowledge Preservation

ROMEIKE identifies two groups of methods for risk identification, analysis and evaluation. The search methods (e.g. checklists, loss databases, SWOT analysis) are particularly suitable for already known or trivial risks. The search methods are suitable for complex and unknown risks and are further subdivided into analytical methods and creativity methods. In the context of this work, the analytical methods will be considered in the following, as they are suitable for "identifying future and previously unknown risk potentials" [19]. The creativity methods are therefore not suitable for this task, as the aim of this paper is to lay out a foundation for an automated determination of risks. Current information systems are not suitable for a creative performance, but are very capable of finding patterns in huge sets of data [20].

The most commonly used and broadly accepted as the tool of choice for risk assessment is the Failure Mode and Effect Analysis (FMEA), which considers a wide range of factors and delivers compelling results. FMEA considers the severity (S), occurrence (O) and detection (D) ratings to determine the risk priority number (RPN) [21].

$$\text{Risk Priority Number(RPN)} = \text{Severity(S)} \times \text{Occurrence(O)} \times \text{Detection(D)} \quad (2)$$

KÖNIG adapted the method, which originally came from quality management, in order to be able to effectively prioritize risks. With the Risk Mode and Effect Analysis (RMEA) approach, the risks are combined into a risk cube, which consists of different risk classes according to the probability of occurrence and detection. [22] There are many other approaches to risk measurement and aggregation like Failure Mode, Effect and Cause Analysis (FMECA) [23], Socio Technical Reliability Analysis (STRA) [24], Fuzzy Fault Tree Analysis (FFTA) [25], Monte Carlo Simulation (MCS) [26] and evaluation laboratory (DEMATEL) [27].

The weak point of all those models still prevails. They all rely on the estimation of the failure rates for the assets [28] or simulate random numbers (e.g. for MCS). In addition, they presume that all possible failure modes are known to the asset owner. It is therefore necessary to develop a data model for risk identification and comparison between companies and production sites. Current ontology-based approaches are limited in the level of detail they provide and do not include a sufficient digital reference shadow for asset risk information.

3   Information Logistics Model for Risks of Production Assets

The current state of the ontology-based risk model is presented in this section, which starts off with a brief description of risk in ontology. Subsequently, the transfer of one example into the information logistics model notation gives an outlook on the results.

3.1   Risk Management Ontology for Production Assets

The application of an ontology-based risk management is not yet sufficiently extended to production assets because of a lacking depth of detail for a reference architecture and comparison of different assets. For example, the models do not take environmental conditions into adequate account, although they are an important factor influencing the wear and tear and the functional efficiency of a machine [29].

For the definition of the risk management ontology for production assets (Fig. 1), the procedure following *STUCKENSCHMIDT* was chosen [30]. The functions of an information system are implemented according to *KRCMAR*: Collect, structure, process, provide, transform, communicate and use data, information and knowledge [31].

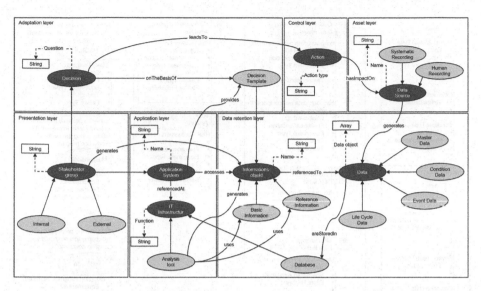

Fig. 1. Risk management ontology for production assets (top level excerpt)

The ontology notation of *MILVICH* is used for Fig. 1 [32]. Accordingly, classes are displayed as dark grey ellipses. Related terms are represented by lighter grey ellipses and are connected by a straight, continuous grey arrow. In order to keep the ontology readable, the classes have been divided into sub-concepts only to the extent necessary for understanding the approach. Accordingly, not every class has assigned terms. Furthermore, in Fig. 1, information containers are displayed with a rectangular grey frame. These are connected to a class by a dotted grey arrow and describe an identi-fication property (displayed on the connection) and its type (string, value, array, and so on). The name and type can be filled with the corresponding values of the application when using the ontology.

3.2 Exemplary Transfer into an Information Logistics Model

For the implementation and future usage, the ontology needs to be transformed into an information logistics model. Figure 2 displays an excerpt of the model for condition monitoring, which has an impact on the occurrence (O) as well as detection (D) of a risk.

The information logistic model notation of *NIENKE* was used for Fig. 2 [33]. It consists of roles that are characterized by the generation of information (source) and the use of or need for information (sink). A vertical line visually separates the two parts of a role. Each role has both elements. A special role is the decision role or target role, which has a certain need for information in order to decide. An oval shape characterizes the role with a dark edge. In addition, the decision questions of the target role are noted above the role. Information objects are exchanged between roles and systems through information flows. The information objects are described under a role or a system on the source side. To improve clarity and structuring, the data records are grouped

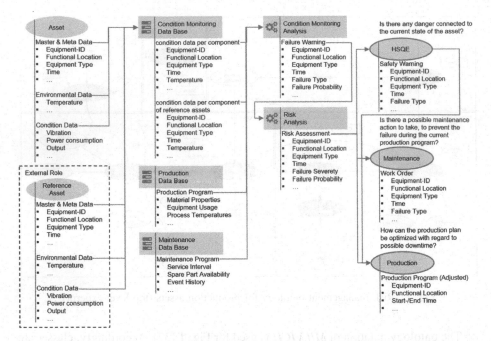

Fig. 2. Information logistics model for condition monitoring (excerpt)

together into information objects and listed accordingly. Figure 2 displays the data transfer from the asset to a data base. The data base is then fed into an analysis system which derives a decision template to present to the specific role. With each step more data is considered, aggregated and analyzed. Since not all data is numerical, available and easy to process, the focus must lie on the possibility to fill the gaps by reference assets. Even if it results in less accuracy for the analysis.

4 Conclusion

Automated risk assessment systems have the potential to contribute to the dissemination and effective use of risk information and analysis. Especially in complex production environments, it provides an effective and efficient way to optimize maintenance and investment spending, as well as the effectiveness of the whole plant. The provided reference digital shadow for risk information linked to a detailed information logistics model will help software companies to improve reliability software, standardize and enable assets owners to establish a customized digital shadow for their production networks. The future goal should be to extend the model with a variety of functions and information. Therefore, further research and case studies need to be conducted. For the moment, the model's functions focus on the process industry, and other industries can be implemented in the future, as they have similar business requirements.

References

1. Wireman, T.: Benchmarking Best Practices in Maintenance, Reliability and Asset Management: Updated for ISO 55000, 3rd edn. Industrial Press, South Norwalk (2015)
2. Nowlan, F.S., Heap, H.: Reliability-Centred Maintenance. Technical Information Service, US Department of Commerce, San Francisco (1978)
3. Bloom, N.B.: Reliability Centered Maintenance (RCM). McGraw-Hill Professional Publishing, Blacklick (2005)
4. Ni, H., Chen, A., Chen, N.: Some extensions on risk matrix approach. Saf. Sci. **48**(10), 1269–1278 (2010). https://doi.org/10.1016/j.ssci.2010.04.005
5. Pollanz, M.: Konzeptionelle Überlegungen zur Einrichtung und Prüfung eines Risikomanagementsystems: droht eine Mega-Erwartungslücke? Der Betrieb(52), 393–399 (1999)
6. Leidinger, B.: Wertorientierte Instandhaltung_ Kosten senken, Verfügbarkeit erhalten-Springer Fachmedien Wiesbaden (2017), Wertorientierte Instandhaltung: Kosten senken, Verfügbarkeit erhalten. Springer, Wiesbaden (2017). https://doi.org/10.1007/978-3-658-04401-5
7. Al-Najjar, B.: A model to diagnose the deviation in the maintenance performance measures. In: Mathew, J. (ed.) Engineering Assessment Management: Proceedings of the 1st World Congress on Engineering Asset Management (WCEAM) 2006 Gold Coast, Queensland, Australia, 11–14 July 2006, vol. 23, pp. 87–93 Springer, London (2006). https://doi.org/10.1007/978-1-84628-814-2_8
8. Porter, M.E.: Competitive Advantage: Creating and Sustaining Superior Performance; with a New Introduction. Free Press, New York (1998)
9. Allee, V.: Reconfiguring the value network. J. Bus. Strategy **21**(4), 36–39 (2000). https://doi.org/10.1108/eb040103
10. British Standards Institution: Asset management: Part 1: Specification for the optimized management of physical assets 03.100.01(55-1) (2008). http://www.irantpm.ir/wp-content/uploads/2014/01/pass55-2008.pdf. Accessed 17 Dec 2019
11. Tupa, J., Simota, J., Steiner, F.: Aspects of risk management implementation for industry 4.0. Procedia Manuf. **11**, 1223–1230 (2017). https://doi.org/10.1016/j.promfg.2017.07.248
12. Geldermann, J., Merz, M., Bertsch, V., et al.: The reference installation approach for the estimation of industrial assets at risk. EJIE **2**(1), 73 (2008). https://doi.org/10.1504/EJIE.2008.016330
13. Kahneman, D., Tversky, A.: Prospect theory: an analysis of decision under risk. Econometrica **47**(2), 263–291 (1979)
14. Green, C.H., Parker, D.J., Tunstall, S.: Assessment of flood control and management options: WCD Thematic Review (2000)
15. Baybutt, P.: Using risk tolerance criteria to determine safety integrity levels for safety instrumented functions. J. Loss Prev. Process Ind. **25**(6), 1000–1009 (2012). https://doi.org/10.1016/j.jlp.2012.05.016
16. Gleißner, W.: Quantifizierung komplexer Risiken – Fallbeispiel Projektrisiken. Risiko-Manager (22), 7–10 (2014)
17. Eruguz, A.S., Tan, T., van Houtum, G.-J.: A survey of maintenance and service logistics management: classification and research agenda from a maritime sector perspective. Comput. Oper. Res. **85**, 184–205 (2017). https://doi.org/10.1016/j.cor.2017.03.003
18. Murè, S., Demichela, M.: Fuzzy Application Procedure (FAP) for the risk assessment of occupational accidents. J. Loss Prev. Process Ind. **22**(5), 593–599 (2009). https://doi.org/10.1016/j.jlp.2009.05.007
19. Romeike, F.: Risikomanagement. Studienwissen kompakt. Springer, Wiesbaden (2018)

20. Oleinik, A.: What are neural networks not good at? On artificial creativity. Big Data Soc. 6 (1), 205395171983943 (2019). https://doi.org/10.1177/2053951719839433
21. Popov, G., Lyon, B.K., Hollcroft, B. (eds.): Risk Assessment: A Practical Guide to Assessing Operational Risks. Wiley, Hoboken (2016)
22. König, R.: Management betrieblicher Risiken bei produzierenden Unternehmen. Dissertation, Rheinisch-Westfälischen Technischen Hochschule, Aachen (2008)
23. Carpitella, S., Certa, A., Izquierdo, J., et al.: A combined multi-criteria approach to support FMECA analyses: a real-world case. Reliab. Eng. Syst. Saf. 169, 394–402 (2018). https://doi.org/10.1016/j.ress.2017.09.017
24. Filho, S.Á., et al.: Management tool for reliability analysis in socio-technical systems - a case study. In: Boring, R.L. (ed.) AHFE 2019. AISC, vol. 956, pp. 13–25. Springer, Cham (2020). https://doi.org/10.1007/978-3-030-20037-4_2
25. Cem Kuzu, A., Akyuz, E., Arslan, O.: Application of Fuzzy Fault Tree Analysis (FFTA) to maritime industry: a risk analysing of ship mooring operation. Ocean Eng. 179, 128–134 (2019). https://doi.org/10.1016/j.oceaneng.2019.03.029
26. Resteanu, C., Vaduva, I., Andreica, M.: Monte Carlo simulation for reliability centered maintenance management. In: Lirkov, I., Margenov, S., Waśniewski, J. (eds.) LSSC 2007. LNCS, vol. 4818, pp. 148–156. Springer, Heidelberg (2008). https://doi.org/10.1007/978-3-540-78827-0_15
27. Si, S.-L., You, X.-Y., Liu, H.-C. et al.: DEMATEL technique: a systematic review of the state-of-the-art literature on methodologies and applications. Math. Probl. Eng. 2018(1), 1–33 (2018). https://doi.org/10.1155/2018/3696457
28. Garg, A., Deshmukh, S.G.: Maintenance management: literature review and directions. J. Qual. Maint. Eng 12(3), 205–238 (2006). https://doi.org/10.1108/13552510610685075
29. Karl, F.: Bedarfsermittlung und Planung von Rekonfigurationen an Betriebsmitteln. Zugl.: München, Techn. Univ., Diss., 2014. Forschungsberichte IWB/ Institut für Werkzeugmaschinen und Betriebswissenschaften, Technische Universität München, vol. 298, Utz, München (2015)
30. Stuckenschmidt, H.: Ontologien: Konzepte, Technologien und Anwendungen, 2. Aufl. Informatik im Fokus. Springer, Berlin (2011)
31. Krcmar, H.: Einführung in das Informationsmanagement, 2., überarb. Aufl. Springer Gabler, Berlin (2015)
32. Milvich, M.: Ein Semantisches Web für die Universitätsbibliothek Heidelberg. Masterthesis, Fachhochschule Karlsruhe (2005)
33. Nienke, S.: Ontologie für Energieinformationssysteme produzierender Unternehmen. Dissertation, 1. Auflage. Edition Wissenschaft Apprimus, Band 156. Apprimus Verlag, Aachen (2018)

Characterization of Energy Consumers in Production Systems with Renewable On-Site Power Generation

Julia Schulz[✉], Felix Rosenberg, Valerie M. Scharmer,
and Michael F. Zaeh

Institute for Machine Tools and Industrial Management (iwb), Technical
University of Munich, Boltzmannstr. 15, 85478 Garching, Germany
julia.schulz@iwb.tum.de

Abstract. The amount of renewable energy is increasing in the German energy system. As a result, grid expansion, consumer regulation (demand response), innovative storage solutions or intelligent grid operation are measures to avoid system instabilities. The development of energy prices and regulatory charges is difficult to predict against this dynamic background. The technological development of small power plants is in progress and many of the offered technologies are reaching grid parity. To increase independency from the grid and to avoid grid supply in periods of high prices, the integration of decentral, renewable power generation technologies is a reasonable solution for manufacturing companies. Therefore, a procedure for industrial companies to use their self-produced energy in a sustainable manner is introduced. This paper focuses on the characterization of industrial energy consumers, which is one of the first steps in the procedure. Different consumer criteria are descripted to define 48 consumer groups. Certain factories include consumers that can be described by a multitude of these consumer groups.

Keywords: Energy consumption · Demand side management · Micro-grid

1 Introduction and State of the Art

It has been noted recently that the energy revolution of the electricity system is proceeding ahead in all corresponding fields. Because of their volatile electricity production, the increasing share of renewable energy will challenge grid operators to establish a stable energy supply. So far, there is no economic solution to store electrical power in the utility grid. Therefore, consumption and production need to be balanced at all times. As a result, the instability of the grid could increase the number of power outages. This can lead to high breakdown costs for manufacturing companies caused by interruptions of the production line. Moreover, the volatile power supply has an impact on the electricity market. Fluctuating prices and power quality issues could lead the manufacturer to become more independent from the utility grid. In addition, the customers' demand for environmentally friendly produced products is on the rise. To increase the independency from the utility grid and to meet the costumers' demands, a reasonable solution is to integrate renewables into the industrial grid. A holistic

© IFIP International Federation for Information Processing 2020
Published by Springer Nature Switzerland AG 2020
B. Lalic et al. (Eds.): APMS 2020, IFIP AICT 591, pp. 19–27, 2020.
https://doi.org/10.1007/978-3-030-57993-7_3

procedure for the integration of suitable technologies within manufacturing companies was introduced recently [1] (Fig. 1). Renewable, decentral power generation technologies include technologies whose energy source is renewable and which are on the scale of the distribution network level. Starting from company-specific goals, the analysis of the consumers, installed in the regarded production systems, is an important step, since its outcome influences all the subsequent activities. The selection and dimensioning of power generation technologies, the choice of the electro-technical micro-grid structure and the development of suitable operation strategies are based on the type of consumers within the system. Against the background of Big Data, several methods from data collection to data processing have also been considered in literature in the field of energy consumption analyses. Liebl et al. [2] provide a review of methods for energy data generation and evaluation differentiated by development depth (concept to prototype) and environmental depth (company to component level). So far, the introduced methods mainly aim at transparency enhancement to improve efficiency and do not pursue the objective of classifying and evaluating individual consumers with regard to the necessary decentral energy supply. Therefore, this paper introduces a qualitative characterization of manufacturing energy consumers considering the subsequent procedure steps.

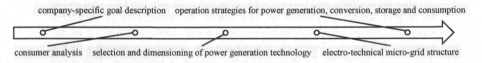

Fig. 1. Procedure for the integration of a renewable, decentral power generation acc. to [1].

2 Electrical and Thermal Consumers in Manufacturing

A broad literature review resulted in the following summary of distinctive criteria of loads in factories divided into functional characteristics and process-related properties.

2.1 Functional Characteristics

Compared to the electrical loads of households, the range of **power requirements** in an industrial application is much higher. Devices in industrial micro-grids considerably exceed the values of power consumption in households, where loads such as instantaneous water boilers or charging stations for electric vehicles (up to 22 kW) represent the highest power requirements. Large electrical loads can strongly influence the industrial grid which is exemplarily shown for an arc furnace by Chang et al. [3]. Depending on the maximum power requirement, industrial loads may be operated either at low or medium **voltage level**. Furthermore, in industrial micro-grids, direct current (DC) and alternating current (AC) loads can coexist [4]. Depending on the type and level of operating voltage, industrial grids may have different requirements concerning grid configuration. In AC-grids, the **power factor** (ratio of effective power and apparent power) is an important functional feature. The idle power in industrial micro-grids is higher compared to conventional grids, e.g. due to a high number of electrical machines. The balance of idle and effective power in an industrial grid is of high relevance to ensure a stable grid operation [5]. A large number of inductive **linear** (e.g. transformers, asynchronous machines) and **non-linear** (e.g. power converters, welding equipment, frequency converters) operating devices are used. The current of linear loads runs approximately sinusoidal. The non-sinusoidal current of non-linear loads can be divided into a base current with grid frequency and several harmonics [6]. These harmonics can lead to thermal overloads and disturbances in electrical systems such as control systems, measuring units, capacitors, or circuit breakers [7]. Since almost every device within a production line is integrated into the control system, a failure of this system can affect the entire electrical, thermal and mechanical energy supply [8] and consequently single machines, the entire process or the product quality. Devices for compensation of the harmonics must be taken into account in the grid planning. Especially in industrial grids with large non-linear loads and low-dimensioned power supply, non-linear loads can cause voltage fluctuations and oscillations [7]. Voltage dips may lead to interruptions in process-relevant devices. A large number of **single-phase loads**, typically at low voltage levels, leads to voltage asymmetries. In industrial grids, rotating electrical machines in particular are influenced by these asymmetries. This leads to counter currents, high thermal losses, torque reduction and vibrations [7]. In contrast to conventional consumers, many industrial consumers are **three phase loads.**

2.2 Process-Related Properties

In micro-grids with a high share of renewable energies and a low share of synchronous generators, the rotating reserve of the grid is low. Therefore, micro-grids are more sensitive to faults than distribution grids. In addition to feed-in voltage and frequency regulation, demand side management is necessary in industrial micro-grids [9]. The potential of consumer-side control in an industrial grid depends, among other things, on the **controllability of the loads**. Controllable loads are characterized, for example, by the adjustment of the power requirement and the starting or shut-down behavior [10]. Energy flexibility describes the ability of production devices to adjust their energy demand to environmental circumstances [11]. Energy-flexible production lines offer organizational energy-flexible measures, whereas single machines provide technical energy-flexible potential for balancing the grid [12]. According to Schenk et al. [13], in a manufacturing factory the energy consumers are considered with different priorities for effective design and planning. Consumers of the first periphery are directly dependent on the production program (e.g. assembling robots, spindle drives). Consumers of the second periphery are not directly dependent on the production program, but on the equipment of the main process (e.g. hydraulic or compressed air units). Within the third periphery, consumers are independent of the production process (e.g. technical building equipment) and are known as cross-sectional technologies as well [14]. Even if their energy demand is mostly lower than the one of the main process consumers, they are considered technologies that are very adjustable and consequently suitable for application in dynamic systems. In these systems, loads have to be specifically removed from the grid in order to avoid load peaks and balance the system [15]. Electrical loads in an industrial environment can have a **uniform** power demand or an **intermittent demand** [16, 17]. Intermittent loads may lead to significant fluctuations in voltage and frequency in the grid, which in turn can lead to instabilities, especially in self-sufficient operation making the integration of distributed energy resources challenging [9]. Electrical loads can cause grid interferences due to functional characteristics and process-related requirements. In contrast, consumers may have certain requirements for **supply reliability** or **voltage quality**. Many consumers, such as motors, just tolerate limited supply quality since fluctuations of the torque can affect the manufacturing process and subsequently the product quality. In addition, low supply quality leads to increased wear or defects of the equipment and may cause decreases in productivity [18].

3 Consumer Characterization

Based on the introduced properties of consumers in industrial (micro-) grids, the characterization of the consumers and the formation of consumer groups can be described.

3.1 Overall Classification

Before characterizing the consumers within production systems, the area of application of the procedure has to be defined. First, the different **industry sectors** are analyzed regarding important features. Gaining independency from the varying and non-transparent electricity price for industry may be one reason for on-site generation. While the electricity price for households undergoes only small price differences, these differences can be significantly higher for industrial customers. This is mainly due to the exemption from various taxes, which relieves the energy-intensive industry in particular. In addition, the absolute electricity consumption and the full-load hours influence the electricity price [20]. The share of energy costs in the gross production value (Fig. 2b) allows more significant conclusions because others than electricity costs are considered and related to the produced outcome. The higher this share, the greater is the incentive for a company to find a more cost-effective alternative than grid procurement. In addition to the energy costs, the share of electricity or heat in the company's energy consumption can be considered as criteria (Fig. 2a). Regarding the required heat, the temperature level is of particular importance since many decentralized and regenerative heat generation processes work at a low temperature level (Fig. 2c). Based on the described criteria, the possibilities for on-site power generation for each industry sector can be evaluated. Figure 2d gives a qualitative evaluation of the sectors regarding the on-site generation of heat and electricity. The qualitative evaluation is based on the data given for each sector. If the electricity share is higher than 50%, the sector is valuated with electricity +. If the temperature level is mainly <500 °C, the sector is valuated with heat +. The share of electricity costs increases the valuation in positive direction if the share is >2.0%.

Sustainable decisions take economic efficiency, the security of supply and the environmental impact into account. In order to assess the economic viability of a power

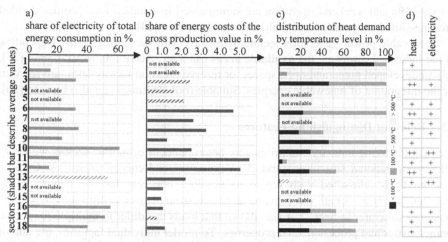

1 mining; 2 quarrying of stone and earth; 3 nutrition, beverage and tobacco; 4 textiles, clothing, leather, leather goods and shoes; 5 wood, wicker and cork products, furniture; 6 paper, cardboard and articles thereof; 7 printed matter, duplication of recorded audio, video and data media; 8 chemical products; 9 other chemical industry (e.g. pharmaceutical products); 10 rubber and plastic goods; 11 glass and glassware, ceramics, stone and earth-work; 12 metal production; 13 metal working and metal products; 14 data processing equipment, electronic and optical products; 15 electrical apparatuses; 16 mechanical engineering; 17 automotive engineering; 18 other sectors.

Fig. 2. Sector-wise characterization for Germany regarding **a)** the share of electricity of total energy consumption according to [27], **b)** the share of energy costs of the gross production value according to [28], **c)** the distribution of heat demand by temperature level according to [29] and **d)** evaluation of the sectors regarding the on-site generation of heat and electricity (sectors are valuated as very suitable (++), suitable (+) for on-site renewable power generation).

plant, a comparison of energy production costs and the procurement costs of electricity and heat is usually carried out. In case of a grid-connected plant, a possible feed-in as well as the associated payments have to be considered in addition [19]. The manufacturing industry in Germany is strongly characterized by medium-sized companies that represent 97.2% of all companies [21]. Despite the dominant number, only about 40% of the total energy consumption in the manufacturing industry is caused by them [22]. Energy costs play a subordinate role for small companies due to their small share in total costs. Energy measures are usually given lower priority than investments in the core business. Therefore, small to medium-sized companies often avoid investing in their own power generation facilities due to a lack of the necessary capital [22]. It can be assumed that the **willingness to invest** in the integration of on-site, renewable energy generation does expand with increasing company size. For high-revenue companies, there are different possibilities for the self-production.

About a quarter of the companies in the German manufacturing sector work in shifts due to high fixed costs for plant and machinery or due to continuous processes [23]. Different **working hours** cause high varying **load profiles** among companies. The range from smaller companies in one-shift operation to large companies in three-to five-shifts and weekend operation are summarized in standard load profiles divided into one-shift load profiles and multi-shift load profiles [24].

Renewable power generation technologies have various requirements. Depending on the industrial company, the **available areas** can vary. According to VDI 3644 [25], only undeveloped green and open spaces, or reserve areas on factory sites, are relevant for the integration of renewable energies. Suitable roof structures can also be used [26].

3.2   Relevant Distinguishing Features

The manufacturing industry comprises very heterogeneous economic sectors with very different operational structures, production processes and energy intensities. Companies are to be classified with regard to possible concepts for the integration of renewable energies. Small, medium and large industrial plants can differ greatly in their consumer structure. In Sect. 2, it was shown that loads can differ in multiple functional characteristics and process-related properties. To model individual factories, the aim of this section is to identify the characteristics of loads that are crucial for the integration of on-site, renewable power generation. The **power demand** of consumers is an essential parameter for the integration of power generators. A classification of the loads into two groups is sufficient to be able to estimate the voltage hierarchies (low-voltage or medium-voltage level) and grid interferences (strong or weak). Accordingly, required generators or storage units can be optimally selected, dimensioned and placed. Small consumers include all loads with a maximum power requirement of up to $P = 100$ kVA. These loads usually have an operating voltage at the low voltage level (400 V/230 V). The loads have a small tendency towards system interferences, which are very small. Large loads have a maximum power requirement of more than 100 kVA. The operating voltages of these loads are usually at the medium-voltage level (1 kV–50 kV) and the system interferences may have large effects on the grid. Due to their characteristics, industrial loads can cause **grid interferences** that consequently may have negative effects on the quality of supply. This danger exists particularly in weak grids in isolated operation. Through a suitable integration of generation technologies and storage, negative influences on the supply quality can be eliminated. Impulsive or intermittent loads, non-linear loads and inductive loads with a low power factor have a high potential for system interferences. Accordingly, loads are classified into loads with high risk of interferences and loads with a low risk of interferences. The classification of loads into the two groups is sufficient to assess the extent to which loads are compatible with sensitive loads and whether measures need to be taken to isolate sensitive loads from loads with a high potential for system interferences. The **organizational classification** serves the purpose of estimating the potential of loads with regard to their use for demand side management. A distinction is made between loads of the main process and peripheral loads. The first group contains loads that are directly related to the main process and that will significantly impair the process in case of supply interruptions. The suitability for load shedding and the controllability is low. Therefore, a low potential for demand side management is attributed. The group of peripheral loads is assigned with a medium and high suitability for load shedding. These loads are either always disconnected from the grid in isolated operation or continue to be operated until there is an imbalance between supply and demand. Then they can be temporarily disconnected from the grid without noticeably affecting the production process. Poor supply quality of the grid can have far-reaching consequences in production and must be taken into account accordingly when integrating power generation and storage facilities. Due to diverse requirements of the consumers for **supply reliability**, the selection of power generation technologies has to be adapted. Consumers can be classified into sensitive loads that allow for supply interruptions of less than one second and insensitive loads that allow for supply interruptions of more than one second. The differentiation of the **required voltage quality** is based on DIN EN 61000-2-4 [30]. Sensitive loads have a high demand on the voltage quality of the network, whereas insensitive loads have standard requirements for the necessary voltage quality of the network. Furthermore, the required **temperature level** has to be considered. Figure 3 summarizes the defined criteria and the distinguishing features with their parametrization. Furthermore, it is described which features relate to which next steps in the procedure for integrating renewable power generation.

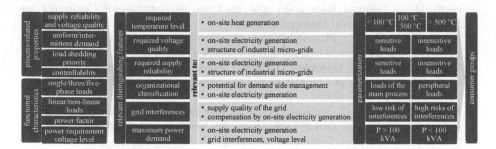

Fig. 3. Characterization of industrial energy consumers in consumer groups.

4 Conclusion and Further Steps

The introduced criteria allow for characterization of the divers consumers in an industrial electrical and thermal grid. Based on the given parametrization, which can be further subdivided, different consumer groups are described. Taking into account invalid combinations of characterization, industrial consumers can be divided into 48 alternative type groups (six features, two or three parametrizations). The consumers within the considered system are typically allocated to several of these groups. Depending on the distribution of consumers among the introduced groups, appropriate generation technologies can be selected and dimensioned. The application of the presented characterization will be carried out exemplarily for a machine tool. Further steps consider a quantitative analysis of the consumers, taking their specific load profile into account.

Acknowledgment. The authors would like to thank the German Federal Ministry of Education and Research (BMBF) and the Project Management Jülich for funding the project *SynErgie* (03SFK3E1-2).

References

Scientific Literature

1. Schulz, J., Scharmer, V., Zaeh, M.F.: Energy self-sufficient manufacturing systems – integration of renewable and decentralized energy generation systems. Procedia Manuf. **43**, 40–47 (2020)
2. Liebl, C., Popp, R.S.H., Zaeh, M.F.: Approach for a systematic energy data generation and evaluation. Procedia CIRP **67**, 63–68 (2018)
3. Chang, G.W., Liu, Y.J., Huang, H.M., et al.: Harmonic analysis of the industrial power system with an AC electric arc furnace. IEEE Power Engineering Society General Meeting (2006)
4. Alfieri, L., Carpinelli, G., Bracale, A., et al.: On the optimal management of the reactive power in an industrial hybrid microgrid: a case study. In: International Symposium on Power Electronics, Electrical Drives, Automation and Motion, pp. 982–989 (2018)
5. Alramlawi, M., Gabash, A., Mohagheghi, E., et al.: Optimal operation of PV-battery-diesel microgrid for industrial loads under grid blackouts. In: International Conference on Environment and Electrical Engineering (2018)
6. Kiank, H., Fruth, W.: Planungsleitfaden für Energieverteilungsanlagen: Konzeption. Umsetzung und Betrieb von Industrienetzen. Publicis, Erlangen (2011)
7. Chhor, J., Schael, M., Einwachter, F., et al.: Modular power conditioner concept for improving quality of supply. In: 41st Annual Conference of the IEEE Industrial Electronics Society, pp. 3497–3502 (2015)
8. Schael, M., Neumann, C., Richmann, S., et al.: Risk evaluation of a chemical production system regarding power quality implications. In: Mediterranean Conference on Power Generation, Transmission, Distribution and Energy Conversion (2016)
9. Mondal, A., Renjit, A.A., Illindala, M.S., et al.: Operation and impact of energy storage system in an industrial microgrid. In: IEEE Industry Applications Society Annual Meeting (2015)
10. Bracale, A., Caramia, P., Mottola, F.: A cost minimization strategy for the control of hybrid AC-DC microgrids in industrial systems. In: International Conference on Clean Electrical Power, pp. 40–47 (2015)
11. Graßl, M.: Bewertung der Energieflexibilität in der Produktion. PhD thesis. Utz, München (2015)
12. Beier, J., Thiede, S., Herrmann, C.: Energy flexibility of manufacturing systems for variable renewable energy supply integration: Real-time control method and simulation. J. Cleaner Prod. **141**, 648–661 (2017)
13. Schenk, M., Wirth, S., Müller, E.: Fabrikplanung und Fabrikbetrieb: Methoden für die wandlungsfähige, vernetzte und ressourceneffiziente Fabrik. Springer, Berlin (2014). https://doi.org/10.1007/978-3-642-05459-4
14. Moog, D., Weber, T., Flum, D., et al.: Energieflexibilitätspotenziale in der Produktionsinfrastruktur. Zeitschrift für wirtschaftlichen Fabrikbetrieb **12**(112), 852–856 (2017)
15. Croce, F., Delfino, B., Fazzini, P.A., et al.: Operation and management of the electric system for industrial plants: an expert system prototype for load-shedding operator assistance. IEEE Trans. Ind. Appl. **3**(37), 701–708 (2001)
16. Haj-ahmed, M.A., Illindala, M.S.: Investigation of protection schemes for flexible distribution of energy and storage resources in an industrial microgrid. IEEE Trans. Ind. Appl. **3**(51), 2071–2080 (2015)

17. Mondal, A., Illindala, M.S., Khalsa, A.S.: Design and operation of smart loads in an industrial microgrid. In: Industrial & Commercial Power Systems Technical Conference (2015)

18. Bayerische Industrie- und Handelskammer: Energiewende im Strommarkt - Chancen für Unternehmen. BIHK-Studie (2017)

19. Matzen, F., Tesch, R.: Industrielle Energiestrategie: Praxishandbuch für Entscheider des produzierenden Gewerbes. Gabler, Wiesbaden (2017)

Statistical Surveys and National Norms

20. Prognose AG: Teilbericht Durchschnittsstrompreise. Forschungsvorhaben: Weiterentwicklung des EEG 2014 im Hinblick auf die Kosten industrieller Verbraucher (2016)

21. Statistisches Bundesamt: Statistisches Jahrbuch Deutschland 2019. Wiesbaden (2019)

22. Bauernhansl, T.: Energieeffizienz in Deutschland - eine Metastudie. Springer, Berlin (2014). https://doi.org/10.1007/978-3-642-55173-4

23. Parent-Thirion, A., Biletta, I., Cabrita, J., et al.: 6th European Working Conditions Survey: 2017 update. Publications Office of the European Union, Luxembourg (2017)

24. Verband der Elektrizitätswirtschaft: Repräsentative VDEW-Lastprofile (1999)

25. Verein Deutscher Ingenieure - Fachbereich Technische Logistik: VDI 3644: Analyse und Planung von Betriebsflächen - Grundlagen, Anwendung und Beispiele (2010)/Analysis and planning of factory areas - Fundamentals, application and examples (2010)

26. Grundig, C.-G.: Fabrikplanung. Carl Hanser Verlag, München (2012)

27. Arbeitsgemeinschaft Energiebilanzen e.V.: Energiebilanz der Bundesrepublik Deutschland 2017 (2019)

28. Statistisches Bundesamt: Produzierendes Gewerbe 2016: Kostenstruktur der Unternehmen des Verarbeitenden Gewerbes sowie des Bergbaus und der Gewinnung von Steinen und Erden. S 4 R 4.3 (2018)

29. Mai, M.: Energieeffizienz in der Wärmenutzung und -erzeugung – ein Langfristprogramm. Ffe-Fachtagung (2015)

30. DIN EN 61000-2-4 VDE 0839-2-4:2003-05 Elektromagnetische Verträglichkeit: Umgebungsbedingungen - Verträglichkeitspegel für niederfrequente leitungsgeführte Störgrößen in Industrieanlagen (2003)/IEC 61000-2-4:2002 Electromagnetic compatibility, 2-4: Environment - Compatibility levels in industrial plants for low-frequency conducted disturbances (2002)

A Simulation Model Supporting
the Production Optimization
for High-Precision Machines Assembly

Andrea Monti, Donatella Corti[(✉)], and Dario Pietraroia

Scuola universitaria professionale della Svizzera Italiana (SUPSI),
Manno, Switzerland
donatella.corti@supsi.ch

Abstract. Simulation has a pivotal role in the Industry 4.0 revolution as a tool to support the decision-making process in the production system. In this paper the model developed for an assembly line of EDM machines is presented and its use to improve the production management approach is described. In particular, simulation has been used to identify a better approach for the dispatching of new job to the line, to optimize the scheduling plan and to develop a training plan for the operators. Obtained results are promising and a further development of the model is foreseen.

Keywords: Modeling and simulation · Planning and control approaches · Smart industry

1 Introduction

In the current competitive scenario, companies producing high-precision machines are facing several challenges such as the high level of customization leading to the need of producing several models and variants or the need to maintain an adequate level of work force occupation and resources saturation in spite of a high demand variability. The exploitation of the advanced technologies brought by the Industry 4.0 provides an enormous support to cope with these multiple requests and to improve the production system performance. Among them, simulation tools are considered a possible decision support system. Aim of this paper is to present the simulation model developed with Arena of an assembly production line of EDM machines of a Swiss company leader in the production of high-precision machines. A recent increase in the number of delays occurred in this line along with the difficulties in efficiently managing the resource allocation led the production manager to believe that a new solution that could take into consideration the evolving dynamics of the relevant parameters is required. Because of the variety of products required by the market, the production mix results to be different month by month. Operators' skills are the key to guarantee high quality standards and the respect of delivery times, yet they feature different individual set of skills. In this context, the use of simulation has been identified as the most promising solution that can provide a complete overview of the system and of the interactions between its elements.

B. Lalic et al. (Eds.): APMS 2020, IFIP AICT 591, pp. 28–36, 2020.
https://doi.org/10.1007/978-3-030-57993-7_4

2   Simulation in the Industry 4.0 Era

A simulation is an approximate imitation of the operation of a process or system [1]: the model represents the system itself, whereas the simulation represents its operation over time [2]. Simulation has been identified as one of the pillars for the Industry 4.0 and should play a central role in industry for the years to come as an enabler of innovative methodologies to plan and control manufacturing systems [3]. In their literature review, [4] identify the main features of the discrete event simulation (DES) that can contribute to the fulfilment of the industry 4.0 agenda, namely automated data exchange, automatic model generation and visualization. On the other hand, as pointed put by [5], industry 4.0 introduces many new modeling demands for DES technology to be able to assess the impact of advanced features, identify areas of risk before implementation, evaluate the performance of alternatives, predict performance to custom criteria, standardize data, systems, and processes, establish a knowledgebase, and aid communication. The use of DES to improve manufacturing performance is widespread (e.g. [6–8]).

3   The Simulation Model

DES has been chosen due to its possibility to simulate the dynamics of a production system in such a way variation in manufacturing processes, assembly times, machine set-ups and breakdowns can be taken into consideration. DES is a kind of simulation involving events (arrival, departure, etc.) that occur at discrete points in time. Often, DES involves random processes (typically, some theoretical statistical distribution). Arena, the simulation software used in this project, is a DES and automation software developed by Systems Modeling and acquired by Rockwell Automation in 2000. It uses the SIMAN processor and simulation language, one of the special-purpose simulation languages (among the others GPSS, Simscript and SLAM).

Main production processes taking place in the production department have been mapped with IDEF0 and their functioning has been discussed with the experts so to start from a shared vision of the system. At the same time relevant data have been prepared integrating existing data bases with missing information (for example the type of options mounted on a machine was not recorded systematically) and *ReadWrite* blocks have been used to read input data from files that are externally editable so to make easier the simulation use by non-experts.

3.1   Assumption and Programming Choices

A set of assumptions on the input data and on the functioning of the system have been introduced to develop and run the model:

- standard values have been used for the process times;
- percentage of non-compliant machines and probabilistic distribution of the associated delays are based on historical data;

- operators' skills have been codified and summarized in a matrix to be used as input file for the Arena environment. The training matrix is binary: each operator is considered to be able or not to perform a certain task, whilst ability can be different depending on the level of expertise
- for each phase, the first free operator is chosen from those able to perform that specific phase (as reported in the relative training matrix);
- at the end of the different lines in the production system there is a shared buffer with a capacity of 6 machines where machines are temporarily stocked waiting for the final test phase.

These assumptions have been introduced to develop the first version of the simulation model, yet most of them can be relaxed in the following versions.

The simulated assembly lines have been graphically represented so that the animation can be used to promote credibility among stakeholders. Given the high relevance of the operators on the line performance a dashboard has been added to monitor some operator's parameters (see Fig. 1).

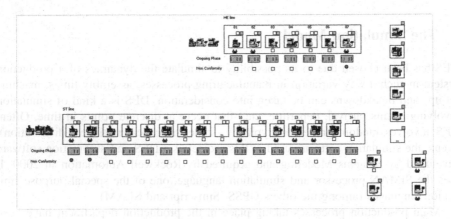

Fig. 1. Simulation model graphics

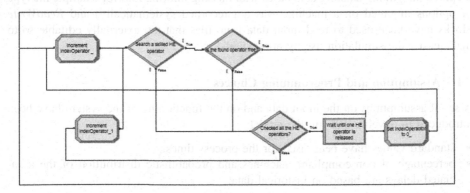

Fig. 2. Operator's search sub-model (Arena code)

The above-mentioned logics of the simulated line have been modelled in Arena by developing differ sub models. As an example, in Fig. 2 the code for the search of and operator able to carry out the considered assembly line is shown. The code crosses data about machine's family and index of the phase to be executed (saved in attributes) with the competence matrix in order to find an operator with the necessary skills. If no adequate operators are the search continues. After having checked all the operators, if nobody is available, the entity stops in a queue waiting a signal informing that an operator has been released and his adequacy is checked.

4 Model Verification and Validation

The criteria to establish the correct number of replications for the model is defined in terms of the percentage difference between two subsequent results that does not have to exceed 3%. This happened from the 10th replication on: the number of replications has been thus set to 10. This number allows to reduce the impact on the results of the main uncertainties of the model that are the statistical distribution of the non-conformities times and the probability of having a non-compliant machine in each assembly phase.

The verification of the model, needed to ensure that the implemented model follows the logic for which it has been designed and it is free of bugs and errors, has been mainly carried out by systematically verifying each logical block of the model, with the Arena debugger and making sure that the machines in the production plan have been processes by the right resources.

The final validation, carried out to confirm that the developed model is suitable for its intended use, has taken into consideration 4 KPIs chosen with the support of experts, namely monthly productivity, assembly and overall lead times, work in progress and resource utilization rates. These KPIs have been validated running the simulation with historical data (production plans of June and July 2019) and all results have been judged as valid by the experts. During the validation it was decided to add the modelling of the periodic absences in the operators' teams (e.g. holidays, illness, medical examinations) given their relevance for the overall process. Based on managers expertise, it has been quantified as one operator per week.

5 Use of the Model to Optimize the Production Management

The developed simulation model allows the company to analyze in a systematic way data coming from the production system taking into account all the sources of variability and, hence, leading to the creation of unprecedented knowledge about the system dynamics. KPIs such as resources utilization rate or average time in queue, that were not measured before, are now made available thanks to the simulation analysis and support the creation of new knowledge for a more informed decision-making process. The model has been tested as a decision support system aimed at optimizing the performance of the assembly line in three different ways: (i) by simulating the efficiency of alternative dispatching rules; (ii) by simulating alternative monthly scheduling plans to minimize bottlenecks and delays; (iii) by developing a training plan for the operators that could optimize the line performance.

The three analysis have been carried out on the line called ST, producing 5 family of products with a volume of around 500 machines/year, that in the last months experienced several delays. The line has 16 stations where 18 assembly tasks, taking from 1.5 to 2 h each, are performed by a team of 11 operators. Each machine can be equipped with up to 5 different options depending on customer's request.

The results are promising and are briefly presented in what follows.

5.1 Comparison of Dispatching Rules

The simulation model has been used to compare the current logic in place (Logic1) to dispatch a job into the line against an alternative one (Logic 2).

Logic 1: As soon as the first station in the line is free, the next machine in the production plan chosen according the earliest shipment date rule is put in the line. As the machine passes through the different stations, the expected delivery date is update. The actual availability of operators and the type of options to be mounted are not considered, thus a time buffer has always to be included in the time estimation. In case of delays, rescheduling of resources is needed and overtime work is requested.

Logic 2: Considering the due date promised to the customer and based on a rough-cut capacity planning analysis, a fixed starting date for each machine is calculated. A new machine enters the line only at the predetermined due date and not when the first station is empty. This logic needs to be supported by the simulation model since it allows to assess more carefully the lead time thanks to the consideration of the different options to be assembled and the different skills of operators. Expected benefits are in terms of better work balancing, reduced WIP and reduced delays.

In order to compare the two logics, a variant of the Arena model for the ST line has been developed and the same production plan of one past month (June 2019) has been used to analyze which of the two performs better. In Table 1 the performance obtained using the two logics are presented. The improvement brought by the use of Logic 2 are evident. In one year time, the time saved (2.7% is around 1 h/machine) can be as high as 400–500 h corresponding to the capacity to produce 10 to 15 additional machines. The reduction of WIP allows to easily manage the work force and the space, whilst avoiding to remove machines form the line before they are complete to meet urgent needs, allows the saving of money and time. The most important benefit is the one related to the saturation of operators: they can be trained in other tasks, can be reassigned to other assembly lines or departments contributing to increase the level of flexibility.

Table 1. Performance comparison between logic 1 and logic 2

Indicator	Logic 1	Logic 2	% difference
Average production LT (hours/machine)	42.38	41.23	−2.71%
WIP (no. of machines)	6.18	5.25	−15.05%
Machines removed before the end	17.2	16.1	−6.40%
Level of operators' saturation	56%	44%	−20.95%

5.2 Comparison of Alternative Scheduling Plans

In the ST line a monthly scheduling plan is currently in use that is developed manually considering the family but not the specific configuration of each machine (set of options is not considered) and individual skills of operators are not considered (the team they belong to is the only information used). Nonetheless, both the production mix and the differential operator's skills have a huge impact on the line performance and, in particular, on the line balancing and the level of saturation of operators that, in turn, influence the generation of possible delays in delivery times.

The simulation considers the number of options and the set of skills of different operators leading in such a way to a more precise and realistic evaluation of the production times. The production plan for the next month (February 2020 at the time the analysis was carried out) has been used to understand how the simulation can support the decision-making process. Differences emerge between the LT provided by the simulation and the LT calculated according to the current approach using average historical data (see Fig. 3). On average, the difference is negative (−0.75) meaning that the more precise calculation of the simulation shows that machines are completed in less time than expected, thus providing a more realistic overview of the finished dates. On the other hand, when the difference is positive, it means that the traditional approach underestimates the actual time it takes (this happens when machines have more options or require particular skills) to complete the machines and possible delays can occur. The simulation tool allows the testing of the feasibility of a production plan taking into account aspects that currently are not considered in the analysis.

KN	Assembly Start	Expected End	Expected LT	Simulated LT	Difference
41622	17.02.2020	25.02.2020	7	6	-1
41623	24.01.2020	03.02.2020	7	7	0
41624	28.01.2020	05.02.2020	7	6	-1
41625	07.02.2020	14.02.2020	6	6	0
41636	03.02.2020	10.02.2020	6	6	0
41637	05.02.2020	12.02.2020	6	8	2
AVERAGE			6.34	5.59	-0.75

Fig. 3. Extract from the scheduling plan of the analyzed month showing differences between expected LT with traditional scheduling and simulated LT

Each month, by simply updating an Excel input file, the company can simulate the production plan of the future month obtaining several interesting inputs (delayed machines, production plan lead time, resources utilization rate) and dynamically improve the production scheduling. Timely identifying the critical machines, it is possible to dedicate to them less saturated resources and shorten their lead time.

Interviewing company's experts, it emerged that on average 3 to 5 machines are behind schedule every month on this line. Using simulation, initially they expect to halve the number of delayed machines resulting in a reduction of 25 units the number of delayed machines per year only for the ST line. Considering the products mix and projecting this result to others lines, the expected reduction of total number of delayed machines (from assembly to test area) can arrive to 35–40 machines per year.

5.3 Optimization of the Training Plan

Delays along the line are often due to lack of operators with the proper set of skills. The time machines spend in a queue is not value-added and needs to be reduced as much as possible. The simulation model has been used to identify for which tasks and operators training is more beneficial in order to reduce queues and, hence, increase the line productivity. Considering again the ST line, a two-month production plan (June and July 2019) has been analyzed focusing on the total waiting time in each of the workstation due to lack of skilled operators (see Fig. 4). Unexpectedly, the main problems are related to the first stations. A matrix has been created where for each operator it is possible to assign up to three skills for each station. The matrix is then used as an input file for the simulation model that can analyze how different training paths impact on the line performance. The definition of the training plan took into consideration some constraints:

- Availability of trainers: for each operator to be trained, an expert operator (trainer) needs to be identified. During training sessions, proper time is needed to transfer the knowledge to the operator.
- Constraints in the training: an operator learns faster if the phases he/she is taught have affinities with those already known. For this reason, defining a plan in advance (without interacting with the line managers) leads to situations that are not feasible.

	Number of Stops	Average Wait Time	Total Wait Time
ST/01	33.7	153.18	5387.4
ST/02	35.5	161.69	6227.848
ST/03	38.1	155.67	6011.577
ST/04	34.2	149.13	5605.6
ST/05	36.9	140.6	5408.064
ST/06	35	139.96	5557.266
ST/07	35.4	87.33	4403.712
ST/08	36.3	92.4	4058.376
ST/09	37.4	82.52	3504.592
ST/10	37.1	88.75	3492.288
ST/11	38.5	82.54	3851.288
ST/12	36.3	77.63	3353.952
ST/13	38	62.05	2405.104
ST/14	37.5	63.55	2272.704
ST/15	37.6	59.27	2497.435
ST/16	38.3	54.7	2333.616
ST/17	35.8	60.06	2316.666
ST/18	38	63.92	2107.926

Fig. 4. Total waiting time (minutes) due to lack of operators in the single stations of the ST line

- System dynamics: given the current logics, it is very difficult to understand if the impact of a proposed solution because of the interactions of lots of elements that generate not predictable results.

Different training plans acting on the set of skills of single operators have been simulated for the same production plan and the resulting waiting time has been recalculated. Improvements have been obtained in terms of average lead time to produce one machine (-2.95%) that is expected to decrease of 1 h. Over a year, such saving can be used to satisfy the demand of additional 10–15 machines.

In the future, the company's experts can modify the operators' training matrix input file of the simulation model in order to simulate alternative training plans and understand the related impact of production's KPIs, non-value-added times and resources utilization. In the short time, company's managers can identify which operators need to be trained on which phases and quantifying the cost-benefit ratio. This tool is extremely powerful because it allows to understand the impact of each change considering the related dynamics and unexpected impacts.

6 Managerial Implications and Conclusions

The current availability of data in the production system makes easier the development of simulation models that can supports the decision-making process. In this paper, the simulation model of an assembly line developed in a company producing high precision machines has been presented and its use in three decisional processes leading to performance improvement has been commented. The simulation tool is first of all a mean to assess production KPIs that allows production managers to dynamically monitor the status of the system and take more informed decisions. Alternative uses of the model to the ones already shown can be identified to support further choices in the production system. Though positive results have been already obtained and corrective actions have been implemented accordingly, the model needs to be further developed and fine-tuned. In particular, additional data collection and programming activities are needed to extend the model to include also the test and metrology phases. Furthermore, additional data sets are needed to analyze the probability distribution of process times to increase the reliability of simulation inputs. So far, performance of the proposed model has been assessed against the current approach in use in the company. Further studies should be carried out to analyze the adequateness of other modelling methods such as queuing theory, Markov chains or casual loops diagrams.

References

1. Banks, J., Carson, J., Nelson, B., Nicol, D.: Discrete-Event System Simulation, p. 3. Prentice Hall (2001)
2. Gómez de Merodio, M., Dodero, J., Mora Núñez, N., Portela Núñez, J.: Innovative Trends in Flipped Teaching and Adaptive Learning, pp. 1–33 (2019)

3. Lugaresi, G., Matta, A.: Real-time simulation in manufacturing systems: challenges and research directions. In: 2018 Winter Simulation Conference (WSC), pp. 3319–3330. IEEE, December 2018

4. Vieira, A.A., Dias, L.M., Santos, M.Y., Pereira, G.A., Oliveira, J.A.: Setting and industry 4.0 research agenda for simulation – a literature review. Int. J. Simul. Model. **17**(3), 377–390 (2018)

5. Sturrock, D.T.: Traditional simulation applications in industry 4.0. In: Gunal, M. (ed.) Simulation for Industry 4.0, pp. 39–54. Springer, Cham (2019). https://doi.org/10.1007/978-3-030-04137-3_3

6. Villagomez, L.E., et al.: Discrete event simulation as a support in the decision making to improve product and process in the automotive industry - a fuel pump component case study. In: Camarinha-Matos, L.M., Afsarmanesh, H., Antonelli, D. (eds.) PRO-VE 2019. IAICT, vol. 568, pp. 572–581. Springer, Cham (2019). https://doi.org/10.1007/978-3-030-28464-0_50

7. Yemane, A., Gebremicheal, G., Hailemicheal, M., Meraha, T.: Productivity improvement through line balancing by using simulation modeling. J. Optim. Ind. Eng. **13**(1), 153–165 (2020)

8. Jurczyk-Bunkowska, M.: Using discrete event simulation for planning improvement in small batch size manufacturing system. In: Królczyk, G.M., Wzorek, M., Król, A., Kochan, O., Su, J., Kacprzyk, J. (eds.) Sustainable Production: Novel Trends in Energy, Environment and Material Systems. SSDC, vol. 198, pp. 19–43. Springer, Cham (2020). https://doi.org/10.1007/978-3-030-11274-5_3

Agent-Based Modeling and Analysis of Dynamic Slab Yard Management in a Steel Factory

Hajime Mizuyama(✉) 📵

Aoyama Gakuin University, 5-10-1 Fuchinobe, Chuoku,
Sagamihara 252-5258, Japan
mizuyama@ise.aoyama.ac.jp

Abstract. The slab yard upstream of a heating furnace in a steel factory has several LIFO buffers and a crane. In managing the yard, slabs are moved from a buffer to another and to the furnace by the crane. Which specific operation should be done and when are determined by the crane operator according to the situation being dynamically changed with arrivals of new slabs to the yard and removals of heated slabs from the furnace. This study models a mathematical aspect of the dynamic decision process for managing the yard, and analyzes the effects of some factors on its performance using a reinforcement learning agent. As a result, it reveals an interaction effect between the arrival rate of slabs and how many steps in the future the agent considers when making decision. The findings obtained by this and similar following studies will be valuable for supporting the actual decision process and for training skills for the process.

Keywords: Slab yard management · LIFO buffers · Reinforcement learning

1 Introduction

There is a heating furnace between casting and rolling processes in a steel factory, and slabs supplied from the casting process are loaded to the rolling process after being adjusted their temperature by the furnace. The yard upstream of the furnace has several stacks, i.e. LIFO buffers, of slabs and a crane, and the slabs are moved by the crane from a stack to another or to the furnace. In the factory considered in this paper, the sequence and timing of arrivals of slabs, those of loading the slabs to the rolling process are not strictly specified in advance. Hence, it becomes a dynamic decision process to determine which slab should be moved to where and when by the crane. This decision process involves quite a few objectives and constraints, such as satisfying the due date assigned to each slab, inserting slabs of similar heating conditions as consecutively as possible, ordering slabs so that the transitions of their width and thickness should fit the requirements of the rolling process. Further, their relative importance depends on the situation. In this factory therefore the dynamic decision process for managing the slab yard is carried out by the operator according to the state of the yard and the furnace, various information exchanged and negotiated with the neighboring processes, etc. Thus, it is an important issue how to effectively support the human decision process

© IFIP International Federation for Information Processing 2020
Published by Springer Nature Switzerland AG 2020
B. Lalic et al. (Eds.): APMS 2020, IFIP AICT 591, pp. 37–44, 2020.
https://doi.org/10.1007/978-3-030-57993-7_5

online as well as how to efficiently train skills necessary for conducting the process offline.

Some authors assumed that the initial arrangement of slabs in the stacks is given and no further slabs will arrive afterwards, and dealt with a planning problem of crane operation for loading the slabs to the furnace and rearranging them in the stacks before loading if necessary. For example, [1–6] proposed how to minimize the number of rearrangement operations (or a certain generalized objective, such as a weighted sum of the number of rearrangement operations and the total moving distance of the crane) with satisfying a specified constraint on the loading sequence. Other authors considered both departures and arrivals of slabs. For instance, [7] minimized the number of crane movements under a given arrival schedule and a specified loading sequence. [8, 9] minimized the number of rearrangement operations under given arrival and loading sequences. [10, 11] minimized the number of crane movements under a given arrival schedule and specified loading due dates. However, all of these earlier studies capture the problem of managing the slab yard as a static optimization problem, which is essentially a different setting from the dynamic decision process to be addressed in this paper. Further, they all aim at automating and computerizing operational planning and lacked the perspective of how to support a human decision-making and how to train skills for it.

Why the task of managing the slab yard is deferred to a human in this factory is not only because it is a dynamic decision process with quite a few objectives and constraints. It is also and more essentially because various conditions and parameters necessary for formulating the decision-making problem underlying the task, such as the relative importance among the objectives and constraints, how to parameterize the uncertain future state, etc. are not fixed a priori and dependent on the changing situation, and hence the human's informal and intuitive estimate on them made on the fly in the shop floor is often helpful and can work favorably. Further, relevant information to the estimate can be attained not only by careful observation of the yard, but also by communicating and negotiating with the managers of neighboring processes. These proactive information collection and intervention can be naturally carried out by a human but are still quite difficult to automate. On the other hand, the decision-making problem itself obtained by setting the parameters and conditions with the help of fuzzy information processing by a human is still a sort of mathematical optimization problem. When considering how to support this decision-making, it will be difficult to take an approach which provides potential solutions to the human in charge, because the problem to be solved cannot be clearly captured a priori and will become complete only after being complemented by the decision maker's intuition. A promising alternative would be to provide an adequate solution framework to be taken when a human cognitively derives a solution to the problem.

Thus, this paper adopts a reinforcement learning model [12] for capturing the framework of the dynamic decision process for managing the slab yard and tries to analyze what factors affect its performance using the model. Due to the sparkling success of recent deep learning techniques and their application to reinforcement learning, (deep) reinforcement learning approaches are actively applied even to manufacturing systems. Most of such applied researches aim at enhancing and automating dynamic scheduling and dispatching [13–24]. This paper can be distinguished against them in that it utilizes a reinforcement learning model as a framework for analyzing how a human addresses a dynamic decision making process. In the remainder, the slab yard and its management task are modelled, and then a reinforcement leaning agent is introduced. Further, numerical experiments and their results are presented, and finally the paper is concluded with potentially fruitful future research directions.

2   A Simple Model of Slab Yard and Its Management

This section provides a model of the dynamic decision process for managing the slab yard, which is considerably simplified but captures essential features of the mathematical aspect of the actual process. The outline of the model is described below.

- The heating furnace and the following rolling process are grouped into a virtual single machine for simplicity, and the slab yard is captured as a set of the machine, several buffers, and a crane.
- The buffers in the yard is classified into an entrance buffer, four intermediate buffers, and a loading buffer to the machine. Further, there is assumed to be an invisible queue upstream of the entrance buffer.
- The entrance and intermediate buffers are LIFO, and the loading buffer and the queue are FIFO. The capacity of the buffers is set to four, except that the queue has an infinite capacity.
- Slabs arrive randomly and enter into the queue. The time between consecutive arrivals follows an exponential distribution with $1/\lambda \in \{10, 11, 12\}$. Slabs in the queue are automatically moved to the entrance buffer one by one and the cycle time of this movement operation is four.
- Each slab has information on its type ($\in \{1, 2, 3, 4\}$) and due (specified by adding a random variable from a uniform distribution $[60, 720]$ to the arrival time).
- Slabs in the loading buffer are automatically loaded to the machine one by one when the machine becomes available. The processing time of each slab is six irrespective of the type.
- A setup operation is necessary before loading a slab if its type is different from that of the immediately earlier one, and its time depends heavily on whether the type is changed in an increasing direction ($= 6$) or a decreasing one ($= 60$).
- The order of processing the slabs is not rigidly specified a priori, but only loosely constrained by their due dates.
- The possible route of the crane is represented by a star graph, whose leaves correspond to the entrance, intermediate and loading buffers. The traveling time of each edge of the graph is the same.
- Every movement cycle of the crane is to start from the center node, move to a buffer, take out a slab from the buffer, travel to another buffer via the center node, release the slab there, and come back to the center node. The cycle time of this movement is four.
- A unitary bonus is given to the operator each time a slab is loaded to the machine.
- A tardiness penalty ($=$ tardiness $\times 1/30$) is incurred for each slab which cannot be loaded to the machine before its due date.

- The objective function to be maximized is the score defined by subtracting the total tardiness penalty from the total bonus attained in a specified period of time ($= 60 \times 24$) starting from a randomly set initial state.

3   Crane Operator Reinforcement Learning Agent

3.1   Actions

The crane operator needs to decide what action to take next in every cycle time. Possible actions are to wait in the center node for a cycle or to move a slab from a buffer (origin) to another (target). When "to move" is chosen, the origin and target buffers need to be specified. Neither the loading buffer nor empty buffers cannot be chosen as the origin. Hence, the origin must be selected among nonempty entrance or intermediate buffers. Similarly, the target must be selected among non-fully occupied intermediate or loading buffers, since neither the entrance nor fully occupied buffers cannot be specified as the target.

3.2   Rewards

How much reward the crane operator receives in each cycle can be defined with the score, i.e. the value calculated by subtracting the tardiness penalty from the loading bonus. More specifically, the reward is defined by the difference of the score between before and after a corresponding action is taken.

3.3   State Features

The state of the yard changes with actions taken by the crane operator, arrivals of new slabs, and accompanied events, such as moving a slab to the entrance buffer, loading one to the machine, starting and finishing a setup operation, starting and finishing processing a slab on the machine, etc. Further, a same state may be perceived differently, and it may affect the performance of the decision process. For simplicity, this paper assumes the operator perceives the state of each buffer with the features below.

The level of the buffer, the number of slab types in it, the number of times the type changes in an increasing direction when taking out slabs one by one, that in a decreasing direction, the average due date, the number of times a consecutive pair of slabs are lined up in the order of their due dates, that in the opposite order, the number of slabs whose due date is earlier than any slab in the loading buffer, their maximum depth from the top, the number of slabs which cannot satisfy their due date without rearranging their position, their maximum depth, the maximum estimated tardiness, the depth of the slab whose estimated tardiness is the longest, the sum of the expected tardiness of all slabs, the sum of the slack times of all slabs

3.4   State Value Function

The discounted sum of the rewards which the crane operator in a specific state will achieve in the future if she/he follows a certain policy from that on is called the state value. This paper approximates the state value function by a standard multi-layer neural network whose input is the state feature vector and output is the state value.

3.5 Myopic and Forward-Looking Policies

If arrivals of new slabs are ignored, the crane operator can envision the state (or afterstate) attained as the result of taking an action from a state. Similarly, the state attained by taking another action from the afterstate, the next state attained by further taking another action, etc. can also be estimated. Thus, it is quite natural to assume that the crane operator chooses an action so that the value of an afterstate be maximized. The question is which afterstate it is. In other words, of how many steps in the future an afterstate is considered?

3.6 Learning Algorithm

This paper utilizes $TD(\lambda)$ algorithm, which learns the state value function according to so called λ return [25]. This algorithm is suitable for a dynamic decision process where afterstates can be defined as described above, and is confirmed to be effective in real-life problems such as backgammon [26].

4 Numerical Experiments

This section conducts numerical experiments using the mathematical models described above and analyzes what factors affect the performance of the decision process of managing the slab yard. Potential factors include how the state is perceived, how much discounting rate is used for calculating the state value, how many future steps are considered in each decision, etc., but this paper focuses on the effects of the number of forward-looking steps with changing the arrival rate of slabs. More specifically, experiments are conducted under nine different conditions obtained by combining three levels of the mean time between arrivals of slabs ($\in \{10, 11, 12\}$) and three levels of the number of future steps considered ($\in \{1, 2, 3\}$).

Other settings are determined according to preliminary experiments. For instance, a standard fully connected multi-layer network with two intermediate layers of 40 nodes is used as the structure of the neural network approximating the state value function. The network uses a sigmoid function as the activation function of every node. The initial value of the learning rate is set to 0.00001 and is decreased exponentially by the ratio of 0.999 in every episode. The learning process is continued up to 1000 episodes. Since the crane operator chooses an action (and a learning step is taken) for about $(60 \times 24)/4 = 360$ times in each episode, this means that the total number of learning steps is about 360,000. The discounting rate for calculating the state value is set to 0.99, and the value of parameter λ for learning is set to 0.7.

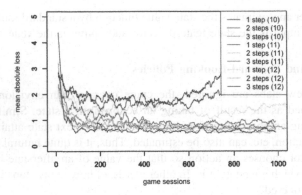

Fig. 1. Mean absolute losses.

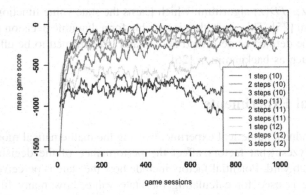

Fig. 2. Mean game scores.

Figure 1 and Fig. 2 show the results. In the figure legends, the number of future steps considered and, in the parenthesis, the mean time between arrivals (i.e. the inverse of the arrival rate) of slabs are indicated. The vertical axis of Fig. 1 shows a moving average of the mean absolute loss of each episode, that of Fig. 2 represents a moving average of the final score of each episode. A most clear result is that the smaller the loss the higher the score. It is also natural that the shorter the mean time between arrivals and the more frequently slabs arrive, the harder the problem and the lower the average score. In addition, it is observed that the average score obtained by the myopic policy with only one step forward-looking is inferior to those obtained by forward-looking policies considering two or more steps in the future irrespective of the mean time between arrivals. Looking into further details reveals that there is no noticeable difference between the policies considering two steps and three steps when the mean time between arrivals is long but, when it is decreased to 10, the superiority of considering three steps appears. These results imply the effectiveness of forward-looking policies and that it depends on the congestion of the yard how many future steps should be taken into consideration.

5 Conclusions

This paper mathematically modelled the dynamic decision process for managing a slab yard in a steel factory and the process of how an operator learns a policy for the decision process. It then analyzed what factors affect the performance of the decision process by conducting numerical experiments using the models. As a result, forward-looking decisions are shown to be effective. Further, it depends on the congestion of the yard how many future steps should be taken into consideration.

The numerical experiments conducted in this paper focused mainly on the effects of the number of forward-looking steps considered. It would be also interesting and valuable to investigate the effects of other factors, such as how the state is perceived, how much discounting rate is used for calculating the state value. Further, it would be important to study how to utilize the findings obtained by this and following studies for supporting the actual decision process and for training skills for the process.

References

1. Tang, L., Liu, J., Rong, A., Yang, Z.: An effective heuristic algorithm to minimise stack shuffles in selecting steel slabs from the slab yard for heating and rolling. J. Oper. Res. Soc. **52**, 1091–1097 (2001)
2. Tang, L., Liu, J., Rong, A., Yang, Z.: Modelling and a genetic algorithm solution for the slab stack shuffling problem when implementing steel rolling schedules. Int. J. Prod. Res. **40**(7), 1583–1595 (2002)
3. Singh, K.A., Tiwari, S.M.K.: Modelling the slab stack shuffling problem in developing steel rolling schedules and its solution using improved parallel genetic algorithms. Int. J. Prod. Econ. **91**, 135–147 (2004)
4. Tang, L., Ren, H.: Modelling and a segmented dynamic programming-based heuristic approach for the slab stack shuffling problem. Comput. Oper. Res. **37**, 368–375 (2010)
5. Cheng, X., Tang, L.: A scatter search algorithm for the slab stack shuffling problem. In: Tan, Y., Shi, Y., Tan, K.C. (eds.) ICSI 2010. LNCS, vol. 6145, pp. 382–389. Springer, Heidelberg (2010). https://doi.org/10.1007/978-3-642-13495-1_47
6. Tang, L., Zhao, R., Liu, J.: Models and algorithms for shuffling problems in steel plants. Naval Res. Logist. **59**, 502–524 (2012)
7. König, F.G., Lübbecke, M., Möhring, R., Schäfer, G., Spenke, I.: Solutions to real-world instances of PSPACE-complete stacking. In: Arge, L., Hoffmann, M., Welzl, E. (eds.) ESA 2007. LNCS, vol. 4698, pp. 729–740. Springer, Heidelberg (2007). https://doi.org/10.1007/978-3-540-75520-3_64
8. Kim, B.-I., Koo, J., Sambhajirao, H.P.: A simplified steel plate stacking problem. Int. J. Prod. Res. **49**(17), 5133–5151 (2011)
9. Lu, C., Zhang, R., Liu, S.: A 0-1 integer programming model and solving strategies for the slab storage problem. Int. J. Prod. Res. **54**(8), 2366–2376 (2016)
10. Rei, R.J., Pedroso, J.P.: Heuristic search for the stacking problem. Int. Trans. Oper. Res. **19**, 379–395 (2012)
11. Rei, R.J., Pedroso, J.P.: Tree search for the stacking problem. Ann. Oper. Res. **203**, 371–388 (2013)
12. Sutton, R.S., Barto, A.G.: Reinforcement Learning: An Introduction, 2nd edn. The MIT Press, Cambridge (2018)

13. Wang, Y.-C., Usher, J.M.: Application of reinforcement learning for agent-based production scheduling. Eng. Appl. Artif. Intell. **18**, 73–82 (2005)
14. Gabel, T., Riedmiller, M.: Distributed policy search reinforcement learning for job-shop scheduling tasks. Int. J. Prod. Res. **50**, 41–61 (2012)
15. Qu, S., Wang, J., Govil, S., Leckie, J.O.: Optimized adaptive scheduling of a manufacturing process system with multi-skill workforce and multiple machine types: an ontology-based, multi-agent reinforcement learning approach. Procedia CIRP **57**, 55–60 (2016)
16. Shahrabi, J., Adibi, M.A., Mahootchi, M.: A reinforcement learning approach to parameter estimation in dynamic job shop scheduling. Comput. Ind. Eng. **110**, 75–82 (2017)
17. Ou, X., Chang, Q., Arinez, J., Zou, J.: Gantry work cell scheduling through reinforcement learning with knowledge-guided reward setting. IEEE Access **6**, 14699–14709 (2018)
18. Stricker, N., Kuhnle, A., Sturm, R., Friess, S.: Reinforcement learning for adaptive order dispatching in the semiconductor industry. CIRP Ann. Manuf. Technol. **67**, 511–514 (2018)
19. Waschneck, B., et al.: Optimization of global production scheduling with deep reinforcement learning. Procedia CIRP **72**, 1264–1269 (2018)
20. Ou, X., Chang, Q., Chakraborty, N.: Simulation study on reward function of reinforcement learning in gantry work cell scheduling. J. Manuf. Syst. **50**, 1–8 (2019)
21. Minguillona, F.E., Lanza, G.: Coupling of centralized and decentralized scheduling for robust production in agile production systems. Procedia CIRP **79**, 385–390 (2019)
22. Kuhnle, A., Röhrig, N., Lanza, G.: Autonomous order dispatching in the semiconductor industry using reinforcement learning. Procedia CIRP **79**, 391–396 (2019)
23. Kuhnle, A., Schäfer, L., Stricker, N., Lanza, G.: Design, implementation and evaluation of reinforcement learning for an adaptive order dispatching in job shop manufacturing systems. Procedia CIRP **81**, 234–239 (2019)
24. Chen, Y., et al.: Can sophisticated dispatching strategy acquired by reinforcement learning?: A case study in dynamic courier dispatching system. In: Proceedings of the 18th International Conference on Autonomous Agents and Multi-Agent Systems, AAMAS 2019, pp. 1395–1403 (2019)
25. Tesauro, G.: Practical issues in temporal difference learning. Mach. Learn. **8**(3), 257–277 (1992)
26. Tesauro, G.: Temporal difference learning and TD-Gammon. Commun. ACM **38**(3), 58–68 (1995)

A Simulation Analysis of Part Feeding to Assembly Stations with Vertical Robotic Storage and Retrieval Systems

Elena Tappia, Emilio Moretti[✉], and Marco Melacini

Department of Management, Economics and Industrial Engineering,
Politecnico di Milano, 20156 Milan, Italy
emilio.moretti@polimi.it

Abstract. The evolution of customer requirements has led companies to pursue mass customization and personalization strategies, increasing the complexity of part feeding operations in assembly systems. At the same time, emerging technologies, based on mobile robots, promise to support material handling activities in an efficient yet flexible manner. This paper studies part feeding to assembly stations with Vertical Robotic Storage and Retrieval Systems (VRSRS), a new technology that allows automating both the storage and the internal transportation activities with the same fleet of mobile robots. We develop a Discrete Event Simulation model of a system made of a Central Warehouse replenishing supermarkets which, in turn, supply mixed-model assembly stations. Through this model, we carry out experiments showing a clear trade-off between the number of robots, which affects the overall investment in the system, and the supermarkets size, which affects space occupation in the shop floor, where space is a critical resource. We also estimate the replenishment lead time and the downtime of assembly stations, showing that this system performs best when small production orders are issued and could therefore be a suitable solution to support part feeding activities in a mass customization context.

Keywords: Parts feeding · Factory logistics · Mobile robots · Supermarket warehouses · Discrete event simulation

1 Introduction

The evolution of customer requirements has led companies to pursue mass customization and personalization strategies. Although beneficial from a sales perspective, the implementation of such strategies may increase the complexity of operations within assembly plants [1]. In fact, it calls for a sharp rise in the number of part variants and it entails assembling goods in small batches, so as to offer a wide product range without overly increasing inventories [2]. In this context, companies are adopting mixed-model assembly lines, where a single line is able to assemble several product variants or models [3]. To cope with these challenges, and since the available space at the border of the lines is normally scarce [4], part feeding systems are shifting towards frequent deliveries of small quantities of parts, like boxes or totes, to assembly stations [5, 6].

© IFIP International Federation for Information Processing 2020
Published by Springer Nature Switzerland AG 2020
B. Lalic et al. (Eds.): APMS 2020, IFIP AICT 591, pp. 45–53, 2020.
https://doi.org/10.1007/978-3-030-57993-7_6

This part feeding policy is often supported by the use of supermarkets, i.e. decentralized warehouses located in the shop floor allowing to reduce delivery lead times [7, 8]. The related academic literature is mainly focused on supermarkets design (e.g. [9, 10]) and on the scheduling, loading, and routing of tugger trains for parts delivery to assembly stations (e.g. [11, 12]). Some research gaps still need to be addressed. In particular, while emerging technologies, based on mobile robots, promise to support material handling activities in an efficient yet flexible manner, there is a gap about the application of such technologies in part feeding systems. Among these technologies, Vertical Robotic Storage and Retrieval Systems (VRSRS) are extremely interesting in this context because they allow automating both the storage and the internal transportation activities with the same fleet of mobile robots, thus seamlessly integrating the two activities. This is possible since the robots, carrying totes, can both roam the shop floor and navigate inside the storage racks, moving horizontally and vertically (Fig. 1). This system has been studied in literature in relation with distribution centers only by [13]: they develop a queuing network-based model of VRSRS, but they neglect the possibility for robots to navigate outside the racks. Only one contribution has addressed the deployment of VRSRS in a factory environment [14], but it models the replenishment of supermarkets from the central warehouse, without considering the transportation of totes to assembly stations.

(a)   (b)

Fig. 1. Mobile robots inside (a) and outside (b) the storage racks (source: Exotec Solutions)

This research aims to assess the performance of a part feeding system to assembly stations based on VRSRS. We study the system through Discrete Event Simulation (DES), and we measure its performances in terms of replenishment lead time and downtime of assembly stations due to lack of materials.

The remainder of this paper is organised as follows. Section 2 gives an overview of the system under analysis, while Sect. 3 describes the developed simulation model. Section 4 reports the results of our analysis: we test alternative configurations of the part feeding system, differing among each other due to the supermarkets size, and we evaluate the impact of production order size (i.e. number of assembled products per order) on system performance. Finally, Sect. 5 includes conclusions and directions for future research.

2 System Description

Figure 2 shows the layout of the system considered in this paper. It consists of a central warehouse (CW) replenishing supermarkets which, in turn, supply mixed-model assembly stations. Each type of stations can make multiple product models. We assume that there are two stations of each type, facing away from each other (e.g. station "A" and station "B" in the figure), and they share the same stock. The product models made by one type of stations cannot be assembled by stations of a different type.

All warehouses are VRSRS made of one aisle (supermarkets) or multiple aisles (CW), with two single-deep storage racks per aisle. Each rack is divided into storage columns and storage levels. Totes are stored randomly within the warehouses, i.e. the probability of accessing any column or level is based on the uniform distribution. Each CW aisle has an input/output (i/o) point for robots, while each supermarket has an input point, facing the CW, and an output point, facing assembly stations.

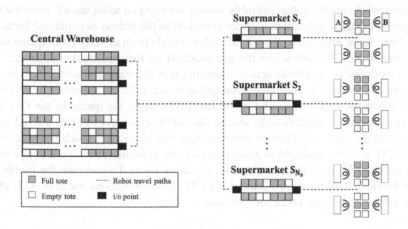

Fig. 2. Part feeding system layout

Robots handle mono-item totes, denoted as "full totes", and perform single-command cycles inside storage racks: they enter the storage aisle input point, travel horizontally to reach the storage column, climb the rack up to the storage level where they retrieve or store the tote, and then travel vertically and horizontally towards the output point. To avoid deadlocks, one robot at a time can access a supermarket or a CW aisle.

Robots can also travel outside the racks, following the bi-directional paths shown in Fig. 2, so as to replenish supermarkets and to feed assembly stations with full totes. Supermarket replenishment works according to the kanban system, as in previous studies (e.g. [5]): whenever a tote is retrieved from the supermarket, its replenishment from the CW is triggered. Similarly, part feeding to assembly stations is controlled through a two-bin inventory system [15]: two totes per each part type are stored between each couple of stations of the same type and, whenever a tote is empty, its replenishment from the supermarket is triggered. Each supermarket supplies four assembly stations.

Finally, we assume that the management of empty totes at the assembly stations is out of scope. For instance, empty totes could be stacked on pallets next to each assembly station and forklift trucks could be used to periodically collect them.

3   Simulation Model

The DES model of the system was implemented in MATLAB-Simulink, using the SimEvents library. As shown in Fig. 3, it is made of four main parts. The first part, highlighted in green, models the generation of robots at the start of the simulation and their travel inside the CW. Robots are modelled as entities of the system: after they are generated, they queue up before the CW in a First In First Out (FIFO) robot queue, waiting to be matched with tote replenishment orders. An order can be issued by either an assembly station or a supermarket. In the former case, if the robot queue in front of the supermarket supplying the assembly station is empty, a robot travels from the CW robot queue to that supermarket, in order to replenish the station as explained further in this section. In the latter case, instead, the robot travels from the CW robot queue to the input point of the CW aisle where the tote required by the supermarket is stored. This travel is modelled as an infinite server, assuming that there are no interferences among robots outside the racks. The same assumption is made for all the other robot movements outside the racks. Thus, the robot travel time from the queue to the CW aisle only depends on the selected aisle and on the robot speed. As in [13], a fixed speed equal to 1 m/s is assumed. Then, to simulate the robot movement inside the racks, each of the 7 CW aisles is modelled as a single server, so as to allow its access to one entity at a time. The CW maximum height is set equal to 10 m. To compute the number of storage levels and all the dimensions of the CW, the assumptions made by [13] about storage locations size are taken into account.

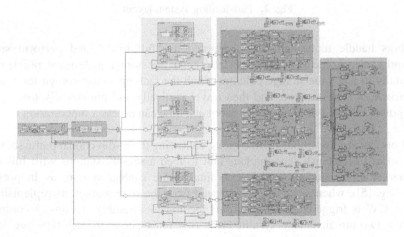

Fig. 3. DES model of the robot-based part feeding system, implemented in Simulink (Color figure online)

The second part of the model, highlighted in yellow in Fig. 3, simulates the travel of the robot from the i/o point of a CW aisle to the input point of a supermarket and inside the supermarket. The travel from the CW to the supermarket is modelled as an infinite server, whose service time depends on the robot speed and on the distance along the path shown in Fig. 2 (120 m for the cross-aisle connecting the CW with the supermarket area, plus the distance from the CW aisle i/o point to this cross-aisle and from this cross-aisle to the supermarket input point). Three supermarkets, evenly distributed along the shop floor, are considered in the model. Supermarkets are modelled as single servers, whose service times depend on the same assumptions made for the CW aisles. After storing the tote and exiting the supermarket from its output point, robots queue up in front of the supermarket, waiting for a replenishment order. When a replenishment order is received from an assembly station, as soon as the supermarket is idle and the required tote is available, the robot enters the supermarket, picks up the tote and exits the supermarket. A signal is sent to the CW to trigger the tote replenishment. The maximum supermarket height is set equal to 5 m, accounting for the real industrial applications. Based on the supermarket storage capacity, the number of storage columns is determined. We assume that the supermarket is full at the start of the simulation.

The model section highlighted in blue in Fig. 3 simulates the travel of the robot between the supermarket output point and the assembly station, the assembly activity and the ensuing consumption of parts. The distance between a supermarket and a station is assumed to be fixed (15 m). After delivering the full tote to the assembly station, the robot either returns to the queue in front of the supermarket, if this queue is empty, or travels to the queue in front of the CW. After a tote is delivered to the assembly station, new entities are generated, corresponding to the parts stored in that tote, that queue up before the station. As regards the assembly activity, we assume that each type of assembly station can make four different product models and each model is made of two parts replenished through the robot-based feeding system: a first part specific of that model and a second one shared with another model assembled at the same station. The assembly of a product may start when three conditions have been verified through a gate: a signal has been received to start the assembly (as explained later in this section) and the two parts are available at the station. These parts are subtracted from the total stock available at the station through an entity terminator, so as to model parts consumption: when all the parts in a tote have been used up, the replenishment from the supermarket is triggered. The number of parts stored in a tote is assumed to be equal to 10, for part types specific of one product model, and to 20, for part types shared by two models. Each couple of stations of the same type is modelled as a dual server, meaning that one product at a time can be assembled at each station. Service times of the assembly stations are exponentially distributed, as in previous simulation analyses of production systems (e.g. [16]), with an average of 30 s.

The model part highlighted in pink in Fig. 3 simulates the arrival of production orders (i.e. the demand). An entity generator creates orders with exponentially distributed inter-arrival times. An order is assigned to one of the product models through an entity output switch, according to a uniform distribution. Then, an entity replicator generates a number of entities corresponding to the production order size, i.e. the number of assembled products per order. The order size is fixed for all the orders during a simulation. Based on the product model, the entities of an order are assigned to an assembly station and wait in a FIFO queue before a single server. When the first entity enters this server, a signal is sent to the assembly station (model section highlighted in blue) to trigger assembly activities. After they exit the single server, entities are terminated.

Each run of the model simulates an 8-h shift. The model was verified and then validated by comparing its output, in terms of assembled products per shift, with the theoretical output, i.e. the overall demand per shift. This comparison was made considering a number of robots high enough to avoid that robots were the bottleneck in the system. It was found that the difference between the simulation output and the theoretical one is always below 5%, thus mostly due to the stochasticity of the assembly time.

4 Results Discussion

4.1 Relationship Between Supermarkets Size and Number of Robots

The main design variables of this system are the supermarkets size, S_s, i.e. the number of totes that can be stored in each supermarket, and the number of robots, N_R, needed to fulfill all the replenishment orders. Once fixed the number of supermarkets, S_s determines space occupation in the shop floor, where space is a critical resource, while robots are the main component of the investment in this system [14]. Thus, the first experiments are aimed at studying the relationship between these two variables.

Figure 4 shows the results when the average demand is 960 orders per shift and the order size is 10 products per order. The colored areas inside the chart represent the difference between the system output, i.e. assembled products per shift, and the required output, i.e. overall demand. In particular, the dark blue area corresponds to the combinations of S_s and N_R for which the system is able to fulfill demand (difference below 5%, that can be ascribed to the stochasticity of demand). Results show a trade-off between S_s and N_R: by increasing N_R, a lower S_s is needed to fulfill demand because the throughput capacity of the system increases; vice versa, the higher S_s the lower the needed N_R, since more totes are stored in the shop floor and thus a lower speed of supermarket replenishment activities has a lesser impact on overall system performances.

Results also show that, given an adequate investment in the robot fleet, the system can fulfill demand with extremely small supermarkets (in the scenario of Fig. 4, even less than 50 totes per supermarket, corresponding to less than 5 m^2 per supermarket).

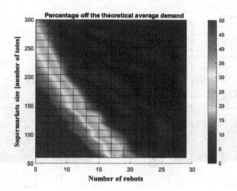

Fig. 4. Relationship between supermarkets size and number of robots (Color figure online)

4.2 Relationship Between Order Size and System Performance

One of the effects of mass customization is a smaller size of production orders. Therefore, with the second group of experiments we study how system performances change when varying the number of assembled products per order and the number of robots. Performance measures encompass the average replenishment lead time (LT) and the average downtime of the assembly stations due to lack of parts (DT). LT is defined as the average time elapsed between a request for tote replenishment by an assembly station and the tote delivery to the station. DT is defined as the percentage of the 8-h shift during which assembly stations are not working due to lack of materials.

In order to plot results and make them comparable, the overall demand in terms of assembled products per shift was fixed for all the scenarios and the number of orders per shift was varied accordingly. For instance, Fig. 5 shows results for a demand equal to 9,600 products per shift and S_S equal to 150 totes: LT and DT improve when decreasing the production order size, going from the red areas (where LT can be as high as 100 s and DT can reach 15% of the 8-h shift) to the dark blue ones (LT close to 30 s and DT close to 0%). Therefore, results show that this system performs better with a lower order size. This is due to the nature of the system itself, which is designed to handle small quantities of several part types: big production orders would overly stress the system since they would require a high quantity of one or few part types, exceeding the quantity stored at the border of the stations and possibly even the quantity stored in the supermarkets.

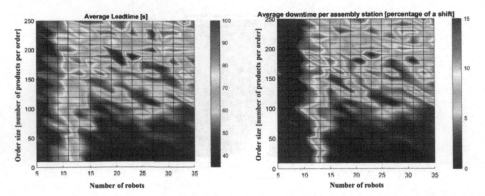

Fig. 5. Relationship between order size and LT (on the left), DT (on the right) (Color figure online)

5 Conclusion

New material handling technologies, based on mobile robots, promise to improve the efficiency of part feeding activities in the context of mass customization and personalization. This paper is the first to study a part feeding system to assembly stations based on VRSRS. We develop a DES model of a system made of a CW replenishing supermarkets that, in turn, supply mixed-model assembly stations.

Through the experiments we conduct, we show the trade-off between the number of robots and the supermarkets size, concluding that, if an adequate investment in the robot fleet is made, this system is able to effectively supply assembly stations even with extremely small supermarkets, thus saving space in the shop floor. Furthermore, we show that this system performs best, in terms of replenishment lead time and downtime of assembly stations, with small production orders, and therefore may be suitable to support part feeding activities in a mass-customized system.

The main limitations of this study are related to the assumptions made in the model development; future research could enlarge the experiments performing sensitivity analyses to understand how our results change when varying parameters. Moreover, future developments could include cost analyses or model extensions to test different layouts of the system, considering a different number of supermarkets or even direct deliveries of totes from the CW to assembly stations.

References

1. Emde, S., Schneider, M.: Just-in-time vehicle routing for in-house part feeding to assembly lines. Transp. Sci. **52**(3), 657–672 (2018)
2. Fathi, M., Rodríguez, V., Fontes, D.B., Alvarez, M.J.: A modified particle swarm optimisation algorithm to solve the part feeding problem at assembly lines. Int. J. Prod. Res. **54**(3), 878–893 (2016)

3. Faccio, M.: The impact of production mix variations and models varieties on the parts-feeding policy selection in a JIT assembly system. Int. J. Adv. Manuf. Technol. **72**(1–4), 543–560 (2014)

4. Faccio, M., Gamberi, M., Bortolini, M., Pilati, F.: Macro and micro-logistic aspects in defining the parts-feeding policy in mixed-model assembly systems. Int. J. Serv. Oper. Manag. **31**(4), 433–462 (2018)

5. Emde, S.: Scheduling the replenishment of just-in-time supermarkets in assembly plants. OR Spectr. **39**(1), 321–345 (2016). https://doi.org/10.1007/s00291-016-0455-x

6. Golz, J., Gujjula, R., Günther, H., Rinderer, S., Ziegler, M.: Part feeding at high-variant mixed-model assembly lines. Flex. Serv. Manuf. J. **24**(2), 119–141 (2012)

7. Battini, D., Boysen, N., Emde, S.: Just-in-time supermarkets for part supply in the automobile industry. J. Manag. Control **24**(2), 209–217 (2013)

8. Sali, M., Sahin, E.: Line feeding optimization for just in time assembly lines: an application to the automotive industry. Int. J. Prod. Econ. **174**, 54–67 (2016)

9. Emde, S., Boysen, N.: Optimally locating in-house logistics areas to facilitate JIT-supply of mixed-model assembly lines. Int. J. Prod. Econ. **135**(1), 393–402 (2012)

10. Nourmohammadi, A., Eskandari, H., Fathi, M.: Design of stochastic assembly lines considering line balancing and part feeding with supermarkets. Eng. Optim. **51**(1), 63–83 (2019)

11. Diefenbach, H., Emde, S., Glock, C.H.: Loading tow trains ergonomically for just-in-time part supply. Eur. J. Oper. Res. (2019). https://doi.org/10.1016/j.ejor.2019.12.009

12. Emde, S., Gendreau, M.: Scheduling in-house transport vehicles to feed parts to automotive assembly lines. Eur. J. Oper. Res. **260**(1), 255–267 (2017)

13. Azadeh, K., Roy, D., De Koster, R.: Design, modeling, and analysis of vertical robotic storage and retrieval systems. Transp. Sci. **53**(5), 1213–1234 (2019)

14. Moretti, E., Tappia, E., Mauri, M., Melacini, M.: A performance model for mobile robot-based part feeding systems to supermarkets. Flex. Serv. Manuf. J. (Submitted)

15. Limère, V., Landeghem, H.V., Goetschalckx, M., Aghezzaf, E., McGinnis, L.F.: Optimising part feeding in the automotive assembly industry: deciding between kitting and line stocking. Int. J. Prod. Res. **50**(15), 4046–4060 (2012)

16. Kundu, K., Rossini, M., Portioli-Staudacher, A.: A study of a kanban based assembly line feeding system through integration of simulation and particle swarm optimization. Int. J. Ind. Eng. Comput. **10**(3), 421–442 (2019)

Process Mining in Manufacturing: Goals, Techniques and Applications

Darko Stefanovic[ID], Dusanka Dakic[✉][ID], Branislav Stevanov[ID], and Teodora Lolic[ID]

Faculty of Technical Sciences, University of Novi Sad,
Trg Dositeja Obradovica 6, 21000 Novi Sad, Serbia
dakic.dusanka@uns.ac.rs

Abstract. Process mining is a discipline positioned between business process management and data mining. It applies algorithms on real event data extracted from information systems that support business processes, to construct as-is process models, and improve them automatically. The benefits can be versatile, from gaining insight into the real execution of a process, to detecting process bottlenecks, activity loops, or social networks of process resources. Several literature reviews have focused on the application of process mining in the healthcare industry and on process mining discipline in general, without the reviews of other application domains. This paper presents the results of a systematic literature review on case studies of process mining projects applied in the manufacturing industry. Case studies are analyzed according to the following aspects: project goals, information systems or devices/equipment that generate event data, particular business processes, event log characteristics, different types and perspectives of process mining performed, tools and techniques used for preprocessing activities, discovery, conformance checking, process enhancement, and social network analysis. Finally, an attempt is made to discover the impact of goals, types of processes, and event log characteristics on the selection of process mining types, perspectives, tools, and techniques.

Keywords: Process mining · Manufacturing · Literature review

1 Introduction

With the increasing availability and lower cost of technology, most manufacturing organizations can manage their business processes with some information system (Enterprise Resource Planning - ERP or Manufacturing Execution System - MES) [1–3]. Furthermore, in the Era of Industry 4.0 and big data [4], modern manufacturing systems generate a large amount of data that has the potential to become actionable information resources. Different data analysis techniques were used for the analysis of processes specific to the manufacturing industry, such as manufacturing and maintenance management processes [5]. Business intelligence, knowledge discovery, and data mining are

© IFIP International Federation for Information Processing 2020
Published by Springer Nature Switzerland AG 2020
B. Lalic et al. (Eds.): APMS 2020, IFIP AICT 591, pp. 54–62, 2020.
https://doi.org/10.1007/978-3-030-57993-7_7

some of the tools that fill the need for automated data analysis. Process mining is a new research field that enables the automatic discovery of business processes and numerous additional process enhancement techniques, such as performance analysis. It is defined by the IEEE Task Force on Process Mining, as follows [6]: "The idea of process mining is to discover, monitor, and improve real processes (i.e., not assumed processes) by extracting knowledge from event logs readily available in today's (information) systems."

Process mining has been mostly applied in the healthcare industry, following with information technology, finance, and manufacturing industries [7]. Literature reviews of case studies in the healthcare industry [8], as well as several reviews of process mining applications [7] and state of the art [9], proved the feasibility and applicability of process mining. However, no study focuses on the applicability and benefits of process mining in the manufacturing industry. This paper aims to discover specific information found in case studies in the manufacturing industry through a systematic literature review that is assumed to be relevant for the future conduction of process mining projects in the manufacturing industry.

Firstly, it is relevant to discover which information systems, manufacturing devices/equipment, and business processes are analyzed in these case studies, as well as project goals. Event log characteristics can also be meaningful, as they can impact the decision on tools and techniques. Preprocessing activities, found to be the most difficult to perform, are also analyzed based on utilized tools and techniques. Furthermore, there are three types of process mining that will be observed: discovery, conformance, and enhancement [6]. Process discovery techniques produce a process model from an event log without using any a priori information about the process. Conformance compares the discovered process model with an event log of the same process and is used to check if event data conforms to the model. Enhancement improves an existing process model by using information about the actual process recorded in the event log. There are also different process mining perspectives [6]. The control-flow or process perspective focuses on the control-flow, i.e., the ordering of activities, and it is equivalent to discovery. The case and time perspectives are usually performed together [7], as they are comparable to process enhancement. The organizational perspective (social network analysis) focuses on information about originators in the log, i.e., which actors \performers are involved and how they are related. These different types and perspectives are used to solve particular problems that occur in real-life processes, and it is essential to outline their share in process mining applications. This paper will also describe different tools and techniques that were applied, grouped by types and perspectives of process mining. The results of this systematic literature review will tackle the benchmarking challenges of process mining and help process analysts in the manufacturing industry gain insight into the detailed possibilities and benefits of process mining applications.

The remainder of the paper is organized as follows. Section 2 describes the design of a systematic literature review. Section 3 presents the results of the review, and Sect. 4 concludes the paper and presents future work.

2   Research Design

A comprehensive and well-structured literature review firstly elaborates on the need for a systematic literature review, then formulates research questions, search strategy, study selection criteria, and performs study quality assessment [10]. Although there are papers that elaborate on the usefulness of process mining in the manufacturing industry, there are no literature reviews that offer summed information and conclusions on the topic, except [7], where authors reviewed process mining in all industries. The following research questions are established:

RQ1: What are the main goals of process mining projects in manufacturing?
RQ2: Which information systems, devices, or equipment are the generators of the event data, and which company processes are being automated?
RQ3: What are the characteristics of analyzed event logs?
RQ4: What preprocessing tools and techniques were used?
RQ5: What types and perspectives were performed, and which tools and techniques were used?
RQ6: Do goals, types of processes, or event log characteristics influence the selection of process mining types, perspectives, tools, and techniques?

The SCOPUS database and Google Scholar were searched with the following search terms: "Process mining" and "manufacturing" and "case studies". The search resulted in 256 papers.

Inclusion criteria applied to papers are:

IC1: Papers have to be published full-text as articles or conference proceedings.
IC2: Paper has to present a case study.
IC3: The paper has to be written in English.

Exclusion criteria applied to papers are:

EC1: Paper presents a case study from other industries.
EC2: Paper presents the same case study, written as a different publication.
EC3: Paper is referencing process mining but is using other technologies in the case study.

After applying defined inclusion and exclusion criteria on available papers, papers were critically appraised based on their relevancy and type of information they contained. Finally, there were 14 primary studies available for data extraction.

Flow diagram of the systematic literature review process is presented in Fig. 1.

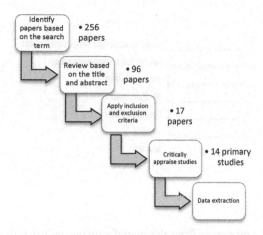

Fig. 1. Systematic literature review flow diagram

3 Data Extraction Results

Besides the process discovery, process mining was successfully applied to detect throughput and waiting times of a process and to discover bottlenecks and feedback loops [12, 14–16, 18, 20, 21, 23, 24]. Moreover, process mining SNA techniques were used for finding the roles and relationships of the resources (e.g., machines, employees) [12, 15, 18, 20, 22], presented through resource networks. Other applications of process mining were focused on detecting compliance issues with the expected behavior of a process [11–13, 16], predicting manufacturing cost based on production volume and time [17], estimating process cycle times [19], and discovering business essential process variants before undergoing an ERP implementation project [23]. Figure 2 presents the types of publications by year.

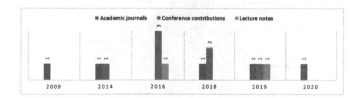

Fig. 2. Types of publications by year

Figure 3 presents the goals of the process mining projects, sorted descendingly by the number of case studies with the same goal.

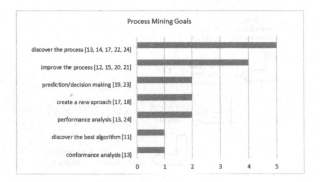

Fig. 3. Number of papers with the same process mining goal

Figure 4 presents processes from the manufacturing industry that were the subject of process mining. The manufacturing process [16–18] and the procurement process [13, 21, 23] were analyzed the most, following with the production planning [15, 20], incident management [12, 24], maintenance management [22, 25], product assembling [11] and product testing process [17]. Mostly used information system was the ERP system [13, 15, 20, 23], which supported all procurement and production planning processes. Other processes were supported by the Supply Chain Management system [11], the MES [17], the Shipbuilding Processing Plan Management system [21], Supervisory Control And Data Acquisition (SCADA) system [24], and a problem handling system [12]. As manufacturing devices and equipment that can generate event data are considered, CNC machine [19], programmable logic controller, and robot stations [22] were analyzed.

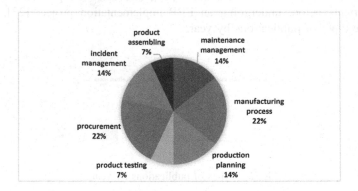

Fig. 4. Analyzed processes in the manufacturing industry

Table 1 presents information about performed techniques, algorithms, and tools in all case studies grouped by different process mining types and perspectives. It can be concluded that all case studies performed process discovery and control-flow perspective. Enhancement was performed in 57% of the case studies [13–18, 20, 24]. Conformance checking was performed in 28% of the case studies [13–16] and SNA in 21% [16, 18, 20].

Table 1. Algorithms/techniques and tools

Techniques/algorithms		Tools					
		ProM	Disco	ProM Import	Manual	KeyPro	New tool
Preprocessing	Attribute filtering		20, 21		12		
	Filter out artificial start and end act		13, 19, 20				
	Filter out incomplete cases		13, 20, 21				
	Filter out infrequent cases		13				
	Convert to MXML, inversion filter	14		14			
	Add attributes to event log				17	23	
Discovery (control-flow)	Heuristic miner	11, 13, 14, 15, 16, 18					12
	Fuzzy miner		19, 20, 21, 24				
	Inductive miner	11, 13, 22					
	ILP miner, Evolutionary tree miner, alpha algorithm	11					
Enhancement (case/time)	Bottleneck analysis	14, 17	20, 22, 24				12
	Calculate throughput time	16, 18	20, 21				
	Detect feedback loops		15, 20, 21, 23				
	Performance analysis plug-in	11, 16					
	Dotted chart analysis	18, 20					
	Process variant analysis		15				
	LTL checker	16					
	Pattern abstraction visualizer	20					
	Process model-enhanced cost plug-in						17

(continued)

Table 1. (*continued*)

Techniques/algorithms		Tools					
		ProM	Disco	ProM Import	Manual	KeyPro	New tool
Conform.	Conformance checking plug-in	11, 16					
	Rule-based conformance checking				13		
	Manual conformance checking				12		
Social network analysis	Social network analysis plug-in	16, 18, 20					
	Originator impact and role analysis						12
	Inductive miner	22					

To answer the RQ6, firstly, it was analyzed if the case studies with the same goal had performed the same process mining types and perspectives. It was concluded that there are patterns by which process mining was conducted based on the overall goal of the case study. Case studies that aimed to discover the process performed control-flow perspective (discovery type) in 100% of the cases and case/time perspective (enhancement) in 80%. The case studies with the goal to perform performance analysis used control-flow and case/time perspectives. The case study with the goal of performing conformance analysis conducted all three types of process mining. Case studies that aimed to develop a new approach for process mining in manufacturing performed discovery and enhancement. The case studies with the goal to improve the process conducted process discovery in 100%, process enhancement in 50%, conformance checking in 25%, and organizational mining in 25% of the cases. The case studies with the goal to predict the process flow or use process mining for decision making, performed only process discovery. Finally, case studies that aimed to discover the best algorithm for process mining in manufacturing performed only process discovery. Secondly, it was analyzed if a process type influences the process mining types and perspectives. Because most process types were discovered and enhanced, there was no significant correlation. However, all production planning processes and 60% of procurement processes were supported by an ERP system. It was discovered that event log characteristics such as event log format, size, and number of cases and activities do not influence types and perspectives of process mining nor chosen tools and techniques.

4 Conclusion

This paper aimed to gain insightful information about the application of process mining in the manufacturing industry. The data extracted from the case studies show an overview of the goals of process mining projects, information systems, analyzed processes, and event log characteristics. More significant is an overview of all techniques, algorithms, and tools, grouped by the process mining types and perspectives. Finally, the paper presented an analysis of the impact that goals, processes, and event log characteristics had on the selection of process mining types, perspectives, and techniques/algorithms. The discovered relationships between the key features of process mining could be tested as hypotheses, by including a higher number of case studies, even considering all industries in which process mining is applied.

References

1. Beric, D., Stefanovic, D., Lalic, B., Cosic, I.: The implementation of ERP and MES Systems as a support to industrial management systems. Int. J. Ind. Eng. Manag. **9**(2), 77–86 (2018)
2. Dakic, D., Sefanovic D., Lolic T., Sladojevic S., Anderla A.: Production planning business process modelling using UML class diagram. In: 17th International Symposium INFOTEH-JAHORINA, pp. 1–6, IEEE, East Sarajevo (2018)
3. Beric, D., Havzi S., Lolic T., Simeunovic N., Stefanovic D.: Development of the MES software and Integration with an existing ERP software in industrial enterprise. In: 19th International Symposium INFOTEH-JAHORINA, pp. 1–6, IEEE, East Sarajevo (2020)
4. Crnjac, M., Veza, I., Banduka, N.: From Concept to the Introduction of Industry 4.0. Int. J. Ind. Eng. Manag. (IJIEM) **8**(1), 21–30 (2017)
5. Lopes, I.S., Figueiredo, M.C., Sa, V.: Criticality evaluation to support maintenance management of manufacturing systems. Int. J. Ind. Eng. Manag. (IJIEM) **11**(1), 3–18 (2020)
6. van der Aalst, W., et al.: Process mining manifesto. In: Daniel, F., Barkaoui, K., Dustdar, S. (eds.) BPM 2011. LNBIP, vol. 99, pp. 169–194. Springer, Heidelberg (2012). https://doi.org/10.1007/978-3-642-28108-2_19
7. Dakic, D., Stefanovic, D., Cosic, I., Lolic, T., Medojevic, M.: Business process mining application: a literature review, In: Katalinic, B. (ed.) Proceedings of the 29th DAAAM International Symposium, pp. 0866–0875. DAAAM International, Vienna, Austria (2018)
8. Rojas, E., Munoz-Gama, J., Sepúlveda, M., Capurro, D.: Process mining in healthcare: a literature review. J. Biomed. Inform. **61**, 224–236 (2016)
9. Tiwari, A., Turner, C.J., Majeed, B.: A review of business process mining: state-of-the-art and future trends. Bus. Process Manag. J. **14**(1), 5–22 (2008)
10. Kitchenham B.: Procedures for undertaking systematic reviews. In: Joint Technical Report, Computer Science Department, Keele University, National ICT Australia Ltd. (2004)
11. Bettacchi, A., Polzonetti, A., Re, B.: Understanding production chain business process using process mining: a case study in the manufacturing scenario. In: Krogstie, J., Mouratidis, H., Su, J. (eds.) CAiSE 2016. LNBIP, vol. 249, pp. 193–203. Springer, Cham (2016). https://doi.org/10.1007/978-3-319-39564-7_19
12. Hidayat, B.N.A., Kurniati, A.P.: Process model extension using heuristics miner: (Case study: Incident management of Volvo IT Belgium). In: 2016 International Conference on Computational Intelligence and Cybernetics, pp. 73–78, IEEE, Makassar (2016)

13. Diba, K., Remy, S., Pufahl, L.: Compliance and performance analysis of procurement processes using process mining. In: International Conference on Business Process Mining, Lecture Notes in Business Information Processing, vol. 362, pp. 116. Springer, Cham (2019)
14. Rozinat, A., de Jong, I.S., Günther, C.W., van der Aalst, W.M.: Process mining applied to the test process of wafer scanners in ASML. IEEE Trans. Syst. Man Cybern. Part C (Appl. Rev.) 39(4), 474–479 (2009)
15. Mahendrawathi, E.R., Arsad, N., Astuti, H., Kusumawardani, R., Utami, R.: Analysis of production planning in a global manufacturing company with process mining. J. Enterpr. Inf. Manag. 31(2), 317–337 (2018)
16. Son, S., et al.: Process mining for manufacturing process analysis: a case study. In: Proceeding of 2nd Asia Pacific Conference on Business Process Management. Springer, Brisbane, Australia (2014)
17. Tu, T.B.H., Song, M.: Analysis and prediction cost of manufacturing process based on process mining. In: 2016 International Conference on Industrial Engineering, Management Science and Application (ICIMSA), pp. 1–5, IEEE, Jeju (2016)
18. Yahya, B.N.: The development of manufacturing process analysis: lesson learned from process mining. Jurnal Teknik Industri 16(2), 95–106 (2014)
19. Ruschel, E., Santos, E.A.P., Loures, E.F.R.: Establishment of maintenance inspection intervals: an application of process mining techniques in manufacturing. J. Intell. Manuf. 31(1), 53–72 (2018). https://doi.org/10.1007/s10845-018-1434-7
20. Dakic, D., Stefanovic, D., Sladoejvic, S., Lolic, T.: Process mining possibilities and challenges: a case study. In: 17th IEEE International Symposium on Intelligent Systems and Informatics. IEEE, Subotica (2019)
21. Rbigui, H., Cho, C.: Purchasing process analysis with process mining of a heavy manufacturing industry. In: 2018 International Conference on Information and Communication Technology Convergence (ICTC), pp. 495–498. IEEE, Jeju (2018)
22. Farooqui, A., Bengtsson, K., Falkman, P., Fabian, M.: From factory floor to process models: a data gathering approach to generate, transform, and visualize manufacturing processes. CIRP J. Manuf. Sci. Technol. 24, 6–16 (2019)
23. Fleig, C., Augenstein, D., Maedche, A.: Process mining for business process standardization in ERP implementation projects-an SAP S/4 HANA case study from manufacturing. In: 16th International Conference on Business Process Management (BPM), pp. 149–155. KIT, Sydney (2018)
24. Feau, B., Schaller, C., Moliner, M.: A method to build a production process model prior to a process mining approach. In: The Fifth International Conference on Intelligent Systems and Applications 2016, pp. 143–146. IARIA XPS Press, Barcelona, Spain (2016)

Bayesian Modelling for Product Testing and Release

John G. Wilson(✉)

Ivey Business School, University of Western Ontario, London,
ON N6G ON1, Canada
jwilson@ivey.uwo.ca

Abstract. Deciding when to release a new product requires a tradeoff between costs, potential profits and the underlying reliability of a product. Many new products go through a "Test Analyze and Fix" process. When a failure occurs, an immediate design "fix" may occur or the product might undergo a minimal fix with design changes being delayed until later when many changes can be introduced at the same time. We introduce a Bayesian model that allows for the introduction of managerial knowledge and experience. Unlike most approaches, we do not build in an assumption that the product always improves throughout the process.

Keywords: Product development · Prototype testing · Product release · Reliability growth

1 Introduction

1.1 Background

The mean time between failures of a new product (MTBF) is an important characteristic that has a direct impact on revenue streams and costs. For products designed for the US military, historically MTBF has to reach a specified level before a product will be accepted. In the commercial world, there is a balance between MTBF and the timing of a new product release: release the product too early and the reliability problems will damage a company's reputation and involve many repair and replacement costs; release the product after extensive and time intensive development to raise MTBF and market advantage and share might be lost. Before formally incorporating costs and revenues into a decision model of how to manage the development phase of a new product and the timing of product release, it is essential to have a flexible statistical process for modelling the phases of test development.

A complex newly designed system generally undergoes several stages of development testing before it is put into operation. After each stage of testing, changes are made to the design with the hope that the new design leads to a longer period of performance. This procedure is referred to as *reliability growth*. It is the result of iterative *Test Analyse and Fix* processes which are conducted to discover deficiencies and to verify that corrective action will prevent recurrence in the further test phases. A "fix" refers to a design change that improves the reliability of the system.

B. Lalic et al. (Eds.): APMS 2020, IFIP AICT 591, pp. 63–70, 2020.
https://doi.org/10.1007/978-3-030-57993-7_8

After fixes have been implemented, the system reliability will jump to a higher value. Usually, the estimate of the reliability jump is not straightforward since the untested fixes require a specific prediction rule for them to "follow" in a growth model. In addition, the test data of a specific test prototype is only one set of data of all possible situations from the same design basis, e.g. design specifications and environmental specifications (Ireson et al. [1]).

1.2   Literature

The first reliability growth model appeared in the late 1950's. Duane [2] analysed the reliability data of five different complex systems and demonstrated that the cumulative failure rate versus the cumulative operation time fell close to a straight line when plotted on a log-log scale. Crow [3] at *Army Materiel Systems Activity* (AMSAA) suggested that Duane's postulate be stochastically represented as a Non-Homogeneous Poisson Process (NHPP) with Weibull intensity $\lambda(t) = \alpha\beta t^{\beta-1}$ where $\alpha, \beta > 0$. This is called the AMSAA model. For $0 < \beta < 1$, $\lambda(t)$ is decreasing implying reliability growth. Bayesian extensions for the AMSAA model were proposed by Higgins and Tsokos [4] and Guida et al. [5]. Yu et al. [6] consider predictions using this model using noninformative priors. A pseudo-Bayes approach has been discussed by Singpurwalla [7] under the stochastic ordering of prior and posterior distributions. Robinson and Dietrich [8, 9] proposed two nonparametric growth models in which no specific functional form is assumed for the change of process failure rate. Crow's *Engineering Judgement Model* [10] (EJM) considered techniques for *projection* of future expected reliability based on a delayed fixes testing plan. In the EJM model it is assumed that the *effectiveness factors* (EF) of fixes for all distinct failure modes in the system are given and all failures observed in RGDT are not fixed until the end of the testing program.

Wayne and Modarres [11] assume that the failure times between fixes are exponential and that a fix results in a known increase in mean time between failures. (MTBF's). Conjugate priors are used to model knowledge of the parameters. Wayne [12] discusses using a beta prior distribution for the factor by which MTBF increases after a fix. Our model generalises this to assuming that the increase in MTBF is itself a random variable and that MTBF's follow a pattern similar to that of AMSAA NHP approach. For software projects, predicting the expected number of software defects is important and Bayesian methods are making inroads. Rana et al. [13] discuss models including the Weibull model which is similar to the NHPP above and discuss finding prior distributions. Chen et al. [14] consider a multi-stage system with NHPP at each stage and models growth factors. Non-Bayesian approaches to modelling RDGT using power law growth models such as NHPP are still areas of active research–see, e.g., Xu et al. [15].

Bayesian methods for estimating the reliability of systems are examined in Li et al. [16] and Ruiz et al. [17]. A comparison of classical versus Bayesian methods can be found in Kamranfar et al. [18]. Pollo et al. [19] introduce an "objective Bayesian prior" that produces a posterior that is a product of gamma functions. Wayne et al. [20] model a posterior distribution for the failure intensity Optimal product release times for a product consisting of subsystems connected in series are modeled in Li et al. [21].

In distinction to the above literature, we don't even require that the reliability grows...some fixes don't work! However, we do assume that on average fixes work and the *expected* reliability grows according to a power law. The parameters of this power law are unknown and we assume that we can obtain prior distributions for the parameters. However, we translate these parameters into quantities that are intuitive and will enable engineers to arrive at reasonable priors. This approach has the advantage of being transparent and intuitive. However, mathematically, arriving at conclusions will now require numerical methods.

2 A Bayesian Product Improvement Model

We will start with a description of the basic model and assumptions. For most of this paper, we consider the model where a fix is incorporated after each failure. Thus, as the machine fails and is repaired, its reliability grows. This is discussed in $2.1, where model assumptions are discussed in detail. The likelihood function for the data is formulated in $2.2. A prior density function $\pi(\alpha, \beta)$ over the parameters α and β of the Weibull intensity $\lambda(t) = \alpha\beta t^{\beta-1}$ is required. Ideally, this should incorporate expert opinion and knowledge. We will provide the likelihood function for the observed data. Then we will describe how to come up with reasonable prior distributions for the underlying parameters. This is an important feature of the model since it allows for the incorporation of expert managerial judgement. This is particularly important in product development where, initially, not much data is available. Most product developers will have a feel for the possible values of the reliability growth parameter β. This is discussed in $2.3. Information about the parameter α is not so intuitive. Instead, in $2.4, we propose the product developer provide information about the expected mean time between failures. This can then be translated into prior information for α. In $2.6, we combine the material from $2.3 and $2.4 to provide a joint prior for the underlying parameter.

2.1 Model Development

After each failure and fix, the time to the next failure is assumed to be exponential but with a new parameter since the machine has been "improved". This is the assumption made in Wayne and Modarres [11].

Suppose the system testing stops at some predetermined number of failures n. Let $t_1, t_2, \ldots, t_n$ be the cumulate test times of n successive failure modes observed up to t_n and let $x_1, x_2, \ldots, x_n$ be the times between failures i.e. $x_1 = t_1$ and $x_i = t_i - t_{i-1}$, for $i = 2, \ldots, n$.

So the number of failures in each stage is limited to one. We note that the test plan of the most popular reliability growth model using NHP belongs to this class of problem.

During a particular stage, the distributions of the times to failure are assumed exponential. The exponential parameters are not assumed to be equal. In Wayne and Modarres [11], the assumption is that each fix results in a known fractional increase in meant time to failure. We generalise this by assuming that exponential parameter for stage i after a fix is assumed to be the value of a gamma random variable with mean $\alpha \beta t_{i-1}^{\beta-1}$ and variance σ^2. We will assume that the value σ^2 is provided—although extension to a prior over this parameter is straightforward. This allows for the incorporation of the major feature of the AMSAA model. In addition, in distinction to other models, the actual failure rate does not necessarily decrease from stage to stage. This is particularly important when considering the development of software products: a fix is new computer code which may itself be faulty and decrease the reliability of the product. However, overall the reliability tends to improve as fixes are incorporated. The parameters α, β and σ will depend on managerial specifications and knowledge and are key components. There are various ways to obtain information that can help set prior distributions. For instance, Wayne [11] discusses developing prior distributions for the factor by which MTBF increases after a fix and suggests the use of historical information such as that found in Trapnell [22] and in Brown [23].

On finding prior distributions, we need to obtain the posterior distributions for the parameters and the posterior expected value of various quantities of interest such as the expected time to failure once all the test data and fixes have been incorporated. Since we are making as few assumptions as possible and trying to capture managerial intuition, these are algebraically messy and ultimately need to be evaluated using numerical methods.

2.2   The Likelihood Function

At the nth failure the data observed will be the times $t_1, t_2, \ldots, t_n$. After simplification, the likelihood function –a constant times the probability of observing the data $t_1, t_2, \ldots, t_n$, can be written as:

$$\prod_{i=2}^{n} \alpha \beta t_{i-1}^{\beta-1} \left\{ 1 + \frac{(t_i - t_{i-1})\sigma^2}{\alpha \beta t_{i-1}^{\beta-1}} \right\}^{-\left(1 + \left(\alpha \beta t_{i-1}^{\beta-1}\right)^2\right)}.$$

Sufficient statistics of fixed dimensionality do not exist for the above likelihood function so that no natural conjugate prior can be found (Schlaifer and Raiffa [24]). Thus, inference based on a continuous joint prior generally requires numerical procedures.

From a practical viewpoint, Bayes methods are attractive because they allow for incorporating experience or technical considerations in the estimation procedure especially when the test data and the test procedure is expensive. This is greatly facilitated when a clear physical meaning can be attached to the model parameters. Generally, for selecting a prior distribution, it must adequately represent the state of prior knowledge about the parameter and not be a computational burden. Based on a technical judgement, if we believe the variability between prototypes will be relatively small it may be reasonable to take σ as a common constant parameter of the model and we do that in the sequel.

2.3   Prior for β

We note that a shape parameter β less than 1 means a system whose expected failure rate is decreasing (small β means rapid reliability growth) whereas a shape parameter β greater than 1 means a system whose expected failure rate is increasing. In many practical situations, bounds for β can follow on the basis of prior knowledge of the underlying failure mechanism. For instance, guidance on practical ranges for β can be found in the following:

- The data collected by Duane [2] and Schafer et al. [25] show that β is "about 0.5 and is rarely less than 0.3 regardless of the initial and final MTBF's"
- For equipment exhibiting a good fit, the Crow's growth parameter β ranged from 0.579 to 0.794 (Gates et al. [26])
- The Duane model provides a reasonably good fit to most of the data sets and the estimated growth rates are within the generally accepted range or 0.3 to 0.9 (Gates et al. [26]).

When no further information exists, it is reasonable to represent prior knowledge by using a uniform prior pdf over the interval (0.3, 0.9), the widest range for β as indicated by Gates et al. [26].

2.4   Prior for α

Since the scale parameter α in this model does not provide a clear physical meaning, we suggest an alternative approach to find a reasonable joint pdf for α and β as follows. For the failure process considered here, the expected failure time at time t is $\alpha\beta t^{\beta-1}$. We note that generally a development test program is never begun without some information regarding potential failure rates. So, the mean life time at some beginning time t_0 can be viewed as a process parameter μ_0. Without loss of generality, suppose that $t_0 = 1$. The physical meaning of μ_0 should allow an engineer to formulate prior knowledge. However, if no prior information is available from a similar system then a commonly used estimate of 10% to 20% of the requirement mean time between failures can be uses as an initial reliability (Morris and MacDiarmid [27]). Using this, the prior for μ_0.can be chosen as uniform over some interval (c_1, c_2):

$$\pi_{\mu_0}(\mu_0) \propto \frac{1}{c_2 - c_1} \text{ for } c_1 < \mu_0 < c_2.$$

2.5   Joint Prior for α and β

Assuming the random variables μ_0 and β are independent, the joint density function of μ_0 and β is given by

$$\pi_{\mu_0,\beta}(\mu_0, \beta) \propto \frac{1}{c_2 - c_1} \frac{1}{\beta_2 - \beta_1} \text{ for } c_1 < \mu_0 < c_2 \text{ and } \beta_1 < \beta < \beta_2.$$

By making a change of variable transformation, this induces an equivalent prior over (α, β) given by

$$\pi(\alpha, \beta) \propto \frac{1}{\beta\alpha^2}$$

over the region $0 < \beta_1 < \beta < \beta_2 < 1$ and $0 < c_1 \leq \frac{1}{\alpha\beta} \leq c_2$.

that μ_0 and β are independent, the joint density function is then equal to $\frac{1}{(c_2-c_1)(\beta_2-\beta)}$. Changing variables the joint distribution of α and β can be shown to be proportional to $\frac{1}{\beta\alpha^2}$ where $0 < \beta_1 \leq \beta \leq \beta_2 < 1$ and $0 < c_1 \leq \frac{1}{\alpha\beta} \leq c_2$.

2.6   Putting It All Together

The likelihood from 2.1 is now multiplied by the prior from 2.5 to form a quantity proportional to the posterior distribution. From this, various posterior quantities such as the posterior MTBF, posterior means of α and β may be obtained via integration. However, the resultant integrals have no closed form and the integrations, of necessity, must be numerical.

3   Applying the Model

To illustrate the application of the Bayesian model, we use the 15 failure data points from Crow's [28] example. These data were generated by the computer simulation of a NHPP with $\alpha = 0.42$ and $\beta = 0.5$. These are (cumulative test times): 0.2, 11.2, 37.2, 39, 48.4, 53.4, 90.2, 91.6, 151.4, 159.4, 197.2, 240.2, 323.6, 361.2, 381.6.

It is important to note that we know a priori that the Bayes model does not fit this data since it was generated assuming the time between failures is non-exponential and there is no variability between prototypes. Thus, the simulated model is at best an approximation to the model which most authors suggest. As will be seen, even for this unfavourable data, the proposed Bayesian model performs well.

We assumed that β was uniform over (0.45, 0.55), μ_0 was uniform over (4.5 and 5) and σ was small.

The table below summarises the estimation results. Included are the results from applying the Bayesian model and the estimated using maximum likelihood estimation of α and β in Crow's model (Table 1).

Table 1. Comparison of Model to Estimates from Crow's Model where underlying data is generated from a known distribution

Model	True σ	True β
True model	0.42	0.5
Bayesian estimates	0.40463	0.522
MLE for crowe model	0.4690	0.5829

4 Conclusions

Planning for new product release requires a reasonable model for the modelling of reliability growth. An approach to product reliability growth modelling that allows for managerial input, variability between prototypes and incorporates historically relevant observations has been presents. In the case of limited data, a Bayesian approach combined with expert judgement, often provides superior results. A limitation of the Bayesian approach is arriving at the prior distributions. This depends on the expert knowledge of the product developers. For cases where development time is short, misspecifications can lean to costly errors. Continuing work involves expanding the model to more general situations and performing extensive numerical comparisons. Now that a feasible model for tracking product reliability growth has been established, a next step is to explicitly incorporate costs and revenues to optimise the testing and fix process.

Acknowledgment. This work was accomplished with the assistance of T. Chu and forms part of his thesis.

References

1. Ireson, W.: Grant and coombs. In: Clyde Jr., F. (ed.) Handbook of Reliability Engineering and Management. McGraw-Hill Book Company, New York (1988)
2. Duane, J.T.: Learning curve approach to reliability monitoring. IEEE Trans. Aerosp. 2(2), 563–566 (1964)
3. Crow, L.H.: Reliability analysis for complex repairable systems US army materiel systems analysis activity. Technical Report 138, Dec. 1975, AD-A020296 (1975)
4. Higgins, J.J., Tsokos, C.P.: A quasi-Bayes estimate of the failure intensity of a reliability-growth model. IEEE Trans. Reliab. 30(5), 471–475 (1981)
5. Guida, M., Calabria, R., Pulcini, G.: Bayes inference for a non-homogeneous Poisson process with power intensity law (reliability). IEEE Trans. Reliab. 38(5), 603–609 (1989)
6. Yu, J.-W., Tian, G.-L., Tang, M.-L.: Predictive analyses for nonhomogeneous Poisson processes with power law using Bayesian approach. Comput. Stat. Data Anal. 51(9), 4254–4268 (2007)
7. Singpurwalla, N.: A Bayesian scheme for estimating reliability growth under exponential failure times. TIMS Stud. Manag. Sci. 19, 281–296 (1982)
8. Robinson, D.G., Dietrich, D.: A new nonparametric growth model. IEEE Trans. Reliab. 36(4), 411–418 (1987)
9. Robinson, D., Dietrich, D.: A nonparametric-Bayes reliability-growth model. IEEE Trans. Reliab. 38(5), 591–598 (1989)
10. Crowe, L.H.: Reliability growth assessments utilizing engineering judgements. Proc. Inst. Environ. Sci. 179–183 (1987)
11. Wayne, M., Modarres, M.: A Bayesian model for complex system reliability growth under arbitrary corrective actions. IEEE Trans. Reliab. 64(1), 206–220 (2014)
12. Wayne, M.: Modeling uncertainty in reliability growth plans. In: 2018 Annual Reliability and Maintainability Symposium (RAMS), pp. 1–6. IEEE (2018)

13. Rana, R., Staron, M., Berger, C., Hansson, J., Nilsson, M., Meding, W.: Analyzing defect inflow distribution and applying Bayesian inference method for software defect prediction in large software projects. J. Syst. Softw. **117**, 229–244 (2016)
14. Chen, G., Li, L., Li, J., Miao, Q.: Multi-stage Bayesian evaluation method of reliability growth for large complex system. In: 2015 Prognostics and System Health Management Conference (PHM), pp. 1–7. IEEE (2015)
15. Xu, J.Y., Yu, D., Xie, M., Hu, Q.P.: An approach for reliability demonstration test based on power-law growth model. Qual. Reliab. Eng. Int. **33**(8), 1719–1730 (2017)
16. Li, Z.S., Guo, J., Xiao, N.-C., Huang, W.: Multiple priors integration for reliability estimation using the Bayesian melding method. In: 2017 Annual Reliability and Maintainability Symposium (RAMS), pp. 1–6. IEEE (2017)
17. Ruiz, C., Heydari, M., Sullivan, K.M., Liao, H., Pohl, E.: Data analysis and resource allocation in Bayesian selective accelerated reliability growth. IISE Trans. **52**(3), 301–320 (2020)
18. Kamranfar, H., Etminan, J., Chahkandi, M.: Statistical inference for a repairable system subject to shocks: classical vs. Bayesian. J. Stat. Comput. Simul. **90**(1), 112–137 (2020)
19. Pollo, M.: Objective Bayesian Inference for Repairable System Subject to Competing Risks. arXiv preprint arXiv:1804.06466 (2018)
20. Wayne, M., Modarres, M.: A Bayesian model for complex system reliability growth under arbitrary corrective actions. IEEE Trans. Reliab. **64**(1), 206–220 (2015)
21. Li, M., Xu, D., Li, Z.S.: A joint modeling approach for reliability growth planning considering product life cycle cost performance. Comput. Ind. Eng. **145**, 106541 (2020)
22. Trapnell, B.: Update on reliability fix effectiveness factors. In: Interim Note R-86. AMSAA, Aberdeen Proving Ground, MD (1984)
23. Brown, S.M.: Development and validation of methodology for fix effectiveness during product development. Ph.D. Dissertation, University of Maryland, College Park (2009)
24. Schlaifer, R., Raiffa, H.: Applied statistical decision theory (1961)
25. Schafer, R.E., Sallee, R.B., Torrez, J.D.: Reliability growth study. Hughes Aircraft Co., RADC-TR-75-253 (1975)
26. Gates, R., Gibson, G., McLain, D.: Reliability Growth Projections. Rome Air Development Study, TR 86-148, September 1986
27. Morris, S., MacDiarmid, P.: Reliability growth testing effectiveness. J. Environ. Sci. **28**(4), 21–28 (1985)
28. Crow, L.H.: A methodology for managing reliability growth during operational mission profile testing. In: 2008 Annual Reliability and Maintainability Symposium, pp. 48–53. IEEE (2008)

Advanced, Digital and Smart Manufacturing

The Use of Organizational Innovation Concepts in Manufacturing Companies

Iztok Palčič[✉][iD], Simon Klančnik[iD], Robert Ojsteršek[iD],
Tone Lerher[iD], Borut Buchmeister[iD], and Mirko Ficko[iD]

Faculty of Mechanical Engineering, University of Maribor,
Smetanova ulica 17, 2000 Maribor, Slovenia
{iztok.palcic, simon.klancnik, robert.ojstersek,
tone.lerher, borut.buchmeister, mirko.ficko}@um.si

Abstract. The main purpose of this paper is to map the adoption of selected innovative organizational concepts in manufacturing companies. A further objective of our research is to find out how different organizational concepts are represented in different manufacturing company's types and how they are related to the use of advanced manufacturing technologies. Based on a sample of 118 Slovenian manufacturing companies collected through the 2018–19 European Manufacturing Survey edition, results give information about the most used organizational concepts, their utilization degree, planned use and average year of implementation. In addition, results give evidence that the use of selected organizational concepts is very positively related to the use of specific advanced manufacturing technologies.

Keywords: Organizational innovation concept · Manufacturing company · Advanced manufacturing technology · European Manufacturing Survey · Slovenia

1 Introduction

The importance of innovation to competitiveness has been acknowledged for many years now. Unfortunately, the term innovation is still sometimes more synonymous with product innovation or technical innovation than process or organizational or managerial innovation. Organizational innovations are often neglected in innovation theory [1]. Keupp et al. [2] made an extensive literature review on innovation management, where analysing more than 342 articles, they found out that there is a low number of articles dealing with the field of non-technical innovation, while the number of articles in the field of technical innovation is much higher.

Although organizational innovation is considered an important contributor and trigger to the product innovation, and ultimately to company success, organizational or non-technical innovation needs further and deeper understanding [3]. Many studies analyse specific organizational innovations. On the other hand, there is a lack of papers that try to identify and measure the organizational innovation in companies [4, 5]. Therefore, our paper contributes to analysis of specific organizational concepts in manufacturing companies from different perspectives.

© IFIP International Federation for Information Processing 2020
Published by Springer Nature Switzerland AG 2020
B. Lalic et al. (Eds.): APMS 2020, IFIP AICT 591, pp. 73–81, 2020.
https://doi.org/10.1007/978-3-030-57993-7_9

Organizational innovation does have an impact on company output, first directly and second, through its interrelationship with technical innovation [1]. Accordingly, several studies exist that emphasize the interdependence of technological and management innovations and their joint, complementary influence on organizational outcomes [5]. These studies usually focus on organizational (and technical) innovation and its impact on innovation and financial performance. On the other hand, there are not many studies that look for relationship between specific organizational concepts implementation and the use of specific advanced manufacturing technologies (AMT).

The main purpose of this paper is to map the adoption of selected innovative organizational concepts in Slovenian manufacturing companies and the relationship with selected AMT. The structure of the remainder of the paper is as follows. Section 2 gives a brief description of organizational innovation. Section 3 describes used research methodology. Section 4 comprises the results of the analysis and discussion, while the conclusions are presented in Sect. 5.

2 Organizational Innovation Concepts

Management innovations, also called organizational, administrative, and managerial innovations, are non-technological innovations that have been conceptualized in contrast to technology-based product and process innovations and pertain to new organizational structures, administrative systems, and management practices [5]. Birkinshaw et al. [6] defined management innovation as 'the generation and implementation of a management practice, process, structure, or technique that is new to the state of the art and is intended to further organizational goals'. OECD Oslo Manual from 2005 [7] defines an organizational innovation as the implementation of a new organizational method in the company's business practices, workplace organization or external relations.

There are several ways to differentiate organizational innovation. The first possibility is into structural organizational innovations and procedural organizational innovations. Structural organizational innovations influence, change and improve responsibilities, accountability, command lines and information flows as well as the number of hierarchical levels, the divisional structure of functions (R&D, production, human resources, financing, etc.), or the separation between line and support functions. Procedural organizational innovations affect the routines, processes and operations of a company. Thus, these innovations change or implement new procedures and processes within the company, such as simultaneous engineering or zero buffer rules. Organizational innovation can be further differentiated along an intra-organizational and inter-organizational dimension. While intra-organizational innovations occur within an organization or company, inter-organizational innovations include new organizational structures or procedures beyond a company's boundaries. These comprise new organizational structures in an organization's environment, such as just-in-time processes with suppliers or customers, supply chain management practices with suppliers or customer quality audits. Intra-organizational innovations may concern particular departments or functions or may affect the overall structure and strategy of the company as a whole. Examples for intra-organizational innovations include the implementation of teamwork, quality circles, continuous improvement processes, certification of a company under ISO 9000, zero-buffer principles, environmental audits etc. [4].

Scholars have started emphasizing that, in order to capture the full benefits of innovation, technological innovation needs to be combined with management innovation [8–10]. Historically research on innovation types has followed a technological imperative. It assumes that companies mainly organize their innovation efforts through R&D activities and has thus focused on a narrow definition of product and process innovations associated with the R&D function in manufacturing organizations [10]. The socio-technical system theory challenged the technological imperative and argued that changes in the technical (operating) system of the organization should be coupled with changes in the social (administrative) system in order to optimize organizational outcome [11–13]. Therefore, our research looks for relationship between technical and organizational innovation concepts.

3 About European Manufacturing Survey

The research data was collected using the EMS, a Consortium of Research Institutions coordinated by the Fraunhofer Institute for Systems and Innovation Research – ISI, the largest European survey of manufacturing activities. The survey's questions deal with manufacturing strategies, application of innovative organizational and technological concepts in production, cooperation issues, production offshoring and backshoring, servitisation, and questions of personnel deployment and qualification. In addition, data on performance indicators such as productivity, flexibility, quality and returns is collected. The survey takes place every three years.

The responding companies present a cross-section of the main manufacturing industries. Included are producers of rubber and plastics, metal works, mechanical engineering, electrical engineering. The survey is conducted among manufacturing companies (NACE Revision 2 codes from 22 to 32) having at least 20 employees. Our research is based on EMS data from a Slovenian subsample from the year 2018/19 round. We sent 778 questionnaires and received 118 responses – a 15% response rate. In our 2018/19 subsample, manufacturing companies from NACE divisions 22, 25 and 28 are represented most widely with around 25% of companies from NACE 25, around 20% from NACE 28, and around 16% from the NACE 22 division. We classified manufacturing companies in three size classed based on the number of employees. The largest share of respondents is from medium sized companies (around 43%), followed by small companies (32%) and large companies (25%).

We present the results of our research with the use of descriptive statistics and linear regression model to analyse the dependency between organizational concepts and AMT.

4 Results and Discussion

4.1 Organizational Concepts in EMS

In EMS 2018, we have divided 11 organizational concepts used in manufacturing companies into 3 groups: Organization of production (OP – 4 concepts); Management/controlling (MC – 5 concepts) and Human resources (HR – 2 concepts).

For each organizational concept, we have asked for the following information:

- Use of organizational concept (yes/no).
- Use planned in the upcoming period of three years.
- Year in which organizational concept has been used for the first time in factory.
- Extent (level) of actual utilization compared to the most reasonable potential utilization in the factory: Extent of utilized potential "low" for an initial attempt to utilize, "medium" for partly utilized and "high" for extensive utilization. High utilization of an organizational concept means, for example, that it involves at least 70% of employees in the company.

Table 1. Characteristics of used organizational concepts.

Organizational concept	Group	Share [%]	Year of introduction	Planned use [%]	Level of use
ISO 900x	MC	83,9	2003	15,8	2,80
Training of employees	HR	83,9	2005	26,3	2,08
Standardised instructions for work	OP	79,7	2002	20,8	2,55
Instruments for promoting staff loyalty	HR	67,8	2005	18,4	2,10
CIP, TPM, TQM, Six sigma	MC	59,3	2009	29,2	2,25
Display boards in production (Visual Manag.)	MC	52,5	2012	41,1	2,44
EN ISO 14001	MC	43,2	2007	34,3	2,78
Value stream mapping	OP	37,3	2010	16,2	1,98
SMED	OP	36,4	2011	34,7	1,98
Production controlling following pull principle	OP	33,9	2011	20,5	2,03
Energy management system (EN ISO 50001)	MC	15,3	2014	17,0	2,37

As we can see from Table 1 both concepts from "Human resources" group have very high adoption rate in manufacturing companies. The age of Industry 4.0 and fast technological pace require that all employees acquire new knowledge and skills in different areas. They are also becoming more and more priceless and scarce, therefore companies must introduce specific instruments to promote staff loyalty (e.g. attractively designed responsibilities, offering learning opportunities, flexible working hours, childcare etc.). Quality standards, such as ISO 9001, have always had a high adoption rate, as they are prerequisite to conduct business in global economy. The pressure of environmental challenges in front of us requires also introduction of specific certified environmental management systems (e.g. EN ISO 14001). As many companies introduced specific organizational concepts in the last few years, the average year of first introduction of organizational concepts differs from previous EMS rounds. Except for Standardized instructions for work, all other three organizational concepts from "Organization of production" group are among the youngest, as well as Visual management from the "Management/controlling" group.

The column "Planned use" presents share of companies that do not possess a specific organizational concept, but are planning to introduce it in the period from 2019 to 2021. We can see that the share of companies that are planning to invest in organizational concepts in the next 3 years is quite high. More than 40% of companies that do not use display boards in production is planning to introduce them by the year 2021. That environmental issues are important is clearly presented also by the fact that one third of companies without environmental systems will introduce them by the end of 2021. CIP and SMED methods are also planned in one third of companies that at the moment do not use them.

Next, we looked at the extent of potential use or actual utilization (low – 1, medium – 2, high – 3) . Both quality and environmental standards have a very high share of companies who claim a high use of the standard (around 80% claim to use them to full potential and with average grade of 2,8 for all analysed companies that use them). As expected from the previous research standardized instructions for work are also used at a high level. There is an increase in share of companies that use visual management at the high level comparing to previous EMS rounds. This means that different display equipment in production is becoming widely used and at the same, it delivers required results. Comparing to previous EMS rounds there is also an increase in the share of companies that use continuous improvement methods to more full potential. It can be seen that both concepts from "Human resources" are often used to a very low potential (grade around 2,1). Pull principle, SMED and value stream mapping methods have the lowest average potential use grade of around "2".

The concept "Certified energy management system (e.g. EN ISO 50001)" has a very low adoption rate (around 15%). Therefore, we have excluded this organizational concept in further analysis.

4.2 Organizational Concepts and Advanced Manufacturing Technologies

In our last EMS 2018/19 research round, we have analysed the use of 16 AMT and ICT. Technologies were divided into four groups Digital factory (9 technologies); Automation and robotics (2 technologies); Additive Manufacturing Technologies (2 technologies) and Energy efficiency technologies (3 technologies).

In this paper, we are focusing on Industry 4.0 specific AMT from the digital/smart factory area, industrial robots and additive technologies (we are skipping energy efficient technologies). Table 2 presents the share of AMT and ICT use. When we looked at the use of both types of discussed robots together, we found that at least one type of robots is present in 64% of companies, making industrial robots the most widely used technology from our list. If we combine both types of additive manufacturing technologies, we can observe that at least one of them is used in around one third of the companies. In this paper we are skipping the more in-detail discussion of AMT and ICT use as the focus is on organisational concepts.

Table 2. AMT adoption in Slovenian manufacturing companies

AMT	Share [%]
Digital factory	
Mobile/wireless devices for programming and controlling facilities (e.g. tablets)	32,2
Digital solutions to provide drawings, work schedules or instructions on the shop floor	54,2
Software for production planning and scheduling (e.g. the ERP system)	62,7
Digital exchange of product/process data with suppliers/customers (EDI)	51,7
Near real-time production control system (MES)	39,8
Systems for automation and management of internal logistics (WMS, RFID)	20,3
Product-Lifecycle-Management-Systems (PLM) or Product Data Management (PDM)	19,5
Virtual reality, or simulation for product design, or product development	38,1
Artificial Intelligence (Deep Learning, Machine Learning or Neural Networks)	5,1
Automation and robotics	
Industrial robots for manufacturing processes (e.g. welding, painting, cutting)	50,0
Industrial robots for handling processes (e.g. assembling, sorting, packing processes, AGV)	35,6
Additive manufacturing technologies	
3D printing technologies for prototyping (prototypes, demonstration models, 0 series)	32,2
3D printing technologies for manufacturing of products, components and forms, tools, etc.	23,7

Our goal was to look for relationship between selected organizational concepts and the use of described AMT. We analysed the following six organizational concepts: Standardized and detailed work instructions (SWI); Measures to improve internal logistics (WMS); Setup time or change-over reductions methods (SMED); Pull principle (KANBAN); Visual management (VM) and Methods of assuring quality in production (Q).

We have used linear regression method to look for relationship between a dependent variable (each organizational concept) and independent variables (each AMT). Table 3 presents (Pearson) correlation coefficients for selected organizational concepts and AMT from the group "Digital factory" and Table 4 presents results for the groups "Automation and robotics" and "Additive manufacturing technologies". Our regression procedure aggregates the empirical results based on the percentage of statistically significant regression coefficients ($p < 0.05$).

Table 3. Organizational concepts and digital factory technologies

Org. con.	Mobi. device	Digital solut.	ERP	EDI	Control	Inter. logist.	PLM, PDM	Virt. real.	AI
SWI	+0,078	+0,170	+0,220	+0,186	+0,067	+0,203	+0,142	+0,137	+0,021
VSM	+0,294	+0,251	+0,232	+0,395	+0,303	+0,438	+0,373	+0,224	+0,141
SMED	+0,270	+0,236	+0,293	+0,344	+0,463	+0,317	+0,472	+0,348	+0,226
Kanban	+0,273	+0,155	+0,182	+0,262	+0,185	+0,305	+0,280	+0,138	+0,160
VM	+0,255	+0,217	+0,320	+0,270	+0,461	+0,227	+0,382	+0,152	+0,220
Q	+0,165	+0,209	+0,289	+0,304	+0,357	+0,247	+0,364	+0,259	+0,192

Table 4. Organizational concepts and, robots and additive manufacturing technologies

Organizational concept	Manufac. robots	Assembly robots	3D protoyping	3D manufacturing
Standardised work instructions	+0,042	+0,112	+0,168	+0,133
Warehouse management systems	+0,210	+0,305	+0,369	+0,353
SMED	+0,123	+0,357	+0,307	+0,406
Kanban	+0,251	+0,328	+0,388	+0,316
Visual Management	+0,170	+0,246	+0,219	+0,251
Quality in production	+0,104	+0,291	+0,275	+0,219

Table 3 and 4 show that in general all six analysed organizational concepts are positively and significantly correlated with majority of AMT. The organizational concept that illustrates work processes and work status (Visual Management) is positively and significantly correlated with all AMT. Digital solutions on the shop floor, ERP, EDI and systems for automation and management of internal logistics are positively correlated with all analysed organizational concepts.

Table 5 presents additional results of linear regression analysis, where we present results for the whole model for each selected organization concept. The model is not significant only for the first organizational concept Standardized instructions for work (Sig. F change is 0,522). For all other organizational concepts, the model is significant, meaning that AMT are relevant predictors for organizational concept use.

Table 5. Results of the regression analysis

Organizational concept	R	R Square	Adjusted R square	Std. error of the estimate	R Square change	Sig. F change
Standardised work instruc.	,323	,105	−,007	,40573	,015	0,522
Warehouse man. systems	,575	,331	,247	,42144	,331	**0,000**
SMED	,632	,399	,324	,39731	,399	**0,000**
Kanban	,499	,249	,155	,43701	,249	**0,003**
Visual Management	,547	,299	,211	,44537	,299	**0,000**
Quality in production	,486	,237	,141	,45716	,237	**0,006**

Predictors: (Constant), Manufac_3D, Internal_log, Virtual_reality, Robots_manuf, AI, ERP, Robots_assem, EDI, Control_system, Mobile_dev, PLM_PDM, Digital_sol, Prototype_3D

5   Conclusion

Since there is not much less research in the area of non-technical innovation than in the area of technical innovation, this paper gives emphasis on this type of innovation. We have analysed how widely selected organisational concepts are used, what is the extent of their potential use, what differences exist in the use and extent of use of these concepts and which are the characteristics of the adopters (company size, technological intensity, OEM/supplier etc.). There is a big difference in the exploitation of organizational concept potential use between analysed concepts. The ones with earlier average year of introduction have higher level of exploiting the potential use. On average, the dispersion of organizational concepts is higher in larger companies, suppliers and within companies from medium or high technological sectors.

The last finding is proved by the analysis of the relationship between organizational concepts and AMT. Our research showed that the use of several organizational concepts, that deal with organization or/and management and controlling of production, are strongly and positively correlated with AMT from "Digital factory" area, robots and additive manufacturing technologies. We can argue that the use of these AMT is not possible without carefully planned and implemented organizational concepts.

Our research has, therefore, practical and managerial implications. Our results show that the use of specific AMT clearly positively affects the need to implement organizational innovation concepts and vice versa. This is a clear message to managers that technical innovation and the use of AMT requires also organizational concepts to support the potential of AMT.

References

1. Gallego, J., Rubalcaba, L., Hipp, C.: Organizational innovation in small European firms: a multidimensional approach. Int. Small Bus. J. **31**(5), 563–579 (2012)
2. Keupp, M.M., Palmie, M., Gassmann, O.: The strategic management of innovation: a systematic review and paths for future research. Int. J. Manag. Rev. **14**, 367–390 (2011)
3. Kocijančič, T., Bikfalvi, A., Llach Pages, J., Palčič, I.: Impact of innovative organisational concepts adoption on manufacturing firms' performance. In: Operations management at the heart of the recovery: collection of presented papers at EurOMA 2013, 20th EurOMA Conference, 7th–12th June 2013, Dublin, Ireland (2013)
4. Armbruster, H., Bikfalvi, A., Kinkel, S., Lay, G.: Organizational innovation: the challenge of measuring non-technical innovation in large-scale surveys. Technovation **28**(10), 644–657 (2008)
5. Damanpour, F.: Footnotes to research on management innovation. Organ. Stud. **35**(9), 1265–1285 (2014)
6. Birkinshaw, J., Hamel, G., Mol, M.: Management innovation. Acad. Manag. Rev. **33**, 825–845 (2008)
7. OECD: Oslo manual. Guidelines for collecting and interpreting innovation data, 3rd edn. OECD EUROSTAT, Paris (2005)
8. Hollen, R.M.A., Van Den Bosch, F.A.J., Volberda, H.W.: The role of management innovation in enabling technological process innovation: an inter-organizational perspective. Eur. Manag. Rev. **10**, 35–50 (2013)
9. Damanpour, F., Aravind, D.: Managerial innovation: conceptions, processes, and antecedents. Manag. Organ. Rev. **8**, 423–454 (2012)
10. Damanpour, F., Walker, R.M., Avellaneda, C.N.: Combinative effects of innovation types and organizational performance: a longitudinal study of service organizations. J. Manag. Stud. **46**, 650–675 (2009)
11. Damanpour, F., Evan, W.M.: Organizational innovation and performance: the problem of organizational lag. Adm. Sci. Q. **29**, 392–409 (1984)
12. Cummings, T.G., Srivastva, S.: Management of Work: A Sociotechnical System Approach. Kent State University Press, Kent (1977)
13. Trist, E., Murray, H.: The Social Engagement of Social Science: A Tavistock Anthology. University of Pennsylvania Press, Philadelphia (1993)

Systems Engineering Approach to Identify Requirements for Digital Twins Development

Ali Gharaei[1] , Jinzhi Lu[1(✉)] , Oliver Stoll[2] ,
Xiaochen Zheng[1] , Shaun West[2] , and Dimitris Kiritsis[1]

[1] EPFL, SCI STI DK ME A1, Station 9, 1015 Lausanne, Switzerland
jinzhi.lu@epfl.ch
[2] HSLU, Technikumstrasse 21, 6048 Horw, Switzerland
shaun.west@hslu.ch

Abstract. Digital Twins (DT) are proposed in industries to support the entire lifecycle of services with different perspectives. Lack of systematic analysis of DT concepts leads to various definitions and services which challenges the DT developers for data integration and integrated service delivery. In this paper, a systems engineering approach is proposed to identify the requirements of DT in order to formalize the DT concepts from a systematic perspective. The conceptual architecture of DT is defined based on ISO standard 42010. Several concepts are captured to recognize DT, to define related terminologies, and to identity concerns and viewpoints in order to provide cues for delivering DT services to industry. This approach is evaluated by multiple industrial use-cases under the Innosuisse IMPULSE project, from which one-use case is selected for further elaboration. It contributes to the development of DT associated to the use-case by addressing the requirements of DT using a semi-formal approach.

Keywords: Digital Twin · Systems Engineering · Architecture design

1 Introduction

With the rapid advancement of Industry 4.0, Digital Twins (DT) are increasingly gaining attention for their potential to support intelligent decision-making for real-time cyber-physical systems. As an emergent technique, many industries from different domains are developing different DT concepts aimed at establishing cost-effective solutions for product development and maintenance. However, the DT concepts are separately defined by different domains, which leads to challenges defining a unified DT concept. Without unified definitions, stakeholders of DT find it difficult to communicate with the same language and thought structure. This negatively impacts the proper delivery of DT services and decision-making identifications.

The DT is a digital duplication of entities, with real-time two-way communication enabled between the cyber and physical spaces [1]. As a DT is developed, four main perspectives need to be considered: i. DT domains; ii., DT organizations; iii., DT models; and, iv., DT decision-making. DT domains refers to the disciplines the DT is used for. DT organizations refer to the group and enterprises providing DT concepts. DT models refer to models constructing virtual entities of DT. DT decision-making to

© IFIP International Federation for Information Processing 2020
Published by Springer Nature Switzerland AG 2020
B. Lalic et al. (Eds.): APMS 2020, IFIP AICT 591, pp. 82–90, 2020.
https://doi.org/10.1007/978-3-030-57993-7_10

the purposes. These perspectives are difficult for DT stakeholders to identify because the systematic view of the DT requires more domain-specific knowledge. Thus, a general architecture description of DT is useful for stakeholders for DT development, implementation and maintenance.

The contribution of this paper is to illustrate a systems engineering approach to formalize architecture descriptions of DT for different domains. Based on ISO standard 42010 as a reference model, DT is defined as a "system" whose architectural entities are formalized including stakeholder concerns and viewpoints. Through these entities, requirements are identified which are used for making decisions about DT service delivery. Finally, an ontology model is developed to visualize the architectural entities from the selected use-case in an Innosuisse project IMPULSE, which aims to provide a unified architecture description of DT.

The rest of the paper is organized as follows. We discuss the related work in Sect. 2 and introduce the systems engineering approach to identify the architecture description of DT in Sect. 3. In Sect. 4, the use case is elaborated to evaluate the approach to identify each requirement of DT development. Finally, we discuss findings and offer our conclusions with a summary in Sect. 5.

Based on the output of this paper an ontology-based approach will be used as a continuation of this works to formalize the architecture entities of DT and visualize a DT concept. This, however, remains beyond the scope of this paper.

2 Literature Review

The concept of digital twins is an emergent technique aiming at providing a rapid and effective solution for product development [2]. The DT concept consists of physical products in real space, virtual products in virtual space and communications between these two spaces [3]. Different domain specialists provide different definitions and technologies to construct digital twins [4]. This brings a new challenge to define and formalize the architecture of DT so stakeholders can make appreciate decisions when developing DT [1].

In systems engineering aspects, an international standard ISO/IEC/IEEE 42010 - Systems and software engineering – architecture description – is officially recommended for describing the system architectures as a reference practice [5]. As R. Capilla et al., [6] explained, the ISO 42010 has provided meta-models for describing systems and software architectures. The specification concluded that most of the key concepts and meta-models in different architectural knowledge management (AKM) tools are consistent. E. Kavakli et al., [7] use the proposed architecture model to produce specifications for a smart system for disruption management. They proposed informational, physical and logical viewpoints to frame the stakeholders' concerns. P. Obergfell et al., [8] used the reference architecture description to specify functional capabilities of modern automobiles from various aspects including services, software, electronics and electrics. They have applied their so-called Electric/Electronic-architecture (E/E-architecture) description method for identifying the Adaptive Cruise Control (ACC) features.

From the literature review, we found DT has been widely proposed by different domains with specific definitions and concepts [1, 9]. A general architecture concept for DT is needed to identify domain-specific requirements for DT development. We found ISO 42010 has been widely used to formalize the architectures of complex systems and can potentially support DT architecture descriptions from different perspectives.

3 Systems Engineering Approach to Identify the Requirements of a Digital Twin

In this paper, a systems engineering approach is proposed to formalize the requirements used for making decisions on DT development. DT developers make use of ISO 42010 to identify the architecture of DT and propose questions to represent views of DT. Then based on an Easy Approach to Requirements Syntax (EARS) [10], requirements are formalized referring to answers to the proposed questions. Figure 1 shows how the requirements are captured in order to make DT development decisions.

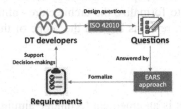

Fig. 1. Workflow of the proposed systems engineering approach

3.1 Identify Questions Using ISO 42010

From literature reviews, we used the international standard ISO/IEC/IEEE 42010 as the reference model, aiming at defining the key architectural concepts and system boundaries for DT from domain-specific perspectives, particularly for the Swiss Innovation Project IMPULSE.

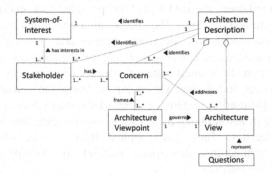

Fig. 2. Reference architecture in ISO 42010 [11]

To focus on the DT requirements, we simplified the model to investigate the core conceptual elements of the DT architecture; System-of-interest, Stakeholder, Concern, Architecture Description, Architecture Viewpoint, and View – as shown in Fig. 2.

The System-of-interest refers to the collection of physical and virtual entities in a DT. Stakeholders interested in the DT (System-of-interest) each have their concerns, for example, DT system developers want to obtain the structure of the physical entities. The architecture description identifies the system-of-interest, the stakeholders and their concerns. It is comprised of more than one architecture view addressing a set of stakeholders' concerns and more than one architecture viewpoint. An architecture viewpoint is a work product that provides a framework for a set of concerns by presenting conventions for constructing, interpreting and using architecture views. An architecture view is a product addressing a (set of) concern(s) raised by the identified stakeholders.

In this paper, the system-of-interest is defined as the collection of physical and virtual entities of the DT which is being developed. The boundary is identified by considering the main stages of the DT system's lifecycle: concept, development, implementation, utilization, support, and retirement [12]. Stakeholders are identified within that boundary while envisioning the phases of the DT's lifecycle. The term 'actor' (with defined roles) is used within Service Dominant logic [13]) and 'beneficiary' identifies where value accrues; these terms are complementary to the Systems Engineering term of stakeholder: stakeholders are actors directly involved with, or one-step-removed from the focus. Stakeholders are identified by the classification of different actors (roles). They provide concerns in order to identify the viewpoints and views. The onion diagram of product stakeholders [14] clearly details the taxonomy of stakeholders and their relationships. The concerns of the Digital Twin's stakeholders can be categorized based on various viewpoints such as performance, asset safety, etc. These viewpoints and views construct an architecture description of DT. Finally, questions for DT development are followed by answers (given by the use case owner) in a semi-formal format and proposed as views to DT developers to identify requirements for DT development.

3.2   Define Requirements Using an EARS Approach

The EARS approach is proposed to formalize the requirement syntax using a semi-formal approach. The requirement is defined as a statement as following:

1. What a system must do (Functional Requirements).
2. A known limitation or constraint on resources or design (non-Functional Req.).
3. How well the system must do what it does (non-Functional Requirements).

The functional requirement is defined as a general syntax for functional requirements:

$$ReqF = \{[Trigger], [Precondition], System, System behavior, [Object]\} \quad (1)$$

Where square brackets (e.g., []) refers to the elements which can be removed. Trigger refers to when a System or others implement actions. Precondition refers to the conditions when a System or others implement actions. System refers to the target system implementing some actions (System behavior) to Objects.

In the EARS approach, requirements are defined as:

1. Ubiquitous refers to the system behavior always occurring.
2. Event-driven refers to the requirements for certain system behaviors.
3. Unwanted behaviors refer to the system behaviors under unwanted conditions.
4. State-driven refers to the system behaviors while in its own states.
5. Optional features refer to the system behaviors under specific conditions.
6. Complex refer to requirements constructed by collections of the above (Table 1).

Table 1. EARS approach for formalizing requirements

Requirement type	Format rules
Ubiquitous	The <system or component> shall <system behavior> ([Object])
Event-driven	WHEN <trigger> <optional precondition> the <system> shall < system behavior > ([Object])
Unwanted behaviors	IF <unwanted condition or event>, THEN the < system or component > shall < system behavior> ([Object])
State-driven	WHILE <system statement>, the < system or component > shall < system behavior> ([Object])
Optional features	WHERE <feature is included>, the < system or component > shall < system behavior> ([Object])
Complex	Combination of the above requirements using first order logic [1]

4 Use Case

In order to evaluate the proposed approach, an industrial use case is investigated. First, stakeholders across the lifecycle of Digital Twin (from Developer, Implementer, User, and Maintainer/Supporter) are identified. By interviewing them, their concerns are collected. Then, four main architecture viewpoints are proposed to frame those concerns.

4.1 Use Case Overview

Company A seeks to add value to its business by offering new asset condition monitoring with control capabilities to its customer (Company C). Company C owns critical rooms and assets including server equipment where their temperature has to be monitored and controlled with special care. Company A has two partner companies: Company B and Company D; the former supports Company A in developing, implementing, and maintaining the DT and the latter in the support phase of the DT lifecycle.

The DT is designed for constant monitoring of temperature profiles in parts of the room as well as the status of specific artifacts such as servers, door/window (being open/closed), HVAC systems, etc. The DT will also be coupled with simulation capabilities to run what-if scenarios and offer potential solutions including control command suggestions to secure proper functioning, and optimal post-failure reaction processes.

4.2 Systems Engineering Analysis

Using the systems engineering approach, we interviewed the stakeholders related to the use case. Figure 3 illustrates the dependencies from stakeholders (blocks in blue) to viewpoints (blocks in green). Blocks in yellow represent categories of stakeholders, and the term 'stakeholder' refers to all the main people/teams involved across the DT lifecycle. Each stakeholder has their own concern(s). The developed viewpoints frame multiple concerns which are raised by one or more stakeholders. By considering all stages of the Digital Twin from concept to retirement, main stakeholders in the use case are identified, followed by the various concerns they have – as shown in Fig. 3.

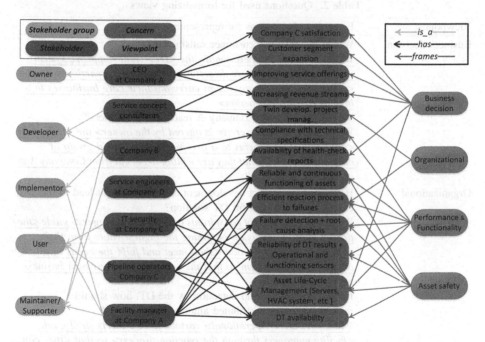

Fig. 3. Dependencies between actors, stakeholders, concerns and viewpoints (Color figure online)

Based on the concerns in each viewpoint, questions are proposed to identify views, then the answers are formalized using the ERAS approach. Proposed examples of questions and answers are shown in Table 2. They are used to capture the requirements of the DT development in the use case.

4.3   Limitations

In the use case, only one service scenario for one customer (Company C) is explored. The stakeholders are identified from actors related to the DT. More stakeholders can be defined in order to capture more complete requirements. However, based on the scope of the IMPULSE project, several key stakeholders were selected to evaluate the approach given in this paper. The whole analysis process demonstrates the systems engineering analysis for the DT required by the use case. More detailed requirements will be analyzed in the future.

This paper is limited to the requirements identifications as one of the earliest efforts prior to initiating the DT development phase. Nevertheless, based on the output of this paper, the work is continued further on to identify all the DT's entities in each use case, classify those entities in relation with each other using ontology languages and finally propose a reference architecture for DTs.

Table 2. Questions used for formalizing views

Viewpoints	Examples of questions for representing views
Business decision	Would the DT raise customer satisfaction? *WHEN <the DT is operational> the <DT> shall <improve system reliability through failure detection and improving reactions> so that <operations of company C can carry out their core businesses to a high degree of satisfaction>* Would the DT help Company A reach new customers? *WHEN <DT solution service is offered by the owner> the <DT> shall <provide further benefits to a previously unidentified group of customers, in a way that they are willing to benefit from Company A in exchange>*
Organizational	How can twin project development and management lead to the execution of a successful DT solution? *When <service concept consultants and project managers> guide <the project work, to focus on obtaining the highest value from their activities> the DT solution <shall meet and fulfil the needs of all actors in the ecosystem so that they can execute their own business goals successfully>* In case of a failure and detection by the DT, how should responsibilities be distributed among various actors? *When <the DT is operational> various failure alerts shall guide <facility managers through the reaction process> so that <they can deliver their service level agreement to the pipeline operators>*
Performance & functionality	Would the DT be able to meet the predefined specifications? *The <sensors> shall <remain continuously operational and functional>* *The <DT> shall <produce automatic periodic reports>* *The <DT results> shall <continuously be displaying monitoring data>* *The <DT> shall <alert when data exceeds boundaries and assist with that specific reaction process>*

(continued)

Table 2. (*continued*)

Viewpoints	Examples of questions for representing views
	How can we be sure the critical assets work continuously and reliably? *The <Digital Twin> shall <constantly provide asset operational data to Company A, Company C and facility managers; additionally, routine physical inspections are carried out.>*
Safety	How can this DT system improve asset safety? *WHEN <the DT is operational> it shall <improve multiple process of MEBAG, various departments of Company C and Company D> so that <all equipment operates as should that supports the other critical reliant equipment in this system to improve overall asset safety>*

5   Conclusion

In this paper, we proposed a Systems Engineering approach to identify requirements, in order to support decision-makings of DT development. The systems engineering approach uses ISO 42010 to identify the architectures of DT and provide questions for capturing the requirements. Based on such questions, requirements are formalized using an EARS approach. Finally, a use case from the IMPULSE project is used to evaluate the approach. From the results, we find the requirements are identified to support decision-making for developing the DT with features to monitor and control the temperature in critical areas.

Acknowledgement. The work presented in this paper is supported by the EU H2020 project (869951) FACTLOG-Energy-aware Factory Analytics for Process Industries and EU H2020 project (825030) QU4LITY Digital Reality in Zero Defect Manufacturing and the Innosuisse (Project 35258.1 IP-SBM) IMPULSE project on Digital Twins. The authors also would like to thank the Lucerne University of Applied Sciences and Arts and the Zurich University of Applied Sciences for supporting this work.

References

1. Lu, J., Zheng, X., Gharaei, A., Kalaboukas, K., Kiritsis, D.: Cognitive twins for supporting decision-makings of Internet of Things systems. In: Wang, L., Majstorovic, V.D., Mourtzis, D., Carpanzano, E., Moroni, G., Galantucci, L.M. (eds.) Proceedings of 5th International Conference on the Industry 4.0 Model for Advanced Manufacturing. LNME, pp. 105–115. Springer, Cham (2020). https://doi.org/10.1007/978-3-030-46212-3_7
2. Bricogne, M., Le Duigou, J., Eynard, B.: Design processes of mechatronic systems. In: Hehenberger, P., Bradley, D. (eds.) Mechatronic Futures, pp. 75–89. Springer, Cham (2016). https://doi.org/10.1007/978-3-319-32156-1_6
3. Tao, F., Zhang, H., Liu, A., Nee, A.Y.C.: Digital twin in industry: state-of-the-art. IEEE Trans. Ind. Inform. **15**(4), 2405–2415 (2019)

4. Lim, K.Y.H., Zheng, P., Chen, C.: A state-of-the-art survey of digital twin: techniques, engineering product lifecycle management and business innovation perspectives. J. Intell. Manuf. **31**, 1313–1337 (2019)
5. IEEE "INTERNATIONAL STANDARD ISO/IEC. IEEE Systems and software engineering — architecture description (2011)
6. Capilla, R., Jansen, A., Tang, A., Avgeriou, P., Babar, M.A.: 10 years of software architecture knowledge management: practice and future. J. Syst. Softw. **116**, 191–205 (2016)
7. Kavakli, E., Buenabad-Chavez, J., Tountopoulos, V., Loucopoulos, P., Sakellariou, R.: WiP: an architecture for disruption management in smart manufacturing. In: Proceedings of the 2018 IEEE International Conference on Smart Computing SMARTCOMP 2018, pp. 279–281 (2018)
8. Obergfell, P., Oszwald, F., Traub, M., Sax, E.: Viewpoint-based methodology for adaption of automotive E/E-architectures. In: Proceedings of the 2018 IEEE 15th International Conference on Software Architecture Companion, ICSA-C 2018, pp. 128–135 (2018)
9. Terzakis, J.: EARS : The easy approach to requirements syntax (2013)
10. Tao, F., Zhang, M., Nee, A.Y.C.: Digital Twin Driven Smart Manufacturing. Academic Press, London (2019)
11. ISO/IEC/IEEE© Std. 4201:2011. INTERNATIONAL STANDARD ISO/IEC/IEEE systems and software engineering — agile environment. ISO/IEC/IEEE 26515. First Edition 2011-12-01; Corrected version 2012-03-15, vol. 2012 (2011))
12. Walden, R.D.H.T.M.S.D.D., Roedler, G.J., Forsberg, K.J.: For INCOSE member, Corporate Advisory Board, and Academic Council use only. Do not distribute (2015)
13. Schmitt, P.H.: First-order logic. In: Ahrendt, W., Beckert, B., Bubel, R., Hähnle, R., Schmitt, P., Ulbrich, M. (eds.) Deductive Software Verification – The KeY Book. LNCS, vol. 10001, pp. 23–47. Springer, Cham (2016). https://doi.org/10.1007/978-3-319-49812-6_2
14. Alexander, I.F.: A taxonomy of stakeholders. Int. J. Technol. Hum. Inter. (2011). https://doi.org/10.4018/jthi.2005010102
15. Vargo, S.L., Lusch, R.F.: Institutions and axioms: an extension and update of service-dominant logic. J. Acad. Mark. Sci. **44**(1), 5–23 (2015). https://doi.org/10.1007/s11747-015-0456-3

Manufacturing Operations Management for Smart Manufacturing – A Case Study

Michael Meyer-Hentschel[1], Oliver Lohse[1(✉)], Subba Rao[2], and Raffaello Lepratti[3]

[1] Siemens AG, Corporate Technology, 81739 Munich, Germany
{michael.meyer-hentschel,oliver.lohse}@siemens.com
[2] Siemens Industry Software Inc., Digital Industries, Troy, MI 48098, USA
Subba.rao@siemens.com
[3] Siemens AG, Digital Industries, 13623 Berlin, Germany
raffaello.lepratti@siemens.com

Abstract. Industry 4.0 was introduced early in the last decade. That introduction spawned related concepts like "Smart Manufacturing" and digitalization, as well as a proliferation of digital manufacturing technologies for supporting systems. The industry experienced widespread puzzlement over how to apply these concepts in practice and which roles "Manufacturing Executions Systems" play and will play in this context.

This paper outlines the change from classical Manufacturing Execution System (MES), with a focus on manufacturing execution including data collection, to monolithic Manufacturing Operations Management (MOM) with an extension of the functionality regarding quality management, planning inclusive scheduling and a collaborative MOM, which stands out from its predecessors through broad horizontal integration and cloud applications.

These parameters lead to an evolution of the Collaborative MOM towards a MOM for Smart Manufacturing, which harmoniously combines, controls and regulates the interaction of technologies such as IIoT, RAD, AI, Edge Computing, Cloud with the MOM functions and therefore enables new production systems like a cyber-physical production system (CPPS).

Keywords: MES · MOM · CPPS

1 Introduction

Due to a variety of external and internal influences, such as increasing globalization, a steadily rising individualization of products and a related increase in complexity, which on the one hand directly affect the products but also have a strong influence on the associated production processes, the requirements on production systems are growing [1]. Concerning the growing requirements of modern production systems, the focus is on the following aspects: self-organization, decentralization, adaptability, networking, closed cycles and resource efficiency, live status of all production resources, customer integration in engineering and production as well as flexible process sequences and an open architecture [1].

B. Lalic et al. (Eds.): APMS 2020, IFIP AICT 591, pp. 91–98, 2020.
https://doi.org/10.1007/978-3-030-57993-7_11

Due to a large number of available solutions, most companies are currently using different technologies, detached from each other, to realize selective improvements in terms of process flexibility and output. Flexibility, agility and efficiency are essential components of future production landscapes. However, companies must go a step further and consider how production landscapes can be holistically and sustainably aligned to dynamic market changes, as this is the only way to fully exploit their potential [1, 3]. This paper describes based on a case study how technologies and systems interact harmoniously via a holistic approach and thus optimally master existing and future requirements.

2   MOM Evolution Towards Smart Manufacturing

2.1   MES Evolution to MOM

The concept of MES has evolved into a broader and more valuable solution: Manufacturing Operations Management. During the 1990 s the focus was on Stand-alone MES for improved manufacturing execution [7]. A best-in-class MES had to provide manufacturing digitalization, standardization, orchestration & collaboration, enforcement and contextualization with a focus on a specific industry. It was (and still is) critical to provide a rich set of industry-specific OOTB functionalities and a vertical integration with the specific production styles of such industry.

During the 2000s the manufacturing scope evolved from pure execution to broader coverage of manufacturing disciplines. From MES to monolithic MOM to digitalize manufacturing execution, quality management, planning and scheduling mostly working as disparate processes & systems under a monolithic MOM umbrella [9]. The traditional MES/MOM functions are defined in IEC 62264-1 [4].

Recently the monolithic MOM evolved even further to an integrated MOM where applications are synchronized through common communication systems (see Fig. 1). This is crucial to connect quality improvements, with manufacturing processes and efficiency logic. Integrated MOM systems must also align with modern technologies: mobility, security, usability, flexibility, agility, etc.

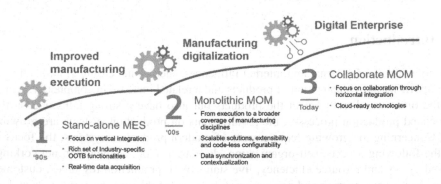

Fig. 1. MES evolution towards MOM

Regardless of the manufacturing industry segment, the manufacturing processes for OEMs or supplier tier, or the maturity of the business, one thing is clear: manufacturing enterprise will go through a continued digital transformation, no matter how digitalized they are today [6]. The question is what, when, and how will that transformation take place? Importantly, the functionality of manufacturing operations management has existed since the second industrial revolution — long before digitalization began. MOM functions always need to occur in any manufacturing setting, irrespective of advancement in production methods, level of automation and supporting systems & technologies – MES/MOM, IIoT, RAD, Edge computing, on-premise vs cloud [4]. What changes is the mechanism or system that performs MOM functions, and the delivery mechanisms for those functions. This calls for more modularity in the MOM functions for flexibility and agility to fulfill the deployment across different technologies and able to meet the transformation and manufacturing data & processes orchestration towards digital excellence in Industry 4.0 and Smart Manufacturing journey.

2.2 MOM Evolution to MOM for Smart Manufacturing

There is an increased transformation in the industry where traditional mass production "make to stock"-environments are transitioning to mass customization modes [5]. In such transformations, the need for flexibility and agility in manufacturing operations is becoming more prevalent.

This need for flexibility & agility is driving the need for increased automation to the line (robots & automated inspection devices), material handling systems (e.g. AGV's). With increased automation and human-machine interactions in shop-floor, how engineering data, manufacturing process, quality and supply chain data is harmonized along with AI principles to orchestrate the data across the systems and processes is more critical for factories of future/smart manufacturing. This calls for a robust connectivity & brokering function as an interoperating module across the systems with streamlined data flows. In the realm of IIoT, cloud and other advanced technologies, MOM for Smart Manufacturing should architecturally address the data orchestration and brokering function.

Specific to MOM, architectural advancements of modular MOM functions towards smart manufacturing functions leveraging IIoT & Cloud is the pivot. As certain functions will remain close to shop-floor data & network latency needs [2, 4], flexibility in architecture is critical.

The gathered information has to be made available for all necessary participants or IT-systems. Therefore, the focus of horizontal integration of a collaborate MOM has to be widened to also include the vertical integration to enable cyber-physical production systems (CPPS) [8]. As in Fig. 2. depicted, MOM must evolve from a "Collaborate MOM" further to a "MOM for Smart Manufacturing" to address the above-mentioned challenges. Current production architectures and IT-systems don't support that high degree of collaboration combined with the functionality to orchestrate those information.

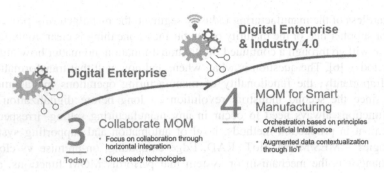

Fig. 2. MOM evolution towards Smart Manufacturing

3 Case Study

A good case study for this aspect is a manufacturer of electric motors, used for the oil and gas industry, paper production, as well as for the use in subways, trains and trams in Germany.

The manufacturer faced the challenge that its products are in direct competition with products on the world market which is currently characterized by overcapacity. This intensified competitive situation requires a cost and time optimized production of the products, with constant high quality. In addition to these external influences, the following factors represent internal motivation drivers. On the one hand, this is the increased variance of the products and the associated complexity concerning order processing and all associated processes and, on the other hand, the insufficient documentation of the "as-built" of the products.

One of the main problems here was excessive processing time, which in turn had a negative effect on costs and the time it took for the customer to receive his order. The reasons for the high processing time were a lack of transparency regarding the workstations and their production resources (e.g. status regarding capacity utilization or availability of production resources and tools and materials) and inefficient detailed planning and order control based on this, which had a particularly serious effect when malfunctions occurred.

From these challenges, concrete requirements and functions for and on the production system have been derived and developed: live status of all production resources, real-time localization, smart products/components, networking, mobile apps, AGVs, flexible adaptation of defined processes, open system architecture.

The idea was to design and implement an innovative production system based on an existing MOM (Mix between Collaborate MOM and a MOM for Smart Manufacturing) by using new technologies and methods (IIoT, RAD, Edge Computing, AI,...), which meets the requirements in a particularly efficient way.

The system now consisted of individual modules, each of which fulfills a specific task. The challenge now was to find an answer to the elementary question: how can such a system, consisting of a multitude of different solutions (hardware and software components), be made to work together and finally be made controllable?

The solution is a new module for the MOM for Smart Manufacturing. The following describes how the developed system is built and how it works. The central element for controlling and regulating such a system is organized communication. All participants in the production system must be enabled to exchange relevant information for specific production tasks with each other. For this purpose, we have implemented a so-called coordinating-app with the help of a RAD platform, which realizes the communication within the system in combination with an MQTT-Broker (Message Queuing Telemetry Transport protocol) which works according to the publish and subscribe principle. This protocol uses topics and payloads to share information among the system participants. We used JavaScript Object Notation (JSON) for the transfer of information via payload linked to the different topics. The system participants e.g. the product, the workstations, the AGVs but also the IT-Systems are managed within the app and their communication is defined and organized and so leveraging IIoT. This application regulates which information can be provided by which participant and for which participants this information could be relevant, for example, for processing a production order. According to this principle, the respective participant (MQTT-Client) publishes its information, which can then be received and processed by the others if required. This approach makes the IT landscape simpler, in particular, the standardized interface and the faster exchange of information between clients are major advantages. Figure 3 shows the implemented communication structure within the production system with all participants. To explain how the system works, this is described in more detail using the processing of production orders. The orders come roughly scheduled from the ERP level and are fed into the control and regulation level together with product information from the PLM level (e.g.: 3D models). In this layer the actual state of work cells, resources, material availabilities will be considered and an optimized manufacturing date, with consideration of all production orders, will be determined. This production date is updated in the production order and triggers the intralogistics for commissioning and in-time supply for production. The result is transferred to the MES which then passes the order information (work plan, including work instructions, required production resources, quality information, skills required for processing, dependencies, pre-conditions regarding the production sequence) on to the individual intelligent products and to other relevant participants (e.g. workstations and operators). The products, therefore, have all the plannable information that is required for production. All other information, such as the status of individual production cells, is obtained by the products independently via the developed communication concept. In addition, process and quality parameters are recorded, linked to the production order and processed in the MES. That information enables the creation of an "as build model" of the product. The previously defined communication forms the framework for efficiently processing the order within the system.

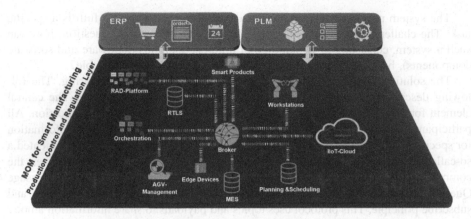

Fig. 3. IT-architecture

In concrete terms, the module consists of two software components. A master app and a client app. Figure 4 contains the definitions of the terms used in the following and shows the relationship between information - topic - category including visual representation.

The master app performs the following tasks:

- System description:
    - Selection and addition of system participants based on predefined categories or creation of new categories
    - Selection of predefined topics depending on the selected category or creation of new topics and assignment to categories

- Manage the system participants:
    - Create and delete categories
    - Create and delete system participants

- Organization of communication:
    - Creation and deletion of information that can be transported using topics
    - Assigning and solving information to topics
    - Creating and deleting topics
    - Assigning and solving topics to categories
    - Selection whether the topic is subscribed by category or published by it.

Whereby the client app covers the following range of functions:

- Installation on the operating system of the system participants or Smart Production Tag
- Initialization: Configuration of the app after installation, with the goal of providing system participants with information

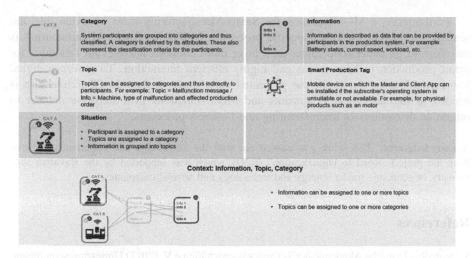

Fig. 4. Relationship between information - topic - category

- Communication from system participant to Client App:
  - Selection of the protocol (OPC UA, MQTT, REST, SOAP, …)
  - Characteristics of the interface: Which data should be propagated?

The result is a concept for the standardized exchange of information and based on this, an organized collaboration across all components within a production system. Furthermore, it can be seen as a preliminary stage of a self-organizing production system. The presented IT-Architecture is a prototype approach in a test environment. To achieve this high degree of communication and collaboration within a production different IT-Systems, like MES, AGV-Management, etc., as well as different system interfaces must be evaluated and implemented. To simplify the implementation of such a production architecture current collaborative MOM systems with an already high degree of horizontal integration must evolve further into a MOM for Smart Manufacturing (see Fig. 2). A MOM for Smart Manufacturing provides functionalities to orchestrate a production system and thus is the foundation of a production architecture with a high degree of horizontal and vertical integration. The described communication principals between the participants could be implemented in a current MOM system to achieve a MOM for Smart Manufacturing.

4 Conclusion

This case study shows how a manufacturing approach according to the Industry 4.0 initiative could be implemented with a holistic IT-structure. Collaborative MOM systems need to further evolve into a "MOM for Smart Manufacturing" to not just ensure a collaboration between different IT-Systems, like IIoT and RAD, but also to orchestrate the data gathered and shared along those data driven self-organizing production systems.

Furthermore, a MOM-solution for Smart Manufacturing must be extensible and scalable to support customer-specific processes. MOM for Smart Manufacturing is therefore to be understood rather as a layer that combines all relevant functions for smart production in harmonious and highly efficient interaction. To realize a digital transformation, as shown in the presented case study, a flexible IT-architecture is needed to introduce new IT-systems and MOM-functions in a stepwise manner to minimize disruptions of manufacturing and business processes.

Acknowledgment. This work was carried out with the knowledge and experience gathered from the project "Road to Digitalization" (R2D), which was supported by the Bavarian state ministry of economy, media, energy and technology and several companies.

References

1. acatech – Deutsche Akademie der Technikwissenschaften e.V. (2013) Umsetzungsempfehlungen für das Zukunftsprojekt Industrie 4.0. https://www.bmbf.de/files/Umsetzungsempfehlungen_Industrie4_0.pdf
2. Alexakos, C., Kalogeras, A.: Exposing MES functionalities as enabler for cloud manufacturing. In: 2017 IEEE 13th International Workshop on Factory Communication Systems (WFCS), pp. 1–4 (31-May-17 – 02-Jun-17)
3. Demartini, M., Galluccio, F., Mattis, P., et al.: Closed-loop manufacturing for aerospace industry: an integrated PLM-MOM solution to support the wing box assembly process. In: Ameri, F., Stecke, KE., Cieminski, G von., et al. (eds) Advances in Production Management Systems. Towards Smart Production Management Systems, vol. 567, pp. 423–430. Springer International Publishing, Cham (2019)
4. Jeschke, S., Brecher, C., Meisen, T., et al.: Industrial Internet of Things and cyber manufacturing systems. In: Jeschke, S., Brecher, C., Song, H., et al. (eds.) Industrial Internet of Things, pp. 3–19. Springer International Publishing, Cham (2017)
5. Kang, H.S., Lee, J.Y., Choi, S., et al.: Smart manufacturing: past research, present findings, and future directions. Int. J. Precis. Eng. Manuf.-Green Tech. 3(1), 111–128 (2016). https://doi.org/10.1007/s40684-016-0015-5
6. Mantravadi, S., Møller, C.: An overview of next-generation manufacturing execution systems: how important is mes for industry 4.0? Procedia Manuf. 30, 588–595 (2019). https://doi.org/10.1016/j.promfg.2019.02.083
7. Qiu, R.G., Zhou, M.: V. IEEE Robot. Automat. Mag. 11(1), 19–40 (2004). https://doi.org/10.1109/MRA.2004.1275947
8. Tritchkov, I., Goetz, H.: Verification and validation of decentralized, self-organizing cyber-physical production systems: a blueprint process for testing cyber-physical production systems with self-properties. In: 2016 IEEE 1st International Workshops on Foundations and Applications of Self* Systems (FAS*W), pp. 112–117. IEEE (2016 – 2016)
9. Filipov, V., Vasilev, P.: Manufacturing operations management - the smart backbone of industry 4.0. Int. Sci. J. "Ind. 4.0" 1(1), 19–24 (2016)

Industry 4.0 on Demand: A Value Driven Methodology to Implement Industry 4.0

Deborah Leone [ID] and Andrea Barni[(✉)] [ID]

University of Applied Sciences and Arts of Southern Switzerland,
Manno, Switzerland
{deborah.leone,andrea.barni}@supsi.ch

Abstract. Technological progress is directing the whole world towards a new way of interacting with information and creating value. From this, the industry (both of products and services) needs to keep up with the times and renew itself. There is talk of *Industry 4.0*, where the digitalization of information through innovative technologies is the key factor for the revolution. In this context, a methodology supporting SMEs in the design and assessment of their I4.0 project portfolio is defined. The methodology adopts a decision making tool exploiting the AHP technique that supports the sorting of the identified projects and the identification of a customized I4.0 roadmap.

Keywords: Industry 4.0 · Digitalization · Roadmap

1 Introduction

The concept of Industry 4.0 was first publicly introduced in 2011 by a group of representatives from different fields, under an initiative to enhance the German competitiveness in the manufacturing industry. The idea of a digitally integrated industry [1] was made public at the Hannover Messe Industrie Fair in which it was demonstrated how cyber-physical systems (CPS) could make possible a paradigm shift in the industrial automation sector [2]. From that moment, the academic and industrial world worked relentlessly to transform that vision in a concrete industrial paradigm shift, extending the concept to what today can be described as the increasing digitization and automation of the manufacturing environment, as well as the creation of a digital value chain enabling communication among products, their environment and business partners [3]. Future value creation is located in digitized, real-time capable, intelligent, connected, and autonomous factories ('smart factories') and production networks [4]. While large companies usually have the resources to define and implement structured roadmaps to support the integration of I4.0 technologies to boost value creation, SMEs are more subject to the risk of addressing this challenge with a scattered and inefficient implementation approach [5], based on a technology push approach to innovation instead of on one based on the analysis of the value creating drivers of technology integration [6].

This paper aims to present a methodology to support SMEs in the path that goes from the identification of inner value drivers that I4.0 technologies can unveil, up to

Published by Springer Nature Switzerland AG 2020
B. Lalic et al. (Eds.): APMS 2020, IFIP AICT 591, pp. 99–106, 2020.
https://doi.org/10.1007/978-3-030-57993-7_12

transforming them into quantitatively assessed and prioritized applied projects. The methodology is then tested within a pharmaceutical company where a roadmap towards the achievement of I4.0 expected goals is defined.

2 Industry 4.0 Implementation and Value Creation Approaches

Recently, the consensus obtained by the expected benefits deriving from I4.0 implementation encouraged practitioners and academia to define approaches driving the deployment of the I4.0 framework at industrial level.

Pessl E. et al. [7] proposed a framework based on the individual application of Industry 4.0 actions consisting of a 6-step approach: (i) general Industry 4.0 analysis, (ii) maturity analysis, (iii) determination of the target state, (iv) development and evaluation of measures for each field of action (v) transfer of the target objectives and measures to a Balance Scorecard and (vi) definition of the final roadmap. Exploiting the main characteristics of the considered company, the research focuses on the need of defining the most appropriate roadmap. Khan R. I. [8] suggests an Industry 4.0 implementation approach for smart manufacturing that consider the development of technology integration prototypes as the main enablers of a successful implementation at industry wide level. The approach follows five different phases: (i) identifying business objectives, (ii) developing prototype, (iii) validation of prototype, (iv) replication of prototype and (v) total rollout.

Extending the scope of the assessment not only to the improvement of production capabilities, but also considering sustainability oriented criteria, Dossou P. [9] developed a framework for implementing Industry 4.0 where the sustainability of future changes is the basis for the future transformation. The framework involves four main steps: (i) brakes detection and analysis, (ii) definition of implementation acceleration levers, (iii) existing SME system modeling and analysis and (iv) definition of the future system and implementation plan. Considering three sub-systems (procurement, manufacturing and logistics) the framework aims at modeling, analyzing and improving each sub-system of the SME being studied and to define best steps for industry 4.0 implementation.

Putting technology at the center, Frank A. G. et al. [10] propose a framework for the identification of adoption patterns of I4.0 technologies in manufacturing firms. After studying how these technologies are used in manufacturing companies and clustering the adoption criteria under two layers of technologies, they argue that the adoption criteria are strictly related to the company dimensions and to capability of integrating a broad number of such technologies.

On the other side, if taking value creation as the main driver of I4.0 implementation, Erol et al. [11] faced the challenge of developing a transition model to I4.0 by developing a three-phase process, guiding companies to understand their specific objectives, the generated value beyond each objective and a series of measures to achieve them. This will lead the company to create a company-specific vision and roadmap. The model includes the following phases: envision (develop a tailored Industry 4.0 vision), enable (roadmapping of Industry 4.0 strategy and identification of the success factors) and enact (preparation of transformation and proposal of Industry 4.0 projects).

Following a more oriented value creation approach, Tonelli F. et al. [12] developed a methodology related to manufacturing value modeling (MVMM) based on 5 steps: Value Map, Maturity Model, Gap and Process Analysis, Validation and Improvement Areas Definition. Through the value map it is possible to establish the current level of the company and to perform a gap analysis, that allows the creation of value with the aim of building a roadmap of the interventions, defining the priorities and activities to be improved.

Overall, the identified methodologies either do not put value creation as the main driver, or fail in providing a method to quantitatively assess the gaps present in the company, and transform them in a prioritized set of projects. This paper aims at filling this gap by proposing a three steps approach that, starting from high level identification of company status and needs, goes down to the identification and prioritization of projects leading to process improvement.

3 Methodological Approach

To address the above outlined issues, we propose a methodological approach as a guiding framework (Fig. 1) for Industry 4.0 strategy design and practical implementation, that takes as main drivers the strategic identification of value creating gaps inside the company and transforms them in managed, quantitatively prioritized, implementation projects. The main goal of the model is to provide companies with a set of methods and tools that are able to guide in the implementation of their I4.0 value driven transition.

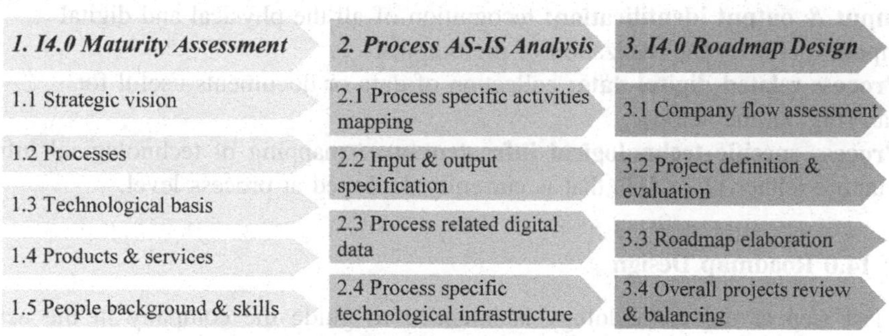

1. I4.0 Maturity Assessment	2. Process AS-IS Analysis	3. I4.0 Roadmap Design
1.1 Strategic vision	2.1 Process specific activities mapping	3.1 Company flow assessment
1.2 Processes	2.2 Input & output specification	3.2 Project definition & evaluation
1.3 Technological basis	2.3 Process related digital data	3.3 Roadmap elaboration
1.4 Products & services	2.4 Process specific technological infrastructure	3.4 Overall projects review & balancing
1.5 People background & skills		

Fig. 1. Methodological framework

The proposed methodology consists in three macro-phases: (i) I4.0 maturity assessment, (ii) Process AS-IS analysis and (iii) I4.0 Roadmap design. Each of the phases is composed of several steps (Fig. 1) that have to be completed in order to provide the necessary input elements to proceed in the analysis and roadmap design path. The details of these steps are reported in the following sections.

3.1   I4.0 Maturity Assessment

The primary step of the methodology aims at assessing the maturity of the company with respect to five main areas influencing the I4.0 transition: strategy, processes, technologies, products & services, and people. The assessment model originates in the work carried out by Canetta et al. [13] has been adapted in order to exploit that methodology as a starting point for the identification of the areas of the company which present the greatest gaps to be solved to foster the transition. The assessment can be carried on either as a remote questionnaire or as an interview, with representatives of the company departments. As output, it provides a radar chart positioning the company under the five mentioned areas and a list of the detected *gaps*. The main *gaps* are those from which the analysis and roadmapping activity should preferably start from (in this regard, the following sections - corresponding to the subsequent phases - cover these gaps). Wherever possible the interview should be conducted with more than one person in the company or in a focus group, in order to mitigate the risk of obtaining a result liable to subjective company vision. Further details about the adopted model can be found in [13].

3.2   Process AS-IS Analysis

Shifting to an operational analysis of the process flows, the second step of the methodology goes into the detail of the identified gaps. The formalization of the AS-IS situation (carried out by means of flowcharts built with the support of managers and operators) is the starting point for the following phases aiming at extracting process related value drivers. To this end, the phase considers the mapping of the following elements for each considered process:

– **Process specific activities mapping:** formalization of the activities within the identified process flow;
– **Input & output identification:** recognition of all the physical and digital
– inputs useful for the realization of the outputs;
– **Process related digital data:** collection of data or documents useful for
– carrying out the activity;
– **Process specific technological infrastructure:** mapping of technological infrastructure (either IT or OT) that is currently deployed at process level.

3.3   I4.0 Roadmap Design

The last step of the methodology is intended to guide the company in the actual identification of the sources of value generated from the gaps existent at process level. The identified gaps are then exploited to identify specific I4.0 projects, prioritized by exploiting a dedicated tool based on AHP methodology.

Phase 1: Company Flow Assessment. Among the different flows within the company (inbound logistics, operations, etc.) the phase aims to select one and begin its evaluation from the mapping carried out in phase 2. By adopting a design thinking approach [14, 15], a workshop with the main internal stakeholders of the process is then organized. Using the selected flow as guidance, the person appointed to manage the workshop stimulates the discussion collecting the problems associated with each activity, "*pains*", and the related desired improvements, "*gains*". Both *pains* and *gains* are appointed on a whiteboard and are used as starting points for the identification of new potential projects. If necessary, this phase can be carried out in an asynchronous fashion by exploiting available online workshopping tools.

Phase 2 - Project Definition & Evaluation. From the inputs gathered through the workshop (pains & gains), a list of innovation projects meant to address area specific or company wide needs is defined. At this point, with an overview of the projects that should be implemented to improve process operations, the risk of being stuck in the project portfolio selection becomes relevant [16]. In this regard, the methodology implements a decision support tool based on the Analytical Hierarchy Process (AHP) technique to guide decision makers in prioritizing the most relevant projects. AHP is a structured technique for organizing and analyzing complicated decisions, based on mathematics and psychology, developed by Thomas L. Saaty in the 1970s [17]. According to the AHP method, the tool proposes a set of evaluation criteria for each project (the criteria of our case are shown in Fig. 2).

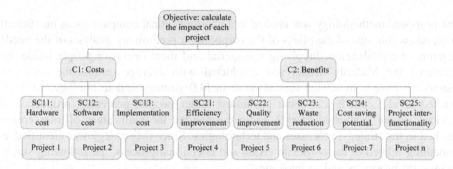

Fig. 2. Criteria adopted

The evaluator assigns a percentage weight to each criterion, then assigns a score that is evaluated by the decision criterion. The score of each decision alternative is the weighted average of the votes of each criterion on the decision for the weight assigned to each criterion. The criteria adopted in our model and shows in Fig. 2 are shortly described in the following table (Table 1).

Table 1. Projects evaluation criteria.

Criteria	Description
SC11	Relevance of the costs related to hardware acquisition
SC12	Relevance of the costs related to software acquisition
SC13	Relevance of the costs related to project implementation
SC21	Potential for Overall Equipment Effectiveness (OEE) improvement
SC22	Potential for quality improvement upon project implementation
SC23	Potential for waste reduction upon project implementation
SC24	Potential for cost reduction upon project implementation
SC25	Extensibility of the project in other company flows

Phase 3 - Roadmap Elaboration. According to the evaluations carried out in phase 2, a list of quantitatively assessed projects is obtained and used to develop the process specific *roadmap*. Passing from the project specific to the overall vision, projects are firstly ordered according to the score obtained in phase 2, then reviewed to integrate strategic decision making. At this point, a reviewed list of projects can be therefore set up.

Phase 4 - Overall Projects Review & Balancing. The last phase can be implemented whenever the methodology is retraced, with the aim of integrating a continuous improvement approach into the process. As the first step of this phase, an extension of Phase 1–3 to the remaining company processes (or to the most strategic ones) should be carried on, with the objective of (i) defining an integrated roadmap composed by the overall company I4.0 projects portfolio and (ii) identifying means of integration or parallelization of the identified projects.

4   Methodology Validation

The proposed methodology was applied in a pharmaceutical company as an instrument to create, within one of the plants of the corporate, a preliminary analysis of the needs in terms of digitalization. Involving managerial and more operative people inside the company, the Maturity Model was conducted with average results: the company resulted to have a somewhat limited score in I4.0 strategy and technology, where it reached level 1, but it was better positioned under people, processes, products and services, where it reached level 2. From the results, the main areas of intervention resulted in the strategy, processes and technologies. Since the strategy was identified as something related to the corporate vision and decisional process, the following stages focused on processes and technologies.

The following step conceived the analysis of the plant and the formalization of its processes. To this end, 4 company flows have been selected as the most impacting on the overall business: production, quality control, logistics and quality assurance. For each of them the related flowcharts were created as input to the analysis of the next phases. One or more representatives of the selected company flows have been therefore involved in two sessions of workshops: the first, carried out with flow responsible and dedicated to identify pain and gains for each specific flow; the second, as a focus group among the different stakeholders, to review the identified value drivers and discuss potential connections. Starting from the identification of the value drivers, a total of 46 I4.0 oriented projects have been identified. Most of them (30) related to the production environment, the remaining almost uniformly divided among the other flows. The potential projects have been then evaluated through the developed analytical tool. Also in this case, the different stakeholders were involved for the assignment of the scores to the decision criteria, then for the evaluation of the projects themselves. For the 46 projects initially identified, three levels of priority were identified. 11 projects resulted to have the highest priority, 24 were in the middle and eventually 11 has been identified as less relevant. Moreover, a particular attention was given to a group of 21 projects which showed potential to be integrated in all the flows (an aspect of fundamental importance for the company). Among the 11 projects considered most relevant, an important number of them was dedicated either to the automated acquisition of production data supporting traceability, or to the transfer of such data to the other involved flows. In particular, the main issues resulting from the carried out the evaluation highlighted the following points to be primarily addressed: the cultural aspect, the available time for the project development and the time dedicated by business experts.

5 Conclusion

In this work we identified a methodology for the identification and assessment of I4.0 related projects within manufacturing companies. It aims to address in particular SMEs that do not have the management processes and/or resources capable of systematically identifying innovation gaps and transforming them into I4.0 integration projects. The results of the methodology envisage therefore a three-phase methodological framework: I4.0 maturity assessment, process AS-IS analysis and I4.0 roadmap design. The third macro-phase provides a "circular" methodology which supports the development of the *roadmap* based on four steps: company flow assessment, project definition and evaluation, roadmap elaboration and overall projects review & balancing. The latter section of the methodology has been designed as a strategy supporting continuous improvement, to be therefore replicated for each corporate process and to be updated periodically. The validation carried out within a pharmaceutical company highlighted the flexibility of the methodology that well applied to the need of identification and prioritization of the I4.0 projects portfolio. As a future development, the impact that the adoption of I4.0 technologies can have on sustainability oriented KPIs will be more explicitly considered. Note that some aspects related to the topic are already considered in this approach: applying the concepts of I4.0 also means less waste, better management of resources, optimization of energy consumption and the use of raw materials and, therefore, emissions.

References

1. Bauernhansl, T., Ten Hompel, M., Vogel-Heuser, B. (eds.): Industrie 4.0 in Produktion, Automatisierung und Logistik: Anwendung-Technologien-Migration, pp. 1–648. Springer, Wiesbaden (2014). https://doi.org/10.1007/978-3-658-04682-8
2. Lu, Y.: Industry 4.0: a survey on technologies, applications and open research issues. J. Ind. Inf. Integr. **6**, 1–10 (2017)
3. Galati, F., Bigliardi, B.: Industry 4.0: emerging themes and future research avenues using a text mining approach. Comput. Ind. **109**, 100–113 (2019)
4. Veile, J., Kiel, D., Müller, J.M., Voigt, K.I.: How to implement industry 4.0? An empirical analysis of lessons learned from best practices. In: Organizational, and Environmental Determinants, International Association for Management of Technology (IAMOT) Conference, Birmingham, UK, April, pp. 22–26 (2018)
5. Matt, D.T., Rauch, E., Riedl, M.: Knowledge transfer and introduction of industry 4.0 in SMEs: a five-step methodology to introduce industry 4.0. In: Analyzing the Impacts of Industry 4.0 in Modern Business Environments, pp. 256–282. IGI Global (2018)

6. Sevinc, A., Gür, S., Eren, T.: Analysis of the difficulties of SMEs in industry 4.0 applications by analytical hierarchy process and analytical network process. Processes **6**(12), 264 (2018)

7. Pessl, E., Sorko, S.R., Mayer, B.: Roadmap industry 4.0–implementation guideline for enterprises. Int. J. Sci. Technol. Soc. **5**, 193–202 (2017)

8. Khan, R.I.: Implementation of Industry 4.0 Smart Manufacturing. ResearchGate. Lancaster Environment Centre, Library Avenue, Lancaster University, UK

9. Dossou, P.E.: Development of a new framework for implementing industry 4.0 in companies. Procedia Manuf. **38**, 573–580 (2019)

10. Frank, A.G., Dalenogare, L.S., Ayala, N.F.: Industry 4.0 technologies: implementation patterns in manufacturing companies. Int. J. Prod. Econ. **210**, 15–26 (2019)

11. Erol, S., Schumacher, A., Sihn, W.: Strategic guidance towards industry 4.0–a three-stage process model. In: International Conference on Competitive Manufacturing, vol. 9, no. 1, pp. 495–501 (2016)

12. Tonelli, F., Demartini, M., Loleo, A., Testa, C.: A novel methodology for manufacturing firms value modeling and mapping to improve operational performance in the industry 4.0 era. Procedia CIRP **57**, 122–127 (2016)

13. Canetta, L., Barni, A., Montini, E.: Development of a digitalization maturity model for the manufacturing sector. In: 2018 IEEE International Conference on Engineering, Technology and Innovation (ICE/ITMC), pp. 1–7. IEEE, June 2018

14. Geissdoerfer, M., Bocken, N.M., Hultink, E.J.: Design thinking to enhance the sustainable business modelling process–a workshop based on a value mapping process. J. Clean. Prod. **135**, 1218–1232 (2016)

15. Tschimmel, K.: Design thinking as an effective toolkit for innovation. In: Proceedings of the XXIII ISPIM Conference: Action for Innovation: Innovating from Experience, Barcelona (2012). ISBN 978-952-265-243-0

16. Archer, N.P., Ghasemzadeh, F.: An integrated framework for project portfolio selection. Int. J. Project Manag. **17**(4), 207–216 (1999)

17. Leal, J.E.: AHP-express: a simplified version of the analytical hierarchy process method. MethodsX **7**, 100748 (2020)

Gamification of Operational Tasks in Manufacturing

A Literature Review

Makenzie Keepers[1], David Romero[2], Jannicke Baalsrud Hauge[3],
and Thorsten Wuest[1(✉)]

[1] West Virginia University, Morgantown, WV 26505, USA
mk0004@mix.wvu.edu, thwuest@mail.wvu.edu
[2] Tecnológico de Monterrey, Monterrey, Mexico
david.romero.diaz@gmail.com
[3] Bremer Institut für Produktion und Logistik GmbH, University of Bremen,
Bremen, Germany
baa@biba.uni-bremen.de

Abstract. Gamification is a growing topic of interest across all industries, including manufacturing. We conducted a literature review to determine the past and current research being conducted in the realm of gamification within manufacturing. We found that significant research is being performed, with growth in recent years. However, our analysis also found that the research is widespread, and not one group of researchers are focused on a niche area for gamification in manufacturing. Gamification in manufacturing research often focuses on three different research areas: knowledge acquisition, training, and operational tasks. Gamification research is conducted in equal parts of in-industry and in-lab settings. Literature reviews, empirical studies, and case studies are commonly used and published, and no specific methodology stands out as being preferred over the other. We found that conducting statistical hypothesis testing is feasible and appropriate when conducting an empirical or case study. Our paper summarizes the analysis by drawing additional conclusions and suggesting future research avenues for other researchers interested in how gamification is and can be incorporated within the manufacturing domain.

Keywords: Gamification · Manufacturing · Operations · Industry 4.0 · Games

1 Introduction

Gamification in manufacturing can often be categorized as focusing on two avenues: education or support for operations. Gamification is a hot and growing topic across many industries but has not yet been thoroughly discussed for operational tasks in manufacturing. Hence, this work aims to identify current research gaps in the field of gamification of operational tasks in manufacturing. It is believed that gamification can assist manufacturing facilities to improve workers' efficiency, motivation, and enjoyment [1]. With recent advancements in technology capabilities, it is feasible and

© IFIP International Federation for Information Processing 2020
Published by Springer Nature Switzerland AG 2020
B. Lalic et al. (Eds.): APMS 2020, IFIP AICT 591, pp. 107–114, 2020.
https://doi.org/10.1007/978-3-030-57993-7_13

desirable to implement gamification into current operating procedures. *Gamification,* "the use of game design elements in non-game contexts" [1], has been a topic of interest in engineering education research for many years, even before the 21st century. However, the term *gamification* itself was not clearly defined until 2010 [1]. Since then, from 2010 and beyond, the use of the word "gamification" in research has grown continuously and significantly, with no evidence of the growth slowing down (see Fig. 1). Between 2000 and 2010, gamification was mentioned in more than 10, but less than 110, research papers annually. Initially focused on education, gamification has branched out into other sectors, including manufacturing. In recent years, we see a large number of publications focused on gamification. Since 2016, exceeding 10,000 papers per year. The histogram depicted in Fig. 1 aims to showcase the growth in overall interest without limiting the domain. The annual numbers are derived from Google Scholar (without accounting for patents and citations).

While we know that gamification has already touched the world of manufacturing, we are interested in determining how much and what has been done concerning gamification in this domain. More specifically, we are interested in the impact of gamification on operational tasks within manufacturing. In other words, we are interested in instances where shop-floor workers are directly interacting with gamification while performing manufacturing tasks. This research aimed to identify promising research gaps for future research opportunities related to manufacturing and gamification.

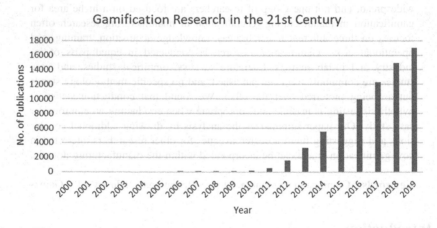

Fig. 1. Histogram: number of publications related to gamification research from 2000–2019

2   Research Methodology and Data Collection

We conducted a literature review to better understand the current state of gamification research within a manufacturing setting. The literature review began with a general search of gamification through two well-known and high-quality databases: Scopus and Web of Science. Since we were specifically focused on how gamification has been used in manufacturing, we added "manufacturing" as part of the search string. We decided on using "gamif*" in our search string to ensure we obtained all versions of "gamification" that are used today. With the search string "gamif* manufacturing" and restrictions to only include conference papers and journal articles, we obtained 46 results from Scopus and 32 results from Web of Science. The results were exported to a spreadsheet for further analyses. After removing duplicates, our initial set of papers forming the basis of this study included 54 papers.

From here, we further reduced the number of papers by closely examining the papers' titles and abstracts. A relevancy score, on a scale from 1–10, one being completely unrelated and 10 being perfectly related to the scope of the research, was assigned to each paper. With at least a score of six, based on our scoring criteria, it was evident that these papers, at a minimum, simultaneously related to both aspects of our topics of interest, "gamification" and "manufacturing". After assigning a relevancy score, we chose to only include papers with a relevancy score of six or above. This resulted in a set of 23 papers remaining in the pool for further analysis.

Of these 23 papers, we were unable to obtain the full English versions of three papers. Therefore, 20 papers were read in their entirety. After reading the papers in detail, we decided to discard four additional papers as they did not fit the scope of the research. At this point, we established the relevant papers and no more papers were removed. The analysis is based on the final group of 16 relevant papers (see Table 1).

In addition to using a *quantitative approach* to analyze the results obtained, a *qualitative approach* was also adopted considering the emerging role of *gamification* in industrial settings. In this sense, a *narrative analysis* of the papers collected was conducted to explore multiple perspectives on the "gamification" topic, with particular focus on gamification usage to improve operational tasks. This complementary qualitative approach is fundamental for our review since it allows us to explore and analyze the trends of the inclusion of gamification in factory shop-floors.

3   Analysis of the Results

The results of this literature review are centered around the type of research methodology used, the research location, the research focus, the utilization of statistical hypothesis testing, and a qualitative analysis of overall content. The results, to the best of our ability, are descriptive and do not include any interpretation but rather factual statements derived and obtained from the literature. The results are critically discussed and interpreted in the following section.

3.1   Type of Research

Each paper was classified into at least one of the following categories: (i) literature review, (ii) empirical study, and/or (iii) case study. In some instances, a paper was classified across multiple categories. Papers were also classified based on their outcome, such as proposing a framework. For this purpose, a *framework* was understood to be a suggestion, or set of suggestions, of basic methods for the use of gamification.

A *literature review* was classified as a paper wherein the purpose of the paper was to examine previous research. An *empirical study* was classified as a paper wherein the research included results through a non-subjective medium, such as hypothesis testing or data collection. Meanwhile, a *case study* was classified as research where results were found through a subjective medium such as individual analysis, discussions and/or interviews. This difference between "empirical studies" and "case studies" is supported by [2].

It was found that of the 16 papers included, there were five literature reviews, six empirical studies, and eight case studies. In addition to their main form of research, four of the 16 papers also included a proposed framework. Of these four papers that proposed frameworks, two conducted empirical studies, while the remaining two conducted literature reviews.

3.2   Location of Research

Papers were classified where the majority of the presented research was conducted, either in an industrial or lab setting. There are two papers which reported on work that was conducted in both settings. A paper was classified as "in-industry" if the research was conducted alongside a company and involved their employees. A paper was classified as "in-lab" if the research was conducted utilizing individuals not specifically associated with a company, such as students at a university lab.

3.3   Focus of Research

We found that all relevant papers could be broken into three main focus areas: knowledge acquisition (knwl. acq.), (ii) training, and (iii) operational tasks. The knowledge acquisition category differs from the training category in that *knowledge acquisition* focuses on gaining knowledge (either from employees or for employees), while *training* focuses on learning a skill or task. *Operational tasks* focus on day-to-day activities with which employees are already familiar. Again, some papers covered multiple categories. Of the 16 papers examined, six focused on knowledge acquisition, five focused on training, and seven focused on operational tasks.

3.4   Statistical Hypothesis Testing

Three papers conducted statistical hypothesis testing. Of these papers, two were empirical studies and the remaining one was a case study. In this work, we understand statistical hypothesis testing as the usage of formal hypotheses, such as H_0 and H_1, to aid in drawing conclusions.

3.5   Overall Content Analysis

From the *empirical and case study* papers examined, there was only one which focused on a paper-based gamification scenario, and all others were digital-based scenarios. For the *training* focused papers, the gamification took place in a scenario off the production line, while the current training trend is incorporating gamification within the scope of work. There was one industry setting which was repeated in more than one article – the automotive industry.

Table 1 Results of literature review

Reference	Research methodology				Research location		Research focus			Hypothesis
	Lit review	Empirical study	Case study	Framework	Industry	Lab	Knwl. acq.	Training	Operations	Statistical
[1]		•	•	•	•				•	•
[3]		•	•		•				•	
[4]				•	•				•	•
[5]		•			•	•	•			•
[6]	•		•		•					
[7]	•			•			•	•		
[8]	•			•	•				•	
[9]		•			•			•		
[10]		•			•		•			
[11]			•		•			•		
[12]			•			•	•			
[13]			•			•	•			
[14]		•	•		•	•			•	
[15]			•		•				•	
[16]			•			•				
[17]				•	•	•			•	

4 Discussion

4.1 Quantitative Observations

In our results, there are more papers reporting work set in an "industrial setting" than those set in a "lab setting". While surprising at first, we believe this may be a bias included via the selection of our search string. Since our search string was small, we believe that we unintentionally pulled only a portion of the results related to gamification in manufacturing. Since we included "manufacturing" in the search term, many of the results are likely biased towards instances where the research was conducted at an actual manufacturing facility.

Of the papers classified with an "operational research" focus, three were conducted in a "lab setting", while four were conducted in an "industrial setting". This near-equal split between lab and industry setting indicates that gamification in manufacturing research is capable of producing significant results in either environment.

For the papers which utilized hypothesis testing, two conducted "empirical studies" while the other one conducted a "case study". The case study which conducted hypothesis testing did not have numerical data to draw conclusions for the hypothesis but did appropriately establish multiple hypothesis statements to assist in drawing conclusions later. It is also important to mention that there were an additional four empirical studies which did not utilize hypothesis testing to draw their conclusions. These papers used basic statistical data such as mean, standard deviation, and percentage of participants (see papers: [3, 9, 10, 14]). In these cases, hypothesis testing may have been beneficial to improve the confidence in the reported findings.

There are a few limitations of this study that need to be taken into consideration when reflecting on the results. First and foremost, like all literature-based studies, this research is limited by the search term used to gather the relevant papers. One might argue that there are complementary terms that should have been included. Potential terms that could have been included in the search include "serious games," "production" and "operations". It is important to note that "serious games" and "gamification" are not as closely related as often assumed.

4.2   Qualitative Observations

Reflecting on the analysis of the quantitative results obtained (see Table 1), and the qualitative analysis of the narrative of the empirical studies and case studies collected, it is possible to observe some coincidences between the rise of the exploration of gamification in manufacturing with the beginning of the Industry 4.0 era, emerging in 2010 and 2011, respectively. *Industry 4.0,* as a novel cyber-physical production paradigm, has challenged the current workforce with an accelerated pace of *knowledge acquisition* and skills development about the new collaborative robotics, intelligent automation, advanced manufacturing, and digitalization technologies. Furthermore, new and innovative visualizations are necessary to enable humans to interact with the many new data-driven tools and interfaces. Among others, this forces operators to quickly go through the different learning curves of these modern technologies and their capabilities for their strategic implementation and immediate operationalization at the factory shop floor as a source of competitive advantage.

Nevertheless, the true source of competitive advantage relies on a knowledgeable and skilled workforce capable of a rapid technology adoption and mastering through "learning by doing". Ideally, no human production resource diverts from the factory shop floor for training or disrupts value-creating production operations. This way, shop floor operators are able to continue to work and learn simultaneously while being trained on how to use these new production and production management technologies to improve the efficiency and effectiveness of their operational tasks. In this sense, from a socio-technical perspective, gamification could help to overcome some of the resistance to change when it comes to the rapid adoption of new technologies and their corresponding new working methods by employing motivational affordances such as points, badges, and leaderboards to drive the workforce to the desired goals and objectives [1]. Utilizing new digital technologies allows leveraging the opportunities of the new gamification paradigm in manufacturing. For example, using augmented reality devices as visualization tools to provide the shop floor operators with "digital assistance systems" (e.g., for assembly tasks) is empowering and, through "learning by doing," can translate into higher job satisfaction and performance.

5   Conclusions and Future Work

The most important conclusion from this research is that manufacturing seems to be severely underrepresented within published gamification research. Given that in 2019 alone, more than 17,000 papers were published where gamification is referenced and that our research only included 16 publications which directly related to manufacturing and gamification, it is evident that only a very small portion of gamification research is related to the manufacturing industry. This minimal representation is in contrast to the very wide range of possible value-adding applications of gamification within the manufacturing field that are theoretically possible.

As aforementioned, the purpose of this paper was to identify research opportunities for future work for individuals interested in gamification in manufacturing. One reoccurring future research opportunity is identifying the long-term effects of gamification. It is unclear if the improvements witnessed in gamification research can be solely attributed to gamification as a technique or gamification as a new and novel tool. If the improvements are mostly related to employees working with a new gamification feature within an operational task, then over time the novelty of gamification will wear out and production will return to its pre-gamification state. Many papers mention limited sample sizes are a potential downfall of their research, so we need large scale studies focused on gamification of operational tasks within manufacturing.

Acknowledgements. This work was performed under the following financial assistance award 70NANB20H028 from U.S. Department of Commerce, National Institute of Standards and Technology and J. Wayne & Kathy Richards Faculty Fellowship at WVU.

References

1. Liu, M., et al.: Gamification's impact on manufacturing: enhancing job motivation, satisfaction and operational performance with smartphone based gamified job design. Hum. Factors Ergon. Manuf. Serv. Ind. **28**(1), 38–51 (2018)
2. Coe, R., Waring, M., Arthur, J.: Research Methods and Methodologies in Education, 2nd edn. SAGE, Thousand Oaks (2017)
3. Lee, J., et al.: A case study in an automotive assembly line: exploring the design framework for manufacturing gamification. In: Schlick, C., Trzcieliński, S. (eds.) Advances in Ergonomics of Manufacturing: Managing the Enterprise of the Future. AISC, vol. 490, pp. 305–317. Springer, Cham (2016). https://doi.org/10.1007/978-3-319-41697-7_27
4. Roh, S., et al.: goal-based manufacturing gamification: bolt tightening work redesign in the automotive assembly. In: Schlick, C., Trzcieliński, S. (eds.) Advances in Ergonomics of Manufacturing: Managing the Enterprise of the Future. AISC, vol. 490, pp. 293–304. Springer, Cham (2016). https://doi.org/10.1007/978-3-319-41697-7_26
5. Stadnicka, D., Deif, A.: A gamification approach application to facilitate lean manufacturing knowledge acquisition. Manag. Prod. Eng. Rev. **10**, 108–122 (2019)
6. Alavesa, P., et al.: Context defined aspects of gamification for factory floor. In: 11th International. Conference on Virtual Worlds & Games for Serious Applications, pp. 1–2. IEEE (2019)
7. Paravizo, E., et al.: Exploring gamification to support manufacturing education on industry 4.0 as an enabler for innovation and sustainability. Proc. Manuf. **21**, 438–445 (2018)
8. Schuldt, J., Friedemann, S.: The challenges of gamification in the age of industry 4.0: focusing on man in future machine-driven working environments. In: IEEE Global Engineering Education Conference, pp. 1622–1630. IEEE (2017)

9. Babu, A.R., Rajavenkatanarayanan, A., Abujelala, M., Makedon, F.: VoTrE: a vocational training and evaluation system to compare training approaches for the workplace. In: Lackey, S., Chen, J. (eds.) VAMR 2017. LNCS, vol. 10280, pp. 203–214. Springer, Cham (2017). https://doi.org/10.1007/978-3-319-57987-0_16

10. Zikos, S., et al.: User acceptance evaluation of a gamified knowledge sharing platform for use in industrial environments. Int. J. Serious Game. **6**(2), 89–108 (2019)

11. Gilotta, S., Spada, S., Ghibaudo, L., Isoardi, M.: A technology corner for operator training in manufacturing tasks. In: Bagnara, S., Tartaglia, R., Albolino, S., Alexander, T., Fujita, Y. (eds.) IEA 2018. AISC, vol. 824, pp. 935–943. Springer, Cham (2019). https://doi.org/10.1007/978-3-319-96071-5_96

12. Tocu, A., et al.: Tool selection: learning pick-and-place operations using smartphone AR technology (2019)

13. Bueno-Delgado, M.V., et al.: IN4WOOD: developing an online and free training course to adapt the curricula of workers and managers of wood and furniture sector to the skills required by industry 4.0. In: 9th International Conference on Education and New Learning Technologies, pp. 536–543 (2017)

14. Lessel, P., et al.: "Don't whip me with your games" investigating "bottom-up" gamification. In: 2016 Conference on Human Factors in Computing Systems, pp. 2026–2037 (2016)

15. Baalsrud Hauge, J., Wiesner, S., Stefan, I.A., Stefan, A., Thoben, K.-D.: Applying gamification for developing formal knowledge models: challenges and requirements. In: Nääs, I., et al. (eds.) APMS 2016. IAICT, vol. 488, pp. 713–720. Springer, Cham (2016). https://doi.org/10.1007/978-3-319-51133-7_84

16. Despeisse, M., Lunt, P.: Teaching energy efficiency in manufacturing using gamification: a case study. In: Lödding, H., Riedel, R., Thoben, K.-D., von Cieminski, G., Kiritsis, D. (eds.) APMS 2017. IAICT, vol. 514, pp. 419–426. Springer, Cham (2017). https://doi.org/10.1007/978-3-319-66926-7_48

17. Markopoulos, A.P., et al.: Gamification in engineering education and professional training. Int. J. Mech. Eng. Educ. **43**(2), 118–131 (2015)

Technology Adoption in the Industry 4.0 Era: Empirical Evidence from Manufacturing Companies

Nenad Medic[1(✉)] ⓘ, Zoran Anisic[1] ⓘ, Nemanja Tasic[1] ⓘ,
Nikola Zivlak[2] ⓘ, and Bojan Lalic[1] ⓘ

[1] Faculty of Technical Sciences, University of Novi Sad, Novi Sad, Serbia
{medic.nenad,anisic,nemanja.tasic,blalic}@uns.ac.rs
[2] Emlyon Business School, Écully, France
zivlak@gmail.com

Abstract. In the process of introducing Industry 4.0 concept into the manufacturing environment companies from emerging countries are lagging behind. The rationale for this could be found in the fact that developed countries are leading this transformation, which includes digitalization and integration of manufacturing processes across the entire value chain. Low technological maturity of companies from emerging countries indicates that their focus should be on the implementation of well-established technologies. The aim of this research is to analyze the trend in implementation of Smart Manufacturing technologies in manufacturing companies from emerging country. For this purpose, data gathered among Serbian manufacturing companies through international project European Manufacturing Survey are used. The results indicate that there is a positive trend in the adoption of Smart Manufacturing technologies, which represents solid ground for Serbian manufacturers to move towards the implementation of the Industry 4.0 concept. Results presented in this research could be of use for managers and practitioners for their strategic orientation concerning improvements of production processes.

Keywords: Industry 4.0 · Smart manufacturing · Technology adoption · Emerging countries

1 Introduction

Technological changes have always been a driving force for the development of the manufacturing sector. Recently, a new trend called Industry 4.0 has been introduced into the manufacturing environment [1]. This new approach is focused on digitalization and integration of processes across the entire value chain. Emerging technologies such as internet of things, big data, and cloud computing are considered as enablers of Industry 4.0, making it become a reality [2]. The main feature of Industry 4.0 is creation of cyber-physical systems in which physical objects and software are interconnected with the purpose of information exchange [3]. In order to achieve these standards, manufacturing companies are adopting various advanced technologies to

© IFIP International Federation for Information Processing 2020
Published by Springer Nature Switzerland AG 2020
B. Lalic et al. (Eds.): APMS 2020, IFIP AICT 591, pp. 115–122, 2020.
https://doi.org/10.1007/978-3-030-57993-7_14

gather and analyze real-time data that can quickly be converted into useful information for the production system [4].

Since the Industry 4.0 is relatively new concept, there is a lot of ambiguity around it. There are a lot of different approaches, focusing on various areas on which Industry 4.0 has impact [5, 6]. One of the concerns lies in the fact that there is no clear understanding about the technologies that are considered as enablers of Industry 4.0 [6]. Research related to Industry 4.0 goes from analyzing widely established technologies such as Enterprise Resource Planning (ERP), to emerging technologies such as blockchain technology [7, 8]. According to Frank et al., Industry 4.0 technologies can be classified into two layers depending on their purpose [9]. One of these layers, called "front-end technologies", is primarily related to operational and market needs of the company. There are four groups of technologies in this layer, namely: Smart Manufacturing [10], Smart Products [11], Smart Supply Chain [12], and Smart Working [13]. The other layer, named "base technologies", is considered as enabler of the Industry 4.0. Technologies in this layer (i.e. internet of things, cloud, big data, and analytics) serve to provide connectivity and information exchange between front-end technologies, thus creating an intelligent manufacturing system [9, 14]. It is worth noting that from all above mentioned layers and groups of technologies, Smart Manufacturing has the crucial role in the early stage of the Industry 4.0 introduction into the manufacturing environment [15].

One more distinctive characteristic of Industry 4.0 is the difference in the approach to the research related to this concept when it comes to the level of development of the region of interest. More specifically, there is a clear distinction of the research conducted in companies from the developed countries compared to those that are focused on emerging countries [16]. This is mainly due to the fact that the idea of Industry 4.0 is born in developed countries which are now transferring their knowledge and expertise to other countries interested in the adoption of this concept [17]. This process of diffusion is relatively slow, thus making a clear distinction between developing and emerging countries concerning adoption of Industry 4.0 concept and related technologies [11]. Therefore, due to low level of maturity concerning implementation of advanced technologies, the research in emerging countries should be focused on the use of well-established technologies that represent a solid starting point for the introduction of the Industry 4.0.

Having this in mind, the aim of this research is to analyze the trend of the implementation of Smart Manufacturing technologies in emerging country (i.e. Serbia). For this purpose, we used data gathered from the European Manufacturing Survey (EMS). More specifically, we did the comparative analyses of the introduction of Smart Manufacturing technologies from two rounds of the survey (years 2015 and 2018) in order to see the trend in implementation of these technologies. This research contributes to the existing literature by presenting empirical evidence on the implementation of Smart Manufacturing technologies in emerging country, thus opening the possibilities for further research in this direction.

The remainder of the paper has the following structure. Section 2 presents the literature review, while Sect. 3 describes methods and data that were used for the purpose of this research. Section 4 presents the results and discussion of this research. Finally, in Sect. 5 we made conclusions along with identified limitations and possibilities for further research in the field.

2   Literature Review

Research related to Industry 4.0 in emerging countries is getting more attention in the last few years. The direction of these studies varies significantly. One of the most common approaches is to analyze the readiness of companies for Industry 4.0, focusing on the barriers for the implementation of this concept [18, 19]. All of these studies are on the conceptual level, using an interview approach as a tool for analysis, without any empirical evidence about the use of Industry 4.0 enabling technologies in companies. There are some attempts to put focus on the use of advanced technologies in manufacturing companies from emerging countries and their contribution to the Industry 4.0 [9, 11, 20]. The analyses in these studies are comprehensive, trying to cover vide range of emerging technologies. There is a lack of studies that are focused on specific group of technologies that form a bundle of complementary technologies. This is an important aspect that is neglected, as prior study shows that investment in emerging technologies do not always lead to expected outcomes [21]. We aim to fill this gap by analyzing one group of technologies identified as one of the enablers of the Industry 4.0. More precisely, our focus is on the adoption of Smart Manufacturing technologies in manufacturing companies from emerging country (i.e. Serbia), which are considered crucial for the implementation of the Industry 4.0 concept [9].

The main function of Smart Manufacturing technologies is to create flexible manufacturing system that is able to adapt to quick changes in the production processes triggered by market demand [4]. One of the expectations from the Industry 4.0 concept, that is enabled by Smart Manufacturing technologies, is to increase flexibility of the production system to the point of mass customization [22]. Furthermore, Smart Manufacturing technologies are focused on operations activities and product processing [10]. It is expected that these technologies contribute to the vertical and horizontal integration, virtualization, automation, flexibility, and energy efficiency [9]. In order to achieve this, the following technologies should be considered [20, 23–25]:

- Mobile/wireless devices for programming and controlling facilities and machinery (e.g. tablets)
- Digital solutions to provide drawings, work schedules or work instructions directly on the shop floor
- Software for production planning and scheduling (e.g. ERP system)
- Digital Exchange of product/process data with suppliers/customers (Electronic Data Interchange EDI)
- Near real-time production control system (e.g. Systems of centralized operating and machine data acquisition, MES)
- Systems for automation and management of internal logistics (e.g. Warehouse management systems, RFID)

- Product-Lifecycle-Management-Systems   (PLM)   or   Product/Process   Data Management
- Industrial robots for manufacturing processes (e.g. welding, painting, cutting)
- Industrial robots for handling processes (e.g. depositing, assembling, sorting, packing processes, AGV)
- 3D printing technologies for prototyping (prototypes, demonstration models, 0 series)
- 3D printing technologies for manufacturing of products, components and forms, tools, etc.)
- Technologies to recuperate kinetic and process energy (e.g. waste heat recovery, energy storage)

In order to analyze the adoption of Smart Manufacturing technologies in manufacturing companies from emerging country (i.e. Serbia) we form the following research questions:

RQ1: What is the current trend in the adoption of Smart Manufacturing technologies in manufacturing companies from emerging country (i.e. Serbia)?
RQ2: What is the expected level of the adoption of Smart Manufacturing technologies in manufacturing companies from emerging country (i.e. Serbia) in the future?

3   Methods and Data

For the purpose of this study we used simple statistics. More specifically, our analysis on the use of Smart Manufacturing technologies in manufacturing companies is based on the descriptive statistics. The data for the analysis is gathered through a survey that is carried out under the international project European Manufacturing Survey (EMS) coordinated by the Fraunhofer ISI Institute from Germany. EMS is mainly focused on technological and organizational innovation in manufacturing companies, but other aspects of manufacturing processes are also considered [26–28]. The survey is performed each three years and targets manufacturing companies (NACE Rev 2 codes from 10 to 33) with more than 20 employees. The dataset used for the analysis in this paper is gathered from Serbian manufacturing companies and includes 285 responses from 2015 and 240 responses from 2018 round of the survey.

In both rounds of the survey (i.e. 2015 and 2018) companies were asked about the technologies that they currently use in their production processes. For our analysis technologies that belong to the Smart Manufacturing dimension are identified. We used this information to compare the use of Smart Manufacturing technologies in 2015 and 2018. In this way, the trend of the adoption of these technologies could be determined. Furthermore, companies that are not implementing Smart Manufacturing technologies were asked whether they plan to use any of these technologies in the next three years. This answer can give us the information about the possible trend of the adoption of Smart Manufacturing technologies in manufacturing companies in near future.

4 Results and Discussion

The results aimed to present current trend in the adoption of Smart Manufacturing technologies in Serbian manufacturing companies are depicted in Fig. 1. We have compared the share of companies that implemented Smart Manufacturing technologies in 2015 and 2018. From the results, it can be seen that for 10 out of 12 technologies there is an increase of the adoption through time. This positive trend of the adoption of Smart Manufacturing technologies represents a solid ground for Serbian manufacturers to move towards the implementation of the Industry 4.0 concept [20]. This is particularly important for companies, since these technologies should be implemented as a bundle in the phase of the maturity growth [9].

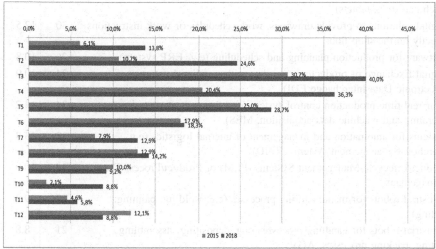

Note: T1 - Mobile devices for programming and controlling; T2 - Digital solutions directly on the shop floor; T3 - ERP system; T4 - EDI; T5 - Near real-time production control system; T6 - RFID; T7 - PLM; T8 - Industrial robots for manufacturing processes; T9 - Industrial robots for handling processes; T10 - 3D prototyping; T11 - 3D technologies for manufacturing; T12 - Technologies to recuperate energy

Fig. 1. The use of Smart Manufacturing technologies in Serbian companies in 2015 and 2018

In order to grasp the full potential of Industry 4.0 and create the environment for the introduction of emerging technologies (i.e. internet of things, big data, and cloud computing), thus creating cyber-physical industrial systems, companies should continue with this positive trend of the adoption of Smart Manufacturing technologies [2]. The results presented in Table 1, which are based on the 240 responses from the 2018 edition of EMS, are showing the intention of manufacturers to implement Smart Manufacturing technologies in near future. Based on these results, we can be confident that there will be continuance of positive trend of the adoption of Smart Manufacturing technologies in the future. Increased implementation of these technologies will create an environment for the implementation of emerging technologies, thus creating greater opportunities for companies [14]. Moreover, it is evident that Serbian manufacturing companies are recognizing the importance of catching up with developed economies in order to be competitive on the global market. If the focus of manufacturing companies is in the right direction, the investments in technologies could lead to expected benefits and increased competitiveness of manufacturing companies from emerging countries. The gradual process of technology adoption will enable companies to adapt smoothly to new manufacturing trends [16].

Table 1. Planned use of Smart Manufacturing technologies in Serbian companies until 2021

Technology	N	Share [%]
Mobile/wireless devices for programming and controlling facilities and machinery (e.g. tablets)	36	15.0
Digital solutions to provide drawings, work schedules or work instructions directly on the shop floor	30	12.5
Software for production planning and scheduling (e.g. ERP system)	26	10.8
Digital Exchange of product/process data with suppliers/customers (Electronic Data Interchange EDI)	24	10.0
Near real-time production control system (e.g. Systems of centralized operating and machine data acquisition, MES)	34	14.2
Systems for automation and management of internal logistics (e.g. Warehouse management systems, RFID)	33	13.8
Product-Lifecycle-Management-Systems (PLM) or Product/Process Data Management	24	10.0
Industrial robots for manufacturing processes (e.g. welding, painting, cutting)	22	9.2
Industrial robots for handling processes (e.g. depositing, assembling, sorting, packing processes, AGV)	21	8.8
3D printing technologies for prototyping (prototypes, demonstration models, 0 series)	16	6.7
3D printing technologies for manufacturing of products, components and forms, tools, etc.	15	6.3
Technologies to recuperate kinetic and process energy (e.g. waste heat recovery, energy storage)	26	10.8

5 Conclusion

The aim of this paper is to investigate the current trend and expected level of the adoption of Smart Manufacturing technologies in near future in Serbian manufacturing companies. In order to obtain results, we used data gathered from EMS. Serbian manufacturers recognize the importance of Smart Manufacturing technologies, as there is a clear empirical evidence of the positive trend in their implementation. Furthermore, we can expect the continuance of this trend in near future.

Our contribution is reflected in the fact that our analyses are focused on specific group of technologies (i.e. Smart Manufacturing technologies) that are considered as vital in the process of introduction of Industry 4.0 in emerging countries. In this way, we opened the field for more narrow and detailed analysis of the adoption of advanced technologies related to Industry 4.0 in emerging countries. Additionally, we provide empirical evidence of the adoption of Smart Manufacturing technologies in manufacturing companies from emerging country. These results could be of use for managers and practitioners for their strategic orientation concerning improvements of production processes.

We have limited this research only to Smart Manufacturing technologies to gain insight on this specific category. However, this is not the only perspective that should be considered when analyzing the use of advanced technologies in manufacturing companies. Other relevant technologies should be analyzed in the context of emerging countries as well [9, 11]. Moreover, we have analyzed the manufacturing sector in general. One of the possible directions for further research is to consider differences between companies based on their size. Furthermore, some other aspects of Industry 4.0, such as new business models and organizational enablers, should be discussed in further research [5].

References

1. Kagermann, H., Wahlster, W., Helbig, J.: Recommendations for implementing the strategic initiative INDUSTRIE 4.0, Frankfurt, Germany (2013)
2. Lu, Y.: Industry 4.0: a survey on technologies, applications and open research issues. J. Ind. Inf. Integr. **6**, 1–10 (2017)
3. Lee, E.A.: Cyber physical systems: design challenges. In: Proceedings - 11th IEEE Symposium on Object/Component/Service-Oriented Real-Time Distributed Computing, (ISORC), pp. 363–369. IEEE (2008)
4. Wang, S., Wan, J., Zhang, D., Li, D., Zhang, C.: Towards smart factory for Industry 4.0: a self-organized multi-agent system with big data based feedback and coordination. Comput. Netw. **101**, 158–168 (2016)
5. Schumacher, A., Erol, S., Sihn, W.: A maturity model for assessing Industry 4.0 readiness and maturity of manufacturing enterprises. Procedia CIRP **52**, 161–166 (2016)
6. Culot, G., Nassimbeni, G., Orzes, G., Sartor, M.: Behind the definition of Industry 4.0: analysis and open questions. Int. J. Prod. Econ. **226**, 107617 (2020)
7. Berić, D., Stefanović, D., Lalić, B., Ćosić, I.: The implementation of ERP and MES Systems as a support to industrial management systems. Int. J. Ind. Eng. Manag. **9**(2), 77–86 (2018)
8. Ahram, T., Sargolzaei, A., Sargolzaei, S., Daniels, J., Amaba, B.: Blockchain technology innovations. In: 2017 IEEE Technology & Engineering Management Conference, TEMSCON 2017, pp. 137–141 (2017)
9. Frank, A.G., Dalenogare, L.S., Ayala, N.F.: Industry 4.0 technologies: implementation patterns in manufacturing companies. Int. J. Prod. Econ. **210**(January), 15–26 (2019)
10. Ahuett-Garza, H., Kurfess, T.: A brief discussion on the trends of habilitating technologies for Industry 4.0 and Smart manufacturing. Manuf. Lett. **15**, 60–63 (2018)
11. Dalenogare, L.S., Benitez, G.B., Ayala, N.F., Frank, A.G.: The expected contribution of Industry 4.0 technologies for industrial performance. Int. J. Prod. Econ. **204**(July), 383–394 (2018)

12. Angeles, R.: Anticipated IT infrastructure and supply chain integration capabilities for RFID and their associated deployment outcomes. In: Proceedings of the 10th International Conference on Information Integration and Web-Based Applications & Services, pp. 634–641 (2008)
13. Stock, T., Obenaus, M., Kunz, S., Kohl, H.: Industry 4.0 as enabler for a sustainable development: a qualitative assessment of its ecological and social potential. Process Saf. Environ. Prot. 118, 254–267 (2018)
14. Büchi, G., Cugno, M., Castagnoli, R.: Smart factory performance and Industry 4.0. Technol. Forecast. Soc. Change 150(October), 119790 (2020)
15. Schuh, G., Anderl, R., Gausemeier, J., Ten Hompel, M., Wahlster, W.: Industrie 4.0 maturity index. managing the digital transformation of companies. acatech STUDY, p. 46 (2017)
16. Da Silva, V.L., Kovaleski, J.L., Pagani, R.N., Silva, J.D.M., Corsi, A.: Implementation of Industry 4.0 concept in companies: empirical evidences. Int. J. Comput. Integr. Manuf. 33, 1–18 (2019)
17. Bernat, S., Karabag, S.F.: Strategic alignment of technology: organising for technology upgrading in emerging economy firms. Technol. Forecast. Soc. Change 145, 295–306 (2019)
18. Türkeş, M.C., Oncioiu, I., Aslam, H.D., Marin-Pantelescu, A., Topor, D.I., Căpușneanu, S.: Drivers and barriers in using Industry 4.0: a perspective of SMEs in Romania. Processes 7 (3), 1–20 (2019)
19. Huang, C.J., Chicoma, E.D.T., Huang, Y.H.: Evaluating the factors that are affecting the implementation of Industry 4.0 technologies in manufacturing MSMEs, the case of Peru. Processes 7(3), 161 (2019)
20. Medić, N., Anišić, Z., Lalić, B., Marjanović, U., Brezocnik, M.: Hybrid fuzzy multi-attribute decision making model for evaluation of advanced digital technologies in manufacturing: Industry 4.0 perspective. Adv. Prod. Eng. Manage. 14(4), 483–493 (2019)
21. Frank, A.G., Cortimiglia, M.N., Ribeiro, J.L.D., de Oliveira, L.S.: The effect of innovation activities on innovation outputs in the Brazilian industry: market-orientation vs. technology-acquisition strategies. Res. Policy 45(3), 577–592 (2016)
22. Fatorachian, H., Kazemi, H.: A critical investigation of Industry 4.0 in manufacturing: theoretical operationalisation framework. Prod. Plan. Control 29(8), 633–644 (2018)
23. Pons, M., Bikfalvi, A., Llach, J., Palcic, I.: Exploring the impact of energy efficiency technologies on manufacturing firm performance. J. Clean. Prod. 52, 134–144 (2013)
24. Koren, R., Palcic, I.: The impact of technical and organisational innovation concepts on product characteristics. Adv. Prod. Eng. Manag. 10(1), 27–39 (2015)
25. Medojevic, M., Medic, N., Marjanovic, U., Lalic, B., Majstorovic, V.: Exploring the impact of Industry 4.0 concepts on energy and environmental management systems: evidence from Serbian manufacturing companies. In: IFIP Advances in Information and Communication Technology, vol. 567, pp. 355–362 (2019)
26. Lalic, B., Rakic, S., Marjanovic, U.: Use of Industry 4.0 and organisational innovation concepts in the Serbian textile and apparel industry. Fibres Text. East. Eur. 27(3), 10–18 (2019)
27. Marjanovic, U., Lalic, B., Medic, N., Prester, J., Palcic, I.: Servitization in manufacturing: role of antecedents and firm characteristics. Int. J. Ind. Eng. Manag. 10(2), 133–144 (2020)
28. Lalic, B., Medic, N., Delic, M., Tasic, N., Marjanovic, U.: Open innovation in developing regions: an empirical analysis across manufacturing companies. Int. J. Ind. Eng. Manag. 8 (3), 111–120 (2017)

Towards the Definition of an Impact Level Factor of SME Features Over Digital Transformation

Melissa Liborio Zapata[1,2(✉)], Lamia Berrah[2], and Laurent Tabourot[1]

[1] Laboratoire Systèmes et Matériaux pour la Mécatronique (SYMME),
Université Savoie Mont Blanc, 74940 Annecy, France
{melissa.liborio-zapata,laurent.tabourot}@univ-smb.fr
[2] Laboratoire d'Informatique, Systèmes, Traitement de l'Information et de la
Connaissance (LISTIC), Université Savoie Mont Blanc, 74940 Annecy, France
lamia.berrah@univ-smb.fr

Abstract. Companies are experimenting change at a fast pace in the business environment due to the evolution of technology. As a result, they require solution approaches designed to guide their Digital Transformation (DT) efforts. However, several factors must be considered in their design, notably how the particular features of companies impact positively or negatively their DT. In the case of Small and Medium Enterprises (SMEs) in manufacturing, this is particularly relevant, as their vulnerabilities, such as the lack of resources, seem to have a significant impact over the success of DT initiatives. Defining this impact as an indicator of this effect will provide valuable information to control the DT to better achieve its objectives. For this reason, the aim of this paper is to introduce the impact level performance indicator for the specific scenario of manufacturing SMEs' DT. An Impact Analysis is presented with this purpose using a qualitative approach. Conclusions of this work lead to further develop the Impact Level indicator using a quantitative approach that enables its use in the control of the DT process.

Keywords: Industry 4.0 · Digital Transformation (DT) · Small and Medium Enterprises (SMEs) · Impact analysis · Impact level performance indicator

1 Introduction

Just some years ago, a company could have periods of stability only interrupted by a few radical changes that required immediate action in order to remain competitive [1]. Nowadays, change is constant and the evolution of technology is an important reason behind its speed [2]. New digital technologies as Artificial Intelligence, along with other trends such as faster Internet service, represent many opportunities for companies searching to lower costs by improving performance or capturing new income by creating value through new products and services [3]. Despite the advantages, companies also face critical challenges in the implementation of these new technologies [2]. In this context, a Digital Transformation (DT), defined as *"the use of new digital technologies to enable major business improvements"* [4], has become the goal for every company. Programs like Industry 4.0, born in Germany in 2011 [5], and other initiatives in

© IFIP International Federation for Information Processing 2020
Published by Springer Nature Switzerland AG 2020
B. Lalic et al. (Eds.): APMS 2020, IFIP AICT 591, pp. 123–130, 2020.
https://doi.org/10.1007/978-3-030-57993-7_15

research and practice, are looking for the right approach to succeed in this transformation. Numerous frameworks and models are also proposed to assist companies of all sizes and sectors with their efforts [6–8]. However, the DT process is highly complex, not only because it involves changes in many business dimensions [9], but also because the degree of the complexity that companies will face depends on their specific situation [3]. Companies, therefore, need to know how their particular features impact positively or negatively their approach of the DT process and the achievement of the associated objectives.

The answer is highly relevant for Small and Medium Enterprises (SMEs), companies with a set of characteristic features related to their size that make them seem vulnerable in the face of a DT [7, 8, 10]. Features, like the lack of financial resources to invest in the new technologies or the human resources with the right skills to implement them, are at the source of those vulnerabilities [3]. Defined by the European Commission as companies with a staff of only 250 people or less [11], SMEs, despite their size, hold great importance as a group, as they account for more than 99% of the businesses in Europe [10]. Consequently, their success is a source of economic growth for the region and their DT is considered as an important avenue to achieving it [10]. Inside the SMEs category, the DT of those in manufacturing is particularly crucial, as they are not only the users but the producers of the new digital technologies. They are also a critical part of supply chains of Business to Business markets that have already started their digitalization process and are demanding the same from their supply chain participants [12].

Given the background, the quantification of the level of impact that manufacturing SMEs features have over the DT is critical in controlling the process and the achievement of its objectives. For this reason, the concern of this work is the introduction of the impact level as an indicator to be used by decision-makers in SMEs with this purpose. To start its development, the aim of this paper is to present the impact level using a qualitative approach that shows its general behaviour. Therefore, the organization of the paper is as follows. In Sect. 2, a brief description of the dimensions of a DT are presented, along with the specific features that characterized manufacturing SMEs. This information is followed by the qualitative analysis of the impact level in Sect. 3. In Sect. 4, feedback from France industry experts regarding the analysis is shared. Finally, conclusions are proposed in Sect. 5, along with the perspectives towards the further development of the Impact Level performance indicator using a quantitative approach.

2   Digital Transformation and Manufacturing SMEs Elements

2.1   DT Dimensions

Solution approaches for DT, in research and practice, propose each a set of business dimensions or aspects that experiment change during the transformation process. Once focused only on the technological side of the change, current works understand the need to have a broad business perspective of the process [7]. However, no consensus has been reached regarding the specific dimensions that must be included, as some works choose a broad and general scope [7], others focus mostly on the operational [8] or technological [3] aspects of the transformation. In consequence, to define a set of dimensions for this work, the following procedure was performed.

1. A literature review was conducted and 21 DT models were identified.
2. An evaluation of the models according to the design principles proposed by Pöppelbuß [13], resulted in the selection of the top 7.
3. A comparative analysis of the different dimensions proposed by the 7 models [3, 5, 7, 8, 14–16] was performed.
4. A proposal of a set of business dimensions affected by a DT was created based on the ones most mentioned by the selected models. This proposal shares a view of the wide scope of the changes involved during a DT.

Table 1 presents the set D of the 12 dimensions $d_j, j \in \{1,2,3,4,5,6,7,8,9,10,11,12\}$, proposed by this work with a brief description of the changes expected in each of them during a DT.

Table 1. DT dimensions.

ID	Dimension	Expected changes
d_1	Strategy	Digital strategy definition and implementation
d_2	Business models	Innovation of the organization's value proposition
d_3	Investment	Planning related to the realization of the Digital Strategy
d_4	Customer	Digital experience definition
d_5	Products and services	Creation of smart and connected products and services
d_6	Business process	Processes creation, redesign and automation
d_7	Culture	Change towards innovation and collaboration
d_8	Organizational structure	Flexibility, agility and cross-functional collaboration
d_9	Leadership	Leaders aware and prepared for the digital era
d_{10}	(Strategic) partnerships	Collaboration with customers and competitors
d_{11}	Employee competences	Digital competences
d_{12}	Technology	Digital technologies selection and implementation

2.2   Features of Manufacturing SMEs

Manufacturing SMEs possess a set of particular characteristics that define their behaviour. Their specific features are enlisted to better understand their particular conditions when they are faced with challenges such as a DT. The definition used in this work (Table 2) is based on a previous research work that assembled a list of their features as a result of a literature review on the subject [6]. The following set F of the ten features $f_i, i \in \{1,2,3,4,5,6,7,8,9,10\}$, conceptualize manufacturing SMEs as companies with low availability of resources and a strong focus on the performance of day-to-day operations.

Table 2. Manufacturing SMEs features.

ID	Feature
f_1	Limited resources (financial, technical, human)
f_2	Organizational structure less complex with informal strategy & decision making
f_3	Culture with low flexibility for change and experimentation
f_4	Personnel engaged in multiple domains of the organization
f_5	Low regard for business processes and standards
f_6	Product development with high levels of customization
f_7	Industry knowledge focused in a specific domain
f_8	Strong customer/Supplier relationships
f_9	Low investment in R&D and lack of alliances with Universities
f_{10}	Low adoption of new technologies

3 Impact Analysis

The proposed approach is to assess, through a qualitative analysis, the level of impact of the effect that SMEs features have over the DT dimensions, based on the theoretical definition of these two elements, respectively, presented in Table 1 and Table 2. For the purposes of this work, the Impact Level $ILij$ is conceptualized as a performance indicator that shows the level of the positive or negative effect that a given feature f_i has over a given dimension d_j. Therefore, IL_{ij} can be defined as the set I and as the result of the following function:

$$ImpLev \;:\; F \times D \to I$$

$$(f_i, d_j) \to ImpLev\,(f_i, d_j) = IL_{ij}$$

The objective of this analysis is to understand the nature and intensity of the Impact Level IL_{ij} using the given set of SMEs features defined by their current stereotypical characterization. This approach provides a point of departure to draw the preliminary conclusions towards the development of the IL_{ij} as a numerical value.

3.1 Methodology

In order to generate the required information for the analysis, a matrix was built with the individual qualification of the impact level of all the possible combinations between features f_i and dimensions d_j. This qualification was performed with a 4-level scale composed by 2 *criteria*, an intensity of the impact, Low "*L*" or High "*H*" and a sense of this impact, Positive "+" or Negative "−". The 4 levels are described as follows.

- **L+:** Low influence of the feature in support of the change in the dimension.
- **L−:** Low influence of the feature against the change in the dimension.
- **H+:** High influence of the feature in support of the change in the dimension.
- **H−:** High influence of the feature against the change in the dimension.

The qualification of IL_{ij} is based on the state of the art on the subject and validated by experts in the related fields. Additional meetings were held when there were conflicting positions in order to reach a consensus. The analysis was performed by the qualification of both criteria for each combination. For example, it is expected that a *Culture with low flexibility for change and experimentation f_3* will be a determinant barrier for the design and especially the implementation of the DT *Strategy d_1*, hence its "$H-$" value, in other words, $IL_{31}= ImpLev\ (f_3,\ d_1) = H-$. The combinations that do not relate or present any impact between them were left empty, as a way to maintain the focus on the real issues during a DT.

3.2   Impact Analysis

Table 3 presents the qualification of the IL_{ij} of the manufacturing SMEs features f_i over the DT dimensions d_j.

Table 3. Impact analysis of DT dimensions vs. Manufacturing SMEs features.

Dimension/ Feature	f_1	f_2	f_3	f_4	f_5	f_6	f_7	f_8	f_9	f_{10}
d_1	H−	H−	H−		H−	H+	H−	H+	H−	H−
d_2			H−	H−			H−	L+		
d_3	H−	H−	H−				H−		H−	H−
d_4	H−		H−		H−			H+	H−	H−
d_5	H−		H−	H−		H+	H−	H+	H−	H−
d_6	H−	H−	H−	H−	H−		H−	H+		
d_7	H−		H−	L+				H+	H−	H−
d_8	H−	H−	H−	L−						
d_9	H−	H−	H−							
d_{10}		H−	H−					H+	H−	
d_{11}	H−		H−	H−			H−		H−	H−
d_{12}	H−	H−	H−			H+	H−	H+	H−	H−

General conclusions of the impact analysis are presented from two perspectives. The first one highlights the dimensions where potential issues can arise during the DT, considering the effect of the given features. The second one, on the other hand, shows the features that hold the most critical influence over the dimensions. The management of these conditions could represent a higher success rate of the DT initiatives.

Dimensions Perspective. The analysis considers the following relevant findings.

- The dimensions that are more impacted by the features are *Strategy d_1*, *Products and Services d_5* and *Technology d_{12}*.
- *Strategy d_1* definition, and particularly its implementation, will challenge almost every feature of SMEs and will require change management tools.
- *Technology d_5* and the *Products and Services d_{12}* that it enables will be the source of the major changes during the DT.

- These 3 dimensions will have the advantage of *Product development with high levels of customization* (f_6) and *Strong Customer/Supplier Relationships* (f_8).

Features Perspective. The analysis considers the following relevant findings.

- The features that make the strongest impact over the dimensions are *Limited resources f_1, Culture with low flexibility for change and experimentation f_3* and *Low investment in R&D and lack of alliances with Universities f_9*.
- *Culture with low flexibility for change and experimentation f_3* and *Limited resources f_1* could have a strong impact as they touch most of the DT dimensions.
- The *Limited resources f_1* of all sorts will affect all the dimensions that need them in order to achieve the necessary changes required by the DT.
- The *Low investment in R&D and lack of alliances with Universities f_9* will demand a significant effort to implement a culture of innovation, crucial in a DT.
- Only 2 features have a positive effect: *Product development with high levels of customization f_6* and *Strong Customer/Supplier Relationships f_8*.

The results of the analysis are not completely surprising as it confirms the disadvantaged position of SMEs in front a DT challenge, but the global view of the IL_{ij} reveals in detail a degree of magnitude of the effect between features and dimensions that it was not evident at the beginning of this work. From this insight, numerous possibilities arise to deepen the understanding of the relationship between them, like, for example, the variations in the IL_{ij} with different configurations of SME features (e.g., a more formal structure, a culture more open to change). As patterns in the table become evident, it becomes clear that the development of this indicator could provide the information to design a DT experience more consistent with the Manufacturing SMEs scenario.

Once collected the necessary insight through this qualitative approach, the next stage of this research will focus on translating this information into a numerical model using a quantitative approach to calculate a more accurate performance expression of the IL_{ij}. The model will provide a quantification of the "High" and "Low" levels in different scenarios and conditions, taking into account the specific factors that define the magnitude of the effect of the features over the dimensions. A model of these characteristics will enable the simulation of different scenarios and, in consequence, will support decision-making when managing DT initiatives, facilitating the achievement of its objectives.

4 Industry Feedback

French manufacturing industry holds a leadership position in Europe [12], however as it happens with many sectors of the economy, in order to boost their growth, the digitalization of manufacturing SMEs is a priority for the region [10]. Accordingly, competitiveness clusters as Mont-Blanc Industries in the French region of Auvergne-Rhône-Alpes, are active in promoting their DT with the participation of a network of universities and other industry actors [17]. As this research work is focused on the participants of this region, a series of interviews were conducted with industry experts to discuss the outcome of the impact analysis, as well as the list of SME features and DT dimensions to verify if those elements correspond to the reality of the sector.

The industry experts confirmed that the findings issued from the analysis make sense according to their practice. They recognize that the limitation of resources is a big issue, but not as big as the type of leadership in the organization that, in their opinion, defines their organizational culture. Often they also see that some types of leadership, present in family-owned SMEs, are a strong barrier to pursue a DT due to a poor vision of the future and lack of willingness to risk their still comfortable positions. These remarks are also consistent with the general characterization of SMEs as companies focused on managing day-to-day operations.

Finally, in addition to their comments regarding the results of the analysis, industry experts stressed the importance to keep in mind that the generalization regarding the manufacturing SME features could not apply to manufacturers in all sectors, as the ones in the automotive and aerospace sectors seem to have a different characterization. Companies in those sectors, as well as those who already started their DT, may have a different level of maturity in their features as a consequence of the changes implemented during their transformation process or because of pressures of their specific environment. This relevant feedback confirms the vision of the design of the future quantitative model that considers the building of a model flexible enough to adapt to the different situations and conditions of manufacturing SMEs.

5 Conclusions and Perspectives

Digital Transformation describes the efforts of the enterprises that want to take advantage of digital technologies to improve their competitive position. However, benefits do not come easy, as the speed in the evolution of these technologies is turning the economic landscape in one full of challenges, especially for manufacturing SMEs. This type of company is struggling to transform, due in theory to the vulnerabilities related to their characteristic features. The contribution of this paper, therefore, is focused on understanding the effect that their features have over the business dimensions of a DT in order to use this insight to improve the success of this process.

Relevant findings include the identification of Strategy d_1 and Culture f_3 as the top critical dimension and feature, respectively. But beyond the obvious, the value of this research is focused on the insight that a global view of the 1 to 1 interaction between features and dimensions provide for the study of the impact level as a performance indicator of the success of a DT. This preliminary work on the subject will be followed by a more in-depth study of the dynamics of the impact between features and dimensions to get the necessary information to translate it into a quantitative approach that provides a model that guides decision-makers to a successful DT. This model will be part of the efforts of a research project whose main objective is to provide manufacturing SMEs in France with a DT framework.

Acknowledgments. The financial support from CONACYT (Grant 707990) is gratefully acknowledged.

References

1. Brown, S.L., Eisenhardt, K.M.: The art of continuous change: linking complexity theory and time-paced evolution in relentlessly shifting organizations. Adm. Sci. Q. **42**(1), 1 (1997)
2. Kagermann, H., Wahlster, W., Helbig, J.: Recommendations for implementing the strategic initiative Industrie 4.0. In: Final Report of the Industrie 4.0 Working Group (2013)
3. Lichtblau, K., Stich, V., Bertenrath, R., Blum, M., Bleider, M., Millack, A., et al.: IMPULS Industrie 4.0 Readiness. VDMA's IMPULS-Stiftung, Aachen, Cologne (2015)
4. Fitzgerald, M., Kruschwitz, N., Bonnet, D., Welch, M.: Embracing digital technology: a new strategic imperative. MIT Sloan Manag. Rev. **55**(2), 1–12 (2014)
5. Schuh, G., Anderl, R., Gausemeier, J., Hompel, M., Wahlster, W.: Industrie 4.0 maturity index: managing the digital transformation of companies. In: Acatech Study, Munich (2017)
6. Mittal, S., Khan, M.A., Romero, D., Wuest, T.: A critical review of smart manufacturing & Industry 4.0 maturity models: implications for small and medium-sized enterprises (SMEs). J. Manuf. Syst. **49**, 194–214 (2018)
7. Schumacher, A., Erol, S., Sihn, W.: A maturity model for assessing Industry 4.0 readiness and maturity of manufacturing enterprises. Procedia CIRP **52**, 161–166 (2016)
8. Akdil, K.Y., Ustundag, A., Cevikcan, E.: Maturity and readiness model for Industry 4.0 strategy. In: Akdil, K., Ustundag, A., Cevikcan, E. (eds.) Industry 4.0: Managing The Digital Transformation. SSAM, pp. 61–94. Springer, Cham (2018). https://doi.org/10.1007/978-3-319-57870-5_4
9. Verhoef, P.C., et al.: Digital transformation: a multidisciplinary reflection and research agenda. J. Bus. Res. (2019)
10. European Commission: European SME Action Programme. https://ec.europa.eu/docsroom/documents/36142/attachments/1/translations/en/renditions/pdf
11. European Commission: What is an SME. https://ec.europa.eu/growth/smes/business-friendly-environment/sme-definition_en
12. Khurana, A., Al-Olama, B., Shaban, M., Wijeratne, D.: The future of manufacturing – france. Global Manufacturing & Industrialization Summit (2018)
13. Pöppelbuß, J., Röglinger, M.: What makes a useful maturity model? A framework of general design principles for maturity models and its demonstration in business process management. In: ECIS 2011 Proceedings, vol. 28 (2011)
14. Geissbauer, R., Vedso, J., Schrauf, S.: Industry 4.0: building the digital enterprise. 2016 Global Industry 4.0 Survey. PwC (2016)
15. Lee, J., Jun, S., Chang, T.W., Park, J.: A smartness assessment framework for smart factories using analytic network process. Sustainability **9**(5), 794–808 (2017)
16. Scremin, L., Armellini, F., Brun, A., Solar-Pelletier, L., Beaudry, C.: Towards a framework to assess the maturity for Industry 4.0 adoption in manufacturing companies. Anal. Impact Ind. **4**, 224–254 (2018)
17. Mont-Blanc Industries Homepage. https://www.montblancindustries.com

Industry 4.0: Maturity of Automotive Companies in Brazil for the Digitization of Processes

Sergio Miele Ruggero[1](✉) , Nilza Aparecida dos Santos[1,2] ,
José Benedito Sacomano[1] , Antonio Carlos Estender[1] ,
and Marcia Terra da Silva[1]

[1] Graduate Studies in Production Engineering, Universidade Paulista,
São Paulo, SP 04026-002, Brazil
miele326@gmail.com, nilzaasantos7@gmail.com,
jbsacomano@gmail.com,
{estender,marcia.terra}@uol.com.br
[2] FATEC, Cotia, SP 06702-155, Brazil

Abstract. This article deals with the level of maturity of companies in the automotive segment in Brazil, to carry out the transition to Industry 4.0, in order to identify the degree of maturity of companies in this segment for the digitalization of processes. The data collection took place through a survey sent to directors, managers, supervisors and leaders of companies in the automotive segment. The results obtained indicated that the transition to Industry 4.0, although considered relevant, does not translate into reality for the companies surveyed. The level of infrastructure of the equipment is insufficient, the level of automation is low and the adaptability of the equipment is not yet technically possible in all companies in the segment. There is also no evidence of the use of digital technologies in the production process in approximately 60% of companies, and the maturity in the digitalization of processes occurs at a slow pace.

Keywords: Industry 4.0 · Digitalization · Technology · Automotive

1 Introduction

The concept of Industry 4.0, considered an integral part of the fourth industrial revolution, encompasses the main technological innovations in the fields of automation, control and information technology applied to manufacturing processes [1]. Characterized by the increasing use of information and automation technologies in the manufacturing environment [2], it brings reflexes to worldwide production, based on cyber physical systems, internet of things, big data and cloud computing.

The new technologies have led companies in the industrial sector of various segments in Brazil and in the world to an intense digital transformation, which can lead to shorter delivery times, greater product reliability and cost reduction.

In developing economies, digitalization can open new markets, leverage innovation and productivity gains. However, for this progress to occur, it is necessary to adopt, on

B. Lalic et al. (Eds.): APMS 2020, IFIP AICT 591, pp. 131–138, 2020.
https://doi.org/10.1007/978-3-030-57993-7_16

the part of governments, incentive programs, improvements in infrastructure, together with policies that challenge the different effects related to the market structure, innovation and divisiveness the benefits of digitalization [3].

Companies will need to adapt their business models to take part in this transformation [4]. The conditions of the companies can be measured by maturity models [5], which describe the stage in which organizations and processes are attaining the transition to Industry 4.0 [6].

In this context, the problem question in this article is: What is the maturity level of companies in the automotive segment in Brazil, in order to make the transition to Industry 4.0? Aiming to identify the degree of maturity of companies in the automotive segment for the digitalization of processes.

2 Literature Review

The concept of Industry 4.0 proposes digitalization from end-to-end of the value chain, through the integration of physical assets in systems and networks linked to a series of technologies to create value [7]. Digitalization can provide efficiency in horizontal integration, access to global manufacturers, suppliers of different raw materials and potential customers [8].

In a smart factory, the production process can promote the communication of workers, machines and inputs, transmitting information in real time [9, 10]. In the search for competitiveness, more and more, companies are looking for improvement and efficiency in their production processes and adaptation to these new technologies.

The transition to Industry 4.0, although the exact consequences for manufacturing operations are not yet known, seems inevitable. Companies need to define their manufacturing model, planning a program for transformation [4]. The digital infrastructure is made up of networks, software and data and precise digital resources to use them efficiently.

Digitalization makes it easier to face growing market challenges [11]. Vertical integration portrays the use of information technology (IT) systems in different hierarchical levels of companies, optimizing the production process, through monitoring and process control in operational and managerial terms [12].

Companies seek to adopt integrated production planning and scheduling solutions that can combine company data with information from partners in the horizontal value chain, controlling inventory and demand levels [13]. The integrated planning of the shop floor, predictive maintenance and horizontal collaboration provides better use of production equipment [14].

Another challenge to promote collaborative activity, within companies, internally and externally, is the interoperability of information systems, which, from the point of view of computer technology, is the ability of two different computer systems to work together and provide access to reciprocal resources [15].

The scenario of each company in relation to the use of new technologies is demonstrated through models of maturity, which can be defined as a conceptual structure, composed of requirements that demonstrate the stage of development to achieve a desired situation [16].

3 Methods

The method used to carry out this research was exploratory, of qualitative and quantitative nature. Interviews were conducted with professionals in the industrial area, belonging to the automotive segment.

The primary data were collected through a survey sent to directors, managers, supervisors and leaders of companies in the automotive segment. Sixty questionnaires with 7 questions were addressed, covering the company's segment; the company's level of knowledge in relation to Industry 4.0; the infrastructure of the equipment in relation to Industry 4.0; automation of equipment in the productive sector; adaptability of equipment; the use of indicators to evaluate productivity and the level of use of digital technologies in the production process.

The questions were prepared based on the professional experience of the authors, in order to portray the resources that the companies surveyed have in relation to the technologies of Industry 4.0, as well as the knowledge of the participants on the subject, mapping the stage of maturity that they are in.

51 responses were obtained from the sample. The questions were presented to respondents at random. Of the responses received, 25% are large assembly companies, 65% small and medium-sized auto parts companies and 10% metallurgical companies. Secondary data were obtained through document analysis and bibliographic references. In parallel with the verification and analysis of results, the professional experience and participation of authors in the segment through the observational method was also considered.

4 Result and Discussion

The results presented below were based on data collection, through research, documentary and observational analysis. In response to the question about the level of knowledge of companies in relation to Industry 4.0, 22% stated that they have little knowledge related to Industry 4.0, 78% answered that they are interested in the subject and consider the topic important, but of these only 9% of companies has a strategy for deploying technologies from Industry 4.0.

The results of the research are presented through in the following figures.

Figure 1 illustrates how the equipment infrastructure is evaluated in the companies of the respective interviewees. The levels of control of the equipment by the network and the communication of the machines with each other are measured on a scale ranging from nonexistent to very high. The non-existent level corresponds to 0%; the very low 1% to 5%; the low of 6% to 10%; the medium of 11% to 40%; the high of 41% to 70% and the very high of 71% to 100%.

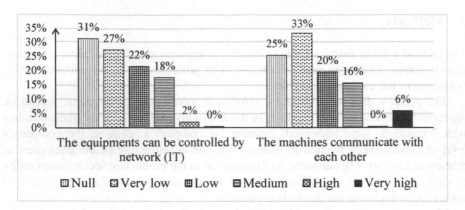

Fig. 1. Infrastructure level of equipment in relation to Industry 4.0 (Source: prepared by the authors).

Regarding the control of the equipment through network (IT), it was found that 31% of companies the level of control is non-existent and 49% levels are low.

In terms of communication between the machines, in 25% of companies the communication is non-existent and in 53% the levels are low. It can be noticed that the equipment infrastructure and the communication between the machines are still embryonic with regard to Industry 4.0.

The level of automation of equipment in the companies' productive sector is shown in Fig. 2.

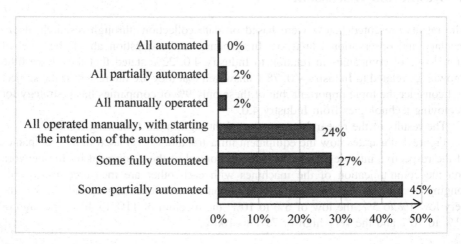

Fig. 2. Automation level of equipment in the productive sector (Source: prepared by the authors).

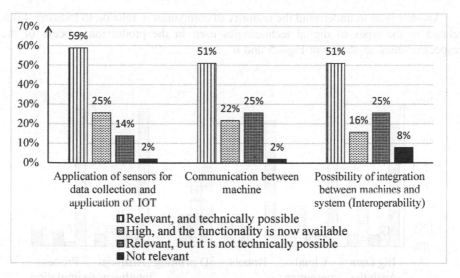

Fig. 3. Adaptability of equipment (Source: prepared by the authors).

The data show that 70% of the equipment still operate manually or are partially automated.

The companies' maturity in terms of equipment adaptability is shown in Fig. 3.

The data indicate that the application of sensors, the communication between machines and the integration between machines and systems are relevant and can be considered technically possible. However, based on the observational method, adaptability of equipment, although relevant, may not be technically possible in part of companies, especially small and medium-sized ones.

It was also asked whether companies use indicators to assess productivity. The results obtained demonstrate that the companies surveyed already use or are in the implementation phase, as shown in Fig. 4 below.

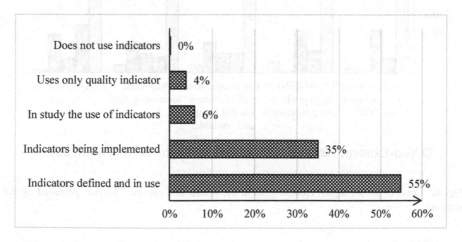

Fig. 4. Use of indicators to evaluate productivity (Source: prepared by the authors).

Another issue to understand the maturity of companies in relation to Industry 4.0 is related to the types of digital technologies used in the production process of the respective ones, as shown in Figs. 5 and 6.

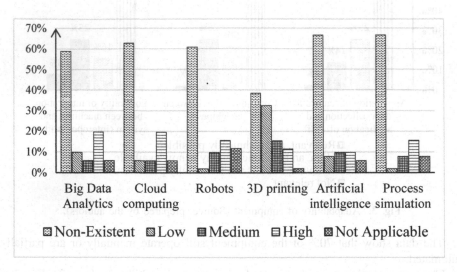

Fig. 5. Level of use of digital technologies in the production process (Source: prepared by the authors).

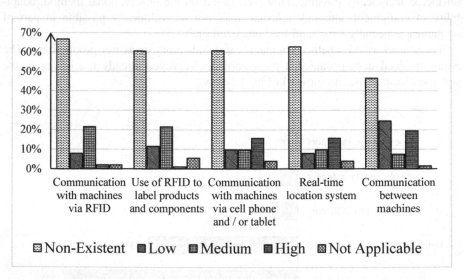

Fig. 6. Level of use of digital technologies in the production process (Source: prepared by the authors).

In the analysis of Figs. 5 and 6, it can be seen that the use of digital technologies in the production process is still non-existent in approximately 60% of the companies surveyed.

5 Conclusion

In seeking to answer the level of maturity of companies in the automotive segment in Brazil, this article sought to identify the degree of maturity of companies for the digitalization of processes.

In the analysis of the data, it was found that 78% of the companies consider the topic relevant, however the significance given to the subject has not yet been translated, in this case, into reality when the focus is on the transition to Industry 4.0. For most of the companies interviewed, the level of equipment infrastructure is insufficient, the level of automation is still low, the adaptability of the machines is considered relevant, but it is not technically possible in all companies in the segment.

The companies pointed out that they already use or are in the implementation phase of some kind of indicator to evaluate productivity.

Regarding the use of digital technologies in the production process, in approximately 60% of the companies there is no evidence of use. The indications of high use of these technologies, when detailing the data, it can be verified that they refer only to the automakers, a situation also found in secondary research [17] that denotes that the auto parts do not follow the same pace of transition, that investments in modernization are restricted in relation to available technologies and that automakers have greater access to new technologies and de-more resources.

Research by PWC [14] points to Industry 4.0 no longer as a trend, but as an epicenter of strategies in global terms, as companies seek to combine advanced connectivity and automation services, cloud computing, sensors and 3D printing, connectivity, computerized processes, artificial intelligence and Internet of Things in transforming your business. On the other hand, they also corroborate the results obtained in this article when they state that Industry 4.0 in Brazil is still at an early stage.

Considering all care in the collection, presentation, analysis and interpretation of the data to ensure the accuracy of the results obtained, the present research does not contain conclusions, but in response to the proposed question it can be stated, based on the results obtained, that in terms process maturity has been taking place in companies in the automotive segment in Brazil, but at a slow pace.

Acknowledgment. This study was financed in part by the Coordenação de Aperfeiçoamento de Pessoal de Nível Superior - Brasil (CAPES) - Finance Code 001.

References

1. Lee, J., Bagheri, B., Kao, H.A.: A cyber-physical systems architecture for Industry 4.0-based manufacturing systems. Manuf. Lett. **3**, 18–23 (2015)
2. Davies, A., Sharp, D.: RICS Strategic Facilities Management. Case studies, International Workplace, Cambridge, Report (2014)

3. IEDI Homepage. https://iedi.org.br/media/site/artigos/20190311_industria_do_futuro_no_brasil_e_no_mundo.pdf. Accessed 15 Feb 2019
4. Almada-Lobo, F.: The Industry 4.0 revolution and the future of manufacturing execution systems (MES). J. Innov. Manag. 3(4), 6–21 (2016)
5. Wendler, R.: The maturity of maturity model research: a systematic mapping study. Inf. Softw. Technol. 54(12), 1317–1339 (2012)
6. Santos, R.C., Martinho, J.L.: An Industry 4.0 maturity model proposal. J. Manuf. Technol. Manag. (2019, ahead-of-print). https://doi.org/10.1108/JMTM-09-2018-0284
7. Görçün, O.F.: Industry 4.0, pp. 1–199. Beta Publisher (2018)
8. Geissbauer, R., Vedsø, J., Schrauf, S. https://www.strategy-business.com/article/A-Strategists-Guide-to-Industry-4.0?gko=a2260. Accessed 10 Jan 2020
9. Rodrigues, L.F., Jesus, R.A., Schützer, K.: Industrie 4.0: a literature review. Rev. Ciên. Tecnol. 19(38), 33–45 (2016)
10. Hermann, M., Pentek, T., Otto, B.: Design principles for Industrie 4.0 scenarios. In: 2016 49th Hawaii International Conference System Sciences (HICSS), pp. 3928–3937 (2016)
11. Zhong, R.Y., Xu, X., Klotz, E., Newman, S.T.: Intelligent manufacturing in the context of Industry 4.0: a review. Engineering 3(5), 616–630 (2017)
12. Dumitrescu, R., et al.: Auf dem Weg zu Industrie 4.0: Erfolgsfaktor Referenzarchtiektur. It's OWL Clustermanagement (2015)
13. Wang, S., Wan, J., Zhang, D., Li, D., Zhang, C.: Towards smart factory for Industry 4.0: a self-organized multi-agent system with big data based feedback and coordination. Comput. Netw. 101, 158–168 (2016)
14. PWC Homepage. https://www.pwc.com.br/pt/publicacoes/servicos/assets/consultoria-negocios/2016/pwc-industry-4-survey-16pdf. Accessed 15 Jan 2020
15. Folmer, E., van Sinderen, M., Oude Luttighuis, P.: Enterprise interoperability: information, services and processes for the interoperable economy and society. IseB 12(4), 491–494 (2014). https://doi.org/10.1007/s10257-014-0246-3
16. Schumacher, A., Erol, S., Sihn, W.: A maturity model for assessing Industry 4.0 readiness and maturity of manufacturing enterprises. Procedia Cirp 52(1), 161–166 (2016)
17. Santos, N.A, Ruggero, S.M., Sacomano, J.B.: A transition to Industry 4.0: a study on the nature of investments in automakers and auto parts. ENEGEP (2019)

General Readiness Assessment of Industry 4.0: Evidence from Serbian Manufacturing Industry

Tanja Todorovic[1]([⊠]) [iD], Bojan Lalic[1] [iD], Vidosav Majstorovic[2] [iD],
Ugljesa Marjanovic[1] [iD], and Nemanja Tasic[1] [iD]

[1] Faculty of Technical Sciences, University of Novi Sad, Novi Sad, Serbia
{ttodorovic,blalic,umarjano,nemanja.tasic}@uns.ac.rs
[2] Faculty of Mechanical Engineering, University of Belgrade, Belgrade, Serbia
vmajstorovic@mas.bg.ac.rs

Abstract. The implementation of Industry 4.0 concepts has significant implications for the manufacturing landscape. The aim of this study is to assess the level of general readiness for Industry 4.0 in the emerging economy of Serbia. The obtained results indicate that the majority of Serbian manufacturing sector has not yet embarked on the path towards transformation and implementation of advanced technologies.

Keywords: Industry 4.0 · Manufacturing industry · Readiness assessment

1 Introduction

The prospects of Industry 4.0 indicate a substantial change in the manufacturing value chain. The introduction of highly flexible and highly productive factories of the future is gaining momentum in industries of developed regions [1]. In order to adapt to the new manufacturing paradigm, emerging markets should analyze their readiness for the implementation of Industry 4.0 concept. The aim of this paper is to evaluate the extent of usage of advanced digital technologies in manufacturing companies in the context of developing countries, i.e. Serbia.

2 Literature Review

Although there is a lack of consensus regarding the Industry 4.0 definition [2], the prevailing terminology of Industry 4.0 concept entails the implementation of digital advanced manufacturing technologies into the manufacturing landscape [3], along with other non-technological enabling factors [4, 5]. Research in this field is primarily focused on companies from developed countries, whilst companies from developing countries are facing different obstacles regarding their technological and organizational capabilities to implement novel concepts [6–8]. Although emerging economies are lagging behind when it comes to implementation of advanced technologies, they have slowly begun to pave a way for inclusion of Industry 4.0 elements [9, 10]. The

B. Lalic et al. (Eds.): APMS 2020, IFIP AICT 591, pp. 139–146, 2020.
https://doi.org/10.1007/978-3-030-57993-7_17

application of various readiness models [5, 11, 12] in order to assess the specific industry's status regarding advanced technologies implementation could indicate the industries with the highest level of Industry 4.0 penetration [13, 14]. Since Industry 4.0 is driven by advanced technologies [15, 16] as core enablers of its implementation, this paper examines the utilization of advanced manufacturing technologies as a first step in analyzing the readiness for Industry 4.0 [17].

To assess the general readiness to digitalize, it is of particular interest whether companies use and combine several technologies at the same time or in which technological fields companies are increasingly active. Regarding the nature of Industry 4.0 enabling technologies, the authors have differing points of view [18]. The Fraunhofer Institute for Systems and Innovation Research ISI developed an I4.0 general readiness assessment methodology [19] that combines the number of digital technologies used with three technological fields and thus provides information on the digitalization readiness of individual companies. The model applied in this study follows the readiness assessment methodology of the Fraunhofer ISI and aims to assess the current situation in terms of implementation of digital advanced manufacturing technologies in the manufacturing sector in Serbia. Based on this assessment, the future steps in further digitalization of economy could be planned and executed both on governmental and individual company's level.

3 Research Questions

Against this background, we investigated how intensively Serbian manufacturing companies are currently implementing Industry 4.0 relevant technologies. Based on the literature review, the following research questions were proposed:

- **RQ1**: What is the level of general readiness for Industry 4.0 in Serbian manufacturing industry?
- **RQ2**: Which industries in Serbia have the highest level of general readiness for Industry 4.0?

4 Data and Methodology

Our analysis used the Serbian dataset from the European Manufacturing Survey (EMS) conducted in 2018. EMS investigates technological and non-technological innovation in the European manufacturing sector. It represents the most detailed and widest survey on industrial value-added processes and modernization strategies of companies in the manufacturing industry and is coordinated by Fraunhofer ISI. The survey is carried out on a triennial basis and targets a random sample of manufacturing companies with more than 20 employees (NACE Rev 2 codes from 10 to 33). The Serbian dataset includes 240 companies. Concerning descriptive statistics, the sampled companies report, on average, a company size of 124 employees (SD = 207). In total, 110 companies are small firms (fewer than 50 employees), 103 companies are medium-sized (between 50 and 249 employees), and 27 companies are large enterprises (more than 250 employees). Table 1 depicts the sample distribution regarding size.

Table 1. EMS database – distribution of firms by size.

Firm size	N	%
20 to 49 employees	110	45.8
50 to 249 employees	103	42.9
250 and more employees	27	11.3
Total	240	100.0

To be able to assess the general willingness to digitalize, it is of particular interest whether companies use and combine several technologies at the same time or in which technological fields companies are increasingly active. For this purpose, the Fraunhofer ISI developed an I4.0 general readiness assessment methodology that combines the number of digital technologies used with three technological fields and thus provides information on the digitalization readiness of individual companies. The Fraunhofer I4.0 Readiness assessment approach is exclusively focused on technology and is based on seven digital technologies:

• Software system for production, planning and control;
• Digital visualization at the work place of the workers;
• Digital data exchange with customers/suppliers;
• Techniques for automation and control of internal logistics;
• Real-time production control system;
• Mobile devices for programming and operation of plants and machines; and
• Product Life Cycle Management Systems.

These are combined into the following technology fields:

1. Digital Management Systems: The first field of technology consists of "Software system for production planning and control" and "Product Lifecycle Management Systems".
2. Wireless human-machine communication: In the second field of technology the "Digital Visualization" is combined with the "Mobile Devices".
3. Cyber-Physical Production System (CPS) related processes: The third field of technology is the "Real-time production control system", the "Automation of internal logistics" and "Digital data exchange with customers and suppliers" together.

While the first two technology fields tend to cover basic digital technologies and still have a clear distance from I4.0, the third technology field already contains the first approaches of digitally networked production. Using this grouping, therefore, those companies that are closer to I4.0 are those who use and combine digital technologies in all three technology fields and use several of the CPS-related processes on the one hand. By contrast, companies that only apply digital technologies in one or two technology fields are less willing to work for digitally networked production in the sense of Industry 4.0

There are six different levels which are summarized graphically on Fig. 1:

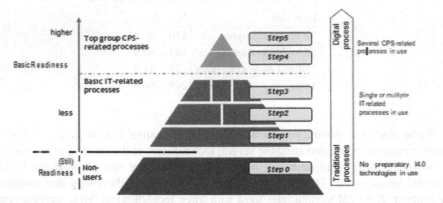

Fig. 1. Levels of I4.0 Readiness [19]

Non-users who do not (yet) have readiness for I4.0:

- Level 0: Companies that do not use any of the digital technologies studied and tend to rely on traditional production processes;

Basic levels, as a base on the way to I4.0, with still less willingness:

- Level 1 (beginners): Companies that use digital processes in one of the three technology fields;
- Level 2 (advanced beginners): Companies that use digital processes in two of the three technology fields;
- Level 3 (advanced): Companies that are active in all three technology fields and use both IT-related processes and a CPS-related process.

Leading group, as a pioneer on the way to I4.0, with higher readiness:

- Level 4: Companies that are active in all fields of technology and use at least two technologies of CPS-related processes;
- Level 5: Companies that are active in all technology fields and use at least three technologies of CPS-related processes.

5   Results

The following Table 2 gives a distribution of general readiness of Serbian manufacturing firms by level of readiness.

Table 2. General readiness assessment of Serbian manufacturing companies – distribution of firms by level of readiness.

Industry	Level 0	Level 1	Level 2	Level 3	Level 4	Level 5	Share on total sample (%)
10	18	4	11		4	2	16.3
11	3	2		1			2.5
12	1						0.4
13	2					2	1.7
14	6	3	1	1	1	2	5.8
15	5		2				2.9
16	6	1	3		1		4.6
17	3		3				2.5
18	2	2	1	1	3		3.8
19	1		1				0.8
20	3	2		1			2.5
21	1		1				0.8
22	6	4	4	2	1	4	8.8
23	7		2	2			4.6
24	3		1	1			2.1
25	14	7	9	5		1	15.0
26	1	1	1	1	1		2.1
27	5	1	4	2	2	1	6.3
28	4	4	6			1	6.3
29	3	4	2	1			4.2
30	2						0.8
31	3	2	1	2		1	3.8
32	1		1	1			1.3
33						1	0.4
% of total	41.7	15.4	22.5	8.8	5.4	6.3	100.0

For RQ1 (What is the level of general readiness for Industry 4.0 in Serbian manufacturing industry?), we conducted descriptive statistics presented in Table 2 and Fig. 2. From the results, we could say that majority (41.67%) of manufacturing companies are still at Level 0 and just a few (6.25%) at the Level 5 of general readiness for Industry 4.0. Furthermore, for RQ2 (Which industries in Serbia have the highest level of general readiness for Industry 4.0?), the most prepared manufacturing industry in Serbia for Industry 4.0 is Manufacture of rubber and plastic products (NACE 22), followed by Manufacture of food products (NACE 10), and Manufacture of wearing apparel (NACE 14), as presented in Table 3.

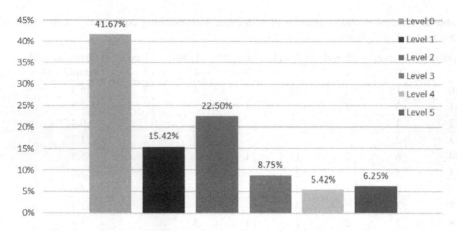

Fig. 2. Distribution of firms by level of general readiness for Industry 4.0.

As for the specific industries, manufacture of rubber and plastic products sector (NACE 22) has four companies at the Level 5, manufacture of food products sector (NACE 10) has two companies at the Level 5 and four companies at the Level 4. Finally, manufacture of wearing apparel sector (NACE 14) has two companies at the Level 5. In terms of readiness levels, it could be observed that there is significant heterogeneity even among companies in the same industry. For example, there are 2 food production companies at level 5, none at level 3 and 18 companies at level 0.

Table 3. General readiness assessment of Industry 4.0 in Serbian manufacturing companies – distribution of firms of top 3 industries.

Industry	Level 0	Level 1	Level 2	Level 3	Level 4	Level 5	Rank
22	6	4	4	2	1	4	1
10	18	4	11	–	4	2	2
14	6	3	1	1	1	2	3

6　Discussion and Conclusion

This study represents the first step in analyzing the readiness of Serbian manufacturing companies for Industry 4.0. It bases on an established methodology of the Fraunhofer ISI from Germany and uses Serbian data of the European Manufacturing Survey representing the most detailed and widest survey on industrial value-added processes and modernization strategies of companies in the manufacturing industry.

The results indicate that the majority of companies in Serbian manufacturing sector have not started the transformation based on advanced digital technologies yet. Even those companies which have started to uptake some digital technologies, are on a very low level of readiness for Industry 4.0. In our sample, we could find only few companies dealing with higher levels of readiness representing rather an exception in

Serbia. One of the reasons for this situation might be the strong market-pool-oriented strategy of the manufacturing sector in Serbia following the needs and requirements of customers instead of a self-initiative in terms of the technological catch-up imitative. In other words, instead of following a technology-based competitiveness, the majority of manufacturing companies follow solely low-price market strategies. An additional argument might be the lack of political instruments for providing technological catch-up in the Serbian manufacturing sector. To identify the barriers for up-taking digital technologies, an in-depth study is to be conducted.

Looking at individual sectors within the manufacturing industry, we could identify three sectors with somewhat higher readiness levels: manufacture of rubber and plastic products, manufacture of food products and manufacture of wearing apparel. The further research should involve the deeper analysis of the underlying factors that positively influence the implementation in these sectors, with the aim to develop policy recommendation for the whole industry.

Despite the solely descriptive characteristic of the methodology, the study gives a first overview of the state of the art in terms of usage of digital technologies. As such, it contributes significantly to the current research on Industry 4.0 in emerging economies. Moreover, giving a first statistical overview, it plays an crucial role for further more comprehensive as well as in-depth studies including additional non-technological areas like human resources and competences in digital surroundings as well as the improvement of organizational and management concepts, new business models and digital innovations.

References

1. Lichtblau, K., et al.: IMPULS-Industrie 4.0-Readiness. Impuls-Stiftung des VDMA, Aachen-Köln (2015)
2. Castelo-Branco, I., Cruz-Jesus, F., Oliveira, T.: Assessing industry 4.0 readiness in manufacturing: evidence for the European union. Comput. Ind. **107**, 22–32 (2019)
3. Kagermann, H., Helbig, J., Hellinger, A., Wahlster, W.: Recommendations for implementing the strategic initiative INDUSTRIE 4.0: Securing the future of German manufacturing industry, final report of the Industrie 4.0 Working Group (2013)
4. Camisón, C., Villar-López, A.: Organizational innovation as an enabler of technological innovation capabilities and firm performance. J. Bus. Res. **67**(1), 2891–2902 (2014)
5. Schumacher, A., Erol, S., Sihn, W.: A maturity model for assessing industry 4.0 readiness and maturity of manufacturing enterprises. Procedia CIRP **52**, 161–166 (2016)
6. Lalic, B., Medic, N., Delic, M., Tasic, N., Marjanovic, U.: Open innovation in developing regions: An empirical analysis across manufacturing companies. Int. J. Ind. Eng. Manag. **8**(3), 111–120 (2017)
7. Medić, N., Anišić, Z., Lalić, B., Marjanović, U., Brezocnik, M.: Hybrid fuzzy multi-attribute decision making model for evaluation of advanced digital technologies in manufacturing: Industry 4.0 perspective. Adv. Prod. Eng. Manag. **14**(4), 483–493 (2019)
8. Delić, M., Beker, I., Cvetković, N., Medić, N., Morača, S.: Assessment of key LEAN dimensions implementation in organisations from developing region. Int. J. Ind. Eng. Manag. **8**(4), 239–245 (2017)

9. Crnjac, M., Veža, I., Banduka, N.: From concept to the introduction of industry 4.0. Int. J. Ind. Eng. Manag. **8**(1), 21–30 (2017)
10. Raj, A., Dwivedi, G., Sharma, A., de Lopes Sousa Jabbour, A.B., Rajak, S.: Barriers to the adoption of industry 4.0 technologies in the manufacturing sector: an inter-country comparative perspective. Int. J. Prod. Econ. **224**, 107546 (2020)
11. Mladineo, M., Horvat, D., Veza, I.: Case study of croatian manufacturing industry. In: 2016 6th International Conference Mechanical Technologies and Structural Materials (2016)
12. Gürdür, D., El-khoury, J., Törngren, M.: Digitalizing swedish industry: what is next?: Data analytics readiness assessment of swedish industry, according to survey results. Comput. Ind. **105**, 153–163 (2019)
13. Horvat, D., Stahlecker, T., Zenker, A., Lerch, C., Mladineo, M.: A conceptual approach to analysing manufacturing companies' profiles concerning Industry 4.0 in emerging economies. Procedia Manuf. **17**, 419–426 (2018)
14. Veza, I., Mladineo, M., Gjeldum, N.: Evaluation of Industrial Maturity Level: A case study of Croatia (2016)
15. Smit, J., Kreutzer, S., Moeller, C., Carlberg, M.: Industry4.0 a study for the European Parliament (2016)
16. Lalic, B., Rakic, S., Marjanovic, U.: Use of industry 4.0 and organisational innovation concepts in the Serbian textile and apparel industry. Fibres Text. East. Eur. **27**(3), 10–18 (2019). https://doi.org/10.5604/01.3001.0013.0737
17. Lalic, B., Marjanovic, U., Rakic, S., Pavlovic, M., Todorovic, T., Medic, N.: Big data analysis as a digital service: evidence form manufacturing firms. In: Wang, L., Majstorovic, V.D., Mourtzis, D., Carpanzano, E., Moroni, G., Galantucci, L.M. (eds.) Proceedings of 5th International Conference on the Industry 4.0 Model for Advanced Manufacturing. LNME, pp. 263–269. Springer, Cham (2020). https://doi.org/10.1007/978-3-030-46212-3_19
18. Pacchini, A.P.T., Lucato, W.C., Facchini, F., Mummolo, G.: The degree of readiness for the implementation of industry 4.0. Comput. Ind. **113**, 103125 (2019)
19. Lerch, C., Jager, A., Maloca, S.: Wie digital ist deutschlands industrie wirklich? Karlsruhe, vol. 71 (2017)

Digital and Virtual Quality Management Systems

Assembly Issue Resolution System Using Machine Learning in Aero Engine Manufacturing

Jörg Brünnhäußer[1(✉)], Sonika Gogineni[1], Jonas Nickel[2],
Heiko Witte[2], and Rainer Stark[1,3]

[1] Fraunhofer IPK, Pascalstraße 8-9, 10587 Berlin, Germany
joerg.bruennhaeusser@ipk.fraunhofer.de
[2] Rolls-Royce Deutschland, Eschenweg 11,
15827 Blankenfelde-Mahlow, Germany
[3] Technische Universität Berlin, Pascalstraße 8-9, 10587 Berlin, Germany

Abstract. Companies are progressively gathering data within the digitalization of production processes. By actively using these production data sets operational processes can be improved, hence empowering businesses to compete with other corporations. One way to achieve this is to use data from production processes to develop and offer smart services that enable companies to continuously improve and to become more efficient. In this paper, the authors present an industrial use case of how machine learning can be implemented into smart services in production processes to decrease the time for resolving upcoming issues in manufacturing. The implementation is carried out by using an assistance system that aids a team which attends to problems in the assembling of turbines. Therefore, the authors have analyzed the assembly problems from an issue management system that the team had to resolve. Subsequently three different approaches based upon natural language processing, regression and clustering were selected. This paper also presents the development and evaluation of the assistance system.

Keywords: Machine learning · Data-driven service · Issue resolution

1 Introduction

An increasing amount of data is stored within enterprise systems and databases of many companies. By introducing Internet of Things (IoT) concepts more and more data throughout the whole product lifecycle are made available every second. This includes the production process where due to the advancing digitalization almost every step within that process leaves data behind. A key aspect for many manufacturing companies is to take advantage of these data to increase competitiveness through machine learning (ML), Smart Services and Data-Driven Applications [1].

The application of ML on existing data is one approach to improve manufacturing processes. This paper shows on an example how one can set up a Smart Service with Machine Learning based on already available data and put it into practice. In the best case it can save time and increase the efficiency, hence saving costs. This is also the

© IFIP International Federation for Information Processing 2020
Published by Springer Nature Switzerland AG 2020
B. Lalic et al. (Eds.): APMS 2020, IFIP AICT 591, pp. 149–157, 2020.
https://doi.org/10.1007/978-3-030-57993-7_18

goal of the COCKPIT 4.0 project (funded by the Berlin Senate, the State of Brandenburg and the European Regional Development Fund – ERDF 1.8/03) in which a consortium of Rolls-Royce Germany, Fraunhofer IPK and the BTU Cottbus are working together to address different challenges in the context of digitalization. This paper is about one work package of the COCKPIT 4.0 project which aims to improve the efficiency of the gas turbine assembly at the Rolls-Royce site in Dahlewitz, Germany. The goal of the work package is to connect various data sources with semantic technologies [2] and support the resulting semantic network with machine leaning techniques to assist in solving production issues efficiently. The learned models enable the creation of an assembly issue resolution system which will aid the fitters to fix manufacturing problems faster. The resulting assistance system improves problem identification, resolution and prevention by the fitters, shop floor management and assembly manufacturing engineering.

2 Problem Description

Modern aerospace products are not only highly complex but are also supplied by an equally complex and globally distributed supply chain. While this approach enables both a cost-effective and flexible product development and production, it also increases the risk of supply chain disruptions and part supply issues for the engine assembly process [3]. Even though many of these risks can be managed upstream of the final engine assembly, it is necessary to quickly react to missing parts and other assembly issues in the build line in order to avoid build stops and delivery delays.

Rolls-Royce Germany has established a small, dedicated "Voice of the Fitter" (VoF) team that focuses on resolving any assembly issues as quickly as possible. As the issues might arise from a number of sources, e.g. supplier production issues, delays in logistics or customs, transport or handling damage, the team needs to access seven data sources and uses different strategies to resolve the issues. Hence, a lot of time is spent on identifying the right data source, accessing the data source, finding the right information, assessing the data, taking a decision and implementing suitable action. In such cases, contextualized data sets assist the users in addressing some of the above tasks such as identifying, accessing, finding and assessing the right data [2]. In addition, ML can be used in enhancing those tasks and also in supporting decision making. This results in saving time for the VoF team.

In this paper, the creation of a smart, ML enabled assistance system that connects all data sources in one location and provides context-related information and resolution strategies to the VoF team is developed. The resulting system can subsequently be expanded to support related tasks in the company, e.g. concession assessments for nonconforming parts.

3   State of the Art

ML is an emerging technology which enables powerful applications and handling of complex data. Production systems are providing a lot of use cases for ML. Wuest et al. [4] outlined the reasons for the increasing importance of ML and mentioned the challenges as well. However, some advantages mentioned are the capability "to handle high-dimensional, multi-variate data, and the ability to extract implicit relationships within large data-sets in a complex and dynamic, often even chaotic environment" [4]. There are already an abundance of applications such as the estimation of the manu-facturing costs of jet engine components [5], the prediction of basic parameters for turbomachinery design based on the load level [6] or approaches to do predictive maintenance [7]. There are also several papers for different systems which support production tasks. In this work [8] an assistance system for operational workers is created which uses simulation and Proper Generalized Decomposition algorithms to provide decision support. Additionally another decision support system [9] uses Case Based Reasoning for scheduling tasks. However, there seems to be no suitable approach which addresses the resolution of single and diverse assembly problem in combination with ML.

4   Solution Definition

The VoF use case was one of several use cases collected in the business understanding phase of the Cockpit 4.0 project. The use case was further detailed by interviews with stakeholders involved in VoF. Opportunities for machine learning were identified as part of the requirements capturing during the interviews. Followed by the next phase of the CRISP-DM [10] process the actual data was fetched and reviewed. The source data for this use case consists of two tables.

One table stores the recent VoF cases (see Table 1). The second table consists of comments (see Table 2) which are linked to the first table. One case can have zero to many comments. These comments describe different things like if a part needs to be reworked, if a part which was missing is ordered or is stuck in delivery. Furthermore, it is noted in the comment table if a VoF case is escalated to a higher level of man-agement. In order to aid the Voice of the Fitter team the authors considered three approaches based on the available data as useful:

1. **Natural language processing (NLP) based approach:** The engineering goal was to identify cases with similar descriptions and similar comments, which might be useful for investigating new VoF case. The available data is not labeled which prevents supervised learning. Therefore, NLP could be applied to show similar cases.
2. **Case length prediction:** The goal here was to generate a model that could predict how long an incoming case will take to be resolved. This information could be helpful to judge the priority. For instance, if a single case would take very long, measures could be taken to reduce the time span like escalating the case or getting

Table 1. Excerpt of VoF table with an exemplary problem case

Id	Vof_case_description	Vof_case_state	Vof_open_date	Vof_close_date	Vof_customer	Vof_category	Vof_priority
41	LAUNCH STOP Due to shortage blades	Closed	03.04.2017 07:42	10.04.2017 12:25	x0036	Delivery	Build stop

Vof_engine_type	Vof_part_number	Vof_problem_ident	Vof_part_description	Vof_organisation	Vof_responsible_id
(engine type)	(affected part number)	Missing component	BLADE, HPT 2	Production	83

Table 2. Excerpt of VoF comments table with comments from VoF team

Vof_case_id	Vof_comment	Vof_comment_update_time	Vof_comment_update_user	Vof_comment_type	Id
1041	11off in transit, expected on dock today 05/04 around noontime	05.04.2017 11:23	x0030	Comment	41

support from other departments. The start and end date of each case is available so the duration of every case can be calculated and supervised learning can be applied.

3. **Clustering:** Unsupervised learning could be used to separate the data into clusters. Those clusters could provide the user with 'similar' cases which can be taken as starting point for their research on how to resolve the current issue

5 Design and Development of the Prototype

The approaches discussed in the previous sectors are further detailed in this section. This is done by explaining the data science aspects of the approaches followed by the implementation in the prototypes architecture.

5.1 Data Science

NLP Based Approach. To select an optimal algorithm to find similar cases, three different algorithms were tested. The first one chosen was the commonly used Jaccard coefficient [11], which is an index for the similarity of two sets by the technique known as shingling [12]. This approach does not take into account the meaning of the words. The second approach was based on word2vec [13]. Word2vec is trained [14] on a large data set like the Google News corpus and calculates vector representations for each word. The vectors for semantic similar words should also be similar. In contrast the self-trained model was trained with a data set of the VoF case descriptions in order to cast the engineering vocabulary and abbreviations into the model. The calculation of the distance was done by the word mover's distance [15].

All models were tested with the same data set and subsequently some examples have been evaluated by an expert. The results provide information about the performance of the approaches to find a similar VoF cases. The evaluation revealed that the self-trained model performed best. This seems reasonable because the data set contains many individual words that are not in common usage. Jaccard delivered the second best result, so the pre-trained model from Google was the least accurate. However, this evaluation was just a first test and further research needs to be conducted.

Case Length Prediction. Initially the label 'duration in hours' was calculated from the start and the end date to be able to train a regression model. After the data preparation of the two tables mentioned in the previous chapter the data was split into a training and a test data set. The evaluation makes it necessary to test the models with unknown data which was not involved in the training. For this purpose the test data set was used. The training data set was used for the training of several different models like linear regression, lasso regression and support vector regression which was taken from the scikitlearn library [16]. Additionally, a model tree (a decision tree with different models on each leaf [17]) was trained. The best model type for the leaf models have been estimated with grid search.

Table 3. Different trained models are compared regarding the root-mean-squared error

Model type	RMSE [in hours]
Linear regression	46.02
Lasso regression	45.83
Support vector regression (SVR)	45.15
Model Tree with (SVR)	43.54

For the evaluation the model made predictions of the VoF case length based on the test data set as input. Those predictions can be compared to the actual values of the duration and the root-mean-squared error can be calculated which gives a metric to evaluate the models (Table 3). In this case the Model Tree approach (with SVR models on each leaf) scored best.

Clustering. The authors compared several combinations of feature reduction methods and clustering algorithms. A subset of six configurations as shown in Table 4 was chosen from the best performing algorithms based on several scores. The subset includes centroid based k-means clustering and a density based DBSCAN clustering. Additionally HDBSCAN was tested as proposed by [18], a combined approach between hierarchical and density based clustering.

The best results were reached with a k-means clustering. The best performing dimensionality reduction method was UMAP which is used for non-linear dimensionality reduction introduced by McInnes et al. [19]. The Silhouette score was proposed in [20]. It measures the separateness and tightness of the clusters found by a clustering and can take values between -1 and 1, whereby a value close to -1 implies that the points are misclassified as, the distance towards the centers of the clusters are larger than the distances to the center of the closest neighboring cluster. A score around 1 implies that the result is very well-classified. The Calinski-Harabasz score was proposed in [21]. It minimizes within-cluster distances and maximizes between-cluster distances, therefore, compact, well-separated clusters get a better score. The larger the Calinski-Harabasz score of a clustering is, the better is the clustering [21]. The Davies-Bouldin score was presented in [22], unlike the other scores it is not maximized, but minimized. It calculates the average similarity of the rated clusters with their most similar cluster [22].

For the application the Kmeans1-clustering was chosen based on the performance metrics introduced above and the intended use. Kmeans2 had the best Silhouette score and Davies-Bouldin score, but the three resulting clusters were not practical for the considered use case. The performance of Hdbscan1, Hdbscan2, Hdbscan3 and Dbscan was worse than that of Kmeans1. After examining whether the contents of the clusters produced by Kmeans1 are sound and realistic it was chosen as the final clustering approach. Furthermore, seven clusters were indeed the number expected by experts. For UMAP the implementation by [23] and for HDBSCAN the one by [24] was used. All other implementations were based on [16].

Table 4. Table shows the evaluation metrics of the different clustering. One of the HDBSCAN cluster always consist out of outliers.

	Clustering	Dimension reduction	Silhouette	Calinski-Harabasz	Davies-Bouldin	Number of clusters
Hdbscan1	HDBSCAN	UMAP	0.6	3472	1.24	7
Hdbscan2	HDBSCAN	UMAP	0.55	3907	1.02	11
Hdbscan3	HDBSCAN	UMAP	0.62	9937	1.02	7
Dbscan	DBSCAN	UMAP	0.62	4308	0.36	8
Kmeans1	K-Means	UMAP	0.64	13732	0.39	7
Kmeans2	K-Means	UMAP	0.7	9542	0.33	3

5.2   Implementation of Models into a Prototype

The prototype for visualizing the ML results to the VoF team was designed based on a microservice architecture. The advantage is the separation of every functionality into a single, atomic web service. The technology stack consists of the Java Spring Boot framework for the backend and vue.js for the frontend. The gateway-service hosts the frontend and serves as controller between the user and the different services. These services take care of the database access or the filtering of the data.

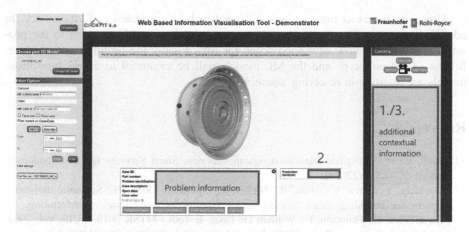

Fig. 1. Screenshot of the current version of the prototype. 1./3. shows the position of the NLP and the clustering. The duration prediction is shown on position 2.

For the voice of the fitter use case the user can see open and closed cases on a 3D model of an engine (see Fig. 1), furthermore, filter options are available in order to handle a larger set of cases. If a case is selected a box pops up with information about the case. If it is an open case the first ML model comes into play which predicts the duration. This gives the user an estimate of how long such a case usually takes, and therefore how critical this case might get. The clustering appears on the right hand side after a click on the "Clustering" button. The individual clusters consist of at least 100 cases. In order to show the user the most suitable case where the NLP approach is used. The cases from the same cluster are sorted by the textual similarity of their case description.

6   Conclusion and Outlook

This paper briefly summarizes the approach and a use case to use ML and generate smart services, which helps reduce time of issue resolution in manufacturing. The significance of this work is also to show how to improve production processes with Machine Learning based on existing data in practice. VoF team and their assembly issue resolution was selected as the initial use case to be enhanced with a smart service and machine learning. Three different approaches of the application of ML were investigated: a NLP approach for text similarity, a prediction of the case duration with regression and a clustering of all the cases. This was further integrated into a prototype system to assist the team. The ML models and the prototype were presented and discussed with the experts from Rolls-Royce Germany. This prototype can be used as an example of how existing data can be turned into a smart service which can improve certain processes. The results show the potential for time savings in solving assembly problems.

However, the exact time savings still need to be investigated in further work. In addition more data from enterprise systems and databases will be added to the prototype which will allow new approaches for ML. Finally the usability and the usefulness of the prototype and the ML models will be evaluated to assess how those models are assisting in resolving assembly issues.

References

1. Stich, V., et al.: Digitale Dienstleistungsinnovationen. Smart Services agil und kundenorientiert entwickeln (2019)
2. Gogineni, S., Exner, K., Stark, R., Nickel, J., Oeler, M., Witte, H.: Semantic assistance system for providing smart services and reasoning in aero-engine manufacturing. In: Garoufallou, E., Fallucchi, F., William De Luca, E. (eds.) MTSR 2019. CCIS, vol. 1057, pp. 90–102. Springer, Cham (2019). https://doi.org/10.1007/978-3-030-36599-8_8
3. Treuner, F., Hübner, D., Baur, S., Wagner, S.M.: A survey of disruptions in aviation and aerospace supply chains and recommendations for increasing resilience. Supply Chain Manag. 14(3), 7–12 (2014)
4. Wuest, T., Weimer, D., Irgens, C., Thoben, K.D.: Machine learning in manufacturing: advantages, challenges, and applications. Prod. Manuf. Res. 4(1), 23–45 (2016)
5. Loyer, J.L., Henriques, E., Fontul, M., Wiseall, S.: Comparison of machine learning methods applied to the estimation of manufacturing cost of jet engine components. Int. J. Prod. Econ. 178, 109–119 (2016)
6. Azzam, M., Haag, J.C., Jeschcke, P.: Application concept of artificial neural networks for turbomachinery design. Comput. Assist. Methods Eng. Sci. 16(2), 143–160 (2017)
7. Susto, G.A., Schirru, A., Pampuri, S., McLoone, S., Beghi, A.: Machine learning for predictive maintenance: a multiple classifier approach. IEEE Trans. Ind. Inf. 11(3), 812–820 (2015)
8. Belkadi, F., Dhuieb, M.A., Aguado, J.V., Laroche, F., Bernard, A., Chinesta, F.: Intelligent assistant system as a context-aware decision-making support for the workers of the future. Comput. Ind. Eng. 139, 105732 (2020)
9. Kocsis, T., Negny, S., Floquet, P., Meyer, X., Rév, E.: Case-based reasoning system for mathematical modelling options and resolution methods for production scheduling problems: case representation, acquisition and retrieval. Comput. Ind. Eng. 77, 46–64 (2014)
10. Wirth, R., Jochen, H.: CRISP-DM: towards a standard process model for data mining (2000)
11. Niwattanakul, S., Singthongchai, J., Naenudorn, E., Wanapu, S.: Using of Jaccard coefficient for keywords similarity (2013)
12. Manna, M., Abdulameer, G.: Web documents similarity using k-shingle tokens and minhash technique. J. Eng. Appl. Sci. 13, 1499–1505 (2018)
13. Mikolov, T., Sutskever, I., Chen, K., Corrado, G., Dean, J.: Distributed representations of words and phrases and their compositionality (2013)
14. Somani, A.K., Shekhawat, R.S., Mundra, A., Srivastava, S., Verma, V.K. (eds.): Smart Systems and IoT: Innovations in Computing. SIST, vol. 141. Springer, Singapore (2020). https://doi.org/10.1007/978-981-13-8406-6
15. Kusner, M.J., Sun, Y., Kolkin, N.I., Weinberger, K.Q.: From word embeddings to document distances. In: Proceedings of the 32nd International Conference on International Conference on Machine Learning - Volume 37 (ICML 2015), pp. 957–966. JMLR.org (2015)

16. Buitinck, L., et al.: API design for machine learning software: experiences from the scikit-learn project. In: ECML PKDD Workshop: Languages for Data Mining and Machine Learning, pp. 108–122 (2013)
17. Github Model Tree project. https://github.com/ankonzoid/LearningX/tree/master/advanced_ML/model_tree. Accessed 21 Feb 2020
18. Campello, R.J.G.B., Moulavi, D., Sander, J.: Density-based clustering based on hierarchical density estimates. In: Pei, J., Tseng, V.S., Cao, L., Motoda, H., Xu, G. (eds.) PAKDD 2013. LNCS (LNAI), vol. 7819, pp. 160–172. Springer, Heidelberg (2013). https://doi.org/10. 1007/978-3-642-37456-2_14
19. McInnes, L., Healy, J., Melville, J.: UMAP: Uniform manifold approximation and projection for dimension reduction (2018)
20. Rousseeuw, P.J.: Silhouettes: a graphical aid to the interpretation and validation of cluster analysis. J. Comput. Appl. Math. **20**, 53–65 (1987)
21. Calinski, T., Harabasz, J.: A dendrite method for cluster analysis. Commun. Stats. Theory Methods **3**(1), 1–27 (1974)
22. Davies, D.L., Bouldin, D.W.: A cluster separation measure. IEEE Trans. Pattern Anal. Mach. Intell. **2**, 224–227 (1979)
23. McInnes, L., Healy, J., Saul, N., Groberger, L.: UMAP: uniform manifold approximation and projection. JOSS **3**(29), 861 (2018)
24. McInnes, L., Healy, J., Astels, S.: hdbscan: hierarchical density based clustering. J. Open Source Softw. **2**(11), 205 (2017)

Introduction to Material Feeding 4.0: Strategic, Tactical, and Operational Impact

Marco Simonetto[(✉)] and Fabio Sgarbossa

Department of Mechanical and Industrial Engineering, Norwegian University
of Science and Technology, S P Andersens V 3, 7031 Trondheim, Norway
marco.simonetto@ntnu.com

Abstract. Mass customization, the process of producing a low-volume high-variety of products, is changing production environments. In Material Feeding (MF) this means a huge increment in the number of parts, and information, that need to be managed during the different MF activities. If companies want to get high performances from their MF activities, they need to be able to manage these changes in the best manner. Industry 4.0 technologies are introducing new opportunities to help companies in the execution and control of the MF activities. It is important for companies to be able to understand how to implement these technologies in their processes and how to take these opportunities. In order to facilitate this, in this paper the concept of Material Feeding 4.0 (MF 4.0) is presented for the first time, as Material Feeding where the Industry 4.0 technologies are introduced. The impact of the identified technologies is studied at a strategic, tactical and operational level.

Keywords: Material Feeding · Industry 4.0 · Assembly system · Strategic · Tactical · Operational

1 Introduction

The demand for customized products is increasing. A high demand of customized products implies that the production and assembly lines require to be fed with an enormous amount of different parts. Material feeding (MF) describes all the activities that are responsible for the provision of components, parts, equipment, etc. to production and assembly systems when needed [1]. If companies want to satisfy the demand of their customers these activities need to be continuously improved and optimized. In this paper the focus will be in the assembly system (AS). MF, in AS, can be performed in different ways, by storing all parts near the assembly line or pre-processing parts and delivering them when needed [2]. In the last years with the so-called Industry 4.0 revolution, both AS and MF are considering the introduction of the technologies that this revolution is offering in their planning and control processes. However, although other works already exist that try to study the effects of these technologies on the AS, [3, 4], still no work exists about their effects in the planning and control processes of the MF systems. Although in literature the terms Supply Chain 4.0 and Logistics 4.0 have been already discussed with a broader perspective, [5, 6], in this paper we focus on the specific process and set of activities related to MF. The idea

© IFIP International Federation for Information Processing 2020
Published by Springer Nature Switzerland AG 2020
B. Lalic et al. (Eds.): APMS 2020, IFIP AICT 591, pp. 158–166, 2020.
https://doi.org/10.1007/978-3-030-57993-7_19

is to understand which are the emerging technologies that can be implemented in the MF activities and how their implementation can impact at three levels: strategic, tactical, and operational. The remainder of this paper is structured as follows. Section 2 provides a review of the existing literature concentrating on the MF activities. Section 3 illustrates and discusses the results obtained from the review of the literature. Finally, in Sect. 4 the paper is shortly summarized.

2 Review of the Existing Literature

Examples of Industry 4.0 technologies in AS are: Internet of Things (IoT), Big data, Cloud Computing, Augmented Reality, Collaborative Robots, and Additive Manufacturing [3]. These technologies affect the performance of the AS activities. In MF it is not yet defined which emerging technologies can be used. The main activities of MF are transportation, preparation, and material management [7]. Transportation implies the process of moving all the components, parts, from a point A where they are stocked to a point B where they are requested. The preparation implies the processes of handling and repacking parts into load carriers used for the corresponding line feeding policy [7]. Material management instead includes all the process related to the storage of components and products. For the storage of components, two of the possible solutions are the central receiving stores and the supermarkets [8]. An extensive review of the existing literature on the subject has been carried out to see what is possible to find about Industry 4.0 technologies that can have an impact on these three activities. We used Scopus database as search engine limiting the research from January 2006 to March 2020, English as language, and journal and conference papers as sources.

2.1 Transportation

In the planning and control of the transportation activity one of the most important decisions is the choice of the transportation devices. Examples of traditional transportation devices are the forklift, tow train, or feeder line [8]. Thanks to the technology development, new solutions have appeared in the last few years [9]. First the Automatic Guided Vehicles (AGVs), driverless vehicles that follow a fixed path in order to move from a point to another [10], and now Autonomous Mobile Robots (AMRs) are getting more popular due to their flexibility [11]. These mobile robots can move without following a fixed path and use cameras and sophisticated software to identify their surroundings and take the most efficient route to their destination [12]. AGVs and AMRs are platforms in which you can implement different additional equipment/resources such as lifting systems and collaborative robot. They can be used as "workstations" to assemble the products [13] or to move shelves from the warehouse to the AS [11]. Based on how companies decide to use them, they will face different problems in order to optimize the performances. For example, if the AGVs/AMRs are used to move the shelves for the picking operations, an example of a possible problem might be when non-completed shelves have to be moved using AGVs/AMRs that usually move complete shelves. A solution to this problem is presented in [14] where the authors proposed a scheduling method to move the shelves even if they are not complete. In [15] a cloud-based architecture that controls and improves the collaboration of the AMRs is presented. Simulations showed that using this cloud-based architecture gives the opportunity to improve energy efficiency and save costs. AMRs seem to be a very prominent technology in order to improve the transportation activity. This is also thanks to the development of more powerful Data Analytics techniques.

2.2 Preparation

In the preparation activity for AS we can find the picking and kitting process [1]. The process of picking can be described as manually seeking a particular item in storage according to a list, taking that object and putting it into a bin/container the appropriate transport vehicle, and bringing the objects to the required location for processing [16]. The kit preparation process instead supplies AS with kits of components. The kits are prepared at a kit preparation workspace apart from the AS [17]. Picking and kitting operation can be facilitated using a AMRs to transport the necessary components from the warehouse to the AS [11]. AMRs are not used only for the transportation. In the last few years many manufacturers have started to develop mobile robots with various functions [9]. If a collaborative robot is integrated with a mobile robot this can be called collaborative mobile robots [18]. In [18] the collaborative mobile robot is used to perform a part-feeding task. The validity of the solution is granted by the successfully performed tests. Another example of a collaborative robot mounted in a mobile robot is presented in [17]. The collaborative robot sorts the components that have been picked by an operator into a batch of kits. The mobile robot gives the opportunity to the collaborative robot to do its operations moving together with the human operator. This is done safely and relieves the human operator of activities associated with sorting components into kits. Kitting preparation in the context of material supply to AS can be performed utilizing augmented reality (AR) [19]. AR is used in single kit-preparation and in batch preparation. The experiment demonstrates how AR is competitive both in terms of time-efficiency and picking accuracy. AR is used also in picking activities. The main improvements that AR can give to picking operations are the errors reduction and time efficiency [16, 20, 21]. The preparation of the different components and parts to deliver at the AS is a very important activity. A mistake in this activity means a reduction in the performances of the AS. The introduction of AR in this activity is made in order to reduce the probability of making mistakes.

2.3 Material Management

Data Analytics techniques, such as data mining algorithms and machine learning algorithm, are becoming more popular and powerful with the advent of Industry 4.0 [22]. These techniques can be used to improve the material management activities of a company. For example, in [23] a machine learning algorithm is proposed to optimize the warehouse storage location allocation. The solution can improve the efficiency of warehouse operations in case of weak correlation between the stock keeping units. Whereas in [24] a positioning big data forecasting model is used in order to predict the trajectory of the mobile robots. This can improve the safety, reliability and stability of the mobile robot navigation. The introduction of mobile robots in the warehouses can mean a change in their design. Mobile robots allow spatial flexibility and expandability. If a warehouse needs more capacity, one simply adds more pods, drives, and stations [11]. In order to manage the inventories of warehouses and ASs it is possible to adopt new smart solutions. Internet of Things (IoT) and Cloud computing can be used to automate inventory systems [25]. An example of a solution that can improve this automation of inventory systems is presented in [26] with the concept of self-optimizing Kanban. Self-optimizing Kanban systems autonomously adjust their capacities as well as the quantity of cards in circulation according to predefined performances. In order to use these systems, it is important to collect all the data of the quantities inside the warehouses in real-time and to use data analytic algorithms to manage the collected data. The data are the most important resource in material management. It is important to know which data need to be collected and how. Once the data are collected, they need to be analyzed in order to obtain valuable information. IoT technologies and Data Analytics techniques will help companies in this MF activity.

3   Material Feeding 4.0

In Fig. 1 we see the results obtained from the review of the literature. From the figure we can see that the most adopted technologies in MF activities are: mobile robots, augmented reality, IoT technologies, Cloud Computing and Data Analytics. These are the technologies that can be present in a MF 4.0 system.

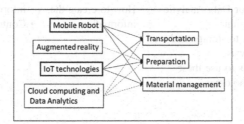

Fig. 1. Industry 4.0 technologies for Material Feeding activities.

Table 1 summarizes where the technologies impact in the different activities at a strategic, tactical, and operational level. The table helps to think about new research challenges that can appear if some of the technologies identified are introduced in the MF system. In order to state the impact of the different technologies at a strategic, tactical, and operational levels in MF 4.0, the scope of every level is shortly explained in the following. Decisions of different levels affect each other and should be considered in an integrated way regarding the intra-organizational decision levels as well as the inter-organizational hierarchy [27]. Due to page restriction, we will use the mobile robots as an example.

Table 1. Decision areas of Material Feeding 4.0. Impact of the different technologies in planning and control.

Industry 4.0 technology	Impact level		
	Strategic	Tactial	Operational
Mobile robots	• Type of mobile robots • Design the guide path system • Warehouse design • Skills to use the sytem	• Feeding polices • Number of mobile robots • Schedulling of the mobile robots • Human-mobile robot interaction	• Routes of the mobile robots • Contol of the system
Augmented reality	• Type of AR devices • Skills to use the AR devices	• Number of workers • Ergonomic of the system	• Real time information sharing → sequencing of kitting and picking information • Control of the system
IoT technologies	• Type of IoT technologies • Type of containers • Skills to use the IoT technologies	• Number of containers in the warehouses and in the AS • Position of the IoT technologies	• Real time control of the capacity of the container • Control of the system
Cloud computing and Data Analysis	• Type of Cloud Computing system and/or Data Analytic techniques • Data to storage and analysis • Skills to use these technologies	• Information to create and share • How to create the information	• Real-time sharing and displaying of the information • Control of the system

3.1 Strategic Level in MF 4.0

Strategic decisions are those decisions that have an influence over the years and a long-term impact on the performance of the MF. Once a strategic decision is made, it is very unlikely to be altered in the short term. They are usually taken at the highest levels of management, include a wide range of uncertainties and carry higher levels of risk. In MF 4.0, the most important decision at this level for all the MF 4.0 activities, is the choice of the technologies to adopt. It is possible to decide gradually which are the technologies to implement in the different activities. Which type of mobile robots to buy will influence all the decisions that a company has to face after their purchase. A mobile robot can be used only as a transportation system or it can be integrated with collaborative robot for picking activities [9, 17]. This together with the flexibility of the guidance system of a mobile robot and its dimensions will influence the design of the possible paths and of the warehouses (central receiving stores or the supermarkets) where it will work [10, 12]. The design of the warehouses can be also influenced by the different types of containers that the mobile robots can transport [11]. The investment that a company makes when it decides to buy the mobile robots is not related only to the purchase of the robots. Someone needs to know how to use them. If the mobile robots are introduced in one or more of the MF activities, it is important to know which skills are needed to use them and what is necessary to do in order to best implement them. This can influence the performance given by the mobile robots. For example, if the company decide to not hire new workers that already know how to use them, it is possible that during the first period, their performance will be lower than the expected. This because a certain amount of time is needed to learn how to use them.

3.2 Tactical Level in MF 4.0

Tactical decisions are decisions and plans that concern the more detailed implementation of the strategic decisions, usually with a medium-term impact on a company. At the tactical level, the decisions about which are the technologies to implement are already made. For the mobile robots this means that the company has decided which type to buy. At this level, for all the MF 4.0 activities, it is important to prepare the different technologies to be used. The first thing to understand is which are the feeding policies to be adopted [1]. The flexibility of mobile robots can change the application of the feeding policies making one policy more convenient than another. For example, it can be more convenient to prepare kits than move entire pallets. Mobile robots are also more flexible with respect to the transported volumes and they can adapt themselves with the variation of the material flow. The chosen policies can influence the number of mobile robots that the company needs and respect with traditional transportation devices it is possible that new algorithms are necessaries to calculate this number. In the scheduling phase of the mobile robots, the company decides when, where and how a mobile robot should act to perform tasks [10]. A new problem to solve during this phase is which mobile robot to use based on the operations needed to perform [9]. This because there are different types of mobile robots that are going to be implemented based on the activities that they must do. In this phase is important to consider also the ergonomic aspect of the system. In fact, the safety precautions that one has to implement can be different in order to use the different type of mobile robots. These can change from a mobile robot that is used only as transportation system from another that works together with human workers, for example when it is used as a workstation or when it helps the human operator in the preparation of the kits [13, 17].

3.3 Operational Level in MF 4.0

Operational decisions are related to day-to-day operations of the companies. They have a short-term horizon as they are taken repetitively. At this level, for all the MF 4.0 activities, it is important to ensure that technology works as best as possible. The vehicle routing problem decides the route a mobile robot should take and the sequence of loads (or jobs) that this vehicle should visit [10]. The routes that a mobile robot can travel are different from those of a traditional transportation devise [8]. The routes change also depending on whether the mobile robots must follow a fixed path or not.

Regardless of the technology, at the operational level it is possible to find the control of the system. This will give the opportunity to continuously improve the MF 4.0 system and to avoid that it stops working. Checking the operation of a mobile robot is more difficult and requires new data to be collected and new knowledge. This is because they are not guided by human workers, and if something is not working properly, no one can be aware of it if a proper control system is not implemented. It is important to create new solutions that can control the mobile robots during the execution of their activities [15]. The data collected from the mobile robots need to be analyzed, and once these data become information these need to be understood before then take any decisions. Not understand the information generated by the execution of the different activities from the mobile robots means not being able to understand if the system is working properly. This means having a system that is not working with the desired performance and that is not possible to change it in order to improve them.

4 Conclusion

This paper focused on the individualization of the most common Industry 4.0 technologies that can be used during the execution of the MF activities. The considered MF activities are transportation, preparation, and material management. This gives us the opportunity to introduce the concept of MF 4.0. MF systems where the different activities are done with the help of the new technologies of Industry 4.0. Moreover, we give some suggestions about the decisions that need to be taken in MF 4.0 with respect to a strategic, tactical and operational impact level. This is only an introduction in the topic of MF 4.0. There seems to be a high potential for future works in this research stream. Future research for example should focus on understanding how to measure the performance of the different technologies implemented in the MF 4.0 activities. This is related to another possible work that is understanding which are the data that need to be collected from the MF 4.0 activities and how to collect them. The technologies are becoming always more powerful and user friendly and their introduction will increase in the next few years. It will be important to know in advance which will be possible issues that companies will face when they decide to implement one of these technologies.

References

1. Battini, D., Faccio, M., Persona, A., Sgarbossa, F.: Design of the optimal feeding policy in an assembly system. Int. J. Prod. Econ. **121**(1), 233–254 (2009)
2. Sali, M., Sahin, E.: Line feeding optimization for just in time assembly lines: an application to the automotive industry. Int. J. Prod. Econ. **174**, 54–67 (2016)
3. Cohen, Y., Naseraldin, H., Chaudhuri, A., Pilati, F.: Assembly systems in industry 4.0 era: a road map to understand assembly 4.0. Int. J. Adv. Manuf. Technol. **105**(9), 4037–4054 (2019)
4. Bortolini, M., Ferrari, E., Gamberi, M., Pilati, F., Faccio, M.: Assembly system design in the industry 4.0 era: a general framework. IFAC-PapersOnLine **50**(1), 5700–5705 (2017)

5. Frederico, G.F., Garza-Reyes, J.A., Anosike, A.I., Kumar, V.: Supply chain 4.0: concepts, maturity and research agenda. Int. J. Supply Chain Manag. 1–21 (2019)
6. Winkelhaus, S., Grosse, E.H.: Logistics 4.0: a systematic review towards a new logistics system. Int. J. Prod. Res. 58(1), 18–43 (2020)
7. Schmid, N.A., Limère, V.: A classification of tactical assembly line feeding problems. Int. J. Prod. Res. 57(24), 7586–7609 (2019)
8. Battini, D., Boysen, N., Emde, S.: Just-in-time supermarkets for part supply in the automobile industry. J. Manag. Control 24(2), 209–217 (2013)
9. Lottermoser, A., Berger, C., Braunreuther, S., Reinhart, G.: Method of usability for mobile robotics in a manufacturing environment. Procedia CIRP 62, 594–599 (2017)
10. Le-Anh, T., De Koster, M.B.M.: A review of design and control of automated guided vehicle systems. Eur. J. Oper. Res. 171(1), 1–23 (2006)
11. Wurman, P.R., D'Andrea, R., Mountz, M.: Coordinating hundreds of cooperative, autonomous vehicles in warehouses. AI Mag. 29(1), 9 (2008)
12. MiR autonomous mobile robot. https://www.mobile-industrial-robots.com. Accessed 30 Mar 2020
13. Here's how Audi plans to scrap the assembly line. https://www.autoguide.com/auto-news/2017/07/here-s-how-audi-plans-to-scrap-the-assembly-line.html. Accessed 30 Mar 2020
14. Yoshitake, H., Kamoshida, R., Nagashima, Y.: New automated guided vehicle system using real-time holonic scheduling for warehouse picking. IEEE Robot. Autom. Lett. 4(2), 1045–1052 (2019)
15. Wan, J., Tang, S., Hua, Q., Li, D., Liu, C., Lloret, J.: Context-aware cloud robotics for material handling in cognitive industrial internet of things. IEEE Internet Things J. 5(4), 2272–2281 (2017)
16. Regenbrecht, H., Baratoff, G., Wilke, W.: Augmented reality projects in the automotive and aerospace industries. IEEE Comput. Graph. Appl. 25(6), 48–56 (2005)
17. Fager, P., Calzavara, M., Sgarbossa, F.: Modelling time efficiency of cobot-supported kit preparation. Int. J. Adv. Manuf. Technol. 106(5), 2227–2241 (2020)
18. Andersen, R.E., et al.: Integration of a skill-based collaborative mobile robot in a smart cyber-physical environment. Procedia Manuf. 11, 114–123 (2017)
19. Hanson, R., Falkenström, W., Miettinen, M.: Augmented reality as a means of conveying picking information in kit preparation for mixed-model assembly. Comput. Ind. Eng. 113, 570–575 (2017)
20. Krajcovic, M., Gabajova, G., Micieta, B.: Order picking using augmented reality. Commun.-Sci. lett. Univ. Zilina 16(3A), 106–111 (2014)
21. Schwerdtfeger, B., Reif, R., Günthner, W.A., Klinker, G.: Pick-by-vision: there is something to pick at the end of the augmented tunnel. Virtual Reality 15(2–3), 213–223 (2011)
22. Choi, T.M., Wallace, S.W., Wang, Y.: Big data analytics in operations management. Prod. Oper. Manag. 27(10), 1868–1883 (2018)
23. Xin, C., Liu, X., Deng, Y., Lang, Q.: An optimization algorithm based on text clustering for warehouse storage location allocation. In: 1st International Conference on Industrial Artificial Intelligence (IAI), pp. 1–6. IEEE, Shenyang (2019)
24. Liu, H., Xu, Y., Wu, X., Lv, X., Zhang, D., Zhong, G.: Big data forecasting model of indoor positions for mobile robot navigation based on apache spark platform. In: 4th International Conference on Cloud Computing and Big Data Analysis (ICCCBDA), pp. 378–382. IEEE, Chengdu (2019)
25. Alwadi, A., Gawanmeh, A., Parvin, S., Al-Karaki, J.N.: Smart solutions for RFID based inventory management systems: a survey. Scalable Comput.: Pract. Experience 18(4), 347–360 (2017)

26. Buer, S.V., Fragapane, G.I., Strandhagen, J.O.: The data-driven process improvement cycle: using digitalization for continuous improvement. IFAC-PapersOnLine **51**(11), 1035–1040 (2018)

27. Bhatnagar, R., Chandra, P., Goyal, S.K.: Models for multi-plant coordination. Eur. J. Oper. Res. **67**(2), 141–160 (1993)

Cloud-Manufacturing

Cycle Time Estimation Model for Hybrid Assembly Stations Based on Digital Twin

Dimitris Mourtzis$^{(\boxtimes)}$ (ID), John Angelopoulos (ID), and Vasileios Siatras

Laboratory for Manufacturing Systems and Automation,
Department of Mechanical Engineering and Aeronautics,
University of Patras, 26504 Rio Patras, Greece
`mourtzis@lms.mech.upatras.gr`

Abstract. Moving towards factories of the future, Human-Robot Interfaces (HRIs) have come to the foreground. HRIs, offer extended potential in terms of flexibility, time and cost reduction, ergonomics, and the overall company's sustainability. What is needed, is the provision of digital tools that will accelerate HRI integration to the existing manufacturing plants as well as render their complex behavior, predictable. Following this rationale, this paper presents, the design of a prediction model, for robot moves in hybrid assembly stations, based on the robot's Digital Twin and a statistical regression model. In addition to that, respect is given to safety standards as well as to robot capabilities. The resulting model is validated against a simulation software, and further implemented in a pilot case derived from the automotive industry.

Keywords: Intelligent manufacturing systems · Production planning and control · Statistical regression · Hybrid assembly stations

1 Introduction

In the Industry 4.0 landscape modern manufacturing plants are constantly evolving. As stated by Chryssolouris in [1], industry is going through an era of market niches. Nowadays, there is an evident need for highly customized products in combination with frugality [2, 3]. Thus, what is needed, is that factories, despite the increased complexity of modern manufacturing systems, can achieve high flexibility along with quick responsiveness. Therefore, industrial robotic arms have been integrated in the production plants. The introduction of robotic arms in a manufacturing cell implies increased repeatability, high motion accuracy and heavier weights lifting with ease. However, the human operator must not be neglected in manufacturing systems. More specifically, special human characteristics, such as adaptation, cognition, problem-solving, fast reaction, and improvisation, are human-related skills that in the current situation cannot yet be replaced by robot workers [4]. Consequently, collaborative cells are used in an attempt to extend the capabilities of both robot workers and human technicians [5]. Therefore, production engineers have to reconsider the existing models regarding process planning, so as to take into consideration the collaborative nature of the modern manufacturing cells [6]. In order to do so, simulation software offer increased capabilities regarding the prediction of the robot workers, at the cost of

B. Lalic et al. (Eds.): APMS 2020, IFIP AICT 591, pp. 169–175, 2020.
https://doi.org/10.1007/978-3-030-57993-7_20

detailed modelling and design, high computational power and time and increased need for historical production data, which in many cases, especially in SMEs (Small Medium Enterprises), are difficult to acquire [7, 8]. However, with the recent technological advances Digital Twins, has enabled engineers to predict the status and constantly monitor a physical system based on their digital counterpart [9, 10] Consequently, the need for a quick and robust estimation emerges. Although collaborative cells offer many advantages over conventional manufacturing cells and robot cells, there is another important factor that increases the complexity of HRIs, regarding human operator's safety that in turn affects cycle time and should be one of the initial considerations during the planning stage, when the required information about the layout is limited.

This paper aims to present a methodology for estimating robot cycle time within a hybrid assembly station which by extension will facilitate production engineers during the early design phase of a production line. Notably, for the accomplishment of this goal, a statistical regression model will be used. In addition to that, the existing safety standards, are also taken into consideration, in order to ensure the applicability of the proposed approach in industrial environments. Accordingly, the created model is validated in a real-life industrial scenario from the automotive industry and a laboratory-based machine shop utilizing robotic arms.

2   Problem Formulation and System Architecture

In an attempt to address the above-mentioned literature gaps, the design, and the development of a framework for predicting robot time for task completion is proposed. The basic concept of this framework relies on the creation of a statistical regression model. The outcome of the regression analysis will provide a polynomial equation with automatically calculated weights for each dynamic variable affecting the system's status, i.e. the robotic arm. Therefore, each time the production engineer is either designing a new production line or is making changes to an existing line, the framework and its services can be recalled from a Cloud platform, in order to get a fast and reliable time estimation regarding the processes undertaken by the robotic arm. Then in continuation, the time estimations can be used in the scheduling software used in the company, so that each collaborative working station is assigned with tasks. In order to accomplish this goal, the production engineer uploads to the Cloud platform a json file containing the tasks and the task sequence for the under-examination production plan. The json file is automatically analyzed by the estimator tool, in order to extract the tasks that can be performed by the robotic arm. Then by using the implemented regression model, the time estimations are extracted for each robot task and are saved within the initial json file. Upon completion of the estimation of all the tasks, the json file is returned to the Cloud platform so as to be further processed by the scheduling tool the company uses.

Since the framework is targeted for use in collaborative environments, safety regulations have to be taken into consideration. Therefore, the guidelines provided by ISO/TS 15066 and relevant research works [11–13] have been examined. The above-mentioned ISO is a technical sheet, for specifying safety requirements in collaborative industrial robot systems. Besides the safety regulations that must be taken into consideration regarding the design of HRIs, the proposed framework is based on the development of a statistical regression model for the robot cycle-time estimation. For the extraction of the regression model, data from the physical robot as well as from the robot's Digital Twin are utilized. The architecture of the framework is presented in Fig. 1.

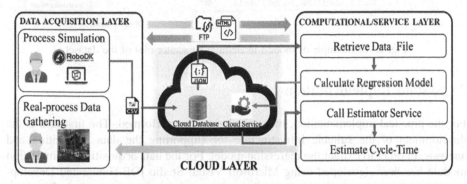

Fig. 1. System architecture for the proposed framework

The data gathered either by the physical robot or the Digital Twin, are uploaded on a Cloud platform. The Cloud platform is responsible for hosting a suitable database where the data are stored and accessed by the end-user application. Besides that, in the Cloud platform, services are also being held, for the data processing.

Statistical regression can be defined as a set of statistical processes for defining the correlation of certain variables affecting a system [14]. Therefore, according to the literature a statistical regression model consists of a dependent variable and one or more independent variables. In this case, the dependent variable is set to be the cycle-time, also denoted as T, for a specific robot motion, whereas the independent variables are the working characteristics of the robotic arm, including its velocity (V), acceleration (A), the distance travelled, in the form of 3D vector (X, Y, Z) and the payload (W) as well. For the extraction of the time prediction equation, an initial dataset has been created, in order to efficiently define and calculate the correlation between the key affecting variables.

In Fig. 2b the scatter plot has been generated for the presentation of the obtained values for both the simulation software and the real robot. In addition to that, the yellow line represents the fitment line as produced by the algorithm. Prior to the generation of the regression model, the visualization of the data has been utilized for the selection of the regression model. Therefore, since the data appear to be linearly correlated, a multiple linear regression model has been chosen.

Taking into consideration that robots are used in a repetitive manner, certain tasks were modelled in order to simplify the process planning phase. A typical example of such tasks is the "Pick and Place". Briefly the robotic arm has to locate a part, grab it from the buffer and position it on the product assembly. In Fig. 2a, a representative example of task modelling is presented.

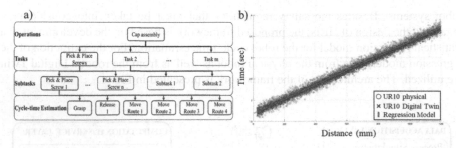

Fig. 2. a) Example of motion modelling; b) scatter plot of the dataset

3 System Implementation

For the practical implementation, two tasks have been performed. The first task is the development of the suitable infrastructure for supporting the data acquisition and analysis, in order to extract the regression model. For the data acquisition, a simulation module has been developed using Microsoft Visual Studio IDE (Integrated Development Environment), which automatically performs simulations in the RoboDk simulation software [15], with the utilization of the RoboDK API (Application Programming Interface) for .NET in C# environment. The simulation data are exported in a CSV (Comma Separated Values) file. The same module has been applied to the real robot, in order to extract time recordings from the real robot. Therefore, the resulted CSV file contained approximately 10000 values. Then, the regression model, was created by using the Python programming language.

$$T = -3.06869 * 10^{-3} * V + 8.67362 * 10^{-19} * A + 1.70749 * 10^{-3} * X + 1.68041$$
$$* 10^{-3} * Y + 1.56752 * 10^{-3} * Z + 1.98345 * 10^{-4} * W + 1.68904$$

$$(1)$$

Where, T is the time estimation, V is the velocity of the robotic arm, A is the acceleration, X, Y, Z the distance travelled in each of the axes, and W is the payload.

The second task was focused on the development of a Cloud service, in the form of a desktop application. For the development of the application, a Windows Form Application has been created by using the Microsoft Visual Studio IDE. The application consists of a single Graphical User interface, which is depicted in Fig. 3. The developed application is realized as a service, which is available from the Cloud platform. The production engineer loads the process plan from the Cloud platform, which in continuation is automatically analyzed by the tool. and the task sequence is displayed in the GUI. What is more, each task that can be performed by the robotic arm, is interactable so that the user can select it and proceed with the time estimation for the robot. Consequently, upon selection of a task, the engineer has to select robot from the dropdown list. Then each task can be described by a list of motions which are input from the user in the form of total distance travelled and payload carried by the manipulator. As soon as the engineer has finished the input of the robot motions, the task details list is updated. When the engineer has reached the final configuration, the initial json file for the process plan is updated and the updated version is uploaded to the Cloud platform.

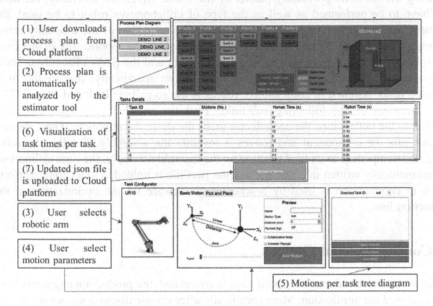

Fig. 3. Estimator's graphical user interface

4 Case Study and Results

The applicability of the developed solution has been tested in a use case coming from the automotive industry. Concretely, the validation process took place in a mimic production line, which uses collaborative robotic arms in conjunction with belt conveyers and human technicians for the simulation of the assembly of an automotive gearbox. The collaborative robots and the human technicians are paired so as to form an individual assembly station. The current situation involves fixed automation layout, designed a priori, during the development phase, where the human technicians works independently from the robotic arms. The aim of the pilot case provider is to make the necessary adaptations to the current layout so as to integrate collaborative cells into their actual production line. Therefore, what is needed, is a tool to provide quick and accurate time estimations, in order for the production engineer to conclude on how the tasks have to be assigned/scheduled, so as to achieve greater productivity. Consequently, the current situation suffers from low adaptability, and by extension this affects adversely the production line's flexibility. The lack of suitable digital tools for predicting cycle-time, poses an inhibitor to the pilot case provider, who aim at the integration of hybrid assembly stations in their production line.

Initially, the robotic arm has to pick the component from the buffer and position it on the assembly, which is located at the conveyor belt. Then, the second step involves again the robotic arm for picking and placing six securing screws. Finally, the third step involves only the human technician, who is responsible for screwing the component, by screwing the six bolts previously placed by the robot. Given the assembly, the tasks that have to be performed as well as the type of collaborative robot to be used, the engineer uses the application, in order to create the sequence of the assembly steps. Through the tool GUI, the engineer first selects the type of the robotic arm, in this case, two robotic arms have been utilized, the UR 10 robot and the SAWYER robot. Then, the engineer creates the list of robot motions. More specifically, one of the most common tasks assigned in collaborative robots is the so called "Pick and Place". This task comprises of the following sub-tasks. First the robot moves from the home position to the buffer, then the end effector grabs the desired component. Then, the end effector lifts the component and moves it towards the assembly. Finally, the robot places the component to its final position on the assembly. Finally, the time estimations are automatically written in a json file and the json file is uploaded to a Cloud platform which in continuation is used by a scheduling software for the optimization of the production line.

5 Conclusions and Outlook

As far as the added value of the application is concerned, the production engineers have well accepted the application. More specifically after on-site discussions, where the as-is situation has been discussed, they responded that with this tool they were able to get a sufficient time prediction with as low input from the user as possible. Having, used the application in order to create a new production plan, the production engineers, could then proceed with designing the process plan in detail, using a dedicated scheduling software. Therefore, from the experimentation on three different scenarios, it has been concluded that the design process has been sped up by 23%, since the production engineers were capable of getting an estimation for the updated process plan. This is backed by the fact that the participating engineers were capable to examine various configurations before proceeding to the detailed design of the pro-duction line. In addition to that, it also has been concluded that a 4.5% increase can be achieved in terms of productivity, since better task assignments to the collaborative assembly stations.

The proposed framework has been tested by comparing the predicted values to the actual values, reflecting a 95% accuracy. In the future, the framework will be enhanced so that the prediction model is automatically updated at a regular basis, ensuring high accuracy at each time. Beyond that, the framework will also be improved by the integration of an Artificial Neural Network (ANN), for the cycle-time estimation and task assignment to the hybrid assembly stations, in an intelligent manner, taking into consideration several production parameters, including the balancing of load between the assembly stations.

Acknowledgement. This research work was performed as part of MANUWORK project, which has received funding from the European Union's Horizon 2020 research and innovation programme under grand agreement no. 723711.

References

1. Chryssolouris, G.: Manufacturing Systems: Theory and Practice, 2nd edn. Springer, New York (2006). https://doi.org/10.1007/0-387-28431-1
2. Mourtzis, D., Doukas, M.: The evolution of manufacturing systems: from craftsmanship to the era of customisation. In: Design and Management of Lean Production Systems, pp. 1–29. IGI Global (2014). https://doi.org/10.4018/978-1-4666-5039-8.ch001
3. Chryssolouris, G., et al.: A perspective on manufacturing strategy: produce more with less. CIRP J. Manufact. Sci. Technol. 1(1), 45–52 (2008). https://doi.org/10.1016/j.cirpj.2008.06.008
4. Krüger, J., Lien, T.K., Verl, A.: Cooperation of human and machines in assembly lines. CIRP Ann.-Manufact. Technol. 58(2), 628–646 (2016). https://doi.org/10.1016/j.cirp.2009.09.009
5. Takata, S., Hirano, T.: Human and robot allocation method for hybrid assembly systems. CIRP Ann.-Manufact. Technol. 60(1), 9–12 (2011). https://doi.org/10.1016/j.cirp.2011.03.128
6. Freitag, M., Hildebrandt, T.: Automatic design of scheduling rules for complex manufacturing systems by multi-objective simulation-based optimization. CIRP Ann.-Manufact. Technol. 65(1), 433–436 (2016). https://doi.org/10.1016/j.cirp.2016.04.066
7. Schröter, D., et al.: Introducing process building blocks for designing human robot interaction work systems and calculating accurate cycle times. Procedia CIRP 44, 216–221 (2016). https://doi.org/10.1016/j.procir.2016.02.038
8. Spena, P.R., Holzner, P., Rauch, E., Vidoni, R., Matt, D.T.: Requirements for the design of flexible and changeable manufacturing and assembly systems: a SME-survey. In: Teti, R. (ed.) 48th CIRP Conference on Manufacturing Systems, vol. 41, pp. 207–212 (2016). https://doi.org/10.1016/j.procir.2016.01.018
9. Mourtzis, D.: Simulation in the design and operation of manufacturing systems: state of the art and new trends. Int. J. Prod. Res. 58(7), 1927–1949 (2020). https://doi.org/10.1080/00207543.2019.1636321
10. Nikolakis, N., Alexopoulos, K., Xanthakis, E., Chryssolouris, G.: The digital twin implementation for linking the virtual representation of human-based production tasks to their physical counterpart in the factory floor. Int. J. Comput. Integr. Manufact. 32(1), 1–12 (2019). https://doi.org/10.1080/0951192X.2018.1529430
11. ISO/TS 15066. Robots and robotic devices – collaborative robots. https://www.iso.org/obp/ui/#iso:std:iso:ts:15066:ed-1:v1:en. Accessed 28 Mar 2020
12. Bjorn, M.: Industrial safety requirements for collaborative robots and applications. In: ERF 2014 – Workshop: Workspace Safety in Industrial Robotics: Trends, Integration and Standards. ABB Corporate Research (2014)
13. Giuliani, M., Lenz, C., Müller, T., Rickert, M., Knoll, A.: Design principles for safety in human-robot interaction. Int. J. Soc. Robot. 2(3), 253–274 (2010)
14. George, E.P., Hunter, J.S., Hunter, W.: Statistics for Experimenters: Design, Innovation, and Discovery. Wiley, Hoboken (2005)
15. RoboDK homepage. https://robodk.com/doc/en/CsAPI/index.html. Accessed 27 Mar 2020

Cyber-Physical Production Systems
and Digital Twins

Digital Shadows as an Enabler for the Internet of Production

Günther Schuh, Andreas Gützlaff, Frederick Sauermann,
and Judith Maibaum[(✉)]

Werkzeugmaschinenlabor WZL der RWTH Aachen, Campus Boulevard 30,
52074 Aachen, Germany
j.maibaum@wzl.rwth-aachen.de

Abstract. Due to increasing atomization, manufacturing companies generate increasing amounts of production data. Most of this data is domain-specific, heterogeneous and unstructured. This complicates the access, interpretation, analysis and usage for efficiency improvement, faster reaction to change and weaknesses identification. To overcome this challenge, the idea of an "internet of production" is to link all kind of production relevant data by a data lake. Based on this data lake, digital shadows aggregate data for a specific purpose. For example, digital shadows in production planning and control help to manage the dynamic changes like delays in production or machine break–downs. This paper examines the existing research in the field of digital twins and digital shadows in manufacturing and gives a brief overview of the historical development. In particular, the potential and possible applications of digital shadows in production planning and control are analyzed. A top–down–bottom–up approach is developed to support the design of digital shadows in production planning and control.

Keywords: Digital shadow · Internet of production · Production planning and control

1 Introduction

The purpose of digital shadows (DS) is to provide all information needed to successfully perform a task and make a decision. The objective is to improve decision-quality and the performance of manufacturing. In practice the use of DS gains relevance as the quantity of information as well as the complexity of information systems increase and DS reduce the complexity for users by providing the relevant information [1, 2].

Advantages in information and communication technologies (ICT) enable companies to collect, use and store data to integrate the physical and the virtual world [3–5]. Using ICT enables e.g. virtual product and process planning or predictive maintenance [6, 7]. In many different industries the use of data analysis to support decision making is increasing [7]. Hence, a goal for producing companies is to identify an efficient way to use data and information [1]. In manufacturing, main benefits are a faster reaction to unexpected events and the identification of weaknesses in order to

© IFIP International Federation for Information Processing 2020
Published by Springer Nature Switzerland AG 2020
B. Lalic et al. (Eds.): APMS 2020, IFIP AICT 591, pp. 179–186, 2020.
https://doi.org/10.1007/978-3-030-57993-7_21

increase the efficiency of manufacturing [8]. This is of high relevance as manufacturing companies face challenges like increasing requirements of the customers on the products, rapidly changing markets, shorter product life cycles and sustainability [1, 4].

Manufacturing companies collect tremendous volumes of structured, unstructured and semi-structured data from different sources along the product life cycle [7, 9]. The increasing speed and volume of data collection simultaneously increase the challenges of data quality [9]. Additionally, in current manufacturing environment there are numerous domains that use different IT-systems, containing specific data and models [10]. This data is stored in different and redundant sources, is heterogeneous and hardly integrated. Therefore, access, interpretation and analysis of production data is difficult [9, 11].

Production planning and control (PPC) allocates activities of employees, production capacities and materials to fulfil customer orders. Therefore, PPC significantly influences the performance of a manufacturing system [12]. One challenge for PPC is the reaction to dynamic changes, e.g. operation times deviating from the plan or machines break-downs [13, 14]. Additionally, the necessary information is collected manually from different IT–systems causing delays, additional search efforts and missing information [3, 15]. Often PPC is dependent on the expertise of the planner [14]. However, even experienced decision makers cannot estimate the full impact of their decisions on the overall manufacturing system, which only achieves local optimization [16]. Therefore, the use of DS in PPS is promising to overcome these challenges and realize dynamic real-time PPC.

In Sect. 2, a literature review on digital shadows is conducted, including a distinction to the related digital twins (DT). Next, the application of DS for PPC and challenges and benefits are described. Section 4 summarizes and discusses the paper.

2 Literature Review on Digital Shadows and Digital Twins in Manufacturing

This section provides a general overview of the historical development of publications and definitions, applications and benefits of DS and DT in manufacturing.

2.1 Historical Development of Publications

In the field of engineering and computer science Google Scholar is the most extensive search engine [17]. Therefore, an analysis of metadata of publications extracted from Google Scholar gives an overview about the historical development of research. DS and DT are a relatively new research field. Prior to 2010, total 208 contributions to the topic DT and 291 contributions to the topic DS were published. Less than 100 each in the context of manufacturing. The development of new publications since 2014 shows that research on the topic of DT has grown strongly. The number of publications per year has grown from under 100 in 2014 to more than 4,500 in 2019. One main research focus is DT in production and manufacturing as Fig. 1. shows. In comparison, the number of publications on the topic of DS has only grown slightly, and has grown from about 100 in 2014 to more than 250 in 2019. The main research focus is also on DS in manufacturing, see Fig. 1. A related field of research is data storage e.g. in data lakes or data warehouses.

Fig. 1. Evolution of research on digital shadows and digital twins

2.2 Characterization of Digital Shadows in Manufacturing

The following paragraphs provide an overview of DS by describing different definitions, the main elements and benefits of DS. DS contain data traces and models [5]. Data traces consists of time-variant data and metadata like information about the source or recording time, which are needed for further data processing [1]. The data is generated by e.g. sensors or simulation and provided in domain–specific real-time [18]. DS contain both information about past and current conditions and provide information about future conditions [19]. DS provide near real-time data and information to enable an organization to control a permanently changing production [18]. When the system changes, DS are updated [5].

DS serve as a platform to integrate information from different sources to overcome semantic heterogeneity [9]. For this purpose, DS link data and models [20]. Data exchange between different domains improve the manufacturing, e.g. the manufacturer creates plant models which the operator needs when operating the plant. Typical tasks supported by DS are order processing, service or production planning. Since DS are task-specific, many different DS exist [13, 21]. Additionally, DS can be used through the whole product life cycle [20].

DS support decision makers and operators by providing the right information at the right place in the right quality in a sufficient way [1, 13]. As DS provide only the task-specific relevant data, the identification of necessary data, selection, aggregating and determination of granularity level of data are core part of designing DS [22, 23]. Data of past and current conditions is analyzed, e.g. for forecasts or simulations, to support decision making [19].

In conclusion a DS is a set of aggregated data traces and models providing the necessary information for a task. As the required information is provided in near real-time, DS enable a fast reaction to the dynamic and complex manufacturing environment.

2.3 Characterization of Digital Twins in Manufacturing

As in the previous paragraph, the following paragraphs provide an overview of DT by describing different definitions, the main elements and benefits of DT. Due to the increasing research in the field of DT, different definitions of a DT exist [24]. NASA provided the initial definition of a DT as "an integrated multi-physics, multi-scale, probabilistic simulation of a vehicle or system that uses the best available physical models, sensor updates, fleet history, etc., to mirror the life of its flying twin" [25].

Likewise, many authors describe the DT in manufacturing as a virtual, computer-based complete representation or counterpart of a physical system which allows various analyses of the system based on real-time production data, e.g. [19, 26–29]. DT support the analysis of static and dynamic systems allowing real-time optimizations, decision support and predictions [27]. DT should improve and shorten production cycles and reveal inefficiencies [26].

The comprehensive literature review on DT by Kritzinger et al. (2018) emphasizes that in existing research the terms digital model, DS and DT are often used synonymously, as all are a digital counterpart of a physical system. Therefore, they are distinguished based on the data flow. Both DT and DS have an automatic data flow from the physical and the digital system. The data flow from the digital to the physical system is automatic for DT and manual for DS [6].

In the newest literature review of DT, Jones et al. (2020) differ between a virtual-to-physical and a physical-to-virtual twinning process. Changes in the physical or virtual entity are registered by metrology methods and lead to a change of the corresponding virtual or physical twin. Jones et al. identify reduction of costs, risk, complexity and reconfiguration time and the improvement of efficiency, decision making, manufacturing processes and competitiveness as perceived benefits described in literature and industry. However, these assumptions are often not based on quantitative evaluations [24].

Summarized, a DT of a manufacturing system consists of a physical and virtual part. Both parts are a complete representation of the counterpart allowing analyses of the original system. The aim is to support decision making and improve the production.

The objective of both DS and DT is to process data in order to support decision making. The comparison of DS and DT shows that they differ in the granularity of the data base. DT are a complete representation of a physical system, whereas DS only represent those parts of a system that are relevant for a specific task. In addition, a core element of DS is the linkage of data from different domains. In the following sections, the focus is on DS as they have similar functionalities as DT but require less data capacity and provide better decision support due to the task-specific information.

3 Application of Digital Shadows in Production Planning and Control

Based on the current research in the following section an approach for designing digital shadows is developed and specified using the example of PPC. Additional potentials of DS for PPC are further analyzed. PPC is chosen as an example because it is a core element in manufacturing companies [12]. Recent trends like volatile markets, increasing complexity and shortened product lifecycles also affect PPC [13]. Therefore, PPC must cope with increasing dynamic and complexity. Existing PPC systems, like Enterprise Resource Planning (ERP) system or Manufacturing Execution System (MES), support different tasks of PPC but the support in everyday, short-term decision-making situations could be further increased [16].

3.1 Approach for Designing Digital Shadows

To extend the existing research on DS a top-down-bottom-up approach to design DS in PPC was developed. The aim is to fulfill the information requirements of production planner and controller by providing the necessary information. As a result the PPC should improve through better decision support and reduced information search efforts. Therefore the information needed (information requirements) of the users are identified top-down. Additionally, the data base is described bottom-up to describe the information provided (information offers). In the following, this approach is presented in detail, Fig. 2 gives an overview of the approach.

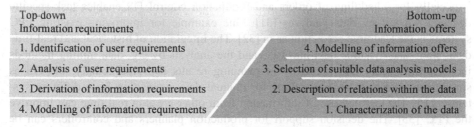

Top-down Information requirements	Bottom-up Information offers
1. Identification of user requirements	4. Modelling of information offers
2. Analysis of user requirements	3. Selection of suitable data analysis models
3. Derivation of information requirements	2. Description of relations within the data
4. Modelling of information requirements	1. Characterization of the data

Fig. 2. Top-down-bottom-up approach for designing DS

In the first step of the top-down analysis, the tasks in the PPC are analyzed to identify the user requirements. According to Schuh et al. the core tasks of PPC are production program planning, production requirements planning and production control [30]. At each of these tasks, production planners and controllers perform different sub-tasks with different requirements. The derived user requirements can be divided in functional and data quality requirements. All user requirements are documented in a specification sheet. In the subsequent user requirements analysis, the customer requirements are evaluated, classified and structured. This serves as the basis for the information requirement derivation. The user requirements are formulated as information requirements for the DS and entered in a requirements specification. This serves as the basis for modelling the information requirements. The result of the top-down analysis is a detailed description of the information requirements from the production planner and controller perspective.

At the same time, the data base is analyzed bottom-up to identify the information offers. For this purpose, the data base and different data analysis methods are investigated. In the first step data is described and characterized (in the context of PPC). The result is a morphology of PPC data describing the data type and context information like unit or change-frequency. In the next step, relations within the data are analyzed and described. The relations simplify the aggregation, linkage, selection and evaluation of the data in a DS. In the next step, suitable data analysis models are selected. First the properties of data analysis methods are described. Based on this, it is investigated which of the described data can be evaluated and how. The aim is to describe the possible analyses and to use them to derive the information offers. Based on the prior steps the information offers are modeled. The result of the bottom-up analysis is a detailed description of the information offers in the context of PPC.

All in all, this procedure enables the description of DS for all tasks of the PPC. These DS provide production planners and controllers with all information they need for their tasks, thus enabling them to make well-founded decisions.

3.2   Potentials of Digital Shadows for Production Planning and Control

The following paragraph analyzes the potential benefits DS offers for PPC. As DS provide real-time data, one potential is the ability to react to dynamic changes [13, 14]. Especially for scheduling of orders and production control DS enables task-specific decision support by data analyses [31]. One example for improving existing PPC systems is the lead time prediction as in [32]. The integration of historical and real-time data, static and dynamic data into PPC and the analysis by e.g. data mining methods increase the quality and reliability of planning results [8]. Additionally, the DS as single source of truth reduces efforts for manual data acquisition from different systems. [15] The targeted use of information from other areas in real time can improve the PPC [33]. The decision support for production planners and controllers can be increased by further analyses and simulation and considering a larger data basis [8, 14]. Another potential of DS for PPC is the development of an autonomous, self-controlling PPC [8].

In summary, the main advantages of DS are an improved decision support for production planners and controllers in short-term decision situations and the reduction of information search efforts and the provision of real-time information. An approach to design DS for PPC must describe how the information can be provided and derived from the data and models in such a way that it increases the decision quality.

4   Conclusion and Further Research

A DS is a set of aggregated data traces and models that provide necessary information for a task. This enables decision support in manufacturing with low latency times. The use of DS in the dynamic and complex PPC therefore offers several potentials for improvement, like enhanced decision support or reduced information search efforts. Additionally, a concept for designing DS in PPC was described. The concept describes a top-down bottom-up approach, with which the information needs and the information offers are linked.

In further research, the procedure for describing specific DS, e.g. in PPC, should be further detailed. Future research should also focus on the further development and application of DS for PPC in industry. This includes the modelling of data structures and information requirements.

Acknowledgement. Funded by the Deutsche Forschungsgemeinschaft (DFG, German Research Foundation) under Germany´s Excellence Strategy – EXC-2023 Internet of Production – 390621612.

References

1. Bauernhansl, T., Hartleif, S., Felix, T.: The digital shadow of production – a concept for the effective and efficient information supply in dynamic industrial environments. Procedia CIRP **72**, 69–74 (2018). https://doi.org/10.1016/j.procir.2018.03.188
2. Cheng, Y., Chen, K., Sun, H., et al.: Data and knowledge mining with big data towards smart production. J. Ind. Inform. Integr. **9**, 1–13 (2018). https://doi.org/10.1016/j.jii.2017.08.001
3. Belli, L., Davoli, L., Medioli, A., et al.: Toward industry 4.0 with IoT: optimizing business processes in an evolving manufacturing factory. Front. ICT **6**, 1–14 (2019). https://doi.org/10.3389/fict.2019.00017
4. Wagner, R., Schleich, B., Haefner, B., et al.: Challenges and potentials of digital twins and industry 4.0 in product design and production for high performance products. Procedia CIRP **84**, 88–93 (2019). https://doi.org/10.1016/j.procir.2019.04.219
5. Brecher, C., Buchsbaum, M., Storms, S.: Control from the cloud: edge computing, services and digital shadow for automation technologies. In: International Conference on Robotics and Automation, pp. 9327–9333 (2019)
6. Kritzinger, W., Karner, M., Traar, G., et al.: Digital twin in manufacturing: a categorical literature review and classification. IFAC-PapersOnLine **51**(11), 1016–1022 (2018)
7. Qi, Q., Tao, F.: Digital twin and big data towards smart manufacturing and industry 4.0: 360 degree comparison. IEEE Access **6**, 3585–3593 (2018). https://doi.org/10.1109/ACCESS.2018.2793265
8. Rosen, R., von Wichert, G., Lo, G., et al.: About the importance of autonomy and digital twins for the future of manufacturing. IFAC-PapersOnLine **48**(3), 567–572 (2015). https://doi.org/10.1016/j.ifacol.2015.06.141
9. Riesener, M., Schuh, G., Dölle, C., et al.: The digital shadow as enabler for data analytics in product life cycle management. Procedia CIRP **26**, 729–734 (2019). https://doi.org/10.1016/j.procir.2017.04.009
10. Schuh, G., Prote, J.-P., Gützlaff, A., et al.: Internet of production. In: Wulfsberg, J, Hintze, W., Behrens, B. (eds.) Proceedings of the 9th congress of the German Academic Association for Production Technology (WGP), Production at the leading edge of technology, 1st edn. pp. 533–542. Springer, Heidelberg (2019)
11. Schuh, G., Jussen, P., Harland, T.: The digital shadow of services: a reference model for comprehensive data collection in MRO services of machine manufacturers. Procedia CIRP **73**, 271–277 (2018). https://doi.org/10.1016/j.procir.2018.03.318
12. Frazzon, E., Kück, M., Freitag, M.: Data-driven production control for complex and dynamic manufacturing systems. CIRP Ann.-Manufact. Technol. **67**(1), 515–518 (2018)
13. Pause, D., Brauner, P., Faber, M., et al.: Task-specific decision support systems in multi-level production systems based on the digital shadow. In: IEEE International Conference on Industrial Engineering and Engineering Management, pp. 603–608 (2019)
14. Yang, S., Arndt, T., Lanza, G.: A flexible simulation support for production planning and control in small and medium enterprises. Procedia CIRP **56**, 389–394 (2016). https://doi.org/10.1016/j.procir.2016.10.062
15. Uhlemann, T.H.J., Lehmann, C., Steinhilper, R.: The digital twin: realizing the cyber-physical production system for industry 4.0. Procedia CIRP **61**, 335–340 (2017). https://doi.org/10.1016/j.procir.2016.11.152
16. Kunath, M., Winkler, H.: Integrating the digital twin of the manufacturing system into a decision support system for improving the order management process. Procedia CIRP **72**, 225–231 (2018). https://doi.org/10.1016/j.procir.2018.03.192

17. Martín-Martín, A., Orduna-Malea, E., Thelwall, M., et al.: Google scholar, web of science, and scopus: a systematic comparison of citations in 252 subject categories. J. Inform. **12**(4), 1160–1177 (2018). https://doi.org/10.1016/j.joi.2018.09.002

18. Landherr, M., Schneider, U., Bauernhansl, T.: The application center industrie 4.0 - industry-driven manufacturing. Res. Dev. Procedia CIRP **57**, 26–31 (2016). https://doi.org/10.1016/j.procir.2016.11.006

19. Stecken, J., Ebel, M., Bartelt, M., et al.: Digital shadow platform as an innovative business model. Procedia CIRP **83**, 204–209 (2019). https://doi.org/10.1016/j.procir.2019.02.130

20. Stark, R., Kind, S., Neumeyer, S.: Innovations in digital modelling for next generation manufacturing system design. CIRP Ann. **66**(1), 169–172 (2017). https://doi.org/10.1016/j.cirp.2017.04.045

21. Kubenke, J., Roh, P., Kunz, A.: Assessing the efficiency of information retrieval from the digital shadow at the shop floor using IT assistive systems. In: Yan, X., Bradley, D., Moore, P. (eds.) Reinventing Mechatronics: Proceedings of Mechatronics 2018, pp. 202–209 (2018)

22. Riesener, M., Dölle, C., Schuh, G., et al.: Framework for defining information quality based on data attributes within the digital shadow using LDA. Procedia CIRP **83**, 304–310 (2019). https://doi.org/10.1016/j.procir.2017.04.009

23. Schuh, G., Dolle, C., Tonnes, C.: Methodology for the derivation of a digital shadow for engineering management. In: IEEE International Conference on Industrial Engineering and Engineering Management, pp. 1–6 (2018). https://doi.org/10.1109/TEMSCON.2018.8488412

24. Jones, D., Snider, C., Nassehi, A., et al.: Characterising the digital twin: a systematic literature review. CIRP J. Manufact. Sci. Technol. (2020). https://doi.org/10.1016/j.cirpj.2020.02.002

25. Shafto, M., Conroy, M., Boyle, R., et al.: Medeling, simulation, information technology & processing roadmap. Technol. Area **11**, 1–38 (2012)

26. Vachalek, J., Bartalsky, L., Rovny, O., et al.: The digital twin of an industrial production line within the industry 4.0 concept. In: International Conference on Process Control, vol. 21, pp. 258–262 (2017). https://doi.org/10.1109/PC.2017.7976223

27. Negri, E., Fumagalli, L., Macchi, M.: A review of the roles of digital twin in CPS-based production systems. Procedia Manuf. **11**, 939–948 (2017). https://doi.org/10.1016/j.promfg.2017.07.198

28. Weyer, S., Meyer, T., Ohmer, M., et al.: Future modeling and simulation of CPS-based factories: an example from the automotive industry. IFAC-PapersOnLine **49**(31), 97–102 (2016). https://doi.org/10.1016/j.ifacol.2016.12.168

29. Brenner, B., Hummel, V.: Digital twin as enabler for an innovative digital shopfloor management system in the ESB logistics learning factory at reutlingen - university. Procedia Manuf. **9**, 198–205 (2017). https://doi.org/10.1016/j.promfg.2017.04.039

30. Schuh, G.: Produktionsplanung und -steuerung: Grundlagen, Gestaltung Und Konzepte. VDI-Buch. Springer, Dordrecht (2007)

31. Fang, Y., Peng, C., Lou, P., et al.: Digital-twin-based job shop scheduling toward smart manufacturing. IEEE Trans. Ind. Inf. **15**(12), 6425–6435 (2019). https://doi.org/10.1109/TII.2019.2938572

32. Schuh, G., Prote, J.P., Sauermann, F., et al.: Databased prediction of order-specific transition times. CIRP Ann. **68**(1), 467–470 (2019). https://doi.org/10.1016/j.cirp.2019.03.008

33. Shao, G., Kibira, D.: Digital manufacturing: requirements and challenges for implementing digital surrogates. In: Proceedings of the 2018 Winter Simulation Conference, pp. 1226–1237 (2018)

The Transformation Towards Smart(er) Factories: Integration Requirements of the Digital Twin

S. Waschull[(✉)] ⓘ, J. C. Wortmann ⓘ, and J. A. C. Bokhorst ⓘ

University of Groningen, PO Box 800, 9700 AV Groningen, The Netherlands
s.waschull@rug.nl

Abstract. The vision of the smart factory with its interconnected systems is based on the seamless (real-time) integration of data across the information system (IS) landscape. Yet, due to the existence of many legacy systems, this task is far from trivial. In industrial practice, the IS landscape comprises systems of different application functionality which can be characterized as technologically heterogeneous, e.g. transaction processing versus real-time systems. Integrating such systems has always been a major challenge and constraining force for many organizations. This problem is receiving renewed attention in the context of the implementation of the digital twin in manufacturing. Due to its central role in the IS landscape, the digital twin needs to communicate with a number of heterogeneous applications to achieve its full potential, i.e. achieving a complete virtual representation of an asset, process or product. This research analyses the integration requirements from the perspective of the digital twins' application functionality. In particular, we provide an explicit mapping of the integrations needed between the digital twin and existing information systems (IS) in manufacturing, which serves as a basis to better understand integration issues. These findings provide an explanation for and a conceptualization of some of the challenges that emerge when transforming towards an interconnected smart factory.

Keywords: Digital twin · Integration requirements · Smart factory · Application functionality · Information systems

1 Introduction

The application of digital twins (DT) in manufacturing presumably leads to better information transparency, which results in better planning, better quality control and improved productivity [1, 2]. The DT is the virtual and computerized counterpart of a physical system (a machine, a product or a whole process). It takes advantage of the real-time synchronization between the virtual and real system, enabled by sensed data and connected smart devices, mathematical models and real time data elaboration [3]. To achieve its full potential, the DT needs to take on a central role in the information system (IS) landscape at companies, yet its integration is certainly not an easy task. It therefore represents a constraining force for many organizations in their quest towards smart factories. New manufacturing systems are rarely planned on a green-field [4].

© IFIP International Federation for Information Processing 2020
Published by Springer Nature Switzerland AG 2020
B. Lalic et al. (Eds.): APMS 2020, IFIP AICT 591, pp. 187–194, 2020.
https://doi.org/10.1007/978-3-030-57993-7_22

This means that in industrial practice, DT usually need to be integrated in existing production system architectures to achieve a complete virtual and accurate representation of the asset, process or product. Such architectures comprise various different types of applications, distinguished by the functionality they exhibit (e.g. transaction processing), the underlying technology (e.g. hardware and software), data formats and addressing different time horizons (seconds versus weeks) [5]. As a result, different types of integrations are presumably required in the context of the DT. For example, integrations between real-time applications and transactional applications are usually completely different from integrations between professional applications, e.g. between different reporting systems. To understand the integration problem in light of the DT better as a whole, and to synthesize the literature primarily addressing single types of integration, in this research we assess different types of integration systematically from the perspective of the application functionality of an information system landscape. We first characterize the application functionality of the components of the DT, thereby restricting ourselves to the DT of products or machines. We then explicitly map the types of integration required between the components of the DT with other information systems. The next section provides the theory, followed by the identification of the data and integration requirements between the digital twin and other IS (Sect. 3). Section 4 concludes the research.

2   Theory

2.1   Concept of the Digital Twin

In the context of smart factories, the convergence of the physical world and the cyber world, as promoted in the Cyber-Physical Systems (CPS) concept, is achieved with the DT [6]. In most definitions, DT refer to virtual models or representations of the physical object or the system [7], which can be a product, machine, or even a whole process or system. Various purposes have been identified for DT, for example decision support, simulation, prediction and optimization [3], applied in different disciplines, e.g. production planning & control [2]. Since the data of the DT are not only from the physical world but also from virtual models, it enables the fusion of data from both worlds [8].

The DT consists of three components that are relevant to identify in this research, as proposed by [4]. First, the digital shadow is the actual data profile that couples with the corresponding physical entity throughout its lifecycle, a structured collection of data generated by operation and condition data, process data, etc. [9]. Second, there is the unique instance of the digital master model of a physical object, e.g. CAD or CAE models, that represent the physical description of the objects as designed, i.e. a set of linked data records [10]. Third, the DT contains the simulation, modeling and analytics part (algorithms, simulation models, correlations), linking the digital master and shadow, and generating meaningful information for various purposes. The models in the analytics and simulation part of the DT, from its individual models to the order structure of the entire production system, may be kept up-to-date by the information in the digital shadows.

2.2 Types of Applications in the IS Landscape

[5] characterized and distinguished information systems in manufacturing according to the application functionality, i.e. the main purpose of an application. In turn, each type of application is then characterized by the specific types of enabling technologies, viz. Software Technology, User-interaction (UI) Technology, Database Technology, etc. The following information systems are distinguished: (a) Systems based on workflow functionality (i.e. workflow-oriented systems) are aware of the sequential structure of a process and the role of actors in executing the processes. They assign and monitor the execution of tasks, while providing access and necessary resources to actors. (b) Transaction processing systems maintain actual states of objects which are relevant for an organization. This transactional data is stored in records centrally in relational databases which is shared among departments and systems, usually by standard software packages labeled as enterprise resource planning systems. (c) Interactive planning systems and (d) analytical systems both provide decision-support, yet they use different algorithms and underlying database technology to achieve their aim. Planning systems usually take a snapshot of objects' states from transactional systems before they start their calculations, whereas analytical systems maintain a series of snapshots in a so-called cube. Both types extract, transform and load (ETL) data from transactional systems. However analytical systems use varying sources to produce aggregated reports but also graphical presentations to users via customized visual user interfaces. (e) A different type of applications are document management systems, such as PDM/EDM systems, which manage and integrate complex product engineering data that originates from working with computer-aided-engineering (CAE) systems. Finally (f) real-time systems on the shop-floor monitor and control different production parameters and variables in real-time, and conduct real-time manipulation of selected production variables through actuators, if necessary.

2.3 Types of Integration Between IS

The exchange of information between different types of systems as classified in the previous section usually requires different types of integration concerning interface development and the development of communication mechanisms. The most common form of integration is data-oriented integration, distinguished into message-oriented integration, and integration based on data sharing [11]. The former can be achieved through various forms, e.g. point-to-point versus bus architectures, each with different triggering mechanisms (push vs. pull, clock- or event-driven) and nature of messages (complete files vs. structured XML messages). Data sharing is based on the development of a unified representation of all data in the enterprise, in which applications exchange information via the shared data schema.

A second form of integration is software-oriented integration on the application level, usually taking the form of a remote procedure call (RPC) for the app being called and the form of an application programming interface (API) for the calling application. An RPC refers to the fact that the app which is being called can be re-used. A typical example is the reuse of a scheduling algorithm or a simulation program. A completely different example is a call to retrieve data from a transactional system via the business logic of that system. A special case of this is a web service, which is an RPC which follows certain standards.

A third form of integration is workflow-oriented integration between workflow functionality on the one hand and transactional, document management, or decisional systems on the other hand. In essence, workflow systems manage the flow of work of a business process [12]. The flow of work consists of activities (or tasks) which can either be a transaction in a session of a transactional system, an update of a document in a document management system (following the check-out and check-in rules and of a vault and the impact analysis of related documents) or a decision in a decisional system. Workflow functionality may be encountered in WfM software, but also in PDM software or on top of transactional software. It enables the (trans)actions needed, it has to be informed about the (trans)actions performed and it informs users that certain tasks are pending, waiting for their action.

Finally, real-time to transactional integration is relevant to mention in this context. The physical asset (either a tool or machine, or a product that is being manufactured) belongs to the real-time world. The transactional system belongs to the information world and is not necessarily strict real-time. Such integrations are in general characterized by sensors producing streaming data with high frequency (e.g. every millisecond), the need to transform these data into meaningful transactions and the choice to transform either at the source (physical asset) or at the target (the transactional part of the digital shadow), or somewhere in between. The transformations are either samples or averages, which lead to transactions. E.g. a temperature measurement is sampled every hour followed by an update in a transactional system, or rates that are summarized over time lead to a periodic volume of liquid or gas which has passed a particular gateway.

The majority of the literature on integration focuses on a specific type of integration in the context of an application functionality, e.g. data integration in the context of ERP and MES (i.e. data integration in transactional systems) [13], or integration between document management systems [14]. We currently lack a systematic analysis of integrations from the perspective of the underlying technology of the applications. We study this in the context of the DT in the next section.

3   Digital Twin – Data and Integration Requirements

3.1   Application Types Within the Digital Twin

To better understand the types of integration required between the components of the DT and other IS, we first need to characterize the DT in terms of its own application functionality. To do so, we distinguish the digital master, the digital shadow and the simulation & analytics part, each with their individual purpose and data requirements:

(1) The digital master is a document-oriented application. The digital master of a machine or tool consists of CAE models of the machine or tool, but also of maintenance guides, operating procedures, etcetera. The digital master of a product to be manufactured consists of CAE models of the product, and also of manufacturing instructions on how to perform the manufacturing operations needed.

These instructions may also refer to measurements and checks to be performed during manufacturing.

(2) The digital shadow has both a *document part* and a *transactional part*. The document part of the digital shadow is derived from the digital master, but now populated with the specific data for the specific asset involved. The transactional part describes the status changes of the physical asset. The digital shadow of a machine or tool consists in its document part of 3D models, maintenance guides, operating procedures, etcetera, for this specific machine or tool as far as these deviate from the digital master. It may have 'as built' documentation in contrast to 'as designed', it may have amendments to operating procedures and maintenance guidelines, and so on. It may use the documents of the digital master, as long as these are fully applicable to the asset concerned. The transactional part describes the status of the tool or machine in terms of number of hours in operation, need for change-overs, cleaning, small or large maintenance, etc. The digital shadow of a product to be manufactured consists in its *document part* mainly of the notes and remarks made during manufacturing, sometimes including non-conformance reports, repair instructions, pictures and videos, etc. The *transactional part* describes the status of the product being manufactured, in terms of actions performed and measurement values obtained.

(3) The simulation and analytics part of the digital twin are *professional* applications, comparable to advanced planning applications and analytical applications respectively, depending on the objective of the data analysis. For example, a program may relate the settings of earlier production parameters (temperature, pressure) on later tolerances achieved in a type of product. This can be based on a data warehouse with past measurements.

3.2 Integration Requirements Between the Digital Twin and Other IS

Next, we describe the types of integrations needed between the components of the DT (i.e. digital shadow, digital master and analytics & simulation part) and other types of applications usually found in the IS landscape of manufacturing organizations.

Integration from the Physical Asset (Real-Time Systems) to the Digital Shadow
The physical asset (either a tool, a machine, or a product which is being manufactured) belongs to the real-time world as outlined in Sect. 2.2, with sensors producing streaming data with high frequency. The real-time data is critical to enable the accurate representation of a DT. Real-time data needs to be transformed into transactional data serving as input for the digital shadow, e.g. temperature measurement every hour, or rates which are summarized over time.

Integration from Transactional Systems to the Digital Shadow
To create and update the DT, various data from legacy transaction processing systems must be downloaded to the digital shadow, e.g. the product type, quantity, specifications or routing. The data are on the one hand stored in the ERP system, such as Bills-of-Material (BoMs) and operations (routings), but also releases of production orders. On the other hand, it includes data from quality management systems, specifying required measurements and controls required during manufacturing. Upon the release

of an order to the shop floor, the data should be pushed from the transactional systems to the digital shadow. These integrations are usually one-way and can be achieved via event-driven data movement, using messages, and be supported by workflow-oriented integration.

Integration from the Digital Shadow to the Transaction Processing System
The digital shadow is required to regularly update relevant transactional systems. Examples can be given for an ERP system or a quality management system. The former shall be informed about e.g. materials used, hours spent on operations and on order progress, whereas the latter is interested in e.g. measurements, quality registrations, possible non-conformance reports or conduced repairs. This is achieved through a one-way integration between the transaction-processing databases of the digital shadow with the other systems' databases. The relevant data can be pushed, or pulled based on some pre-defined trigger, e.g. an event or a specific time interval. Events would have to be predefined in the process digital shadow, which could be, for example, the occurrence of a reject.

Integration from Document Management Systems to the Digital Master
In this integration we assume that the digital master is implemented as a separate system, which means that the relevant documents need to be downloaded from their source. These systems are usually CAE systems linked to PDM systems, i.e. product development or work preparations systems used by manufacturing engineers. The digital master must be provided with means to read and display these documents. This can be achieved by a call to the original software, if such a call is enabled by a SaaS architecture, or the handling software can be made available at the digital twin platform.

Integration from the Digital Twin (Analytics and Simulation Part) to the Physical Asset
A key characteristic of the digital twin is that a change in the state of the digital object also triggers a change in the state of the physical object and vice versa, yet in practice automating this is far from trivial. Its success heavily depends on the digitization of the process steps and the machines. The machine would need to be programmed in such way that it understands the message of the analytical application and is able to changes settings automatically based on a message. This solution would require customization, since different machines often are based on different technology and are controlled by different control systems. Also, contractual and legal restrictions should be taken into account when deciding whether this is an option. Therefore, in practice this integration would most likely be achieved manually by humans. Via the dashboard of the analytics software, feedback can be given to the operator at the machine, e.g. an alert to an operator or technical service when analytics software predicts a break down based on (transactional records of) sensor data.

In Fig. 1, the described data flows and required integrations within the DT, and between the DT and other IS, are illustrated.

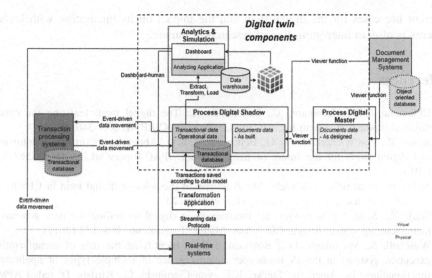

Fig. 1. Integration requirements of the DT in an IS landscape [15]

4 Conclusion

Considering that organizations want to protect their investment in existing legacy systems, a critical problem faced at the IT level is the integration of legacy systems with the components of the DT. In that light, a number of questions emerge and whose answer have a great impact upon technological features (e.g. databases, system architectures). For example, questions are related to the position of the data, the synchronization of systems (e.g. what triggers the creation of the DT) or the location of procedures (e.g. use DT optimization engines or legacy analytical systems). To increase our understanding, this paper contributes by systematically analyzing different types of integrations based on the intrinsic technological differences of the application. We studied the digital twin due its central position in the IS architecture, allowing us to assimilate and analyze different types of integrations required in this context. Therefore, we characterized the DT, and its individual components (i.e. digital shadow, digital master and analytics & simulations part) in terms of their main purpose (i.e. application functionality). For example, transaction processing functionality in the digital shadow is needed to describe and record the status changes in the physical object, document management functionality in the digital master enables the access to as-designed document of the physical system, or functionality similar to analytical systems is needed for optimization purposes. Due to differences in e.g. data formats, time horizons (frequencies), or the type of analysis, integrations can become difficult on the technological level. To further explore these technological issues, but also managerial issues related to such integrations (e.g. allocation of various functions to different systems and avoidance of redundancy), future research should be conducted to explore the individual integrations in-depth, and in practice. The exploration of different use cases for the digital twin and the impact on its integration with legacy systems is also an interesting line of research to pursue.

References

1. Uhlemann, T.H.J., Lehmann, C., Steinhilper, R.: The digital twin: realizing the cyber-physical production system for industry 4.0. Procedia CIRP **61**, 335–340 (2017)
2. Rosen, R., Von Wichert, G., Lo, G., Bettenhausen, K.D.: About the importance of autonomy and digital twins for the future of manufacturing. IFAC-PapersOnLine **48**(3), 567–572 (2015)
3. Negri, E., Fumagalli, L., Macchi, M.: A review of the roles of digital twin in CPS-based production systems. Procedia Manuf. **11**, 939–948 (2017)
4. Stark, R., Kind, S., Neumeyer, S.: Innovations in digital modelling for next generation manufacturing system design. CIRP Ann. Manuf. Technol. **66**, 169–172 (2017)
5. Waschull, S., Wortmann, J.C., Bokhorst, J.A.C.: Identifying the role of manufacturing execution systems in the IS landscape: a convergence of multiple types of application functionalities. In: Ameri, F., Stecke, K.E., von Cieminski, G., Kiritsis, D. (eds.) APMS 2019. IAICT, vol. 567, pp. 502–510. Springer, Cham (2019). https://doi.org/10.1007/978-3-030-29996-5_58
6. Qi, Q., Tao, F.: Digital twin and big data towards smart manufacturing and industry 4.0: 360 degree comparison. IEEE Access **6**, 3585–3593 (2018)
7. Ríos, J., Hernández, J.C., Oliva, M., Mas, F.: Product avatar as digital counterpart of a physical individual product: literature review and implications in an aircraft. Adv. Transdisc. Eng. **2**, 657–666 (2015)
8. Tao, F., Cheng, J., Qi, Q., et al.: Digital twin-driven product design, manufacturing and service with big data. Int. J. Adv. Manuf. Technol. **94**, 3563–3576 (2018)
9. Kritzinger, W., Karner, M., Traar, G., et al.: Digital twin in manufacturing: a categorical literature review and classification. IFAC-PapersOnLine **51**, 1016–1022 (2018)
10. Hoffman, C.M., Joan-Arinyo, R.: CAD and the product master model. CAD Comput. Aided Des. **30**, 905–918 (1998)
11. Giachetti, R.E.: A framework to review the information integration of the enterprise. Int. J. Prod. Res. **42**, 1147–1166 (2004)
12. Vernadat, F.B.: Interoperable enterprise systems: principles, concepts, and methods. Ann. Rev. Control **31**, 137–145 (2007)
13. Moones, E., Vosgien, T., Kermad, L., Dafaoui, E.M., El Mhamedi, A., Figay, N.: PLM standards modelling for enterprise interoperability: a manufacturing case study for ERP and MES systems integration based on ISA-95. In: van Sinderen, M., Chapurlat, V. (eds.) IWEI 2015. LNBIP, vol. 213, pp. 157–170. Springer, Heidelberg (2015). https://doi.org/10.1007/978-3-662-47157-9_14
14. Figay, N., et al.: Model based enterprise modeling for testing PLM interoperability in dynamic manufacturing network. In: van Sinderen, M., Chapurlat, V. (eds.) IWEI 2015. LNBIP, vol. 213, pp. 141–153. Springer, Heidelberg (2015). https://doi.org/10.1007/978-3-662-47157-9_13
15. Antonides, L.: Integration requirements of a process digital twin within an existing information system landscape. University of Groningen (2019)

IIOT Interoperability

Towards Inter-Operable Enterprise Systems – Graph-Based Validation of a Context-Driven Approach for Message Profiling

Elena Jelisic[1]($\boxtimes$), Nenad Ivezic[2], Boonserm Kulvatunyou[2], Scott Nieman[3], Hakju Oh[2], Sladjan Babarogic[1], and Zoran Marjanovic[1]

[1] Faculty of Organizational Sciences, University of Belgrade, Belgrade, Serbia
{elena.jelisic, sladjan.babarogic, zoran.marjanovic}@fon.bg.ac.rs
[2] National Institute of Standards and Technology, Gaithersburg, MD, USA
{nivezic, serm, hakju.oh}@nist.gov
[3] Land O'Lakes, Shoreview, MN, USA
stnieman@landolakes.com

Abstract. Providing the business context has a potential to become a powerful mechanism for the interoperable usage and efficient maintenance of message standards. In the literature, there are multiple techniques for its representation and application. Industry use cases have identified multiple issues that come with currently used techniques, which can represent that context. Initial assessment of a logic-based technique for doing so has been conducted and showed that some of the identified issues can be resolved. This paper presents plan for validation of the logic-based technique where proposed algorithms will be assessed in realistic integration scenarios. The paper gives details of the validation steps, goals that need to be met, and indicates issues that guide our future research plans.

Keywords: Business context · Services integration · Enterprise interoperability

1 Introduction

Distributed and autonomous services are increasingly becoming components of the manufacturing and logistics enterprises. To achieve efficient integration of these services, message standards are needed. Messages (i.e., payload or business document specifications) define types of transaction-related information that need to be exchanged among different services. Messages are necessarily standardized because of the wide variety of inputs to those services. Inputs come from numerous business sectors, business processes, business contexts, and business representatives.

However, traditional message standards have been only partially successful. We have identified four major issues inhibiting the adoption of messaging standards. First, "out-of-the-box" message standards are necessarily generic, making them difficult to adapt to specific use cases. Second, the standards are typically documented in text form to facilitate human interpretation and do not have a computational form that can be

© IFIP International Federation for Information Processing 2020
Published by Springer Nature Switzerland AG 2020
B. Lalic et al. (Eds.): APMS 2020, IFIP AICT 591, pp. 197–205, 2020.
https://doi.org/10.1007/978-3-030-57993-7_23

processed by validation tools to assure integration and interoperability. Third, over time the standards become large supersets of duplicative data elements contributed by various industries making the standards difficult to implement. And, fourth, as more elements are added, detailed refinement or profiling of a message standard is necessary to recapture the original business intent and business context.

On-going work by the Open Application Group [1], industry, and National Institute of Standards and Technology (NIST) [2] continues to explore the concept of using business context to improve 1) the enablement of new syntax-neutral message standards and 2) the resolution of the identified issues [3–5]. Some of the currently implemented context schemas and management approaches, however, have proved to be inadequate [6]. On the other hand, some newly proposed, promising approaches are introduced [7] but must be tested with realistic industry situations to establish their capability and feasibility. Yet, such testing is resource-intensive and requires commitment and engagement of industry and standardization communities.

We have started to validate a newly proposed approach using existing scenarios already contributed to OAG-i by industry stakeholders [1, 6]. Further industry adoption of the proposed context management approach depends on its capability to address all real-world use cases. Accordingly, the theme for this paper is our proposed approach to validate a promising, context-management technique for cross-industry use cases. Since the outcome of our approach depends on the validation process, this paper provides a detailed description of that process. That description identifies the goals and steps needed to achieve those goals. To the best of our knowledge, there are no research papers that deal with validation of a proposed, business-context-management approach.

In the following, Sect. 2 introduces background information about important concepts that are used in the paper, Sect. 3 describes the validation process through steps needed to achieve identified validation goals, Sect. 4 describes validation domain, and, finally, and Sect. 5 discusses the expected results and future research steps.

2 Background

Message standards are expressed in terms of message components. Message components are developed and offered as parts of a message standard suite where they are used to form multiple types of messages. An important, international standard, Core Component Technical Specification (CCTS), has been proposed to enable uniform and consistent development of message components and message standards. The goal of CCTS is to advance interoperability among applications and services [8].

A key concept in CCTS is *business context*, which is used to describe the business intent of using a message component or message profile, which is a subset of a corresponding message standard. In our view, capturing that intent is essential to finding and reusing the right message components and profiles, which will enable interoperability of corresponding data and services. Following CCTS, a specific business context is represented as a set of context values that are associated with their corresponding context categories (e.g., business process party profiles, geo-political location, tasks with a business process, resources available, and industry).

While the business context can indeed identify situations in which some components will be reused, we found this to be insufficient for interoperability. This is because semantic interoperability must also consider what happens in the background (e.g., transformation of the data into the database). Hence, in this paper, we assume that business context must also provide semantic definitions and validation rules that may be triggered when choosing the components in the business context. Providing those definitions and rules requires business-context knowledge.

Business-context knowledge can be represented using multiple, modeling techniques including graphical, object-oriented, logic-based, and ontology-based. For the purpose of this paper, we will employ a logic-based modeling technique - Enhanced UN/CEFACT's Context Model (E-UCM) [7]. E-UCM represents business-context knowledge using decentralized, directed, acyclic graphs. Each business-context category has at least one such graph that represents a list of possible values (or nodes) in the corresponding category. Then, a specific business context for a specific, information-exchange situation corresponds to a collection of nodes belonging to specific categories in the E-UCM graph.

E-UCM methodology for creating these graphs has two main parts. First, there is an infrastructure for (a) business-context presentation and expression and (b) contextualization of existing message profiles. Contextualization is supported by algorithms that can detect message components that are either relevant or irrelevant for a *Requested business context*. Second, there is a set of algorithms that can be used to generate the structure of new message profiles using existing message components that are relevant for *Requested business context* of a new message profile.

To determine a business context for a specific, information-exchange situation, we identify a collection of graph nodes that make up that business context. A list of specific nodes can be identified from E-UCM graph using E-UCM-provided expressions that are built using available operators and predicates. Every message component and profile has an associated E-UCM expression that captures its usage intent. This expression is called *Assigned business context*.

Along with the *Assigned business context*, E-UCM introduces terms *Overall* and *Effective business context* and provides directives for calculation of these terms for all situations and components, ultimately resulting in *Effective business context* for each component. The *Overall business context* can be understood as cumulative business context of some compound message component, while the *Effective business context* should reveal message component's relevancy in a *Requested business context*.

The process of assigning contexts to a message profile and its components, and calculation of *Overall* and *Effective business contexts* is called *contextualization*.

3   E-UCM Approach – on-Going Validation

Our initial validation [6] concluded that E-UCM methodology provides a powerful mechanism for business context presentation and expression. Our goal in this paper is to validate the algorithms that E-UCM proposed for both *contextualization* of existing message profiles and profile generation. Our approach to achieve that goal involves two steps. The first step is to assesses *Effective business context* as sufficient evidence of message component's relevancy or irrelevancy in the defined business context. The second step assesses the algorithms for message profile generation as capable of constructing a valid, message profile for a *Requested business context*. The key difference between those two goals is whether message profile structure is available or not. If it is available, profile refinement occurs for new integration scenarios. Otherwise, message profile structure should be generated using E-UCM algorithms on the basis of existing message profiles.

We made two important assumptions in completing the validation study. First, we assumed *contextualization* would be realized by a specialized service provider. Such a service provider would need domain knowledge needed for the development (or selection from an existing standard library) and use of message components. Such domain knowledge would typically be obtained through 1) business analysis of existing business processes and 2) information exchanges that rely on documentary standards and standard operating procedures.

Second, we assumed that there is one contextualized *Initial profile* upon which all others are based. To obtain the *Initial profile*, a service provider would construct a special kind of domain knowledge that contains an *initial collection of document components* and a *set of business rules* that govern the usage of those components. Using this domain knowledge, the service provider would generate an output in the form of a contextualized *Initial profile* with its components assigned intended business context, corresponding to the business rules.

Our validation process is shown in Fig. 1. First three steps are prerequisite and the same for both validation goals, fourth and fifth steps reveal our validation goals, while the sixth step is an assessment of validation results. The third step gathers validation cases that will be used to accomplish our, two, identified, validation goals. Each validation case is described using *Requested business context*.

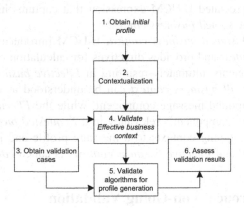

Fig. 1. Validation process

3.1 Validation of *Effective Business Context*

The input for this validation step is semi-contextualized *Initial profile* with defined *Assigned business context* and calculated *Overall business* context and a set of validation cases. The output is a set of identified message profiles obtained through refinement of an *Initial profile*. The first step in our validation approach is to put the *Initial Profile* to use in a variety of validation cases, both boundary and normal, where business context is adequately and precisely expressed. For each validation case, *Effective business contexts* for each component will be calculated in order to identify irrelevant components. *Effective business context* is calculated as intersection between component's *Overall business context* and business context in which corresponding component is supposed to be used (*Requested business context*). Intersection is conducted for each business context category separately.

In general, there are three possible outcomes: *Effective business context* is equal to null, *Effective business context* is narrower than component's *Overall business context* and *Effective business context* is equal to component's *Overall business context*. *Effective business context* can be equal to null if intersection of the *Overall business context* and *Requested business context* expressions across any of their business context categories gives an empty set. This outcome informs us that the corresponding component or field is not relevant for the *Requested business context*. Other two outcomes inform us that the corresponding component is relevant, but it might undergo additional considerations (because *Effective business context* of the component is narrower).

The refinement of an *Initial profile* results in the identification of new message profiles for a specific set of integration scenarios, where only components that are relevant for the *Requested business contexts* are included. Message profiles' refinement results in recalculation of *Overall business contexts*. New message profiles will have *Assigned business context* equal to *Requested business context*. Figure 2 presents a reusable Contextualization and profile refinement subprocess that can be applied to any domain. Since the calculation of *Overall business context* depends on message component's type it is represented currently as a subprocess and details are neglected.

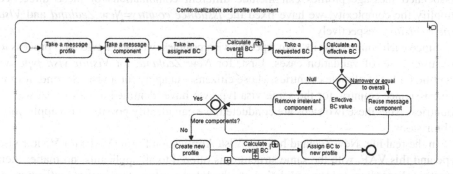

Fig. 2. Contextualization and profile refinement process

3.2   Validation of Algorithms for Message Profile Generation

A set of refined message profiles, obtained from the previous step, and a set of validation cases provide the input for this validation step. An output is a set of generated new message profiles constructed using E-UCM proposed algorithms. In this validation step, we will take one by one validation case, and compare *Requested business context* with business contexts assigned to existing profiles that we got as the output from the previous validation step. If there is a match, we will reuse it, otherwise, we will employ E-UCM algorithms to obtain components, from the repository of contextualized ones, that are relevant for a new validation case. E-UCM proposes an algorithm with five processing steps. The first step gathers all components from an existing standard component library, while each of the next steps has the goal to filter message components applicable to the *Requested business context* regarding different matching indexes, such as complete or partial matching. Details of this algorithm are out of scope of this paper and will be discussed in our future work.

3.3   Results Assessment

To achieve the identified goals, the structure of resulting profiles, both from the first and the second step, will be compared with expected outcomes by consulting human expert or developer. Important remark is that the fifth validation step is conducted under assumption that the output of the fourth step is valid.

4   Validation Domain

We demonstrate our validation process using a case study from a Visa application domain. Afterwards, all conclusions will be verified in other domains, such as a Small-and-Medium-Enterprise (SME) and its procure-to-pay scenarios. We have identified three variables in Visa application domain: *Issuance country*, *Visa type* and *Applicant's country*. Moreover, we use these three variables as our business-context categories. Associated message profiles can include different combinations of these three. To simplify the complexity, we have fixed the *Issuance country=New Zealand* and *Visa type = Visitor*, respectively.

Since each country has its own, specific visa policies, we used a two-step process to construct a set of validation cases. First, for *New Zealand*, for *Visitor visa type* we identified a list of eligible countries whose citizens can apply for a visa. Second, for the same issuance country, for the same visa type we have identified a list of visa waiver countries. After these two steps are conducted, we can identify possible visa application submissions.

In the real life, New Zealand has one Visa Application Form (VAF) for Visitor visa type and this VAF, with the same structure, is offered to all applicants, no matter their country. According to our validation methodology setup, this *initial collection of document components* will be analyzed by the service provider, along with the set of New Zealand's specific business rules. As the output, we will get the contextualized *VAF Initial profile*. By studying the structure of visa applications for different visa types and different countries, we have concluded that there is a great chance that irrelevant fields will be proposed to a certain applicant. Korean application form has the field *Kanji Name* that is applicable for a few applicants' countries only. New Zealand's application form has the field *SWITCH card* which is the United Kingdom-specific credit card type, to name a few. These examples clarify the purpose of our first goal - to approve *Effective business context* as enough to identify relevant fields from the *VAF Initial profile*. The output of this validation step would be a set of *VAF profiles* that would contain only components relevant to the *Requested business contexts*. Consequently, each applicant would get a customized VAF that contains only relevant set of fields, which will ultimately lead to less error-prone application process.

When a new visa application is recorded, first, we will compare *Requested business context* with business context assigned to existing profiles using the E-UCM business-context, matching algorithms. If there is a match, we will reuse it; otherwise, we will employ the E-UCM algorithm to construct a new message profile. That construction is based on relevant, obtained components from the repository of contextualized ones. The structure of resulting *VAF profiles* will be compared with expected outcomes by consulting human expert or developer. These conclusions contribute to the identified validation goals.

5   Discussion and Future Work

So far, first three validation steps have been conducted. Analysis of *Initial profile* and validation cases show that, in most situations, *Effective business context* can be used to identify irrelevant components from existing message profiles. However, there are some boundary scenarios where *Effective business context* is insufficient to make conclusions. We have identified the following types of unsuccessful validation cases. They justify the purpose of our validation process. From those example scenarios, E-UCM validation must be conducted prior to its industry adoption.

Time-dependent - Values assigned to business-context categories denote the current state of an object. We identified scenarios where it was necessary to remember the history, not just the current state. For example, keeping history of applicant's country transitions might be important to decide whether some field is applicable to the integration situation at hand. In this case, *Applicant's country* business-context category would be used to denote transition of the applicant's country, not just his current citizenship. Example transitions include changes in citizenship, holidays, temporary work, and student-exchange programs. In practice, this means that the result of *Effective business context* might vary through time. Hence, considering only one state, without considering history of change, may not be sufficient to communicate needed information for the relevant integration situation.

Unpredictable - There are scenarios that lack the logic needed to determine whether some field is relevant to the applicant or not. For example, field *Passport book number* can often be found in VAFs. The *Passport Book Number* may appear in a passport in addition to the *Passport Number*. Some countries may have this detail in some versions of their passports, while others may not. There is no traceable guideline that will inform us which passport versions contain this detail, so defining *Assigned business context* for such component would be a challenge. Further, it means that calculation of *Effective business context* might be impossible.

Insufficient - There are scenarios where business context does not give us enough information. For example, *Applicant's country* may not be enough because applicant's current residence or applicant's nationality, to name a few, may also affect appearance of some field. This means that the business-context categories that are chosen to describe business context are not enough; and, other relevant categories should be introduced. In practice, *Effective business context* can be calculated, but it can lead to conclusions that are inadequate for the specific integration situation.

If our validation process proves *Effective business context* as insufficient, which we believe is the case, future research will be needed. We plan to consider using new context categories and employing data mining techniques for business context definition to resolve those failing scenarios and enable adequate calculation of *Effective business context*. These approaches may help identify combinations of context categories expected to adequately define a specific business context [4]. Also, there is a possibility for extension of E-UCM methodology to capture history data through business context categories. A possible solution would be introducing state-machine diagrams for business context definition that would enable capturing multiple states (values for specific business context category) through time.

The described on-going validation covers algorithms that can be employed for profiles' generation when there is only one document type considered. Also, E-UCM offers other algorithms that can be applied for profiles' generation when there are two, or more, paired document types. Future research will consider validation of this aspect of E-UCM methodology as well.

Disclaimer
Any mention of commercial products is for information only; it does not imply recommendation or endorsement by NIST.

References

1. The Open Applications Group Inc. https://oagi.org
2. The National Institute of Standards and Technology (NIST). https://www.nist.gov
3. Ivezic, N., Ljubicic, M., Jankovic, M., Kulvatunyou, B., Nieman, S., Minakawa, G.: Business process context for message standards. In: CEUR Workshop Proceedings, vol. 1985, pp. 100–111 (2017)
4. Jelisic, E., Ivezic, N., Kulvatunyou, B., Anicic, N., Marjanovic, Z.: A business-context-based approach for message standards use - a validation study. In: Welzer, T., et al. (eds.) ADBIS 2019. CCIS, vol. 1064, pp. 337–349. Springer, Cham (2019). https://doi.org/10.1007/978-3-030-30278-8_35
5. Jelisic, E., Ivezic, N., Kulvatunyou, B., Jankovic, M., Marjanovic, Z.: A two-tiered database design based on core components methodology. In: Welzer, T., et al. (eds.) ADBIS 2019. CCIS, vol. 1064, pp. 350–361. Springer, Cham (2019). https://doi.org/10.1007/978-3-030-30278-8_36

6. Jelisic, E., et al.: Knowledge representation for hierarchical and interconnected business contexts. In: Enterprise Interoperability IX, pp. 17–20, Tarbes (2020)
7. Novakovic, D.: Business context aware core components modeling. Publikationsdatenbank der Technischen Universität Wien. (2018). https://publik.tuwien.ac.at/. Accessed 28 Sept 2018
8. UN/CEFACT Core Components Technical Specification CCTS, version 3.0. https://www. unece.org. Accessed 10 Mar 2020

Supply Chain Planning
and Optimization

Software-Based Assistance System for Decision Support on Supply Chain Level

Maria Linnartz[✉] and Volker Stich

Institute for Industrial Management, RWTH Aachen University, Aachen,
Germany
maria.linnartz@fir.rwth-aachen.de

Abstract. In recent years, the complexity of the management of supply chains has increased significantly due to the growing individualization of products and dynamics of the market environment. To remain competitive, ensuring efficient and flexible processes and procedures along the entire supply chain are of particular importance for companies. Especially in the inter-company context, decisions must be made as quickly and correctly as possible. To enable good decision-making processes data must be processed and provided in a targeted manner. Currently, however, the necessary transparency is often lacking within the supply chains. In this article, a software-based assistance system for decision support on supply chain level is presented that aims to increase the transparency and efficiency of the decision-making process. A concept for decision support on supply chain level is presented. This paper focuses on the conceptual linkage of relevant decisions and data. Therefore, indicators are identified and linked with the relevant decisions. Moreover, a suitable way of visualizing the identified indicators for each decision in a user-friendly manner is defined. These results are then used to implement the software tool.

Keywords: Supply chain management · Decision support · Software tool

1 Introduction

Many companies are facing an increasingly dynamic and volatile market environment. Various factors like increasing customer expectations, demand for individual products, shorter product life cycles and intensified cost pressure have led to an increase in complexity in managing supply chains. In this environment, efficient and flexible processes along the whole supply chain are necessary. At the same time, more and more data is generated along the supply chain. Utilizing this data holds the potential to increase transparency and improve processes and decisions. [1–3] Currently, however, the necessary transparency is often lacking within the supply chain. A reliable and up-to-date basis for decision-making is often not available. [4] The required data is often not available or not available in sufficient quality [2]. Companies need to be able to extract useful information from huge amounts of data and provide this information to decision-makers to stay successful [1].

To face these challenges, assistance systems for decision-makers in supply chain management and logistics are needed. Such systems can ensure a structured provision

© IFIP International Federation for Information Processing 2020
Published by Springer Nature Switzerland AG 2020
B. Lalic et al. (Eds.): APMS 2020, IFIP AICT 591, pp. 209–216, 2020.
https://doi.org/10.1007/978-3-030-57993-7_24

of required data and thereby increase the transparency. Therefore, assistance systems lead to faster decision making.

The aim of the software-based assistance system for decision support on supply chain level presented in this paper is to increase the transparency and efficiency of the decision-making processes on the strategic, tactical and operative level through a demand-oriented provision of data. The decision support is achieved through the analysis and linkage of data in indicators and the visualization of these indicators within a software-based assistance tool.

2 State of the Art

There is a wide variety of existing approaches used for decision support in different tasks within supply chain management. To provide decision support assistance systems need to be based on a sufficient database, process and utilize data and contain comprehensive technical solutions [2, 5]. To achieve the above-mentioned goal, the assistant system should address concrete decisions in the area of sourcing and delivering, contain a data model, provide the relevant evaluated data through a user interface and be implemented in a software tool.

A general framework for decision support along the whole product life cycle is the **Internet of Production** (see Fig. 1) which was introduced at the Aachen Machine Tool Colloquium in 2017.

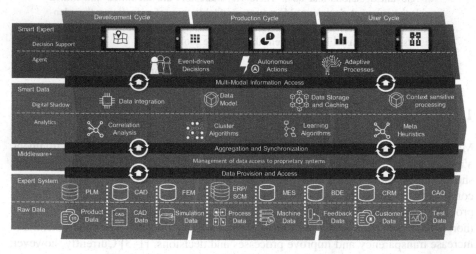

Fig. 1. Infrastructure of the Internet of Production [6]

It covers the different phases of the product life cycle (development, production and use). The basis for analysis and decision support is raw data from different business application systems like Enterprise Resource Planning (ERP) systems. Raw data is processed using algorithms and business analytics to create smart data which contains a high information content. This information is then used to provide decision support for the decision-maker through assistance systems. [6] In the framework of the research project Cluster of Excellence "Internet of Production" several decision support apps within the different cycles are developed. So far, it does not contain a specific assistance system for decision support on supply chain level.

According to a systematic literature review by TENIWUT AND HASYIM [7], decision support systems in the context of supply chain management often focus on specific tasks like determining delivery routes or choosing a supplier.

IVANOV [8] presents an adaptive framework for aligning (re)planning decisions on supply chain strategy, design, tactics, and operations. While this framework identifies specific decisions and relevant data, it does not provide a data model or advise on the data provision for the decision-maker. BISWAS AND NARAHARI [9] present generic supply chain objects to model a variety of supply chains. MUKKADES ET AL. [10] identify information categories for a demand-oriented provision of data on supply chain level. SCHUH AND BLUM [11] develop a data structure for order processing as a basis for data analytics. These works offer data structures to model supply chains but they do not link these data to specific decisions. Moreover, they do not focus on the design of the user interface for data provision.

Existing software tools and business application software for different tasks along the order processing process contain user interfaces for decision support but often focus on a few specific decisions. As an example, any Logistix uses optimization and simulation results to support decisions in the area of location and capacity planning, procurement and transport guidelines and order consolidation. Moreover, the tool uses key indicators to measure the quality and effects of the decisions. [12] However, the tool does not cover all relevant decisions. SAP APO (Advanced Planning and Optimization) as an example for business application software in supply chain management contains different modules amongst others for demand or network planning. Moreover, it includes a Supply Chain Cockpit that offers an overview of the entire supply chain as well as a view of all products, resources, locations, production process models and transport relationships. [13] Even though SAP APO enables decision support, it is system-oriented and requires high implementation effort.

Existing conceptual contributions only cover some of the derived requirements. The approaches focus either on concrete decisions or on general data models. The provision of the relevant evaluated data through a user interface and implementation in a software tool is mostly missing. Existing software tools provide user interfaces but usually focus on individual and specialized tasks. Moreover, these systems are often not efficiently linked with each other.

Thus, a software tool that offers a comprehensive picture of the status of the sourcing and delivering processes on supply chain level by linking data from different sources is currently missing. To increase transparency on supply chain level, such a system should cover decisions on strategic, tactical and operative level and ensure the demand-oriented provision of data for decision-makers in a software tool.

3 Software-Based Assistance System

The software-based assistance system presented in this paper systematically links data from different sources to generate information that supports the decision-maker in sourcing and delivering decisions on different decision levels. It has been developed as part of the research project Cluster of Excellence "Internet of Production" and thus uses the above-described framework of the Internet of Production which ensures systematic linkage and processing of data and user-friendly decision support.

The concept comprises five modules (see Fig. 2). To utilize the increasing amount of data to support decisions, a systematic linkage of decisions and data (Module 3) and a demand-oriented provision of evaluated data (Module 4) is needed. This is achieved through a systematic comparison of information needs and offers. Identifying relevant decisions (Module 1) and the development of a data model (Module 2) serve as the basis for modules 3 and 4. Module 1 uses a process reference model to identify relevant decisions. Module 2 applies a standardized notation to ensure a structured and formal data model. Module 5 combines the developed content of modules 1 to 4 and implements them within a software tool. This ensures the applicability of the results. The paper focuses on the linkage of decisions and data, the demand-oriented provision and the implemented software tool.

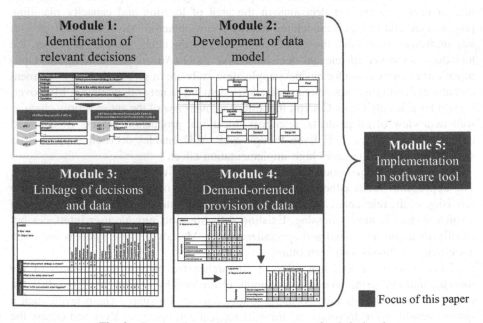

Fig. 2. Concept for decision support at supply chain level

A detailed description of the results of the first modules can be found in [14] and thus will only be summarized shortly. The **identification of relevant decision** is based on planning, sourcing and delivering processes described in the SCOR model [15]. Strategic sourcing decisions concern the definition of the procurement strategy and long-term planning of the required articles and stock. In the tactical decisions, the material program is detailed, whereby, among other things, the required quantities are specified. The operational decisions concern specific procurement orders. Strategic delivery decisions include determining the distribution strategy, the distribution channels and the distribution concept. Within the tactical decisions, carriers are selected and the capacities of the vehicle fleet are determined. Decisions on concrete transport orders and route planning are made within the operational decisions. The result of the second module is a UML-based **data model** containing the data which is needed in order to provide decision support. It consists of data classes, attributes and links between different data classes.

To **link decisions and data** an impact matrix is developed to analyze which data classes are needed for which decisions. This impact matrix is iteratively developed further. On one side, the influence matrix serves as a basis for identifying relevant indicators for decision support and, on the other side, existing literature-based indicators enable the revision of the influence matrix. Thus relevant indicators in the context of sourcing and delivering are identified using a literature analysis. These indicators are then linked to different decisions. Indicators condense information and enable statements about quantifiable facts in the past or future [16]. To cover the different decision levels absolute and relative indicators, as well as financial and non-financial indicators, are used. While relative indicators represent a ratio of two variables, absolute indicators are absolute values that summarize data. Moreover, indicators can be evaluated by company-wide or periodically comparisons. Absolute indicators are mostly non-financial indicators that will be used for decisions on strategic level. Moreover, the absolute indicators can be used to analyze the development over defined time horizons and are thus used for periodical comparisons. Examples for absolute indicators for the sourcing area are number of suppliers, number of procurement orders and number of procurement order items. For decisions in the area of delivering examples for absolute indicators are the number of distribution points, the number of means of transport and the number of customer orders. Relative indicators serve as decision support on all decision levels. Moreover, they comprise several financial indicators. Examples for indicators in the area of sourcing are stock turnover capability, stock range and costs per stock movement. Examples for indicators that are relevant for delivering processes are means of transport utilization rate, delivery service level and average transport distance. The indicators are calculated using the data model.

To ensure a **demand-oriented provision of data**, a suitable way of visualizing the indicators to support the decision-maker is defined. Characteristics for sufficient data visualization are a target group-specific and context-related presentation in an easily understandable, quickly comprehensible and precise form [17]. For the visualization of the indicators, different diagram types are used in the context of this work (bar chart, line chart and network diagram). The application of each diagram depends on the indicator type, the unit of the indicator and the type of indicator comparison. For each decision, the indicators that support the decision and a suitable way of visualization are identified. Moreover, the time horizons for the calculation of the indicators are determined.

4 Presentation of the Software Tool

To provide decision support, user-friendly and context-dependent information visualization and interaction formats are of particular importance [18]. Thus, the above-described results are implemented in a software tool to ensure the practical use of the developed results. In doing so various software components are utilized. The most important components are a scripting language (Python), a web framework (Django) and a relational database management system (PostgreSQL).

The foundation for the implementation of the developed concept in a software-based solution is a relational database. This database is derived from the above-described data model. The database integrates data from different data sources like ERP systems and Supplier Relationship Management systems.

The software tool consists of various screens. Figure 3 shows the welcome screen and a detailed screen for operative sourcing decisions of the software tool.

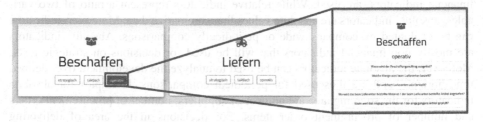

Fig. 3. Structure of the software tool

Fig. 4. Screen for operative sourcing decision "which supplier is ordered from?"

The welcome screen of the software tool summarizes the main decision areas (sourcing and delivering) and the decision levels (strategic, tactical, operative). Choosing one of the decision levels for sourcing or delivering leads to the list of decisions that are covered within the tool. For each listed decision the tool then contains detailed screens that summarize the necessary information to support the decision-maker. These screens comprise visualized indicators that have been identified in Module 3 and Module 4.

The operative decision from which supplier a material should be ordered serves as an example of the visualization (see Fig. 4). This decision is strongly influenced by supplier evaluations. For the five best-rated possible suppliers their service level, the response time and the delay rate are visualized. Moreover, the average price and the average procurement time for these suppliers are compared.

5   Summary and Need for Further Research

To increase the transparency and efficiency of decision-making processes in the area of sourcing and delivering a software-based assistance system is developed. The decision support is reached through the visualization of data and indicators. Relevant decisions on strategic, tactical and operative level and a data model serve as the basis. The paper focused on the linkage of decisions and data through indicators and the definition of a suitable way of visualizing the selected indicators in the context of specific decisions. Moreover, it is demonstrated how these results are implemented in a software tool.

The concept systematically links data from different sources to provide a comprehensive overview of relevant sourcing and delivering decisions. The software tool ensures the demand-oriented provision of evaluated data and practical feasibility. In doing so, the presented concept and software tool bridge the described research gap.

The tool will be validated using real company data and conducting expert interviews with different user groups. In the developed software tool the different decisions are currently dealt with separately. Further research is thus needed to link the decisions. In doing so, interdependencies between the decisions need to be analyzed. These results can then be integrated into the software tool for instance through overview dashboards or push messages for the user. Another additional functionality for the software tool is the integration of analytical methods to gain even more information from existing data.

Acknowledgments. Funded by the Deutsche Forschungsgemeinschaft (DFG, German Research Foundation) under Germany's Excellence Strategy – EXC-2023 Internet of Production – 390621612.

References

1. Biswas, S., Sen, J.: A proposed architecture for big data driven supply chain analytics. Int. J. Supply Chain Manag. (2016). https://doi.org/10.2139/ssrn.2795906
2. Kersten, W., Seiter, M., See, B.V., Hackius, N., Maurer, T.: Trends und Strategien in Logistik und Supply Chain Management. Chancen der digitalen Transformation. DVV Media Group GmbH, Hamburg (2017)

3. Dombrowski, U., Richter, T.: Ganzheitliche Produktionssysteme und Industrie 4.0. ZWF (2016). https://doi.org/10.3139/104.111651
4. Brecher, C., et al.: Nutzen und Potenziale modellbasierter Datenanalyse. In: Brecher, C., Klocke, F., Schmitt, R., Schuh, G. (eds.) Internet of Production für agile Unternehmen. AWK Aachener Werkzeugmaschinen-Kolloquium, 1st edn., pp. 163–195. Apprimus Verlag, Aachen. 18. bis 19. Mai (2017)
5. Klocke, F., et al.: Assistenzsysteme in der Produktionstechnik. In: Brecher, C., Klocke, F., Schmitt, R., Schuh, G. (eds.) Internet of Production für agile Unternehmen. AWK Aachener Werkzeugmaschinen-Kolloquium, 1st edn., pp. 287–313. Apprimus Verlag, Aachen. 18. bis 19. Mai (2017)
6. Klocke, F., et al.: Vernetzte adaptive Produktion. In: Brecher, C., Klocke, F., Schmitt, R., Schuh, G. (eds.) Internet of Production für agile Unternehmen, AWK Aachener Werkzeugmaschinen-Kolloquium, vol. 18, pp. 263–285 (2017)
7. Teniwut, W.A., Hasyim, C.L.: Decision support system in supply chain: a systematic literature review (2020). https://doi.org/10.5267/j.uscm. https://doi.org/10.5267/j.uscm.2019.7.009
8. Ivanov, D.: An adaptive framework for aligning (re)planning decisions on supply chain strategy, design, tactics, and operations. Int. J. Prod. Res. (2009). https://doi.org/10.1080/00207540902893417
9. Biswas, S., Narahari, Y.: Object oriented modeling and decision support for supply chains. Eur. J. Oper. Res.(2004). https://doi.org/10.1016/S0377-2217(02)00806-8
10. Mukaddes, A.M.M., Rashed, C.A.A., Malek, A.B.M.A., Kaiser, J.: Developing an information model for supply chain information flow and its management. Int. J. Innov. Manag. Technol. 1, 226–231 (2010)
11. Schuh, G., Blum, M.: Design of a data structure for the order processing as a basis for data analytics methods. In: Kocaoglu, D.F. (ed.) Technology Management for Social Innovation. PICMET 2016: Portland International Conference on Management of Engineering and Technology Proceedings, pp. 2164–2169. IEEE (2016)
12. Ivanov, D.: Supply chain simulation and optimization with anylogistix. Decision-oriented teaching notes for model-based management decision making (2019)
13. Kurbel, K.: Enterprise resource planning and supply chain management. In: Functions, Business Processes and Software for Manufacturing Companies. Progress in IS. Springer, Dordrecht (2013). https://doi.org/10.1007/978-3-642-31573-2
14. Pause, D., Fischer, M., Linnartz, M.: Assistenzsystem zur Entscheidungsunterstützung in der Supply Chain. ZWF (2019). https://doi.org/10.3139/104.112135
15. Supply Chain Council: Supply Chain Operations Reference Model. Revision 11.0, United States of America (2012)
16. Alpar, P., Alt, R., Bensberg, F., Weimann, P.: Anwendungsorientierte Wirtschaftsinformatik. Springer Fachmedien Wiesbaden, Wiesbaden (2019)
17. Kahl, T., Zimmer, F.: Kontextspezifische Visualisierung von Prozesskennzahlen. In: Barton, T., Müller, C., Seel, C. (eds.) Geschäftsprozesse. AW, pp. 75–97. Springer, Wiesbaden (2017). https://doi.org/10.1007/978-3-658-17297-8_5
18. Bauernhansl, T., Krüger, J., Reinhart, G., Schuh, G.: WGP-Standpunkt Industrie 4.0, Darmstadt (2016)

Integration of Triple Sustainable Management by Considering the Multi-period Supply Chain for Next-Generation Fuel

Waqas Ahmed[1]([⊠]), Biswajit Sarkar[2] [iD],
and Mujtaba Hassan Agha[1] [iD]

[1] Department of Operations and Supply Chain, NUST Business School,
National University of Sciences and Technology (NUST), H-12,
Islamabad 44000, Pakistan
engrwaqas284@gmail.com
[2] Department of Industrial Engineering, Yonsei University, 50 Yonsei-ro,
Sinchon-dong, Seodaemun-gu, Seoul 03722, South Korea

Abstract. Energy sources depending on biofuel have a positive impact on the environment, economy, and society. To use this next-generation fuel appropriately at a developed scale, well-designed and efficient supply chain management are desired. Therefore, it is necessary to design and develop a sustainable biofuel supply chain that is economical, minimizes environmental threats, and improves social benefits. In this study, a multi-period multi-objective sustainable supply chain management is developed. This long-term planning horizon is divided into an equivalent number of sub-periods in which all objectives are executed simultaneously. The objective is to make a framework of the multi-period sustainable supply chain management that reduces the carbon emission and take full advantage of the new job opportunities in the entire period. The parameters in this model are needed to extend during the time to meet the upward demand for markets. The augmented ε-constraint approach with an improved way of computing the step size is used to make a trade-off between contending objectives. The findings will help the organizations to respond accordingly for different parameters and regulations while designing the long-term planning for second-generation biofuel supply chain management.

Keywords: Triple sustainable management · Multi-period supply chain · Sustainable fuel · Carbon emissions · Augmented ε-constraint

1 Introduction

In the current era, a sustainable development under the umbrella of environmental and social concerns is more focus than cost reduction, because experts believe that direction on these concerns is necessary due to an elevated level of global warming and for the betterment of society. Today's business organizations face pressure to develop sustainable actions from several sources, including government regulations, environmental advocacy groups, non-availability of natural resources, stakeholders, customers, and

© IFIP International Federation for Information Processing 2020
Published by Springer Nature Switzerland AG 2020
B. Lalic et al. (Eds.): APMS 2020, IFIP AICT 591, pp. 217–226, 2020.
https://doi.org/10.1007/978-3-030-57993-7_25

society [1]. According to Elkington [2], to grasp sustainability, social and environmental aspects are also needed with the addition to the economic dimension.

Nowadays a new paradigm of a triple bottom line approach is introduced by sustainable value creation with the incorporation of the social aspects in addition to economic and environmental measures. Second generation biofuel (SGB) is a compelling source for next-generation energy because of concerns related to ecological safety and energy means. The SGB is a cost-effective sustainable fuel that bounds the expenditure of fossil fuel [3]. The production and supply of second-generation biofuel have not been commercialized on a large scale until now [4]. To achieve sustainability is a comprehensive and efficient optimization of a residual biomass (RB) based second-generation biofuel supply chain management (SGBSCM) is necessary. Developing a sustainable supply chain management SSCM system for SGB is one of the foremost challenges in this scenario. This study is a blend of the "triple sustainable management" (TSM) approach as shown in Fig. 1. It uses a sustainable raw-material for sustainable energy with sustainable supply chain management. As the residual biomass is an agricultural waste and natural source of raw material. Additionally, the end-product which is sustainable energy in the form of biofuel is a potential source of fuel for next-generation vehicles. Lastly, in this study, the three dimensions of sustainability i.e., environmental, economic, and social are optimized during SCM activities.

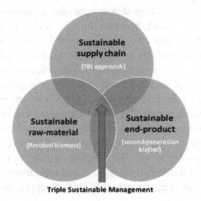

Fig. 1. Blend of triple sustainable management approach.

2   Literature Review

To deal with the uncertainties in the development of the biofuel market, the SCM of RB plays an important part [5]. Xie and Huang [6] formulated a multistage, mixed-integer stochastic model for biofuel SCM with evolving uncertainties. This model is an expansion in the biofuel SCM with demand uncertainty. Bairamzadeh et al. [7] modeled some uncertainties in the planning and design of the biofuel supply network under a robust optimization approach. In the condition of uncertainty, a robust model is established to optimize the biomass SCM network [8]. The fuzzy goal programming approach is used to deal with uncertainties in a biomass SCM [9]. The carbon tax, as well as carbon cap, is one of the main emission policies, started by different countries to restrict emissions. Ahmed and Sarkar [10] designed an incorporated economic and environmental structure for a multi-stage SCM following the carbon tax policy scheme. Ghosh et al. [11] considered a collaborative model to minimize carbon emissions for a two-echelon SCM with the carbon tax and uncertain demand. Their study and model benefit the organizations to minimize carbon emissions and total cost, also it will help authorities to regulate the proper carbon tax rate. Consequently, consideration of carbon rules and policies during optimizing supply chain management actions has become imperative as regulatory bodies all over the globe have implemented different schemes to reduce emissions of GHG's.

The simple ε-constraint approach has no assurance of the efficiency of the generated solution, particularly when there are more than two objectives [12]. To resolve this issue, a methodology is developed by Mavrotas and Florios [13] named as an augmented ε-constraint approach. Several authors applied this methodology to get an efficient solution in multi-objective optimization [14–18]. Du et al. [15] stated that in augmented ε-constraint approach inefficient solutions are transferred to one efficient solution. Also from this approach efficient Pareto optimal solutions are generated and it evades inefficient ones. This technique considers all conflicting objectives simultaneously without involving weights [19]. The discussion and literature review concluded that a carbon tax policy scheme should be incorporated out in the planning and design of second-generation biofuel supply chain management. It is also concluded that uncertain factors should be present while optimizing the mathematical models for second-generation biofuel supply chain management. So, the consideration of carbon tax policy and uncertain parameters are important. Moreover, the integration of second-generation biofuel and sustainable supply chain management makes a blend of "TSM" and has a big contribution to literature.

In the TSM approach, sustainable raw-material in the shape of residual biomass is utilized, the performance of sustainable supply chain management by adopting a triple bottom line approach, and sustainable energy in the shape of second-generation biofuel is obtained. To advance this study, an improved augmented ε-constraint methodology using lexicographic optimization is proposed.

3 Problem Description and Notation

3.1 Problem Description

A multi-period mathematical model for SGBSCM that simultaneously optimizes the multiple-objectives under the triple bottom line is developed. The long-period, which is ten years, is equally divided into ten number of the one-year planning horizon. All dimensions of sustainability are executed in the same structure for this long-term divided horizon. The impact of inflation on an annual basis is also implemented on all cost parameters, including carbon emission cost to demonstrate the actual scenarios. Residual biomass harvesting area, as well as carbon cap on agricultural zones, biorefineries and transportation nodes, need to be extended for a specific period to meet the upward demand of markets.

The uncertain parameters along with that carbon tax and cap policy scheme are also incorporated in the model. As a result, the optimal SGBSCM decisions for the individual period are connected with the entire period. The objective of this study is designing the multi-period multi-objective SGBSCM based on (i) development of the SGBSCM for long-term planning (ii) new job opportunities and carbon emission estimation for planning horizon (iii) allocation of extended quota in carbon cap and tax policy scheme for designed horizon (iv) extension of residual biomass cultivation agricultural zone to meet market demand (v) distribution of biofuel by meeting the demands of multiple particular markets. As the model considers the trade-offs between total supply chain management cost, carbon emissions, and opportunities of job employment for the individual planning period, so findings will help the organizations and government agencies to respond accordingly for different regulations and parameters while designing the long-term decisions.

3.2 Notation

Indices
C number of total agricultural regions c
I number of total biorefinery plants i
N number of total market centers n
T total planning horizon t

Decision variables
Q_{cit} amount of biomass transported
Q_{int} amount of the biofuel transported
T_{cit} trips for shipment of biomass
T_{int} trips for shipment of biofuel

Parameters
A_{ct} area for residual biomass (Acres)
C_t^{tx} carbon tax ($/ton)
C_{ct}^{ha} harvesting & baling cost ($/ton)
C_{ct}^{co} collection cost for unit of biomass ($/ton)
C_{ct}^{st} storage cost for unit of ($/ton)
C_{ct}^{ld} loading cost for unit of biomass ($/ton)
C_{it}^{P} production cost for unit of biofuel production ($/gallon)
θ_{cit}^{tr} fixed transportation cost loaded/unloaded in a truck ($/Ton)
C_{cit}^{tr} variable transportation cost ($/ton.km)
θ_{int}^{tr} fixed transportation cost of biofuel loaded/unloaded in a truck ($/gallon)
C_{int}^{tr} variable transportation cost of biofuel for a unit distance ($/gallon.km)
cp_{it} maximum production ability (gallons/year)
D_{nt} demand for biofuel in planning period t from market center n (gallons)
ds_{cit} distance between agricultural region c to biorefinery plant i (km)
ds_{int} distance between biorefinery plant i to market n (km)

e_{ct} emission for unit amount biomass in an agricultural region (g of CO_2/ton)

e_{cit} emission for transporting unit of per unit distance (g of CO_2/ton.km)

e_{it} emission for production unit amount of biofuel (g of CO_2/gallons)

e_{int} emission for transporting unit of biofuel (g of CO_2/ton.km)

E_{ct}^{cap} fixed carbon cap on emission for agricultural zone (tons of CO_2)

E_{cit}^{cap} fixed carbon cap on emission at transport route (tons of CO_2)

E_{it}^{cap} fixed carbon cap on emission for biorefinery (tons of CO_2)

E_{int}^{cap} fixed carbon cap at transport from biorefineries to market (tons of CO_2)

j_{ct} number of jobs in agricultural zone c (jobs/year)

j_{cit} number of transporting residual biomass for unit distance (jobs/year)

j_{it} number of jobs in biorefinery i (jobs/year)

J_{int} number of jobs in transporting unit amount of biofuel (jobs/year)

γ_{it} conversion rate at biorefinery plant i (gallons/ton)

V_{cit} truck maximum capacity from agricultural region c to biorefinery i (ton)

V_{int} truck maximum capacity from biorefinery i to market n (gallons)

y_{ct} yield of residual biomass at agricultural region c (tons)

4   Mathematical Model for a Multi-period Multi-objective SSCM

The long-term multi-period multi-objective function for SSCM, is explained as follows:

4.1   Multiple Objectives

The economic objective is the first objective of this multi-period model. Additionally, to represent the actual scenario, the annual inflation rate i is applied with the cost parameters of operational activities at agricultural zones, biorefineries, and transportation sectors for this study. The next objective for this multi-period multi-objective SSCM study for SGB is environmental and social. For this multi-period study, all parameters of these objectives are functioned according to planning period t as shown in Eqs. 1–3.

$$
\begin{aligned}
Min\,TC = \sum_{r=1}^{R}\sum_{f=1}^{F}\sum_{t=1}^{T}\Bigg[& \left(\begin{array}{l} \left(C_{rt}^{ha}\times(1+i)^t\right)+\frac{1}{4}\left(\Delta_{2rt}^{ha}-\Delta_{1rt}^{ha}\right)+\left(C_{rt}^{co}\times(1+i)^t\right)+\frac{1}{4}\left(\Delta_{2rt}^{co}-\Delta_{1rt}^{co}\right) \\ +\left(C_{rt}^{st}\times(1+i)^t\right)+\frac{1}{4}\left(\Delta_{2rt}^{st}-\Delta_{1rt}^{st}\right)+\left(C_{rt}^{ld}\times(1+i)^t\right)+\frac{1}{4}\left(\Delta_{2rt}^{ld}-\Delta_{1rt}^{ld}\right) \end{array} \right) + \left(e_{tr}\times\left(C^{\alpha}\times(1+i)^t\right)\times\alpha_{rt}\right)\Bigg]Q_{rft} \\
& +\sum_{f=1}^{F}\sum_{s=1}^{S}\sum_{t=1}^{T}\left[C_{ft}^{p}\times(1+i)^t+\left(e_{ft}\times\left(C^{\alpha}\times(1+i)^t\right)\times\beta_{ft}\right)\right]Q_{fst}+\sum_{r=1}^{R}\sum_{f=1}^{F}\sum_{t=1}^{T}\left[\left(\left(C_{rft}^{tr}\times(1+i)^t ds_{rft}\right)+\theta_{rft}^{tr}\right)\times V_{rft}\right]T_{rft} \\
& +\sum_{r=1}^{R}\sum_{f=1}^{F}\sum_{t=1}^{T}\left[\left(e_{rft}\times\left(C^{\alpha}\times(1+i)^t\right)\times\psi_{rft}\right)\times V_{rft}\times ds_{rft}\right]T_{rft}+\sum_{f=1}^{F}\sum_{s=1}^{S}\sum_{t=1}^{T}\left[\left(\left(C_{fst}^{tr}\times(1+i)^t ds_{fst}\right)+\theta_{fst}^{tr}\right)\times V_{fst}\right]T_{fst} \\
& +\sum_{f=1}^{F}\sum_{s=1}^{S}\sum_{t=1}^{T}\left[\left(e_{fst}\times\left(C^{\alpha}\times(1+i)^t\right)\times\phi_{fst}\right)\times V_{fst}\times ds_{fst}\right]T_{fst}
\end{aligned}
$$

(1)

$$Min\, TE = \sum_{r=1}^{R}\sum_{f=1}^{F}\sum_{t=1}^{T} e_{rt} \times Q_{rft} + \sum_{r=1}^{R}\sum_{f=1}^{F}\sum_{t=1}^{T} e_{rft} \times Q_{rft} + \sum_{f=1}^{F}\sum_{s=1}^{S}\sum_{t=1}^{T} e_{ft}$$

$$\times Q_{fst} + \sum_{f=1}^{F}\sum_{s=1}^{S}\sum_{t=1}^{T} e_{fst} \times Q_{fst} \tag{2}$$

$$Max\, TJ = \sum_{r=1}^{R}\sum_{f=1}^{F}\sum_{t=1}^{T} j_{rt} \times Q_{rft} + \sum_{r=1}^{R}\sum_{f=1}^{F}\sum_{t=1}^{T} j_{rft} \times Q_{rft} + \sum_{f=1}^{F}\sum_{s=1}^{S}\sum_{t=1}^{T} j_{ft}$$

$$\times Q_{fst} + \sum_{f=1}^{F}\sum_{s=1}^{S}\sum_{t=1}^{T} j_{fst} \times Q_{fst} \tag{3}$$

4.2 Constraints of the Model

The constraints of this multi-period model consist of resource availability, production capacity, mass balance, transportation capacity, carbon cap constraint, and demand constraint for the planning horizon. For this multi-period study, all constraints are functioned according to planning period t as shown in Eqs. (4–14)

$$\sum_{i=1}^{I} Q_{cit} \leq A_{ct}\left(y_{ct} + \frac{1}{4}(\Delta_{2ct} - \Delta_{1ct})\right) \qquad \forall c, \forall t \tag{4}$$

$$\sum_{c=1}^{C} Q_{cit} \times \gamma_{it} = \sum_{n=1}^{N} Q_{int} \qquad \forall i, \forall t \tag{5}$$

$$\sum_{n=1}^{N} Q_{int} \leq cp_{it} \qquad \forall i, \forall t \tag{6}$$

$$T_{cit} = \frac{Q_{cit}}{V_{cit}} \qquad \forall c, \forall i, \forall t \tag{7}$$

$$T_{int} = \frac{Q_{int}}{V_{int}} \qquad \forall i\, \forall n\, \forall t \tag{8}$$

$$\sum_{i=1}^{I} Q_{int} = D_{nt} + \frac{1}{4}(\Delta_{2nt} - \Delta_{1nt}) \qquad \forall n, \forall t \tag{9}$$

$$e_{ct} \times \sum_{i=1}^{I} Q_{cit} \leq E_{cit}^{cap} \qquad \forall c, \forall t \tag{10}$$

$$\sum_{i=1}^{I} e_{cit} \times ds_{cit} \times Q_{cit} \leq \sum_{i=1}^{I} E_{cit}^{cap} \qquad \forall c, \forall t \tag{11}$$

$$e_{it} \times \sum_{n=1}^{N} Q_{int} \leq E_{it}^{cap} \ \forall i, \forall t \tag{12}$$

$$\sum_{n=1}^{N} e_{int} \times ds_{int} \times Q_{int} \leq \sum_{n=1}^{N} E_{int}^{cap} \qquad \forall i, \forall t \tag{13}$$

$$Q_{cit}, Q_{int}, T_{cit}, T_{int}, \geq 0 \qquad \forall c, i, n, t \tag{14}$$

4.3 Solution Methodology

The solution methodology used in this long-term multi-period multi-objective sustainable supply chain is the augmented ε-constraint method, additionally with some improvement in computing the step size for iterations. Furthermore, after finding the ranges of ε1 and ε2 by using the pay-off table generated from lexicographic optimization, the step size of iterations is calculated by a different method as mentioned in Mavrotas and Florios [13].

5 Comparative Analysis Based on Different Solution Methodologies

The comparative and gap analysis based on different solution methodologies has been done for a long- term horizon to analyze the optimal values for all objectives. The result shows that augmented ε-constraint is the best method, as the difference of gap from this approach is less from target values following with goal programming and weight- sum approach. The gap between the target value and the results from augmented ε-constraint for optimal total cost is 0.005%, for optimal total emissions is 0.002%, and for the optimal total number of jobs is 0.013%. Table 1 shows the gap percentage resulted from different methodologies and target values.

6 Discussion

The key results and observations for multi-period multi-objective SSCM for SGB study show that the long- term planning period for second-generation biofuel can be well elaborated by dividing the planning horizon into an equal number of sub-periods. It determines the optimal long-period (i.e., through total horizon) and short-period (i.e., individual sub-period) decisions necessary for efficient SSCM for SGB to meet the market demand.

The findings show that for the long-term planning period, the total cost increases as the carbon emissions decrease for a specific job target. An intuitive relationship between them exists. Furthermore, as by increasing the number of new job opportunities by making it a pioneer priority, the total cost increases as well. The increment in a number of jobs thus increases the transport cost of biofuel per unit. Hence, on the other

Table 1. Comparative analysis of results from different methodologies.

Methodology	Augmented ε-constraint	Goal programming	Weight-sum approach
Gap % for cost (+)	0.05	1.518	2.164
Gap % for emissions (+)	0.02	4.344	5.884
Gap % for jobs (−)	0.03	11.489	22.275

side, the optimal emissions and jobs can be minimized and maximized, respectively by a marginal increase in the total cost of the SCM. The multi-period study will also benefit from reviewing the allotted quota of a carbon cap in different sectors. As it is observed that in the seventh year of the planning period instead of increasing the number of carbon emissions which was 5.18% averagely increment annually, it is decreased by 1.4%. This is due to the reason that allocated carbon cap quota is reviewed and increased, to satisfy the market demand. The total optimal emissions for the individual period, except for the seventh year, increased linearly.

The implementation of carbon cap restricted carbon emissions for a certain amount, as it helps to control emissions for a specific route and sector. But if the same value of carbon cap exists for the next period, it restricts emissions for that route but will increase the total emissions of the SCM. It is a result of the fact that as demand increase more carbon is emitted as transportation and operational activities increase to satisfy that demand under the same carbon cap. Similarly, the optimal total cost and optimal total jobs are also increased linearly for the whole planning horizon.

The comparative analysis between the target value of objectives with different methodologies shows that augmented ε-constraint is the best suitable approach. The resulted gap percentage of this approach from the target value is very small as compared to goal programming and weight-sum approach.

7 Conclusions

In this research, the long-term multi-period multi-objective SSCM for SGB is presented. This study considered that the long-term horizon is permitted to divide into an identical sub-terms. The multi-period multi-objective model determines the decisions required for optimal long-term planning horizon and short-term individual planning period in second-generation biofuel supply chain management under all dimensions of sustainability. The objective was to maximize the number of job opportunities and minimizes the carbon emissions and cost for this long-term planning horizon.

The annual inflation rate on cost parameters of operational activities and the transportation sector is incorporated to make a real scenario. The decisions throughout the whole planning period will lower the uncertainty connected with sub-period planning. The study shows that the implementation of a carbon cap scheme regulates carbon emissions for specific sectors and routes. But in contrast, if the allocated quota of carbon cap is not reviewed after a specific period, then it may disrupt satisfying the market demand. The optimal cost, emissions, and the number of new job opportunities increased linearly along the planning horizon. The integrated cost of biofuel per gallon also increases by the end of the planning period as compared with the initial period.

The literature is familiarized with a new terminology named "triple sustainable management". A multi-period multi-objective SSCM for SGB under uncertain parameters and carbon tax policy scheme will, therefore, turn out to be an efficacious supporting tool which can be used for decision-making within TSM. This research shows the application of the improved augmented ε-constraint approach in the context of second-generation biofuel supply chain management, it will be valuable to consider this approach in any supply chain management for future direction i.e., food supply chain management or steel supply chain management, where multi-objective optimization problems are considered.

References

1. Dey, P.K., Cheffi, W.: Green supply chain performance measurement using the analytic hierarchy process: a comparative analysis of manufacturing organisations. Prod. Planning Control **24**(8–9), 702–720 (2013)
2. Elkington, J.: Enter the triple bottom line, in The triple bottom line. pp. 23–38. Routledge (2013)
3. Ghafoor, A., ur Rehman, T., Munir, A., Ahmad, M., Iqbal, M.: Current status and overview of renewable energy potential in Pakistan for continuous energy sustainability. Renew. Sustain. Energy Rev. **60**, pp. 1332–1342 (2016)
4. Ahmed, W., Sarkar, B.: Impact of carbon emissions in a sustainable supply chain management for a second generation biofuel. J. Cleaner Prod. **186**, 807–820 (2018)
5. Ghaderi, H., Pishvaee, M.S., Moini, A.: Biomass supply chain network design: an optimization-oriented review and analysis. Ind. Crops Prod. **94**, 972–1000 (2016)
6. Xie, F., Huang, Y.: A multistage stochastic programming model for a multi-period strategic expansion of biofuel supply chain under evolving uncertainties. Transp. Res. Part E: Logistics Transp. Rev. **111**, 130–148 (2018)
7. Bairamzadeh, S., Saidi-Mehrabad, M., Pishvaee, M.S.: Modelling different types of uncertainty in biofuel supply network design and planning: a robust optimization approach. Renew. Energy **116**, 500–517 (2018)
8. Kim, J., Realff, M.J., Lee, J.H.: Optimal design and global sensitivity analysis of biomass supply chain networks for biofuels under uncertainty. Comput. Chem. Eng. **35**(9), 1738–1751 (2011)
9. Balaman, Ş.Y., Selim, H.: A fuzzy multiobjective linear programming model for design and management of anaerobic digestion based bioenergy supply chains. Energy **74**, 928–940 (2014)
10. Ahmed, W., Sarkar, B.: Management of next-generation energy using a triple bottom line approach under a supply chain framework. Resour. Conserv. Recycl. **150**, 104431 (2019)
11. Ghosh, A., Sarmah, S.P., Jha, J.K.: Collaborative model for a two-echelon supply chain with uncertain demand under carbon tax policy. Sādhanā **43**(9), 1–17 (2018). https://doi.org/10.1007/s12046-018-0899-6
12. Khorram, E., Khaledian, K., Khaledyan, M.: A numerical method for constructing the Pareto front of multi-objective optimization problems. J. Comput. Appl. Math. **261**, 158–171 (2014)

13. Mavrotas, G., Florios, K.: An improved version of the augmented ε-constraint method (AUGMECON2) for finding the exact pareto set in multi-objective integer programming problems. Appl. Math. Comput. **219**(18), 9652–9669 (2013)

14. Nezhad, A.E., Javadi, M.S., Rahimi, E.: Applying augmented ε-constraint approach and lexicographic optimization to solve multi-objective hydrothermal generation scheduling considering the impacts of pumped-storage units. Int. J. Electr. Power Energy Syst. **55**, 195–204 (2014)

15. Du, Y., Xie, L., Liu, J., Wang, Y., Xu, Y., Wang, S.: Multi-objective optimization of reverse osmosis networks by lexicographic optimization and augmented epsilon constraint method. Desalination **333**(1), 66–81 (2014)

16. Rossit, D.G., Tohmé, F.A., Frutos, M., Broz, D.R.: An application of the augmented ε-constraint method to design a municipal sorted waste collection system (2017)

17. Keshavarz Ghorabaee, M., Amiri, M. Turskis, Z.: A new approach for solving bi-objective redundancy allocation problem using DOE, simulation and ε-constraint method. Informatica **28**(1), pp. 79–104 (2017)

18. Yu, H., Solvang, W.D.: An improved multi-objective programming with augmented ε-constraint method for hazardous waste location-routing problems. Int. J. Environ. Res. Public Health **13**(6), 548 (2016)

19. Amirian, H., Sahraeian, R.: Augmented ε-constraint method in multi-objective flowshop problem with past sequence set-up times and a modified learning effect. Int. J. Prod. Res. **53** (19), 5962–5976 (2015)

Potential Benefits of Reverse Blending in the Fertilizer Industry

Latifa Benhamou[1,2(✉)], Pierres Fenies[1,2(✉)], and Vincent Giard[1,3(✉)]

[1] EMINES School of Industrial Management, UM6P, Benguerir, Morocco
{Latifa.Benhamou,Pierre.Fenies,
Vincent.Giard}@emines.um6p.ma
[2] Paris II Panthéon Assas University, Paris, France
[3] University Paris-Dauphine, PSL Research University, Paris, France

Abstract. Delayed differentiation, one of the key techniques of mass customization, has proven to be a high-performance strategy in the discrete industry. In the process industry, however, it remains poorly explored, especially when differentiation relates to product composition rather than form. Reverse Blending is a new OR blending problem based on a quadratic formulation, where output requirements are similar to those of classical blending, but here inputs are not preexisting and must be defined simultaneously with their use in the blending process while exactly meeting output requirements. These may then be used to obtain a wide variety of custom fertilizers (outputs) from a small number of Canonical Basis Inputs that can be blended outside the chemical plant, close to the endusers. This would avoid production of a wide variety of small batches of final products through a small number of large batches of intermediate products, resulting in valuable logistical streamlining and substantial cost savings. Accordingly, our paper investigates the potential benefits of implementing Reverse Blending in the fertilizer industry.

Keywords: Reverse Blending · Delayed differentiation · Fertilizer industry

1 Introduction

Increasing global food production by maximizing crop yields while preserving soil fertility is critical to sustaining food security and keep pace with population growth. To this end, soil nutrient concentration must be optimal to ensure high nutrient use efficiency [1]. This requires using customized fertilizers complying with specifically adapted formulas whose nutrients and proportions differ according to the pedological characteristics and the crops. In addition to the principal nutrients (nitrogen N, phosphorus P, potassium K), such fertilizers can be supplemented by several secondary nutrients (such as sulfur), resulting in hundreds or even thousands of formulas to match the actual needs for these different nutrients. For a fertilizer manufacturer, this means producing a large number of batches of different customized fertilizers on continuous production lines, and a major challenge in managing the production, storage and distribution of a wide variety of continuous flow products. However, such very wide variety, especially in the context of continuous production, should be avoided since

© IFIP International Federation for Information Processing 2020
Published by Springer Nature Switzerland AG 2020
B. Lalic et al. (Eds.): APMS 2020, IFIP AICT 591, pp. 227–236, 2020.
https://doi.org/10.1007/978-3-030-57993-7_26

production and delivery performance are undermined by a greater product variety that increases direct labour and material costs, manufacturing overheads, delivery lead time and inventory levels [2]. Concerning discrete production, extensive literature reviews are available as to which industrial organization is most suitable to handle a wide product variety. For example, through their review of 60 papers (80% of which concern discrete production and 20% of which deal with the service sector), Reis et al. [3] identified seven strategies capable of mitigating the negative effects of product variety. The most recurring strategy consists in using common components [3]. According to Johnson and Kirchain [4] this turns out to be the most effective way of reducing costs. This strategy, also known as standardization, is commonly associated with Delayed Differentiation (DD), the objective of which is to delay the differentiation processes, where the combination of common products occurs as late as possible so as to achieve supply chain cost-effectiveness [5]. In discrete production, DD refers to the successive production of different products obtained by combining alternative components in an assembly line allowing for thousands of product combinations with a high level of reactivity (e.g. automotive industry). To our knowledge, no research was ever conducted on the management of very high diversity in continuous production, save where this diversity derives from customized shapes (e.g. packaging in the coffee industry [6] or product shape/cutting in the steel industry [7]). We hold the view that in the process industry, Reverse Blending (RB) (an extension of classical blending where the inputs are to be defined), can be a disruptive approach to implementing effective delayed differentiation by adding to mere packaging a dimension concerning actual product internal composition [8]. By showing a major impact on Supply Chain (SC) organization, our paper discusses the potential benefits of RB for those fertilizer producers who are prepared to redesign their supply chain.

Following this brief introduction, our paper is structured as follows: Sect. 2 describes RB fundamentals before discussing; in Sect. 3, the potential benefits of a RB-based organization; Sect. 4 presents the main findings of our case study and to conclude, Sect. 5 highlights important guidelines for future research.

2 Reverse Blending Fundamentals

To achieve a wide variety of customized fertilizers, RB seeks the optimal chemical specifications of the smallest set, called "canonical base (CB)", of blending inputs, called "Canonical Basis Inputs (CBIs)", whose blend combinations form a bill of materials (BOM) used to produce any quantity of any output belonging to the variety of fertilizers under consideration [8]. Other additional fertilizer formulae may be obtained from these CBIs by a classical blending linear problem aiming at minimizing deviations from the specifications of these formulae. In terms of OR, RB is a new one-stage blending problem where input characteristics are decision variables as opposed to classical blending where input specifications are parameters. Our literature review, set forth in [8], proves the originality of our approach versus the blending problems as dealt with in various industries (the agri-food, mining, petroleum, and chemical sectors) and the fertilizer industry in particular. [8] points the differences between the modeling of RB and classical blending.

As non-pre-existing, some of the CBIs are composite materials that may have to be created from scratch, and laboratory experiments may, therefore, be required to obtain chemically stable reactions for the development of the new target formulas. An alternative is to produce the CBIs by blending pre-existing composites available on the market. This approach amounts to a two- stage blending problem where existing composites are blended to obtain the CBIs (first stage) and where the CBIs are blended to obtain the customized fertilizers (second stage). This method, called Adapted Pooling Problem (APP), differs from the Pooling Problem (PP), which also refers to multistage blending problems [10]. The reasons for this difference are set forth in [8]. They include the fact that chemical specification of existing composites may preclude the simultaneous use of some of them in producing a CBI, thereby preventing the free combination of all CBIs in producing a fertilizer (the differences between the APP and the PP models are outlined in [8]). Due to these chemical constraints, it is most likely that a number of composites in the set we studied is not suitable to produce a CB capable of satisfying all needs for fertilizers. We accordingly opted for an extended version of RB consisting in producing a subset of CBIs by mixing existing composites through APP while completing the manufacture of the remaining subset through RB.

Regardless of how CBIs are created, this approach allows for massive flow concentration since it can reduce the flows to be managed from 100% down to only 1% as shown by the results of our case study reported in [8] where 700 fertilizer solutions could be delivered with no more than 10 CBIs.

3   Reverse Blending Potential Benefits

An extensive literature review assesses the best production policy of Make-To-Order (MTO), Make-To-Stock (MTS), and hybrid MTS/MTO. Overall, MTS is used when production can be based on forecasted demand [7, 11] which usually involves few, low-cost, standard products. While this approach induces streamlined production costs, reduces customer lead-time, increases production capacity and reduces changeover costs, few systems fully use MTS. This results from the fact that to remain competitive, industries must now fulfill customer expectations [7]. In fertilizer industry, these refer to customized fertilizers to maximize crop yields. MTO policy, where production is launched following customer orders, on the other hand, while delivering a large variety of products, induces longer customer lead times and higher changeover costs [12]. An alternative is to combine these two approaches in a hybrid MTS/MTO, involving a hierarchical approach (e.g., priority to MTO, and using MTS for remaining capacity) [13], or storing semifinished products in intermediate warehousing (MTS) and assembling pursuant to customer orders (MTO) [11, 12, 14]. The choice of the optimal production strategy is influenced by several factors depending on products, processes, and market characteristics [6] (e.g., discrete/process industry, product variety, product expiry/contamination, market competitiveness, supply chain structure, flexible/rigid processes...). Yet, as many researchers argue [11, 12, 15, 16], where the industrial context is conducive, the most effective policy is hybrid MTS/MTO as it delivers customized products with lower customer order fulfillment lead time [16]. The idea is to develop lean approaches based on efficiency, waste elimination, cost-saving in the upstream phases of SC, and design agile processes that enable quick response to real-time changes in demand in downstream phases [17]. To do so, many researchers see DD as the best option [6, 11, 12, 16]. However, if DD has proven to be very relevant to the discrete industry (e.g., Hewlett Packard reported double-digit savings on supply chain costs by applying DD [6]), in the process industry, it is more challenging, as it is difficult to decouple processes at an intermediate stage [6].

The difficulty lies in finding commonalities between different product varieties to be able to design a common platform to which specific bricks can be added to obtain customizable products for specific segments [18]. Also, in the process industry, when customization affects a product's inner composition and is not a mere packaging/labeling issue, it becomes tough to postpone the Product Differentiation Point (PDP) to the SC downstream stages, which limits flexibility and responsiveness to customer demand [8]. In the fertilizer industry, RB is a solution that overcomes these difficulties as: *i*) it provides a robust common platform which can serve an extensive base of customized fertilizers; *ii*) it ensures an effective and efficient DD since differentiation may be performed close to farmers, rather than at production sites, in small blending units that can produce, at similar costs (through a common blending process), any required fertilizer using the relevant CBI formula. RB can thus become a key lever for the successful implementation of a hybrid MTS/MTO system in the process industry. With an RB-based configuration, at the chemical plant level, production is MTS and involves very few CBIs. In addition to harnessing MTO's main strength, through high responsiveness and sales loss prevention, such RB transformation offers several benefits. It simplifies the production system as it enables a continuous flow with no (or very few) production line changeovers. Indeed, as changeover operations can result in significant burdens in chemical plants (e.g. product and time losses, additional water, and energy use, creation of wastewater, chemical use for cleaning purposes... [19]), improving changeover times is very crucial to meeting customer demand as well as productivity targets [9, 19–21]. A continuous flow production of few CBIs (one/two CBIs per production line) would thus significantly enhance the performance of production lines compared to a pull production involving small quantities of a broad diversity of products (e.g., Grundermann *et al.* assessed the impact of converting from batch to continuous production and concluded that this conversion might reduce the use of detergent and water by up to 95% [22]). Eliminating shutdowns due to changeovers would also increase production capacity and avoid losing market share to competitors.

Moreover, it is admitted that MTS production leads to high storage costs and entails risks that forecasted orders will not materialize [13, 23]. RB almost eliminates such risks since the few CBIs to be stored correspond to a universal common platform for any custom-made fertilizer, ensuring strong demand for these CBIs. RB would also simplify storage shed management (one or two inputs per shed) thus doing away with the storage issues arising from increased diversity (vacant space due to small production batches, contaminated fertilizers due to poor product segregation, production shutdown due to stock saturation, etc.). At shipment level, RB-related standardization would simplify routing operations by facilitating flow segregation (as the same CBIs are used for all customers), reduce conveyor line cleaning process costs, as well as delivery costs and all issues to do with loading fertilizers onto the ships, to name but a few. From a commercial standpoint, RB ensures high flexibility and responsiveness to individual customer demand as differentiation is implemented: *i)* close to the farmers and *ii)* through a straightforward mixing process in mostly pre-existing blending units. Note that remote blending is indeed already per- formed though not with very good results: it is limited to mixing a few existing fertilizers that hardly meet the full range of nutrient requirements. In short, RB will greatly improve customer satisfaction and increase the customer base, especially as such customization will be more cost-effective than MTO-based customization. In addition to these economic benefits, RB would pre- serve soil fertility in the long term, thus ensuring sustainable agriculture and global food security.

4   Case Study

4.1   Case Description

OCP Group, one of the world leaders in the fertilizer sector, is seeking to increase its share of the world fertilizer market and to win over new customers by offering them customized fertilizer solutions. Increasing the diversity of its product portfolio is a strategy that OCP Group has been pursuing for many years. Indeed, since 2000, OCP Group has expanded the variety of its fertilizers to 50 different fertilizers.

This growing diversity improves agility and flexibility, and comforts the Group's leadership. However, in an MTO-dominated approach, the greater the diversity, the more difficult it is to manage production, storage, and distribution. The aim of our case study, therefore, was to show that OCP's production diversity-related issues could be solved by RB through a shift from MTO to MTS production. To this end, we started from OCP's daily 2019 production program, and reviewed the list of relevant CBIs as discussed below.

In 2019, OCP's order book included 28 fertilizers whose overall production on 7 production lines is provided in the Annual_Production.xlsx file included in the Mendeley link (http://dx.doi.org/10.17632/zfp6nzy87w.1) used to store our large tables so as to keep the text within the prescribed format. We applied the RB model to this annual dataset before analyzing its results on a monthly mesh. OCP's monthly fertilizer production is shown in the Monthly_Production.xlsx file.

4.2   Findings

Applying RB to the 28 different fertilizers revealed that all can be produced using a mere 8 CBIs. Table 1 describes the chemical composition of each CBI in terms of N, P, K, B2O3, Zn, and *filler* (a neutral component added for chemical stabilization purposes having no impact on the nutritional structure).

Table 1. The optimal composition of RB CBIs

	Canonical Basis Inputs (CBIs)								
	CBI 1	CBI 2	CBI 3	CBI 4	CBI 5	CBI 6	CBI 7	CBI 8	*filler*
%N	46.00%	11.86%	12.70%	19.00%	0.00%	2.34%	2.14%	0.00%	0.00%
%P	0.00%	56.08%	16.11%	38.00%	0.00%	56.00%	56.00%	51.24%	0.00%
%K	0.00%	0.00%	16.11%	0.00%	63.60%	0.00%	0.00%	0.00%	0.00%
%S	0.00%	0.00%	0.00%	7.00%	25.27%	11.78%	7.06%	19.67%	0.00%
%B_2O_3	0.00%	0.00%	0.00%	0.00%	6.13%	3.15%	0.00%	0.00%	0.00%
%Zn	0.00%	0.00%	0.00%	0.00%	0.00%	0.00%	0.00%	7.79%	0.00%
filler	54.00%	32.06%	55.07%	36.00%	5.00%	26.72%	34.81%	21.30%	100.00%

In addition to identifying the CBIs, RB shows the quantities of each CBI required to produce the exact volume needed for each fertilizer and to match their precise chemical composition (see details for this solution in the RB_Annual_Results.xlsx file). Please remember that the filler must be used in combination with the CBIs to obtain the desired quantities.

Annualized Results

Finer study of RB results showed that OCP's annual production volume of 4,440,150 tons comprising at least 28 fertilizers (see corresponding % share in the left box of Fig. 1) can be fully obtained by producing just 4,290,687 tons broken down into 8 CBIs (see % share in the right-hand box of Fig. 1) the first four of which account for more than 96% of total production.

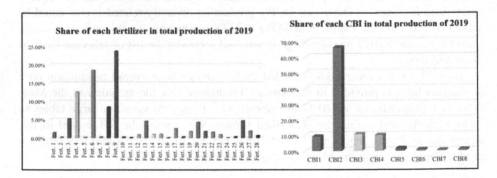

Fig. 1. Current OCP production vs. CBI-based production

The above flow consolidation would have been even more significant had we dealt with a greater variety than just 28 fertilizers. Note for example in [8], that RB matched the requirements for more than 480 NPK formulas with no more than ten CBIs. To meet growing trends towards precision agriculture, particularly in Africa, we believe that OCP will need to increase its portfolio diversity in the next few years, so significantly strengthening the value of RB-based production.

Monthly Results

The value of RB is even clearer on the basis of monthly results. Indeed, using the current production system (see Fig. 2), we observe that product diversity and output volumes vary from month to month and that volumes correspond to small batches (the production system being driven by actual orders (MTO)).

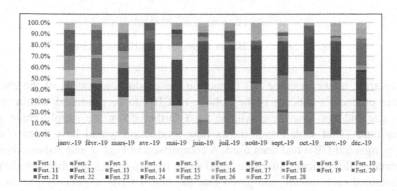

Fig. 2. Fertilizer share of OCP aggregate monthly production (Color figure online)

The different colors (for each different fertilizer reference) in each stick (overall monthly production) illustrate the diversity and provide an indication as to the number of production line changeovers that had to be carried out in 2019. Considering the daily production schedule, the total number of changeovers for all 7 production lines amounted to 175. As launch time depends on the nature of the "previous reference/following reference" couple, and knowing that the shortest launch time is of nearly two hours, then production had to be stopped for at least 350 h (175*2). Furthermore, OCP has two types of production lines (lines 107 and 07 with production rates of 108.3 tons/hour and 80.82 tons/hour, respectively). In terms of production capacity, on lines 107, where production shutdown amounted to 200 h, lost production capacity reached 2,1660 (108.3*200) tons and on lines 07, where production was stopped for at least 150 h, lost production capacity was 12,123 (80.82*150) tons. Moreover, OCP experiences arduous inventory management in its 9 storage sheds, due, among other reasons, to its production system which is based on the irregular launch of small batches.

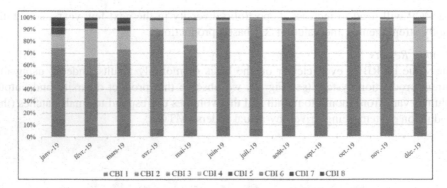

Fig. 3. Share of CBIs in aggregate monthly production

In contrast, as we examine RB impact on the production system of the chemical plant, the producer's concern is the volume of CBIs to be produced within its production site and not how these will be used further down the supply chain in the blending units. That said, Fig. 3 shows how production would have been obtained month by month if CBIs had been used. A comparison of Figs. 2 and 3 shows how this transformation dramatically simplifies production management since the same formulas are maintained each month, and given that the first 4 CBIs, especially the 2nd one, account for more than 90% of monthly production.

The above flow consolidation points to the opportunity of designing a new production system based on MTS. Using seven production lines, three of which have an annual throughput of about 897, 000 tons, and four an annual throughput of about 669,000 tons, managing the production of 8 CBIs is quite straightforward. Indeed, considering the respective shares of CBIs (cf. Figure 1) and taking into account the throughputs of OCP's production lines, we recommend allocating CBIs to dedicated production lines to ensure continuous production to the fullest possible extent (one CBI per production line) and so reap the benefit of streamlined, cost-saving production. Moreover, since CBI2 accounts for more than 66% of the annual production volume, we recommend dedicating three full production lines to it. CBIs 1, 3 and 4, each accounting for about 10%, we recommend allocation of a production line to each one of them. Finally, with the remaining CBIs accounting for less than 4% of the total production, we recommend the allocation of a single production line.

By producing continuously, mono-product lines would eliminate launch time stoppages, so boosting production capacity. Turning to the only remaining multi-product line, it could retain an order-point production rationale (production starts when a given stock level is reached) to produce CBI 5 that accounts for almost 2% of annual production. Concerning CBIs 6, 7 and 8 (each representing less than 1% of annual production), production could be triggered when inventory drops below the safety stock and stopped when the storage capacity is fully used.

OCP's current product portfolio covers a limited set of fertilizers with 5 references accounting for more than 60% of sales. With this in mind, RB's contribution does not appear to be crucial. Nevertheless, we are not looking to replace the production of 28 fertilizers by that of 8 CBIs, but rather to demonstrate the impact on production and storage of a CB enabling hundreds of fertilizer formulas to be manufactured on demand. The case for our solution becomes highly compelling if OCP implements its strategy of conquering emerging markets by offering them customized fertilizers, as it will then have to dramatically increase product diversity (to the tune of hundreds of fertilizers): in these circumstances, RB's contribution becomes obvious.

5 Conclusion

Through delayed differentiation (a MTS/MTO hybrid), Reverse Blending, a technique that can be used in industries operating in blending contexts, offers the advantages of both MTS (i.e., facilitate production, storage and distribution management, increase production capacity and reduce customer lead-times) and MTO (i.e., offer customized products and retain competitive edge), while doing away with their main disadvantages namely high storage costs and long delivery lead times respectively. Our case study shows that significant savings can be made at production system level alone while the impact at inventory and shipment levels has yet to be studied. Note that this approach may require thorough reengineering of the production and distribution processes, since industries looking to implement RB may have to change their decoupling points. Indeed, while several RB potential benefits are explored in this paper, the next step of this research should be to consider the challenges facing producers on the road to implementing RB.

References

1. Incrocci, L., Massa, D., Pardossi, A.: New trends in the fertigation management of irrigated vegetable crops. Horticulturae 3(2), 37 (2017)
2. Salvador, F., Forza, C., Rungtusanatham, M.: Modularity, product variety, production volume, and component sourcing: theorizing beyond generic prescriptions. J. Oper. Manag. 20(5), 549–575 (2002)
3. Da Cunha Reis, A., Scavarda, L.F., Pancieri, B.M.: Product variety management: a synthesis of existing research. Afr. J. Bus. Manag. 7(1), 39 (2013)
4. Johnson, M.D., Kirchain, R.E.: Quantifying the effects of product family decisions on material selection: a process-based costing approach. Int. J. Prod. Econ. 120(2), 653–668 (2009)
5. Boone, C.A., Craighead, C.W., Hanna, J.B.: Postponement: an evolving supply chain concept. Int. J. Phys. Distrib. Logistics Manag. 37, 597–611 (2007)
6. Van Hoek, R.I.: The rediscovery of postponement a literature review and directions for research. J. Oper. Manag. 19(2), 161–184 (2001)
7. Kerkkänen, A.: Determining semi-finished products to be stocked when changing the MTS-MTO policy: case of a steel mill. Int. J. Prod. Econ. 108(1–2), 111–118 (2007)
8. Benhamou, L., Giard, V., Khouloud, M., Fenies, P., Fontane, F.: Reverse blending : an economically efficient approach to the challenge of fertilizer mass customization. Int. J. Prod. Econ. 226, 107603 (2019)

9. Karam, A.-A., Liviu, M., Cristina, V., Radu, H.: The contribution of lean manufacturing tools to changeover time decrease in the pharmaceutical industry. A SMED Proj. Procedia Manuf. **22**(886), 892 (2018)

10. Chang, J.C., Graves, S.C., Kirchain, R.E., Olivetti, E.A.: Integrated planning for design and production in two-stage recycling operations. Eur. J. Oper. Res. **273**(2), 535–547 (2019)

11. Sharda, B., Akiya, N.: Selecting make-to-stock and postponement policies for different products in a chemical plant: a case study using discrete event simulation. Int. J. Prod. Econ. **136**(1), 161–171 (2012)

12. Gupta, D., Benjaafar, S.: Make-to-order, make-to-stock, or delay product differentiation? A common framework for modeling and analysis. IIE Trans. **36**(6), 529–546 (2004)

13. Agra, A., Poss, M., Santos, M.: Optimizing make-to-stock policies through a robust lot-sizing model. Int. J. Prod. Econ. **200**, 302–310 (2018)

14. Morikawa, K., Takahashi, K., Hirotani, D.: Make-to-stock policies for a multistage serial system under a make-to-order production environment. Int. J. Prod. Econ. **147**, 30–37 (2014)

15. Soman, C.A., Van Donk, D.P., Gaalman, G.: Combined make-to-order and make-to-stock in a food production system. Int. J. Prod. Econ. **90**(2), 223–235 (2004)

16. Jewkes, E.M., Alfa, A.S.: A queueing model of delayed product differentiation. Eur. J. Oper. Res. **199**(3), 734–743 (2009)

17. Fornasiero, R., Macchion, L., Vinelli, A.: Supply chain configuration towards customization: a comparison between small and large series production. IFAC- PapersOnLine **48**(3), 1428–1433 (2015)

18. Tyagi, S.: Optimization of a platform configuration with generational changes. Int. J. Prod. Econ. **169**, 299–309 (2015)

19. Gungor, Z.E., Evans, S.: Understanding the hidden cost and identifying the root causes of changeover impacts. J. Clean. Prod. **167**, 1138–1147 (2017)

20. Ferradás, P.G., Salonitis, K.: Improving changeover time: a tailored SMED approach for welding cells. Procedia CIRP **7**, 598–603 (2013)

21. Meixell, M.J.: The impact of setup costs, commonality, and capacity on schedule stability: an exploratory study. Int. J. Prod. Econ. **95**(1), 95–107 (2005)

22. Grundemann, L., Gonschorowski, V., Fischer, N., Scholl, S.: Cleaning waste minimization for multiproduct plants: transferring macro batch to micro conti manufacturing. J. Clean. Prod. **24**(92), 101 (2012)

23. Karasu, M.K., Cakmakci, M., Cakiroglu, M.B., Ayva, E., Demirel-Ortabas, N.: Improvement of changeover times via Taguchi empowered SMED/case study on injection molding production. Measurement **47**(741), 748 (2014)

Effectiveness of Vendor Managed Inventory - VMI: A Study Applied in a Mining Company

Alexandre Formigoni[1,2] ⓘ, João Gilberto Mendes dos Reis[1,3](✉) ⓘ,
Roberto Padilha Moia[1,4] ⓘ, Caio Flávio Stettiner[1,4] ⓘ,
and João Roberto Maiellaro[1,5] ⓘ

[1] RESUP - Research Group in Supply Chain Management, São Paulo, Brazil
[2] Gestão de Tecnologia em Sistemas Produtivos,
Centro Paula Souza, São Paulo, Brazil
[3] Graduate Studies in Production Engineering,
Universidade Paulista, São Paulo, Brazil
betomendesreis@msn.com
[4] Centro Paula Souza - College of Technology Sebrae, São Paulo, Brazil
[5] Centro Paula Souza - College of Technology Zona Leste, São Paulo, Brazil

Abstract. The large mining companies usually outsource the blasting service. There are two options regarding the management of the stocks of the explosives: first, the mining company management; second using Vendor Managed Inventory [VMI], which means that the supplier responsible for the management of the stock and all the logistics of delivery of the material. The present work has the objective of studying the effectiveness of this VMI in a supplier of a transnational mining company. Logistics costs are accounted for the period from January to September 2018. They are compared to the cost that the miner would have if the material requests were made on their account. The VMI in this mining company is very effective with a total saving of BRL 676.801,92 concerning logistics and BRL 7,356,295.36 about inventories. Furthermore, it was identified that there was no supply disruption, the stocks were in equilibrium according to the maximum and minimum limits and there was a low obsolescence percentage of products.

Keywords: Cost reduction · Logistics · Freight · Inventory · Explosive · Production management

1 Introduction

Mining is an important activity in modern life whose objective is the extraction of minerals of interest for various purposes [1]. From smartphones to autonomous cars, from the structures in civil construction to the money we use, ores are the basis for a multitude of essential items for everyday life. Most of the mineral extractions use explosives of different types for the fragmentation and dismantling of the rock in the production process [2].

© IFIP International Federation for Information Processing 2020
Published by Springer Nature Switzerland AG 2020
B. Lalic et al. (Eds.): APMS 2020, IFIP AICT 591, pp. 237–242, 2020.
https://doi.org/10.1007/978-3-030-57993-7_27

One of the main challenges in large mining companies is to manage the inventory of the explosives used to carry out the rock dismantling. The control and management of explosives stock is an essential activity because the lack of material or the non-compliance with any of the conditions of the army, the body office that regulates and supervises the use of this type of product, can impact on all activities subsequent to dismantling and in mining can cause losses in the order of millions.

Inventory management and planning are matters of extreme importance in a business environment once the investment is a substantial part of an organization's operating budget. In Supply Chain Management one of the most important issues is the inventory management [3]. Managing stocks economically consists essentially in the search for rationality and balance with consumption, in such a way that: the effective needs of its consumers are met with minimum cost and the lowest possible risk of shortages [4].

Mining companies are aware of the importance of explosives inventory management and their correct application usually outsource this type of service, that is, they hire a company to supply the explosives and/or carry out the dismantling and control the inventories.

When mining companies hire the rock dismantling service, there are two options regarding inventory management, the first option is the mining company itself to do all the inventory management by making its own explosive orders according to its demand. The second option is to leave the entire inventory management to the supplier (Supplier Managed Inventory) where the supplier plans orders according to the monthly demand informed by the customer.

According to Freitas et al. [5] the Vendor Managed Inventory (VMI), which assigns a company the task of managing the stock of the sequential link in its production chain, determining when and how much of each product should be sent to its immediate customer, one of the most discussed collaborative practices for improving the efficiency of the supply chain. The idea revolves around the manufacturer directly manages the inventory at the client [6].

Inventory management by the supplier - VMI, according to Santos and Alves [7] has been used to minimize inventories, without reducing the service level. It is an inventory initiative managed by supplier, where he assumes responsibility for planning and managing the customer's inventory, based on an agreed replacement service contract.

This study aims to assess the effectiveness of inventory management carried out by an explosive supplier in a large multinational in the mining industry.

2 Methodology

As mentioned previously, the objective of the study is to investigate the effectiveness of the VMI to manage inventory in a large mining company. The VMI optimize supply chain performance since the supplier has access to the customer's inventory data being responsible for maintaining the inventory level required by the customer [8]. To do so, the vendor through regularly scheduled reviews of the on-site inventory to counter and restocked to predefined levels [8].

The VMI system will be evaluated in this study from the perspective of two main points: (1) logistics costs; and (2) costs with a mobilized inventory.

The mining company has three units located in Para state, north of Brazil: S11D, Sossego and Carajás. The supplier responsible for the VMI is established in Paraná, south region of Brazil.

The products are manufactured and shipped to the three subsidiaries, based on the mining demand and stock availability. Therefore, logistics and inventory management is a hard activity and requires very effective planning.

To analyse logistics costs, the expenses in escort and freight during the period from January to September 2018 were collected. After, we predicted the theoretical values of escort and freight implementing the VMI, and calculate the differences regarding the real values.

The costs of mobilized inventory were calculated based on how much is spent in BRL (Brazilian Reis) to maintain inventories at the end of each month about 4 types of explosive: Initiators, Cord, Reinforcers and Wrapped.

3 Results

Table 1 presents the stock at the end of each month, from January to September, of the four categories of explosives: Initiator, Cord, Reinforcer and Wrapped.

Table 1. Stock of explosives

Month	Initiator (parts)	Cord (m)	Reinforcer (pars)	Wrapped (kg)
January	12,525	61,135	4,258	13,100
February	13,187	50,511	4,879	6,600
March	13,199	41,362	3,710	4,100
April	12,673	30,543	2,022	2,975
May	11,170	33,552	2,319	8,075
June	13,883	65,251	8,520	13,775
July	10,792	43,786	5,998	12,975
August	12,301	17,572	3,752	4,900
September	12,238	65,239	2,756	10,375
Maximum storage	18,250	100,000	11,500	16,300
Minimum storage	9,000	20,000	2,000	3,000

The maximum stock of explosives is established by the Brazilian Army's while the minimum is agreed between the supplier and the mining company. Therefore, occurs a disruption due to lead time and consumption of the products.

During the period of this study, there was the consumption of 24,985 initiators as can be seen in Table 2. Moreover, 110 initiators are discarded by obsolescence which represents 0.44% of the total.

Table 2. Month consumption

Month	Initiator (parts)	Cord (m)	Reinforcer (pars)	Wrapped (kg)
January	2,197	48,090	3,010	3,516
February	1,858	51,124	3,471	9,500
March	2,148	52,899	3,759	6,500
April	1,966	55,819	3,768	9,125
May	3,705	65,741	5,043	8,900
June	2,669	54,301	3,674	9,900
July	4,099	71,465	4,072	14,800
August	2,831	66,214	4,836	14,075
September	3,512	57,333	4,004	14,125
Total	24,985	522,986	35,637	90,441

Analyzing the required amount of transportation that would be required to meet the units, Table 3 shows the total of trips that would be required was reduced from 77 to 54 trips while Table 4 presents sharing cargo of the plants in Brazilian Reais (BRL).

Table 3. Number of trips

Month	Amount required			Freight total		Difference
	Plant sossego	Plant carajás	Plant S11D	Required (no sharing)	Used (sharing)	
January	3	4	1	8	5	3
February	4	2	3	9	5	4
March	2	2	2	6	3	3
April	2	4	3	9	6	3
May	3	2	3	8	5	3
June	2	4	2	8	6	2
July	4	4	2	10	9	1
August	2	5	3	10	9	1
September	3	4	2	9	6	3
Total	77	77	77	77	54	23

Table 5 shows the value predicted in BRL with the stock of explosives. The stock was used as a basis at the end of each month and multiplied by the average price of each of them and reached the actual value in the period.

The budgeted value was calculated by the mining company considering the amount necessary to maintain the deposit with its maximum capacity of each

Table 4. Cost and freight

Month	Total required (no sharing)	Total used (sharing)	Diference
January	135,818.64	84,886.65	50,931.99
February	152,795.67	84,886.65	67,909.02
March	101,863.98	50,931.99	50,931.99
April	152,795.97	101,863.98	50,931.99
May	135,818.64	84,886.65	50,931.99
June	135,818.64	101,863.98	33,954.66
July	169,773.30	152,795.97	16,977.33
August	169,773.30	152,795.97	16,977.33
September	152,795.97	101,863.98	50,931.99
Total	1,307,254.11	916,775.82	390,478.29

Table 5. Real versus budget

Item	Real	Budget
Initiator	4,938,908.48	7,245,067.50
Cord	2,650,002.48	5,832,000.00
Reinforcer	826,186.68	2,237,670.00
Wrapped	502,762.50	959,418.00
Total	8,917,860.14	16,274,155.50

material, therefore the maximum capacity value of each item is multiplied by the respective average price.

Making a general analysis the [VMI] presents a cost reduction for the mining company with logistics of BRL 676,801.12 and with inventories of BRL 7,356,295.36.

4   Final Remarks

Supplier Managed Inventory - VMI in an explosive supplier company to a multinational mining company is effective in showing considerable savings in both logistics and capital mobilized in stock in relation to the option of traditional inventory management. On the other hand requires special attention in relation to cargo sharing because the greater the amount of loads the greater the cost reduction with freight and escorts and also management should be attentive to keep stocks at levels avoiding mobilising high amounts of capital without need.

It is noticeable that the [VMI] allows a balance of inventories within the maximum and minimum limits and there was no disruption of supply something that is extremely critical for this branch of activity. Efficient management by the supplier allows a minimum disposal of products by obsolescence presenting a small financial impact to the customer.

References

1. Alves, W., Ferreira, P., Araújo, M.: Challenges and pathways for Brazilian mining sustainability. Resour. Policy, 101648 (2020). https://linkinghub.elsevier.com/retrieve/pii/S0301420717304877
2. ANEPAC: Estudo dos custos operacionais do desmonte de rocha por explosivo tipo encartuchado e emulsão bombeado (2018). http://www.anepac.org.br
3. Sadeghi, J., Sadeghi, S., Niaki, S.T.A.: A hybrid vendor managed inventory and redundancy allocation optimization problem in supply chain management: an NSGA-II with tuned parameters. Comput. Oper. Res. 41, 53–64 (2014). https://linkinghub.elsevier.com/retrieve/pii/S0305054813002049
4. Viana, J.: Administração de Materiais, Saraiva, São Paulo (1999). https://www.saraiva.com.br/administracao-de-materiais-um-enfoque-pratico-437358/p
5. Freitas, D., Tomas, R., Alcantara, R.: Estoque Gerenciado pelo Fornecedor (VMI): Análise das Barreiras e Fatores Críticos de Sucesso em Empresas de Grande Porte. Revista de Administração da Unimep 11(3), 221–252 (2013)
6. Whipple, J.M., Russell, D.: Building supply chain collaboration: a typology of collaborative approaches. Int. J. Logist. Manag. 18(2), 174–196 (2007). https://www.emerald.com/insight/content/doi/10.1108/09574090710816922/full/html
7. Santos, R., Alves, J.: Proposta de um modelo de gestão de cadeia de suprimentos com o apoio da Teoria das Restrições, VMI e B2B. In: The Industrial Engineering and the Sustainable Development: Integrating Technology and Management, Salvador (2009)
8. Blackstone, J.H., A.T.E.S. for Resource Management (eds.): APICS Dictionary, 13 (revised edn). APICS, The Association for Operations Management, Chicago, Illinois (2010)

Value Chain Integration – A Framework for Assessment

Inger Gamme[1], Bjørn Andersen[2], Håkon Raabe[1],
and Daryl Powell[1,2(✉)]

[1] SINTEF Manufacturing AS, Raufoss, Norway
hakon.raabe@sintef.no
[2] Norwegian University of Science and Technology, Trondheim, Norway
daryl.j.powell@ntnu.no

Abstract. Despite an abundance of research on the topic, firms continue to struggle with integrating their value chains in order to create and deliver more value to customers. Silo-thinking (rather than systems-thinking) is a typical symptom of poorly integrated value chains. In this paper, we explore the enablers of better value chain integration, before developing and presenting a framework that can be used for assessing the maturity of value chain integration in organizations. We draw on practical insights from a multiple case study of several diverse companies currently working with the systematic integration of their value chains.

Keywords: Value chain integration · Maturity assessment · Multiple case study

1 Introduction

Organizations often struggle to integrate their value chains due to specific factors, such as the presence of a "silo-culture" as well as a lack of documentation or systematization [1, 2]. For example, defending silos over teamwork has emerged as a symptom of big company disease [3]. Moreover, having little flexibility in written descriptions and infrastructure could also lead to unreliable integration processes, particularly if employees choose to create their own routines besides those described in the system. Value creating processes must act together and there should be aligned and balanced intra-organizational coordination capabilities, in order to achieve a value chain that is well-managed [4]. Such a well-managed value chain is referred to as an *integrated value chain* that provides optimized value for the customer [5, 6]. As such, focusing on the interfaces between functions or process steps has been relevant for decades. Literature has various interpretations of the term "integration", the content and framing are varying, and few authors present a formal definition [2, 7]. The main purpose of this article is to extend existing knowledge identifying the enablers and disablers of integration within the value chain for different sectors. By studying what enables value chain integration, and which mechanisms are used to facilitate integration in five different organizations within different sectors in Norway, the following research questions will be addressed:

© IFIP International Federation for Information Processing 2020
Published by Springer Nature Switzerland AG 2020
B. Lalic et al. (Eds.): APMS 2020, IFIP AICT 591, pp. 243–249, 2020.
https://doi.org/10.1007/978-3-030-57993-7_28

Research question (RQ) 1: *What are the enablers of better value chain integration?*
RQ2: *How can firms increase the degree of integration throughout the value chain?*

2 Theoretical Background: Enablers for Achieving Integration in Value Chains

To answer RQ1, we carried out a review of the extant literature. The following seven enablers for achieving integration in value chains were formally identified during the literature search, and provide the basis for the rest of the investigation (Table 1):

Table 1. Enablers of value chain integration

Enablers of value chain integration	Identified in:
Culture (social mechanisms and the creation of lateral relations)	[8, 9]
Management support (vertical integration)	[1, 2, 5, 9–14]
Consensus	[2]
Formalization (standardization)	[15, 16]
Information systems	[17, 18]
Facility and layout	[19, 20]
Measurements and rewards	[21, 22]

3 Research Design

Guided by the research questions, the research approach adopted for this study is a multiple case study design that builds on the identification of enablers for value chain integration that were identified in the previous section. Partly to serve as illustrative cases and partly to demonstrate practical usage of the integration theory, the case studies were conducted in different industries and different types of companies. The cases also serve to provide empirical insights into enablers and disablers of better integration in internal value chains. The main reason for choosing a case-study approach, according to [23], is its distinct advantage in situations wherein "how", "what" and "why" type questions are posed in order to understand a complex phenomenon. When selecting cases for studying, there are several criteria to consider, i.e. what data are accessible, type of context and if the data is suitable for testing for the chosen approach. Within this study, the dominant criteria for selecting the case organizations has been the convenience sample [24]. We chose to study the phenomena within different industries in order to have the possibility to illustrate the topic from different perspectives and to build a foundation for the research to be generalizable for different industries. To increase the robustness of the research [25], data triangulation was ensured by using multiple sources when collecting the data, such as documents and direct observations in the field [26].

3.1 Case Study Overview

The case companies in this study are two mass producers (MPI & MPII), a craft producer (CP), a hospital (H) and a service provider (SP), each of which are presented below. The units of analysis in these different organizations are the value-adding elements of their internal value chains. As stated in [2], "the only way to truly assess the level of integration is by collecting data from respondents responsible for different value creating processes." Consequently, this research focuses on ensuring that at least two employees were interviewed within each process step of the value-adding elements of the value chain. Interviewees ranged from operators and team leaders to more senior managers, as well as trade union representatives. A summary of the case studies can be found in the following Table 2:

Table 2. Case study overview

	MPI	MPII	H	CP	SP
Main Product/area of study	Auto components	Aluminium billets	Thrombolysis ward	Leisure boats	Insurance & banking
No of employees	37	513	265	20	1200
No of interviews	11	16	15	12	8

4 Discussion: Towards a Theoretical Framework for Value Chain Integration

Based on the theory from the literature study and the observations made during the case study research, we have been able to construct a model that provides insight into the relationships of each of the enablers for value chain integration. The model is illustrated in Fig. 1:

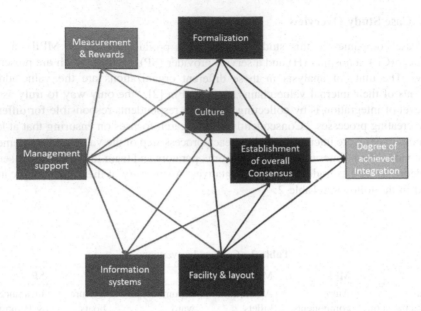

Fig. 1. Theoretical framework for value chain integration

We suggest that the model can be used as the basis for a value chain integration maturity assessment tool, to help improve the integration of value chains in and across organizations. To exemplify how this could be applied to improve the integration of a value chain, we provide a theoretical example using data from MPII. The mechanisms were rated according to the extent to which the researchers found evidence for each mechanism during the case study, following the scale defined. (It should be noted that this rating should normally be performed by the company representatives themselves, who would rate the mechanisms according to their own experiences with them). After the rating procedure, the average rating per category is calculated. Table 3 presents an overview of the distribution and scoring of several examples within the given categories *Consensus, Culture,* and *Facility & Layout*:

Table 3 Maturity model for value chain integration

	Low Definitely not		Somewhat		High Definitely	
Use of mechanisms within each category	1	2	3	4	5	Average
Consensus integration						
The overall strategy is transferred down to individual measures				x		4
The employees are involved in the process of deriving KPI's (to avoid mistrust)			x			3
The overall strategy is well known					x	5
The employees support the overall strategy				x		4
There is a correlation between management focus and employee focus				x		4
All the managers agree upon the business strategy			x			3
Count per score value	0	0	2	3	1	3,83
Culture, social mechanisms and creation of lateral relations						
The personell are available at the value chain				x		4
The employees have confidence in systems				x		4
Degree of acknowledgement of colleagues				x		4
Degree of focus on customer among the employees				x		4
Degree of openness among the employees				x		4
Degree on focus on the entire value chain				x		4
The employees have focus on the interrelation of the process steps				x		4
There exists an informal culture				x		4
The employees have an information sharing mentality				x		4
The use of job rotation is consistent when possible throughout the value chain				x		4
The employees have knowledge of other departments				x		4
The employees have team work experience					x	5
The transfer of managers is used to increase the integration					x	5
There is a use of cross functional teams				x		4
The employees are used to standardized work				x		4
Count per score value	0	0	0	13	2	4,13
Facility and layout						
The employees are co-located			x			3
The plant layout is small and transparent				x		4
The layout contains no partitions				x		4
Count per score value	0	0	1	2	0	3,67

The result is a maturity level on the scale 1–5, where 1 indicates a very poor level of value chain integration and 5 indicates very good level of value chain integration.

5 Conclusion and Further Research

The results of this research support the view of [27] in that integration is a multidimensional concept. This may explain why, when studying an individual category, it is often seen that it can directly or indirectly influence one or more other categories. It can also be observed that some enablers or disablers might be placed under several categories and that an enabler could be a disabler, or vice versa, depending on circumstances. Despite several years of research on the topic of integration, there remains a need for further research to achieve a greater understanding of this concept [7, 28]. Many different terms and definitions are used within this field, and some authors do not even use any definitions. Given that such inconsistency exists within this area of study, this research was intended to address the need for greater clarification and to provide a holistic overview of integration measures in the value chain. Furthermore, this article contributes to providing an enhanced understanding of which enablers can influence the levels of integration between two or more process steps. As an initial step toward gaining a more generic understanding of the topic, five case companies were studied. Moreover, a value chain integration maturity assessment model was constructed. This can be used to support practitioners when attempting to improve the value chain integration through identifying actions to strengthen such integration.

Acknowledgements. The authors acknowledge the support from the Research Council of Norway through the research program *SFI Manufacturing*.

References

1. Basnet, C., Wisner, J.: Nurturing internal supply chain integration. Oper. Supply Chain Manag. **5**(1), 27–41 (2012)
2. Pagell, M.: Understanding the factors that enable and inhibit the integration of operations, purchasing and logistics. J. Oper. Manag. **22**(5), 459–487 (2004)
3. Ballé, M., et al.: The Lean Sensei. Go. See. Challenge. Lean Enterprise Institute Inc., Boston (2019)
4. Stank, T.P., Keller, S.B., Daugherty, P.J.: Supply chain collaboration and logistical service performance. J. Bus. Logist. **22**(1), 29–48 (2001)
5. Morash, E.A., Clinton, S.R.: Supply chain integration: customer value through collaborative closeness versus operational excellence. J. Mark. Theor. Pract. **6**(4), 104–120 (1998)
6. Stock, G.N., Greis, N.P., Kasarda, J.D.: Logistics, strategy and structure. Int. J. Oper. Prod. Manag. **18**(1), 37–52 (1998)
7. Frankel, R., Mollenkopf, D.A.: Cross-functional integration revisited: exploring the conceptual elephant. J. Bus. Logist. **36**(1), 18–24 (2015)
8. Griffin, A., Hauser, J.R.: Integrating R&D and marketing: a review and analysis of the literature. J. Prod. Innov. Manag.: Int. Publ. Prod. Dev. Manag. Assoc. **13**(3), 191–215 (1996)
9. Braunscheidel, M.J., Suresh, N.C., Boisnier, A.D.: Investigating the impact of organizational culture on supply chain integration. Hum. Resour. Manag. **49**(5), 883–911 (2010)
10. Lawrence, P.R., Lorsch, J.W.: Organization and environment (1967)
11. Chen, I.J., Paulraj, A.: Towards a theory of supply chain management: the constructs and measurements. J. Oper. Manag. **22**(2), 119–150 (2004)
12. Barki, H., Pinsonneault, A.: A model of organizational integration, implementation effort, and performance. Organ. Sci. **16**(2), 165–179 (2005)
13. Drupsteen, J., van der Vaart, T., Van Donk, D.P.: Operational antecedents of integrated patient planning in hospitals. Int. J. Oper. Prod. Manag. **36**(8), 879–900 (2016)
14. Le Meunier-FitzHugh, K., Massey, G.R., Piercy, N.F.: The impact of aligned rewards and senior manager attitudes on conflict and collaboration between sales and marketing. Ind. Mark. Manag. **40**(7), 1161–1171 (2011)
15. Bowersox, D.J., Closs, D.J., Stank, T.P.: 21st Century Logistics: Making Supply Chain Integration a Reality (1999)
16. Malone, T.W., Crowston, K.: The interdisciplinary study of coordination. ACM Comput. Surv. (CSUR) **26**(1), 87–119 (1994)
17. Gattiker, T.F.: Enterprise Resource Planning (ERP) systems and the manufacturing–marketing interface: an information-processing theory view. Int. J. Prod. Res. **45**(13), 2895–2917 (2007)
18. Galbraith, J.R.: Competing with Flexible Lateral Organizations. Addison-Wesley Reading, Boston (1994)
19. Pinto, M.B., Pinto, J.K., Prescott, J.E.: Antecedents and consequences of project team cross-functional cooperation. Manag. Sci. **39**(10), 1281–1297 (1993)
20. Pagell, M., LePine, J.A.: Multiple case studies of team effectiveness in manufacturing organizations. J. Oper. Manag. **20**(5), 619–639 (2002)

21. Coombs Jr, G., Gomez-Mejia, L.R.: Cross-functional pay strategies in high-technology firms. Compens. Benefits Rev. **23**(5), 40–48 (1991)
22. Galbraith, J.R.: Designing Organizations: An Executive Guide to Strategy, Structure (2002)
23. Karlsson, C.: Researching Operations Management. Routledge, New York (2009)
24. Marshall, M.N.: Sampling for qualitative research. Fam. Pract. **13**(6), 522–526 (1996)
25. Patton, M.Q.: Qualitative Evaluation and Research Methods. SAGE Publications, Inc., Thousand Oaks (1990)
26. Yin, R.K.: Case Study Research: Design and Methods, 4th edn. Sage Publications, Thousand Oaks (2009)
27. Turkulainen, V., Ketokivi, M.: Cross functional integration and performance: what are the real benefits? Int. J. Oper. Prod. Manag. **32**(4), 447–467 (2012)
28. Autry, C.W., Rose, W.J., Bell, J.E.: Reconsidering the supply chain integration–performance relationship: in search of theoretical consistency and clarity. J. Bus. Logist. **35**(3), 275–276 (2014)

A Dynamic Hybrid Berth Allocation Problem with Routing Constraints in Bulk Ports

Hamza Bouzekri[1,2]([✉]) [iD], Gülgün Alpan[1,2] [iD], and Vincent Giard[1,3] [iD]

[1] EMINES - School of Industrial Management,
Mohammed VI Polytechnic University, 43150 Ben Guerir, Morocco
hamza.bouzekri@emines.um6p.ma
[2] Université Grenoble Alpes, Grenoble INP, CNRS, G-SCOP,
38000 Grenoble, France
gulgun.alpan@grenoble-inp.fr
[3] Université Paris-Dauphine, PSL Research University, 75016 Paris, France
vincent.giard@dauphine.psl.eu

Abstract. The Berth Allocation Problem (BAP) is considered as one of the most important operational problems in the seaside area of ports. It refers to the problem of assigning a set of vessels to a given berth layout within a given time horizon. In this paper, we study the dynamic and hybrid case of the BAP in the context of bulk ports with multiple quays, different water depths, and heterogeneous loading equipment, considering routing constraints (routes between storage hangars and berths). This study is motivated by the operations of OCP Group, a world leader in the phosphate industry, at the bulk port of Jorf Lasfar in Morocco, recognized as the largest ore port in Africa. The objective of the problem is to enhance the coordination between the berthing and yard activities, besides maximizing the difference between the despatch money and the demurrage charges of all berthed vessels. We propose an integer linear programming model formulated with predicates, which ensures maximum flexibility in the implementation of the model. Finally, the proposed model is tested and validated through numerical experiments based on instances inspired by real bulk port data. The results show that the model can be used to solve to optimality instances with up to 40 vessels within reasonable computational time.

Keywords: Berth Allocation Problem · Conveyor system · Bulk ports

1 Introduction

Although containerization has played a significant role in developing the port sector and maritime transport, bulk cargoes are still the essential and enduring trades that support the dynamism of maritime shipping. It has to be noted that bulk port operations are very different from container port operations. Indeed, in bulk ports, it is necessary to consider the cargo type and to model the interaction between the storage locations of goods on the yard and the berthing locations of vessels. Hence, establishing a set of feasible routes between berths and storage locations to guarantee that goods are shipped on schedule when making berth allocation decisions, is critical.

© IFIP International Federation for Information Processing 2020
Published by Springer Nature Switzerland AG 2020
B. Lalic et al. (Eds.): APMS 2020, IFIP AICT 591, pp. 250–258, 2020.
https://doi.org/10.1007/978-3-030-57993-7_29

Our analysis considers the bulk port of Jorf Lasfar where a complex conveyor system, composed of different routes that share one or more conveyor belts, is used to transport goods from storage hangars to berths. In addition, we consider the draft restrictions on vessels that limit the feasible berthing positions to only those berths having a water depth higher than their draft. To solve this problem, we propose an integer linear programming model. The spatiotemporal constraints of the problem are formulated as disjunctive constraints, thanks to the use of spatiotemporal binary variables. Moreover, all the conditions of the problem are expressed as predicates, which ensures maximum flexibility in the implementation of the model and significantly improves its computational performance. Indeed, it is no longer necessary to introduce the conditions of the problem as constraints in the model, and the space search of solutions becomes smaller.

The rest of the paper is organized as follows: Section 2 provides a literature review. In Sections 3 and 4, the problem and the mathematical formulation are introduced. The results of the numerical experiments are reported in Section 5. Finally, conclusions and future research directions are addressed in Section 6.

2 Literature Review

The BAP in bulk ports has received little attention in Operations Research literature compared to container ports. In this section, we present a brief review of past research on the BAP in the context of bulk ports. There is a multitude of BAP formulations depending on the spatial and temporal constraints involved in the problem. The spatial attribute concerns the berth layout (discrete, continuous or hybrid) and the draft restrictions, while the temporal one includes the arrival process and the handling time of vessels. Umang et al. [1] studied the dynamic hybrid BAP taking into account the cargo type and the draft of each vessel. Ernst et al. [2] solved the continuous BAP with tidal constraints that limit the departure of fully loaded vessels from the terminal. In contrast, Barros et al. [3] solved the discrete BAP considering homogeneous berths with tide and stock level constraints, prioritizing vessels related to the most critical mineral stock level.

Since the problems of berth allocation and yard management are interrelated, some authors have integrated the BAP with the Yard Assignment Problem. Indeed, Robenek et al. [4] extended the dynamic hybrid BAP to account for the assignment of yard locations, with the assumptions that each vessel has only one single cargo type. To solve this integrated problem, the authors proposed an exact solution algorithm based on a branch and price framework and a metaheuristic approach based on critical-shaking neighborhood. Unsal and Oguz [5] proposed a MILP model for an integrated problem that consists of three operations: berth allocation, reclaimer (a large machine used to recover bulk material from a stockpile) scheduling and stockyard allocation, considering tide constraints. In the same logic of integrating problems, Pratap et al. [6] developed a decision support system to solve the integrated problem of berth and ship unloader allocation. Menezes et al. [7] integrated production planning and scheduling problems with a First In, First Out (FIFO) policy for berthing vessels. This integrated problem defines the amount and destination of each input or output order between reception, stockyards and piers, establishing a set of feasible routes between these three subsystems, to guarantee that goods are stored and shipped on schedule and to minimize operational costs.

In our paper, we solve the dynamic and hybrid BAP under routing constraints, considering the type of cargo and the capacity limits of the equipment. The storage locations of goods are provided as input parameters to the model. To reduce the gap between the abstract representation of the studied problem and its applicability in real situations, we consider many aspects such as draft restrictions, the heterogeneity of equipment, Charter Party clauses and multiple cargo types on the same vessel.

3 Problem Description

We consider a bulk port with multiple quays and heterogeneous loading equipment linked to storage hangars by a conveyor system. This latter is composed of different routes that share one or more conveyor belts (see Fig. 1a). Each quay has as hybrid layout where large vessels may occupy more than one berth, however, small vessels cannot share a berth (see Fig. 1b). Each berth is characterized by a length, a fixed loading equipment and a water depth. All the berths of a quay can have the same water depth, or the water depth increases seaward by berths. We assume dynamic vessel arrivals (i.e. Fixed arrival times are given for the vessels; hence, vessels cannot berth before the expected arrival time). Each vessel is characterized by a length, a draft, a maximum waiting time in the harbor and a number of cargo types with different amounts to be loaded in it. These amounts of cargo types can be expressed as batches. Each batch has an availability date and is stored in a hangar. It has to be noted that the batches to be loaded in a single vessel can be stored in different hangars. Handling times of vessels depend on their berthing position due to the productivity of the loading equipment at the berth. We assume that two (or more) batches cannot be loaded at the same time, but they can be loaded in any order, with no downtime. We also consider technical constraints of vessels that prohibit their berthing at some berths or oblige them to berth at a specific berth. Finally, we consider Charter Party clauses by defining for each vessel the laytime (i.e. contractual handling time), the despatch money (i.e. the bonus payment offered by the shipowner to the charterer if the vessel completes loading before the laytime has expired), and the demurrage charges (i.e. the fees paid by the charterer to the shipowner for exceeding the laytime). These contractual clauses are more detailed in Bouzekri et al. [8].

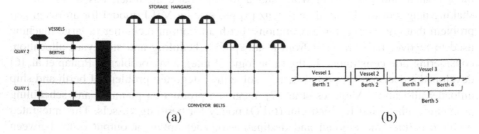

(a)   (b)

Fig. 1. a. Port conveyor system. b. Hybrid berth layout.

4 Model Formulation

4.1 Notation

Indices, sets, parameters and decision variables are detailed in Table 1.

Table 1. BAP mathematical notation.

Index	Description
v	Index of vessels $\mathcal{V} = \{1, \ldots, V\}$.
b	Index of berths $\mathcal{B} = \{1, \ldots, B\}$.
t	Index of time periods $\mathcal{T} = \{1, \ldots, T\}$.
p	Index of pairs of berths that share a berth and cannot be used simultaneously $\mathcal{P} = \{1, \ldots, P\}$ (e.g. in Fig. 1b, the pair of berths 3 and 5 share the berth 3, so they cannot be used at the same time).
i_v	Index of batches to be loaded in vessel v $\mathcal{I}_v = \{1, \ldots, I_v\}$.
r	Index of routes $\mathcal{R} = \{1, \ldots, R\}$. Each route links a storage hangar to a berth.
g	Index of groups of routes that share at least one conveyor belt of the conveyor system to transport batches $\mathcal{G} = \{1, \ldots, G\}$. Hence, the routes in a given group cannot be used all at once.
Parameter	Description
L_b	Length of berth b.
W_b	Minimum water depth of berth b.
E_b^p	Boolean parameter that equals 1 if berth b belongs to the pair p of berths that share a berth, 0 otherwise.
A_v	Expected time of arrival of vessel v.
M_v	Maximum waiting time in the harbor of vessel v.
λ_v	Length of vessel v.
D_v	Draft of vessel v when it is fully loaded.
N_{vb}	Boolean parameter that equals 1 if vessel v can berth at berth b, 0 otherwise.
J_v	Contractual handling time of vessel v.
δ_v	Contractual finishing time of vessel v: $\delta_v = A_v + J_v - 1, \forall v \in \mathcal{V}$.
α_v	Contractual demurrage by hour of vessel v.
β_v	Contractual despatch by hour of vessel v.
$\theta_{vb}^{i_v}$	Loading time of batch i_v in vessel v when this latter is berthed at berth b.
O_{vb}	Loading time of vessel v, which equals the sum of loading times of all the batches loaded in this vessel: $O_{vb} = \sum_{i_v \in \mathcal{I}_v} \theta_{vb}^{i_v}, \forall v \in \mathcal{V}, \forall b \in \mathcal{B}$.
$K_v^{i_v}$	Date of availability of batch i_v to be loaded in vessel v.
$H_v^{i_v}$	Storage hangar of batch i_v to be loaded in vessel v.
Q_r	Index of the berth linked to route r.
S_r	Index of the storage hangar linked to route r.
F_r^g	Boolean parameter that equals 1 if route r belongs to group g of routes that share at least one conveyor belt of the conveyor system, 0 otherwise.
U^g	Maximum number of routes that can be used simultaneously in group g of routes.
Variable	Description
x_{vbt}	1 if vessel v starts berthing at berth b in time period t, 0 otherwise.
$y_{vbtr}^{i_v}$	1 if batch i_v starts to be loaded in vessel v at berth b in time period t using route r, 0 otherwise.
u_v	Integer, delay of vessel v.
w_v	Integer, advance of vessel v.

4.2   Mathematical Model

The existence of the decision variable x_{vbt} is subject to four conditions:

1. Vessel v must be able to berth at berth b: $N_{vb} = 1$.
2. The length of vessel v must not exceed the length of berth b: $\lambda_v \leq L_b$.
3. The draft of vessel v must not exceed the water depth of berth b: $D_v \leq W_b$.
4. Vessel v can berth only after its expected time of arrival without exceeding its maximum waiting time in the harbor: $A_v \leq t \leq A_v + M_v$.

The existence of the decision variable $y_{vbtr}^{i_v}$ is subject to seven conditions:

1. Conditions 1, 2 and 3 of the existence of the decision variable x_{vbt}.
2. Batch i_v can be loaded in vessel v between the expected time of arrival of this vessel and its finishing time as it reaches its maximum waiting time in the harbor, minus the loading time of this batch: $A_v \leq t \leq A_v + M_v + O_{vb} - \theta_{vb}^{i_v}$.
3. Batch i_v can be loaded in vessel v only after its date of availability: $t \geq K_v^{i_v}$.
4. The route used to load the batch i_v in vessel v must be linked to the berth b of this vessel: $Q_r = b$.
5. The route used to load the batch i_v in vessel v must be linked to the storage hangar of this batch: $S_r = H_v^{i_v}$.

We define the intermediate variables μ_v and $\eta_v^{i_v}$, which give for each vessel v, respectively, the berthing position in both decision variables x_{vbt} and $y_{vbtr}^{i_v}$.

$$\mu_v = \sum_{b \in \mathcal{B}|N_{vb}=1 \wedge \lambda_v \leq L_b \wedge D_v \leq W_b} \sum_{t \in \mathcal{T}|A_v \leq t \leq A_v + M_v} b \cdot x_{vbt}, \forall v \in \mathcal{V}$$

$$\eta_v^{i_v} = \sum_{b \in \mathcal{B}|N_{vb}=1 \wedge \lambda_v \leq L_b \wedge D_v \leq W_b} \sum_{t \in \mathcal{T}|A_v \leq t \leq A_v + M_v + O_{vb} - \theta_{vb}^{i_v} \wedge t \geq K_v^{i_v}} \sum_{r \in \mathcal{R}|Q_r = b \wedge S_r = H_v^{i_v}} b \cdot y_{vbtr}^{i_v},$$

$$\forall v \in \mathcal{V}, \forall i_v \in \mathcal{I}_v$$

Similarly, we set for each vessel v, the berthing and finishing time ε_v and τ_v by replacing $b \cdot x_{vbt}$ in μ_v, respectively, by $t \cdot x_{vbt}$ and $(t + O_{vb} - 1) \cdot x_{vbt}$. Likewise, we define for each batch i_v to be loaded in vessel v, the loading start and finishing time $\rho_v^{i_v}$ and $\sigma_v^{i_v}$ by replacing $b \cdot y_{vbtr}^{i_v}$ in $\eta_v^{i_v}$, respectively, by $t \cdot y_{vbtr}^{i_v}$ and $(t + \theta_{vb}^{i_v} - 1) \cdot y_{vbtr}^{i_v}$.

The model for the BAP with routing constraints can be formulated as follows:

$$Max \sum_{v \in \mathcal{V}} (\beta_v \cdot w_v - \alpha_v \cdot u_v) \tag{1}$$

$$\text{s.t.} \quad \sum_{b \in \mathcal{B}|N_{vb}=1 \wedge \lambda_v \leq L_b \wedge D_v \leq W_b} \sum_{t \in \mathcal{T}|A_v \leq t \leq A_v + M_v} x_{vbt} = 1, \forall v \in \mathcal{V} \tag{2}$$

$$\sum_{b \in \mathcal{B}|N_{vb}=1 \wedge \lambda_v \leq L_b \wedge D_v \leq W_b} \sum_{t \in \mathcal{T}|A_v \leq t \leq A_v + M_v + O_{vb} - \theta_{vb}^{i_v} \wedge t \geq K_v^{i_v}} \sum_{r \in \mathcal{R}|Q_r = b \wedge S_r = H_v^{i_v}} y_{vbtr}^{i_v} = 1,$$

$$\forall v \in \mathcal{V}, \forall i_v \in \mathcal{I}_v$$

$$\tag{3}$$

$$\mu_v = \eta_v^{i_v}, \forall v \in \mathcal{V}, \forall i_v \in \mathcal{I}_v \tag{4}$$

$$\rho_v^{i_v} \geq \varepsilon_v, \forall v \in \mathcal{V}, \forall i_v \in \mathcal{I}_v \tag{5}$$

$$\sigma_v^{i_v} \leq \tau_v, \forall v \in \mathcal{V}, \forall i_v \in \mathcal{I}_v \tag{6}$$

$$\sum_{i_v \in \mathcal{I}_v} \sum_{b \in \mathcal{B}|N_{vb}=1 \wedge \lambda_v \leq L_b \wedge D_v \leq W_b} \sum_{t'=A_v|t' \geq K_v^{i_v} \wedge t' + \theta_{vb}^{i_v}-1 \geq t}^{t'=t|t' \leq A_v+M_v+O_{vb}-\theta_{vb}^{i_v}} \sum_{r \in \mathcal{R}|Q_r=b \wedge S_r=H_v^{i_v}} y_{vbt'r}^{i_v} \leq 1,$$
$$\forall t \in \mathcal{T}, \forall v \in \mathcal{V} \tag{7}$$

$$\sum_{v \in \mathcal{V}} \sum_{i_v \in \mathcal{I}_v} \sum_{b \in \mathcal{B}|N_{vb}=1 \wedge \lambda_v \leq L_b \wedge D_v \leq W_b} \sum_{t'=A_v|t' \geq K_v^{i_v} \wedge t' + \theta_{vb}^{i_v}-1 \geq t}^{t'=t|t' \leq A_v+M_v+O_{vb}-\theta_{vb}^{i_v}} \sum_{r \in \mathcal{R}|F_r^g=1 \wedge Q_r=b \wedge S_r=H_v^{i_v}} y_{vbt'r}^{i_v} \leq U^g,$$
$$\forall t \in \mathcal{T}, \forall g \in \mathcal{G} \tag{8}$$

$$\sum_{v \in \mathcal{V}|N_{vb}=1 \wedge \lambda_v \leq L_b \wedge D_v \leq W_b} \sum_{t'=A_v|t' + O_{vb}-1 \geq t}^{t'=t|t' \leq A_v+M_v} x_{vbt'} \leq 1, \forall t \in T, \forall b \in \mathcal{B} \tag{9}$$

$$\sum_{v \in \mathcal{V}} \sum_{b \in \mathcal{B}|E_b^p=1 \wedge N_{vb}=1 \wedge \lambda_v \leq L_b \wedge D_v \leq W_b} \sum_{t'=A_v|t' + O_{vb}-1 \geq t}^{t'=t|t' \leq A_v+M_v} x_{vbt'} \leq 1, \forall t \in \mathcal{T}, \forall p \in \mathcal{P} \tag{10}$$

$$u_v \geq \tau_v - \delta_v, \forall v \in \mathcal{V} \tag{11}$$

$$w_v \geq \delta_v - \tau_v, \forall v \in \mathcal{V} \tag{12}$$

$$u_v - w_v = \tau_v - \delta_v, \forall v \in \mathcal{V} \tag{13}$$

$$u_v, w_v \geq 0, \forall v \in \mathcal{V} \tag{14}$$

Objective function (1) maximizes the difference between the despatch money and the demurrage charges of each vessel v. Equation (2) ensures that each vessel v starts berthing at a unique berth b and in a unique time period t. Equation (3) ensures that each batch i_v starts its loading in vessel v at a unique berth b, in a unique time period t, and is transported in a unique route r. Equation (4) ensures that berth b in both decision variables x_{vtb} and $y_{vtbr}^{i_v}$ is the same. Equation (5) ensures that the loading of each batch i_v can only begin once vessel v has been berthed. Equation (6) ensures that each vessel v can only leave the port when all batches have been loaded. Equation (7) ensures that two (or more) batches cannot be loaded at the same time in each vessel v. Equation (8) avoids simultaneous use of routes that share at least one conveyor belt of the conveyor system. Equation (9) avoids the overlapping of vessels in each berth b. Equation (10) ensures that only one berth can be used from each pair of berths that share a berth since the berth layout of each quay is hybrid. Equations (11)–(14) determine the delay and the advance of each vessel.

5 Numerical Experiments

The experiments were conducted using a computer with a core Intel® Xeon® CPU E3-1240 v5 @ 3.50 GHz - 64 Go RAM, running a 64-bit version of the commercial solver Xpress-IVE 1.24.24. The method used for solving the problem is the primal simplex algorithm. The detailed characteristics of test instances and results can be found at Mendeley in Bouzekri et al. [9].

5.1 Input Data

Test instances were generated based on a sample of data obtained from OCP group. This latter operates six quays in the port of Jorf Lasfar to import raw materials (sulfur and ammonia) and export raw materials and products (phosphate rock, phosphoric acid and fertilizers). We focus on the first two quays that are dedicated to the export of fertilizers and partitioned into five berths each (1, 2, 3, 4, and $5 = 3 \cup 4$). Each berth has a minimum water depth and a fixed quay crane with a specific productivity. The produced fertilizers (around 50 different types) are stored in 9 hangars. All the hangars are linked to all the berths by a conveyor system composed of 90 routes. The data sample received provides information about all the vessels that were berthed during the year 2019. We consider 3 sets of 5 instances each for $V = \{20, 30, 40\}$, generated from the data sample, for a planning horizon of 20 days (480 h).

5.2 Computational Results

The output of the model refers to the scheduling of vessels and batches. These decisions can be illustrated in a same Gantt chart (see Bouzekri et al. [9]). For each set of 5 instances of a given size, Table 2 shows the number of instances solved, the number of instances solved to optimality, the average computation time in seconds, and the average and maximum gap in percentages. For each instance, the computation time was limited to 1 h and the gap was provided by the solver as $100 \cdot (ub - lb)/ub$, where ub is the best upper bound obtained within the time limit, and lb is the value of the objective function corresponding to the best integer solution achieved. Overall, from the results, we can observe that the computation time increases with the number of vessels and the solver can solve to optimality most of the cases.

Table 2. Computational results.

V	Solved	Optimum	Avg. time	Avg. gap	Max. gap
20	5	5	5.9	0	0
30	5	5	203.6	0	0
40	5	3	1734.2	2.4	7.4

6 Conclusions and Future Research

In this paper, we study the Berth Allocation Problem with routing constraints in bulk ports. Our study is motivated by the port of Jorf Lasfar, but it is also valid for any bulk port. A new integer linear programming model is proposed to solve this problem. The formulation proposed herein is flexible thanks to the use of predicates and it can be used to solve real cases in bulk ports. Computational experiments show that our model is able to solve the problem instances of realistic size (up to 40 vessels, 10 berths, 9 storage hangars, and 90 routes) in a reasonable computation time.

Further improvements are intended to be made such as considering tide constraints and extending our model to integrate storage locations decisions under the restrictions that forbid two or more cargo types to be stored in adjacent yard locations to avoid intermixing. Also, a heuristic could be developed to obtain faster results.

References

1. Umang, N., Bierlaire, M., Vacca, I.: Exact and heuristic methods to solve the berth allocation problem in bulk ports. Transp. Res. Part E: Logistics Transp. Rev. **54**, 14–31 (2013). https://doi.org/10.1016/j.tre.2013.03.003
2. Ernst, A.T., Oğuz, C., Singh, G., Taherkhani, G.: Mathematical models for the berth allocation problem in dry bulk terminals. J Sched. **20**, 459–473 (2017). https://doi.org/10.1007/s10951-017-0510-8
3. Barros, V.H., Costa, T.S., Oliveira, A.C.M., Lorena, L.A.N.: Model and heuristic for berth allocation in tidal bulk ports with stock level constraints. Comput. Ind. Eng. **60**, 606–613 (2011). https://doi.org/10.1016/j.cie.2010.12.018
4. Robenek, T., Umang, N., Bierlaire, M., Ropke, S.: A branch-and-price algorithm to solve the integrated berth allocation and yard assignment problem in bulk ports. Eur. J. Oper. Res. **235**, 399–411 (2014). https://doi.org/10.1016/j.ejor.2013.08.015
5. Unsal, O., Oguz, C.: An exact algorithm for integrated planning of operations in dry bulk terminals. Transp. Res. Part E Logistic Transp. Rev. **126**, 103–121 (2019). https://doi.org/10.1016/j.tre.2019.03.018
6. Pratap, S., Nayak, A., Kumar, A., Cheikhrouhou, N., Tiwari, M.K.: An integrated decision support system for berth and ship unloader allocation in bulk material handling port. Comput. Ind. Eng. **106**, 386–399 (2017). https://doi.org/10.1016/j.cie.2016.12.009
7. Menezes, G.C., Mateus, G.R., Ravetti, M.G.: A branch and price algorithm to solve the integrated production planning and scheduling in bulk ports. Eur. J. Oper. Res. **258**, 926–937 (2017). https://doi.org/10.1016/j.ejor.2016.08.073

8. Bouzekri, H., Alpan, G., Giard, V.: Integrated Laycan and Berth allocation problem. In: 2019 International Conference on Industrial Engineering and Systems Management (IESM), pp. 1–6, Shanghai, China (2019). https://doi.org/10.1109/IESM45758.2019.8948110

9. Bouzekri, H., Alpan, G., Giard, V.: A dynamic hybrid berth allocation problem with routing constraints in Bulk Ports: Data sets and results. Mendeley Data, v2 (2020). http://dx.doi.org/10.17632/bzmgbjttv3.2

Blockchain-Based Secured Collaborative Model for Supply Chain Resource Sharing and Visibility

Tarun Kumar Agrawal[1(✉)] [ID], Ravi Kalaiarasan[1,2] [ID], and Magnus Wiktorsson[1] [ID]

[1] Department of Sustainable Production Development, KTH Royal Institute of Technology, Södertälje, Sweden
tkag@kth.se
[2] Scania CV AB, Södertälje, Sweden

Abstract. Globalization, escalating competition, and demand for sustainable practices have required supply chain and production managers to consider various capabilities and value creation strategies for the customers. Rapid technological advancement in the current production environment calls for integrative and collaborative efforts for effective resource utilization and better visibility to gain competitive advantages. However, privacy risks and trust have always been a significant barrier for organizations' efforts towards supply chain integration. Supply chain stakeholders fear these collaborate practices might weaken their bargaining power, accelerate risk of data manipulation and result in loss of information advantages. Addressing these issues, the study proposes a Blockchain-based collaborative model for production visibility and resource sharing. It demonstrates the framework for stakeholders' interaction over a central procurement system backed with blockchain technology. The study further lays down the notion of production capacity backed smart contract rules. These smart contracts will run on the proposed blockchain network to reduce the possibilities of fraudulent transactions and capacity overbooking- leading to illegitimate subcontracting. The overall network will stimulate visibility and develop a technology-based trust among partners which ensuring sustainability by effective utilization of resource.

Keywords: Blockchain · Resource sharing · Supply chain collaboration · Visibility

1 Introduction: Supply Chain Collaboration

Recent studies highlight the importance and demand for sustainable initiatives in the production and supply chain environment [1]. Constant pressure from customers, governments, and stakeholders' groups has stimulated firms to efficiently incorporate sustainability issues into their strategic and operational planning [2]. Nevertheless, these initiatives can only lead to sustainable supply and production when all the individual firms in the supply network collaborate and integrate to possess or develop the necessary resources as requisites for realizing sustainable production and supply

© IFIP International Federation for Information Processing 2020
Published by Springer Nature Switzerland AG 2020
B. Lalic et al. (Eds.): APMS 2020, IFIP AICT 591, pp. 259–266, 2020.
https://doi.org/10.1007/978-3-030-57993-7_30

chain. In this way, they can facilitate environmentally and ethically sound organizational and supply chain behaviors [1–3].

Numerous studies in the past have advocated the benefits of collaborative alliances and inter-organizational resource sharing [3, 4]. Collaboration has multiple advantage: ranging from network expansion to better insights and visibility in production units, from accessing new talent, skills/techniques and processes to potentially increased productivity, better utilization of resources, faster growth and increased global reach [2, 3]. These collaborations can include both material flow and information flow. Wherein information flow includes not only the process, and product transformation data but also the knowledge creation and transfer among organizations in the forms of new products, processes and technology development [2, 3].

While it is true that many managers have attempted to form collaborative alliances with other partner organizations, such strategies are tough to implement. Usually, they fail as implementation and management of an alliance is much harder than the decision to collaborate [5]. It is found that building consensus among organizations is often difficult. As collaboration involves material and information flow, partner organizations often do not trust each other and perceive a strong risk of losing strategic/competitive advantage. They believe information sharing among partners can lead to risk of manipulated data, loss of know-how and expertise, weakening of bargaining power and information disadvantage [5]. At the same time, collaboration leads to a revelation of the whole supply network and easier tracing of unethical practices, which happens to be a major concern for dishonest partners.

In fact, lack of collaboration among partners has made the supply chain quite unsustainable. There is lack of transparency in supply chain, ineffective utilization of resources, issues of capacity overbooking - leading to illegitimate subcontracting and inefficient production planning and synchronization. Hence, there is a need for further development of digital collaborative platforms that can facilitate information sharing and develop mutual trust among partners without risking their competitive and information advantage.

In this direction, the paper proposes blockchain as a potential technology that can address the above challenges. Several studies in the past have advocated blockchain application for supply chain digitalization, traceability and visibility enhancement, improving forecasting, demand based supply planning, fraud prevention, reducing negative impact on environment [6–8]. Nevertheless, [9] identifies blockchain for supply chain integration as a potential field lacking substantial research contribution. Besides, it is important to consider and examine the blockchain operations based on its applications in supply chain requirements [10]. Therefore, based on literature and understanding of blockchain technology, the study introduces a work-in-progress solution contributing to improve supply chain collaboration at operational level. It follows a pearl growth search strategy to explore literature (initiating from few sources to identify and understand appropriate terminologies that could be used in search queries) [11]. Thereafter, the paper primarily focuses on information flow between actors and illustrates a blockchain-based collaborative network that can ensure privacy of individual partners, promote visibility in the network and ultimately develop a technology-based trust among partners. Finally, smart contract rules for the proposed system have been explained that can lead to efficient resource sharing and reduce fraudulent transactions. The potential effects and consequence of the proposed solution are explained in the discussion section followed by conclusions and future research areas.

2 Proposed Collaborate Network Platform

Based on literature, the proposed collaborate platform is presented by introducing general aspects on blockchain technology, followed by an example where two key features are described: Supply chain partner integration and Capacity based smart contract.

2.1 Blockchain Technology

Blockchain is defined as:

A shared, immutable ledger that facilitates the process of recording transactions and tracking assets in a business network. An asset can be tangible (a house, a car, cash, land) or intangible (intellectual property, patents, copyrights, branding). Virtually anything of value can be tracked and traded on a blockchain network, reducing risk and cutting costs for all involved [12].

Blockchain can be public (open to anyone and everyone with access to internet [12]. Anyone can join the network and perform transactions) and private (only authorized participants can join the network and their rights are defined by network accessibility rules) [13]. Due to text limitation, the paper explains four key features of blockchain technology that makes it unique and secure. These features play a vital role in the proposed collaborative framework. Subsequently, a detailed overview of the technology and its application in logistics and manufacturing industry can be found in [14–17].

First is distributed network, which makes it ideal for multi-tier supply chain applications where the partners are usually located at large geographical distances with limited amount of trust. It encourages partners with differences in governance rule to share essential information on a shared platform. Second, smart contract, which contains transaction rules agreed among partners, written and stored as computer programs over the network. It ensures validity of transaction and trust that that everyone is playing fairly. Third, data immutability, which is achieved through cryptographic function and block linking mechanism. It ensures traceability and accountability of each transaction. Fourth, is consensus, which is the process of reaching an (automatic) agreement among all the involved partners for each transaction by verifying it with each individual copy of shared ledger. It helps in reducing fraudulent and inaccurate transactions and overcome the Byzantine fault problem [12, 13, 18].

2.2 Blockchain-Based Collaborative Model: Supply Chain Partner Integration

For effective communication, a simplified example of supply chain of two suppliers (A and B) and one buyer (focal firm) the framework explains partner interactions over the network. Buyer is downstream manufacturing unit in the supply chain that procures the same kind of intermediate products from supplier A and B. It can be noted that the described network can be complicated with certain modifications and following similar network rules to fit in real case examples and/or more complex supply chain networks. Production at buyer site is highly dependent on flow of intermediate products from suppliers. In usual situations, both suppliers compete to secure more orders to keep their production running and gain more profit. This leads to over-booking of capacity, irregular utilization of resources and illegitimate subcontracting. Additional, sharing information lead to security and privacy issue.

Hence, in the proposed framework, as shown in Fig. 1, the individual suppliers can be connected over different channels over a same blockchain network managed by a focal firm, in this example, the buyer. Each channel is a subnet/subnetwork of the global blockchain network, having their separate smart contract and a shared ledger that runs transaction rules as agreement between buyer and respective supplier. Individual channels also have their own-shared ledger to recode different transactions between the buyer and supplier and ensure traceability and visibility. However, on the global network scale, each channel is connected to central procurement unit that only records and maintains shareable real-time capacity data. Thus, the central procurement unit ledger can be referred for order procurement to ensure fair and efficient utilization of resources. It can be further observed from Fig. 1 that each production unit (buyer and suppliers) has an internal traceability system that is connected with sensors at each work station, tracking and recording material flow at each stage of the production system. This enables better visibility within the production unit and is helpful to identify bottleneck. Nevertheless, as shown, and if administered properly, it is not necessary to link each of these data collection points directly to a blockchain network. Direct linking can make the network cumbersome.

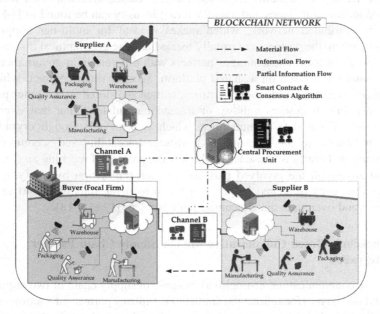

Fig. 1. A simple illustration of supply chain partners' (one focal firm as buyer and two suppliers) interactions over a blockchain-based collaborative network.

2.3 Blockchain-Based Collaborative Model: Capacity Based Smart Contract

A capacity-based smart contact would be an apt solution to prevent fraudulent transactions and overbooking of capacity in the proposed collaborative model. The shared ledger on the central procurement unit will connect real-time data of the capacity of individual supplier from individual channels. These real-time data, for instance, could include information related to number of operational machine, shift hours, product SAM, line efficiency, machine downtime, operators' attendance etc. Even factors related to multi criteria decisions including factors of the triple bottom line to reach the sustainability of the supply chain. In a situation of another new demand from the buyer, it will verify and distribute order according to the available resources as shown in Fig. 2.

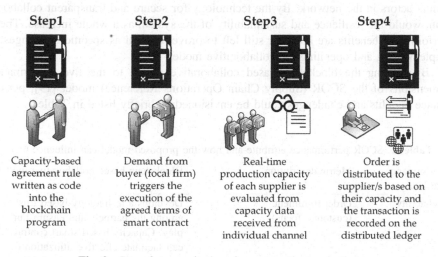

Step1	Step2	Step3	Step4
Capacity-based agreement rule written as code into the blockchain program	Demand from buyer (focal firm) triggers the execution of the agreed terms of smart contract	Real-time production capacity of each supplier is evaluated from capacity data received from individual channel	Order is distributed to the supplier/s based on their capacity and the transaction is recorded on the distributed ledger

Fig. 2. Steps for capacity-based smart contract execution

3 Discussion

3.1 Characteristics of the Blockchain-Based Collaborative Model

The proposed collaborative model utilizes the four key features of Blockchain technology, the distributed network, smart contract, data immutability and consensus. The distributed network and capacity based smart contract is explained in the previous sections. Data immutability is ensured by the cryptographic SHA function, Merkle tree and linking the chain of hashes with the newly formed block, as in case of bitcoin. A detail about the explanation about the data immutability feature can be found in [12, 13]. As the proposed model is a permissioned network, actors can only access the network based on their accessibility condition and consensus algorithm need not to be as complex as the proof-of-work in case of bitcoin. Proof-of-stake or proof-of-elapsed time can be used to test and achieve consensus among the actors. Additionally, being a permissioned network, not all actors can perform all type of task on the blockchain. For instance, an actor with read only permission can only access the distributed ledger to check the transactions, whereas an actor with write permission can read as well as record a transaction on the ledger. Similarly, only limited actors will have the permission to actually perform transactions on the blockchain. This characteristic makes the system secure but also eliminates the possibility of unwanted transactions in a distributed network.

3.2   Potential Effects of the Blockchain-Based Collaborative Model

The hypothesis behind the proposed blockchain based collaborative model is that the distributed database technology for secure data responds well to the increasing complexity of global supply chains, with high requirements on security, privacy and trust amongst actors, while still enabling high visibility and resource utilization for individual actors in the network. By the technology for secure and transparent collaboration, would the resilience and sustainability of the system as a whole increase. These performance benefits are however still left to prove, as well as specific challenges in implementing and operating the collaborative model.

By relating the blockchain-based collaborative model to the five performance dimensions of the SCOR (Supply Chain Operations Reference) model [19], performance benefits and challenges could be envisioned as briefly listed in Table 1.

Table 1. SCOR performance attribute and how the proposed model can influence them

Performance attribute	Metric description	Blockchain-based collaborative model
Reliability	Order fulfilment. (customer focus)	Develops a technology-based trust among the partners and ensure fair play. Capacity based smart contract can facilitate effective utilization of resources for on-time order fulfilment
Responsiveness	Order fulfilment cycle time. (customer focus)	Optimum order allocation based on real time capacity knowledge can ensure quick response and shorter order fulfilment cycle
Agility	Upstream adaptability. Downstream adaptability. Value-at-Risk. (customer focus)	Secured information sharing mechanism can enhance supply chain visibility, which facilitate swift adaptability in unforeseen situations
Cost	Total SCM costs. Cost of goods sold	Effective resource utilization reduces production cost
Asset Management Efficiency	Cash-to-cash cycle time. Return on fixed assets. Return on working capital. (internal focus)	Collaboration and resource sharing helps in effective utilization of available assets and working capital (resources). Thus, helpful to attain return on investment

4   Conclusions

Taking an example of buyer and suppliers' interaction, the paper explains a blockchain-based secured collaborative model for visibility and resource sharing. A network framework using channel/subnet has been demonstrated that can ensure security and at the same time privacy, in the blockchain network. Further, a capacity-based smart contract has been proposed that can ensure efficient utilization of resources and prevent fraudulent transactions. Thus assuring a technology-based trust among the partners in a multi-tier supply chain. The proposed model ensure effective utilization of resources, ensuring economical sustainability. It can be noted that this study is work-in-progress and in future works, the model will be complicated to include other stages of supply chain. Further, a discussion with companies could enable a first step towards validation of the still theoretical model. The proposed smart contract would be developed on an example blockchain network to test with a simulated situation of the demonstrated framework. Followed by development of a consensus algorithms that would facilitate validation and broadcasting of transactions on blockchain. Beside, further research can be carried out to identify key factors that can influence the collaborative models (including those related with social and environmental sustainability), which, can be input for the smart contract and useful for multi criteria decision making for optimum order distribution. Moreover, as data sharing among partners is a major concern due to privacy issues; therefore, the data components and their accessibility and visibility to the specific actors would be identified and segregated. Further, for coherent and seamless data communication and sharing data nomenclature would be defined.

Acknowledgement. We gratefully acknowledge the funding from Produktion2030 and Vinnova for this research, as part of the research project Production Logistic Visibility (LOVIS).

References

1. Grzybowska, K., Awasthi, A.: Literature review on sustainable logistics and sustainable production for industry 4.0. In: Grzybowska, K., Awasthi, A., Sawhney, R. (eds.) Sustainable Logistics and Production in Industry 4.0: New Opportunities and Challenges, pp. 1–18. Springer International Publishing, Cham (2020)
2. Chen, L., Zhao, X., Tang, O., Price, L., Zhang, S., Zhu, W.: Supply chain collaboration for sustainability: a literature review and future research agenda. Int. J. Prod. Econ. **194**, 73–87 (2017)
3. Soosay, C.A., Hyland, P.: A decade of supply chain collaboration and directions for future research. Supply Chain Manag. Int. J. **20**, 613–630 (2015)
4. Duong, L.N.K., Chong, J.: Supply chain collaboration in the presence of disruptions: a literature review. Int. J. Prod. Res. **58**(11), 1–20 (2020)
5. Eurich, M., Oertel, N., Boutellier, R.: The impact of perceived privacy risks on organizations' willingness to share item-level event data across the supply chain. Electron. Commer. Res. **10**, 423–440 (2010)
6. Korpela, K., Hallikas, J., Dahlberg, T.: Digital supply chain transformation toward blockchain integration. In: The Digital Supply Chain of the Future: Technologies, Applications and Business Models Minitrack, Waikoloa, HI (2017)

7. Dujak, D., Sajter, D.: Blockchain applications in supply chain. In: Kawa, A., Maryniak, A. (eds.) SMART Supply Network, pp. 21–46. Springer International Publishing, Cham (2019)

8. Saberi, S., Kouhizadeh, M., Sarkis, J., Shen, L.: Blockchain technology and its relationships to sustainable supply chain management. Int. J. Prod. Res. **57**(7), 1–19 (2018)

9. Queiroz, M.M., Fosso Wamba, S.: Blockchain adoption challenges in supply chain: an empirical investigation of the main drivers in India and the USA. Int. J. Inf. Manag. **46**, 70–82 (2019)

10. Umeh, J.: Blockchain double bubble or double trouble? ITNOW **58**, 58–61 (2016)

11. Rowley, J., Slack, F.: Conducting a literature review. Manag. Res. News **27**, 31–39 (2004)

12. Gupta, M.: Blockchain for Dummies. John Wiley & Sons, Incorporated, Hoboken (2018)

13. Swan, M.: Blockchain: Blueprint for a New Economy. O'Reilly Media, Inc., California (2015)

14. Venkatesh, V.G., Kang, K., Wang, B., Zhong, R.Y., Zhang, A.: System architecture for blockchain based transparency of supply chain social sustainability. Robot. Comput. Integr. Manuf. **63**, 101896 (2020)

15. Francisco, K., Swanson, D.: The supply chain has no clothes: technology adoption of blockchain for supply chain transparency. Logistics **2**, 2 (2018)

16. Lee, J., Lee, J., Azamfar, M., Singh, J.: A blockchain enabled cyber-physical system architecture for industry 4.0 manufacturing systems. Manuf. Lett. **20**, 34–39 (2019)

17. Liu, X.L., Wang, W.M., Guo, H., Barenji, A.V., Li, Z., Huang, G.Q.: Industrial blockchain based framework for product lifecycle management in industry 4.0. Robot. Comput. Integr. Manuf. **63**, 101897 (2020)

18. Abeyratne, S.A., Monfared, R.: Blockchain ready manufacturing supply chain using distributed ledger. Int. J. Res. Eng. Technol. **5**(9), 1–10 (2016)

19. SCOR 12.0 | New SCOR Model for the Modern Supply Chain | APICS. http://www.apics.org/apics-for-business/frameworks/scor12. Accessed 31 May 2020

Gripper Types and Components in Robotic Bin Picking

Patrik Fager[1(✉)], Stefano Rossi[2], Robin Hanson[1], Lars Medbo[1],
Omkar Salunkhe[1], Mats I. Johansson[1], and Åsa Fast-Berglund[1]

[1] Chalmers University of Technology, Gothenburg, Sweden
fagerp@chalmers.se
[2] University of Padova, Vicenza, Italy

Abstract. While automation is increasingly applied in production processes, it is still rarely used for the core picking activity in kitting and order picking. As picking activities often involves a large number of stock-keeping units (SKUs) with different characteristics, what gripper to use is a central aspect when robotics is applied. The aim of this paper is to improve the understanding of the relationship between gripper types and component characteristics in robotic applications for preparation of component kits. The aim is addressed by means of an experiment in a laboratory setting where a two-finger gripper and a vacuum-gripper are applied for grasping a variety of components in a kit preparation process. The two gripper types are studied with respect to important component characteristics for their suitability, and how the two gripper types compare from an efficiency standpoint. The paper's findings are useful for practitioners when introducing robotic bin picking. The paper also makes an important contribution to academia in studying the effects of robot picking applications empirically, laying grounds for focused future studies within this area.

Keywords: Kit preparation · Robot grippers · Order picking

1 Introduction and Aim of the Study

In mixed-model assembly settings, where there is a large number of stock-keeping units (SKUs) that need to be handled, picking activities are often performed in the materials supply. For component kitting, in which components are picked and placed into kits and each kit supports one or more assembly operations for one product, the use of robotic picking could be an option for performing these processes, potentially enabling a lowered operating cost as well as a high reliability, as suggested by [1]. However, in component kitting for mixed-model assembly, components are often heterogeneous, differing in terms of, e.g., size, shape, weight and material. It is therefore difficult to find a robot gripper that has sufficient flexibility to achieve efficient and reliable picking for all components, which has been pointed out by [1]. Accordingly, recent studies within the industry still mostly report on manual component kitting in the materials supply to assembly [4].

© IFIP International Federation for Information Processing 2020
Published by Springer Nature Switzerland AG 2020
B. Lalic et al. (Eds.): APMS 2020, IFIP AICT 591, pp. 267–274, 2020.
https://doi.org/10.1007/978-3-030-57993-7_31

There exist several types of grippers. According to [5], grippers can be based on three different actuating principles: mechanical, vacuum or magnetic, and universal. It is possible to change grippers between different picks, thus utilising the advantages of the different grippers, even though this can be time consuming and may accordingly reduce the capacity of the picking operation. Another option is to allocate only certain SKUs to robotic picking while other components are still being picked by a human.

The use of robot grippers has been addressed in research. Topics that have been dealt with include vision-supported bin picking [8] and robot agility architecture [1, 6] and [3] recognise the complexity of picking heterogenous components in component kitting and study the division of labour between robot and human pickers in this context. The relationship between gripper types and component characteristics has received a fair amount of attention within literature dealing with robot applications in manufacturing settings. [2] suggests design guidelines for various types of grippers that in part consider component characteristics, while [9] point out component character-istics as central when selecting gripper for assembly applications. [7] focus on assembly operations, including picking of components, and propose a methodology for the division of labour between human and robot for such contexts. Materials handling in assembly operations share similarities with component kitting, but the latter also imposes unique requirements with respect to robotic picking. In component kitting, picking and placing of components are central activities which are repeated for all components of a kit and the applicability of knowledge from assembly operations is not obvious. To design processes for component kitting that effectively utilise robotic support, it is of central importance to understand which type of gripper, if any, fits which component characteristics, and which option should be used when multiple options appear feasible. The current paper expands on the research by [7] in a com-ponent kitting context, and aims to improve the understanding of the relationship between gripper types and component characteristics in order to improve setup and processing times for component kitting.

This aim is addressed by means of a laboratory experiment where components of varying characteristics are kitted by means of robotic grippers. Here, it is important that the grippers considered in the study can grasp components with characteristics that often appear in kit preparation. Based on the reviewed literature, the two gripper types two-finger servo-electric gripper and a vacuum gripper are focused upon in the paper. This is because 1) they are based on two principally different actuating principles [7], and 2) they have frequently been considered in theoretical studies dealing with robotic kit preparation (e.g. [1, 3]).

The experiment is set up to answer two research questions that both address the relationship between gripper types and component characteristics in kit preparation. As noted above, it is important when dealing with robotic kit preparation to know for which component characteristics different gripper types are suitable to use. A first question is therefore expressed as: *which component characteristics are important for graspability with a two-finger servo-electric gripper and a vacuum gripper, respec-tively, in components kit preparation?*

When a component can be grasped by several types of grippers, it necessary to know which gripper type should be used, and whether it is worthwhile from an effi-ciency standpoint to perform a tool change. A second research question can be expressed as follows: *for components with characteristics that are suitable both for a two-finger servo-electric and a vacuum-gripper, which gripper type should be used?*

The remainder of the paper is structured as follows. Section 2 presents the experimental settings and research method. Section 3 presents the results and an analysis of the results. Finally, Sect. 4 presents a discussion of the paper's findings and conclusions.

2 Experimental Settings

The research questions that were identified as important with respect to the paper's aim, as presented above, were used as basis for the design of an experiment. As explained in the introduction, the paper considers two gripper types: a two-finger servo-electric gripper and a vacuum gripper.

In terms of components, the component characteristics shown in Table 1 were derived from previous studies on the topic (e.g. [5, 7]). Components were selected from a set of automotive components, aiming to establish variability with respect to the component characteristics in Table 1. The factor levels in Table 1 were determined based on the variability with respect to the component characteristics among the selected components. In total, 18 components were selected for the experiment, ranging from bolts and nuts to rear-view mirror caps and bearings. Each component was classified according to the component characteristics in Table 1. An overview of the component selection is shown in Table 2.

A three-level shelf was created to simulate storage racks in an industrial kit preparation process, and a UR10 robot arm was placed in front of the shelf. The shelf was built in proportion with the UR-10 robot arm, and the components to pick were put into plastic boxes stored on the shelf, see Fig. 1.

The experiment was carried out in two stages relating to the research questions. In the first stage, grasping attempts were made with the two gripper types for the components shown in Table 2.

The grasping attempts were made at various resting positions (lying self-supported on a flat surface) of each component. If the component was possible to grasp in at least one resting position, the grasping activity was considered successful and noted as a 'Success'. If the component could not be grasped in any resting position, the gripping activity was considered unsuccessful and noted as 'Fail'. Grasping attempts were performed with both grippers for 9 components, while grasping attempts of 4 components were made only with the two-finger gripper, and for 5 components only with the vacuum gripper. That is, for 9 of the components it was deemed obvious that one of the gripper types could not be used, which were denoted as "Not tested". The grasping attempts that were performed for each gripper individually were performed in order to clarify the results from the grasping attempts that were made with both grippers.

In the second stage, addressing the second research question, the components suitable to kit with either a two-finger gripper or a vacuum gripper, as determined from the first stage, were compared in terms of the time required to grasp and place components in the kit package with the two different gripper types.

Table 1. Factor levels among the component characteristics.

Name	Description	Level 1	Level 2	Level 3
F1: Size	Longest straight line L through the component [mm]	$L < 20$	$20 < L < 70$	$L > 70$
F2: Weight	Weight W of the component [kg]	$W < 0.1$	$0.1 < W < 1$	$W > 1$
F3: Regularity	Refers to whether all components of the same type have the same shape, e.g. metal plates (regular) or wires (irregular)	Irregular	Regular	
F4: Flatness	Refers to the diameter of the largest planar surface D on the component's surface relative to the diameter of a vacuum gripper d_{vac}	$D < d_{vac}$	$d_{vac} < D < 2d_{vac}$	$D > 2d_{vac}$
F5: Fullness	Refers to whether the component has holes (hollow) or not (full) that can help grasping	Hollow	Full	
F6: Stiffness	Refers to how easily the component deforms when compressed	Deformable	Stiff	

Table 2. The 18 components considered and their characteristics in terms of the six factors of Table 1.

No.	Description	F1	F2	F3	F4	F5	F6
1	Thick sheet-metal plate	3	3	2	2	1	2
2	Plastic seal	3	1	1	2	1	1
3	Bent metal bracket	2	3	2	2	2	2
4	Angled girder	2	2	2	2	2	2
5	Plastic cabin-interior detail	2	1	2	1	2	2
6	Plastic pipe	3	1	2	3	1	2
7	Screw	1	1	2	1	2	2
8	Towing hook cap	2	1	2	2	1	1
9	Plastic electric connector box	2	1	2	3	2	2
10	Plastic bracket	3	2	2	1	2	2
11	Large bearing	3	3	1	3	2	2
12	Sheet-metal bracket	3	2	1	1	2	2
13	Wide hose half-clamp	2	1	2	2	2	2
14	Bent plastic pipe	2	1	2	2	2	2
15	Bolted plate	1	1	2	3	2	2
16	Hose clamp	3	1	2	3	1	2
17	Sheet-metal cover	3	2	2	3	2	2
18	Rear-view mirror cap	3	1	2	3	1	2

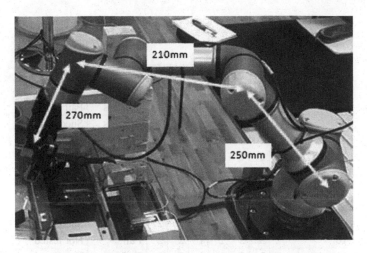

Fig. 1. The UR10 robot-arm when picking components from the shelf.

3 Results and Analysis

3.1 Suitable Gripper Type Given Component Characteristics

The outcome of the first stage of the experiment is shown in Table 3 for each of the two gripper types.

Vacuum-Gripper and Important Component Characteristics: Looking at the suitable component characteristics for a vacuum-gripper in Table 3, it seems that components that have a large- or medium-sized planar surface, and a low to moderate weight, are suitable. This is represented by, for example, component number 2 (plastic seal), 5 (plastic cabin-interior detail), 6 (plastic pipe), 8 (towing hook cap), 9 (plastic electric connector box), and 13 (wide hose half-clamp). For components with higher weight, similar conditions seem to apply, although it is crucial that there is a planar surface available near the component's centre of gravity, as with component number 3 (bent metal bracket).

From Table 3, the vacuum gripper appears not to be suitable with components of small size or irregular shape, thereby displaying small planar surfaces to grip. This is represented by, for example, component number 7 (screw), 10 (plastic bracket), 12 (sheet-metal bracket), and 14 (bent plastic pipe). Furthermore, with components 1 (thick sheet-metal plate) and 4 (angled girder), which both have planar surfaces for the vacuum-gripper to grip, these cannot be grasped successfully owing to their relatively high weight and the fact that there is no planar surface available near their centre of gravity.

Finger-Gripper and Important Component Characteristics: From Table 3, it can be seen that the two-finger gripper appear suitable with a multitude of component characteristics. Overall, most components with a thickness smaller than the maximal gap opening of the gripper could be grasped successfully.

Table 3. Gripping outcomes for the two gripper types.

Component no.	Component characteristics						Gripping outcome	
	F1	F2	F3	F4	F5	F6	Vacuum	Two-finger
1	3	3	2	2	1	2	Fail	Fail
2	3	1	1	2	1	1	Success	Fail
3	2	3	2	2	2	2	Success	Success
4	2	2	2	2	2	2	Fail	Success
5	2	1	2	1	2	2	Success	Success
6	3	1	2	3	1	2	Success	Success
7	1	1	2	1	2	2	Fail	Success
8	2	1	2	2	1	1	Success	Success
9	2	1	2	3	2	2	Success	Success
10	3	2	2	1	2	2	Fail	Not tested
11	3	3	1	3	2	2	Fail	Not tested
12	3	2	1	1	2	2	Fail	Not tested
13	2	1	2	2	2	2	Success	Not tested
14	2	1	2	2	2	2	Fail	Not tested
15	1	1	2	3	2	2	Not tested	Success
16	3	1	2	3	1	2	Not tested	Success
17	3	2	2	3	2	2	Not tested	Success
18	3	1	2	3	1	2	Not tested	Fail

As shown in Table 3, the two-finger gripper was unable to grasp components that had a larger size than the maximum grip opening, and for which it was not possible to enter a hole or cavity, such as with component number 18 (rear-view mirror cap). The two-finger gripper could also not grasp component number 1 (thick sheet-metal plate) due to its high weight and slippery surface generating too little friction to grip the component. Furthermore, as with component number 2 (plastic seal), the component deformed extensively when gripped and was not possible to grip firmly without damaging.

3.2   Time Requirement for Different Grippers with the Same Components

In the second stage of the experiment, addressing the second guiding question, the kitting activity time is considered with respect to components that could be gripped by either a two-finger gripper or a vacuum-gripper. The results are shown in Table 4.

As shown in Table 4, the vacuum gripper generally requires less time to kit a component when compared with a two-finger gripper. This is because a two-finger gripper often needs some positioning in order to access the gripping points on a component. On the contrary with a vacuum-gripper, as long as there is a gripping point exposed when a component is at rest, there is a straight line towards the gripping point.

Table 4. Time required for picking the same components with two gripper types.

Gripper type	Time to grasp [s/component]	Time to place [s/component]	Time to kit [s/component]
Two-finger	3.4 ± 0.25	3.48 ± 0.28	18.4 ± 0.65
Vacuum	1.93 ± 0.1	2.37 ± 0.2	14.2 ± 0.27

4 Discussion and Conclusions

The paper has addressed typical issues in designing and planning of robot applications for preparation of component kits. The findings contribute to an understanding of problems related to choice of gripper type in robotic kitting of components, but illuminate also choice between robotic and manual kitting of components. The findings are important as working conditions in picking systems make automation is highly desirable.

In the experiment, two types of grippers were tested: vacuum grippers and servo-electric two-finger grippers. The results show that the two-finger gripper is more versatile with respect to variable component characteristics compared to a vacuum gripper. Two-finger grippers can be used with most of the considered component characteristics, as long as the gap between the fingers is large enough and the component is stiff enough.

Vacuum-grippers are suitable for light components that have planar surfaces larger than the vacuum-gripper's opening. Heavier components with planar surfaces can also be gripped, but the planar surface must then be near the component's centre of gravity.

With components that can be gripped by either a two-finger gripper or a vacuum gripper, the experiment results demonstrated that the vacuum-gripper generally is the faster alternative. This is important during the kit preparation work cycle, as it can be worthwhile to change gripper when the faster alternative is applicable. The time saved from the higher gripping efficiency must, of course, be weighed against the additional time required to perform a tool change.

Accordingly, the results related to the fast vacuum gripper and the flexible two-finger gripper provide input to planning of kit preparation activities. Here, a conscious choice of the sequence by which components are kitted can decrease the time required to prepare kits. However, the kit would need to be structured with separate space for each component in order for the sequence to be freely chosen. With unstructured kits, the assemblers' consumption sequence of components would instead control the sequence.

The components considered in the experiment represent typical components used in assembly of automotive products. The paper shows that all components, in that type of industry, are not feasible for robot picking with the two gripper types considered. In design of kit preparation processes where both manual and robotic picking will be applied, the findings can contribute to better allocation of components between an operator and a robot.

The current paper has presented an experimental analysis of the relationship between gripper types and components in component kitting. The results highlight important aspects of this relationship that are useful for effectively implementing robotic picking in a component kitting context. Future studies should account for the relationship also from a statistical standpoint, potentially by use of a full-factorial experimental approach. Here, the findings of the current paper would constitute a useful starting point.

The experiment show that the orientation of the component is essential for the grippers being able to pick the component. In a future real picking system, there is a need to find ways to control, or to obtain information about, the orientation of components. Possible solutions may include choice of component packages from suppliers, handling of component packages by robots and their associated grippers, and involvement of operators.

References

1. Boudella, M.A., Sahin, E., Dallery, Y.: Kitting optimisation in Just-in-Time mixed-model assembly lines: assigning parts to pickers in a hybrid robot–operator kitting system. Int. J. Prod. Res. **56**(16), 5475–5494 (2018)
2. Causey, G.C., Quinn, R.D.: Gripper design guidelines for modular manufacturing. In: Proceedings of 1998 IEEE International Conference on Robotics and Automation (Cat. No. 98CH36146), vol. 2, pp. 1453–1458 (1998)
3. Fager, P., Calzavara, M., Sgarbossa, F.: Modelling time efficiency of cobot-supported kit preparation. Int. J. Adv. Manuf. Technol. **106**(5), 2227–2241 (2019)
4. Hanson, R., Medbo, L.: Man-hour efficiency of manual kit preparation in the materials supply to mass-customised assembly. Int. J. Prod. Res. **57**(11), 3735–3747 (2019)
5. Hugo, P.O.: Industrial grippers: state-of-the-art and main design characteristics. In: Carbone, G. (ed.) Grasping in Robotics. Springer, London (2013)
6. Kootbally, Z., Schlenoff, C., Antonishek, B., Proctor, F., Kramer, T., Harrison, W., Downs, A., Gupta, S.: Enabling robot agility in manufacturing kitting applications. Integr. Comput. Aided Eng. **25**, 193–212 (2018)
7. Malik, A.A., Bilberg, A.: Complexity-based task allocation in human-robot collaborative assembly. Ind. Robot. **46**(4), 471–480 (2019)
8. Martinez, C., Boca, R., Zhang, B., Chen, H., Nidamarthi, S.: Automated bin picking system for randomly located industrial parts. In: Proceedings of the 2015 IEEE International Conference on Technologies for Practical Robot Applications (TePRA), Woburn, USA, 11–15 May 2015 (2015)
9. Pham, D.T., Yeo, S.H.: Strategies for gripper design and selection in robotic assembly. Int. J. Prod. Res. **29**(2), 303–316 (1991)

A Stochastic Model for a Two-Level Disassembly Lot-Sizing Problem Under Random Lead Time

Ilhem Slama[1], Oussama Ben-Ammar[2], Alexandre Dolgui[1(✉)], and Faouzi Masmoudi[3]

[1] IMT Atlantique, LS2N-CNRS, La Chantrerie, 4 Rue Alfred Kastler, B.P. 20722, 44307 Nantes, France
{ilhem.slama,alexandre.dolgui}@imt-atlantique.fr

[2] Department of Manufacturing Sciences and Logistics, Mines Saint-Etienne, University Clermont Auvergne, CNRS, UMR 6158, LIMOS CMP, Gardanne, France
oussama.ben-ammar@emse.fr

[3] Engineering School of Sfax, Laboratory of Mechanic, Modeling and Production (LA2MP), University of Sfax, Sfax, Tunisia
masmoudi.fawzi@gmail.com

Abstract. The purpose of this research is to propose an optimization method for the stochastic disassembly lot-sizing problem under uncertainty of lead time. One type of end-of-life (EoL) product is disassembled to satisfy a dynamic and known demand of items over a planning horizon. The tactical problem is considered as a random optimization problem in order to minimize the expected total cost. A sample average approximation (SAA) approach, is developed to model the studied random optimization problem and minimize the average total cost. The effectiveness of the solution approach has successfully tested and proved.

Keywords: Disassembly lot-sizing · Random lead time · Stochastic programming · Monte Carlo simulation

1 Introduction

Managing uncertainty is becoming one of the most important challenge in optimizing the disassembly process. Uncertainty leads to several difficulties in production planning and inventory management. The sources of uncertainty are diverse and can be found at several levels of the disassembly process: variability of demand, probabilistic recovery rates of items, delivery times, quality problems, etc. In this paper we consider the situation where demand on items/parts must be satisfied from the disassembly of EoL products. According to the classification proposed by [2], the studied problem enters into the classification of disassembly lot sizing problem (DLS) problem that consists in finding when and how much EoL products to disassemble to meet demand for the items while minimizing the costs associated with the disassembly system.

© IFIP International Federation for Information Processing 2020
Published by Springer Nature Switzerland AG 2020
B. Lalic et al. (Eds.): APMS 2020, IFIP AICT 591, pp. 275–283, 2020.
https://doi.org/10.1007/978-3-030-57993-7_32

Without trying to do an exhaustive review of the literature, we highlight the works on DLS problem under uncertainty. The stochastic literature review can be split into four different cases: (i) the uncertainty of demand [1, 5], (ii) the uncertainty of disassembly yield (see for example the paper of [3, 4]), (iii) the uncertainty of yield and demand [7] and (iv) the uncertainty of disassembly lead time (DLT) [9, 10]. This latter can be defined as the time difference between placing a disassembly order and receiving the disassembled items. The DLT is crucial parameter in disassembly planning. However, their variability strongly affect the disassembly system efficiency and it can affect the customer orders with a random availability of disassembled items.

Managing disassembly operation under uncertainty of DLT is very challenging in practice. Indeed, when an EOL product is disassembled, it is fundamental to ensure that it is the right model to be supplied under uncertain DLT in order to manage disassembly and delivery process. In order to position our research in the existing literature, we will only review in detail the previous works on the stochastic DLS problem under uncertainty of DLT. Only two papers populated this category. The paper in [9] is the first to treat this problem type. The case of two-level disassembly system is studied under unlimited disassembly capacity. The problem is formulated as a minimization problem and then converted to a Monte Carlo-mixed integer programming model. The Model is used to determine the optimal quantity for EoL products in order to minimize the average total cost over the planning horizon. Recently, [10] proposed a generalization of the discrete Newsboy formulae to find the optimal release date when the disassembly lead time of the EoL product is random variable. This study deals with a single-period disassembly to-order problem with known and fixed demand for components, when the disassembly capacity is unlimited.

To close to real industrial planning approach, the capacity restriction on disassembly resources is an important consideration. As for approach, a sample average formulation is necessary to approximate the expected objective value. This paper is a continuation of our previous preliminary work [9]. The contributions of this study are as follow:

1. The problem is extended to a capacitated disassembly lot sizing (CDLS) problem and formulated as a minimization problem and converted to a Monte Carlo-Mixed-Integer Programming model (MC-MIP);
2. The sample average approximation algorithm based on Monte Carlo (MC) optimization approach is proposed.

In this article, we study the case of a two-level disassembly system with a lot-sizing policy. The disassembled item requests are known and must be delivered on predefined delivery dates. To meet the items requirements, a quantity of EoL product Zt is ordered at the period t. Once the disassembly order is released, a random real Lt is found in that period and the disassembled items are received at period $t' = t + L_t$. Note that, a setup cost is generated if any disassembly operation is released in period t. The DLT at each period are independent random discrete variables with known probability distributions and varying between L− and L+ . The randomness of the lead time is a classic problem for industrial companies. If the date of recovery of an item during the disassembly of the EoL product is lower than its planned delivery time, this item will be stored until this date. This situation usually occur in companies and generates holding costs. In the same manner, if an item is not received in time, a backlogging cost is incurred for it. Regarding the capacity, the disassembly quantity is limited by a certain capacity time in each period over the planning horizon. The rest of this paper is organized as follows. In Sect. 2, the proposed stochastic programming model of the CDLS problem is described. MC optimization approach is presented in Sect. 3. Section 4 reports some preliminary results. Our conclusions are drawn in the final section.

2 Problem Formulation

To solve the studied problem under random lead time, a stochastic MIP is proposed to minimize the expected total cost $(E(T\ C))$. The list of notations used in this paper is given in Table 1:

Table 1. Notation.

• Index	
t	Index of period t, $t \in T$
i	Index of item i, $i \in N$
ω	Index of scenario ω, $\omega \in \Omega$
• Parameters	
T	Set of time periods of the planning horizon
N	Set of items
Ω	Set of possible scenarios
R_i	Yield of leaf item i from disassembling the parent item
L_t^ω	Random disassembly lead time in period t under scenario ω
$D_{i,t}$	External demand for leaf item i in period t
I_{i0}	Beginning inventory of leaf item i
h_i	Per period inventory holding cost of one unit of leaf item i
b_i	Per period backlogging cost of one unit of leaf item i
s_t	Setup cost for parent item in period t
C_t	Disassembly capacity time in period t
G	Disassembly operation time for end-of-life product
M	A large number
• Functions	
$E(.)$	Expected value
P_w	Probability distribution for scenario ω
• Decision variable	
Z_t	Disassembly quantity ordered in period t
• Variables	
Y_t	Binary indicator of disassembly order in period t
$H_{i,t}^\omega$	Inventory level of leaf item i at the end of period t and scenario ω
$B_{i,t}^\omega$	Backordered quantity of leaf item i at the end of period t and scenario ω
$I_{i,t}^\omega$	Inventory level at the end of period t it is equal to $H_{i,t}^\omega - B_{i,t}^\omega$

We note that the total number of the possible scenarios is $|\Omega| = \prod_{t \in T} (L^+ - L^- + 1)$ Thus, $E(T\,C)$ can be calculated by considering all possible values of L_t^ω and the objective function, expressed in Eq. (1), can be modeled as follows:

$$\text{Min}\,E(TC) = \sum_{t=1}^{T} \left(\sum_{i=1}^{N} \sum_{\omega=1}^{|\Omega|} \frac{1}{|\Omega|} (h_i.H_{i,t}^\omega + b_i.B_{i,t}^\omega) + s_t.Y_t \right) \quad (1)$$

Equation (2) defines the inventory balance for each item i at the end in each period t under scenario ω

$$H_{i,t}^\omega - B_{i,t}^\omega = I_{i,0} + \sum_{\tau=1}^{t-L_\tau^\omega} R_i Z_\tau - \sum_{\tau=1}^{t} D_{i,\tau} \quad \forall i \in N, \forall t \in T, \forall \omega \in \Omega \quad (2)$$

Constraints (3) represents the modeling constraint for disassembly indicator of the EOL product in period t:

$$Zt \le Yt.M \quad \forall t \in T \quad (3)$$

Constraints (4) represents the capacity constraint in each period t:

$$G.Zt \le Ct \quad \forall t \in T \quad (4)$$

Constraints (5 to 7) provides the conditions on the decision variables:

$$Zt \ge 0 \quad \forall t \in T \quad (5)$$

$$H_{i,t}^\omega - B_{i,t}^\omega \ge 0 \quad \forall i \in N, \forall t \in T, \forall \omega \in \Omega \quad (6)$$

$$Yt \in \{0, 1\} \quad \forall t \in T \quad (7)$$

The complexity of the problem may increase exponentially if a large set of $|\Omega|$ is considered to represent the stochastic DLT and the resolution of (1) to (7) becomes impossible. The total cost can be estimated by an empirical average $(\overline{TC})$ using: Monte Carlo (MC) simulation. It can provide an estimate of the criterion that converge to $E(T\,C)$ calculated by the stochastic MIP.

Proposition 1. *The MIP model can be converted to the following MC-MIP model:*

$$\text{Min}\,(\overline{TC}) = \sum_{t=1}^{T} \left(\sum_{i=1}^{N} \sum_{\omega=1}^{k} \frac{1}{K} (h_i.H_{i,t}^\omega + b_i.B_{i,t}^\omega) + s_t.Y_t \right) \quad (8)$$

$$H_{i,t}^\omega - B_{i,t}^\omega = I_{i,0} + \sum_{\tau=1}^{t-L_\tau^\omega} R_i Z_\tau - \sum_{\tau=1}^{t} D_{i,\tau} \quad \forall i \in N, \forall t \in T, \forall \omega \in k \quad (9)$$

$$H_{i,t}^{\omega}, B_{i,t}^{\omega} \geq 0 \quad \forall i \in N, \forall t \in T, \forall \omega \in K \tag{10}$$

subject to (3), (4), (5) *and* (7).

Proof. The MC-MIP is implemented with the following steps:

- Step 1: $\forall t \in T$, generate the random samples for L_t^{ω} for $\omega \in \vartheta$ where ϑ is a set of random samples such that $\vartheta \subset \Omega$ and $|\vartheta| = K$;
- Step 2: Each expected inventory level is estimated by $\overline{I_{i,t}}$ based on L_t^{ω} which is generated in step 1 using expressions (9) *and* (10).

Of particular interest is to study the Monte Carlo optimal solution convergence, we describe in the next section the convergence provided by the SAA algorithm based on MC optimization approach.

3 "Exact" Monte Carlo Optimization Method

In this section we present an almost exact method to solve the stochastic problem, referred to as the true optimization problem using MC-MIP. This approach is also known as the stochastic counterpart or the sample path method [8]. The evidence from this study points towards the idea incorporates an optimal algorithm to solve the problem under a large set of samples [6]. Thus, the excepted total cost developed in Eq. (1) can be approximated by SAA based on MC optimization steps:

- Step 1: Solve the MC-MIP model: Let X^* be the optimal solution and $\overline{TC}^*$ the obtained optimal average cost,
- Step 2: $\forall t \in T$, generate B large random samples of $L_t \quad \forall t\omega \in B$,
- Step 3: Evaluate the "Exact" optimal cost $\widehat{TC}_B$ of the optimal solution X^*, using Eq. (11)

$$\text{Min } \widehat{TC}_B = \sum_{t=1}^{T} \left(\sum_{i=1}^{N} \sum_{\omega=1}^{B} \frac{1}{B} (h_i.H_{i,t}^{\omega} + b_i.B_{i,t}^{\omega}) + s_t.Y_t \right) \tag{11}$$

subject to (9) and (4).

Remark 1. According to [6], "By the law of large numbers, the approximated total cost $(\widehat{TC}_B)$ converges with probability 1 to the excepted total cost $(E(T\,C))$ as B increases".

4 Computational Experiments and Result

In order to investigate the speed convergence of the solution provided by the MC optimization, this section presents numerical results that prove our findings. All approaches were solved using optimization software for small instances. All formulations are implemented in C using Concert Technology and are solved by

IBM CPLEX 12.4 on a PC with processor Intel (R) Core™ i7-5500 CPU @ 2.4 GHz and 8 Go RAM under Windows 10 Professional.

We considered a finite planning horizon with 5 periods and a disassembly system with 3 items (See Fig. 1). The number in parentheses represents the number of items obtained from the EoL product. The number of scenarios K takes a value in [2, 10, 30, 50, 150, 200, 400, 600, 1000]. For each K, we performed 100 independent runs of the MC-MIP to provide 100 optimal solutions X^* and the related average costs. The "exact" cost of each X^* was evaluated using a bigB number of scenarios (10^5 samples), i.e., $\overline{TC} \approx E(TC)$ with B = 10^5 (See [6]). To obtain E(T C), the stochastic MIP was solved with $|\Omega|$ = 3125 scenarios and the E(T C) takes a value equal to 70955 (see Fig. 2).

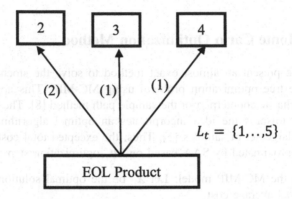

Fig. 1. Example of two-level disassembly system.

The tests are carried out under the parameter costs listed in Table 2. The inventory and backlogging costs of one unit of item i are 3 and 87, respectively. Starting inventory for each item is assumed to be zero. We note that the capacity is 180 for all periods.

Table 2. Characteristics of the data set.

(a) Demands and setup costs

Period	1	2	3	4	5
Demand A1	17	28	34	15	9
Demand A2	56	25	0	76	12
Demand A3	12	58	74	13	69
St	100	0	200	100	300

(b) Disassembly lead time probability distribution

ω	1	2	3	4	5
$Pr(Lt = \omega)$	0.245	0.48	0.255	0.01	0.01

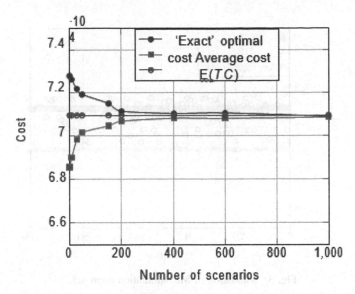

Fig. 2. Convergence cost.

Let us now compare the convergence of the average total cost $(\overline{TC})$. Figure 2 shows that $\widehat{TC}_B$ decreases when K is increasing. The findings of this study support the idea that $\overline{TC}$ converges to the exact solution $E(TC)$ and is quite robust if a large number of samples is used, for example if $K \geq 200$. Our work has led us to conclude that our proposed optimization method can provide the convergence of the solution to the optimal one as the set of scenarios increases.

As expected, our experiments show that for $K = 10^3$, the MC-MIP approach can generate a good approximate solution for the stochastic problem. As previously noted, we realized 100 independent runs of the same data set of the MC-MIP with 10^3 scenarios. Then, 100 optimal solutions are obtained. Among these solutions, the Best-Known Solution (BKS) is selected. As Fig. 3 witnesses, the results founded are stable and the average gap from BKS is no more than 4% for all runs.

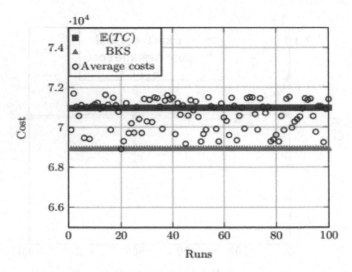

Fig. 3. Validation of MC simulation approach.

5 Conclusion

In this work, we studied a stochastic CDLS problem with several items disassembled from one type of EoL. We assumed that the items-demand is known. The DLT are an independents random variable whose probability distribution is known and bounded. The combination of MC-MIP approach has been developed. A SAA based on MC optimization provides almost optimal solutions using a modest number of scenarios in order to minimize the average total cost. Our model can easily be implemented in practice to define the DLT in a disassembly planning and control system. Our experiments show clear that the average total cost can be tends to the expected one as the number of scenarios increases. The stability of the proposed model is also verified. In the future, we will try to treat the randomness of demand and/or disassembly yield in the study of the multi-level disassembly systems and multi type EOL product.

References

1. Barba-Gutiéerrez, Y., Adenso-Díaz, B.: Reverse MRP under uncertain and imprecise demand. Int. J. Adv. Manuf. Technol. **40**(3–4), 413–424 (2009)
2. Ilgin, M.A., Gupta, S.M.: Environmentally conscious manufacturing and product recovery (ECMPRO): a review of the state of the art. J. Environ. Manag. **91**(3), 563–591 (2010)
3. Inderfurth, K., Langella, I.M.: Heuristics for solving disassemble-to-order problems with stochastic yields. OR Spectr. **28**(1), 73–99 (2006)
4. Inderfurth, K., Vogelgesang, S., Langella, I.M.: How yield process misspecification affects the solution of disassemble-to-order problems. Int. J. Prod. Econ. **169**, 56–67 (2015)

5. Kim, H.J., Xirouchakis, P.: Capacitated disassembly scheduling with random demand. Int. J. Prod. Res. **48**(23), 7177–7194 (2010)
6. Lamiri, M., Xie, X., Dolgui, A., Grimaud, F.: A stochastic model for operating room planning with elective and emergency demand for surgery. Eur. J. Oper. Res. **185**(3), 1026–1037 (2008)
7. Liu, K., Zhang, Z.H.: Capacitated disassembly scheduling under stochastic yield and demand. Eur. J. Oper. Res. **269**(1), 244–257 (2018)
8. Ruszczynski, A., Shapiro, A.: Handbooks in operations research and management. Science **10**, 1–64 (2003)
9. Slama, I., Ben-Ammar, O., Masmoudi, F., Dolgui, A.: Scenario-based stochastic linear programming model for multi-period disassembly lot-sizing problems under random lead time. IFAC-PapersOnLine **52**(13), 595–600 (2019)
10. Slama, I., Ben-Ammar, O., Dolgui, A., Masmoudi, F.: Newsboy problem with two- level disassembly system and stochastic lead time. In: ROADEF (2020)

Digital and Smart Supply Chain Management

ERP in Industry 4.0 Context

Vidosav Majstorovic[1(✉)] [iD], Slavenko Stojadinovic[1] [iD],
Bojan Lalic[2] [iD], and Ugljesa Marjanovic[2] [iD]

[1] Faculty of Mechanical Engineering, University of Belgrade, Belgrade, Serbia
vmajstorovic@mas.bg.ac.rs
[2] Faculty of Technical Science, University of Novi Sad, Novi Sad, Serbia

Abstract. Industry 4.0 (I4.0) is a new model of technology systems automation, based on the convergence of technologies that make up the concept of intelligent manufacturing, integrated with information and communication technologies that have been applied in a new way (cloud computing, big data analytics and AI), and the basis of distributed control. This approach has brought unprecedented opportunities to manufacturing systems, especially in the fields of planning and control, from resource to supply chains levels. For this reason, enterprise resource planning (ERP) is being researched and developed, which is based on the use of I4.0 elements: internet of things (IoT), big data analytics (BDA), AI and cloud computing (CC), which in this paper show.

Keywords: Industry 4.0 · ERP · Smart factory · Smart ERP

1 Introduction - The Need for New ERP Paradigms for Industry 4.0

Industry 4.0 is today and strategic national program of scientific and technological development of the most developed countries around the world, which has been implemented since 2011. Today, thirty-seven countries have this program, whose primary objective is to increase the competitiveness, productivity and efficiency of national industries [1, 2]. On the other hand, this model is the basic framework for research, development, designing and implementation of the next generation of technological systems, smart factories. One of the most important elements within them is the ERP model, which is considered in this paper from the following aspects: (i) historical development of the concept of planning and production control in the context of automation of manufacturing systems and the nature, type and volume of data in them, (ii) ERP data management and integration model in I4.0 concept, (iii) structure of the smart manufacturing model I4.0 with the place of the ERP model in it, and (iv) modeling with case studies for SMEs. Finally, some aspects of the future development of the ERP model for the I4.0 concept are given, especially from the perspective of new paradigms such as designing and production control.

Industry 4.0 model is based on data-driven technology which is networked and decentralized, and realized in cyber space. Therefore, it is very important for the smart manufacturing model to explore nature, the type and size of databases used to plan and manage at the plant, factory and supply chain levels [5–7], from the perspective of the

B. Lalic et al. (Eds.): APMS 2020, IFIP AICT 591, pp. 287–294, 2020.
https://doi.org/10.1007/978-3-030-57993-7_33

six technologies on which this production is based, and which containing elements of the ERP model. This overview is given in Table 1, with special reference to additional characteristics related to Industry 4.0.

Table 1. Characteristics of data in smart manufacturing (adopted according [6])

	Nature of data	Data type	Data volume
Automation and manufacturing technology	Prediction technology	Numerical, string, bits, symbolic	Medium. (Very large – big volume)[a]
Data storage technology	Status and history of production equipment	Numerical, symbolic, string, time series, text	Very large. (Cloud computing)[a]
Digitization technology	Artifact characterization, status	Numerical, symbolic, text	Large. (Digital twin)[a]
Cloud computing technology	As-is data, transformed data, integrated data, models, algorithms	Potentially data of types determined by the cloud design	Very large. (SaaS)[a]
Agent technology	Application specific	Application specific	Low. (AI)[a]
Prediction technology	Application specific	Numerical, categorical, time series	Medium. (Intelligent Maintenance)[a]

Note: [a]Add characteristics of I4.0 approach.

Information content and level connectivity in smart manufacturing is high and is implemented through 2M (man-machine) - computer communication, which is monitored by AI algorithms. In the smart manufacturing model, information flows are realized through cloud and physical layers. Cloud layer includes models and algorithms related to: operations and configuration management, process and service models and condition monitoring. ERP covers this last layer. The physical layer includes equipment and sensors. In this way, divided virtual-physical systems through cloud computing perform resource sharing, managed through the ERP model.

The planning of production and technological resources in the production control model (MRP/ERP) has a long history, and this development has taken two directions: (i) business aspect (from stock planning at the plant level to the whole chain (request for offer - delivery of the finished product) at the company level, and (ii) technological aspect (from the software package to the client server architecture). An overview of the development of this model is given in Table 2 [3, 9].

Information system for control the appropriate level of stock in a warehouse (material, spare parts) was been the first level in this area [9]. Material requirement planning (MRP I) used software applications for scheduling manufacturing processes and for operations raw material purchases, level two. Now, for the first time, they are introducing into production planning and control bill of structure, materials (BOM) and quantity. Manufacturing Resource Planning (MRP II) used software for coordinating

Table 2. History of ERP model development [3, 9]

Year/model/level	Characteristics of MRP/ERP model	Aspects of function
1960s/IC/I level	Inventory management and control	Warehouse control
1970s/MRP I/II level	Material Requirements Planning	Bill of product
1980s/MRP II/III level	Manufacturing Resources Planning	Bill of manufacturing process
1990s/ERP/IV level	Enterprise Resource Planning	Integrate business activities across organization units
2000s/ERP II/V level	Enterprise Resource Planning by Internet	Services Oriented Architecture (SOA)
2010s/Cloud based ERP/VI level	Cloud based ERP	ERP as software a service (SaaS) model
2020s/I4.0 ERP/VII level	ERP of Industry 4.0 model	I4.0 concept introducing

manufacturing processes from product planning, parts purchasing, inventory control to product distribution, level III. Enterprise resource planning (ERP) uses a multi-module application software system, for improving the performance of the internal business processes, based on integrate business activities (planning, purchasing and distribution) across functional departments (marketing, design, accounting, HR), level IV. ERP II using internet web-browsers, with Services Oriented Architecture (SOA) and mobile devices were made possible, is level V. Cloud ERP, level VI are business applications are delivered as a service (SaaS) model, suitable for SMEs as well. Finally, the last seventh level refers to the ERP model for Industry 4.0. The previous analysis shows that the development of the first four levels of the ERP model was based on the development of information systems, and after that IT technologies involved in the development of this model. The latest model is an internet-oriented networking concept, based on cloud computing and AI tools in Industry 4.0 model.

2 ERP Model for Industry 4.0

Digitized and networked technology systems, with Internet of Things as per Industry 4.0 concept, have the ability to assign production control tasks to "intelligent" objects: machines, products and parts [10]. In this way, greater flexibility and adaptability of the manufacturing system itself, through the ERP model, is achieved. This approach defines new paradigms of production planning and control, which is based on a hybrid model of transition at centralized to a decentralized management concept. On the other hand, the optimization of ERP parameters is performed at a centralized (supply chain) and/or distributed (part) control level, which means that decisions regarding production planning and control are made globally or locally, according to Kanban (pull) or holon model.

Data became the key elements in planning, control and executing all activities along supply chain in I4.0 model. For these reasons, an organization must carefully treat and properly use all data to create an effective basis for decision making [11]. The main challenge is innovative data management on the Industry 4.0 platform, which includes storage, exchange and use of data. The development and implementation of such concepts must be stimulated because only data that is error-free, up-to-date, accessible and usable can contribute to the success of the company, Table 3.

Table 3. Framework of ERP model for Industry 4.0 (extended approach according [11])

Characteristics/I4.0 challenge	Desirable features of an ERP systems	Example	Goals	I4.0 approach
Data storage/balance centralized and decentralized approach	Simplification of data model	Simple table structures for the logical data model	Data on time	Cloud computing
	Decentralized data management	Distributed storage of data in different systems	Bidirectional (ERP-MES[a]-PLC[b]) loading of data	
Data flow/the connection of the ERP system in two directions – horizontal and vertical	Linkage to previous systems	Exchange data (vertical and horizontal) and processing of different systems	Integration of systems for a flexible planning and control	Interoperability
	Speed of data access	ERP system should deliver requested data within short response times	Fast reaction to changes	
Data used/virtual and real models of intelligent products	Visualization	The user interface of the ERP systems should display information adequately	Improvement of human-machine interaction	Big data analytics, AI
	Integration and Intelligence	ERP system should connect data from different sources and hence create new information	Generation of new information	
	Automation	ERP system should use the data to trigger automated processes	Reduction of errors and increase in efficiency	

Note: [a]MES – Manufacturing execution system; [b]PLC - Programmable logic controller.

The ERP model for smart factories is used to manage all business and technology processes in real time across the whole supply chain, based on a fast and flexible response to its customers' requirements. For the first time the Industry 4.0 model allows us do this, and the ERP model permeates the infrastructure of the entire model shown on Fig. 1 [8].

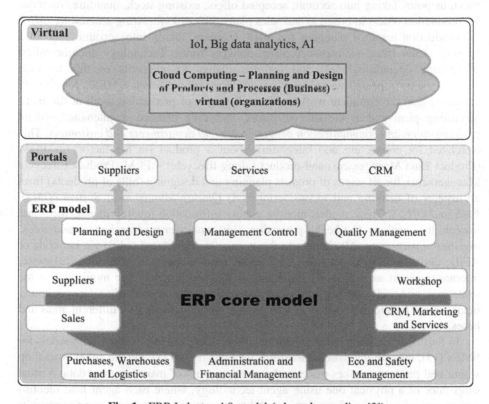

Fig. 1. ERP Industry 4.0 model (adopted according [3])

The model has three parts: (i) virtual whole, which is based on the cloud computing (SaaS) model. It contains a virtual model of an ERP system, linked through IoT all business (procurement, sales, management, finance), production (workshop) and technological (designing) processes, with large databases that are generating. Their analysis, optimization and decision making are perform using AI and machine learning techniques; (ii) interfaces (suppliers, services and CRM). Their function is to provide to user the on-line user necessary information related to procurement, sales and other services (for example maintenance) that help us track the dynamics of smart manufacturing, and (iii) core model, which includes the business-technological and managerial functions of the organization as well as the production itself, a total of ten units.

In the smart factory model, the following functions are realized using an intelligent ERP system [4, 7, 12, 13]: *(i) management of customer requirements.* Real time creating the information content of request or offer using: Electronic Data Interchange (EDI) tools, web portals, forecasts and customer MRPs. Also managing the "Master Production Schedule" (MPS), with open orders and framework agreements, the procurement activities can be scheduled (purchases and production of finished or semi-finished goods); (ii) *production planning (MRP 1)*. The model calculates the needed quantities of raw materials to be procured for the accepted requirements from the previous point, taking into account: accepted offers, existing stock, quantities reserved for production orders in progress and sales plans; (iii) *manufacturing scheduling (MRP 2)*. Production resource planning for MRP 1 orders, taking into account: machines capacity, labor force, maintenance plans, delivery times. Technology documentation (machining operations, tools and controls plans) are elements of this module; (iv) *management production (Manufacturing Execution System – MES)*. Monitoring and managing the complete work order at all stages of production, both at the manufacturing plant and at the subcontractors, including planned maintenance orders; (v) *integration and communication between technical departments and customers*. This is related for connecting and integrating about a product (in the factory) – PDM (Product Data Management) and product (along lifecycle) – PLM (Product Lifecycle Management), for all stages of product planning and designing (bills of products) from all aspects of defining and reconsidering; (vi) *Quality Management System (QMS), EMS and OH&S*. These models manage quality information (quality management and traceability), ecology and health protection; (vii) *management warehouses and stock, logistics management*. All changes to the storage are monitored online via bar code or RFID, and the ERP model takes care about required/planned quantities. Likewise, internal transport as well as all shipments of finished products, are monitored in the same way, and (viii) *administration and financial management*. Production accounting management to determined all costs and productivity parameters, by different areas and bases.

In Serbia, intensive work is being done to develop and implement ERP models for SMEs [13], through the national Platform for Industry 4.0 [1]. On the smart workshop where real production takes place as the creating point of manufacturing data. Virtual shop floor of a physical one using agent technology, where each agent has: identification, authorization, configuration, capability, operation and status data, and transmits them and their metadata. Data warehouse is an information hub that stores and exchanges manufacturing data. Data analytics center is the model creation, storage, retrieval and uncertainty which provides machine learning, statistical, or stochastic based models that build on mathematical functions needed to create data driven models. Each agent retrieves such models through a broker agent and decides predictive operations and controls, based on the results that models output. Manufacturing application include applications, such as CAD, CAM, CAQ, ERP systems. These applications communicate with the platform through their application interfaces because they eventually supervise and manage all activities and events occurring on the physical workshop. Agent manager searches adequate agents, and manages them during their lifecycles. Data governor manages master data as well as the lifecycle and quality of raw data. Workflow manager controls workflows to automate the tasks performed on the platform, manages the rules designed to handle workflow appropriately, and engages in model representation. Security controller protects against computer viruses and hacking, and controls electronic authorization and authentication, because data and models that incorporate manufacturing experience and knowledge are valuable and, thus, must be protected.

Integration center is an intelligent product, with added value; and (iii) supply chains and sustainable production with a customer relationship management (CRM) integration center. Thus the organization builds a new business model of its Industry 4.0 concept, the center of which is a large database and its reporting. The ERP model plays a key role in this [14].

3 Conclusions

The concept of Industry 4.0 has a special place and role for the design engineer and production planner, which is still irreplaceable, but now has a different role, namely a new paradigm. It is particularly reflected in the construction and management of the digital twin model of the smart factory, and thus of the ERP module. In [15, 16], this approach is explored in detail, and a five-level model of the pyramid of the industrial internet is proposed: (i) smart object (physical objects and embedded intelligence), (ii) industrial internet of things (level 1 and network, (iii) cyber-physical production system (level 2 and integration previous levels), (iv) service-oriented digital twin (ubiquitous knowledge and level 3), and (v) smart factory (manufacturing employees and level 4). From an ERP perspective, the specificities of executives monitoring CPSs, facility managers and engineer resource planners are specifically referenced and used here, as outlined in Levels 4 and 5. One of the future directions of ERP development is the open source model.

Research on the project [13] in the forthcoming period will focus on the development of demonstration models for individual I4.0 segments for SMEs (designing - digital twin, procurement, customers, MES, etc.). The limitations on the development and application of this model in SMEs primarily relate to the lack of resources in them, and in particular finance (ICT infrastructure and cloud services) and experts knowledge from SMEs for the used of ERP.

References

1. Majstorovic, V.D., Mitrovic, R.: Industry 4.0 programs worldwide. In: Monostori, L., Majstorovic, V.D., Hu, S.J., Djurdjanovic, D. (eds.) AMP 2019. LNME, pp. 78–99. Springer, Cham (2019). https://doi.org/10.1007/978-3-030-18180-2_7
2. Majstorović, V.D., et al.: Cyber-physical manufacturing in context of industry 4.0 model. In: Ni, J., Majstorovic, V.D., Djurdjanovic, D. (eds.) AMP 2018. LNME, pp. 227–238. Springer, Cham (2018). https://doi.org/10.1007/978-3-319-89563-5_17
3. N.N.: ERP and Industry 4.0. https://www.centrosoftware.com/en/erp-and-industry-4.0. Accessed Mar 2020
4. Ahmad, M., Cuenca, R.: Critical success factors for ERP implementation in SMEs. Robot. Comput. Integr. Manuf. 29, 104–111 (2013). https://doi.org/10.1016/j.rcim.2012.04.019

5. Cadavid, J.P.U., Lamouri, S., Grabot, B., Fortin, A.: Machine learning in production planning and control: a review of empirical literature. IFAC Papers Online 52(13), 385–390 (2019). https://doi.org/10.1016/j.ifacol.2019.11.155

6. Kusiak, A.: Fundamentals of smart manufacturing: a multi-thread perspective. Ann. Rev. Control 47, 214–220 (2019). https://doi.org/10.1016/j.arcontrol.2019.02.001

7. Usuga Cadavid, J.P., Lamouri, S., Grabot, B., Pellerin, R., Fortin, A.: Machine learning applied in production planning and control: a state-of-the-art in the era of industry 4.0. J. Intell. Manuf. 31(6), 1531–1558 (2020). https://doi.org/10.1007/s10845-019-01531-7

8. Osterrieder, P., Budde, L., Friedli, T.: The smart factory as a key construct of industry 4.0: a systematic literature review. Int. J. Prod. Econ. 211, 35–51 (2019). https://doi.org/10.1016/j.ijpe.2019.08.011

9. N.N.: A brief history of ERP – since 1960 and the future of ERP. https://www.erp-information.com/history-of-erp.html. Accessed Mar 2020

10. Bendul, J.C., Blunck, H.: The design space of production planning and control for Industry 4.0. Comput. Ind. 105, 260–272 (2019). https://doi.org/10.1016/j.compind2018.10.010

11. Hochmuth, C.A., Bartodziej, C., Schwägler, C.: Industry 4.0 is your ERP system ready for the digital era? (2017). https://www2.deloitte.com/content/dam/Deloitte/de/Documents/technology/Deloitte_ERP_Industrie-4-0_Whitepaper.pdf. Accessed Feb 2020

12. Panetto, H., Iung, B., Ivanov, D., Weichhart, G., Wang, X.: Challenges for the cyber-physical manufacturing enterprises of the future. Ann. Rev. Control 47, 200–213 (2019). https://doi.org/10.1016/j.arcontrol.2019.02.002

13. Majstorovic, V., et al.: I4.0 for SMEs. Project, Faculty of Mechanical Engineering, Belgrade (2019)

14. Lalic, B., Medic, N., Delic, M., Tasic, N., Marjanovic, U.: Open innovation in developing regions: an empirical analysis across manufacturing companies. Int. J. Ind. Eng. Manage. 8 (3), 111–120 (2017)

15. Olson, D.L., Johansson, B., De Carvalho, R.A.: Open source ERP business model framework. Robot. Comput. Integr. Manuf. 50, 30–36 (2018). https://doi.org/10.1016/j.rcim.2015.09.007

16. Longo, F., Nicoletti, L., Padovano, A.: Ubiquitous knowledge empowers the smart factory: the impacts of a service-oriented digital twin on enterprises' performance. Ann. Rev. Control 47, 221–236 (2019). https://doi.org/10.1016/j.arcontrol.2019.01.001

Identifying the Opportunities for Enhancing the Digital Readiness Level of the Supply Chain

Chiara Cimini[✉] ⓘ, Fabiana Pirola ⓘ, and Sergio Cavalieri ⓘ

Department of Management, Information and Production Engineering,
University of Bergamo, Viale Marconi 5, Dalmine, BG, Italy
{chiara.cimini,fabiana.pirola,
sergio.cavalieri}@unibg.it

Abstract. Assessing the digital readiness of companies is becoming crucial to undertake a successful journey towards the digitalization of industry. Recently, the attention of both scholars and practitioners has turned to an extension of the assessment to the whole Supply Chain (SC). Given the importance of reaching a high level of integration and digital readiness in all the various actors that collaborate in the SC, some Digital Supply Chain (DSC) assessment models have been proposed mainly in the consulting field. However, to fully exploit the benefits of measuring the digital readiness of a SC, companies need also to be supported in the identification and prioritization of the most relevant opportunities triggered by the deployment of DSC projects. To this purpose, this paper presents a framework that links the potentials of DSC implementations with the SC operation processes, highlighting the most suitable technologies to deploy them. The framework has been conceived starting from a literature review and aims at providing a valuable tool to all the stakeholders involved in the transformation towards Digital Supply Chains.

Keywords: Digital supply chain · Readiness assessment · Digital transformation

1 Introduction

The business landscape has been heavily broken out by the emergence of the COVID-19 pandemia which is affecting all the societies and economies at the global level, changing promptly and profoundly the lifestyle of people, altering the market dynamics, disrupting dramatically the operations of companies and, at a large extent, of the supply chains. These extreme and severe changes have further fueled some needs and opportunities which were already nurturing in the last years, regarding in particular the digital transformation of the organizations to enable smart working of white collars, on-line controlling and monitoring of production systems, remote assistance of machines, thus mitigating the downfall effects triggered by reduced mobility of people, workers and goods. However, the appropriate adoption and use of these new technologies are not immediate, but require a deep understanding and companies must be prepared for them [1].

© IFIP International Federation for Information Processing 2020
Published by Springer Nature Switzerland AG 2020
B. Lalic et al. (Eds.): APMS 2020, IFIP AICT 591, pp. 295–303, 2020.
https://doi.org/10.1007/978-3-030-57993-7_34

One of the main requirements is the achievement of a certain level of digital readiness and this clearly makes it extremely important to identify a valid and reliable model for measuring it. Several digital readiness assessment and maturity models have been developed, mainly in the consulting and academic contexts [2]. Nevertheless, they tend to focus on the single firm and not on the value chains in which it operates. This is the reason why the attention has been shifting to an extension of the analysis at a supply chain (SC) level, encompassing the upstream and downstream sides of a focal company.

This new vision stems from the idea that significant advantages, such as an additional increase in efficiency, competitiveness and mitigation of risks, can only be achieved with a high level of integration and digital readiness of all the various actors collaborating in the SC.

This paper devotes its focus on the phase after Digital Readiness Assessment (DRA), that is when companies are required to define the main improvement areas in the SC. After briefly defining the basic concepts of Digital Supply Chain (DSC) and readiness assessment (Sect. 2), the paper presents a framework, which merges the technological perspective with the operational one, providing a tool for practitioners that want to enhance the digital readiness of their SC (Sect. 3). Some limitations and further improvements of the conducted research are finally discussed (Sect. 4).

2 Background

2.1 Digital Supply Chain

Industry 4.0 is a new industrial trend in which process integration and product connectivity allow to increase performance [3]. After e-commerce, which has completely changed the way people buy and sell products all over the world, the SC is evolving towards DSC, that in literature is considered according to two main definitions.

The first definition concerns the digital product ecosystem, or the chain of companies interested in providing digital products that were originally physical, such as eBooks and MP3s. The physical product must pass through the SC to reach the consumer; in the same way, the digital products must pass processing phases before the final consumer can use them [4]. This definition focuses more on the product: in fact, its digital nature contributes to the creation of "digital supply chains"; consequently, their construction derives from the needs and characteristics of the product.

In the second definition, instead, the digital nature is not in the product, but in the process of designing, producing and supplying goods. Alicke et al. [5] define the DSC as the next-generation SC which relies at the field level on interconnected systems, automatization of plants, collaborative digital platforms.

For these reasons, the second definition of DSC represents an integration between the traditional concepts of SC and the digital transformation, as enabling technologies generate new opportunities and trigger new managerial SC models and processes. In literature, it has been shown that the use of technologies is positively correlated to the joint performance of the supplier and the focal company; familiarity with new digital trends allows companies' openness to share core information with their suppliers, and vice versa [6].

In a nutshell, the digital transformation of the SC is based on new innovative approaches and new features, such as:

- Speed, which allows the delivery of goods in useful times and faster movements in internal and external logistics, and in the long term even to possible "predictive shipment" (patented by Amazon) [5].
- Global connectivity, i.e. the creation of effective global hubs to provide goods and services locally, supporting integration [7], collaboration [8] and coordination [9].
- Intelligence, which allows converting digital data into useful information (automated execution, actionable insights and accelerated innovation) [10, 11].
- Flexibility, which consists in using the information to react to problems or changes instantaneously; for example, planning becomes a continuous process that reacts dynamically to the constraints and requirements of evolution [5].
- Transparency, that allows anticipating disruptions thanks to a wide information visibility [10].
- Scalability and Granularity, that allows to adapt the capacity of the SC to the "peak and trough" volumes of market demand [5].
- Sustainability, supporting the compliance and responsibility with environmental and social norms [5].

2.2   DSC Readiness Assessment

To develop such a DSC, Büyüközkan et al. [12, p. 168] proposed a framework considering three different steps that are "vital for organizational alignment". The first step for digitalization is the definition of a digital strategy that exactly indicates what the company wants to achieve in terms of DSC features. Depending on the goal and its vision, as a second step, the company formulates the implementation strategy that allows it to achieve its objective(s) [13]. It considers "how, where, when and who" for the realization of the objective(s). Different aspects of SCM are affected by digital transformation and need to be defined in this step (e.g., integration, processes, automation, and analytics). The technological infrastructure must support the company strategy. Defining the nature of the infrastructure means better understanding the technological priorities and requirements (step 3) [14].

In order to support companies in these steps, DRA represents a valuable tool to suggest both the digital strategy definition and implementation.

Readiness is defined as the state of "being both psychologically and behaviorally prepared to take action (i.e., willing and able)" [15] and is strictly connected to a change process. The systemic analysis of an organization's ability to cope with transformational process or change is defined as measuring or assessing readiness, since readiness assessment aims at identify the risks, the opportunities, and the potential challenges that might arise when change processes (concerning new processes, procedures, organization, etc.) are implemented within an actual organizational context [16]. Changing readiness means having the right conditions and resources to support certain company initiatives, to have clear goals and visions of change and to have objectives and the motivation to face it. As a result, assessing the readiness is fundamental, as companies often do not know their position towards their competitors and changes in general. Moreover, readiness assessment models can be used for comparison and benchmarking.

In the Industry 4.0 context, both scholars and consultancy groups have proposed several readiness assessment tools or maturity models (e.g., [16, 17]). However, they often focus on a single enterprise, maybe with a distinction between SMEs and large companies. So far, few researches deal with the DSC readiness. The assessment developed by the Digital Supply Chain Institute [18] has been applied to some companies operating in the manufacturing and service industry. The objective of this assessment is to analyze the SC from an internal focus to a customer-supplier focus. The assessment is divided into four areas (Demand, People, Technology and Risk), each area containing three levels. The DSC assessment developed by the consulting group Tecsys [19] aims at analyzing the critical milestones for an end-to-end SC, i.e. Executive Buy-In, Financial Foundations, Infrastructure Essentials, SC Operations, Cross-Functional Collaboration and Strategic Momentum. These ones are used to develop a roadmap to support digital transformation. Other assessment tools have been provided by the other consulting groups as well, such as Gartner [20] and McKinsey [5].

All these DRA represent significant tools for companies to identify their current level of digital readiness, but they lack in providing a clear view of the improvements that companies need to implement to increase their readiness level. Given this gap, further reflections about the post-assessment phase are required. For this reason, in the next paragraph a framework for recognizing the most interesting opportunities offered by the new technologies to improve the digital supply chain readiness is proposed.

3   The DSC Improvements Framework

In the McKinsey assessment [5], a Compass map with a series of improvement levers classified in six categories (planning, strategy, collaboration, order management, performance management and physical flow) originating from the DSC is presented.

To conceive our framework, we took the Compass map as a starting point to identify the main improvement areas, merging this perspective with other two dimensions: the Industry 4.0 technologies and the SC processes as defined by the Supply Chain Operations Reference (SCOR) model [21]. Similar approaches have been used in literature to build systematic literature mapping [22]. In this way, the framework provides the company with an overview of the digital results that can be potentially reached, indicating at the same time the processes that would benefit it and the technological solutions necessary to implement them successfully.

The resulting framework (represented in Fig. 1) has been developed based on academic articles, conference proceedings, and the SCOR model (version 12.0).

It is composed by three dimensions:

- The digital achievements (in orange) represent the opportunities and possible implementations of DSC in different areas of business management. They have

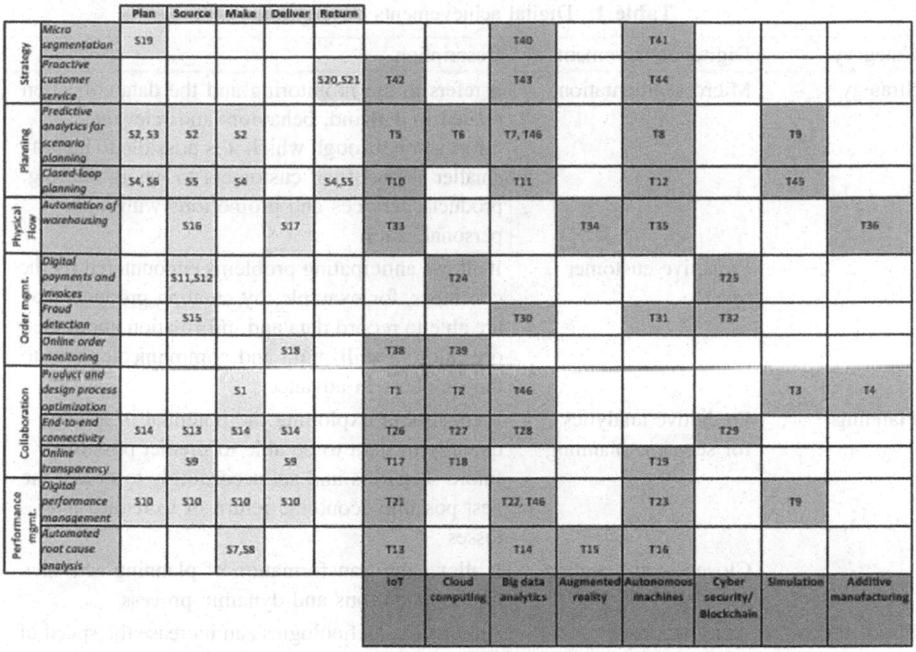

		Plan	Source	Make	Deliver	Return	IoT	Cloud computing	Big data analytics	Augmented reality	Autonomous machines	Cyber security/ Blockchain	Simulation	Additive manufacturing
Strategy	Micro segmentation	S19								T40	T41			
Strategy	Proactive customer service					S20,S21	T42		T43		T44			
Planning	Predictive analytics for scenario planning	S2, S3	S2	S2			T5	T6	T7, T46		T8		T9	
Planning	Closed-loop planning	S4, S6	S5	S4		S4,S5	T10		T11		T12		T45	
Physical Flow	Automation of warehousing		S16	S17			T33			T34	T35			T36
Order mgmt.	Digital payments and invoices		S11,S12						T24			T25		
Order mgmt.	Fraud detection		S15						T30		T31	T32		
Order mgmt.	Online order monitoring				S18		T38	T39						
Collaboration	Product and design process optimization			S1			T1	T2	T46				T3	T4
Collaboration	End-to-end connectivity	S14	S13	S14	S14		T26	T27	T28			T29		
Collaboration	Online transparency		S9		S9		T17	T18			T19			
Performance mgmt.	Digital performance management	S10	S10	S10	S10		T21		T22, T46		T23		T9	
Performance mgmt.	Automated root cause analysis			S7,S8			T13		T14	T15	T16			

Fig. 1. DSC improvements framework (Color figure online)

been identified from different sources such as the McKinsey's Compass discussed above, but also from academic articles (in particular the ones used to build the framework) in which results, practices and improvements brought by the digitalization of the SC are described. The digital achievements are briefly described in Table 1.

- The SC processes (in green) refers to the SCOR model and allow to easily identify which aspects of the supply chain and companies' operations are directly affected by digital changes. In the SCOR model, six processes are described, while in the framework only five are considered. In fact, the process named Enable has not been reported, since, referring to the management of company rules, performance, data, resources, structures, contracts, network and risks, it is strictly connected to every other process. For this reason, it is possible to assume that all the digital achievements that affect the first five processes, also contribute to an improvement in the Enable dynamics.

- The enabling technologies (in blue) are the most relevant innovative technologies of Industry 4.0, as described by [23], which support the realization of the SC digital achievements.

Each cell of the framework is based (and therefore justified) on an academic contribution or, rarely, on a web article, which explain the correlation between the three elements described above. The sources that have been used are marked in the cells with an acronym (letters S for SCOR or T for technologies and a sequential number) and can

Table 1. Digital achievements description

Category	Digital achievements	Description
Strategy	Micro segmentation	It refers to the monitoring and the data collection related to demand, behaviors and relevant information through which it is possible to identify smaller segments of customers to whom offering products, services and promotions with high personalization
	Proactive customer service	It allows anticipating problems encountered by the consumer, for example, by creating products that are able to record data and information about their operation or utilization and communicate them to the suppliers in advance
Planning	Predictive analytics for scenario planning	It consists in exploiting the potential of a large quantity of data to be able to predict possible future scenarios and act accordingly to obtain the best possible economic return or to reduce any losses
	Closed-loop planning	It allows the transformation of planning activities into a continuous and dynamic process
Physical flow	Automation of warehousing	Automation technologies can increase the speed of picking operations, optimize the space and the layout of the warehouse and reduce human error in inventory operations, transforming the warehouse from a cost center to a source of competitive advantage
Order mgmt.	Digital payments and invoices	They allow companies to capitalize on aspects such as repayments and discounts due to upfront payments, adequately manage their supplier base and reduce invoice processing and payment costs
	Fraud detection	It deals with the identification of possible frauds such as failure by suppliers to comply with contractual conditions, billing of non-delivered material or even corruption, thanks to the availability and correct analysis of a huge quantity of data
	Online order monitoring	It allows companies to improve the service offered to customers who are able to monitor at any time different types of information constantly updated on their orders
Collaboration	Product and design process optimization	It refers to the potential of new technologies in increasing the coordination and cooperation both internally with company functions such as marketing and production, and externally by involving suppliers in the product development cycle

(*continued*)

Table 1. (continued)

Category	Digital achievements	Description
	End-to-end connectivity	It allows that different actors at different levels of the supply chain can obtain data and visibility in real-time, enhancing communication and coordination of activities and processes.
	Online transparency	It concerns the sharing of information with the partners in the SC, referring to Key Performance Indicators (e.g., service level) or real-time data (e.g., the position of a truck carrying a specific order)
Performance mgmt.	Digital performance management	It refers to the use of models that automatically and continuously process data and detect real-time performances to analyze and improve inefficiencies
	Automated root cause analysis	It refers to the implementation of machine learning techniques to automatically identify problems, their causal dependencies and their root causes

be consulted at the link: https://drive.google.com/open?id=1h9ZHJ7pqzcCzn_cTxRMNiPIT52ohvZEJ.

Observing the framework, it is possible to notice that the proposed digital achievements affect mainly four out of the five SCOR processes. The process Return can be improved introducing only IoT technologies and data analytics to obtain data from the products' lifecycle, enabling improved customer assistance and planning activities.

Actually, it is quite evident that IoT and Big Data analytics, along with Autonomous machines, are the technologies more relevant to the realization of almost all the digital achievements. Also Simulation seems to support several digital achievements and can affect notably the companies' planning activities, potentially increasing in a significant way the performances of all the SC. Conversely, technologies such as Augmented Reality or Additive manufacturing seem to have less application in the DSC.

4 Conclusion

The paper presents a framework on the adoption of digital solutions for the optimization of SC processes, showing the advantages that they would entail and the business processes that would be involved and would benefit from it. Some limitations and further development of this research can be envisioned. First, the framework is conceived as a tool to be used in a following phase respect to a DRA of the SC. To this purpose, the digital achievements could be enriched and reorganized according to specific assessments, refining the framework also according to different perspectives (e.g., suppliers, customers). Future research will test the validity of the framework, evaluating how it could be applied jointly with a readiness assessment. In a second instance, the framework can be improved merging financial aspects of the technology implementations, evaluating technical feasibility along with returns on investments.

References

1. Nasution, R.A., Rusnandi, L.S.L., Qodariah, E., Arnita, D., Windasari, N.A.: The evaluation of digital readiness concept: existing models and future directions. AJTM. **11**, 94–117 (2018) https://doi.org/10.12695/ajtm.2018.11.2.3
2. Colli, M., Berger, U., Bockholt, M., Madsen, O., Møller, C., Wæhrens, B.V.: A maturity assessment approach for conceiving context-specific roadmaps in the Industry 4.0 era. Annu. Rev. Control **48**, 165–177 (2019). https://doi.org/10.1016/j.arcontrol.2019.06.001
3. Dalenogare, L.S., Benitez, G.B., Ayala, N.F., Frank, A.G.: The expected contribution of Industry 4.0 technologies for industrial performance. Int. J. Prod. Econ. **204**, 383–394 (2018)
4. Hines, T.: From analogue to digital supply chains: implications for fashion marketing. In: Fashion Marketing: Contemporary Issues, pp. 26–47. Routledge (2001)
5. Alicke, K., Rachor, J., Seyfert, A.: Supply chain 4.0 – the next-generation digital supply chain. McKinsey (2016)
6. Scuotto, V., Caputo, F., Villasalero, M., Giudice, M.D.: A multiple buyer – supplier relationship in the context of SMEs' digital supply chain management. Prod. Plan. Control **28**, 1378–1388 (2017). https://doi.org/10.1080/09537287.2017.1375149
7. Rai, A., Patnayakuni, R., Seth, N.: Firm performance impacts of digitally enabled supply chain integration capabilities. MIS Q. **30**, 225–246 (2006)
8. Min, S., et al.: Supply chain collaboration: what's happening? Int. J. Log. Manag. **16**, 237–256 (2005). https://doi.org/10.1108/09574090510634539
9. Iddris, F.: Digital supply chain: survey of the literature. Int. J. Bus. Res. Manag. **9**, 47–61 (2018)
10. Hanifan, G., Sharma, A., Newberry, C.: The digital supply network: a new paradigm for supply chain management. In: Accenture Global Management Consulting, pp. 1–8 (2014)
11. Trkman, P., McCormack, K., de Oliveira, M.P.V., Ladeira, M.B.: The impact of business analytics on supply chain performance. Decis. Support Syst. **49**, 318–327 (2010). https://doi.org/10.1016/j.dss.2010.03.007
12. Büyüközkan, G., Göçer, F.: Digital supply chain: literature review and a proposed framework for future research. Comput. Ind. **97**, 157–177 (2018)
13. Pradabwong, J., Braziotis, C., Tannock, J.D.T., Pawar, K.S.: Business process management and supply chain collaboration: effects on performance and competitiveness. Supply Chain Manag. **22**, 107–121 (2017). https://doi.org/10.1108/SCM-01-2017-0008
14. Townsend, M.A.Y.A.: Priorities for building organizational infrastructure (2006)
15. Weiner, B.J.: A theory of organizational readiness for change. Implement. Sci. **4**, 67 (2009)
16. Pirola, F., Cimini, C., Pinto, R.: Digital readiness assessment of Italian SMEs: a case-study research. J. Manuf. Technol. Manag. (2019). https://doi.org/10.1108/JMTM-09-2018-0305
17. Vivares, J.A., Sarache, W., Hurtado, J.E.: A maturity assessment model for manufacturing systems. J. Manuf. Technol. Manag. **29**, 746–767 (2018). https://doi.org/10.1108/JMTM-07-2017-0142
18. DSCI: Digital Supply Chain Transformation Guide: Essential MetricsD (2017). https://www.dscinstitute.org/assets/documents/Digital-Supply-Chain-Transformation-Guide-Essential-Metrics_DSCI_Oct2.pdf

19. Tecsys: IDN Supply Chain Transformation (2018). https://infohub.tecsys.com/idn-supply-chain-transformation-readiness-assessment-tool
20. Poole, C., et al.: Gartner's Demand-Driven Model for Supply Chain Maturity (2015)
21. APICS: SCOR Supply Chain Operations Reference Model (2017). https://www.apics.org/docs/default-source/scc-non-research/apicssccc_scor_quick_reference_guide.pdf
22. Wolf, H., Lorenz, R., Kraus, M., Feuerriegel, S., Netland, T.H.: Bringing advanced analytics to manufacturing: a systematic mapping. In: Ameri, F., Stecke, K.E., von Cieminski, G., Kiritsis, D. (eds.) APMS 2019. IAICT, vol. 566, pp. 333–340. Springer, Cham (2019). https://doi.org/10.1007/978-3-030-30000-5_42
23. Rüßmann, M., et al.: Industry 40: the future of productivity and growth in manufacturing industries. Boston Consult. Group **9**(1), 54–89 (2015)

Intelligent Logistics Networks Management

The Role of Last-Mile Delivery in the Future of E-Commerce

Fernanda Alves de Araújo[1]([⊠]) [iD],
João Gilberto Mendes dos Reis[1,2] [iD],
and Paula Ferreira da Cruz Correia[1] [iD]

[1] RESUP/PPGEP - Universidade Paulista, São Paulo, Brazil
fernanda.logistica@gmail.com,
joao.reis@docente.unip.br, paulafecruz@gmail.com
[2] Postgraduate Program in Agribusiness, Universidade Federal da Grande
Dourados, Dourados, Brazil

Abstract. Last-Mile delivery has attracted considerable interest from the logistics suppliers and retail industry in the last few years. New technologies and approaches are being discussed both professional and academic side. The trend of new technologies developed for transportation will not stop and the reason is not hard to explain: The increase of online commerce and app-based ordering of almost everything from books to food, requires a large capacity, speed, and flexibility. Following the importance of last-mile delivery, this paper intends to investigate the expectations of consumers and parcel logistics provides regarding last- mile delivery. To do so, we conducted a literature review of last-mile to identify the main gaps found in the literature so far, aiming to extend the current literature. Our results showed that advances in last-mile delivery will depend on the capacity of logistics parcel services and consumers to align their expectations.

Keywords: City logistics · Urban freight · Parcel freight distribution

1 Introduction

In the last few decades, the future of transportation has been revolving around science fiction ideas such as flying cars, floating bridges, teleportation. However, although our transport systems are a little bit far from this futuristic world, nowadays there is much more technology applied to the transport segment than ever before.

The most recent innovation in urban transportation is autonomy Drones. The first official tests with Drones started in 2013, performed by Amazon. According to the CEO company, the Drones could deliver packages weighing up to 2,3 kg to customers within 30 min of them placing order [1]. In the following year, DHL launched its initial operation for research purposes with Drones focused in remote areas with restricted access [2].

Currently, drone delivery is a reality. The "Prime Air" Amazon service is available in the US where drones cover up to 15 miles and delivery packages less than 30 min counting with the FAA (Federal Aviation Administration) approval and certification

Published by Springer Nature Switzerland AG 2020
B. Lalic et al. (Eds.): APMS 2020, IFIP AICT 591, pp. 307–314, 2020.
https://doi.org/10.1007/978-3-030-57993-7_35

[3]. The German company DHL also launched in May 2019 their first regular service of Drones delivery in China, with a partnership with EHang an autonomous aerial vehicle company [4]. Another American parcel company – UPS – also performs Drone delivery for medical samples, but is going to expand the service for regular operations pushed by the competition and for the growth of online shopping [5]. Floreano and Wood [6] estimated that Drones will have an important socio-economic impact in society in many areas such as: Volumetric data collection; Inspection; Humanitarian Organizations, Transportation and others. In addition, they pointed out the Transport application affirming that Drones will also help developed countries to improve the quality of service in congested or remote areas and will enable rescue organizations to quickly deliver medical supplies in the field and on demand.

The trend of new technologies developed for transportation will not stop and the reason is the increase of online commerce and app-based ordering of almost everything from books to food, requires a large capacity, speed, and flexibility. In this context, last-mile delivery has grown exponentially in importance globally and is getting attention from the biggest companies around the world.

Besides drones, another trend for last-mile is shared mobility, Shaheen and Chan [7] explain that it will be possible in the future including the use of trip planning mobile apps, multi-modal integration, and potential opportunities with automation applied to last-mile delivery and not only for people mobility.

In this context, note that logistics service providers, who used to be almost invisible to final consumers, are now the first physical contact on the sales experience that consumers have. Moreover, more than ever, logistics and last-mile delivery are an active part of the whole customer experience journey. For Rai et al. [8] in the omnichannel environment, where products are delivered to the store and to the home, logistics service providers have become important links between retailers and their customers.

Indeed, the e-commerce sector was the first to realize the importance of last- mile delivery, nonetheless, the growth of sector create a gap between consumers and logistics parcel services companies. While the former are seeking alternatives to cost reduction and increase of the delivery efficiency, the latter are interested in more convenience to receive their products.

With those ideas in mind, this work intents to identify the expectations of logistics parcel providers and consumers and discuss the implications from e- commerce marketing. To this end, a literature review was conducted.

This paper is organized as follows. Section 2 represents the fundamental concepts for last-mile. Section 3 we delve into discussions considering expectations and implications of the last mile delivery in e-commerce. The last section closes with an initial conclusion and wonders for future researches.

2 Last-Mile

In recent years, logistics evolve from supporting role to the protagonist in the management scenario, replacing the notion that transportation is a necessity following production. Logistics turns out a paradigm referring to the integrated management of the whole supply chain, encompassing the entire cycle of production, circulation and, increasingly, consumption as something to be planned and analyzed [9].

Logistics always pursue the development from industry and market trends, emerging from a cost center to an innovative player, being crucial for the success of any retail company. Competitiveness can be improved through better management of logistics networks and can lead to the development of new models for different sectors [10].

Regarding last-mile delivery, it is necessary an overview of City Logistics topic. Taniguchi and Shimamoto [11] define city logistics as the process for totally optimizing the logistics and transport activities by private companies with the support of advanced information systems in urban areas considering the traffic environment, its congestion, safety, and energy savings within the framework of a market economy. In addition, Savelsbergh and Woensel [12] explain there are many definitions of city logistics, but common to all of them is that city logistics is about finding efficient and effective ways to transport goods in urban areas while taking into account the negative effects on congestion, safety, and environment.

Another important aspect of city logistics, it has been coined to emphasize the need for an optimized consolidation of loads of different shippers and carriers within the same delivery vehicle and coordination of freight transportation activities within the city [13].

Part of city Logistics' concerns is last-mile delivery. Lim and Srai [14] explains that the term "last-mile" originated in the telecommunications industry and refers to the final leg of a network. Today, last-mile logistics denotes the last segment of a delivery process, which is often regarded as the most expensive, least efficient aspect of a supply chain and with the most pressing environmental concerns.

Last-mile deliveries are one of the major effectors of heavy traffic on commercial vehicles in the whole city area. Their essential features, significantly lowering the rational functioning of the transport system, include a high degree of fragmentation and a low range of use of the cargo load compartment of vehicles [15]. Boysen et al. [16] brings to light that traditional last-mile delivery by trucks faces several problems, due of the human driver and the large fraction of unproductive work (e.g., due to absent customers or traffic holdups), truck deliveries are costly and, furthermore, seen as a major source of negative effects on congestion, safety, and environment in large city centers. However, according to Mackinnon [17] the amount and efficiency of freight movement in urban areas will be influenced more strongly by wider technological and business trends than by the localized actions of government agencies. One such trend is the growth of online retailing.

In the environment of e-commerce, Irakleous [18] says that although the provision of delivery service for e-shopping is an issue between e-retailer and transport service provider, the services to be developed need to identify consumers' demand and especially under what conditions a customer is willing to pay for these services.

It is a complex chain, to meet expectations from different stakeholders, such as consumers, retailers, parcel service companies among others. According to Irakleous [18], e-shopping can be fulfilled by a delivery system that can satisfy both consumers' and retailers' needs.

Consumers care about last-mile delivery because it offers convenience and flexibility. For those reasons, same-day and on-demand delivery services are gaining traction for groceries (e.g. Deliv Fresh, Instacart), pre-prepared meals (e.g. Sun Basket).

3 Results and Discussion

3.1 Last-Mile Expectations

Based on the literature review was possible to identify five aspects of interest from the e-commerce consumer perspective: (1) Delivery point; (2) Delivery time and speed; (3) Track and trace; (4) Value-added services and (5) Delivery Price:

- **Delivery point:** is the first thing that consumers will determine after purchase something online. There are two main obvious options: at home or at the workplace or if available pick-up in a point provided by the e-retailer.
- **Delivery time and speed:** are regarding the total time between order confirmation and final delivery, as mentioned previously is the main factor that impacts on the choice of delivery services attribute.
- **Track and trace:** are services based automatic communication between parcel providers and e-shoppers, thought RFID bar codes or number of orders, guarantee end-to-end tracker is very important for the final consumer has the feeling of control of their package.
- **Value-added:** is difficult to measure, because depends on consumer perception, can be a different package, an electric vehicle, a bike delivery, a call from provider among others. The price of delivery is the most sensitive aspect of this relationship, preferably should be lower than product price, but also cover all transportation and information costs, some companies still offering "free shipment" sometimes absorbing part of freight cost, sometimes embedding in the final cost [18].

Each one of those five attributes above are connected more to the consumer perspective, but online retailers are striving to offer consumers evermore responsive (and costly) last-mile delivery services in their efforts to increase sales and gain market share from their competitors, and as a result, often fail to cover the costs of these operations. The most significant impact of e-commerce on freight transportation is the increase in direct home delivery of smaller shipments, which may stimulate greater complexity in distribution system management, potentially causing higher costs in carrier's fleet operations [19, 20].

On the other hand, three aspects from parcel service providers were also identified, being: (1) the "not at home" problem; (2) Unattended delivery and (3) Last-mile collection. From the last-mile provider side, we can summarize those three aspects in one unique concern: Operational Cost.

- **The not at home:** issue is a growing concern for logistics providers, the rise of home deliveries of very small packages, increases the freight cost and makes the flow more complex. When the customer is not at home at the time of delivery, it generates a future attempt and a lower satisfaction from the consumer as well.

- **Unattended delivery** may offer an option for not at home situation, is cheaper and no need a person to receive the package, leaving the package in the doorstep, garden shed, concierge; but it can cause some security implications mostly when are high-value packages.
- **last-mile collection** consists in giving the consumer the option to pick-up their package at some convenient location, such as retail shops, petrol stations, etc., but this option is only reasonable if the pick-up point concentrates a certain number of orders to justify the cost transportation, even though is the same cost as home delivery [20]. Endorsing those challenges Wang et al. [21] argues that in urban logistics, the last-mile delivery from the warehouse to the consumer's home has become more and more challenging with the continuous growth of E-commerce. It requires elaborate planning and scheduling to minimize the global traveling cost but often results in unattended delivery as most consumers are away from home.

Figure 1 summarizes the disproportional scale between parcel service providers and final consumers, in the middle is the online companies that must administrate and balance the operational costs of delivery with the final price of their products.

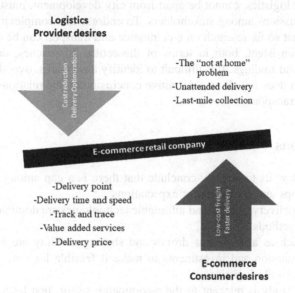

Fig. 1. Logistics desires × consumer desires

3.2 Last-Mile Implications

According to our research is possible to infer that there is a saturation of urban centers in terms of logistics flows, but there is a lack of an efficient and sustainable framework to deal with many challenges and expectations from different stakeholders along the last-mile in e-commerce supply chains.

Altenried [9] argues that the rise of logistics to a position in which it has become a central discipline of contemporary capitalism and sketches its digitally- driven saturation of urban spaces as the expression of new logistical urbanism.

Lim and Srai [14] endorse this idea saying that the development of these experimental last-mile logistics models, not surprisingly, created uncertainty within increasingly complicated and fragmented distribution networks. Without sustainable delivery economics, last-mile service provision will struggle to survive retailers increasingly challenged to find an optimal balance between pricing, consumer expectations for innovative new channels, and service levels.

Furthermore, is important to note that last-mile itself is a challenge for the majority of urban territories nowadays. Altenried [9] brings a reflection that with a glance at the streets of most cities brings to light the ubiquity of logistical operations: These streets are swarming with delivery vans of all sorts, bicycle messengers, food delivery drivers on scooters and many others trying to deliver all kinds of products to customers with maximum speed. Contemporary cities can no longer be understood primarily in relation to static objects, but increasingly through their logistical systems and procedural flows, claiming that time is now 'the most critical attribute of city making'.

In this sense logistics, cannot be apart from city development, must be an essential part of any discussions among stakeholders. To endorse this complexity Bjerkan et al. [22] conclude that so far research on e-commerce and transport can be characterized as diverse and inconsistent, both in terms of theoretical approaches, definitions, data, methodologies and findings. It is difficult to identify an obvious, overall direction, and existing research does not allow a definitive conclusion on the relationship between e-commerce and transport.

4 Conclusions

The research allow us to initially conclude that there is a gap among logistics parcel providers, e-Shops and e-Consumers expectations.

The limited delivery options and affordable technologies are dominated by standard home delivery methods.

Solutions such as autonomous drones and sharing mobility are embryonic; still, need a clear regulation and investments to make it feasible for most parcel delivery companies in last-mile logistics.

Finally, this study is relevant to the e-commerce sector, first because brings light that last-mile delivery is becoming a more significant factor that may affect online sales expansion in the future.

Acknowledgments. This study was financed in part by the Coordination of Improvement of Personal Higher Education - Brazil (CAPES) - Finance Code 001.

References

1. BBC: Amazon testing drones for deliveries. https://www.bbc.com/news/technology-25180906
2. DHL: DHL | press release | english. https://www.dhl.com/en/press/releases/releases_2014/group/dhl_parcelcopter_launches_initial_operations_for_research_purposes.html
3. D'onfo, J.: Amazon's new delivery drone will start shipping packages' in a matter of months (2019). https://www.forbes.com/sites/jilliandonfro/2019/06/05/amazon-new-delivery-drone-remars-warehouse-robots-alexa-prediction/#44921c7f145f
4. E-commerce: quantas lojas virtuais existem por aí? https://www.ecommercebrasil.com.br/artigos/quantos-e-commerce-existem-por-ai/
5. UPS: UPS plans to expand drone deliveries - CBS news. https://www.cbsnews.com/news/ups-plans-to-expand-drone-deliveries/
6. Floreano, D., Wood, R.J.: Science technology and the future of small autonomous drones. Nature **521**(7553), 460–466 (2015). http://www.nature.com/articles/nature14542
7. Shaheen, S., Chan, N.: Mobility and the sharing economy: potential to facilitate the first- and last-mile public transit connections. Built Environ. **42**(4), 573–588 (2016). https://doi.org/10.2148/benv.42.4.573
8. Rai, H.B., Verlinde, S., Macharis, C.: How are logistics service providers adapting to omnichannel retail? IFAC-PapersOnLine **51**(11), 588–593 (2018). https://doi.org/10.1016/j.ifacol.2018.08.382
9. Altenried, M.: On the last mile: logistical urbanism and the transformation of labour. Work Organ. Labour Glob. **13**(1), 114–129 (2019). www.jstor.org/stable/10.13169/workorgalaboglob.13.1
10. Juhász, J., Bányai, T.: Last mile logistics: an integrated view, vol. 448, p. 012026 (2018). http://stacks.iop.org/1757-899X/448/i=1/a=012026?key=crossref.c07a3066cca27eeb30a245e85c4aa373
11. Taniguchi, E., Shimamoto, H.: Intelligent transportation system based dynamic vehicle routing and scheduling with variable travel times. Transp. Res. Part C Emerg. Technol. **12**(3), 235–250 (2004). https://doi.org/10.1016/j.trc.2004.07.007
12. Savelsbergh, M., Van Woensel, T.: 50th anniversary invited article—city logistics: challenges and opportunities. Transp. Sci. **50**(2), 579–590 (2016). http://pubsonline.informs.org/doi/10.1287/trsc.2016.0675
13. Crainic, T.G., Ricciardi, N., Storchi, G.: Models for evaluating and planning city logistics systems. Transp. Sci. **43**(4), 432–454 (2009). https://doi.org/10.1287/trsc.1090.0279
14. Lim, S.F.W., Jin, X., Srai, J.S.: Consumer-driven e-commerce: a literature review, design framework, and research agenda on last-mile logistics models. Int. J. Phys. Distrib. Logist. Manage. **48**(3), 308–332 (2018). www.emerald.com/insight/content/doi/10.1108/IJPDLM-02-2017-0081/full/html
15. Iwan, S., Kijewska, K., Lemke, J.: Analysis of parcel lockers' efficiency as the last mile delivery solution – the results of the research in poland. Transp. Res. Proc. **12**, 644–655 (2016). https://doi.org/10.1016/j.trpro.2016.02.018
16. Boysen, N., Briskorn, D., Fedtke, S., Schwerdfeger, S.: Drone delivery from trucks: drone scheduling for given truck routes. Network **72**(4), 506–527 (2018). https://doi.org/10.1002/net.21847
17. Mckinnon, A.: The possible impact of 3D printing and drones on last-mile logistics: an exploratory study. Built Environ. **42**(4), 617–629 (2016). www.ingentaconnect.com/content/10.2148/benv.42.4.617

18. Irakleous, A.: Modeling framework for last-mile logistics services, p. 12. University of the Aegean (2018)
19. Allen, J., et al.: Understanding the impact of e-commerce on last-mile light goods vehicle activity in urban areas: the case of london. Transp. Res. Part D Transp. Environ. **61**, 325–338 (2018). https://doi.org/10.1016/j.trd.2017.07.020
20. Xu, M., Ferrand, B., Roberts, M.: The last mile of e-commerce – unattended delivery from the consumers and eTailers' perspectives. Int. J. Electron. Market. Retail. **2**(1), 20–38 (2008). www.inderscience.com/link.php?id=16815
21. Wang, Y., Zhang, D., Liu, Q., Shen, F., Lee, L.H.: Towards enhancing the last- mile delivery: an effective crowd-tasking model with scalable solutions. Transp. Res. Part E Logist. Transp. Rev. **93**, 279–293 (2016). https://doi.org/10.1016/j.tre.2016.06.002
22. Bjerkan, K.Y., Bjørgen, A., Hjelkrem, O.A.: E-commerce and prevalence of last mile practices. Transp. Res. Proc. **46**, 293–300 (2020). https://doi.org/10.1016/j.trpro.2020.03.193

Production-Storage and Transport Integrated Planning for a Multi-site Mining Industry

Asma Rakiz[1,2(✉)] and Pierre Fenies[1,2]

[1] Emines - Mohammed VI Polytechnic University, 43150 Benguerir, Morocco
{asma.rakiz,pierre.fenies}@emines.um6p.ma
[2] Paris II Panthon-Assas University, 75006 Paris, France

Abstract. Assuming that local planning usually leads to sub-optimal solutions, this work aims to solve an integrated production, storage and distribution problem as part of a global supply chain system. The problem we address combines a lot sizing and distribution problem in a multi-level, multi-product, multi-period production network. To solve it, we propose a MILP (Mix Integer Linear Program) taking into consideration the local constraints of the different subsystems, but also the global ones that express the interactions between subsystems. This model proposes simultaneously a production, storage and transport plan that satisfies a known demand while minimizing total production, storage and distribution costs. Finally, the solutions found within this approach have the advantage of considering the system's overall decisional cohesion as well as the constraints propagation in the various links of the chain. The originality of the work comes from the fact that we have addressed a multi-level lot-sizing problem, combined with a single rail transport problem. This integrated problem, to the best of our knowledge, has not been previously addressed. The model is tested and validated on a real mining industry, it proposes an integrated solution for simultaneous production, storage and distribution planning.

Keywords: Intergated lot sizing · Transportation · Linear optimisation · Mining industry

1 Introduction

This work takes place at OCP group, one of the world's leading companies in the phosphate market. OCP has a complex supply chain structure that starts with the mining phosphate deposits and reaches customers all over the world. The present study concerns Youssoufia site, located in the central axis, one of the three independent parallel axes of OCP's supply chain. This site produces three products (P1, P2, P3) delivered for two types of customers: local customers who refer to chemical transformation sites where acids and fertilizers are produced, and international ones from around the world. Youssoufia site is composed of three plants (laundry, calcining, and drying plant) that are interconnected by conveyors and separated by stocks upstream and downstream of each transformation process. This research focuses on supply chain planning problems as a whole. It considers an integrated planning approach where production, inventory, and transportation decisions are integrated. It adopts a global approach aiming to achieve an integrated flow planning that considers all the supply chain components including their

© IFIP International Federation for Information Processing 2020
Published by Springer Nature Switzerland AG 2020
B. Lalic et al. (Eds.): APMS 2020, IFIP AICT 591, pp. 315–322, 2020.
https://doi.org/10.1007/978-3-030-57993-7_36

respective constraints and specifications. The aim is to propose a single optimisation model taking into consideration (i) the characteristics of each subsystem composing the global production system, but also (ii) the different interactions that interconnect these subsystems in order to guarantee their synergy in the global logistics system. Classical models address supply chain planning problems sequentially or independently. The most classical approach starts with production and storage planning decisions, and establishes later transport decisions in an independent way. Though, it is now demonstrated that production and distribution decisions are mutually related problems and need to be dealt with simultaneously in an integrated manner [9]. According to [3], integrating these decisions lead definitely to a considerable increase in efficiency and effectiveness.

In addition, this paper addresses a real industrial problem posed by OCP. The studied system is a complex mining industrial system consisting of a multi-level, multi-product supply chain. This supply chain is composed by a multi-site production system, several storage sites and a train transport system within a single railway. This railway is used sequentially for passengers transport and for finite products transport, which imposes fixed time windows for finite products transport. This said, this paper addresses a capacitated lot sizing problem, combined with a hybrid transport problem using conveyors (for inter-site transport) and a single rail with time windows (for finished product delivery). All the production, storage and transport resources are limited by finite capacities. The remainder of this paper is organized as follows: Sect. 2 presents a literature review of the main themes addressed by this work. The proposed MILP to answer the problem is detailed in Sect. 3 before illustrating it with a practical case study in Sect. 4. Finally, some conclusions are addressed in Sect. 4.

2 Literature Review

Many researchers have been interested in production and stock planning using the lot sizing problem which has led to a literature proposing diverse and varied models to solve this kind of problems. The main objective of these models is determining the quantities of products to be manufactured in order to meet the demand while minimizing production, set up and storage costs [8]. Other costs may be added such as stock shortage cost. One of the reasons for interest in these models is their wide scope. Indeed, these models can be applied for the uncapacitated lot sizing [5], scheduling and lot sizing (small bucket) [12], and flow control [15]. They can also be associated with other supply chain planning problems [2] such as distribution problems to form the Integrated lot sizing with direct shipment models class, or to routing problems to form the class of models called Inventory Routing Problem (IRP), or even include all supply chain planning problems (production, storage, distribution, and routing) to create the Production Routing Problem (PRP) class. The extension of lot sizing models to multi-level supply chain structure is called multi-level lot sizing problem (MLLSP). The basic multi-level model, called the Multi-Level Capacitated Lot Sizing Problem (MLCLSP), was proposed by [6]. Its purpose is to link the end-products demand with the needs for internal components using the Goz-into matrix. This matrix is composed of the coefficients $a_{i,j}$ which represent the number of products i necessary to produce a product j, where i is the immediate predecessor of j in the product bill of material.

Based on the research that we analyzed, we could not find a paper that combines the problem of multi-level lot sizing with that of transport using a single railway track with time windows. To the best of our knowledge, little attention has been given to the problem of variable transport capacity and minimum quantity to be transported. Moreover [13] indicate that the most of industrial lot sizing literature is interested on discrete production problems, which makes production planning in the process industry a promising area for new research. All of these and other differences were synthesized in Table 1 containing the comparison between our MILP model and the reviewed ones that are dealing with a multi-level modeling.

Table 1. Comparison of the proposed MILP and reviewed models

	[20]	[16]	[17]	[14]	[19]	[11]	[18]	[6]	[1]	[3]	[4]	[10]	[7]	MILP
Parameters														
Production capacity	X		X		X	X	X	X	X	X		X		X
Dynamic stock capacity														X
Variable transport capacity		X												X
Transport capacity					X	X			X	X		X		X
Minimum quantity to be transported														X
Product structure		X	X		X			X	X		X			X
Inter-site travel time								X	X					X
Set up time							X	X	X					X
Maximum number of trains per period														X
Holding stock cost	X	X	X	X	X	X	X	X	X		X	X		
Variable production cost	X		X	X	X	X	X	X	X	X		X	X	X
Set up cost			X				X	X	X	X	X	X	X	X
Transport cost	X	X	X	X							X	X		X
Decision variables														
Hline multi-level production	X	X	X	X	X	X	X	X						X
Storage	X	X	X	X	X	X	X	X	X	X	X	X	X	X
Train transport														X

3 Multi-level Integrated Planning Model

The considered production network Fig. 1 is inspired by a real case industrial problem, it is composed of several manufacturing plants producing N products intended to meet two types of demand: an independent final demand known for a finite horizon, and an intermediate one of a product being a component of another downstream product in the supply chain. Shortages are not allowed and manufactured product have general type structure. The planning horizon is discrete and is composed by T periods. One product can be manufactured in several plants. Each plant is limited by a maximum production capacity and has a downstream stock in which the manufactured products can be stored. Each stock is limited by a maximum stock capacity. The different plants are inter-connected by conveyors characterized by $z_{u,u'}$: which refer to time required for a product to be transferred from plant u to plant u′, u′ being a downstream plant of the plant u in the supply chain structure. All finished products are transported via a single railway track to two different destinations: the port from which products are exported to international customers, and the local customers (chemical manufacturing sites). Products can be stored at the train unloading stations. Each train can ship only one product at a time and requires time to travel between production sites and destination sites. There are fixed time windows (train paths) in which the transport of finished products is possible; outside these hours, the railway is reserved for passenger transport. The delivery of the finished products must therefore respect these train paths.

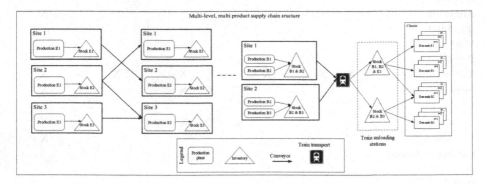

Fig. 1. Multi-level, multi product supply chain structure

In order to solve this problem, we propose a multi-level multi-product linear model where the shipment of end-products to the final stocks is provided by trains respecting the transport time windows. The objective of the model is to identify the periods in which production takes place as well as the production quantities, the amount that has to be stored and the quantity to be transported by train and the time windows to exploit. The production of each product generates a variable production cost, a set up cost and a set up time are incurred whenever a production batch starts. A holding cost is incurred per unit held in inventory per period. In addition, transport by train of a product generates a train transport cost. The considered notations of the mathematical model are detailed in Table 2. The formulation of the mathematical model is as follows:

Table 2. Parameters and variables

N	Number of products ($i = 1..N$)
T	Number of periods in the planning horizon ($t = 1..T$)
J	Number of days ($j = 1..J$) composing the planning horizon
H	Number of hours considered per days
S^p	Set of production sites
S^f	Set of final stocks
$D_{i,t}$	Final demand for product i in period t
X_u^{max}	Maximum production capacity at the plant u
$a_{i,j,u}$	The quantity of i needed to produce a unit of j at the plant u. $a_{i,j,u} = 0$ if $j < i$ (j predecessor of i)
$db_{i,t,u}$	Hourly production rate of product i in the plant u at the period t
$I_{max,u}$	Maximum storage capacity at the site u
Q_{max}	Maximum train transport capacity
Q_{min}	Minimum train transport capacity
λ_t	Binary parameter equals to 1 if train transport is possible at period t, 0 otherwise
$z_{u,u'}$	Time required for a product to be shipped from the plant u to the plant u'
ts_i	Set up time of the product i
$\beta_{i,u}$	Binary parameter equals to 1 if the product i can be produced at the plant u, 0 otherwise
h_i	Unit holding cost of product i
p_i	Unit production cost of product i
s_i	Set up cost of product i
t_u	Train transport cost from the plant u
M	Large number
R	Maximum number of trains allowed per day
$X_{i,t,u}$	Quantity of product i, to be produced at plant u in period t
$I_{i,t,u}$	Inventory level of product i at the end of period t for plant u
$Q_{i,t,u}$	Quantity of product i delivered by train from site u to final stocks, at the end of period t
$\gamma_{i,t,u}$	Binary set-up variable equal to 1 if and only if $X_{i,t,u} > 0$
$\omega_{i,t,u}$	Binary transport variable equal to 1 if and only if $Q_{i,t,u} > 0$

Minimize

$$\sum_t \sum_u \sum_i \left(p_i \cdot X_{i,t,u} + s_i \cdot \gamma_{i,t,u} + h_i \cdot I_{i,t,u} + t_u \cdot \omega_{i,t,u} \right) \tag{1}$$

Subject to:

$$I_{i,t-1,u} + X_{i,t,u} - Q_{i,t,u} - \sum_j a_{i,j} \cdot X_{j,t+z_{u,u'};u'} - I_{i,t,u} = 0$$
$$\left(\forall i, t, u \in S^p, u' \in S^f \right) \tag{2}$$

$$I_{i,t,u} = I_{i,t-1,u} - D_{i,t} \quad \left(\forall i, t < z_{u';u}, u \in S^f \right) \tag{3}$$

$$I_{i,t,u} = I_{i,t-1,u} + \sum_{u'} Q_{i,t-z_{i,u';u},u'} - D_{i,t} \quad \left(\forall i, t \geq z_{i,u';u}, u \in S^f\right) \tag{4}$$

$$ts_i \cdot \gamma_{i,t,u} \cdot db_{i,t,u} + X_{i,t,u} \leq X_u^{\max} \quad (\forall i, t, u) \tag{5}$$

$$\sum_i I_{i,t,u} \leq I_u^{\max} \quad (\forall t, u) \tag{6}$$

$$X_{i,t,u} < \beta_{i,u} \cdot X_u^{\max} \quad (\forall i, t, u) \tag{7}$$

$$I_{i,t,u} < \beta_{i,u} \cdot I_u^{\max} \quad (\forall i, t, u) \tag{8}$$

$$Q_{i,t,u} \leq Q^{\max} \cdot \lambda_t \quad (\forall i, t, u) \tag{9}$$

$$Q_{i,t,u} \geq Q^{\min} \cdot \omega_{i,t,u} \quad (\forall i, t, u) \tag{10}$$

$$\sum_{t\in H} \omega_{i,t+((j-1).H),u} \leq R \quad (\forall i, j \in J, u) \tag{11}$$

$$X_{i,t,u} - M \cdot \gamma_{i,t,u} \leq 0 \quad (\forall i, t, u) \tag{12}$$

$$Q_{i,t,u} - M\omega_{i,t,u} \leq 0 \quad (\forall i, t, u) \tag{13}$$

$$I_{i,t,u} \cdot X_{i,t,u} \geq 0 \quad (\forall i, t, u) \tag{14}$$

$$\gamma_{i,t,u}, \omega_{i,t,u} \in 0, 1 \quad (\forall i, t, u) \tag{15}$$

Objective function (1) minimizes total costs. Constraint (2) is stock balance equation of stocks downstream the production plants. Constraints (3) and (4) are stock balance equations of final stocks. Constraints (5) and (6) ensure the respect respectively of the maximum production and inventory capacity. Constraints (7) and (8) assign the products respectively to the plant/stocks in which they are produced/stored. Constraints (9) and (10) ensure maximum and minimum quantity limitations for transport by train. Constraint (11) limits the maximum number of trains per day. Constraints (12) and (13) bind binary variables to corresponding decision variables. Constraints (14) and (15) define the domain of the decision variables.

3.1   Case Study

In what follows, we illustrate the model previously described by a numerical example. The model is solved on a one week horizon with a temporal mesh of one hour (168 periods). The daily demand has been converted to hourly demand by assuming it is evenly distributed during the day. The program has been solved in few minutes using Xpress solver. The model has calculated an integrated plan of all components of the overall production system. These plans have enabled a demand satisfaction rate of 100%. For each period, product and site, the model proposes: (i) A production plan defined by the quantity to be produced per period and per product in each site where the fact that product P2 can be manufactured in two different sites has been considered. (ii) An inventory plan for the whole stock of the productive system. (iii) A transport plan, which identifies the quantity to be transported from the production sites to the final stocks. This plans respects travel time required to transport products to final stocks which is 2 h. The results of the products P1, P2 are respectively presented in Table 3, 4. These plans have enabled a demand satisfaction rate of 100%. We have found a global solution applicable in a global supply chain context.

Table 3. Production, storage and transport plans for product P1

Period	Quantity to produce	Inventory level	Quantity to transport by train	Inventory level at final stock	Demand
1	68	1068	0	0	0
2	91	1159	0	0	0
...	...	...	...	...	...
20	91	2803	0	0	0
21	91	519	2376	0	0
22	91	610	0	0	0
23	91	701	0	2376	0
24	91	793	0	2376	0
25	91	884	0	2268	108
26	91	975	0	2160	108
...	...	...	...	...	...
...	...	...	...	...	...
164	0	0	0	828	83
165	0	0	0	745	83
166	0	0	0	662	83
167	0	0	0	579	83
168	0	0	0	496	83

Table 4. Production, storage and transport plans for product P2

Period	Calcining plant			Drying plant			Inventory level at final stock	Demand
	Quantity to produce	Inventory level	Quantity to transport by train	Quantity to produce	Inventory level	Quantity to transport by train		
1	91	1091	0	0	0	0	4583	417
2	258	1349	0	0	0	0	4166	417
3	258	1607	0	0	0	0	3749	417
4	258	1865	0	0	0	0	3332	417
5	258	2123	0	0	0	0	2915	417
6	258	2381	0	0	0	0	2498	417
7	258	2639	0	272	272	0	2081	417
8	258	2897	0	272	545	0	1664	417
9	258	1066	2089	272	817	0	1247	417
10	258	1324	0	272	1089	0	830	417
...	...	...	...	...	...	...	...	...
167	0	0	0	0	0	0	417	417
168	0	0	0	0	0	0	0	417

4 Conclusion

In this paper, we propose a MILP to perform simultaneous planning of production, storage and transport over a finite horizon composed of discrete periods. This planning takes place in the context of a multi-level, multi-period, multi-product supply chain structure, while taking into account all the different capacities. Also, the transport of the finished products is ensured by a single railway track, with fixed time windows. This model has been tested on a mining system in order to achieve an overall flow optimization, that takes into account the characteristics of the different subsystems, their interactions and the propagation of constraints all along this chain.

References

1. Absi, N., Archetti, C., Dauzère-Pérès, S., Feillet, D.: A two-phase iterative heuristic approach for the production routing problem. Transp. Sci. **49**(4), 784–795 (2014)
2. Adulyasak, Y., Cordeau, J.F., Jans, R.: Optimization-based adaptive large neighborhood search for the production routing problem. Transp. Sci. **48**(1), 20–45 (2012)
3. Adulyasak, Y., Cordeau, J.F., Jans, R.: Formulations and branch-and-cut algorithms for multivehicle production and inventory routing problems. INFORMS J. Comput. **26**(1), 103–120 (2013)
4. Aghezzaf, E.H., Zhong, Y., Raa, B., Mateo, M.: Analysis of the single-vehicle cyclic inventory routing problem. Int. J. Syst. Sci. **43**(11), 2040–2049 (2012)
5. Bahl, H.C., Ritzman, L.P., Gupta, J.N.: Or practice—determining lot sizes and resource requirements: a review. Oper. Res. **35**(3), 329–345 (1987)
6. Billington, P.J., McClain, J.O., Thomas, L.J.: Heuristics for multilevel lot-sizing with a bottleneck. Manag. Sci. **32**(8), 989–1006 (1986)
7. Brahimi, N., Aouam, T.: Multi-item production routing problem with backordering: a MILP approach. Int. J. Prod. Res. **54**(4), 1076–1093 (2016)
8. Brahimi, N., Dauzere-Peres, S., Najid, N.M., Nordli, A.: Single item lot sizing problems. Eur. J. Oper. Res. **168**(1), 1–16 (2006)
9. Fahimnia, B., Farahani, R.Z., Marian, R., Luong, L.: A review and critique on integrated production–distribution planning models and techniques. J. Manuf. Syst. **32**(1), 1–19 (2013)
10. Federgruen, A., Tzur, M.: Time-partitioning heuristics: application to one ware-house, multiitem, multiretailer lot-sizing problems. Naval Res. Logist. (NRL) **46**(5), 463–486 (1999)
11. Fran,ca, P.M., Armentano, V.A., Berretta, R.E., Clark, A.R.: A heuristic method for lot-sizing in multi-stage systems. Comput. Oper. Res. **24**(9), 861–874 (1997)
12. Graves, S.C.: A review of production scheduling. Oper. Res. **29**(4), 646–675 (1981)
13. Jans, R., Degraeve, Z.: Modeling industrial lot sizing problems: a review. Int. J. Prod. Res. **46**(6), 1619–1643 (2008). https://doi.org/10.1080/00207540600902262
14. Kaminsky, P., Simchi-Levi, D.: Production and distribution lot sizing in a two stage supply chain. IIE Trans. **35**(11), 1065–1075 (2003)
15. Kuik, R., Salomon, M., Van Wassenhove, L.N.: Batching decisions: structure and models. Eur. J. Oper. Res. **75**(2), 243–263 (1994)
16. Lin, J.T., Chen, Y.Y.: A multi-site supply network planning problem considering variable time buckets–a TFT-LCD industry case. Int. J. Adv. Manuf. Technol. **33**(9–10), 1031–1044 (2007)
17. Pibernik, R., Sucky, E.: An approach to inter-domain master planning in supply chains. Int. J. Prod. Econ. **108**(1–2), 200–212 (2007)
18. Tempelmeier, H., Derstroff, M.: A lagrangean-based heuristic for dynamic multi- level multiitem constrained lotsizing with setup times. Manag. Sci. **42**(5), 738–757 (1996)
19. Timpe, C.H., Kallrath, J.: Optimal planning in large multi-site production networks. Eur. J. Oper. Res. **126**(2), 422–435 (2000)
20. Van Hoesel, S., Romeijn, H.E., Morales, D.R., Wagelmans, A.P.: Integrated lot sizing in serial supply chains with production capacities. Manag. Sci. **51**(11), 1706–1719 (2005)

Artificial Intelligence and Blockchain Technologies in Logistics and DSN

Evaluating a Blockchain-Based Supply Chain Purchasing Process Through Simulation

Geraldo Jose Dolce Uzum Martins[1] ⓘ,
Jacqueline Zonichenn Reis[2](✉) ⓘ, Benedito Cristiano A. Petroni[2] ⓘ,
Rodrigo Franco Gonçalves[1,2] ⓘ, and Berislav Andrlić[3] ⓘ

[1] Politecnic School, University of Sao Paulo, Sao Paulo, Brazil
geraldo.martins@gmail.com, rofranco212@gmail.com
[2] Graduate Studies in Production Engineering, Universidade Paulista,
Sao Paulo, Brazil
zonichenn@hotmail.com,
benedito.petroni@docente.unip.br
[3] Polytechnic in Pozega, Pozega, Croatia
bandrlic@vup.hr

Abstract. Tracking financial data is a task that usually involves intermediaries and this issue has not been totally covered by information systems. Blockchain has been presented as a potential solution though. The aim of this paper is to perform a proof of concept of purchasing management that makes use of blockchain technology in order to track financial data. The adopted methodology was simulation to compare two different scenarios: a traditional purchasing process (As-Is) and another using blockchain (To-Be). The output of the simulations was used to compare the transactional costs of each model measured through two variables: the execution time of placing orders and the number of service stations required. It could be verified that the blockchain network alternative had a superior performance according to the type of architecture employed. In the present study, the private blockchain with proof of work adjusted to seek hashes that begins with two consecutive zeros had the best achievement.

Keywords: Blockchain · Purchasing process · Economic decision · Simulation

1 Introduction

The financial information sharing frequently requires a trustful intermediary to confirm the transaction. Public authorities, registry offices and banks are the main stakeholders. The transactional costs associated with these intermediaries reduce the operational efficiency of the process. Numerous technologies were developed to solve this confidence issue in order to automate and connect activities executed traditionally by people, in an individual manner or in groups, but without success [1].

Similarly, the purchasing process has many agents to validate transactional data in all stages. These transactions could be tax registrations, accounting and financial records that attribute monetary values to the products or services. Information systems

© IFIP International Federation for Information Processing 2020
Published by Springer Nature Switzerland AG 2020
B. Lalic et al. (Eds.): APMS 2020, IFIP AICT 591, pp. 325–332, 2020.
https://doi.org/10.1007/978-3-030-57993-7_37

applied to the purchasing process are unable to provide real-time and checked tracking data during the manufacturing and distribution stages. The data privacy is also a strategic issue when the finished products trade is concerned [2].

The blockchain has the potential for application in value chains that demand the record of operational or financial data in an authentic and incorruptible form. It was suggested that automation with blockchain could be viable in workflows that spend considerable time to be executed [3].

Since the blockchain application in the industry is seen as an alternative to increase the process automation and reduce the transactional costs, the performance comparative analyzes between scenarios without and with blockchain are pertinent to evaluate its adoption.

Regarding simulation, Sabounchi and Wei [4] use this approach to evaluate trading of electricity model distributed peer-to-peer in the Ethereum blockchain. Engelmann et al. [5] also use this method to assess the financial performance of adjacent connections between pairs of computers and the blockchain network, with the aim of storing the bilateral payment transactions outside the network.

The objective of this research is to evaluate the blockchain feasibility as a potential substitute of integrated information system applied to a purchasing process among organizations. The effectiveness of this proposition was done through the comparison of transactional costs linked to the operational times measured in the traditional condition and in a scenario which the blockchain is used.

2 Background

The blockchain is an architecture of data blocks tied by cryptography. The blocks are organized in a temporal sequence and validated by an algorithm with hash functions. Hash functions are small computer codes that convert any class of data in a string of fixed size, independently of the input data size [6].

Wright [7] suggested a database framework composed with addresses combined to balance amounts, with copies distributed in all nodes of a network, and some nodes could offer computational efforts to record a new block of data in exchange for a fraction of the amount traded. This was the first application of the blockchain, the Bitcoin cryptocurrency. The blockchain can be also used to record, track and control asset transfers as an inventory system. Therefore, any tangible or digital asset could be stored in the blockchain [8].

2.1 Blockchain Operation

Each block in the blockchain contains all system transactional data since its beginning and the unique fingerprint used to confirm the information. The blocks are connected linear and chronologically through a hash with the next block as a real chain. The creation of a new block depends on proof of work that are mathematical problems which demand the computing power to be solved [6].

The blockchain can be configured in two types of architectures: public or private. In the public blockchain, all users can read, send transactions and cooperate in the proof of work without any authorization. All transactions are public, and the users remain anonymous. On the other hand, private blockchain is run by a single entity that authorizes access to selected users [2].

2.2 Proof of Work

The central feature in the block validation is the running of the proof of work that is a resolution of a hash puzzle. Only blocks that hold an accurate solution of a single hash will be processed. This confirmation is an answer to a mathematical problem that makes uses of unidirectional hash functions. In a simplified form, the problem is to determine a variable that produces a result whose beginning be a specific sequence pre-determined, when it is combined with data of the former and the actual blocks and processed by a hash function [9]. For example, the effort could be discovering a string value whose result starts with three zeros on the left. Since this function is one-way, this resolution needs to be done by trial and error and as far as the network expands, the blockchain system calibrates the difficulty of finding the answer for the problem by increasing the number of zeros.

2.3 Blockchain Applications

It can be found in scientific literature, there are researches about potential application of blockchain in several areas of knowledge.

Dujak e Sajter [10] discuss, broadly, the application of blockchain in logistics and supply networks. Petroni et al. [11] present a particular application in this context using Big Data Analytics.

Sikorski, Haughton, and Kraft [12] present an example where blockchain is employed to facilitate M2M interactions and establish a M2M electricity market in the context of the chemical industry.

Huckle et al. [13] explore combining use of smart contracts in the blockchain with IOT for three sharing economy examples: an autonomy vehicle rent system, a foreign exchange contract and automation of royalties payable for the licensing of copyrights.

França et al. [14] present a blockchain application using a social cryptocurrency to improve recycling and solid waste management, with social and environmental benefits in a small municipality. The presented blockchain payment system can provide transaction security among all the stakeholders.

3 Method

The adopted methodology was simulation to compare two different scenarios. Simulation is one of the most useful techniques in Operational Research and it facilitates the design of scenarios to orientate the decision-making procedure [15].

The method adopted for the research was:

1) Definition of a purchasing process scenario among organizations:
   a. An As-is scenario with manual payment system.

b. A To-be scenario using blockchain.

2) Simulation program modelling and construction, considering as fundamentals variables the public or private blockchain and proof of work effort.

3) Run simulation to compare the As-is scenario with the To-be scenario.

In this sense, four scenarios were simulated:

a) A manual purchasing order;
b) A private blockchain with two zeros proof-of-work;
c) A public blockchain in the Ethereun network;
d) A private blockchain with three zeros proof-of-work;

In the As-Is process, the transaction data are manually recorded in four different databases. Countless inconsistencies during conciliation are identified due to imprecise registers or incomplete integration and it causes delays in manufacturing and erroneous orders executed. In contrast, in the To-Be process, the shop floor data are saved solely in a blockchain which is accessible to the buyer and seller as well. Each agent is responsible for making the consults and executing the required transactions confirmations in the blocks. In this model, it is assumed that agents were the machines themselves and the interactions occurred uniquely in the blockchain.

The transactional cost is the expenses included in the process. In the purchase process As-Is, these costs could be related to these activities: demand identification, preparation of the purchase order, supplier order confirmation, tax invoice issue, manual registration of the product in the inventory system and manual recording of the tax invoice in account books. In the To-Be process, these costs comprise the data recording in blockchain by the buyer and the subsequent blocks query to verify the status of the goods in transit. In both situations, the transactional efforts were statistically analyzed by two variables: the execution time of placing orders and the number of service stations required. The As-Is and To-Be processes are represented through flow charts detailed in Figs. 1 and 2.

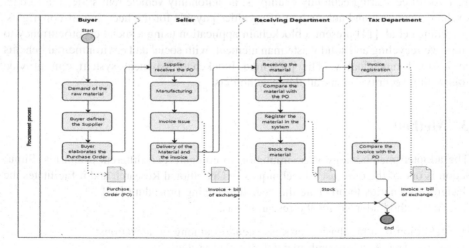

Fig. 1. As-Is process (prepared by the author in Bizagi software)

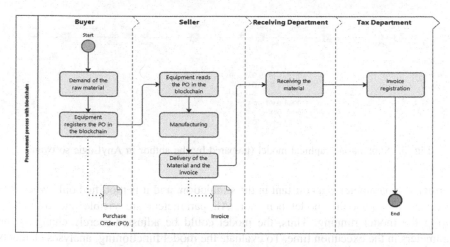

Fig. 2. To-Be process (prepared by the author in Bizagi software)

The historical data of Ethereum block creation time from 11/12/2017 to 11/18/2018 were used to simulate the public blockchain [16]. In the private blockchain, it was necessary to develop a mechanism to measure the time to discover a final hash that began with two and three consecutive zeros.

The model's source code and data simulated are available in https://github.com/gdolce/blockchain.

Both models were simulated as discrete events modeling because the objective was exactly the process model, in other words, it is a sequence of operations that agents perform. In this simulation, the agents are the purchase orders and the material in transit along the As-Is and To-Be processes. The operations in the modeling can be delays, multiple resources services, process ramification selections, separations, among others. Once the agents compete for limited resources and they might delay, queue generation is inherent to most of the discrete event models.

The discrete events models are stochastics since the arrival times of the agents and service times are usually stochastics, that is, they have resulted from a probabilistic distribution. It means that the model must be run for a determined time or carry out enough number of replications until an output relevant be generated. The most common outputs in the discrete events are resource utilization, time spent in the whole system or in part of it, waiting times, queues, system performance, and bottlenecks identification. The activities of purchasing process modeled in the AnyLogic software were consolidated in three consecutive steps: purchase order issue, manufacturing, and material receiving. These elements are graphically presented in Fig. 3.

Four variables were used in the simulation: demanded quantity, operational time to issue the purchase order, operational time to manufacture and operational time to the material receiving. The parameters are frequently used to represent some characteristics of the modeled object and could express for example time, velocity, quantity, acceleration, size, area, etc. They are appropriate when the objects have the same behavior described in their class and they are usually used to specify the objects statically.

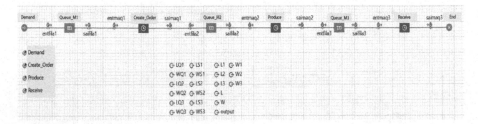

Fig. 3. Simulation graphical model (prepared by the author in AnyLogic software)

Normally, a parameter is a constant in the simulation, and it is modified only when it is necessary to adjust the model behavior. All parameters are visible and oscillating during the model running. Thus, the model could be adjusted merely changing the parameters in the execution time. To evaluate the model functioning, analyses elements were used to collect, visualize and test the outputs data. These elements can store the statistical data of a queueing network such as queue size, queue time, average customer number in the system, average customer number in service, average time spent in the system and service time. The output element was used to store a unique scalar data vector and exhibit after finishing the run.

4   Discussion and Results

The summary of the results is presented in Table 1. In the comparison among the four scenarios, it could be observed that the private blockchain, with proof of work adjusted to seek hashes that begins with two consecutive zeros, had the best performance.

Table 1. Summary of the simulation results.

As-Is		To-Be (Blockchain)		
Recording type	Manual	Private 2 zeros hashes	Public	Private 3 zeros hashes
Probablity distribution	Uniform	Exponential	Lognormal	Exponential
Output quantity (thousand)	718,3	718,3	717,3	445,4
Average queue size in the system (units)	29,4	29,1	1.150	136.470
Average time spent in the system (min)	24	22,7	820	99.828
The utilization rate of Create_Order block	40,50%	13,60%	65,20%	100,00%
Service capacity of creating orders (unit)	5	1	1	1

The private blockchain with proof of work adjusted to seek hashes that begin with three consecutive zeros had the service level of 100% and it resulted an average queue size and average time in system higher than the other conditions. The As-Is performance was similar to the best To-Be scenario with regard to the variables output quantity, average queue size in the system and average time in the system. However, As-Is needs a service capacity of five units while To-Be needs only one.

The different creation time between public and private blockchain can be explained by the hardware used in the processing. In public blockchain, powerful equipment such as dedicated graphics processing unit (GPUs) and application-specific integrated circuit (ASIC) are used and they facilitate the scale gain.

The proof of work demands a growing energetic consumption which limits the scalability of the network and in a certain moment, the transactional cost, that includes the costs of computational infrastructure and energy, will be so high that the network will become so costly to be used. For example, the Bitcoin could consume in a near future, 7.7 GWe of electricity which is comparable to the demand of countries such as Ireland (3.1 GWe) and Austria (8.2 GWe) [17].

Alternative algorithms are being developed at this moment. In contrast to the proof-of-work, the great emphasis is the proof-of-stake that chooses the miner of the block randomly and restricted. Only miners that deposit a guarantee in the network are eligible to participate in the efforts to solve the problem. But, in case that other miners decide that the block validation was not done according to the rules, the miner loses its deposit. By this way, the value in risk is higher than the compensation received by the block validated. So, fraudulent authentications are not attractive which ensure the network security [18].

5 Conclusion

This research showed, through simulation, the feasibility of blockchain to be the medium of register and the operator of the purchase orders among companies, considering the limitation of a theoretical study.

Technical conditions at present, as computational capacity and energy consumption, defines the limits of use of the public blockchain or private blockchain scenarios. The core factor of this limitation is the proof of work, adjusted to seek hashes that begins with three consecutive zeros. Therefore, it is unlikely that these two scenarios reach productivities equivalent to the As-Is scenario and to private blockchain with proof of work adjusted to seek hashes that begins with two consecutive zeros.

The blockchain industry is in its initial stages of development and consequently, potential limitations are recognized, but nothing that interferes in the technology diffusion. Thus, this work contributes to revealing the understandability of the technology and its feasibility to a purchasing process among organizations. Future works can apply this simulation at the shop floor level, considering M2M transactions, as well to conduct field studies about real implementations.

References

1. Glaser, F., Bezzenberger, L.: Beyond cryptocurrencies - a taxonomy of decentralized consensus systems. In: Presented at the 23rd European Conference on Information Systems (ECIS), Münster, Germany (2015)
2. Wu, H., Li, Z., King, B., Ben Miled, Z., Wassick, J., Tazelaar, J.: A distributed ledger for supply chain physical distribution visibility. Information **8**, 137 (2017). https://doi.org/10.3390/info8040137
3. Christidis, K., Devetsikiotis, M.: Blockchains and smart contracts for the Internet of Things. IEEE Access. **4**, 2292–2303 (2016). https://doi.org/10.1109/ACCESS.2016.2566339
4. Sabounchi, M., Wei, J.: Towards resilient networked microgrids: blockchain-enabled peer-to-peer electricity trading mechanism. In: 2017 IEEE Conference on Energy Internet and Energy System Integration (EI2), pp. 1–5. IEEE, Beijing (2017). https://doi.org/10.1109/EI2.2017.8245449
5. Engelmann, F., Kopp, H., Kargl, F., Glaser, F., Weinhardt, C.: Towards an economic analysis of routing in payment channel networks. In: Proceedings of the 1st Workshop on Scalable and Resilient Infrastructures for Distributed Ledgers - SERIAL'17, pp. 1–6. ACM Press, Las Vegas (2017). https://doi.org/10.1145/3152824.3152826
6. Buchmann, J.: Introduction to Cryptography. Springer Science & Business Media, Berlin (2013)
7. Wright, C.S.: Bitcoin: a peer-to-peer electronic cash system. SSRN J. (2008). https://doi.org/10.2139/ssrn.3440802
8. Swan, M.: Blockchain: Blueprint for a New Economy. O'Reilly Media Inc, Sebastopol (2015)
9. Tapscott, D., Tapscott, A.: Blockchain Revolution: How the Technology Behind Bitcoin is Changing Money, Business, and the World. Penguin, New York (2016)
10. Dujak, D., Sajter, D.: Blockchain applications in supply chain. In: Kawa, A., Maryniak, A. (eds.) SMART Supply Network. E, pp. 21–46. Springer, Cham (2019). https://doi.org/10.1007/978-3-319-91668-2_2
11. Petroni, Benedito C. A., Reis, J.Z., Gonçalves, R.F.: Blockchain as an Internet of services application for an advanced manufacturing environment. In: Ameri, F., Stecke, Kathryn E., von Cieminski, G., Kiritsis, D. (eds.) APMS 2019. IAICT, vol. 567, pp. 389–396. Springer, Cham (2019). https://doi.org/10.1007/978-3-030-29996-5_45
12. Sikorski, J.J., Haughton, J., Kraft, M.: Blockchain technology in the chemical industry: machine-to-machine electricity market. Appl. Energy **195**, 234–246 (2017). https://doi.org/10.1016/j.apenergy.2017.03.039
13. Huckle, S., Bhattacharya, R., White, M., Beloff, N.: Internet of Things, blockchain and shared economy applications. Procedia Comput. Sci. **98**, 461–466 (2016). https://doi.org/10.1016/j.procs.2016.09.074
14. França, A.S.L., Amato Neto, J., Gonçalves, R.F., Almeida, C.M.V.B.: Proposing the use of blockchain to improve the solid waste management in small municipalities. J. Cleaner Prod. **244**, 118529 (2020). https://doi.org/10.1016/j.jclepro.2019.118529
15. Pereira, C.D., da Cunha, G.F., da Silva, M.G.: A simulação na pesquisa operacional: uma revisão literária. Presented at the IX EEPA - Encontro de Engenharia de Produção Agroindustrial, Campo Mourão (2015)
16. Team, Etherscan: Etherscan: The Ethereum Block Explorer. https://etherscan.io/tokens
17. de Vries, A.: Bitcoin's growing energy problem. Joule **2**, 801–805 (2018). https://doi.org/10.1016/j.joule.2018.04.016
18. Siim, J.: University of Tartu - Institute of Computer Science courses. https://courses.cs.ut.ee/MTAT.07.022/2017_fall/uploads/Main/janno-report-f17.pdf

Questionnaire Model for Paraconsistent Quality Assessment of Software Developed in SalesForce

Luiz Roberto Forçan(✉) ⓘ, Jair Minoro Abe ⓘ,
Luiz Antônio de Lima ⓘ, and Samira Sestari Nascimento ⓘ

Paulista University, São Paulo, Brazil
luforcan@gmail.com.br, jairabe@uol.com.br,
luiz@wcisp.com.br, samirasestari@gmail.com

Abstract. The article suggests the use of the Paraconsistent Decision Method (MPD) to improve the analysis of data captured in a standardized SUS-System Usability Scale questionnaire. The paraconsistent evaluation allows you to measure the usability quality of the provider registration software developed on the SalesForce platform. The data obtained through the questionnaire must be processed to be submitted to the Para-analyzer algorithm of The Paraconsistent Annotated Logic Evidential Eτ - Logic Eτ. Logic Eτ is used as a non-classical logic that allows analyzing the opinions of users considering their uncertainties, inaccuracies, ambiguities, and subjectivities that are inherent to human values. Through the Para-analyzer algorithm, we intend to obtain a consensus of the opinions of the experts on the usability of the software. The model with Logic Eτ allows being used in addition to the statistical treatment provided by the SUS method, improving the analysis of the data. With the result of this analysis, it is intended to diagnose usability problems contributing to the improvement of software development.

Keywords: Software usability quality · Paraconsistent logic annotated Eτ · Cloud computing · Salesforce

1 Introduction

To be successful in this competitive market one vital point is the usability assessment. It is essential to measure the degree of user satisfaction that uses the software product developed in the SalesForce tool in your daily life.

There are several approaches to assess the usability of the software: the System Usability Scale (SUS) questionnaire is widely used for usability testing, reliability, learning capacity, appearance, and other aspects. A newer scale for measuring usability is the usability metric for user experience with few items that determine reliability and usefulness.

For the present study, we will use the SUS questionnaire format, and the main advantages of using these instruments for distance evaluation are objectivity in the

© IFIP International Federation for Information Processing 2020
Published by Springer Nature Switzerland AG 2020
B. Lalic et al. (Eds.): APMS 2020, IFIP AICT 591, pp. 333–340, 2020.
https://doi.org/10.1007/978-3-030-57993-7_38

collection of information, replicability of the instrument in other studies and quantification of results from the participants' responses [11].

Logic Eτ because it is a non-classical logic, allows the analysis of the subjective opinions of experts considering their uncertainties, inaccuracies, ambiguities, and subjectivities that are inherent to human values [2]. Other approaches allow you to do this analysis, such as the AHP Analytic Hierarchy Process. It is observed that the AHP method, although with peculiarities that aim to solve these possible problems, is based on the classical methods of decision-making, which consider the human opinions accurate and well defined (false and true) [7, 14].

Considering that it is proposed of the ISO/IEC 25010 standard [12] complements the study as qualitative attributes distributed in eight main characteristics: Functional adequacy, Performance efficiency, compatibility, usability, reliability, safety, maintenance, and portability. The standard recommends the qualitative feature of usability, which is divided into six sub characteristics: Accessibility, Apprehension, Aesthetics of the user interface, Operability, Protection against user errors, and Appropriate Recognition.

This article presents the results of a survey, applying the SUS questionnaire, to the specialists who use the software registration of providers, measuring the favorable and contrary evidence for each question of the questionnaire.

The research presents a model to assist in the decision-making process of evaluating the data collected on usability using Logic Eτ, through the Para-analyzer algorithm, using logical criteria that enable technical validation, and the input parameters are established by the opinions of the experts, consolidating a collective logic of these opinions, converted into mathematical terms.

2   Literature Revision

2.1   SalesForce

Salesforce (SF), which stands for "SalesForce" was founded in 1999 in California, USA by Marc Benioff and Parker Harris, and its main predominant point is the customer relationship management or Customer Relationship Management (CRM) system. It proposes to offer a platform in the clouds where the entire computational resource is located [9]. The SF platform has become attractive with the relationship management solution due to outsourcing CRM on the Internet, providing the CRM Web Service where it offers customizable, easy-to-implement software that easily engages the user, ensuring data integrity and security [15].

2.2   Software Usability

According to the iso/IEC 25010 usability standard is the ability of the software to be easily operated, understood, easy to learn, and with an attractive user interface. ISO/IEC25010 [12] defines the following usability characteristics of software product quality: Accessibility, Apprehension, User Interface Aesthetics, Operability, User Error Protection, and Intelligibility or appropriate recognition.

To evaluate the usability of software, questionnaires such as SUMI, SUS, WAMMI, SUPR-Q, CEG, and NPS are used. With these questionnaires, usability, reliability, and learning capacity and appearance tests are performed in software. For this article, we opted for the System Usability Scale - SUS questionnaire because it is the most popular choice for evaluating software usability [11].

2.3   System Usability Scale (SUS)

The Usability Scale System - SUS [8] questionnaire is used to assess the level of usability of the system. The SUS scale consists of 10 specific questions to allow an analysis of the usability and ease of learning characteristics of a system. Each question has five answer options that follow the 5-point Likert scale: from 1 (I totally disagree) to 5 (I totally agree) where 3 means neutrality. This instrument allows objectivity in the collection of information and evaluation of the results of the experts' answers, through statistical calculations [6, 11].

2.4   Analytical Hierarchical Process (AHP)

The Analytical Hierarchical Process (AHP) method is used to assist in decision making, evaluating multiple objectives and criteria in problems characterized by complexity and subjectivity. Alternatives are evaluated in the face of a complex decision problem [16].

The AHP assumes that the decision-makers can provide accurate answers by comparing criteria and alternatives. However, due to the uncertainty, incompleteness, and subjectivity of the information, it is difficult to provide accurate judgments [7, 14].

2.5   Paraconsistent Annotated Evidential Logic Eτ

Paraconsistent logic is a category on non-classical logics that the Contradiction (or Non-contradiction) Principle is not valid in general. So, in this type of logic, theories based on it, there are propositions p and ¬p (the negation of p) both true [1]. One category of paraconsistent logic, namely the paraconsistent annotated evidential logic Eτ, besides being paraconsistent, it is also paracomplete. Such logic is capable of handling inconsistent, imprecise, and paracomplete data.

In everyday life, the data from various sources can be contradictory, making room for uncertainties, resulting in contradictions that prevent decision-making.

In the Paraconsistent annotated evidential Logic Eτ, each Proposition P associates a Favorable Degree of Evidence (μ) and a Contrary Degree of Evidence (λ). The Degrees of Evidence are real values between 0 and 1 that denote, in the case of the Favorable Degree of Evidence, the evidence that proposition P is true, and in the case of the Contrary Evidence Degree denotes contrary when proposition P is not true.

It is called Degree of Uncertainty Gin (μ, λ) of an annotation (μ, λ) to any of the degrees of inconsistency or paracompleteness.

It is called Gce Degree of Certainty (μ, λ) of an annotation (μ, λ) to any of the degrees of truth or falsehood. Depending on the Values of the Degrees of Evidence, four extreme states can be: true, false, inconsistent, and paracomplete as shown in Fig. 2.

The Para-analyzer algorithm is composed of a set of information collected through a research questionnaire for decision-making analysis [5]. The definition of the Para-consistent Decision Method (MPD), proposed in the studies, reflects the method, through Paraconsistent Logic, to use contradictory information, obtaining results that help in decision making [1, 4]. Figure represents the Unitary Square of the Cartesian Plan (QUPC), the degrees of certainty and contradiction, grouped into twelve states, which graphically presents the Para-analyzer algorithm.

Extreme states	Symbol	Non-extreme states	Symbol
True	V	Quasi-true tending to Inconsistent	QV→T
False	F	Quasi-true tending to Paracomplete	QV→⊥
Inconsistent	T	Quasi-false tending to Inconsistent	QF→T
Paracomplete	⊥	Quasi-false tending to Paracomplete	QF→⊥
		Quasi-inconsistent tending to True	QT→V
		Quasi-inconsistent tending to False	QT→F
		Quasi-paracomplete tending to True	Q⊥→V
		Quasi-paracomplete tending to False	Q⊥→F

Fig. 1. Unitary square of the cartesian plane (Source: [1])

It is observed, then, that with the Para-analyzer algorithm, in addition to the four extreme states, it is possible to determine eight more non-extreme states. The Fig. 1 shows the states that represent the non-extreme states in the para-parser algorithm. The Para-analyzer algorithm works with four external control values defined in the application environment, represented in Fig. 3: V_{cve} - Veracity control value, $0 \leq V_{cve}$ 1. V_{cfa} - Falsehood control value, $-1 \leq V_{cfa} \leq 0$. V_{cic} - Inconsistency Control Value, $0 \leq V_{cic} \leq 1$ e V_{cpa} - Paracompleteza control value, $-1 \leq V_{cpa} \leq 0$.

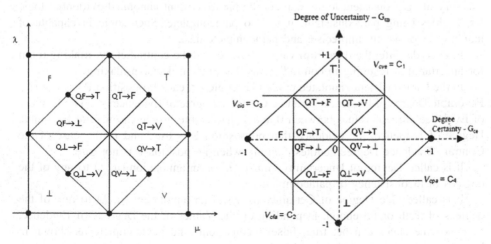

Fig. 2. Lattice τ (Source: [2])   **Fig. 3.** Control values (Source: [3])

3 Methodology

This research intends to evaluate the usability through the data collected through the AHP questionnaire. The users' responses will be submitted to the algorithm para-analyzer, the results of which will be published in an upcoming article after application and analysis of the results. The objective of this research is exploratory because it is intended to build knowledge about the application of Logic Et in the evaluation of usability, through the process of presenting them to a group of specialists who work with the software registration of providers, is based on the research as a survey.

The target audience of interest in this research is the professionals in the area of registration of providers who work with the software in their daily lives, hereinafter called specialists. Participants are not identified with personal data in this research. The questionnaire will be forwarded to the selected specialists via e-mail and telephone contact for the acceptance of participation.

Nine specialists working in a health care company in the city of São Paulo were selected, divided into three groups, adopting the position as a grouping criterion, according to Table 1.

Like Logic Eτ, it works with values between 0 and 1. The experts' answers will be mapped to logic Eτ's values. The value 0 is assigned to the answer "I totally disagree" and the value 1 to the answer "I totally agree", where 0.5 means "Indifferent" and so on, according to Table 2.

Table 1. Classification of expert groups (Source: Authors)

Group	Occupation	Number of Interviewees
A	Coordinators	3
B	Senior Registry Analysts	3
C	Junior Registry Analysts	3

Table 2. Conversion of values (Source: Authors)

Answer	Score	Value Logic Eτ
I totally agree	5	1
Agree	4	0,75
Indifferent	3	0,5
Disagree	2	0,25
I totally disagree	1	0

The research instrument was composed of ten closed questions based on the SUS questionnaire, with a Likert scale [10, 13] according to Table 3. The questions for usability evaluation were mapped to the factors of Logic Eτ, according to Table 3.

With the result of the questionnaire, we obtain the agreement or degree of favorable evidence (μ) and the disagreement or evidence contradicts (λ) for each opinion of a specialist regarding the usability of the software. With the data collected from the groups of specialists, through the questionnaire, it is intended to feed a database to be submitted to the Algorithm Para-analyzer of Logic Eτ, according to the model in Table 4.

As an example of an application of Logic Eτ's MPD method, the following simulation is produced, considering that the 9 experts, who are called Expert 1, Expert 2, ..., Expert 9 in the database, answered two questions: Factor 1 (F1) - I think I would like to use this application frequently and F2 - I found this application unnecessarily complicated. Data entries are obtained for the Algorithm Para-analyzer, according to the database shown in Table 4.

By applying the Para-analyzer algorithm, developed in an Excel spreadsheet, the result is obtained according to Figs. 4 and 5. The result of the Global Analysis of the Para-Analyzer algorithm (0.87; 0.25) indicates that it is in the "Totally True" region resulting in a viable result. The Para-analyzer algorithm processed a consensus in the opinion of the nine experts, presenting the following results for the factors: F1 (0.75; 0.25) and F2 (1.00; 0.25). It is understood that the usability of the software is within a viable quality standard.

Table 3. SUS questionnaire (Source: Adapted from [8])

Factor - Question	Factor - Question
F1 - I think that I would like to use this system frequently. ( ) I totally disagree ( ) Disagree ( ) Indifferent ( ) Agree ( ) I totally agree	F6 - I thought there was too much iconsistency in this system. ( ) I totally disagree ( ) Disagree ( ) Indifferent ( ) Agree ( ) I totally agree
F2 - I found the system unnecessarily complex. ( ) I totally disagree ( ) Disagree ( ) Indifferent ( ) Agree ( ) I totally agree	F7 - I felt very confident using the system. ( ) I totally disagree ( ) Disagree ( ) Indifferent ( ) Agree ( ) I totally agree
F3 - I thought the system was easy to use. ( ) I totally disagree ( ) Disagree ( ) Indifferent ( ) Agree ( ) I totally agree	F8 - I found the system very complicated to use. ( ) I totally disagree ( ) Disagree ( ) Indifferent ( ) Agree ( ) I totally agree
F4 - I think that I would need the support of a technical person to be able to use this system. ( ) I totally disagree ( ) Disagree ( ) Indifferent ( ) Agree ( ) I totally agree	F9 - I would imagine that most people would learn to use this system very quickly. ( ) I totally disagree ( ) Disagree ( ) Indifferent ( ) Agree ( ) I totally agree
F5 - I found the various functions in this system were well integrated. ( ) I totally disagree ( ) Disagree ( ) Indifferent ( ) Agree ( ) I totally agree	F10 - I needed to learn a lot of things before I could get going with this system. ( ) I totally disagree ( ) Disagree ( ) Indifferent ( ) Agree ( ) I totally agree

Table 4. Database model formed μ and λ assigned by the experts for each factor of SUS questionnaire (Source: Authors)

Factor	Group A						Group B						Group C					
	Expert 1		Expert 2		Expert 3		Expert 4		Expert 5		Expert 6		Expert 7		Expert 8		Expert 9	
	μ	λ	μ	λ	μ	λ	μ	λ	μ	λ	μ	λ	μ	λ	μ	λ	μ	λ
F1	0,75	0,25	1,00	0,25	0,75	0,25	0,50	0,25	0,75	0,25	1,00	0,25	0,75	0,25	0,50	0,25	0,75	0,75
F2	1,00	0,25	0,75	0,25	1,00	0,25	0,75	0,25	1,00	1,00	1,00	0,25	0,75	0,00	0,75	0,25	1,00	1,00

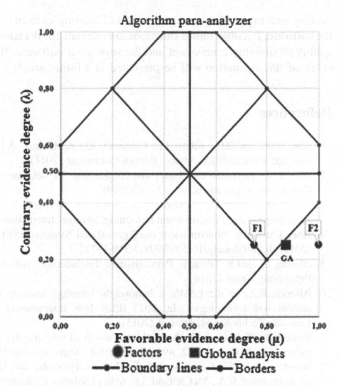

Fig. 5. Overall analysis of questionnaires (Source: Authors)

Factor	Resulting degrees		Decision
	μ	λ	
F1	0,75	0,25	Not conclusive
F2	1,00	0,25	Viable
Global analysis	0,87	0,25	Viable

Fig. 4. Final result of the questionnaire analysis (Source: Authors)

4   Conclusions

Current usability assessment processes do not take into account inconsistency or contradiction. In a real situation, both contradiction and inconsistency appear due to the conditions of the environment in which the questionnaire was applied.

Therefore, the existence of conflicts is part of the usability evaluation process. The greater the involvement of specialists with the software to solve their work processes daily, the higher the levels of conflicts, contradictions, and inconsistencies to which they will be subject.

The research presents a paraconsistent model to assist in the decision-making process of usability evaluation using Logic Eτ, through the Para-analyzer algorithm, using logical criteria that allow a technical validation, and the input parameters are established by the opinions of the experts consolidating the input values into a collective logic of all, converted into mathematical terms.

The research presents a paraconsistent model based on the perspectives that provide satisfaction to the specialists, assisting in the decision-making process of usability evaluation using logic Eτ. That can be used to validate and present a new technique of dealing with expert opinions in situations of blurring or even inconsistency in the use of the software. Possible future situations are relevant for decision making that ensure the quality of usability assessment and the success of software. Both the analysis and the result of this evaluation will be presented in a future article.

References

1. Abe, J.M., Da Silva Filho, J.I., Celestino, U., de Corrêa, A.H.: Lógica Paraconsistente Anotada Evidential Eτ. Santos, Editora Comunicar (2011)
2. Abe, J.M.: Paraconsistent logics and applications. In: 4th International Workshop on Soft Computing Applications, pp. 11–18 (2010)
3. Abe, J.M., Akama, S., Nakamatsu, K.: Introduction to Annotated Logics: Foundations for Paracomplete and Paraconsistent Reasoning. Springer International Publishing, Cham (2015)
4. Abe, J.M. (ed.): Paraconsistent Intelligent-Based Systems. ISRL, vol. 94. Springer, Cham (2015). https://doi.org/10.1007/978-3-319-19722-7
5. Akama, S. (ed.): Towards Paraconsistent Engineering, vol. 110. Springer International Publishing, Cham (2016)
6. Alamer, R.A., et al.: L3MS: a lightweight language learning management system using mobile web technologies. In: 2015 IEEE 15th International Conference on Advanced Learning Technologies, pp. 1–2 (2015)
7. Bolturk, E., Kahraman, C.: A novel interval-valued neutrosophic AHP with cosine similarity measure. Soft. Comput. **22**, 4941–4958 (2018). https://doi.org/10.1007/s00500-018-3140-y
8. Brooke, J.: SUS: A 'quick and dirty' usability scale. In: Jordan, P.W., Thomas, B., Weerdmeester, B.A., McClelland, I.L. (eds.) Usability Evaluation in Industry, pp. 189–194. Taylor and Francis, Abingdon (1996)
9. Buyya, R., Broberg, J., Goscinski, A.M.: Cloud Computing: Principles and Paradigms. Wiley, Hoboken (2011)
10. Derham, P.A.J.: Using preferred, understood, or effective scales? How to scale presentations effect online survey data collection. Australas. J. Mark. Soc. Res. **19**(2), 13–26 (2011)
11. Sauro, J., James, R.L.: Quantifying the User Experience, 2nd edn. Elsevier, Amsterdam (2016). ISBN 978-0-12-802308-2
12. ISO/IEC 25010:2011. Systems and software engineering—Systems and software Quality Requirements and Evaluation (SQuaRE)—System and software quality models. https://www.iso.org/standard/35733.html. Accessed 25 May 2020
13. Likert, R.: A technique for the measurement of attitudes. Arch. Psychol. **22**(140), 1–55 (1932)
14. Saeedpoor, M., Vafadarnikjoo, A.: Corrigendum to multicriteria renewable energy planning using an integrated fuzzy VIKOR & AHP methodology: the case of Istanbul. Energy **79**, 536–537 (2015)
15. Manchar, A., Chouhan, A.: Salesforce CRM: a new way of managing customer relationships in a cloud environment. In: 2017 Second International Conference on Electrical, Computer and Communication Technologies (ICECCT), pp. 1–4 (2017). https://doi.org/10.1109/ICECCT.2017.8117887
16. Vaidya, O., Sushil, K.: Analytic hierarchy process: an overview of applications. Eur. J. Oper. Res. **169**, 1–29 (2006). https://doi.org/10.1016/j.ejor.2004.04.028

Novel Production Planning and Control Approaches

Supporting the Decision of the Order Processing Strategy by Using Logistic Models: A Case Study

Janine Tatjana Maier[1]([✉]), Tammo Heuer[2], Peter Nyhuis[2], and Matthias Schmidt[1]

[1] Institute of Product and Process Innovation, Leuphana University of Lüneburg, Universitätsallee 1, 21335 Lüneburg, Germany
{janine_tatjana.maier, matthias.schmidt}@leuphana.de
[2] Institute of Production Systems and Logistics, Leibniz University Hannover, An der Universität 2, 30823 Garbsen, Germany
{heuer, nyhuis}@ifa.uni-hannover.de

Abstract. The selection of a suitable order processing strategy from an economic and logistic point of view plays a fundamental role in the achievement of efficient and waste-free production processes. Many factors influence the order processing strategy and the choice of the order processing strategy affects many variables. The problem for companies that has not yet been solved is the holistic selection of the best possible order processing strategy for each product or product group and, if necessary, subordinate components.

The authors present an approach to analyze the effects of the choice of the order processing strategy on the economic and logistic objectives. The description and modeling of the interdependencies between the order processing strategies and the influenced objectives refer to existing logistic models. A case study to evaluate the impact of different order processing strategies on costs shows the practicality of the proposed approach. The exemplary application of the presented approach showed a potential of an average reduction of 30% of the variable costs resulting from the change of the order processing strategy. The savings varied between 1% and 62% depending on the order quantity and frequency for the individual products.

Keywords: Order processing strategy · Interdependencies · Logistic models

1 Introduction

The increasing amount of data resulting from digitalization and increasing networking offers both opportunities and challenges. Efficient use of data is discussed often in the context of improving production planning and control (PPC) or work operations. In the literature, numerous approaches related to the decision-making processes in the PPC exist. Scheduling [1], capacity planning [2] and lot sizing [3] are examples of widely discussed decision-making processes. In the last years, the use of methods such as data mining techniques increased in the PPC [4]. Especially for forecasting behavior [5] and planning of sales [6], such methods prove to be very suitable. The availability of data

© IFIP International Federation for Information Processing 2020
Published by Springer Nature Switzerland AG 2020
B. Lalic et al. (Eds.): APMS 2020, IFIP AICT 591, pp. 343–350, 2020.
https://doi.org/10.1007/978-3-030-57993-7_39

also holds great potential in upstream decision-making processes. A decision prior to the above tasks is the selection of the order processing strategy. This decision interacts both with downstream PPC tasks and with upstream strategic aspects. Primary strategic decisions interacting with the order processing strategy can be found in areas such as product design and customer relationship management. Due to the high level of knowledge required and the lack of practice-oriented approaches, the systematic selection of the most suitable order processing strategy is a major challenge for companies.

This calls for a holistic decision support model to select a suitable order processing strategy from an economic and logistic point of view. Realizing this vision is a step-by-step process that requires continuous validation of the results through practical applications in industry. The approach presented in this paper is a first step in this direction and shows the practicability of the underlying idea. Section two describes the selection of the order processing strategy in the literature and in the industrial practice. The economic and logistic objectives are investigated with regard to the choice between make-to-order and make-to-stock in section three. Based on this, the general concept to determine the order processing strategy by using logistic models is presented. A case study in section four supports the practicality of the presented approach. Lastly, the conclusions of the paper are summarized and future research possibilities are outlined.

2 Decision-Making in Theory and Industrial Practice

The literature usually distinguishes between the order processing strategies engineer-to-order production (ETO), make-to-order (MTO), assemble-to-order (ATO) and make-to-stock (MTS) [7]. In case of an engineer-to-order strategy, the product prescribes this strategy and does not offer any alternatives. This is different for the other strategies. Companies have the choice between MTO, ATO and MTS. The problem of selecting the order processing strategy and the associated positioning of the customer order decoupling point have been intensively studied for many years. The high amount of approaches dealing with the decision on the order processing strategy indicates the complexity of this problem. Considering the numerous interactions of the order processing strategy, a number of approaches focus on the optimization of a system for a given order processing strategy [8]. Other approaches deal with the decision between MTO and MTS [9]. According to a recent survey, MTO and MTS are currently the most commonly used order processing strategies [10]. To simplify matters, many authors severely restrict the decision criteria. In some cases, products are grouped together with the help of a few differentiating features. However, there are no rules in the literature for determining the criteria and their characteristics. The wide variety of characteristics leads to different results for the individual approaches. Furthermore, the results are only recommendations with regard to just a few or even only one objective, such as short delivery times. Approaches based on numerous criteria face the problem of not being able to make a uniform statement for the products. Simulation-based models can support the decision-making, but result in a high computational and modelling effort.

In practice, various combinations of MTO and MTS exist [11]. Besides ATO, there are other hybrid strategies such as configure-to-order. Due to variety of options and the time pressure in industrial practice, companies often tend to simplify problems or rely on empirical values to make decisions. The selection of the order processing strategy usually relies on qualitative criteria or experience, either as a lump sum for certain articles and order types or on a case-by-case basis for individual orders [12]. Lacking transparency about the reasons, it looks as if the decision highly depends on intuition or experience of the product management. Despite higher costs or a higher risk, there are strategic reasons for choosing a certain strategy. For example, the stock in a finished goods store provides an opportunity to differentiate from the competitors. Shorter delivery times and higher delivery capability enable companies to secure or expand market shares. Outsourcing is another important aspect in this context. The use of external capacities allows shorter delivery times. However, many companies prefer to build up stocks to protect in-house knowledge. In addition, regulatory constraints and dependence on suppliers can be key factors.

3   Make-to-Stock Versus Make-to-Order

3.1   Economic and Logistic Objectives

Manufacturing companies aim to be economic, but they also have to satisfy their customers. To achieve this, companies must find the best possible position in the triangle of costs, time and quality [13]. Companies state that they could not compromise on the quality of their products and the choice of order processing strategy does not directly relate to the quality of products or processes. Therefore, the following analysis focuses only on costs and time. These two dimensions reflect themselves in the form of key figures in the economic and logistic objectives and in the organization of the production processes.

In the following, the focus lies on the two opposing strategies MTO and MTS. This helps to highlight the effects of different order processing strategies on the manufacturing and logistics costs as well as the logistics performance. From an economic and logistic point of view, both strategies have their individual advantages and disadvantages. For example, MTS has the benefit of producing a cost optimal lot size for the respective product. Production orders flow into a storage level, which makes them more flexible to control than MTO orders. This can indirectly have a positive impact on the utilization of production capacity. As the finished products are in stock, very short delivery times are possible. Operating a finished goods store generates costs and ties up capital for goods and infrastructure. Maintaining a high safety stock helps to ensure a high level of delivery reliability even during fluctuations in demand. This increases the risk costs for unsaleable products [14]. In MTO production, this risk does not exist, but therefore the delivery times increase. The quantities requested by the customer directly transform into production orders. Thus, the realization of economic production orders is not possible [15]. As shown in ETO industry, real-time capable production planning and control can decrease complexity [16]. This indicates new trends, like industry 4.0 and self-controlling processes can reduce the effort required in MTO production.

A change in the cost-benefit ratio could make MTO production profitable for many companies.

The objectives are not only influenced by the chosen order processing strategy, they also influence the strategy itself. An example of this is the logistic objective delivery time. In MTS production, the delivery time equals the time in the dispatch process plus the transportation time. Whereas in the case of MTO production the throughput time is added on top of that. If the customer demands a very short delivery time and this is the primary purchasing criteria, the company will most likely choose MTS production. However, which order processing strategy is more beneficial always depends on the company's intentions and the particular product. Considering the numerous qualitative and strategic influences, it is necessary to decide on the order processing strategy individually for each product or product family.

3.2 Decision-Making Based on Logistic Models

Multiple authors used abstract, time-consuming mathematical models to tackle the problematic of the order processing strategy. For example, Hadj Youssef et al. [17] analyzed the effects of the priority allocation on the efficiency of the decision between MTO and MTS and the associated costs. Approaches like this and the observation in the context of previous research projects led to the basic idea of this project. Logistic models support the decision-making process by evaluating the effects of different order processing strategies on the economic and logistic objectives. As a first step, an analysis of the influencing factors related to the choice of the order processing strategy is required. The modelling builds on the assumption, that the costs per product are the determining criteria for companies. The influencing cost factors derive from literature search, interviews with companies from various industries and observations from previous research projects. The choice of the order processing strategy influences the cost per product resulting from the following aspects: storage costs in the produced goods store, purchasing costs, set up costs, storage costs in the finished goods store and costs for delays in delivery.

These influencing factors can be modelled using logistic models and simple calculations. The selected logistic models differ for the individual order processing strategies. For MTS production, on-time delivery is primarily a result of the service level in the finished goods store. In turn, the inventory in the finished goods warehouse has a considerable influence on the service level. The characteristic curve for stock-on-hand describes this interrelationship mathematically [18]. In the case of MTO production, on-time delivery results from the schedule reliability in the sales order-specific production area. The implementation of safety times can compensate for delays in production. However, this is at the expense of delivery time and the stock of completed orders. The underlying cause-effect relationships between the schedule compliance, the delivery time and the stock of finished orders can be modelled mathematically using schedule compliance operating curves [19]. Lot-sizing models can be used to map the effects of the order processing strategy on set up costs, purchasing costs and storage costs in the produced goods store [20]. Figure 1 illustrates the general modeling approach by positioning existing logistic models. The exemplary operating points show the different cost distributions for a similar amount of on-time deliveries in MTO and MTS production.

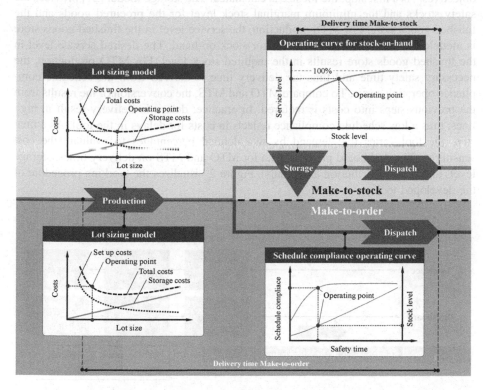

Fig. 1. Approach for the decision-making process by using existing logistic models

4 Case Study

4.1 Application of the Approach

At a manufacturer for construction industry components, the proposed approach helped to support the decision between MTO and MTS. The determining objectives in this single-stage production were delivery time, adherence to delivery dates and product costs. The analysis contained operating data as well as two years of historical data on production performance, schedule reliability and customer demand. The focus lay on quantitative values for the static evaluation of production performance and determination of the required stocks in the supply chain. The conversion of the influencing factors and interactions into accruing costs enabled an allocation according to the cause for the 63 individual products.

The developed tool determines the cost of an individual product in six steps. Figure 2 visualizes the working procedure of the developed tool. The user needs to enter operating data and if available data on the demand, the storage costs and the schedule adherence through the interface. The operating data contains data on the performance of suppliers, general company and manufacturing conditions (e.g. working days per year), cost rates, customer demand and desired values of the logistic objectives. As a first step, the lot size is calculated. The storage model [21] provides the safety stocks and the minimum marginal stock level for the procured goods and the finished goods store. For MTS production, the service level in the finished goods store is modeled by the characteristic curve for stock-on-hand. The desired service level in the finished goods store results in the required stock level. For MTO production, the necessary safety time and thus the delivery time is derived from the schedule compliance operating curve. To compare MTO and MTS, the conversion of the results from the previous steps into costs is required. In practice, delays in delivery result in high fines, thus a low schedule compliance reflects in costs for delays in the tool. As a final step, the tool varies the demand by two defined percentages to evaluate the cost sensitivity. The dashboard provides data for MTO and MTS on delivery times, storage levels and costs (distribution and trends). Figure 2 visualizes the working procedure of the developed tool.

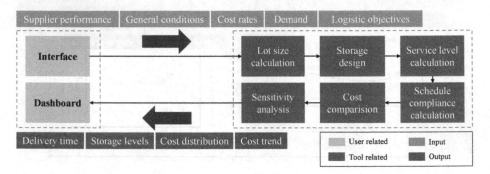

Fig. 2. Principle of the developed tool

4.2 Results

The comparison of a service level of 95% for MTS production and 95% adherence to delivery dates for MTO production, revealed on average a reduction of 30% of the variable costs resulting from the change of the order processing strategy. Depending on the order quantity and frequency, the savings varied between 1% and 62% for the individual products. The analysis of all 63 products showed a nearly equal distribution between MTS products (28) and MTO products (35). It is therefore necessary for companies to make the decision for each product individually. Due to the non-optimal lot sizes, MTO production generates higher set-up costs. The varying lot size causes difficulties in planning, thus purchasing costs are higher and more capital is tied up in the produced goods store. In addition, MTO results in higher costs for delays. These costs correspond to the costs of operating the finished goods store in MTS production. For higher quantities, the costs for MTO production increase considerably. Near the intersection point of the MTS and MTO cost curves, the detailed cost analysis highlights saving potentials. The delivery time acts as the elimination criteria for MTO production. The developed tool provides the base for an analysis of different scenarios by changing the desired values of delivery time and schedule compliance. In this way, the savings potential resulting from a change in the order processing strategy is comparable with the costs of implementing possible measures to increase schedule compliance or shorten delivery times. As a result of the numerous company-specific qualitative and strategic aspects, the distribution proposed by the tool was not directly incorporated. Instead, the original workflow for determining the order processing strategy was modified by adding a new step. The developed tool is used to evaluate the cost of previously made decisions on the order processing strategy. In case the costs of the selected order processing strategy are too high, the decision is reviewed.

5   Conclusion and Future Research

The economic and logistic objectives influenced by the choice of order processing strategy are essential for the success of a company. Adherence to delivery dates and delivery times are directly decisive purchasing criteria for customers [22]. This paper presents an approach to support the decision of the order processing strategy by using logistic models. A case study to evaluate the impact of different order processing strategies on costs showed the general practicality of the approach.

The variety of qualitative and strategic influencing variables revealed some limitations of the presented approach. To achieve the vision of a holistic model, further development in an iterative process is required. As a next step, the validity of the identified correlations needs to be examined regarding hybrid order processing strategies. Therefore, the characteristic curves of logistic models have to be examined. Additionally, it is necessary to integrate more logistic models and, if necessary, modify the models. A simulation model can be used to validate the modelling work. A possible other extension of the developed tool could be the implementation of the utilization and management efforts, such as workload balancing, associated with the order processing strategy. Analyzing the interactions with additional downstream decisions such as the order generating process or order releasing process can provide some interesting insights.

Acknowledgements.   The research project was carried out in the framework of the industrial collective research programme (IGF no. 20906 N). It was supported by the Federal Ministry for Economic Affairs and Energy (BMWi) through the AiF (German Federation of Industrial Research Associations eV) and the BVL (Bundesvereinigung Logistik eV) based on a decision taken by the German Bundestag.

References

1. Branke, J., Nguyen, S., Pickardt, C.W., Zhang, M.: Automated design of production scheduling heuristics: a review. IEEE Trans. Evol. Comput. **20**(1), 110–124 (2015)
2. Aarabi, M., Hasanian, S.: Capacity planning and control: a review. Int. J. Sci. Eng. Res. **5**(8), 975–984 (2014)

3. Jans, R., Degraeve, Z.: Modeling industrial lot sizing problems: a review. Int. J. Prod. Res. **46**(6), 1619–1643 (2008)
4. Cheng, Y., Chen, K., Sun, H., Zhang, Y., Tao, F.: Data and knowledge mining with big data towards smart production. J. Ind. Inf. Integr. **9**, 1–13 (2018)
5. Altintas, N., Trick, M.: A data mining approach to forecast behavior. Ann. Oper. Res. **216** (1), 3–22 (2014)
6. Maaß, D., Spruit, M., de Waal, P.: Improving short-term demand forecasting for short-lifecycle consumer products with data mining techniques. Decis. Anal. **1**(1), 1–17 (2014)
7. Hoekstra, S., Romme, J., Argelo, S.M.: Integral Logistic Structures Developing Customer-Oriented Goods Flow. Industrial Press, New York (1992)
8. Stevenson, M., Hendry, L.C., Kingsman, B.G.: A review of production planning and control: the applicability of key concepts to the make-to-order industry. Int. J. Prod. Res. **43**(5), 869–898 (2005)
9. Rajagopalan, S.: Make to order or make to stock: model and application. Manage. Sci. **48**(2), 241–256 (2002)
10. Mundt, C., Winter, M., Heuer, T., Hübner, M., Seitz, M., Schmidhuber, M., Maibaum, J., Bank, L., Roth, S., Scherwitz, P., Theumer, P.: PPS-Report 2019. TEWISS, Garbsen (2019)
11. Rafiei, H., Rabbani, M.: Order partitioning and order penetration point location in hybrid make-to-stock/make-to-order production contexts. Comput. Ind. Eng. **61**(3), 550–560 (2011)
12. Gudehus, T., Kotzab, H.: Comprehensive Logistics, 2nd edn. Springer, Berlin, Heidelberg (2012)
13. Westkämper, E., Decker, M.: Einführung in die Organisation der Produktion. Springer, Berlin, Heidelberg (2006)
14. Syska, A.: Produktionsmanagement. Das A - Z wichtiger Methoden und Konzepte für die Produktion von heute (engl. title: Production management: important methods and concepts for today's production). Gabler, Wiesbaden (2006)
15. Schmidt, M., Münzberg, B., Nyhuis, P.: Determining lot sizes in production areas – exact calculations versus research based estimation. Procedia CIRP **28**, 143–148 (2015)
16. Rauch, E., Dallasega, P., Matt, D.T.: Complexity reduction in engineer-to-order industry through real-time capable production planning and control. Prod. Eng. **12**(3–4), 341–352 (2018)
17. Hadj Youssef, K., van Delft, C., Dallery, Y.: Priority optimization and make-to-stock/make-to-order decision in multiproduct manufacturing systems. Int. Trans. Oper. Res. **25**(4), 1199–1219 (2018)
18. Nyhuis, P.: Lagerkennlinien - ein Modellansatz zur Unterstützung des Beschaffungs- und Bestandscontrollings. In: Baumgarten, H. (eds.): RKW-Handbuch Logistik. 2nd edn., 1–30. Erich Schmidt, Berlin (1996)
19. Schmidt, M., Bertsch, S., Nyhuis, P.: Schedule compliance operating curves and their application in designing the supply chain of a metal producer. Prod. Plan. Control Manag. Oper. **25**(2), 123–133 (2014)
20. Münzberg, B.: Multikriterielle Losgrößenbildung (engl. title: Multicriterial lot sizing). Berichte aus dem IFA. PZH, Garbsen (2013)
21. REFA-Verband für Arbeitsstudien und Betriebsorganisation: Methodenlehre der Planung und Steuerung. Carl Hanser, München (1985)
22. Schuh, G., Westkämper, E.: Liefertreue im Maschinen- und Anlagenbau: Stand - Potenziale - Trends. Forschungsinstitut für Rationalisierung an der RWTH Aachen, Stuttgart, Fraunhofer-Institut für Produktionstechnik und Automatisierung (2006)

Order Acceptance and Scheduling
with a Throughput Diagram

Christopher Mundt$^{(\boxtimes)}$ and Hermann Lödding

Hamburg University of Technology, Hamburg, Germany
{christopher.mundt,loedding}@tuhh.de

Abstract. Determining realistic delivery times is difficult for make-to-order manufacturers, especially due to uncertainties such as future production capacity utilization. Nevertheless, delivery times have to be stated in new offers. In this paper, we show a simple procedure for determining delivery times using the throughput diagram and determining a likely future situation by including early available information such as the acceptance of offers in the planning process. In a first simulative evaluation, the procedure is examined for its basic effect on the order lateness.

Keywords: Production planning · Order scheduling · Throughput diagram

1 Introduction

Order acceptance and scheduling has the task to determine a realistic delivery time when customers request an offer. The delivery time, a company offers is an important decision criterion for the customer, along with the price and the quality of a product. Therefore, order acceptance and scheduling is a particularly important task for make-to-order companies, which has an impact on sales, profits and capacity utilization in production. Also, good order scheduling protects production from overload by scheduling orders for a later date or even rejecting them, if necessary.

The challenge is to acquire as many orders as possible without overloading production, building up backlogs and causing late delivery. Measured by the importance of the task, the implementation in many companies is inadequate: It is common for companies to use standard delivery times or to systematically accept more orders than the production capacity can handle, especially when the economy is prospering [1].

Due to a high number of variants and varying delivery time demands from customers, it is difficult for make-to-order manufacturers to perform reliable production planning. Another difficulty is that at the time of order acceptance and scheduling, realistic work plans with detailed target times are usually not available. In addition, other open offers are usually not sufficiently taken into account when scheduling offers. It is therefore not surprising that customers of make-to-order manufacturers complain about a low delivery reliability [2] and that the make-to-order manufacturers themselves rate high delivery reliability as the most important logistical goal [3].

This article shows a simple procedure for scheduling and capacity planning using throughput diagrams.

© IFIP International Federation for Information Processing 2020
Published by Springer Nature Switzerland AG 2020
B. Lalic et al. (Eds.): APMS 2020, IFIP AICT 591, pp. 351–359, 2020.
https://doi.org/10.1007/978-3-030-57993-7_40

2 Fundamentals and Current State of Research

Already with the offer, contractors usually must state not only technical specifications but also a binding delivery date. In many cases, the offer is only valid for a limited period of time, during which the customer can accept it. At the time of the offer preparation, usually neither work plans nor order times are available as input to calculate the delivery time. Moreover, it is also unclear whether the customers will accept the open offers or not. The reliability of the load of open offers therefore is very low, which makes scheduling and capacity planning more difficult [4].

Based on their experience, some companies can estimate the probability that offers for their most important products or from long-term customers will be accepted. This acceptance rate can help to better estimate the future load on production. For a systematic assessment of this acceptance rate, it is necessary to keep statistics on accepted and rejected offers. However, the planning software often does not support this, so that many companies fail to keep track of these statistics [5].

Often companies therefore neglect requests, offers and even orders prior to product design and work planning. In many cases, the sales department promises delivery times without first carrying out a sufficient capacity check of production. The customers are instead given standard delivery times, which cannot be guaranteed to be met. Because Sales and Distribution is rewarded for winning orders, this can lead to a systematic overload of production capacity, especially under good economic conditions. Various authors suggest procedures for integrating offers in the scheduling and capacity planning process.

Already in the 1960s, Brankamp suggested to take offers into account in capacity planning. His proposal is based on multiplying unplanned capacities by a factor for the probability of acceptance. This acceptance rate is the reciprocal of the probability that customers will accept an offer [6].

Kingsman and Hendry propose to multiply the work content of the offers by their probability of acceptance. They then calculate a range of coverage that includes not only the orders in production, but also orders waiting to be released and the open offers. This range of coverage can be used for scheduling, but also for rejecting customer inquiries or adjusting capacity [7, 8].

Wiedemann proposes to determine the possible delivery date by simulating future capacity requirements [9].

However, these procedures have not been established as common practice in industry so far, possibly because the procedures take a very detailed look at the loads of individual workstations, thus becoming complex and also requiring the knowledge of the work content for the required processes. Our approach aims to cover less detailed information to make the procedure easier to apply in an earlier stage of the order process. The question is if that is sufficient to meet the requirements for the accuracy of scheduling.

There are some basic requirements for an effective scheduling procedure. Such a procedure should be simple to use, which may be even more important than the accuracy of the procedure. Nevertheless, it has to deliver good and robust results. Furthermore, the procedure should be comprehensible in order to increase the insight into the cause-effect relationships of production. In addition, the procedure should take into account the various order states (request, offer and order in design and work preparation) before a production order is generated.

Throughput diagrams show the cumulative actual and planned output of a work system or the entire production over time. The work can be measured in number of orders, in hours or similar capacity equivalents. The throughput diagram is often used in the analysis or controlling of work processes. It is used to visualize the existing situation of the logistic target values or to compare it with a target state [10]. Another application is the visualization during production planning [11].

3 Scheduling Offers and Orders in a Throughput Diagram

3.1 General Considerations

The proposed order acceptance and scheduling procedure does not take into consideration individual operations and workstations an order will pass through, but is restricted on the entire manufacturing department and the entire order. This makes it easy to apply, but also reduces the transparency over relevant information on workstation level. Therefore, in contrast to other procedures, it requires less information, especially workstation related information is not necessary.

The workload can be considered in different ways to align the planned output with the capacity of the production. The unit of output should be chosen in a way that it reflects the capacity requirements of the orders as accurately as possible. Standard hours are often well-suited to reflect the capacity requirements of an order in a work system. However, the effort required to estimate the standard hours at the time of offer processing is usually considerable. If a company produces a large number of orders, large and small orders balance each other out. In this case, it is often sufficient to measure the output in number of orders. This simplifies the calculation of the planned output, especially for open offers. Alternatively, the average work content can be used as a basis.

In all cases, open offers should be discounted with the likely acceptance rate to calculate the planned output from offers following the suggestion of Kingsman and Hendry [8]. In this way the planned output represents its likely future value at the current day.

Some values have a crucial impact on the planned due date and therefore on the scheduling procedure itself. The throughput time by its definition forms a lower boundary for the delivery time and needs to be considered respectively. The customer usually needs time for his decision on a placed offer. The customer response time can be considered in different ways. The validity of the offer is an upper limit. For the sake of simplicity, we assume that there is no difference in the customer response time between accepted and unaccepted offers. In order to prevent minor disturbances in production from directly leading to a delayed delivery, it is also useful to use a delivery time buffer.

3.2   Construction of a Throughput Diagram with Planned Data

Figure 1 shows a throughput diagram with planned data. The following quantities are shown cumulatively over time:

- Actual output
- Planned output
  - from requests and offers
  - from confirmed orders in different states
- Possible output with planned capacity

The planned output might be detailed further, e.g. according to the order status, for example orders after release, orders after work preparation but before release, orders after design but before work preparation. For reasons of clarity, however, this paper does not present these different planned outputs individually.

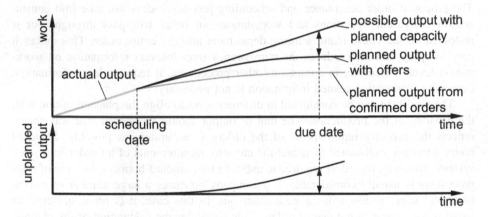

Fig. 1. Throughput diagram for scheduling purposes

3.3   A Generic and Simple to Use Scheduling Procedure

The scheduling of incoming requests and the determination of the delivery time is generally made by checking three conditions. Firstly, the planned delivery time has to be at least the throughput time, because this is the shortest time the product can be produced under standard conditions (1). Secondly, the promised delivery time does not need to be shorter than the customer requests (2). Lastly, the unplanned output at the possible due date has to be larger than the work content of the offer (3).

$$TT_{poss} \geq TT_m \tag{1}$$

$$TT_{poss} \geq TD_{req} - T_{Buffer} \tag{2}$$

$$OUT_{up}(D_{scheduling} + TT_{poss}) > WC_i \tag{3}$$

With: TT_{poss} *possible throughput time* TT_m *mean throughput time*
         TD_{req} *requested delivery time* T_{Buffer} *delivery time buffer*
         OUT_{up} *unplanned output* $D_{scheduling}$ *scheduling date*
         WC_i *work content of offer i*

The possible throughput time is now calculated by determining its maximum value in the above stated conditions. To compensate minor disturbances, the delivery time buffer is added to get the delivery time that can be communicated to the customer (4).

$$TD = TT_{poss} + T_{Buffer} \tag{4}$$

With: TD *delivery time* TT_{poss} *possible throughput time*
         T_{Buffer} *delivery time buffer*

3.4 Consideration of Offers and Orders in the Planned Output

Basically, the planned output from confirmed orders is considered at the time of their planned completion and the planned output from offers is considered at their likely completion date. Comparing the planned output with the capacity in a throughput diagram (Fig. 2) illustrates the above stated scheduling and works as follows.

Order requests from customers and open offers are added to the planned output from confirmed orders with an expected value. The expected share of offers that are converted into an order is calculated by multiplying the offers by an acceptance rate. In the simplest case, the acceptance rate can be calculated based on historical data from the ratio of the number of accepted offers to the total number of submitted offers (5).

$$AR = \sum O_{acc} / \sum O_{sub} \tag{5}$$

With: AR *acceptance rate* $O_{acc.}$ *accepted offers*
         $O_{sub.}$ *submitted offers*

In practice, the acceptance rate can be estimated individually for each offer. Possible differences result from the consideration of different customers, products, projects

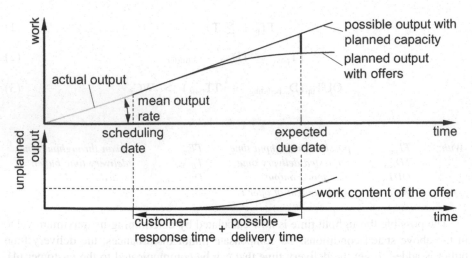

Fig. 2. Adding offers to the planned output

or similar criteria. The workload of an offer is then multiplied by the acceptance rate. For the planned output in number of orders the considered workload equals the acceptance rate (6). If the order times are also to be taken into account, Eq. (7) is obtained.

$$OUTO_{plan,off,j} = AR_i \qquad (6)$$

$$OUT_{plan,off,j} = AR_i \cdot WC_m \qquad (7)$$

With: $OUTO_{plan,off,j}$ *planned output of offer j* AR_i *acceptance rate of*
                                   [number of orders]   *offer i*
           $OUT_{plan,off,j}$ *planned output of offer j [h]* WC_m *mean work content*

To determine the likely due date of an offer, three factors are taken into account: the current scheduling date, the customer response time for accepted offers and the previously calculated possible delivery time. The customer response time is considered with its mean value (8). If the customer response behaviour differs for various customers individual values might be considered here.

$$EDD = D_{scheduling} + TCR_m + TT_{poss} \qquad (8)$$

With: *EDD*   *expected due date* $D_{scheduling}$ *scheduling date*
           TCR_m *mean customer response time* TT_{poss} *possible throughput time*

The discounted workload from the offer calculated with (6) or (7) is added to the output at the due date calculated with Eq. (8).

To determine the possible output with the planned capacity the procedure is as follows. The curve starts at the end of the actual output on the scheduling date. If the capacity remains unchanged, the average output rate of the previous planning period can be used to estimate the possible output. Accordingly, the curve of the possible output proceeds linearly with the output rate as gradient.

The unplanned output is the difference between the two curves, if the planned output is below the possible output or displays the overload when it is the other way around.

After the customers decision there might be an accepted or rejected offer. If the offer is accepted, it will be scheduled with their whole workload and the promised delivery time. The earlier scheduled status as offer will be removed from the planned output. If the offer is not accepted, then its scheduled output will just be removed.

The throughput diagram also allows the initial backlog of production to be included. In this case the actual output and the planned output deviate at the scheduling date.

4 Evaluation by Simulation

Production disturbances and uncertainties can lead to production performance deviating from capacity. Usual disturbances are for example machine failures, sick employees, sequence deviations of orders or other issues. Uncertainties with regard to the procedure which might vary over time are the acceptance rate, the customer response time or the workload. Varying these variables in the throughput diagram visualizes this overload to support decisions about increasing the capacity.

The presented scheduling procedure was compared to scheduling with standard delivery times in a simulation to evaluate the basic effect. Therefore, a simplified simulation model was built with a linear material flow of five workstations and a situation with fifty percent overload. Also, short-term fluctuations in offer request rate, acceptance rate and customer response time have been implemented. A delivery time buffer of one day was used. The simulation was conducted for both procedures with 1000 offer requests each. The resulting throughput diagrams for the backwards scheduling procedure and the throughput diagram scheduling procedure are shown in Fig. 3.

The planned output for the backwards scheduling procedure (Fig. 3b) is mostly above the capacity limit. The difference between the planned and actual output, which represents the backlog, is large and increases over time. This results in a mean lateness of four shop calendar days with a standard deviation of more than two days. The schedule reliability with limits of plus minus one day is only 18 percent.

The planned output for the presented procedure (Fig. 3a) is below the capacity limit and close to the actual output all the time. On average the orders are finished slightly early with a mean lateness of minus one-third shop calendar days and a standard deviation of one shop calendar day. The schedule reliability is 87 percent, in the limits of plus minus one day for this procedure.

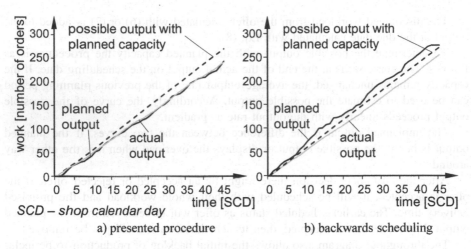

a) presented procedure

b) backwards scheduling

Fig. 3. Resulting throughput diagrams of the evaluated procedures

However, the presented procedure comes along with the cost of a slightly lower output rate of five percent compared to the backwards scheduling. A WIP regulating order release such as CONWIP could compensate for this effect, by utilizing unused capacity.

5 Summary and Outlook

The presented paper shows how companies can visualize the future load situation in production using a throughput diagram, determine their unplanned output and schedule orders. The throughput diagram enables companies to schedule offers taking into account backlogs, previous orders and the expected load of open offers. Compared to other procedures it works without information on workstation level, therefore needs less information and is easier to apply. This makes the procedure particularly suitable for practical application.

In a first simple evaluation we were able to show its general effectiveness. Under the considered conditions this comes with a slightly lower output rate. These downsides of the procedure appear to be uncritical under the considered conditions. Our procedure generally aims to be sufficient for a wide variation of make-to-order situations, as long as the required acceptance statistics are available. Nevertheless, the greater the offer backlog, the greater is the procedure's impact. To prove this, further simulations with different situations will be performed and an implementation in practice is planned. Furthermore, we will extend the procedure to include special order types, such as rush orders.

Acknowledgement. The Authors would like to thank Deutsche Forschungsgesellschaft (DFG) for funding the project "Model-based order acceptance and scheduling" (Project No. 405645389).

References

1. Bretzke, W.-R.: Logistische Netzwerke. Springer, Berlin, Heidelberg (2020). https://doi.org/10.1007/978-3-662-59757-6
2. Schuh, G.: Produktionsplanung und-steuerung: Grundlagen Gestaltung Und Konzepte. Springer, Dordrecht (2007)
3. Nyhuis, P., (ed.) : Aktuellen Herausforderungen der Produktionsplanung und -steuerung mittels Industrie 4.0 begegnen: Studienergebnisse, PZH Verlag, Garbsen (2016)
4. Schuh, G., Schmidt, C.: Produktionsmanagement: Handbuch Produktion und Management 5. Springer Vieweg, Berlin (2014). https://doi.org/10.1007/978-3-642-54288-6
5. Hentschel, D.: Kunde "droht" mit Auftrag: Risiko Auftragswahrscheinlichkeit. PPS-Manage. **13**(1), 55–58 (2008)
6. Brankamp, K.: Ein Terminplanungssystem für Unternehmen der Einzel- und Serienfertigung, Aachen (1967)
7. Kingsman, B.G., Tatsiopoulos, I.P., Hendry, L.C.: A structural methodology for managing manufacturing lead times in make-to-order companies. Eur. J. Oper. Res. **40**(2), 196–209 (1989). https://doi.org/10.1016/0377-2217(89)90330-5
8. Hendry, L.C., Kingsman, B.G.: Customer enquiry management: part of a hierarchical system to control lead times in make-to-order companies. J. Oper. Res. Soc. **44**(1), 61–70 (1993). https://doi.org/10.1057/jors.1993.7
9. Wiedemann, M.: Methodik zur auslastungsorientierten Angebotsterminierung für hochvariante Produkte mit kundenindividuellen Leistungsanteilen, München (2016)
10. Nyhuis, P., Wiendahl, H.-P.: Logistische Kennlinien. Springer, Berlin, Heidelberg (2012). https://doi.org/10.1007/978-3-540-92839-3
11. Lödding, H.: Verfahren der Fertigungssteuerung. Springer, Berlin, Heidelberg (2016). https://doi.org/10.1007/978-3-662-48459-3

Machine Learning and Artificial Intelligence

Machine Learning-Supported Planning of Lead Times in Job Shop Manufacturing

Kathrin Julia Kramer[1(✉)], Carsten Wagner[2], and Matthias Schmidt[1]

[1] PPI, Leuphana University Lueneburg, 21335 Lueneburg, Germany
{kathrin.kramer,matthias.schmidt}@leuphana.de
[2] HAWK University of Applied Sciences and Art
Hildesheim/Holzminden/Goettingen, Buesgenweg 1a,
37077 Goettingen, Germany
carsten.wagner@hawk.de

Abstract. In order to ensure adherence to schedules, knowledge of planned lead times (LT) is crucial for success. In practice, however, rigid planning methods are often used which cannot adequately reflect constantly changing environmental influences (e.g. fluctuations in the daily workload). Particularly in job shop production, precise planning of LT is difficult to implement. This paper therefore examines whether existing machine learning (ML) approaches, in particular supervised learning methods, in production planning can support LT scheduling in job shop production to generate added value. The paper enhances existing research by comparing deep artificial neural networks with ensemble methods (e.g. random forest, boosting decision trees). The applied approach bases on the Cross Industry Standard Process for Data Mining (CRISP-DM), which was created by a consortium of companies. Finally, the evaluation through an exemplary job shop production shows that the present work contributes to mastering the planned LT. In particular, the ML model, boosting decision trees and deep artificial neural networks show significant improvements in planning quality. This practical reference has not yet been addressed comprehensively in the literature.

Keywords: Machine learning · Production planning & control approaches · Job shop production · Lead times

1 Introduction

In production companies, the lead time (LT), inventory, capacity utilization and adherence to delivery dates are the production logistical objectives. However, it is not possible to improve all objectives at the same time, as some of them are contradictory. For example, high capacity utilization can be achieved through high stocks, which in turn results in long LT. Long LT usually fluctuate strongly and thus have a negative influence on adherence to delivery dates [1–3]. The mutual influence underlines the importance of precise planning of the respective logistical objectives.

In times of increasing customer requirements and thus a high level of adherence to delivery dates, realistic planned LT are necessary in order to be able to confirm a feasible date to the customer. The correct determination of planned LT is also important

© IFIP International Federation for Information Processing 2020
Published by Springer Nature Switzerland AG 2020
B. Lalic et al. (Eds.): APMS 2020, IFIP AICT 591, pp. 363–370, 2020.
https://doi.org/10.1007/978-3-030-57993-7_41

for the determination of capacities within the production system and for procurement [4]. For instance, as Shaw and Whinston [5] outline, more precise LT have a positive effect on the accuracy of scheduling decisions and vice versa. Incorrect LT planning can lead to low adherence to delivery dates and high inventories. In practice, however, rigid methods are often used that cannot adequately reflect constantly changing environmental influences (e.g. short-term sick leave of employees or fluctuations in daily workload). Classically used methods often base their prediction on historical data or estimations. Generally, none or limited data is being used in relation to these methods and the actual status of the production system is not reflected. For instance, the average order LT, the sum of the average LT of operations or the sum of the average execution times of the relevant operations of the orders plus a lump sum of the transition time of these operations is used for LT prediction of a new order [1, 2]. In addition, precise planning of LT is particularly difficult in job shop production, because the length of orders, the use and sequence of workstations per order varies: In a job shop a job follows an individual and predefined sequence or route for its processing on one or more existing machines [1, 3]. Machine learning (ML) methods could potentially improve prediction quality, as research has outlined its potential benefit for production planning and control tasks [6]. Therefore, this paper examines whether existing ML methods can provide benefit to the planning of LT in job shop manufacturing.

The structure of the paper foresees four further sections: Sect. 2 provides an overview about ML in general and the current state of research concerning the prediction of LT with ML methods in a complex production system. Section 3 presents the methodology for applying ML to LT planning and Sect. 4 deploys the process to real data of a job shop manufacturing company. The last section outlines the key findings and a possible future research agenda.

2 Current State of Research

2.1 Definition of ML and Its Types

Statements by Arthur Samuel [7] define ML as the field of study in which humans do not dictate every step to the computer and instead facilitate computers to learn independently. One possible way of clustering ML methods is according to their learning method. Following Russel et al. [8], commonly known learning methods are supervised learning (SL), unsupervised learning and reinforcement learning. This paper focuses on regression methods as part of SL methods, thus a function should be identified that predicts LT of orders based on a labelled data set. The model learns to recognize and generalize the relationship between given input and output data and uses it to predict outputs for unknown examples.

2.2 LT Prediction Supported by ML Methods

The use of regression methods for the planning of LT has been carried out using case studies of different production environments. For complex production systems like job shop manufacturing, researchers have explored the use of different input factors, ML methods and data sources. So far, a generalized model selection does not exist and depends on the production environment and the taken model parameters [9]. Hence, it is not suitable to focus on just one model. Instead, a comparison of different models should take place. The current research has used linear regression (LR), decision tree (DT), random forest (RF), k-nearest neighbor and support vector regression (SVR). Further lasso regression, ridge regression, artificial neural networks (NN), multivariate adaptive regression, deep neural networks (DNN), bagging decision trees and boosting decision trees (BDT) were used for determining planned lead times of orders. In regards, to a suitable choice of a regression model, the case studies show that more complex regression models (e.g. RF or BDT) often outperform simple regression models (e.g. LR or DT) in regards to prediction accuracy. However, within the field of more complex regression models, the current literature does not compare DNN with ensemble methods (e.g. RF, BDT).

Gyulai et al. [9] compare the prediction accuracy of LR, DT, RF and SVR using the normalized root mean square error (NRMSE). The modelling is based on data of a real flow-shop environment in the optic industry, where complexity of the LT prediction exists due to a large number of process parameters and uncertainties within foreseeing the client order stream. Input factors are e.g. time of order's arrival in the production system, product type or material. The RF model shows the best performance with a NRMSE that is in average 10.1 percentage points lower than the other models [9]. Lingitz et al. [10] explore the prediction accuracy of LR, lasso regression, ridge regression, NN and multivariate adaptive regression. Further, they examine SVR, k-nearest neighbor, DT, RF, bagging decision trees and BDT. The models use real data (e.g. work in progress of process step or weekday of order's arrival time) of a job shop manufacturing from the semiconductor industry. The RF model and the BDT show the best performance using evaluation metrics like root mean square error (RMSE) or NRMSE [10]. Wang et al. [11] examine the prediction of completion times and not LT by using NN and DNN. The models use real data like the work in progress of each process step within a complex job shop from an equipment manufacturing enterprise. The applied evaluation metrics like RMSE or mean value of the relative errors show that DNN outperforms NN [11].

In contrast to the presented research, this paper aims at covering all aspects of a data mining process to predict LT in a comprehensible way as Cadavid et al. [12] underpins this as essential. A comparison of the state-of-the-art in regards to model selection takes place. This is applied to a real job shop, since simulation data is not suitable for making general assumptions for a real production environment [13].

3 Research Methodology

The research methodology follows the Cross Industry Standard Process for Data Mining (CRISP-DM), a widespread, industry-independent life cycle process [14]. The process contains six phases: "business understanding", "data understanding", "data preparation", "modelling", "evaluation" and "deployment" [14]. This chapter explains each step of CRISP-DM in the context of predicting LT in a job shop environment.

The business-understanding phase covers the set-up of the project by determining business and data mining goals as well as an assessment of the current situation in order to define the scope of the project [14]. As described in the previous chapters, the goal is to examine if a regression model could improve the prediction accuracy of planned LT in a job shop-manufacturing environment. In addition, the complexity of the models should also be taken into consideration. The data-understanding phase foresees to collect initial data and then to describe, examine and to check the data quality [14]. According to Kuepper [15] data can be collected through an analysis of documents or the organisation. Further, stated by Loos [16], data types to be captured are master data or variable data, which can be analyzed e.g. by visualization or statistics [17]. The data preparation phase chooses the relevant data for the modelling phase and prepares the data by cleaning, adding further data or integrating different data sources as well as adjusting the data format [14]. Feature selection or the creation of more suitable features can occur e.g. with regression methods or expert insights [12]. Ludwig and Nyhuis [3] state that the consideration of the order-specific situation by characterizing the orders, recording the current work in progress and capacity situation of the production system and the processing sequence is relevant for the LT prediction. In general, LT consists of the components transition time and execution time. Transition time corresponds to the transportation time, post- and pre-processing waiting time. Execution time is equivalent to the set-up and processing time [1, 2, 18]. Typically, the transition time, especially the waiting time, reflects up to 90% of the overall LT in a job shop [1]. Therefore, especially the present state of influencing factors from the waiting time should contribute to the accuracy of the prediction model. According to Nyhuis [2, 19] the current work in progress at each workstation has a major impact on transition time.

During the modelling phase, chosen regression methods are modelled and a generated test design evaluates the models [14]. Based on the current research LR, DT, RF, BDT and DNN are chosen. DNN is based on a multi-layer feed-forward artificial neural network that is using back-propagation [20]. On the one hand, RF, BDT and DNN show in different studies the best performance, despite a direct comparison between RF/BDT and DNN. On the other hand, LR and DT are less complex, hence easier to understand and implement [8]. The final tradeoff between model complexity and prediction accuracy depends on the business and data mining goals. The test design consists of 40% from the overall data set and measures with RMSE, a commonly used evaluation metric [21]. The tool RapidMiner [20] is applied due to its straightforwardness application of ML models [12].

The evaluation phase evaluates the results, conducts a review process and determines the next steps in regards to a potential deployment [14]. Hence, this phase compares the results of the modelling phase with the originally set goals of the business-understanding phase. The evaluation of the results can either lead to adjustments of the previous phase and therefore to a repetition of the modelling or to an approval of an appropriate model. In the case of an approval, the deployment phase begins by planning the deployment and runtime management as well as by preparing a final project report and conducting a project assessment [14]. For deployment, e.g. considerations of database requirements or the implementation in existing processes need to be conducted. Generally, the characteristics of the manufacturing system or process can change over time [22]. Therefore, a ML model needs to be updated regularly, as the relationships between the features can change unforeseeable [23]. Hereafter, CRISP-DM corresponds to a continuous improvement process [14].

4 Application

The research methodology is applied to manufacturing enterprise system data from a German job shop manufacturer, who is responsible for the maintenance of complex investment goods. The job shop consists of 14 shop sections, each with three to six workstations of the same kind and has nine main production routes with different work contents and recursion loops. Typically, the order characteristics vary for each maintenance order because the complex capital goods are exposed to different external factors such as environmental conditions or degree of capacity utilization, resulting in different maintenance efforts. Hence, maintenance orders usually differ in their duration and the workstations they pass through, which is consistent with the definition of a job shop. Currently, the planned LT equals to the operation-specific execution time plus a generalized transition time. In an investigation period of about one year, the current method deviates on average by -12.17 days with a standard deviation of 12.95 days from the actual LT. The typical variance of the characteristics from the maintenance orders in a job shop and the prediction deviations of the current method underpin the need for an alternative approach to determine the planned LT. For the modelling phase, thus, the initial data set with the maximum available 66 features describing these orders is examined. The provided data set of approx. 7,900 orders from the ERP system is of sufficient quality and consists of features, which characterize the orders (e.g. business unit, client type, part type, order quantity, and planned working hours per workstation), the order's process (e.g. actual start of processing) or the job shop (e.g. work in progress per workstation). The feedback was accurate to the day, which is sufficient for predicting LT of orders. Statistical and visual analysis do not show strong patterns for deviating LT or any outliers. However, the data set excludes 13 attributes, because they are not available at the time of forecasting a new order's LT (e.g. actual start of processing) or they reflect the planned working hours of a workstation, which is not used in the majority of orders and thus has insufficient quality of information for the prediction. Further feature selection is conducted through an algorithm-based approach, whereas the choice also depends on the set parameters of the models. Referring to Table 1, the models all have the originally planned LT as one of their top features, which ranges from 1.6 to 233.9 days with an average of 27.6 days and a standard deviation of 10.1 days. In four of the five models, the planned working hours of the workstation 131 is a major feature. Each order uses this workstation with varying planned working hours of 0.10 to 78.00 h with an average of 2.89 h and a standard deviation of 4.11 h. The workstations 81, 91, 21 and the overall planned working hours are only in some of the chosen models a major factor. Not amongst the top three features, nevertheless the work in progress of some specific workstations has also an influencing effect and underpins Nyhuis's hypothesis [2, 19].

As stated in Table 1, a comparison of the RMSE values from the different approaches shows that all chosen models outperform the original procedure and DNN has overall the best accuracy. However, the method is only slightly better than BDT. The RMSE of LR, DT and RF is roughly one day higher than from BDT and DNN. Overall, the RMSE of the DNN model, which is not as traceable as simpler models, is currently 9.6 days lower than the original procedure and 1.1 days lower than the LR model. In addition, DNN deviates in average by 0.43 days with a standard deviation of 7.98 days from the actual LT.

Table 1. Overview of results from LT planning.

Model	Top 3 features	RMSE [days]
LR	Originally planned LT, planned working hours of workstation 131 and 81	5.9
DT	Originally planned LT, overall planned working hours, planned working hours of workstation 131	6.0
RF	Originally planned LT, planned working hours of workstation 131 and 91	6.1
BDT	Originally planned LT, overall planned working hours, planned working hours of workstation 91	5.0
DNN	Originally planned LT, planned working hours of workstation 131 and 21	4.8
Original	Operation-specific execution time, generalized transition time	14.4

Moreover, Fig. 1 visualizes the model accuracy by showing the distribution of deviations between actual and planned LT from the test data set of LR, DNN and the original procedure.

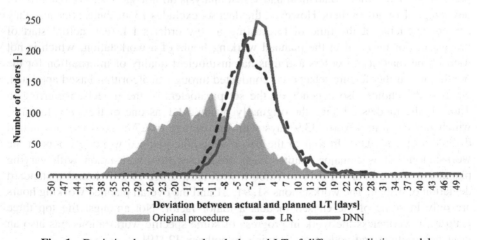

Fig. 1. Deviation between actual and planned LT of different prediction models

The average deviation between actual and planned LT of the test data set has decreased by 11.83 days for LR and 12.61 days for DNN in comparison to the original procedure. In order to decrease the overall range of deviations, a further balancing of the data set could be carried out, as currently the majority of orders consist of short LT. In addition, as Ludwig and Nyhuis [3] state, information about the processing sequence of operations could further add value to the accuracy of the models.

Within the scope of a feasibility study of the company, the applicability was examined and evaluated based on actual data. Due to the high programming effort in the ERP system used, an approach has not yet been integrated into the ongoing operation.

5 Conclusion and Future Research Agenda

This paper has shown a comprehensive approach to predict LT in a job shop environment. Overall, more precise LT planning reduces the effort of downstream process steps (e.g. capacity coordination) in job shop production and enables a more reliable promise of customer appointments. The paper contributes to the current research by highlighting the different state of the art of regression model selection and the associated input characteristics. The application to a real job shop production shows that DNN has the best prediction accuracy, closely followed by BDT. RF's accuracy is slightly worse than the simpler models, LR and DT. However, in current literature RF has often shown the best results, which cannot be proven for this case.

Further investigations should be carried out in an additional research project to identify generally valid statements along the modelling process for LT prediction. The aim is to study the different influence factors in LT planning and to identify the key influence variables. This would also facilitate the introduction of SL approaches, as correspondingly targeted priorities could be set within the data-mining project. The research project could also be further specified by additional analyses of other regression models or modifications with regard to parameter setting. Besides the research about ML-supported LT planning, there is also a need for further research on the general handling of ML in the production domain. For example, practically relevant research questions concern ethics, data protection, and the traceability of the solution or the integration of ML models into existing organizational structures. In a further step, these findings can be applied to the determination of planned LT.

Acknowledgements. Funded by the Lower Saxony Ministry of Science and Culture under grant number ZN3489 within the Lower Saxony "Vorab" of the Volkswagen Foundation and supported by the Center for Digital Innovations (ZDIN).

References

1. Wiendahl, H.-P.: Betriebsorganisation für Ingenieure, 8th edn. Carl Hanser, Muenchen (2014)
2. Nyhuis, P., Wiendahl, H.-P.: Logistic production operating curves – basic model of the theory of logistic operating curves. CIRP Ann. **55**(1), 441–444 (2006)

3. Ludwig, E., Nyhuis, P.: Verbesserung der Termineinhaltung in komplexen Fertigungsbereichen durch einen neuen Ansatz zur Plandurchlaufzeitermittlung. In: Görke, W., Rininsland, H., Syrbe, M. (eds.) Information als Produktionsfaktor. INFORMAT, pp. 473–483. Springer, Heidelberg (1992). https://doi.org/10.1007/978-3-642-77810-0_43

4. Lödding, H.: Handbook of Manufacturing Control – Fundamentals, Description, Configuration. Springer, Berlin and Heidelberg (2016). https://doi.org/10.1007/978-3-642-24458-2

5. Shaw, M., Whinston, A.B.: An artificial intelligence approach to the scheduling of flexible manufacturing systems. IIE Trans. 21(2), 170–183 (1989)

6. Bullers, W.I., Nof, S.Y., Whinston, A.B.: Artificial intelligence in manufacturing planning and control. AIIE Trans. 12(4), 351–363 (1980)

7. Samuel, A.L.: Some studies in machine learning using the game of checkers. IBM J. Res. Dev. 3(3), 210–229 (1959)

8. Russel, S., Norvig, P.: Artificial Intelligence: A Modern Approach, 3rd edn. Pearson Education, Upper Saddle River (2010)

9. Gyulai, D., Pfeiffer, A., Nick, G., Gallina, V., Sihn, W., Monostori, L.: Lead time prediction in a flow-shop environment with analytical and machine learning approaches. IFAC-PapersOnLine 51(11), 1029–1034 (2018)

10. Lingitz, L., et al.: Lead time prediction using machine learning algorithms: a case study by a semiconductor manufacturer. In: 51st CIRP Conference on Manufacturing Systems, vol. 72, pp. 1051–1056 (2018)

11. Wang, C., Jiang, P.: Deep neural networks based order completion time prediction by using real-time job shop RFID data. J. Intell. Manuf. 30(3), 1303–1318 (2019)

12. Cadavid, J.P.U., Lamouri, S., Grabot, B., Pellerin, R., Fortin, A.: Machine learning applied in production planning and control: a state-of-the-art in the era of industry 4.0. J. Intell. Manuf. 31, 1531–1558 (2020)

13. Mourtzis, D., Doukas, M., Fragou, K., Efthymiou, K., Matzorou, V.: Knowledge-based estimation of manufacturing lead time for complex engineered-to-order products. In: 47th CIRP Conference on Manufacturing Systems, vol. 17, pp. 499–504 (2014)

14. Chapman, P., et al.: CRISP-DM 1.0 step-by-step data mining guide. The CRISP-DM consortium (2000)

15. Kuepper, H.-U.: Controlling. Konzeption, Aufgaben und Instrumente, 4th edn. Schaeffer-Poeschel, Stuttgart (2005)

16. Loos, P.: Grunddatenverwaltung und Betriebsdatenerfassung als Basis der Produktionsplanung und -steuerung. In: Corsten, H., Friedl, B. (eds.) Einführung in das Produktionscontrolling, pp. 227–252. Vahlen, München (1999)

17. Witten, I., Frank, E., Hall, M.: Data Mining – Practical Machine Learning Tools and Techniques, 3rd edn. Elsevier, Burlington (2011)

18. Bechte, W.: Methoden und Hilfsmittel der Durchlaufzeit- und Bestandsanalyse in Klein- und Mittelbetrieben. Beuth, Berlin (1979)

19. Nyhuis, P.: Practical applications of logistic operating curves. CIRP Ann. 56(1), 483–486 (2007)

20. Mierswa, I., Klinkenberg, R.: RapidMiner Studio. 9.3. RapidMiner Inc. (2019)

21. Kuhn, M., Johnson, K.: Applied Predictive Modelling, 1st edn. Springer, New York (2013). https://doi.org/10.1007/978-1-4614-6849-3

22. Deep, K., Singh, P.K.: Design of robust cellular manufacturing system for dynamicpart population considering multiple processing routes using geneticalgorithm. J. Manuf. Syst. 35, 155–163 (2015)

23. Hammami, Z., Mouelhi, W., Said, L.B.: On-line self-adaptive framework for tailoring a neural-agent learning model addressing dynamic real-time scheduling problems. J. Manuf. Syst. 45, 97–108 (2017)

Connected, Smart Factories
of the Future

Identifying Key Business Processes that Can Benefit from Industry 4.0 in the Gas Sector

The Public Gas Distribution Networks Case in Greece

Nikolaos A. Panayiotou(✉), Vasileios P. Stavrou,
and Konstantinos E. Stergiou

National Technical University of Athens, 15780 Zografou, Athens, Greece
panayiot@central.ntua.gr

Abstract. The Natural Gas Distribution sector is considered one of the most critical areas in which Industry 4.0 methodologies can be applied, as they form a part of critical infrastructure management where automation, information technology and high-tech solutions can offer high-level service. The paper aims to identify critical business processes that can substantially benefit from Industry 4.0 and Information Technology solutions in a Natural Gas Distribution Company which distributes Natural gas in Greece in Medium and Low Pressure.

The research conducted identified the company's business processes and highlighted these which are critical to its operation. Having identified the technological advancements in the Gas sector, the business processes that can benefit from Industry 4.0 and Information and Communication Technologies were recognized.

The results revealed three critical business processes that can be radically improved: management of new customers' connections, project management of works projects and network maintenance. Technological approaches that can transform these processes were identified to be a real-time collaborative CRM system, a real-time collaborative project management system integrated with an appropriate document management system, smart meters, sensors and actuators for real-time monitoring of important operational variables and a monitoring system which collects and generates consolidated information in a Control Room.

Identification of the processes into which Industry 4.0 and information technologies can lead to the introduction of corresponding solutions, can increase operational efficiency of company's network and minimise running costs. The research effort should be continued in order to achieve higher integration between business processes, Industry 4.0 concepts and Information Systems.

Keywords: Industry 4.0 · Key business processes · Utilities · Gas sector · Maintenance

© IFIP International Federation for Information Processing 2020
Published by Springer Nature Switzerland AG 2020
B. Lalic et al. (Eds.): APMS 2020, IFIP AICT 591, pp. 373–380, 2020.
https://doi.org/10.1007/978-3-030-57993-7_42

1   Main Characteristics of Industry 4.0 Integration in a Utility Company Business Processes

Industry 4.0 defines a methodology in order to transform machine dominant manufacturing to digital manufacturing (Oztemel and Gursev 2018). Its products or services are considered the results of deep integration between industrialization and informatization (Gilchrist 2016). The concept was introduced in Germany in 2011 (Xu et al. 2018) making up an innovative effort by the German government in order to gain a strategic competitive advantage over their key industrial competitors. In the utilities sector, Industry 4.0 can find a number of discrete applications.

In the context of Industry 4.0, utility companies are trying to implement a number of innovative solutions, incorporating Information and Communication Technologies (ICTs), Cyberphysical Systems (CPS) and Internet of Things. In this way, they are able to monitor and control their processes in a more efficient, flexible, reliable, sustainable, decentralized, secure and economic manner, using a number of suitable tools (Faheem et al. 2018). In this context, a new concept, Oil and Gas 4.0 has also been put on the agenda as an instantiation of Industry 4.0. Oil and Gas 4.0 has the potential to completely change oil and gas industry, accelerating, digitalizing and reengineering its processes (Lu et al. 2019). This concept has gained ground in recent years among businesses in the industry.

2   Main Concepts and Tools Used in Oil and Gas 4.0

Oil and Gas 4.0 in oil and gas companies is implemented with the aid of several methods and tools. Although certain techniques can be identified in oil and gas upstream sector (smart oilfield) and others can be found in the last steps of the supply chain (sales), many of the most important applications arise mainly in the midstream (intelligent pipeline, equipment maintenance, smart metering), in which special emphasis will be given in this article.

First of all, oil and gas pipelines and networks are usually centrally managed by a control room using computer-aided control, monitoring systems, sensors and actuators. In recent years, the control room's communication with pipeline points of interest (equipment, sensors and end-users) has been upgraded with more modern tools (pipeline surveillance software). In order to implement this communication, different wired and wireless communication technologies are used (Faheem et al. 2018).

Currently, most of the smart pipelines critical applications are relying on wired networks, using optical fiber technologies. On the other side, microwaves technology provides secure and high-speed wireless connection for sending and receiving a huge amount of information. In addition, wireless solutions are preferred due to higher data rates, while satellite communication is preferred due to extremely long-distance coverage (Lu et al. 2019). Sensors and actuators are located at specific preselected points of the oil or gas smart pipeline. Specific sensors are positioned along the smart pipeline in order to detect malfunctions and activate respective maintenance mechanisms. In addition, sensors can also detect leakage in specific areas of the network and supply interruption can be ordered. Finally, advanced sensors can collect weather data, helping operators to implement actions and handling risks (Qarabash et al. 2020).

A key element of Oil and Gas 4.0 is the use of smart meters. Smart metering enables the remote control, in order to accurately measuring consumption and fuel flow at precise time windows, extracting consumption statistics, while avoiding leakage or fraud. In addition, demand-side management is generally considered a critical parameter, as changes in consumption are usually managed by altering the loads on the distribution grid (Lu et al. 2019). As regards Oil and Gas 4.0 under the prism of maintenance of intelligent pipeline, sensors and actuators are considered key parameters. By building digital twins of equipment, oil and gas companies can detect early signs of failure in advance, enabling them to take maintenance measures ahead of time, which allows them to save costs, given the fact that repair after failure is always more expensive than maintenance in advance.

Creation of digital files containing materials, consumables and equipment matrices (catalogs of equipment needed to be changed, maintained, upgraded) are also considered main aims in Oil and Gas 4.0, based on principles of automation and digitization. In addition, security plays a vital role in order to ensure stability and avoiding unwanted situations. A large amount of raw data from heterogeneous devices may contain a variety of vulnerabilities, allowing attackers to enter to the system and manipulate metering data, cause data management chaos or destabilizing oil and gas networks (Faheem et al. 2018). Based on the above, it is easily understood that the use and management of big data in an IoT environment is a matter of major importance for Oil and Gas industry.

Additional techniques can also be identified in the literature, as they are used in Oil and Gas 4.0 context. For example, the use of Augmented Reality (AR) technology in the training of operators can guide experts before the actual maintenance operation, reducing the probability of operational errors, while blockchain technology can be used in order to secure data, increase transparency, and provide tracking for goods (Lu et al. 2019).

The use of ICT Information Systems in collaboration with industrial automations and cyberphysical systems (CPS) in Oil and Gas 4.0 aims mainly to enhance smart pipelines efficiency and reliability. At first, customer relationship management tools (CRM) are used closely associated with smart pipelines in order to secure better communication with customers and subcontractors (Panayiotou et al. 2019 [a]). In terms of in-company communication, modern ERP's and Document Management Systems can help companies, with the aim of document controlling. ICT implementation in Oil and Gas industry can provide user-friendly services to customers, bringing economic benefits to both sides. In addition, information systems aim to operate in conjunction with industry partners in a single framework in order to optimize business processes, customer service and cost savings (Merlin 2010).

Business process collaboration with Industry 4.0 (and Oil and Gas 4.0) is accomplished using Process Modeling and similar methods, providing stakeholders with adequate means in order to control processes efficiently and effectively (Rehse et al. 2018). Under the Industry 4.0 concept, systematic attempts have been made in order to adopt industrial digitization and transformation under a single architecture. For example, Panayiotou et al. (2019 [b]) established an Industry 4.0 architecture in order to integrate business automations, information systems, business processes and the physical world.

In the following paragraphs, a case of a Natural Gas Distribution company is presented and the approach it followed for the introduction of Oil and Gas 4.0 technologies driven by its business processes specific needs. Although Natural Gas as a product can be classified as "non-intelligent" as it cannot add embedded information or connectivity to it, Natural Gas Distribution companies place particular emphasis on Oil and Gas 4.0 concept, as smart pipelines, maintenance and metering are their main area of activity. In this context, Oil and Gas 4.0 is widely applied to Natural Gas Distribution companies, and its relation with business processes will be demonstrated in the following case study.

3   The Case of a Natural Gas Distribution Company

During the implementation and integration of Industry 4.0 in a natural gas distribution company, the design and modeling of business processes is of particular value. Without proper planning of company's business processes, it is not easy to identify the fields in which Oil and Gas 4.0 can be implemented. The current effort aims to implement certain Oil and Gas 4.0 tools and techniques in a natural gas company operating in Greece (DEDA S.A.). DEDA (Public Gas Distribution Networks) SA is a newly established company, founded in 2017 having as its main activity to operate as the Distribution Network Administrator (in Medium and Low Pressure) for Natural Gas in Greek Territory (with the exception of Attica, Thessaloniki and Thessaly regions). In particular, the company's core business includes planning, study, development, maintenance, operation and management of the natural gas distribution network in the abovementioned geographic areas. Monitoring of the whole distribution process is one of its key responsibilities, in addition to the measurement of natural gas quantities delivered at delivery points. In addition, maintenance and upgrading of the distribution network remains a major priority, as DEDA's network is designed not only to support the transfer of natural gas from high-pressure network, but also to ensure the safe distribution from medium and low pressure network to the final consumers. DEDA is aiming to develop a network of above 1,200 km in the next few years.

During the case study, the company's business processes were initially identified and grouped into distinct groups, with the help of the company's staff, while a Value Added Chain Diagram was created. A total of 10 personal and group interviews took place involving 12 DEDA employees (senior executives and company officers). Subsequently, a literature review was implemented in order to record existing technologies which could help the company to transform its processes. As a final step, an effort was made in order to identify business processes in which the abovementioned techniques could be applied, while a detailed study was implemented in order to plan the future situation (TO BE) of these processes and the way they could be improved using Oil and Gas 4.0 technologies. The research question can be stated as follows:

- In which business processes of a natural gas distribution company can Industry 4.0 be implemented, and which tools or techniques can be exactly applied?

The VACD diagram which resulted is depicted in Fig. 1. In conclusion, 93 processes have been recorded, divided into 7 process groups. As regards the literature review, regarding Oil and Gas 4.0 technologies, results are summarized in the second part of this article. Concerning the identification of processes in which Oil and Gas 4.0 could be used, a total of 38 processes were found in which such technologies could be used in an integrated way (indicated with an asterisk in Fig. 1).

Regarding **client's management** of the company, as a complex process with many stakeholders, requires a huge workload and its automation will save a lot of resources which could be allocated to other tasks. It will also reduce the mistakes on the part of the company. Concerning this process, a new CRM software, which is about to be installed, will handle new connection requests, in order to be completed smoothly. The same system will handle customer complaints, in order to have a unified view of the customer's behavior during their lifecycle. Concerning the **Financial Management**, which is critical for the overall operation of the company and has increased oversight needs, invoices will be managed through an integrated system with full visibility of the end-to-end "sell to collect" process group, while employees will have the ability to monitor invoices throughout their life cycle.

In addition, **Project and Network Management** is considered a critical area in the natural gas network operation, for a company such as DEDA that aims to expand its network in the coming years and serve a larger amount of clients. For that reason, a number of procedures related to the development of the company's network are going to be reengineered (project bidding, monitoring of the contract and monitoring of the financial part of the project, monitoring of DEDA and subcontractor's performance, delivery of materials, project completion) using a Project Management System supported by a Document and Workflow Management system.

Based on the current processes, **network maintenance** takes place either in a preventive or in a corrective method. In the near future, based on the new Oil and Gas 4.0-based techniques (implementation of a control room, in which all information from the pipelines and end users will be directed using appropriate sensors, actuators and smart meters, through the operation of a parallel data network), real time network status and malfunctions will be detected. In case of emergency, a vehicle (terrestrial or UAV) may be sent and transmit image by satellite from the damage area so that appropriate personnel and equipment can be dispatched. All of the aforementioned procedures may be carried out in collaboration with subcontractors who undertake part of the network maintenance. All data are recorded in a network surveillance information system implemented in the control room.

Concerning the **network operation** processes which involve Industry 4.0 techniques, the company has to take a series of measurements at various points of the pipeline. All of these metrics will be monitored by the control room. Real-time monitoring of the pipeline status (using sensors) will also be performed. Finally, the company is obliged to regularly check the facilities of gas consumers using specialized equipment, while the results have to be sent to DEDA's control room.

Finally, in the **Corporate Governance** processes group, three processes could be supported by an appropriately designed Document and Workflow Management system (Management Review, Corporate Knowledge Management, Document and File Management). Especially the Management Review process was completely

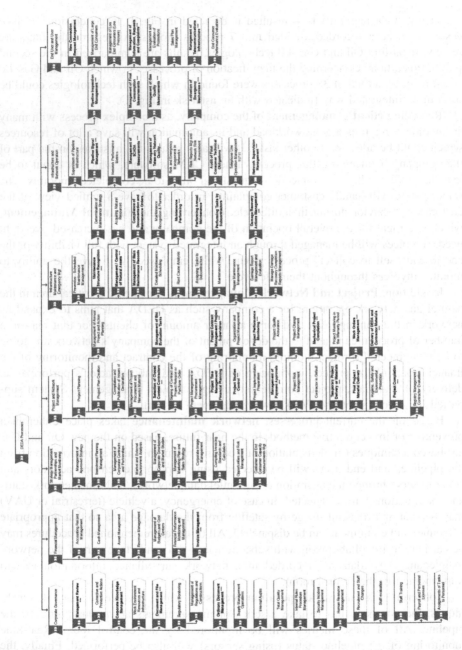

Fig. 1. DEDA Value Added Chain Diagram (the selected processes are indicated with an asterisk)

reorganized in order that all stakeholders have the ability to monitor process real time metrics. It should be emphasized that the technologies which have been prioritized at this stage are not the only Oil and Gas 4.0 technologies which can be applied in a gas distribution company, and possibly the next implementation step in DEDA's case is to adopt some of the technologies which have not been adopted in this step of the company modernization.

4 Conclusions

It became evident that Industry 4.0 in combination with the cooperating Information Technology solutions are issues of primary importance for the gas sector in general and for gas distribution companies in particular. Maintenance and operations management, project management, as well as day-to-day customer management are important activity areas, interconnected around the Factory of the Future concept.

While the identification of critical business processes is considered the first major step, the contribution of Industry 4.0 in processes such as network maintenance and invoicing became immediately evident in the analysis. However, it was also clear that the introduction of supportive information systems (a collaborative CRM and a Project Management System supported by a Document and Workflow Management system) were additionally needed in order to achieve fully streamlined and integrated business processes. CRM proved to play a key role regarding the communication of the company with other stakeholders, while the Project Management software facilitates the monitoring of works and maintenance projects. These two software solutions are fully integrated with the Industry 4.0 solutions for gas metering and real time monitoring of the gas network operation that provides all the necessary data in a Control Room in order to be transformed to information and decisions.

The gas distribution companies are expected to benefit from the introduction of Industry 4.0 solutions and Information Technology. However, in order for the necessary investment to really pay-off, the selection of the technological solutions must be driven by business processes needs. In the future, emphasis should be placed on designing business processes taking into account all actors involved. In addition, the impact of the implementation of the abovementioned technologies should be assessed in order to aid decision makers in their decision regarding their final adoption.

Acknowledgments. This research has been co-financed by the European Union and Greek national funds through the Operational Program Competitiveness, Entrepreneurship and Innovation, under the call RESEARCH – CREATE – INNOVATE (project code: T1EDK-01825).

References

Faheem, M., et al.: Smart grid communication and information technologies in the perspective of industry 4.0: opportunities and challenges. Comput. Sci. Rev. **30**, 1–30 (2018)

Fang, X., Misra, S., Xue, G., Yang, D.: Smart grid –the new and improved power grid: a survey. IEEE Commun. Surv. Tutor. **14**, 944–980 (2012)

Gilchrist, A.: Industry 4.0: The Industrial Internet of Things. Apress, New York City (2016)

Lu, H., Guo, L., Kun, M.: Oil and Gas 4.0 era: a systematic review and outlook. Comput. Ind. **111**, 68–90 (2019)

Merlin, S.: Smart utilities and CRM: The next phase of customer management in utilities. J. Database Market. Customer Strategy Manag. **17**, 49–58 (2010)

Oztemel, E., Gursev, S.: Literature review of industry 4.0 and related technologies. J. Intell. Manuf. **31**, 127–182 (2018)

Panayiotou, N., Stavrou, V., Stergiou, K.: Reengineering of the new customer gas connection process utilizing industry 4.0 technologies. In: The Greek Case of Public Gas Distribution Networks S.A., ISCSIC 2019, 25–27 September 2019, Amsterdam, Netherlands (2019) [a]

Panayiotou, N., Stergiou, K., Stavrou, V.: The Role of Business Process Modeling & Management in the Industry 4.0 Framework. In: INAIT 2019 – Industry 4.0 and Artificial Intelligence Technologies, Cambridge, UK, 19–20 August 2019 [b]

Qarabash, N., Sabah, S., Qarabash, H.: Smart grid in the context of industry 4.0: an overview of communications technologies and challenges. Indonesian J. Electr. Eng. Comput. Sci. **18**(2), 656–665 (2020)

Rehse, J.-R., Dadashnia, S., Fettke, P.: Business process management for industry 4.0 – three application cases in the DFKI-smart-lego-factory. It – Inf. Technol. **60**(3), 133–141 (2018)

Xu, L.D., Xu, E.L., Li, L.: Industry 4.0: state of the art and future trends. Int. J. Prod. Res. **56**(8), 2941–2962 (2018)

The Impact of Industry 4.0 Connectivity on the Collaboration Along Brazilian Automotive Supply Chain

Nilza Aparecida dos Santos[1,2](✉) ⓘD, Sergio Miele Ruggero[1](✉) ⓘD,
José Benedito Sacomano[1](✉) ⓘD, Antonio Carlos Estender[1](✉) ⓘD,
and Marcia Terra da Silva[1](✉) ⓘD

[1] Graduate Studies in Production Engineering, Universidade Paulista, São Paulo,
SP 04026-002, Brazil
nilzaasantos7@gmail.com, miele326@gmail.com,
jbsacomano@gmail.com,
{estender,marcia.terra}@uol.com.br
[2] FATEC, Cotia, SP 06702-155, Brazil

Abstract. Industry 4.0 presents a new manufacturing model through the intensive use of new technologies in the pursuit of improving processes in the value chain. The use of digital technologies and the application in the industry in general influence the value chain of products, business models and commercial integration, which can improve the competitiveness of companies. This text seeks to understand the importance of data connectivity in the value chain processes of the automotive sector, in order to identify and analyze the relevance of data connectivity between the company, suppliers, customers and partners. The data were collected through a survey applied to professionals in the automotive segment, the observational method and bibliographic research. The results showed that although the use of data to define the business is relevant, investments in digital technologies are insufficient. Data connectivity between companies, suppliers, customers and partners were identified as essential, but it still does not occur as expected.

Keywords: Connectivity · Industry 4.0 · Investments · Value chain ·
Automotive

1 Introduction

The concept of Industry 4.0 is seen as a trend towards automation and data exchange during the manufacturing process [1]. The use of new technologies seeks to meet an advanced manufacturing system and the integration of the value chain, transforming the physical, digital and biological pillars, promoting changes that affect the economy as a whole [2].

Technological advances can reconfigure the industrial sector, boosting productivity, modifying business models and skills necessary to add value throughout the value chain operations. Digitalizing and integrating processes vertically, from product development and purchase, to manufacturing, logistics and services.

© IFIP International Federation for Information Processing 2020
Published by Springer Nature Switzerland AG 2020
B. Lalic et al. (Eds.): APMS 2020, IFIP AICT 591, pp. 381–388, 2020.
https://doi.org/10.1007/978-3-030-57993-7_43

Industry 4.0 integrates various technologies, enabling smarter and more efficient factories and production models, capable of leveraging growth and economic development [3]. In Brazil, the transition to Industry 4.0 can generate new manufacturing models and the evolution of production processes. It is necessary to make investments for the adaptation of infrastructure and qualification of labor [4].

Connectivity, artificial intelligence and flexible automation are considered key technologies for Industry 4.0 [5]. Connectivity creates connections between devices, sensors, machines and software. Regarding the value chain, connectivity optimizes communication with all stakeholders [6].

Considering aspects related to the transition to Industry 4.0, the object of study of this article is: What is the importance of data connectivity in the automotive industry's value chain processes? Aiming to identify and analyze the relevance of data connectivity between the company, suppliers, customers and partners.

2 Literature Review

Industry 4.0 proposes a new manufacturing model through the intensive use of new technologies in the pursuit of improving industrial processes in the value chain [7]. In the context of industrial production, it comprises a variety of cutting-edge technologies characterized by Cyber-Physical systems (CPS) [8]. Cyber-Physical systems are computational and collaborative systems composed of interconnected physical and computational elements [9]. In addition to the interaction between workers and machines [10], CPS also have potential for planning, controlling and organizing production processes and supply chains [11].

Intelligent factories, considered the epicenter of Industry 4.0, operate in a network and show characteristics such as: the vertical integration of production systems; the horizontal integration of networks and the global value chain; engineering in the value chain and acceleration through exponential technologies [12]. The main requirements for the construction of these factories are process control, real-time data and product tracking, setting a new manufacturing standard [13], whose objective is to achieve a higher level of automation, operation, efficiency and productivity [14].

The widespread use of digital technologies and application in industry in general influences the value chain of products, business models and commercial integration. The combination of these new technologies can provide important productivity gains, improving the competitiveness of companies [15].

Industry 4.0 also brings opportunities for the development of new products, in companies and research institutions. On the other hand, the lack of adaptation to the new technological challenges can lead to difficulties in the development of new products, services, innovation and technological models, considering that competitiveness is also supported by cost reduction [16]. Regarding data connectivity, surveys [17] show that 91% of national companies are not connected.

In the conception of Industry 4.0, digitalization in industries has a broader approach, considering new technologies and concepts relevant to the management of the value chain, decentralizing operational decision making through the creation of smart factories [10]. The horizontal integration of the value chain, network production system and vertical integration and the final digitalization of projects along the value chain are requirements for the implementation of Industry 4.0 supported by emerging technologies, comprising IOT (Internet of Things), networks wireless sensors, big data, cloud-based services, embedded systems and mobile Internet [18].

3 Methods

This article was made using an exploratory, qualitative and quantitative methodology. The collection of primary data occurred through the application of a survey, for professionals in the automotive segment.

The research included 07 questions, based on the professional experience of the authors in the segment. One question designed to qualify the sample (type of company and function) and other 06 questions that asked about the use of data for the definition of the business model, level of data connectivity between the company, suppliers, customers and partners, the collaboration of companies with suppliers, customers and partners, the bottlenecks for the use of new technologies and level of investments.

In the selection of participants, we chose those who exercise leadership functions in the industrial area. The automotive segment was chosen due to its relevance to the Brazilian economy, as it represents 22% of Industrial Gross Domestic Product (GDP) [15]. The companies were selected because they are part of the supply chain of the researched sector. Of the 60 questionnaires sent, 51 were answered and 9 did not justify the absence of an answer.

The surveyed sample was composed of 65% of auto parts companies, 25% of assembly companies and 10% of metallurgical companies, the respondents occupy leadership roles (directors, managers and supervisors). Secondary data were determined by documentary analysis and bibliographic references. The observation method was also used to determine and analyze the results, based on professional experience and the participation of the authors in the segment.

The validity of the research is ensured by the description, by the understanding of the aspects related to connectivity and the adherence of the collected and interpreted data, added to the construction of reality by the participants. Considering that everyone involved has professional experience in the industrial area and that the companies are members of the automotive industry value chain.

4 Result and Discussion

The results obtained are shown by the following figures.

Figure 1 demonstrates the level of importance that the surveyed companies give to the use of data to define the business model. It was used for measuring an intensity scale ranging from 1 (null) to 6 (fundamental). It can be seen that for more than 80% of companies the use of data is fundamental.

The level of data connectivity that currently sets between companies, suppliers, customers and partners is illustrated in Fig. 2. It was found that for 94% of the

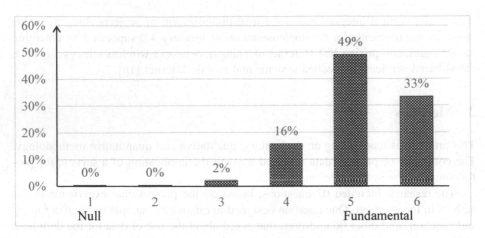

Fig. 1. Use of data to define the business model (Source: prepared by the authors).

companies surveyed, the level of connectivity established between the members of the value chain is considered low.

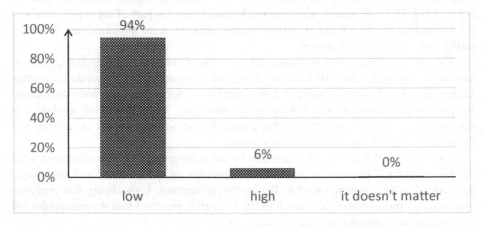

Fig. 2. Current level of data connectivity between the company, suppliers, customers and partners (Source: prepared by the authors).

Another question raised at the companies surveyed, it was about what would be the expected level of data connectivity between the company, suppliers, customers and partners. The answers to that question are shown in Fig. 3.

Comparing the results presented in Figs. 2 and 3. It is observed that the desired level of connectivity by companies is far from what is expected, which indicates that the established connectivity today among value chain components still does not meet the needs of companies.

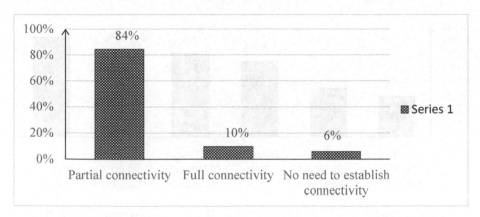

Fig. 3. Expected level of data connectivity between company, suppliers, customers and partners (Source: prepared by the authors).

Figure 4 shows the level of cooperation of companies with suppliers, customers and partners for business development using digital technologies.

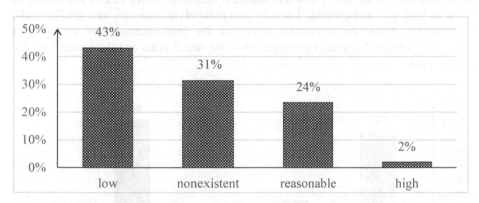

Fig. 4. Your company's level of collaboration with suppliers, customers and partners for business development using digital technologies (Source: prepared by the authors).

The level of collaboration between members of the value chain for the use of digital technology is pointed out as low and non-existent for 74% of the companies interviewed, which is in line with the situation presented in Figs. 2 and 3. Although the companies aim to connectivity along the value chain is greater, the scenario set points to a shortage in the use of digital technology in a collaborative way.

The difficulties in using new technologies, according to the companies surveyed, are presented in Fig. 5.

The lack of connection between the participants in the business chain is the most cited impediment to the use of new technologies. Availability of financial resources and indicators to measure the return on investments are also highlighted in a significant way

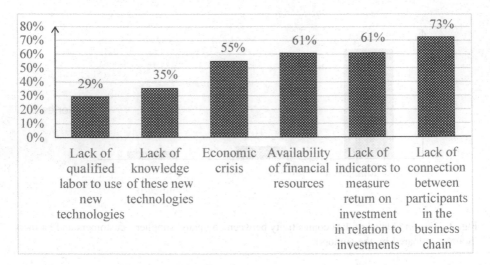

Fig. 5. Impediments to the use of new technologies (Source: prepared by the authors)

as impediments to the use of new technologies. Economic crisis, lack of knowledge of these technologies and qualified labor are also pointed out, however on a smaller scale.

Figure 6 shows the investment levels for the implementation of technologies related to Industry 4.0 made by companies in the last 2 years and the forecast for the next 5 years.

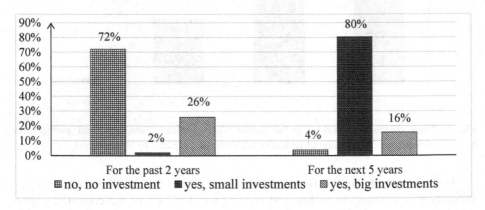

Fig. 6. Investments levels for the implementation of technologies (Source: prepared by the authors)

The data show that 72% of the companies have not made any investment to implement technologies related to Industry 4.0 in the last 2 years. For the next 5 years, 80% of companies intend to make small investments. In detailing the data, it was found that the 26% of companies that made high investments in the last 2 years, as well as the 16% that they intend to make in the future correspond only to assembly companies.

5   Conclusion

The aim of this study was to identify and analyze the importance of data connectivity between the company, suppliers, customers and partners. Based on the results obtained, it was found that this issue is paramount for more than 80% of the companies surveyed. The level of connectivity is below expectations, as well as the level of collaboration between members of the value chain for the use of digital technology.

The low collaborative connectivity was identified by the interviewees as the main impediment to the use of new technologies. Other impediments such as available financial resources, indicators to measure the return on investments are also highlighted. Aspects related to the lack of knowledge about new technologies and labor appear as impediments but to a lesser extent. Regarding the level of investments, the data pointed to a low level of investments made and future estimates of small investments.

Research carried out by PWC [19] emphasizes that connectivity between suppliers is necessary, which must communicate integrating all components of the value chain, a situation that is in line with the results obtained by this research.

Considering the level of investments made and to be made by the companies surveyed, it can be said that the impediments to the use of digital technologies tend to continue to occur over the next 5 years.

Technologies related to Industry 4.0 can fundamentally transform industry value chains, production value chains and business models [20]. Bearing in mind that companies point to the lack of connectivity between members of the value chain as a major impediment to the use of digital technologies, the low level of investment made and proposed further aggravates this situation, culminating in greater difficulties for collaborative integration of members of the value chain.

In response to the question proposed in this study, it can be seen that data connectivity in the value chain processes of the automotive sector is relevant, and data connectivity between companies, suppliers, customers and partners proved to be essential for companies surveyed, although connectivity and collaboration between members of the value chain is still not as expected.

Even with great care in carrying out data collection and analysis, this research has limitations, due to the sample size and the complexity of the factors involved. Other answers can be found in different samples and even by the same companies at different times and scenarios. In future articles we suggest comparative studies of the Brazilian case with other countries.

Acknowledgment. This study was financed in part by the Coordenação de Aperfeiçoamento de Pessoal de Nível Superior - Brasil (CAPES) - Finance Code 001.

References

1. Kagermann, H., Wahlster, W., Helbig, J.: Recommendations for implementing the strategic initiative industrie 4.0. Final report of the industry 4.0 WG (2013)
2. Schwab, K.: The Fourth Industrial Revolution, 1st edn. World Economic Forum (2017)

3. Brettel, M., et al.: How virtualization, decentralization and network building change the manufacturing landscape: an industry 4.0 perspective. Int. J. Mech. Aerosp. Ind. Mechatron. Manuf. Eng. **8**(1), 37–44 (2014)
4. Lorenz, M., Küpper, D., Rüßmann, M., Heidemann, A., Bause, A.: Time to accelerate in the race toward industry 4.0. Boston Consulting Group (2016)
5. World Economic Forum homepage. http://www3.weforum.org. Fourth Industrial Revolution: Beacons of Technology and Innovation in Manufacturing. Accessed 21 Mar 2020
6. Büyüközkan, G., Göçer, F.: Digital supply chain: literature review and a proposed framework for future research. Comput. Ind. **97**, 157–177 (2018)
7. Pilloni, V.: How data will transform industrial processes: crowdsensing, crowdsourcing and big data as pillars of industry 4.0. Future Internet **10**, 34 (2018)
8. Colombo, A.W., Karnouskos, S., Kaynak, O., Shi, Y., Yin, S.: Industrial cyber-physical systems: a backbone of the fourth industrial revolution. IEEE Ind. Electron. Mag. **11**(1), 6–16 (2017)
9. Lee, J.D., Bagheri, B., Kao, H.A.: A cyber-physical systems architecture for industry 4.0-based manufacturing systems. Manuf. Lett. **3**, 18–23 (2015)
10. Hermann, M., Pentek, T., Otto, B.: Design principles for industry 4.0 scenarios. In: 2016 49th Hawaii International Conference on System Sciences (HICSS), pp. 3928–3937 (2016)
11. Hirsch-Kreinsen, H.: Digitalization of industrial work: development paths and prospects. J. Labour Market Res. **49**, 1–14 (2016)
12. Macdougall, W.: Industry 4.0 smart manufacturing for the future. Germany trade and invest (2014)
13. Bahrin, M.A.K., Othman, M.F., Nor, N.H., Azli, M.F.T.: Industry 4.0: a review on industrial automation and robotic. Jurnal Teknologi (Sci. Eng.) **78**, 6–13 (2016)
14. Abbas, S.A.: Entrepreneurship and information technology businesses in economic crisis. Entrepreneurship Sustain. Issues **5**, 682–692 (2018)
15. CNI - CONFEDERAÇÃO NACIONAL DA INDÚSTRIA – CNI. Industry 2027 risks and opportunities for Brazil in the face of disruptive innovations, Brasília (2018)
16. Khan, A., Turowski, K.: A perspective on industry 4.0: from challenges to opportunities in production systems. In: Proceedings of the International Conference on Internet of Things and Big Data (IoTBD) (2016)
17. ABIMAQ – Associação Brasileira de Máquinas e Equipamentos. Full General Report, São Paulo (2018). http://abimaq.org.br/COMUNICACOES/2018/PROJETOS. Accessed 15 Feb 2020
18. Wang, S., Wan, J., Zhang, D., Li, D., Zhang, C.: Towards smart factory for industry 4.0: a self-organized multi-agent system with big data based feedback and coordination. Comput. Netw. **101**, 158–168 (2016)
19. PWC homepage. https://www.pwc.com.br/pt/publicacoes/servicos/assets/consultoria-negocios/2016/pwc-industry-4-survey-16.pdf. Accessed 15 Feb 2020
20. Xu, X., Klotz, E., Newman, S.T., Zhong, R.Y., et al.: Intelligent manufacturing in the context of Industry 4.0: a review. Engineering **3**, 616–630 (2017)

Manufacturing Systems Engineering:
Agile, Flexible, Reconfigurable

Towards a Reference Model for Configuration of Reconfigurable Manufacturing System (RMS)

Erica Capawa Fotsoh[1,2]($\boxtimes$), Nasser Mebarki[2], Pierre Castagna[2],
Pascal Berruet[3], and Francisco Gamboa[1]

[1] IRT Jules Verne (French Institute in Research and Technology in Advanced
Manufacturing), 44340 Bouguenais, France
erica.fotsoh@irt-jules-verne.fr

[2] LS2N, Nantes University, IUT of Nantes, BP539, 44475 Carquefou Cedex,
France
erica.fotsoh@ls2n.fr

[3] Lab-STICC Research Center, University of South-Brittany, BP 92116,
56321 Lorient, France

Abstract. Reconfigurable Manufacturing Systems (RMSs) offer the ability to
change organizations to fit changing contexts. Modularity, both physical and
logical, is an essential feature of RMS. Not only because it allows a wide variety
of use of the system, but also because it allows to determine the other characteristics of RMS. We propose in this article a new way of defining a configuration for RMS, based on modularity. The module-based view includes four
aspects: physical, control, performance and simulation, taken at different levels:
system, machines or component. The introduction of the virtual view of the
module aim to align the proposition with the requirement of industry 4.0 (The
RAMI 4.0 architecture). Simulation and performance concern the technical,
ecological or even economical aspect of the system. The module-based view of
the system allows a decomposition, a description and an accurate analysis of the
system, that leads to a better knowledge of the system, its components and
allows a better approach to the reconfiguration process: an industrial case study
is presented for illustration. A reference data model emerged from module-based
view of the system. The purpose of this reference model is to create a configuration database that can be used as input to a reconfiguration decision process.

Keywords: Modularity · Module-based configuration · Reference model ·
Reconfiguration process · Industry 4.0

1 Introduction

Within the context of Industry 4.0, production systems have to adapt to different
context changes. Reconfigurable Manufacturing Systems (RMSs) are designed to fit
these challenges. Reconfiguration consists in the transition from one *configuration* to
another at a given time to match with the needs that arise. This requires an in-depth
knowledge of the system, and a clear definition of the concept of configuration. The
more complex the system, the more the difficult it is to cover this task, due to the many

© IFIP International Federation for Information Processing 2020
Published by Springer Nature Switzerland AG 2020
B. Lalic et al. (Eds.): APMS 2020, IFIP AICT 591, pp. 391–398, 2020.
https://doi.org/10.1007/978-3-030-57993-7_44

parameters: the physical aspect of the system has to be considered, as well as the logical aspect [1] and performances (due date, cost, environmental criteria, etc.). One of the most common techniques used to support complex system analysis is simulation, as it faithfully replicates situations as close to reality as possible [2]. Yet, one drawback remains, the definition and description of RMS *configuration*. Many research exists in this area and each one gives a particular consideration to the *configuration*. [3] and [4] consider configuration as the result of the process of determining which machines should be added or removed in case of sudden changes. They address a layout-based method to choose the suitable configuration for a system. According to this perspective, the configuration of a system is the layout of the machines in this system (the physical structure). Other research take into account the logical aspect [5, 6], whereas [7] use KPIs such as production and quality rate to identify and define a configuration. [8] argue that the energy consumption or the cost of implementation and maintenance of the system have also to be taken into account. These different considerations are useful in the configuration description as they give decisional information about the system. However, they need to be consider simultaneously, i.e. the configuration definition and description should formally involve the previous mentioned (physical, logical, performances, etc.). As far as we know, research undertaken in reconfiguration area has been more focused on technologies of design and decision-making tools. Up to now, very few research has proposed formal definition, including both physical, logical and related KPIs description, that could support the decision-making. The focus was to propose informational model to formally represent the configuration. An ontology-based model proposed by [9], a model for control logic by [10] and an informational model provides by [11] are some example. Still, a formal definition and description are lack.

This paper aims to address this issue, by proposing a new way to formally define and describe a configuration for RMS, based on modularity. The proposed definition involves physical and logical aspects, as well as KPIs, and virtual aspects. In digital manufacturing simulation is widely used to evaluate configuration alternatives. We believe that for reconfiguration decision process it is important to relate this virtual aspect to the real world situation through simulation, as it offers god alternatives of previewing and evaluation [2]. Moreover, it allows our proposition to get align with the RAMI4.0 architecture [12], especially the second layer (the need to have a transition between real to digital world). The simulation model could include both shop floor simulation, ecological impact simulation and also economical simulation- as far as these three dimension are essential in reconfiguration decision process [8]. The remainder of the paper is as follows: a module-based view of configuration is introduced and used within a case study. This module-based view leads to a reference model used to formalize the description and characterization of configuration. The main purpose of the reference model is to achieve to a database of configurations, that will be used in the process of reconfiguration decision-making.

2 The Module-Based View of Configuration

2.1 Modularity as a Basic Requirement for RMS

Modularity both physical and logical enables large variety in utilization of the system. It is essential for reconfigurability and constitutes a basic requirement for RMS, that leads to the determination of the other RMS characteristics. Indeed, elements can be put together either to adjust the production volume (scalability), or to add functionality to the system (convertibility), or to produce more customized products (customization). Moreover, the part-to-part analysis of the system ensures the discovery of the real causes of potential problems (diagnosticability), and of the possible solution to implement (reconfiguration strategy). Additionally, putting modules together involves either common interfaces between these modules, or intermediary element to join it. In the first case, modules are considered integrable, because they share common interfaces (integrability).

2.2 A Module-Based View of Configuration of RMS

[13] describes configuration as a set of resources connected together with a control logic. We propose to see configuration as an aggregation of modules (physical, control, simulation and KPIs) taken on different levels. According to the precision degree wanted for the description, the level could refer to the system level, machine level, component level or even sub component level description. The module-based view of the configuration shows that system components are fractal- each module is made of another module, and both has the four mentioned aspects (physical, control, KPIs, and simulation) (Fig. 1).

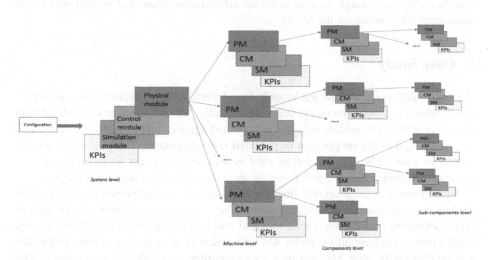

Fig. 1. Module-based view of configuration

The Physical Module (PM). The physical module represents the resources of the system. It can refer to workstation, operators, transportation system, storage system, etc. Each PM is managed by a control module. The use of a configuration leads to some KPIs related to the PM. Moreover, when the PM cannot be implemented, the associate simulation module can be used to evaluate those KPIs.

The Control Module (CM). It is the location of the system's intelligence and decision-making. Here, decisions are made to satisfy production goals under constraints. The control module is in charge of the management of the physical module.

The Simulation Module (SM). This module is the virtual representation of the physical module. As far the simulation is a faithful representation of the real system, this module may allow to evaluate the module as it would be in real situation. The replication of the real world in the virtual world could be a tricky process due to the complexity of the system. The idea of using modularity in real world could then be applied on the simulation model. Thus, the simulation model will be built modularly by adding or removing virtual module parts. We then assume that, each physical part of the system has its virtual representation. The simulation here can refer to mathematical models, discrete event simulation, energy consumption simulation, carbon footprint and cost evaluation.

The KPIs Module. This is the measurement made either on the physical module or the simulation module or both. They allow to compare the real situation (or simulated situation) to the production goals, therefor a reconfiguration point. As KPIs depend on the use of the physical module, the module-based decomposition of the system allows to facilitate the diagnostic of each module. KPIs, as well as the simulation are not only related to the technical aspect of the system, but also concern any other measurement data that relevant enough to give accurate information about the system and or its component (depending on the level).

3   Case Study

The case study presents how the module-based view of an assembly line can help to rapidly identify possible reconfigurations. Especially, we will show how the simulation module and the KPIs module help in the system diagnosis, and how the use of module simulation lead to the proposition of potential reconfiguration. The case study will be limited to two KPIs, the simulation used is the discrete event simulation with the software FlexSim©, and we will focus on the system and machine level diagnosis.

The example is an assembly line where products are transported on pallets. The product is a four colored disks arrangement. The current configuration is made of four (04) workstations named: ws1, ws2, ws3 and ws4 (ws stands for workstation). On ws1 a robot places the base on the pallet. On ws2 and ws3 an automatic system places the colored disk on the base, and ws4 uses a vision camera to verify that each color is well placed (the sequence of color is verified). The control logic of ws4 is the following: *if the product is non-compliant, it is from the system without being adjusted, even if the*

non-compliance could be easily corrected. When analysing the assembly line performances, the production manager found that there is a high non quality rate.

The system analysing regarding the module-based decomposition and a simulation
of the assembly line was built. It reveals that, the non-quality rate is due to the error on
ws2 and ws3 (Table 1). Using the simulation model as a forecasting -previewing tool,
the target then was to reduce the non-quality the assembly line (achieve the 100%
quality), since the non-quality rate of ws2 and ws3 cannot be changed. By using
modularity of the simulation module, many possibilities where tested by changing
control modules of work stations, adding/removing workstations; obtained quality rate
where compared with the target one. The simulated KPIs show that, even with error on
ws2 and ws3 the quality rate reaches the 100% (i.e. non-quality of 0%) is achieved by
adding a workstations ws5 and ws6, and changing the control logic of ws4. Although
the quality issue seems to be solved, it would be more relevant to analyse the economical aspect of the proposition to ensure its feasibility.

Table 1. Module decomposition of the assembly line

Level	Module	Measured non-quality	Simulated non-quality
system	Assembly line	30–40%	30–40%
Machine	Ws1	0%	0%
	Ws2	–	5–10%
	Ws3		5–10%
	Ws4	0%	0%

This example shows how the module-based view, especially the use of simulation
and KPIs modules could be use in reconfiguration process. The example highlighted the
fact that, the reconfiguration can either concern physical aspect of the system (addition
of ws5 and ws6), or logical changes (the added control logic to ws4). This is easily
possible because the system has a modular structure as well as the related simulation
model. The module-based decomposition of the system helps to clearly identify the
problem, and to propose an accurate solution, without changing the entire system.

4   Towards Reference Model to Describe Configurations

For a company, the reconfiguration management is not always an easy task. Finding
and applying a configuration could be a waste of time and money especially if the
searched solution is close to an already existing configuration. Thus, the ideal scenario
would be to identify each configuration, to keep a history of different configurations
used, and to store them in a database that can be used as a support for decision-making
during the reconfiguration process. The reference model (Fig. 2) based on concepts of
modularity aims to fit this target. The proposed model provides an overview of system
needs, focusing on data and their interactions. The purpose of this reference model is
formalize the definition and description of a configuration, and to reach a generic

database of configurations. The issues address by the model concern the following question: *What a configuration is made of? How physical module are arranged and control within this configuration? Which product could be manufactured on this configuration, following which logical range? What are the KPIs related to this configuration?* As each manufacturing system differ from one to another they cannot be satisfactorily designed from pre-existing solutions. We do not pretend the proposed model will be a cure-all solution that will give answer to all manufacturing context, it would be illusory. However, we believe that this objective becomes possible and realistic in the case of modular reconfigurable systems. Our proposition is therefore limited to this class of production systems. The proposed model is built using the UML class diagram (Unified Modeling Language). The main classes of the model are describing bellow:

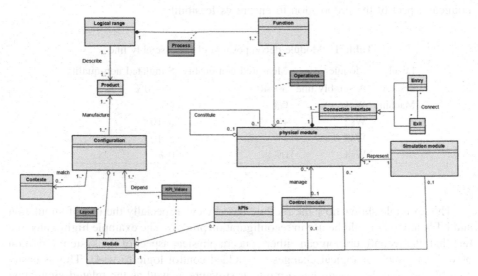

Fig. 2. Reference model of a configuration

Module: It represents the set of physical, simulation, control and KPIs. It can refer to the system, machine or component level. The highest module is the system itself. Each module has related KPIs, which values can either be measured on the real system, simulated or required by the production manager. Comparing the KPIs values of each level of the system could lead to a reconfiguration decision.

Function: This class describes the services the system delivers. It represents the response of the system or a component when it operates under normal conditions and independently from the environment in which it is required [14]. When a function is assigned to a physical element of the system that consumes time and has a limited capacity, it becomes an operation. Thus, for the same system function, there can be several associated operations, i.e. several resources capable of performing the same function. For example, "Drilling ø = 20 mm" is a function in a system that can be assigned either to a CNC machine or to a traditional machine. Drilling ø = 20 mm by the CNC machine and Drilling ⌀ = 20 mm on conventional machine are two different operations as operating time and other data related to the operation may vary. The function describes the capability of the system, while the operation describes how the function is performed by the system. From the management point of view, it is necessary to know for each configuration its potentiality. This information could be useful during the reconfiguration process, in particular when defining the reconfiguration strategy (i.e., how the system could adapt to a variation).

Product: This class describes the main element for which configurations are designed. A product is defined by a manufacturing process and could be achieved in different manner; different functions sequence so call logical range could be used to manufacture the same product. Thus, it is possible to know in term of functionality (functions and operations), whether a new product could easily be added to the system or not.

Configuration: This class represent the aggregation of modules, and could be related to a particular manufacturing context (the situation that triggers the reconfiguration process). Modules are arranged following a particular layout within the configurations.

5 Conclusion

The module-based view of the system at different levels has inspired the reference model proposed in this paper to describe a configuration. The module-based view of the system allows a quite precise decomposition and description of the system. That leads to a better knowledge of the system and its components. Note that this reference model gets align with some layers of the RAMI 4.0 (2nd, 3rd and 4th layer). Hence the proposed reference model could be seen as a part of industry 4.0 enabler. The case study shows how this module-based analysis of the system could be helpful in the reconfiguration process, especially the simulation and KPIs modules. Using the module- based view, we proposed a reference data model to describe configurations, the fact of including the simulation in the model is to align our proposition with the developing industry 4.0 paradigm. Moreover, we propose to take into account both technical, ecological (through energy consumption for example) and economical parameters while describing the configuration. The database obtained from this reference model would be rich in useful information and can easily be used as an input for the reconfiguration decision process. Indeed, the layout, the KPIs, the control module associated to each part of the system, and even the simulation data of the system could now be found in the same database. However, it is important to well define the level at which the decomposition must end: the greater the number of modules, the greater the volume of data, and the greater the time to put them together. The module-based vision permits an evaluation of a configuration "reconfiguration degree" aligned with the eight RMSs characteristics proposed in [15]. Thus it will be possible to compare configurations (in terms of characteristics) before choosing the best one. Future work will be to implement the model through a database, that will be used as an input of the reconfiguration decision process. As configurations can be considered in terms of the formation of holarchies [16], the module-based description seems to be quite similar to the holonic paradigm [17], a novel research issue could be to investigate an holonic description of RMS.

Acknowledgments. This research work is supported by funding of the PhD program PER-FORM (Fundamental research and development program resourcing on manufacturing) from the IRT Jules Verne (https://www.irt-jules-verne.fr/).

References

1. Koren, Y., et al.: Reconfigurable manufacturing systems: introduction. CIRP Ann. **48**(2) (1999)
2. Lateef-Ur-rehman, A.: Manufacturing configuration selection using multicriteria decision tool. Int. J. Adv. Manuf. Technol. **65**(5–8), 625–639 (2013)
3. Tang, L., Koren, Y., Yip-Hoi, D.M., Wang, W.: Computer-aided reconfiguration planning: an artificial intelligence-based approach. J. Comput. Inf. Sci. Eng. **3**(6) (2016)
4. Wang, W., Koren, Y.: Design principles of scalable reconfigurable manufacturing systems. IFAC **46**(9), 1411–1416 (2013)
5. El Maraghy, H.: Flexible and reconfigurable manufacturing systems paradigms. Flex. Serv. Manuf. J. **17**(4 Special issue), 261–276 (2006)
6. Kanso, M., Berruet, P., Philippe, J.L.: A framework based on a high conception level to generate configurations in production systems. In: ICINCO 2010 - Proceedings of the 7th International Conference on Informatics Control, Automation Robotics, vol. 1, pp. 244–248 (2010)
7. Bhargav, A., Sridhar, C.N.V., Deva Kumar, M.L.S.: Study of production scheduling problem for Reconfigurable Manufacturing System (RMS). Mater. Today Proc. **4**(8), 7406–7412 (2017)
8. Azab, A., ElMaraghy, H., Nyhuis, P., Pachow-Frauenhofer, J., Schmidt, M.: Mechanics of change: a framework to reconfigure manufacturing systems. CIRP J. Manuf. Sci. Technol. **6** (2), 110–119 (2013)
9. Alsafi, Y., Vyatkin, V.: Ontology-based reconfiguration agent for intelligent mechatronic systems in flexible manufacturing. Robot. Comput. Integr. Manuf. **26**(4), 381–391 (2010)
10. Michalos, G., Sipsas, P., Makris, S., Chryssolouris, G.: Decision making logic for flexible assembly lines reconfiguration. Robot. Comput. Integr. Manuf. **37**, 233–250 (2016)
11. Mabkhot, M.M., Al-Samhan, A.M., Darmoul, S.: An information model to support reconfiguration of manufacturing systems. IFAC-PapersOnLine **49**(5), 37–42 (2016)
12. Adolphs, P., et al.: Reference architecture model industrie 4.0 (rami4.0) (2015)
13. De Lamotte, F.F., Berruet, P., Philippe, J.L.: Using model engineering for the criticality analysis of reconfigurable manufacturing systems architectures. Int. J. Manuf. Technol. Manag. **11**(3–4), 315–337 (2007)
14. Toguyeni, A.K.A., Berruet, P., Craye, E.: Models and algorithms for failure diagnosis and recovery in FMSs. Int. J. Flex. Manuf. Syst. **15**(1), 57–85 (2003)
15. Capawa Fotsoh, E., Mebarki, N., Castagna, P., Berruet, P.: A classification for reconfigurable manufacturing systems. In: Benyoucef, L. (ed.) Reconfigurable Manufacturing Systems: From Design to Implementation. SSAM, pp. 11–28. Springer, Cham (2020). https://doi.org/10.1007/978-3-030-28782-5_2
16. Chacón, E., Cardillo, J., Chacón, R., Zapata, G.: Planification en ligne pour les systèmes de production distribués: une approche par les systèmes holoniques (2012)
17. Gamboa Quintanilla, F., Cardin, O., L'Anton, A., Castagna, P.: A modeling framework for manufacturing services in Service-oriented Holonic Manufacturing Systems. Eng. Appl. Artif. Intell. **55**, 26–36 (2016)

Automatic Design of Dispatching Rules with Genetic Programming for Dynamic Job Shop Scheduling

Salama Shady(✉), Toshiya Kaihara, Nobutada Fujii,
and Daisuke Kokuryo

Graduate School of System Informatics, Kobe University,
Kobe, Hyogo 6578501, Japan
shady.salama@kaede.cs.kobe-u.ac.jp

Abstract. Traditionally, scheduling experts rely on their knowledge and experience to develop problem-specific heuristics that require a considerable amount of time, experience, and code effort. Through this tedious process, experts must follow a trial-and-error cycle by evaluating the generated rules in a simulation model for the problem under consideration until achieving satisfactory results. Recently, hyper-heuristic approach has emerged as a powerful technique that uses artificial intelligence to automatically design efficient heuristics for various optimization problems. Genetic programming (GP) is the most popular hyper-heuristic approach to automate the design of production scheduling heuristics. In this paper, a genetic programming framework is proposed to generate efficient dispatching rules in a dynamic job shop. The proposed framework integrates the reasoning mechanism of GP with the ability of discrete event simulation in analyzing the performance of generated rules under dynamic conditions. Afterward, the evolved heuristics are compared to human-tailored literature rules under different dynamic settings using mean flow time and mean tardiness as performance measures. The achieved results prove the ability of the proposed approach in generating superior scheduling rules rapidly, within a few hours, compared to the conventional literature rules commonly adopted in the industry.

Keywords: Dynamic job shop · Scheduling · Dispatching Rules · Hyper-heuristic · Genetic Programming

1 Introduction

Job Shop Scheduling Problem (JSSP) is a well-studied problem in combinatorial optimization literature that has proven to be NP-hard. JSSP can be defined as there are a number of jobs and each job has a predefined set of operations (tasks) that need to be processed for specific processing time on a limited number of machines (resources) while optimizing some performance criteria [1]. Due to the complex nature of the JSSP, several solution approaches have been developed to provide satisfactory solutions for both static and dynamic scenarios. Although many solution approaches are proposed for solving JSSP, most of these approaches mainly focus on relatively small problem

© IFIP International Federation for Information Processing 2020
Published by Springer Nature Switzerland AG 2020
B. Lalic et al. (Eds.): APMS 2020, IFIP AICT 591, pp. 399–407, 2020.
https://doi.org/10.1007/978-3-030-57993-7_45

instances or moderate to large instances with over-simplified assumptions. Dispatching Rules (DRs) have been widely employed for solving Dynamic Job Shop Scheduling Problem (DJSSP) in a practical time due to its flexibility, scalability, and fast response to real-time events. There are several comparative studies in the literature for analyzing the performance of traditional scheduling rules under different conditions, for example, reference [2] and [3]. The common conclusion in these studies is that human-designed rules are developed to address specific job shop settings using a certain objective function, and usually perform poorly under other system configurations or performance measures. Moreover, literature rules experience a myopic nature by considering only local and current shop conditions that lead to poor quality solutions compared to global optimization methods.

In order to tackle these limitations, many scholars have used Artificial Intelligence (AI) techniques to automatically develop competitive scheduling rules that are trained under different scenarios. In recent years, Genetic Programming (GP) has proven its superiority compared to other AI techniques to generate DRs for different production scheduling problems [4]. Miyashita [5] is perhaps the first study that proposed GP approach to evolve DRs for job shop scheduling problems using a multi-agent model. Geiger et al. [6] employed the GP approach to obtain high-quality DRs for a single-machine scheduling problem. After evaluating the generated rules against 6 DRs from the literature, the generated rules revealed competitive results in minimizing completion time, total tardiness, and maximum tardiness. In the same context, the authors in [7] employed a decision tree to classify the available machines in a job shop as bottlenecks or not, then the GP approach is used to generate scheduling heuristic on a given machine based on its classification. The evolved rules provided better performance compared to seven literature rules. In [8], single-machine and static job-shop scheduling problems are considered. For the single machine problem, the authors examined the ability of the GP approach under both static and dynamic conditions as well as with or without setup times. While for JSSP, the GP approach used to minimize weighted job tardiness and total makespan. Their findings are consistent with previous studies in supporting the superiority of GP rules against literature rules. A two-stage hyper-heuristic is suggested in [9] by adopting the GP approach to generate DRs and an evolutionary algorithm to assign the developed rules to different work centers. In [10], the authors investigated the use of GP hyper-heuristic approach to evolve DRs for a two-machines job shop in both static and dynamic conditions. For the dynamic case, two GP representations were examined, including a single rule in both machines and evolving a specific rule for each machine. The GP approach achieved the optimal makespan in the static problem and good results in the dynamic problem.

The aim of this paper is to propose a GP framework for generating competitive DRs for DJSSP under different system scenarios. There are different sources of randomness considered in this study, such as job arrival, operations processing time, the number of operations per job, operation-machine compatibility, and due dates. To verify the effectiveness of the proposed framework, the GP evolved heuristics are compared to 12 human-tailored rules in minimizing mean flow time and mean tardiness under various dynamic settings. The remainder of this paper is organized as follows. The proposed framework is presented in Sect. 2. Also, the experimental details are given in Sect. 3.

Section 4 provides a summary of the obtained results. Conclusions and some suggestions for future work are addressed in Sect. 5.

2 Genetic Programming Framework

The proposed framework consists of two main modules, a GP-based reasoning module, and a performance evaluation module to automatically generate dispatching rules for DJSSP. As shown in Fig. 1, the GP module starts by generating an initial population of candidate heuristics using predefined functions, terminals (attributes), and a specific representation. In this study, we adopted a tree-based representation which is the most popular data structure to represent any priority function. Moreover, it is worth noting that there are three random techniques widely used to create the initial population, namely grow, full, and ramped-half-and-half. The grow method generates trees in variable sizes, while all trees have the same shape and size using the full method. Ramped-half-and-half combines both the full and the grow methods to produce a diverse population of trees with various shapes and sizes.

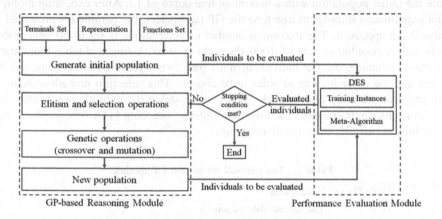

Fig. 1. The genetic programming framework

Afterward, the solution quality of generated heuristics will be assessed in the performance evaluation module using a Discrete Event Simulation (DES) model. The DES model includes a pre-defined set of training instances and a meta-algorithm. The meta-algorithm encapsulates the GP evolved rule and possible system constraints to produce valid schedules for a specific scheduling environment. The Giffler & Thompson (GT) meta-algorithm is widely used to create active and non-delay schedules [1]. The employed non-delay GT algorithm can be briefly described as follows. While there are unprocessed operations and there is an idle machine, the GT algorithm calculates the priority value for queued operations and schedules the operation with the highest priority. Then, the evolutionary process starts by selecting fit individuals from the population. The selection process determines which individuals can survive (copy the fittest heuristics to the new population) and which individuals are allowed to reproduce (apply genetic operations). After selecting the mating pool, genetic operators are employed to combine existing individuals (crossover operator) or introduce diversity (mutation operator) in order to form offspring for the next generation. The population evolves over a specified number of generations until the stopping criteria are satisfied. Finally, the algorithm terminates, and the best dispatching rule is obtained.

3   Numerical Experiments

3.1   The Genetic Programming Module

For the sake of evaluating the effectiveness of the proposed GP framework, it is used to generate competitive dispatching rules in minimizing mean flow time and mean tardiness for DJSSP. Then, the fittest rule for each objective is compared with 12 human-made rules under different system configurations. Tables 1 and 2 demonstrate the set of terminals and functions used in the GP module to create priority functions. The first part of the terminal set represents the local job shop attributes, while the second part refers to the global attributes. The ramped-half-and-half method is employed to generate the initial population with a maximum tree depth of 12. After executing multiple pilot experiments in order to fine-tune the GP parameters, the parameters presented in Table 3 are approved. The maximum number of generations is set to 50 generations each with a population size of 1000 dispatching rules. Using a double tournament selection technique, the GP individuals must pass two layers of tournaments, one by fitness and the other by size in order to be chosen. This selection procedure helps in mitigating the bloating effect which usually slows down the evolutionary search process, consumes extra memory, and restricts effective breeding [11]. Afterward, genetic operations are employed to create offspring.

Table 1. The terminal set for the GP module.

Node Name	Description
rJ	The release date of job (j)
RJ	The operation release date
RO	Number of remaining operations within the job
RT	Work remaining of the job
PR	Operation processing time
DD	Job due date
CT	Current time (Machine ready time)
WT	Current waiting time of the job $(t - RJ)$
#	Ephemeral constant (Random number between 0 and 1)
NPT	Processing time of next operation
WINQ	Work in the next queue
APR	Average operation processing time of jobs in the queue

Table 2. The function set for the GP module.

Node Name	Description
+	Binary addition operator
−	Binary subtraction operator
*	Binary multiplication operator
/	Protected binary division/(a, b) returns "1" if b = 0, else "a/b"
IF ternary	IF (a, b, c) returns "b" if a $\geq$ 0, else "c"
MIN	MIN (a, b) returns "a" if (a < b), else "b"
MAX	MAX (a, b) returns "a" if (a > b), else "b"

Table 3. The GP parameters.

Parameter	Description
Initialization	Ramped-half-and-half
Crossover rate	85%
Mutation rate	10%
Elitism	5%
Maximum depth	12
Number of generations	50
Population size	1000
Selection	Double tournament selection (size = 5)

One-point leaf biased crossover is used to create children by randomly selecting a crossover point (with 10% probability to choose terminal nodes) in each individual and the parts below crossover points are exchanged. Also, uniform mutation operator randomly selects a point in an individual and replaces the subtree at this point with a randomly generated tree (with tree depth equals three). The best 5% of individuals are copied across generations to prevent the fittest heuristics from getting lost during the evolution process.

3.2 The Performance Evaluation Module

A DES model for a commonly used symmetrical job shop was developed to assess the steady-state performance of the evolved heuristics [4]. The job shop has 10 machines and each machine can process only one operation at a time. The interarrival times between jobs are generated using an exponential distribution, and each job consists of a random number of operations between 2 and 14 operations. The processing time for each operation is randomly distributed U [1, 49] and U [1, 99]. The job due date is assigned using the total work content method, i.e. job due date = job release date + (allowance factor × total job processing time). The model is analyzed under three levels of utilization, including 70%, 80%, and 90%. In each simulation replication, the shop starts empty. Then, the obtained data between the beginning of the simulation until the arrival of the 1500th job is discarded, and the statistics are collected from the 1500th job to the next completed 5000 jobs. The triplet (p, u, c) represents the system settings by defining the average processing time, the job utilization level, and the tightness factor (to determine the tightness of job due date). Changing the values of "p" and "u" significantly affects the mean flow time, while varying the "c" values greatly affects the mean tardiness. The training and testing scenarios are illustrated in Table 4. Two simulation scenarios are employed to train the evolved rules in minimizing mean flow time and mean tardiness. Also, the 6 testing scenarios for each objective are used to compare the performance of the GP evolved rules with 12 rules from the literature. The benchmark rules are described as follows; SPT: Shortest Processing Time, LPT: Longest Processing Time, FIFO: First In First Out, LIFO: Last In First Out, WINQ: Work In Next Queue, SL: Slack, NSL: Negative Slack, SPT + WINQ + SL, MWKR: Most Work Remaining, COVERT: Cost Over Time, EDD: Earliest Due Date, and MOD: Modified Due Date, for more details please refer to [3].

Table 4. Simulation configurations for the training and testing sets.

Parameters	Training	Testing
Processing time	U [1, 49] and U [1, 99]	U [1, 49] and U [1, 99]
Shop utilization	70% and 90%	70%, 80%, and 90%
Tightness factor	3 and 5	3, 4, and 5
Mean flowtime scenarios	(25, 70, 3), (50, 90, 3)	(25, 70, 3), (50, 70, 3), (25, 80, 3), (50, 80, 3), (25, 90, 3), (50, 90, 3)
Mean tardiness scenarios	(25, 70, 5), (50, 90, 3)	(25, 70, 3), (50, 70, 3), (25, 80, 4), (50, 80, 4), (25, 90, 5), (50, 90, 5)

4   Results and Discussion

The proposed framework was executed on a PC with 2.7 GHz CPU and 16 GB RAM. The GP module was trained on the training set for minimizing the mean flow time and the mean tardiness. Then, the fittest GP rule was compared with the 12 human-tailored rules on the 6 testing scenarios for each performance indicator. For the sake of convenience, we referred to the best GP rule for the mean flow time as FGP, and the best GP rule for mean tardiness as TGP. Tables 5 and 6 show the mean flow time and mean tardiness for each rule on different problem instances.

Regarding the mean flow time, it is obvious that the evolved GP rule outperforms the literature rules for all the test instances. The relative change was calculated using the following equation:

$$Relative change = \frac{P_{ref.} - P_{GP}}{P_{ref.}} * 100$$

Where $P_{ref.}$ denotes the performance value of the best literature rule in a specific problem instance, and P_{GP} denotes the performance value of the GP rule for the same

Table 5. Performance of all rules for mean flow time.

Rules	Case 1	Case 2	Case 3	Case 4	Case 5	Case 6
SPT	394.2	792.58	526.28	1039.33	862.2	1687.42
LPT	636.37	1265.64	1073.51	2153.54	2634.44	5184.4
FIFO	482.54	961.23	689.75	1375.78	1278.46	2489.33
LIFO	479.55	945.38	676.84	1357.58	1266.19	2478.04
WINQ	437.35	870.25	598.22	1193.64	1032.13	2018.64
SL	457.15	906.1	654.36	1292.04	1233.28	2409.71
NSL	476.98	948.80	660.03	1323.17	1232.90	2389.51
SPT + WINQ + SL	440.3	888.38	631.62	1273.64	1210.19	2360.26
MWKR	567.54	1116.51	899.80	1761.97	1975.12	3847.52
COVERT	479.79	965.82	679.78	1371.5	1259.02	2483.99
EDD	454.16	897.46	644.57	1279.12	1225.65	2383.55
MOD	449.96	897.08	628.36	1247.36	1049.82	2043.90
FGP	**383.45**	**775.87**	**502.04**	**995.8**	**762.6**	**1519.96**
Relative change (%)	**2.73**	**2.11**	**4.61**	**4.19**	**11.55**	**9.92**

Table 6. Performance of all rules for mean tardiness.

Rules	Case 1	Case 2	Case 3	Case 4	Case 5	Case 6
SPT	29.79	57.91	64.09	125.49	248.16	470.32
LPT	188.51	375.65	451.01	919.35	1780.28	3489.27
FIFO	45.02	86.82	85.75	166.14	393.78	731.4
LIFO	87.68	170.15	177.27	356.3	598.27	1153.94
WINQ	38.43	74.01	71.44	137.53	275.59	510.57
SL	19.58	38.57	39.14	71.87	306.65	562.62
NSL	24.04	46.03	39.8	79.03	282.02	524.05
SPT + WINQ + SL	15.95	32.12	33.58	63.39	288.09	526.25
MWKR	151.2	291.25	343.15	667.36	1222.67	2344.97
COVERT	42.71	84.99	82.73	161.73	381.02	727.08
EDD	23.17	44.05	42.45	81.3	308.73	575.72
MOD	21.78	42.21	38	72.52	240.47	448.61
TGP	**12.13**	**23.7**	**16.71**	**32.23**	**91.86**	**170.41**
Relative change (%)	**23.94**	**26.20**	**50.24**	**49.16**	**61.80**	**62.00**

instance. As shown in Table 5, the performance of the FGP dominates the best literature rule, and the average relative change is 5.85%. Moreover, the gap between the performance of FGP and the best literature rules in each instance widens by increasing the system usage and processing time interval i.e. when the problem instance becomes more complex and dynamic. The FGP rule was analyzed to understand how this role works and what parameters have the highest impact on the mean flow time. We noticed that all the global features are used in the evolved rule, while only some local features are considered. This finding manifests the importance of global attributes in mitigating the myopic nature of scheduling rules. Also, the top 4 features used in descending order based on the number of occurrences are the operation processing time, the work in the next queue, the processing time of the next operation, and the number of remaining operations within the job. This observation is consistent with the superiority of SPT and WINQ in being the best literature rules which proves the reasoning ability of GP to choose the most important job shop attributes for a specific objective. Excluded features include job release date, due date, and operation waiting time. Using these results, we concluded that the excluded features do not have a significant impact on average job flow time, which explains the disappointing performance of LPT, FIFO, and LIFO rules in reducing the mean flow time.

Regarding the mean tardiness, the TGP showed substantially better performance compared to the best literature rule with an average relative change of 45.56%. Also, the superiority of the GP approach was revealed as the job shop becomes more random, and due dates become tighter, as shown in case 1 compare to case 6. After investigating the features employed in the TGP rule and sorting them in descending order of importance, the following results were obtained. The most significant attributes for minimizing the mean tardiness are operation processing time, work in the next queue, number of operations within the job, and job due date. Furthermore, we gained a solid understanding of why the TGP achieved the best results, as well as why MOD, SPT +WINQ+SL, and SPT are the top literature rules in minimizing the mean tardiness. Similar to the FGP rule, all the global features are included in the TGP rule which demonstrates its great impact on enhancing the performance of DRs.

5   Conclusions and Future Research

This paper proposed a GP framework to automatically generate scheduling policies in dynamic job shops. The main building blocks of this approach were presented with a detailed explanation of the internal mechanism. Also, the proposed approach was employed to minimize mean flow time and mean tardiness under different dynamic scenarios. The experimental results demonstrated the ability of the proposed framework to automatically design effective dispatching rules with respect to the considered performance measures. Moreover, the GP reasoning mechanism was able to select the most significant attributes to include them in evolved heuristics and exclude insignificant attributes. In future research, the proposed approach will be extended to generate scheduling rules that can handle multiple objectives. Also, the framework is expected to be evaluated using real-world data to assess its practical effectiveness.

References

1. Pinedo, M., Khosrow, H.: Scheduling: theory, algorithms and systems development. In: Gaul, W., Bachem, A., Habenicht, W., Runge, W., Stahl, W.W. (eds.) Operations Research Proceedings 1991. ORP, vol. 1991, pp. 35–42. Springer, Berlin (2012). https://doi.org/10. 1007/978-1-4614-2361-4_1

2. Rajendran, C., Holthaus, O.: Comparative study of dispatching rules in dynamic flowshops and jobshops. Eur. J. Oper. Res. (1999). https://doi.org/10.1016/S0377-2217(98)00023-X

3. Sels, V., Gheysen, N., Vanhoucke, M.: A comparison of priority rules for the job shop scheduling problem under different flow time- and tardiness-related objective functions. Int. J. Prod. Res. **50**, 4255–4270 (2012). https://doi.org/10.1080/00207543.2011.611539

4. Nguyen, S., Mei, Y., Zhang, M.: Genetic programming for production scheduling: a survey with a unified framework. Complex Intell. Syst. **3**, 41–66 (2017). https://doi.org/10.1007/s40747-017-0036-x

5. Miyashita, K.: Job-shop scheduling with genetic programming. In: Proceedings of the 2nd Annual Conference on Genetic and Evolutionary Computation, pp. 505–512 (2000)

6. Geiger, C.D., Uzsoy, R., Aytuğ, H.: Rapid modeling and discovery of priority dispatching rules: an autonomous learning approach. J. Sched. **9**, 7–34 (2006). https://doi.org/10.1007/s10951-006-5591-8

7. Jakobović, D., Budin, L.: Dynamic scheduling with genetic programming. In: Collet, P., Tomassini, M., Ebner, M., Gustafson, S., Ekárt, A. (eds.) EuroGP 2006. LNCS, vol. 3905, pp. 73–84. Springer, Heidelberg (2006). https://doi.org/10.1007/11729976_7

8. Jakobović, D., Marasović, K.: Evolving priority scheduling heuristics with genetic programming. Appl. Soft Comput. J. **12**, 2781–2789 (2012). https://doi.org/10.1016/j.asoc.2012.03.065

9. Pickardt, C.W., Hildebrandt, T., Branke, J., Heger, J., Scholz-Reiter, B.: Evolutionary generation of dispatching rule sets for complex dynamic scheduling problems. Int. J. Prod. Econ. **145**, 67–77 (2013). https://doi.org/10.1016/j.ijpe.2012.10.016

10. Hunt, R., Johnston, M., Zhang, M.: Evolving machine-specific dispatching rules for a two-machine job shop using genetic programming. In: Proceedings of the 2014 IEEE Congress on Evolutionary Computation, CEC 2014, pp. 618–625. Institute of Electrical and Electronics Engineers Inc. (2014). https://doi.org/10.1109/CEC.2014.6900655

11. Luke, S., Panait, L.: Fighting bloat with nonparametric parsimony pressure. In: Guervós, J.J.M., Adamidis, P., Beyer, H.G., Schwefel, H.P., Fernández-Villacañas, J.L. (eds.) PPSN 2002. LNCS, vol. 2439, pp. 411–421. Springer, Berlin (2002). https://doi.org/10.1007/3-540-45712-7_40

A Literature Review on the Level of Automation and New Approach Proposal

Hasnaa Ait Malek[1,2(✉)], Alain Etienne[1], Ali Siadat[1], and Thierry Allavena[2]

[1] LCFC, Arts et Métiers Paristech, Metz, France
{alain.etienne,ali.siadat}@ensam.eu
[2] Groupe PSA, Vélizy Villacoublay, France
{hasnaa.aitmalek,thierry.allavena}@mpsa.com

Abstract. This paper sheds light on various definitions of the term automation. On the basis of a bibliographical study it hands out a state of the art in terms of the level of automation. The aim of the said paper is to study, analyze and discuss several definitions of the LoA proposed in the literature. On the grounds of this analysis, a set of requirements that ought to be respected by an accurate indicator were given out in order to propound a new definition of the LoA aimed at application in the manufacturing domain and its interest in order to optimize workstations. At the end of this bibliographical study, a table summarizing the list of different definitions, and the requirements that each of them meet is drawn. A proposal for a new definition of LoA as a time ratio is also presented. Furthermore, the application on an academic case study on an assembly line with 13 operations helped us demonstrate its interest.

Keywords: Automation · Requirements · Indicator · Level of automation · Time

1 Introduction

The word "automation"appeared in April 1947 in the department of Ford's vice-president, Del Harder, who wanted to use technology to change production rates and increase the productivity of automotive assembly lines [1]. In 1997, Parasuraman and Riley [2] defined automation as the performance by a machine (usually a computer) of a function previously performed by a human. Thus, according to Claverie [3], the automation of processes has changed working conditions and the role of human in industry. The latter has become, instead of an actor, a designer, maintenance agent or supervisor. In 2016, Vagia, Transeth and Fjerdingen [4] presented another definition of automation. For them, this term refers to a system that will perform the tasks for which it is programmed without having the choice or possibility to act differently. Its actions are predefined from the beginning and it has no possibility to change them in the future.

Today, the technological challenge for manufacturers is to have a versatile production line, flexible to the product and volume [5]. Therefore, choosing a good level

© IFIP International Federation for Information Processing 2020
Published by Springer Nature Switzerland AG 2020
B. Lalic et al. (Eds.): APMS 2020, IFIP AICT 591, pp. 408–417, 2020.
https://doi.org/10.1007/978-3-030-57993-7_46

of automation will avoid unnecessary investments in inadequate technological solutions. Establishing a good level of automation from the design phase of the line will avoid the enormous costs of changing the production line in case we realize the unsuitability after its implementation. So the objective of our work is to group together the operations that can be automated in order to make the investments profitable and optimize the workstations. Which leads to this scientific question: **"How to qualify the level of automation of a work station?"**.

The purpose of this paper is to present and analyze the different approaches proposed in recent years on the level of automation in order to finally propose a new quantitative approach.

2 The Level of Automation

Currently, there is no consensus on the definition of the level of Automation. In fact, the decision about automation should be driven based on several parameters and decision criteria. Therefore, this section introduces this concept by addressing the different approaches found in the literature. The objective is to come up with a new scale proposal for evaluating this indicator.

There are many definitions of the LoA concept. The method of evaluation is not the same, some studies propose a quantitative evaluation while others are moving towards a qualitative approach.

2.1 LoA Defined as a Degree of Evolution of the Expert System in Decision-Making

One of the oldest definitions that can be found in the literature is proposed by Sheridan and Verplank [6] and repeated in various works [7, 8]. The authors [6] identified six functions that a human operator or computer could perform during an operation: Requests, Gets, Selects, Approves, Starts and Tells. The authors explain how the human operator and the computer are supposed to cooperate under different LoAs for each of these commands. In this sense, the authors define automation as a total or partial replacement of a function previously performed by the human operator. This implies that automation is not total or non-existent, but that it can vary according to different levels. The Table 1 presents the 10 levels of LoA, defined by Sheridan and Verplank [6].

For example, at low level 2 (Table 1), several options are offered to humans, but the system has no say in the decision. At level 4, the computer suggests an alternative decision, but the human being retains the power to execute this alternative or choose another one. At a higher level 6, the system gives human only a limited amount of time to exercise his right of veto before making a decision.

Table 1. Definition of LoA proposed by Sheridan and Verplank [6]

LoA	Description
Level 1	Fully manual control, the computer offers no assistance
Level 2	The computer offers a complete set of alternatives. Several options are offered to human who decides
Level 3	The computer reduces the number of alternatives, and it is always the human who decides
Level 4	The computer suggests only one option, human can decide whether or not to follow it
Level 5	The computer executes the option if the human approves it. The approval of human is necessary
Level 6	The computer leaves a limited time to the human to decide before executing the action
Level 7	The computer executes the action automatically and informs the human
Level 8	The computer informs the human if he requests the information
Level 9	The computer informs if it considers it necessary
Level 10	Full control of the computer. It decides everything and acts independently

In this definition, the authors proposed a very broad and detailed explanation on computer and human operator cooperation under different LoA degrees from fully manual to fully automated. However, this definition is more oriented towards the control of systems than the operational part.

2.2   LoA Defined as a Degree of Automation of Physical and Cognitive Operations

In 2008, Frohm, Lindström and Winroth [9] defined the level of automation as the allocation of physical and cognitive operations between humans and technology. Indeed, for them, LoA is presented in two degrees: one for physical operations, and the other for cognitive operations. The Table 2 presents the seven LoA levels proposed by the authors.

Table 2. Definition of LoA proposed by Frohm, Lindström et Winroth [9]

LoA	Physical operations	Cognitive operations
Level 1	**Totally Manual**	**Totally manual**
Level 2	**Static hand tool**: Manual work with support of static tool	**Decision giving**: The user gets information on what to do, or proposal on how the task can be achieved
Level 3	**Flexible hand tool**: Manual work with support of flexible tool	**Teaching**: The user gets instruction on how the task can be achieved
Level 4	**Automated hand tool**: Manual work with support of automated tool	**Questioning**: The technology question the execution, if the execution deviate from what the technology consider being suitable
Level 5	**Static machine/workstation**: Automatic work by machine that is designed for a specific task	**Supervision**: The technology calls for the users' attention
Level 6	**Flexible machine/workstation**: Automatic work by machine that can be reconfigured for different tasks	**Intervene**: The technology takes over and corrects the action
Level 7	**Totally Automated**	**Totally automated**

The degree of description is fairly accurate and complete. However, the scale can lead to confusion. We don't understand the value of establishing two levels; a static hand tool (LoA = 2) and a totally manual (LoA = 1). Using a manual tool (such as a screwdriver or hammer) doesn't change the decision about automation. The level for us should always be manual. Another problem concerns levels 3 (Flexible hand tool) and 4 (Automated hand tool). In fact, a flexible hand tool can be automated, such as an automatic screwdriver for which the drills calibers can be changed to deal with different screw sizes or types. The last point concerns level 7 (fully automatic). It can be flexible, such as robotic or reconfigurable stations. We believe that this scale describes the levels excluding new advanced robotic solutions that cannot be exclusively classified in a single category of the proposed scale. In addition, level 5 of static machine can in some cases be confused with level 7 of fully automatic. In fact, a dedicated static machine can operate autonomously and can be fully automatic.

2.3 LoA Defined as a Degree of Intelligence and Autonomy

In 1989, Riley defined a general model of human-machine interaction. His model presents factors that define 7 levels of intelligence (Table 3) and 12 levels of autonomy (Table 4) [10]. Each combination of an intelligence level and an autonomy level is called an automation state and each state corresponds to a predefined and unique form [11].

Table 3. Riley's proposed intelligence levels [4]

Intelligence level	Description
Level 1	Manual operations
Level 2	Processing of available information
Level 3	The system cannot perform any action by itself, unless it advises the operator
Level 4	Recommendations: The machine has no power to act and is limited to communication with the operator
Level 5	Recommendations with interaction: The machine does not have the power to act and is limited to communication with the operator
Level 6	Adaptive recommendations: The machine has no power to act and is limited to communication with the operator
Level 7	The machine is a servant and has the possibility to perform actions

Table 4. Riley's proposed autonomy levels [4]

Autonomy level	Description
Level 1	Manual operations
Level 2	Processing of available information
Level 3	The system cannot perform any action by itself, unless it advises the operator
Level 4	Recommendations: The machine has no power to act and is limited to communication with the operator
Level 5	Recommendations with interaction: The machine does not have the power to act and is limited to communication with the operator
Level 6	Adaptive recommendations: The machine has no power to act and is limited to communication with the operator
Level 7	The machine is a **servant** and has the possibility to perform actions
Level 8	The machine is an **assistant** and can perform actions but requires operator approval
Level 9	The machine is **associated** and can perform actions autonomously without explicit authorization from the operator, but the operator can always replace it
Level 10	The machine is a **partner** and has the same rights as the operator
Level 11	The machine is a **supervisor** and can replace the operator who has no authority
Level 12	Fully autonomous operation

In the first six levels of autonomy (Table 4), the machine has no authority to act; it is limited to communication with the operator. The last six levels give the machine the possibility to act. The distinctions between these levels of autonomy are based on the sophistication of the machine's information processing functions and the authority to manipulate the operator's screens. For example, an Associated machine is autonomous and able to perform actions without the explicit authorization of the operator, but the operator can always cancel it. A Partner machine has the same derogation power as the operator, and a Supervisor machine can replace the operator, but the operator cannot ignore it [11].

2.4 LoA Defined as a Cost Ratio

The level of automation L_{auto} can be calculated based on the operating costs of equipment C_{eqh} (€/h) and Labor costs C_{Lab} (€/h) [12], as shown in Eq. (1)

$$L_{auto} = \frac{C_{eqh}}{C_{eqh} + C_{Lab}} \qquad (1)$$

When the ratio L_{auto} is zero, it is assumed that production is entirely manual; the operating cost of the equipment is negligible compared to the cost of Labor. When this ratio is equal to 1, it is the Labor cost that is negligible compared to the operating cost of the equipment, so production is fully automated.

This approach has the advantage of describing the LoA in a quantitative way. However, it does not provide a true picture of the rate of automation in a workshop. The definition of cost is not sufficiently representative. For example, if we consider a workshop of 8 workstations, with 2 automated workstations at a high cost. The ratio L_{auto} will be close to 1, without a high automation rate. This limit more significant in countries where investment and operating costs are significantly higher than Labor costs. Thus, this approach does not reflect the actual level of automation of a production line.

An analysis of the various works in the literature shows that most of the proposed approaches address the entire process and lack precision in describing the Level of automation of each workstation or operation.

3 Requirements and Suggested LoA Definition

The purpose of the bibliographic study that was carried-out is to analyze the different definitions of levels of automation presented in the literature. An appropriate definition and scale must first be established to be able to describe all possible automation scenarios before making a decision.

3.1 Requirements

Our scale must be **applicable** for existing production systems **(R1)** and **applicable** for future production systems **(R2)**. A good indicator should be **quantitative (R3)**, measurable data that can be easily monitored to maximize or minimize our LoA as needed. The scale must concern the **operating mode (R4)**, i.e. the physical operations that the machine or human can perform. A good definition of LoA must be **objective (R5)** and can allow decision making according to a methodology rather than intuition. The indicator must allow **partial automation (R6)**, and therefore have levels between fully manual and fully automatic. And finally, the scale must give a **clear vision to decision-**

makers on the operator and machines load (R7), which allows to study the line balancing and take into account the profitability aspect. The Table 5 summarizes the different approaches identified with the requirements they meet.

Table 5. Table summarizing the different approaches identified in the literature with and the requirements they meet

Authors	Requirements						
	R1	R2	R3	R4	R5	R6	R7
Sheridan and Verplank	X					X	
Frohm, Lindström and Winroth	X			X		X	
Riley	X			X		X	
Windmark, Gabrielson, Andersson and StŒhl	X	X	X	X	X	X	

It can be noted that none of the proposed definitions in the literature respect all the requirements. Nevertheless, all definitions are applicable. Most of them are qualitative and allow partial automation. There is only one definition that is quantitative, but unfortunately, it takes cost as a criterion, which really does not give a clear vision of the level of automation. However, none of the definitions found in the literature take into account the operator and machines load aspect.

3.2 Suggested LoA Definition

We appreciate defining a good level of automation as the best allocation of resources and their associated levels of automation. The indicator chosen to quantify the LoA is Time, which makes it possible to study the load of operators and the load of automated tools, in order to get a clear vision of line balancing.

To improve decision support methods for assembly line automation, it is necessary to develop a new definition of the LoA. Therefore, the definition proposed will be at the workstation level and not at the level of the entire process. This allows us to analyze all operations and suggest several automation scenarios to choose the optimal one. The level of automation must be quantitative and must vary from fully manual to fully automated with intermediate levels to represent human-machine collaboration. The indicator chosen to quantify the LoA is Time. Hence, the proposed LoA is defined as a time relationship between the time of automated operations T_{auto} (min) and the cycle time T_c (min) as shown in Eq. (2).

$$LoA = \frac{T_{auto}}{T_c} \qquad (2)$$

If the LoA $\approx$ 0%, the workstation is completely manual; the only resource is human. If the LoA $\approx$ 100%, the workstation is fully automated; the only resource is the machine. Between the two levels, the station is semi-automated; the two resources present are human and machine.

4 Case Study

For reasons of confidentiality, we have presented in this paper an academic case study. The Fig. 1 shows a production line with several workstations. The analysis is done on the first workstation with a cycle time equal to 1.86 min.

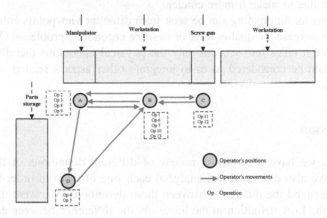

Fig. 1. Fictive production line and presentation of the operations and the different operator's positions

The tasks done by the operator are presented in Table 6 which also shows the time (in min) for each of the operations.

Table 6. Description of the operations done by the operator, his position and the duration of each one of them

Operation	Description	Position	Time (min)
Op 1	Move to the manipulator's zone	B	0.1
Op 2	Take the manipulator	A	0.02
Op 3	Move to parts storage	A	0.2
Op 4	Pick up the part with the manipulator	D	0.08
Op 5	Move to the workstation 1	D	0.2
Op 6	Drop the part	B	0.02
Op 7	Move to the manipulator's zone	B	0.1
Op 8	Put down the manipulator	A	0.02
Op 9	Move to the workstation 1	A	0.1
Op 10	Move to the screw gun	B	0.1
Op 11	Take the screw gun	C	0.02
Op 12	Move to the workstation 1	C	0.1
Op 13	Screw	D	0.8

According to this configuration, $LoA = 0\%$; the station is totally manual. If we decide to automate the picking and dropping of parts, Op1, Op2, Op7, Op8 and Op9 will be suppressed. Op3, Op4, Op5 and Op6 will be fully automated so $T_{auto} = 0.5$ min. In this case, $LoA = 27\%$. The indicator shows that 27% of the operations on the first workstation are automated. Therefore, we know the availability of the operator which allows us, not only, to optimize and improve the workstation, but also to balance the line to make it more efficient.

The reasons for automating can be seen from different viewpoints either to reduce labor costs, to increase the quality level or to solve ergonomic problems. Our approach is limited since it takes into account only the physical operations therefore a second approach should be considered so as to integrate other aspects related to work conditions such as mental workload, ergonomics etc.

5 Conclusion

In this paper, we have presented a review of different definitions of the Level of automation. We also discussed and analyzed each one of them in order to allow the reader to understand the difference between these definitions. We went through three main points: the LoA definition in the literature, the difference between each of these definitions and the chosen criteria for an appropriate definition. Finally, we have listed a set of requirements that a good definition of LoA must respect, and based on these requirements, we proposed a quantitative definition of the LoA that was applied on an academic case study.

Acknowledgments. This work took place in the framework of the OpenLab Materials and Processes combining Arts et Métiers network, GeorgiaTech Lorraine and Groupe PSA.

References

1. Lorre, B.: L'automatisation industrielle, quel avenir pour les usines du futur? Transhumanisme et Intelligence Artificielle, 9 January 2018
2. Parasuraman, R., Riley, V.: Humans and automation: use, misuse, disuse, abuse. Hum. Factors: J. Hum. Factors Ergon. Soc. **39**, 230–253 (1997). https://doi.org/10.1518/001872097778543886
3. Claverie, B.: COGNITIQUE - Science et pratique des relations à la machine à penser, Bernard Claverie - livre, ebook, epub. L'Harmattan (2005)
4. Vagia, M., Transeth, A.A., Fjerdingen, S.A.: A literature review on the levels of automation during the years. What are the different taxonomies that have been proposed? Appl. Ergon. **53**, 190–202 (2016). https://doi.org/10.1016/j.apergo.2015.09.013
5. Wiendahl, H.-P., et al.: Changeable manufacturing - classification, design and operation. CIRP Ann. **56**, 783–809 (2007). https://doi.org/10.1016/j.cirp.2007.10.003
6. Sheridan, T.B., Verplank, W.L.: Human and Computer Control of Undersea Teleoperators. Massachusetts Institute of Technology, Cambridge (1978)

7. Parasuraman, R., Sheridan, T.B., Wickens, C.D.: A model for types and levels of human interaction with automation. IEEE Trans. Syst. Man Cybern. Part A: Syst. Hum. **30**, 286–297 (2000). https://doi.org/10.1109/3468.844354
8. Lintern, G., Hughes, T.: Development of a supervisory control rating scale, p. 35 (2008)
9. Frohm, J., Lindström, V., Winroth, M., et al.: Levels of automation in manufacturing. Ergonomia – Int. J. Ergon. Hum. Factors **30**(19) (2008)
10. Adams, J.A., Rani, P., Sarkar, N.: Mixed-initiative interaction and robotic systems, p. 8 (2004)
11. Riley, V.: A general model of mixed-initiative human-machine systems. In: Proceedings of the Human Factors Society Annual Meeting, vol. 33, pp. 124–128 (1989). https://doi.org/10.1177/154193128903300227
12. Windmark, C., Gabrielson, P., Andersson, C., StŒhl, J.E.: A cost model for determining an optimal automation level in discrete batch manufacturing. Procedia CIRP **3**, 73–78 (2012). https://doi.org/10.1016/j.procir.2012.07.014

De-risking Investments in Industrial Systems Using Real Options Analysis: Case of Phosphates Fertilizer Firm

Imane Essaadi[1]([⊠]) [iD] and Richard de Neufville[2] [iD]

[1] EMINES – Mohammed VI Polytechnic University,
43150 Benguerir, Morocco
imane.essaadi@emine.um6p
[2] Institute for Data, Systems and Society, Massachusetts Institute of Technology,
Cambridge, MA 02139, USA
ardent@mit.edu

Abstract. Many industrial firms adopted a deterministic irreversible investment plans without any pro-active risk management strategy. The existing literature of the Supply Chain Design does not value the managerial flexibility as enabled by the Real Option (RO) theory. However, this latter considers only single project and not adapted to supply chain investments. This opens a new area of research. Thus, this paper is concerned with providing a practical and novel framework for de-risking future investments of large-scale, capital-intensive interdependent industrial projects, in an uncertain and risky environment. The suggested framework is based on real option analysis and aims to integrate managerial flexibility in terms of "real options" to efficiently adjust the investment plans to the evolution of uncertainties over time, considering interdependencies between projects, while reducing downside risks and increasing potential opportunities. This framework has been tested to assess potential risks, define and value flexible strategies to deal with the construction delays and the cost overruns in the investment planning of phosphates fertilizer firm. The insights indicate that flexibility lead to higher expected performance while reducing downside risks and raising potential upside gains.

Keywords: Managerial flexibility · Real Option Analysis · Uncertainties · Risks · Real options

1 Introduction

Complex industrial systems strategic planning involves capitalistic investments expenditures and depends upon the future evolution of the global market which is highly risky. Many firms adopt a deterministic irreversible investment plan without any proactive risk management strategy. This could lead the firm to considerable economic losses. This paper is concerned with providing a practical framework for de-risking future investments of complex industrial systems in an uncertain and risky environment, especially cost overruns and time construction delays. This problem may be significantly critical when investing in a commodity-based integrated chemical supply

© IFIP International Federation for Information Processing 2020
Published by Springer Nature Switzerland AG 2020
B. Lalic et al. (Eds.): APMS 2020, IFIP AICT 591, pp. 418–426, 2020.
https://doi.org/10.1007/978-3-030-57993-7_47

chain such as oil and gas or phosphates-based mining and chemical industry. These industries invest in capital intensive projects whose value chains are usually vertically integrated from mining to distribution and include complex logistic infrastructure and multi-products chemical transformation facilities and infrastructures that are hieratically dependent.

The most common approaches to deal with uncertainty in the strategic investment planning are the Stochastic Programming and Robust Optimization (RO). RO provides reliable but too conservative solutions [1] since it either maximizes the profit of either the worst-case scenario or the profit of the scenario with highest deviation. SP assumes a risk-neutral decision-maker and focuses only on finding the best design that performs best on average; by optimizing the expected economic value. Thus, the optimal stochastic design could be over-sized and generates losses or under-sized and miss opportunities when the future departs significantly from expectations. This is because, the value of the overall distribution of uncertainties is different than the value associated to the average [2]. Some studies [3–7] have integrated risks measures into their design, but these concern mainly the minimization of downside risks. In short, they are reactive to risks and do not provide proactive measures to increase the flexibility of the system for future to deal with unexpected events. However, good strategic investment planning will not only recognize the distribution of possible futures but also proactively take steps to de-risk and future-proof the investments. It will take steps to reduce the possible downsides, investing in ways to deal effectively with eventualities and to unlock future market opportunities. The design should integrate managerial flexibility into the system in terms of "real options" to efficiently adjust the supply chain to the evolution of uncertainties/risks over time. Real options provide the "right, but not the obligation, to change the system easily in the face of uncertainty, such: option to abandon, to defer, to relocate and to expand/contract the capacity.

Despite the flexibility in engineering systems being promising approach to deal with uncertainty [2], its effective deployment into the system can be a challenge. It depends highly on the choice of the future alternatives actions (real options); the timing and the location of flexibility in the system. The most common forms of Real Option Analysis (ROA) used in the literature are based on analytical methods (based on dynamic programming) or on lattices (binomial or multinomial). These are typically used to analyze and price financial options. But they do not apply to physical systems for which there is no ready market, in which arbitrage-enforced pricing does not apply, and for which managerial independence invalidates potential assumptions about path independence. To cope with these challenges in valuing flexibility, novel approaches based on decision rules, linking the observations of uncertainty data to decisions, were recently proposed, as by [2]. However, many applications are limited, for example to one type of flexibility (single real options) [10] or to a single project/supply chain component [8, 9] which cannot be applied to multiple interdependent projects/components.

Considering the background above, the main contribution of this research paper is to provide a practical approach to flexibility analysis that effectively integrates real options in large-scale complex systems involving interdependent projects. Its novelty lies in the scope and its approach:

As for Its scope: We particularly interested in de-risking investment in dependent industrial projects, operating in a commodity based global market, characterized by the need for large capital resources, and where the impact of uncertainties on one potential project will consequently impact the operational functioning of her projects that depend on it.

As for Its Approach: To make the best use of managerial flexibility on proactively dealing with uncertainties in the chemical supply chain investments, we first model uncertainties considering their correlation, then we quantitatively evaluate their impact including financial risks underlying an investment plan. Based on this evaluation, we explore the options on investments that could be susceptible to increase the expected value from the industrial investments and reduce downside risks.

The remainder of this paper is organized as follows: Sect. 2 provides the details of the proposed approach. In Sect. 3, illustrates the use of the suggested approach to the case of an integrated chemical company. The final section summarizes the major findings by providing conclusions and future research perspectives.

2   Proposed Framework: Real Compound Option Analysis

The proposed framework demonstrates how to adapt investment plans to future uncertainties based on proactive and flexible strategies. It aims to avoid future downside risks and take advantage of new opportunities. It involves 5 steps as shown in Fig. 1:

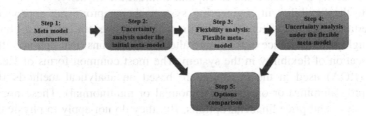

Fig. 1. Real compound options analysis framework

2.1   Step 1: Meta-model Construction

As many investment planning models are complex in nature, the evaluation of comprehensive flexibility to incorporate into the planning requires the use of meta-models. They could be developed in three ways [2]: **Bottom-up approach**: the metamodel is built upon the aggregation of the detailed description of the model by reducing the inputs and simplifying the formulation of the model without omitting interesting details. **Simulator models**: mimic detailed descriptions of the system or the model responses. It considers the model as a black box, does not consider its technical details.

Top-down approach: it consists in defining conceptual representations of the overall pattern of the system behavior, such as systems dynamics.

2.2   Steps 2 and 4: Uncertainty Analysis

These steps model potential input uncertainties and investigate the consequent uncertainty of the performance of the investment plan. They enable us to assess the risk-reward of different investment strategies (initial and flexible investment). The risk of loss could be evaluated by the Value at Risk – indicating the 5 or 10% probability of low returns or the complementary Value at Gain, the possible gain for given level of probability.

2.3   Step 3: Flexibility Analysis

This step explores proactive strategies and ways to reduce risks (assessed in step 2) and increase opportunities given of the investment plan. This can be done by responding systematically to the questions: where, when and how the flexibility should be incorporated into the design? What flexibility? The answer to the "where" comes by analyzing the most interdependent projects in the alternative design, this comes with the deep knowledge of the supply chain/value chain. The answer to "when" is related to the timing of the risk occurrence. For example, if the potential risk is the project execution delay, then we could distinguish two delay periods: either in the design or in construction phase of the critical project. The answer to the "how" comes by defining the combination of flexible options and the decision rules ("If…Then") that will structure the use of these flexibilities. These rules both state the conditions under which designers would choose to act and implement the decisions in the meta-model/the initial model to change the design. According to [1], these rules should mimic what management would do if they had to deal with a changing situation.

2.4   Step 5: Options Comparison

Finally, we have to assess the value of flexibility underlined with these compound options and appreciate the risk-reward trade-off between candidate options. One measure of the option value is the difference between the overall design value with and without compound options as calculated in Step 2, as Eq. 1 indicates:

$$Flexibility\ Value = max\ (0\ ,\ ENPV\ \underset{\iota}{\iota}\ Best\ Flexible\ design - EN \qquad (1)$$

3   Case Study

The presented framework has been tested in the case of our industrial partner (OCP.SA) leader in the phosphate mining and chemical production industry in Morocco. Its logistics chain is spread over three independent axes "northern axis", "central axis" and "southern axis". Each axis is vertically integrated: from the extraction of phosphate ore through the chemical valorization (phosphoric acid and fertilizers). The Group has embarked on an ambitious investment program for the period 2008 to 2030. The first wave of investments focused on the extension of mining and chemical capacities located on its northern axis. The second wave of investments concerns the reconfiguration of the central axis by implanting: a new port in Safi, new acid and fertilizer plants and an acid pipeline that will link acid plants in Youssoufia with fertilizer plants in Safi. For confidentiality reasons, we will consider a fictious investment plan and normalize real data by taking the expected performance of the initial investment plan (Table 1). For the space limit, we do not present the meta-model.

3.1 Step 1: Uncertainty Analysis Under Fixed Design

Among potential uncertainties that may lead to significant losses if proactive actions are not considered, are: prices of fertilizer products and raw materials inputs (Ammonia and Sulfur), the acid pipeline construction delays and cost overruns (Table 2). By simultaneously varying different uncertain parameters within their possible range of variation (Table 3), we obtain the distribution of the possibilities of the investment plan performance (Fig. 2). This curve represents the cumulative chance of obtaining a result below any specific target value, according to ascending manner. We notice that there is 10% chance of losing respectively about 2092 MMAD or more, that is of missing

Table 1. Potential new projects

Asset	Opening date	CAPEX (MMAD)
Complex site 1	2023	358
Complex site 2	2023	358
Complex site 3	2024	358
Complex site 4	2025	358
Complex site 5	2026	358
Acid pipeline	2023	116
New port	2023	268

Table 2. Delays and cost overruns

Years of delays	Cost overruns
1 year	25%
2 years	50%
3 years	70%
4 years	85%

Table 3. Statistical distribution of potential uncertainties

Commodity price	Statistical distribution[a]	Parameters Sulfur
Price ($)	Triangular	(33, 83, 806)
Ammonia price ($)	Triangular	(125, 705, 884)
Fertilizer price ($)	Triangular	(200, 263, 1280)
Acid pipeline delays	Uniform	(0, 4)

[a]The observation of the historical data shows that the annual price, for a given commodity, is an independent variable that follow a statistical non-skewed distribution.

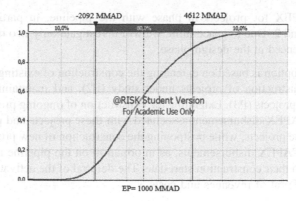

Fig. 2. Cumulative distribution function of the investment plan value (without option)

around −2092 MMAD Target. This investment plan has about 40% chance of breaking (investment value = 0) and could realize 1000 MMAD on average.

3.2   Step 2: Flexibility Analysis

To counteract the risk of the acid pipeline construction delay, a distinction must be made between two cases depending, on the location of the delay in the progress of pipeline development (Fig. 3). Similarly, a distinction will be made between ongoing projects (P1), those whose arrival date coincides with that of the pipeline, projects under study (P2), those whose arrival date is later than the initial arrival date of the pipeline (without delay) and the new projects (P3), those whose arrival date is later than the new arrival date of the pipeline (with delay) (Fig. 3). If the delay is identified at the design phase of the acid pipeline, in our example in 2020, the firm will have disbursed

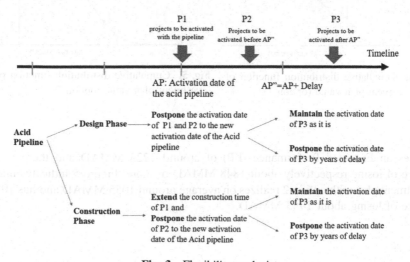

Fig. 3. Flexibility analysis

part of the CAPEX for projects in phase with the pipeline, in particular the two complex site 1 and 2. Due to space limit, we will investigate only two options to limit the delay experienced at the design phase:

Option 1: This option is based on extending the construction of existing projects (P1), deferring the construction of projects under study (P2), and maintaining the arrival dates of the new projects (P3). Extending the construction of ongoing projects results in extending the CAPEX disbursement associated with these projects and postponing the activation of these projects, while postponing the construction of new projects results in postponing the CAPEX disbursements, as information on the pipeline arrival delay is identified prior to their construction start date. The deferral of the activation of projects results in the deferral of revenues and costs.

Option 2: This option carries forward the same rules applied in Option 1 except for the maintenance of new projects. In this second option, we will postpone their activation date, in order to lighten the financial commitments in CAPEX.

3.3   Step 3: Uncertainty Analysis Under Flexible Designs

By running 10000 Monte Carlo Simulations of the meta-model, using @Risk excel add-in, including option 1 and 2, separately, we obtain the cumulative distribution functions in Fig. 4 and 5. Figure 4 indicates that the investment plan with option 1

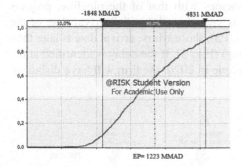
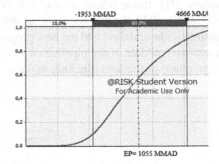

Fig. 4. Cumulative distribution function of the investment plan value (option 1)

Fig. 5. Cumulative distribution function of the investment plan value (option 2)

realizes an Expected Performance (EP) of around 1223 MMAD and there is 10% chance of losing respectively about 1848 MMAD or more. Figure 5 indicates that the investment plan with option 2 realizes on average around 1055 MMAD and has 10% of chance of losing about 1953 MMAD.

Table 4. Statistical distribution of potential uncertainties

Commodity price	Without option	Without option 1	Without option 2
Exacted performance (MMAD)	1000	1223	1055
Option value (MMAD)		216	55
10% VAR (MMAD)	−2092	−1848	−1953
10% VAG (MMAD)	4612	4831	4666

3.4 Step 4: Options Comparison

Table 4 resumes the statistical metrics of each investment plan. We can conclude that the integration of the flexibility in investment planning provides better reward while reducing downside losses (Fig. 2, 4, 5). Indeed, both options lead to greater expected value. They lower VAR and raise VAG. More remarkably, maintaining future projects dates is more interesting than postponing them, thus option 1 outperforms option 2 at all levels. Finally, the implementation of option 1 depends upon the trade-off between the option value and the cost underlying the postponement of projects type 1 and 2. This insight will support the industrial development department during its negotiation with its contractor, considering potential delays.

4   Conclusion and Research Perspectives

Major long-term investments are inherently risky, because future market, economic, and political conditions are highly uncertain. However, the literature has focused on finding the best design optimizing the expected performance and risks without integrating proactive measures to increase the flexibility of the system for future to deal with unexpected events. In order to address this problem, we suggested a proactive practical framework that integrates and value flexibility -real options- in large-scale complex systems involving interdependent projects. Given the complexity of the studied systems, we considered compound options, each option was applied on a specific project following a specific decision rule. Overall insight from our case study confirms that flexibility is an effective way to improve the expected performance of systems in uncertain environments. In our future work, we will provide guidance for supply chain decision makers on how and when to exercise flexibility to mitigate pandemic crisis.

References

1. Kirilyuk, V.S.: Risk measures in stochastic programming and robust optimization problems. Cybern. Syst. Anal. **51**(6), 874–885 (2015)
2. de Neufville, R., Scholtes, S.: Flexibility in Engineering Design. The MIT Press, Cambridge (2011)

3. Dal-Mas, M., Giarola, S., Zamboni, A., Bezzo, F.: Strategic design and investment capacity planning of the ethanol supply chain under price uncertainty. Biomass Bioenergy **35**(5), 2059–2071 (2011)

4. Kostin, A.M., Guillén-Gosálbez, G., Mele, F.D., Bagajewicz, M.J., Jiménez, L.: Design and planning of infrastructures for bioethanol and sugar production under demand uncertainty. Chem. Eng. Res. Des. **90**(3), 359–376 (2012)

5. Gebreslassie, B.H., Yao, Y., You, F.: Design under uncertainty of hydrocarbon biorefinery supply chains: multiobjective stochastic programming models, decomposition algorithm, and a comparison between CVaR and downside risk. AIChE J. **58**(7), 2155–2179 (2012)

6. Ribas, G.P., Hamacher, S., Street, A.: Optimization under uncertainty of the integrated oil supply chain using stochastic and robust programming. Int. Trans. Oper. Res. **17**(6), 777–796 (2010)

7. Santibañez-Aguilar, J.E., Guillen-Gosálbez, G., Morales-Rodriguez, R., Jiménez-Esteller, L., Castro-Montoya, A.J., Ponce-Ortega, J.M.: Financial risk assessment and optimal planning of biofuels supply chains under uncertainty. Bioenerg. Res. **9**(1), 1053–1069 (2016)

8. Sharma, P., Romagnoli, J.A., Vlosky, R.: Options analysis for long-term capacity design and operation of a lignocellulosic biomass refinery. Comput. Chem. Eng. **58**, 178–202 (2013)

9. Zhang, S., Cardin, M.-A.: Flexibility and real options analysis in emergency medical services systems using decision rules and multi-stage stochastic programming. Transp. Res. Part E: Logistics Transp. Rev. **107**, 120–140 (2017)

10. Cardin, M.-A., Xie, Q., Ng, T.S., Wang, S., Hu, J.: An approach for analyzing and managing flexibility in engineering systems design based on decision rules and multistage stochastic programming. IISE Trans. **49**(1), 1–12 (2017)

Data-Driven Replenishment Method Choice in a Picking System

Simon Hummelshøj Sloth, Magnus Abildsten Bøgh,
Christian Møller Nielsen, Konstantinos Panagiotis Konstantinidis,
and Inkyung Sung(✉) ⓘ

Department of Materials and Production, Aalborg University, Aalborg, Denmark
{ssloth16, mbagh16, cmnil16, kkonst19}@student.aau.dk,
inkyung_sung@mp.aau.dk

Abstract. Designing the operating policies of picking systems, which connect inventory and production/assembly lines in a manufacturing system, involves determining replenishment methods for individual items. These replenishment methods affect the overall labor cost and flexibility of the picking system by determining the frequency and quantity of item picking. To design the replenishment method, in this paper, we propose a data-driven decision support framework that provides guidance in comprehending features in a picking system based on demand, size, and value of individual items. The proposed framework is then applied to a real-world case for validation.

Keywords: Order picking · Continuous replenishment · Replenishment methods · Data-driven decision support · Principal component analysis

1 Introduction

Many companies, especially manufacturers, have seen increasing pressures on cost reduction during the past decades. To cope with this, they often focus on efficient production processes to reduce the operating cost. Furthermore, manufacturing systems have been increasingly challenged by short product life cycles, frequent product introductions and ever changing product mix. These trends force manufacturing companies to focus on a flexible and responsive manufacturing system [1].

One of the system elements contributing to the desired production and manufacturing systems is a picking system, which conducts the process of retrieving items from storage and fulfilling the order of internal or external customers. By nature, the picking system plays a key role as an interface between inventory and production. Importantly, the picking system accounts for a large part of operating costs related to inventory due to the labor-intensive nature of the activities involved in the system. In general, labor cost accounts for upwards of 55% of the total inventory operating cost [2], therefore, the cost for inventory operations can be reduced dramatically by designing an efficient picking system.

The complexity of picking system design is mainly determined by the target system characteristics. These include mechanization level of a system, information availability, scale of operations, and organizational/operating policies for storage, routing, batching

© IFIP International Federation for Information Processing 2020
Published by Springer Nature Switzerland AG 2020
B. Lalic et al. (Eds.): APMS 2020, IFIP AICT 591, pp. 427–432, 2020.
https://doi.org/10.1007/978-3-030-57993-7_48

and order release [3]. In this paper, we focus on designing an operating policy especially for a replenishment method that governs overall picking processes. Specifically, a replenishment method specifies (1) how a picking order for a specific item is generated, (2) how the picking orders are batched, (3) how the items are picked, and (4) how the items are delivered.

A replenishment method is generally designed by following the conventional discrete order picking (COP) method or the continuous replenishment (CR) method. In the COP method, the items are picked to an order generated with a fixed time interval, whereas in the CR method, the items are continuously picked by re-order point logic following a pull type control mechanism [3–6]. While the CR method lowers picking labor cost and increases the picking flexibility in general [6], the performance of the methods varies depending on the characteristics of the item to be picked [7].

Let us note that the replenishment method choice is not straightforward due to the complicated relationships involved in a picking system and picking operations. For example, human factors such as learning, fatigue and ergonomics [8] are critical to the choice but difficult to measure. The real-life conditions, e.g. safety constraints and picker blocking [9], also increase the complexity of relevant planning problems including the replenishment method choice. As a result, an analytical framework for the replenishment method choice in a picking system has not yet materialized properly and the choice often relies on human expertise in practice.

To address the issue, we propose a data-driven replenishment method choice framework that guides a manager to identify a suitable replenishment method for an item, i.e. whether an item is replenished by the COP method or the CR method. Given a data set containing various items and their specifications, we first determine the attributes of the items that explain the data set, and classify the items based on their replenishment methods (COP or CR), resulting in two data clusters. Given an item of interest, closeness of the item to the clusters of the replenishment methods is evaluated with respect to the attributes determined and, finally, the corresponding replenishment method of the cluster with higher closeness to the item is proposed for the item.

2 Proposed Replenishment Method Choice Framework

In this section, the proposed framework is explained with connection to its implementation in a large Danish manufacturing company. The framework consists of six steps as visualized in Fig. 1.

Fig. 1. Visualization of the replenishment method choice framework

Step 1 is to identify the attributes of items that would affect the replenishment method choice. Through interviews with the relevant decision-makers in the manufacturing company and considering the commonly available attributes of an item in the database of companies, we identify the following attributes of an item, which will be used to classify the replenishment method of the item: *size, weight, price* and *demand*.

For a physical item to be picked, it is critical to consider its *size* to evaluate if the item violates space constraints in the picking system. Similarly, the *weight* of an item is essential for the replenishment method choice as the total weight of items carried on a shelf or a pallet is limited. The size and weight of an item are also important as they are closely linked with ergonomic challenges for system operators.

Price is another attribute that affects the desired replenishment method for an item. Note that the CR method tends to pick an item in larger batches, allowing the following assembly or production process to stock the item for convenience. However, this practice could increase the risk of the item being lost or damaged during the stock period. Therefore, the COP approach that would reduce the batch size of the item will be suitable for an expensive and valuable item.

Last, the *demand* of an item, and in particular the demand rate of the item, are keys to sustain a flow of items in a system. Obviously, an item with low demands is not suitable to be managed by the CR method. We further consider the *demand variation*, which affects the safety stock level of an item.

It should be noted that the impact of the selected attributes of an item on the replenishment method choice would vary depending on the picking system of interest. To address this issue, further analysis can be performed to see how well the picking item data of the system is explained by the selected attributes.

For this purpose, the principal component analysis (PCA) can be used to evaluate whether the identified attributes are able to explain the variation between the replenishment method choices of items. The PCA is a tool for dimension reduction with the aim of reducing several variables into fewer principal components (PC) that captures a decreasing amount of the variation between the given observations [10].

A Danish manufacturing company investigates their choice of replenishment method for the items to be picked in relation to their internal logistics between inventories and several assembly lines. At the time of investigation, 1777 items and 274 items are being replenished by the COP and CR methods, respectively.

Considering the item attributes proposed in the framework, the company set the *weight, price, yearly demand,* and *demand variation* of an item as the attributes of interest for the replenishment method choice.

To verify the attributes identified, the PCA is performed on the data set of the items, which contains all the attribute values of the items covered in the picking system. The result shows that the selected attributes are able to explain the variation between the items. The PCA result is summarized in Table 1. The PC 1, which is the direction of the data where the most variation in the data is explained, is mainly contributed by the weight, price and the coefficient of variation (CV) of demand.

In *Step 2*, after identifying the attributes, they are normalized to a range between 0 and 1 to eliminate the impact of units of measurement on the replenishment method choice.

In *Step 3*, weights can be applied to the attributes to scale the importance of them, thereby emphasizing parameters with high impacts on the replenishment method

Table 1. Cumulative variation explained by the principle components

Attribute	PC 1	PC 2	PC 3	PC 4
Yearly demand	0.041	0.984	0.174	0.001
Unit price	−0.661	0.064	−0.201	−0.720
Unit weight	−0.641	0.085	−0.330	0.688
CV	−0.388	−0.144	0.906	0.091
Cumulative proportion	0.513	0.764	0.968	1.000

choice. The weights can be guided by the loading scores from the principal components of the PCA (see Table 1) or by the experience of a manager of the target picking system.

In **Step 4**, ideal candidate items, which represent items most suitable for the COP and CR methods, respectively, are found based on the current replenishment method choices for the items. One feasible way of finding the ideal candidate item is to examine the items that are currently replenished by the same method (COP or CR). Specifically, given the item cluster grouped based on their replenishment method choice, an item positioned in the center of the cluster can be considered as the ideal item for the method. Following the idea, with k item attributes, the centroid C of n items in a cluster can be calculated by

$$C = \left(\frac{\sum_{i=1}^{n} x_{i1}}{n}, \frac{\sum_{i=1}^{n} x_{i2}}{n}, \ldots, \frac{\sum_{i=1}^{n} x_{ik}}{n} \right), \tag{1}$$

where x_{ik} is the kth attribute value of item i.

The company groups all items in the picking system according to the replenishment method of the items (COP or CR) and the centroids of the groups are calculated accordingly. To visualize the grouping, the PCA result is re-called. Figure 2 shows the plot where all items are presented with respect to the first and second PC of the analysis with a log-transformation applied for better visualization of data. In the figure, the items are color coded according to their methods and the vectors (arrows) represent the directions the values of the attributes are varied along.

From the figure, it is first observed that in the picking system of the company an item with high demand, a low price, a low weight and a low CV tends to be managed by the CR method, aligned with common practice. Moreover, it is also observed that items with a PC 1 value greater then 0 are most likely managed by the COP method.

In **Step 5**, after identifying the ideal candidate item for a replenishment method in Step 4, the relevance of an item of interest to a replenishment method is measured. For measuring, the weighted Euclidean distance between the item of interest and the ideal item of the method (the centroid of the data cluster of the method) can be calculated by

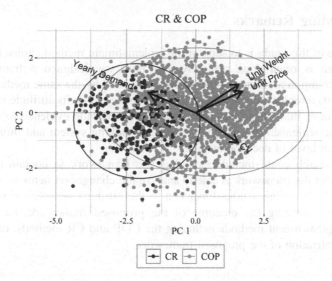

Fig. 2. Log-transformed biplot of PC 1 and PC 2 with confidence ellipses containing 95% of observations

$$\sqrt{w_1 \cdot (x_1 - c_1)^2 + w_2 \cdot (x_2 - c_2)^2 + \cdots + w_k \cdot (x_k - c_k)^2}, \qquad (2)$$

where w_k is the weight of the kth attribute determined in Step 3, and x_k and c_k are the kth attribute value of the target item and the ideal item, respectively.

In **Step 6**, based on the distance measured, the replenishment method of an item is determined. If the distance of an item to the centroid of a certain replenishment method is close enough, the item might can be replenished by the method.

Note that the replenishment method choice made based on the distance should be used as a guidance because the suitable replenishment method for an item would depend on picking system, item-specific characteristics and other practical conditions. However, such a guidance dramatically lessens the burden of a manager, especially when there are many items and attributes of the items to consider for the replenishment method choice.

The distances of all the items in the picking system to the centroids of the COP and CR method clusters are measured by Eq. (2). Based on the distances, 67 items, currently replenished by the COP method, are identified as potential items to be replenished by the CR method. From our analysis, it was estimated that replenishing the 67 items by the CR method would yield a reduction in the total number of picks by 3.8% for the three-month period assessed.

3 Concluding Remarks

The objective of this study is to support the replenishment method choice in a picking system, which is often done manually. For this, we designed a framework that investigates common attributes of the items replenished by the same method (steps 1–3) and suggests a replenishment method for an item based on its attribute values (steps 4–6). We believe that the proposed framework can provide evidence to validate the practice in the replenishment method choice in a picking system and further increase the automation level of decision-making.

Future research could include extending the framework to contain a predictive function, so that the framework is able to analyze the changes on items over time. This could be done by adding a time dimension to the attribute set of an item. Also, the possibility of extending the outcome of the proposed framework, i.e. supporting additional replenishment methods including the COP and CR methods, can be tested for the generalization of the proposed framework.

References

1. Wiendahl, H., ElMaraghy, H.A., Nyhuis, P., et al.: Changeable manufacturing- classification, design and operation. CIRP Ann.-Manuf. Technol. **56**(2), 783–809 (2007)
2. Le-Duc, T., de Koster, R.: Travel distance estimation and storage zone optimization in a 2-block class-based storage strategy warehouse. Int. J. Prod. Res. **43**, 3561–3581 (2005)
3. de Koster, R., Le-Duc, T., Roodbergen, K.J.: Design and control of warehouse order picking: a literature review. Eur. J. Oper. Res. **182**, 481–501 (2007)
4. Karaesmen, F., Dallery, Y.: A performance comparison of pull type control mechanisms for multi-stage manufacturing. Int. J. Prod. Econ. **68**, 59–71 (2000)
5. Liberopoulos, G., Dallery, Y.: A unified framework for pull control mechanisms in multi-stage manufacturing systems. Ann. Oper. Res. **93**, 325–355 (2000). https://doi.org/10.1023/A:1018980024795
6. Nash, M.A., Evans, C.: Warehouse order picking process at pelco products, Inc. In: Proceedings of the 2011 Industrial Engineering Research Conference, Reno, Nevada, USA, pp. 1–8 (2011)
7. Goetschalckx, M., Ashayeri, J.: Classification and design of order picking. Logist. World **2**(2), 99–106 (1989)
8. Grosse, E.H., Glock, C.H., Jaber, M.Y., Neumann, W.P.: Incorporating human factors in order picking planning models: framework and research opportunities. Int. J. Prod. Res. **53**(3), 695–717 (2015)
9. van Gils, T., Caris, A., Ramaekers, K., Braekers, K., de Koster, R.: Designing efficient order picking systems: the effect of real-life features on the relationship among planning problems. Transp. Res. Part E: Logist. Transp. Rev. **125**, 47–73 (2019)
10. James, G., Witten, D., Hastie, T., Tibshirani, R.: An Introduction to Statistical Learning: with Applications in R. Springer Texts in Statistics. Springer, New York (2013). https://doi.org/10.1007/978-1-4614-7138-7

Business Process Management for MES Deployment: Some Lessons from a Bearings Manufacturer Experience

Hervé Verjus[1], Vincent Clivillé[1(✉)], Lamia Berrah[1], Romain Gandia[2], and Claude Chapel[3]

[1] Laboratoire d'Informatique, Systèmes, Traitement de l'Information et de la Connaissance, Université Savoie Mont Blanc, 74940 Annecy, France
{herve.verjus, vincent.cliville, lamia.berrah}@univ-smb.fr

[2] Institute de Recherche en Economie et en Gestion, Université Savoie Mont Blanc, 74940 Annecy, France
romain.gandia@univ-smb.fr

[3] NTN SNR Roulements, 1 rue des Usines, 74010 Annecy, France
claude.chapel@ntn-snr.fr

Abstract. Industrial company's physical production and information systems have to be adapted in the digital transition context from the automatized Industry inherited from the 70's to the Industry 4.0. The information system must namely be completed by the deployment of new software solutions such as the Manufacturing Execution System (MES). Controlling this MES deployment is a critical point where structuring frameworks such as the Business Process Management (BPM) can be a solution. Indeed, the BPM allows managers to deal with the company changes, and allows to control them thanks to an iterative cyclic approach. Moreover, recent developments introducing agility in BPM have enabled it to take into account a high level of uncertainty as well as the promoting of team collaboration. Starting from this idea, this article explores this method in an industrial context given by an aeronautics bearings supplier company. This company is deploying a MES solution for a new high-tech manufacturing plant. After a first informal MES deployment for a pilot plant, the company would like to deploy this MES in a systematic way to all its other plants. Starting from some observations made during the ongoing MES deployment, this paper proposes to explore BPM as a means to assist managers and key users in optimizing the existing knowledge and improving the current practice for its further reuse. Then some recommendations coming from this experience are made for helping companies involved in such a MES deployment.

Keywords: MES deployment · Business process management · Case study

1 Introduction

Digital transition is today a key point for industrial companies [1]. The corresponding challenges concern global sustainability, process reproducibility despite the growing customization, induced manufacturing flexibility, product genealogy management,

© IFIP International Federation for Information Processing 2020
Published by Springer Nature Switzerland AG 2020
B. Lalic et al. (Eds.): APMS 2020, IFIP AICT 591, pp. 433–440, 2020.
https://doi.org/10.1007/978-3-030-57993-7_49

human-sensitivity and responsibility, team collaboration... Thus, companies have to adapt their physical production and information systems according to the innovation possibilities provided by the Industry 4.0 context, while experiencing a high level of uncertainty about the suitability of these innovations [2]. To do this companies have to develop the intermediate level of their information system located between the strategic level ensured by the Enterprise Resource Planning ERP and the operational level ensured by SCADA as shown in the Computer Integrated Manufacturing pyramid. It is the role of the MES as mentioned by the MESA definition: *"The MES delivers information that enables the optimization of production activities from order launch to finished goods. Using current and accurate data, the MES guides, initiates, responds to, and reports on plant activities as they occur. The resulting rapid response to changing conditions, coupled with a focus on reducing non-value-added activities, drives effective plant operations and processes."* [3]. Even though MES is not a recent information system element, there is now a renewed interest in it for numerous companies which are today seeing it as a prerequisite for their digital transition. Thus they have to deploy this system according to more or less precise requirements due to their lack of maturity concerning the digital transition. In this context how can they do this to change in a controlled way? To do this they need a formal framework to anticipate the problems, to control the deployment and to continuously improve the results. By focusing on enterprise processes, BPM [4] can be considered as such a framework. Indeed, it has been applied to other parts of the information system such as the ERP for instance [5]. BPM applied to MES deployment process in a company has not been really documented, very few papers have been published dealing with both MES and BPM approaches [6, 7]. Our idea is that BPM can help to understand the critical MES aspects and to manage its deployment until its further improvements. Moreover, applying agility facet to BPM can be a way for dealing with changes and uncertainties that are generally associated with the operational MES deployment. Agile BPM also allows the company to continuously adapt the deployment given the difficulty to have a complete overview of the problem since the deployment start. As a first step of this association MES-BPM, the proposed approach is based on the analysis of a current industrial practice, namely the one of a bearing manufacturer and aeronautics supplier in its digital transformation. Such an analysis will lead to deduce some lessons and recommendations.

This study subscribes to the general issue of relevance of using information system tools for the manufacturing systems control. In particular, this paper deals with the following question: *"How (agile) BPM does benefit to a MES deployment in a manufacturing company?"* In this sense, this paper is organized as follows. Section 2 presents the BPM general principles with a particular focus on the agility aspects. Then, the testimony of the NTN-SNR company regarding the MES deployment is given Sect. 3. This deployment is thus revisited by BPM and agile BPM. Recommendations and benefits related to agile BPM enactment within MES deployment process are discussed Sect. 4, before concluding on this preliminary work.

2   Business Process Management and Agile BPM

Business process management (BPM) is a discipline in *"operations management in which people use various methods to discover, model, analyze, measure, improve, optimize, and automate business processes"* [8]. There has been a growing interest in BPM during these last decades, because BPM allows to assist organizations to increase productivity, improve operational quality and efficiency or save costs [9]. Business analysts often consider BPM as an *"enabler of enterprise digital transformation"* [10, 11]. Research results in BPM coming from different domains (*i.e.* computer science, management science and information systems) [12], and have proposed a large variety of models, methods and tools that support the design, enactment, management and analysis of business processes.

There are various BPM process lifecycles proposed in the literature [13], most of them being based on the DMEMO (Design, Model, Execute, Monitor, and Optimize) cycle. When unplanned events occur, dynamic feedback from process practitioners is required and process has to be dynamically adapted [14], since DMEMO-based life-cycles are inappropriate. In this case BPM must be adapted, such as the Agile BPM coming from the software development lifecycle management methodology (SDLC). It is an iterative approach where actions are taken in many smaller iterations in all phases in a similar way to the PDCA cycle [15]. Agile BPM promotes collaboration among process stakeholders, multiple iterations resulting in several versions of a given process and tries to avoid organization silos. Agile BPM aims to combine strengths of traditional BPM approaches (process control, process consistency and repeatability, customer satisfaction) and needs for adjusting business processes to a constantly changing context of conditions and customer demands. Agile BPM frameworks are proposed combining pillars from both the Scrum method and BPM [16, 17]. Authors highlighted that *"...the controlling of indicators plays an important part in order to evaluate the changes and from this to derive new follow-up steps. Agility requires continued intensive communication between all participants, creates transparency on the progress, transfers responsibility to the team, forcing radical prioritization"*. In agile BPM the Define, Model and Execute phases can be merged into one, and thus the cycle is divided in a series of smaller development cycles [18]. So this brief review shows that BPM can be adapted when an agile approach is relevant to deal with the addressed problem. Let us now illustrate these ideas through the MES deployment in the NTN-SNR company.

3   The NTN-SNR Case Study

The NTN-SNR company is a bearings supplier for the aeronautics and automotive industry and produces a large variety of bearings in about 15 manufacturing plants. Involved in its digital transition, it had begun with the MES deployment in a traditional project management method in a pilot plant. From this first experience's limits (delay, lack of functionalities, over budget, non-quality), company wished to control the further plant MES deployment thanks to BPM. In order to do this, key users and managers were interviewed in order to *a posteriori* infer the BPM from their first deployment using the BPMN 2.0 models[1] (due to the complexity of such models, they cannot be detailed in this paper). Figure 1 shows the MES macro-process deployment model.

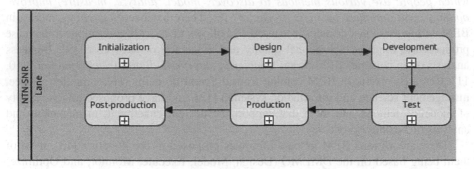

Fig. 1. The MES deployment macro-process model.

Figure 2 details a Production phase sub-process fragment with back and forth between MES software editor and NTN-SNR. The overall macro-process reveals a traditional (sequential) engineering process revealing two main lacks: it is less efficient than concurrent engineering such as the SDLC [20], results are unpredictable knowing that BPMN 2.0 cannot anticipate the diversity of situations that may arise.

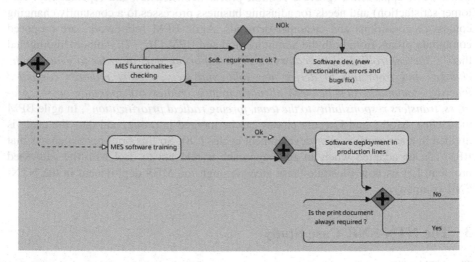

Fig. 2. Back and force between the NTN-SNR company and the software editor (extract of a BPMN 2.0 process fragment of the AS-IS Production activity).

---

[1] BPMN 2.0 is an ISO standard notation for process modeling [19].

BPM exposes another problem concerning relationships between the MES software editor and the NTN-SNR teams: during the deployment process, editor had to adapt and improve the software several times in response to NTN-SNR needs. There were numerous unplanned and unanticipated demands that were empirically managed, resulting in delays, with time consuming and unsatisfactory situations. According to this diagnosis, BPM shows that the MES deployment process should be considered as a flexible process which must be dealt in an agile way.

4 Recommendations and Benefits

Some recommendations and benefits can be seen as a consequence of this industrial practice: the MES deployment in the aeronautics plant and its analysis, and though the use of agile BPM. These recommendations resulting from our work are listed in Table 1 and permit to answer to the question *"How (agile) BPM does benefit to a MES deployment in a manufacturing company?"*.

Table 1. Proposed recommendations and benefits.

Recommendation benefit	Details
Consider process modeling	The process modeling will help the company for knowledge capturing, process standardization: processes can be more robust, optimized and reproductible, and also help teams in understanding the entire process, favoring uses to be agreed upon in the required activities, necessary resources, assets, collaboration between actors, etc.
Consider the TO-BE process as an agile process	Deployment process has to integrate agility principles using management precepts of the Scrum method. Knowing the strong background of NTN-SNR IT unit in the Scrum, this agile method must be considered as a framework for the MES deployment process. MES design, development, test, production and post-production phases (see Fig. 2) must be managed, using itcrative Scrum workflows (product backlog, sprint planning, daily Scrum, sprint review, sprint retrospective, backlog refinement). Moreover, the team must be organized according to the Scrum roles (*i.e.* product owner, development team, Scrum master)
Consider the BPM lifecycles diversity	Agile BPM approach [18] is well adapted for dealing with unanticipated, unplanned and unknown situations. By merging the Model, Define and Execute phases, agile BPM may facilitate relationships between NTN-SNR and the MES software editor, and the alignment between the

(continued)

Table 1. (*continued*)

Recommendation benefit	Details
	NTN-SNR IT and manufacturing services. Once the first deployment instance is sufficiently improved, other process instances will be started, each corresponding to a specific NTN-SNR plant. For these other processes, it will be probably better to follow the traditional BPM lifecycle
Consider globally the organization and human resources management	Agile BPM enables team collaboration, increases actors' responsibilities and implication, develops new actors' skills and knowledge. Applying agile BPM in a MES deployment process will also avoid silos; instead, agile BPM facilitates the convergence between the manufacturing, the IT and the organization management services. Agile BPM may also help in enacting some liberated company aspects in a traditional and hierarchical company
Consider the norms and standards enactment	BPM and BPMN are key factors favoring continuous improvement [21], ISO/IEC 19510:2013 when MES is a means for the ISA 95 implementation that allows to control manufacturing by exploiting real-time manufacturing data. Combining these two aspects promotes agility, flexibility and adaptability of the company required for the context changes and the customer satisfaction improvement according to the current standards
(Re) Consider process description languages	Introducing flexibility in MES deployment is a key issue. BPMN is not suitable when agility is mandatory and for processes that work in environments where participants have a large autonomy. Thus, other process description languages may be more relevant (*i.e.* CMMN [22], Declare [23], pi-Diapason [24]) and be used either in conjunction with BPMN, or as BPMN replacement

From these recommendations, the company can now deploy the MES to the other manufacturing plants, avoiding past mistakes and being able to control this deployment.

5   Concluding Remarks

The renewed interest for the MES, viewed as a prerequisite of digital transition, leads companies to deploy it to address both customer and manufacturing company expectations which are new. This paper presents some recommendations that should benefit to companies engaged in a MES deployment process; these recommendations are the contribution of this case study analysis and they invite companies to consider both BPM and agile BPM as a means for assisting them in their MES deployment processes.

Very few similar works address both BPM and MES deployment in a manufacturing company. Based on our study and analysis, we believe that agile BPM for MES deployment may be a new trend for digitally aware manufacturing companies. In this perspective, some prerequisites are necessary: (1) the manufacturing company is aware of BPM and agile methods, (2) the MES software editor has to be implicated in the MES deployment process, and has agreed to act as a very close partner in an agile spirit; (3) manufacturing company is ready to move forward to a less hierarchical organization, encouraging collaboration and task sharing between teams, and (4) manufacturing company employee positions are involved, with more autonomy and responsibility. It is then challenging to consider and manage both the needs of flexibility in processes and organization, and the needs of process standardization.

Acknowledgments.   The authors would like to thank Ms Selcan Buba, Ms Ophélie Gaucher and Mr Théophile Trouvé, Master's students at the Université Savoie Mont-Blanc for their contribution to the NTN-SNR deployment process, BPMN modeling and NTN-SNR employee interviews.

References

1. Kagermann, H., Wahlster, W., Helbig, J.: Recommendations for implementing the strategic initiative Industrie 4.0 – securing the future of german manufacturing industry. Final report of the industrie 4.0 working group, acatech – National Academy of Science and Engineering, München (2013)
2. Oztemel, E., Gursev, S.: Literature review of Industry 4.0 and related technologies. J. Intell. Manuf. **31**, 127–182 (2018). https://doi.org/10.1007/s10845-018-1433-8
3. MESA, MES explained: A High Level Vision, White paper #6. MESA International (1997)
4. BPM Resource Center Homepage. http://www.what-is-bpm.com/get_started/bpm_methodology.html. Accessed 1 Apr 2020
5. Kraljić, T., Kraljić, A.: Process driven ERP implementation: business process management approach to ERP implementation. In: Johansson, B., Møller, C., Chaudhuri, A., Sudzina, F. (eds.) BIR 2017. LNBIP, vol. 295, pp. 108–122. Springer, Cham (2017). https://doi.org/10.1007/978-3-319-64930-6_8
6. Kannengiesser, U., Neubauer, M., Heininger, R.: Integrating business processes and manufacturing operations based on S-BPM and B2MML. In: Proceedings of the 8th International Conference on Subject-Oriented Business Process Management, pp. 1–10. ACM Press, Erlangen (2016). https://doi.org/10.1145/2882879.2882881

7. Michalik, P., Štofa, J., Zolotová, I.: The use of BPMN for modelling the MES level in information and control systems. QIP J. **17**, 39–47 (2013). https://doi.org/10.12776/qip. v17i1.68
8. van der Aalst, W., van Hee, K.M.: Workflow management: models, methods, and systems. ISBN 0262011891, 9780262011891 (2002)
9. van der Aalst, W.M.P.: Business process management: a comprehensive survey. ISRN Software Engineering, pp. 1–137 (2013)
10. CIO Homepage. https://www.cio.com/article/3176077/why-bpm-is-now-taking-a-central-role-in-digital-transformation.html. Accessed 01 Apr 2020
11. Fischer, M., Imgrund, F., Janiesch, C., Winkelmann, A.: Strategy archetypes for digital transformation: defining meta objectives using business process management. Inf. Manag. **57**, 103262 (2020). https://doi.org/10.1016/j.im.2019.103262
12. van der Aalst, W.M.P., ter Hofstede, A.H.M., Weske, M.: Business process management: a survey. In: van der Aalst, W.M.P., Weske, M. (eds.) BPM 2003. LNCS, vol. 2678, pp. 1–12. Springer, Heidelberg (2003). https://doi.org/10.1007/3-540-44895-0_1
13. Szelągowski, M.: Evolution of the BPM lifecycle. Presented at the 2018 Federated Conference on Computer Science and Information Systems, pp. 205–211 (2018). https://doi. org/10.15439/2018F46
14. Verjus, H., Pourraz, F., Fakhfakh, N.: Cadre conceptuel pour la modélisation et la supervision d'architectures à base de services. Une approche pour l'ingénierie des SI à base de services. Développement des SI à base de modèles: exigence, traçabilité et co-conception - Ingénierie des Systèmes d'Information - Revue des sciences et technologies de l'information (RSTI-ISI) **16**, 43–72 (2011). https://doi.org/10.3166/isi.16.5.43-72
15. Deming, E.: Out of the Crisis. MIT Press, Cambridge (1982)
16. Thiemich, C., Puhlmann, F.: An agile BPM project methodology. In: Daniel, F., Wang, J., Weber, B. (eds.) BPM 2013. LNCS, vol. 8094, pp. 291–306. Springer, Heidelberg (2013). https://doi.org/10.1007/978-3-642-40176-3_25
17. Paschek, D., Rennung, F., Trusculescu, A., Draghici, A.: Corporate development with agile business process modeling as a key success factor. Procedia Comput. Sci. **100**, 1168–1175 (2016). https://doi.org/10.1016/j.procs.2016.09.273
18. Bider, I., Jalali, A.: Agile business process development: why, how and when—applying Nonaka's theory of knowledge transformation to business process development. Inf. Syst. E-Bus. Manag **14**, 693–731 (2016). https://doi-org.camphrier-1.grenet.fr/10.1007/s10257-014-0256-1
19. ISO/IEC. ISO. https://www.iso.org/cms/render/live/en/sites/isoorg/contents/data/standard/ 06/26/62652.html. Accessed 1 Apr 2020
20. Taylor, J.: Managing information technology projects, p. 39 (2004)
21. ISO 9001:2015 ISO. https://www.iso.org/cms/render/live/en/sites/isoorg/contents/data/ standard/06/20/62085.html. Accessed 1 Apr 2020
22. OMG, CMMN 1.1 (2016). https://www.omg.org/cmmn/
23. Pesic, M., Schonenberg, H., van der Aalst, W.M.P.: DECLARE: full support for loosely-structured processes. In: 11th IEEE International Enterprise Distributed Object Computing Conference, p. 287 (2007). https://doi.org/10.1109/EDOC.2007.14
24. Pourraz, F., Verjus, H.: Diapason: an engineering environment for designing, enacting and evolving service-oriented architectures. In: International Conference on Software Engineering Advances (ICSEA 2007), pp. 23–30. IEEE Computer Society, France (2007)

An Application of a DSML in Industry 4.0 Production Processes

Marko Vještica[1]([⊠]) [iD], Vladimir Dimitrieski[1] [iD], Milan Pisarić[2] [iD],
Slavica Kordić[1] [iD], Sonja Ristić[1] [iD], and Ivan Luković[1] [iD]

[1] University of Novi Sad, Faculty of Technical Sciences, Novi Sad, Serbia
{marko.vjestica,dimitrieski,slavica,
sdristic,ivan}@uns.ac.rs
[2] Industrial Automation, KEBA AG, Linz, Austria
pisa@keba.com

Abstract. One of the goals of Industry 4.0 is to enable mass customization of products and to satisfy specific needs of customers. This goal is often hard to achieve in traditional manufacturing systems. To enable fast production changes, an automatic and flexible production is needed. In this context we propose a Model-Driven Software Development (MDSD) approach and a Domain-Specific Modeling Language (DSML) to model production processes. The language supports two levels of abstraction. A Master-Level (ML) model is used by a process designer to model process steps. A Detail-Level (DL) model is used by Orchestrator, a cluster of industrial computers that manages production, to fill existing ML models with a specification of production logistic and smart resources. A code generator is used to generate machine-readable or human-readable instructions from DL models. Generated code is used for automatic execution of production processes within a simulation or a shop floor. In this paper we provide an application of a DSML, which is capable of modeling production processes that are ready for automatic code generation.

Keywords: Production process modeling · Domain-Specific Modeling Languages · Model-Driven Software Engineering · Industry 4.0 · Process execution

1 Introduction

Industry 4.0 aims to establish a flexible production in the traditional manufacturing [1], moving from mass production to mass customization [2]. Introducing variability to the production process in traditional manufacturing systems requires either stopping the production to reconfigure machines or having multiple production lines for every product variant. To achieve aimed production flexibility, production process variability need to be enabled during manufacturing, without a need to stop the production [3]. Thus, a customized product's price could be lower, as one of the key aspects of the mass customization is to provide products with prices that are near to mass production prices [4]. In order to establish production flexibility at the lower cost and to enable automatic production, we proposed a Model-Driven Software Development (MDSD)

© IFIP International Federation for Information Processing 2020
Published by Springer Nature Switzerland AG 2020
B. Lalic et al. (Eds.): APMS 2020, IFIP AICT 591, pp. 441–448, 2020.
https://doi.org/10.1007/978-3-030-57993-7_50

approach to model and automate the execution of production processes [5]. The overview of the approach is given in Fig. 1 and described in short below.

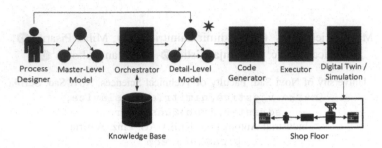

Fig. 1. The proposed MDSD approach

In the presented MDSD approach, a process designer uses a Domain-Specific Modeling Language (DSML) to specify production processes. This production process specification is a technical description of a production process, which we call a Master-Level (ML) model. It includes specification of: (i) process steps, (ii) required capabilities, i.e. skills to execute the step, (iii) input and output products, i.e. transformed resources like raw materials, components or finished goods, (iv) constraints and (v) capability parameters. In order to use such a production process model for automatic code generation and execution, additional information needs to be added. This information includes: (i) specific smart resources, e.g. storage, machines, robots and humans, which execute process steps, (ii) logistic information for product and resource movement and (iii) configuration tasks of smart resources, e.g. software setup, changing grippers, plugging into a charger or a workstation. This enrichment is automatically performed by Orchestrator and we denote the enriched process model as a Detail-Level (DL) model. It is up to process designers to either mark the process model for execution or perform manual interventions and optimization where they deem necessary.

Orchestrator is a software run on top of a cluster of industrial computers that is able to orchestrate smart resources and assign them to process steps for their execution [6]. It also needs to detect and configure new smart resources or reconfigure existing ones [7]. Each process step is specified with a required capability, a skill required to execute the process step. On the other hand, each resource offers a set of capabilities, i.e. skills it is able to perform. Using a knowledge base and the required and offered capabilities, Orchestrator is able to identify smart resources which are able to execute specific process steps. It is also able to identify storages that contain required products and process steps that need to be changed or added, e.g. transportation or machine configuration process steps, in order to execute the production process with the available resources. A DL model is used by the code generator to automatically generate instructions that are to be performed by humans or machines. The executor sends generated instructions to the digital twin that comprises both the simulation and the command proxies to the shop floor. In our case, the digital twin can be used as the simulation only or it can forward instruction to shop floor smart resources via the built-in proxies.

As a DSML is an integral part of the proposed MDSD approach which aims to improve flexibility and automation of a factory, and as no appropriate DSML has been found for modeling all the aspects of a production process, we decided to create a new one which fits this need. In this paper we present basic concepts of the proposed DSML that is used to model production processes. In this paper an application of this DSML in an assembly use case is presented. The DSML is used by domain experts to model production processes using familiar, domain concepts. This should result in faster, easier and comprehensive modeling of production processes which are suitable for automatic execution that yields less faults. Using the DSML within our MDSD approach should also improve the manufacturing flexibility and the level of overall automation of production.

Apart from Introduction, this paper is structured as follows. An overview of the related work is presented in Sect. 2. Basic concepts of the proposed DSML for production process modeling and an assembly production use case are described in Sect. 3. Conclusions and future work are given in Sect. 4.

2 Related Work

Modeling production processes in Industry 4.0 is an important industrial informatics research topic [8], as production processes are digitally supported, and they need to be integrated with Cyber-Physical Production Systems [9].

There are many process modeling languages, but most of them are neither tailored for production processes, nor ready to model execution-ready production processes. There is the manufacturing process chart standard named KS A 3002 [10], however it lacks a tooling support for modeling and automatic execution [11]. Companies often utilize process charts or Bill of Materials (BOM) specifications, but none of them can fully describe production processes that could be automatically executed. BOM specifications are not sufficient to understand a production flow [11]. Bill of Materials and Operations (BOMO) specifications include the production flow, but cannot specify the selection and iteration patterns or smart resources.

Conceptual process modeling languages like Business Process Modeling and Notation (BPMN), Unified Modeling Language (UML) Activity Diagram, Petri Nets and Event-Driven Process Chains usually cannot support the material flow concept, which makes modeling production processes very difficult. To model production processes, BPMN extensions have been created [12], but a depiction of material flow is still hard to achieve [13] and there was an absence of uniformity [11]. Also, BPMN extensions were created for production process similarity measurements [11], but it is not possible to model selection or iteration patterns or smart resources. Using Systems Modeling Language (SysML) or Petri Nets to model production processes usually lack to model complex production processes or the material flow. To overcome usual lack of the material flow concept, a new material flow-oriented process modeling language – GRAMOSA has been created using UML profiles, but the material flow-oriented approach was complex [13]. Some languages lack production logistic specifications like DELMIA Process Engineer (DPE), while others are limited to simple linear process sequences like Value Stream Design (VSD) [13]. We have identified the lack of a modeling language capable to specify all relevant aspects of a production process in the context of its formal definition suitable for automatic execution. That is the main reason why we have decided to create a new DSML instead of applying an existing one in our MDSD approach. The main goal of introducing such a DSML is to improve the production process flexibility and to enable formal specification of production processes that will allow automatic generation of program code aimed at automation of process execution.

3   Application of the DSML in an Assembly Use Case

In our previous work [5], we discussed a DSML usage for modeling production processes in Industry 4.0. We also identified concepts that must be supported by a DSML for production processes modeling that will enable automatic code generation and execution from such models. In this section, we present a use case to demonstrate the application of the developed DSML. For each DSML concept we provide an example of its use in the presented use case. The language is created by using Ecore meta-meta-model, while the graphical syntax and the modeling tool are created by using Eclipse Sirius. Concepts of the graphical syntax are presented on the left side of Fig. 2.

The presented use case describes an assembly process of a custom LEGO flag. The process is modeled by our DSML and the model is then passed for code generation which is executed both in the simulation and on the shop floor. Bricks of various colors are stored in a smart shelf while a human worker and an industrial mobile robot pick different bricks in parallel and assemble the flag on a brick pedestal at an assembly table. A human worker is using a tablet or a smart watch in order to receive instructions and to send feedback when an activity is finished.

Our DSML supports modeling at two levels of abstraction in order to make the modeling easier for process designers. They are creating higher-level abstraction models, i.e. ML models. An ML model can be extended with additional specifications of execution details. In that way a DL model, at a lower level of abstraction, is created. Execution details can be added to an ML model manually or automatically by means of Orchestrator, as it is illustrated in Fig. 1. Based on these two abstraction levels, we have classified the language elements into two groups: (i) elements that are needed to model ML production processes and (ii) elements that are needed to be added into existing ML models to create DL models. The ML model of our LEGO use case is presented in the central part of Fig. 2, while the DL model is presented on the right side of Fig. 2.

At the higher level of abstraction, process designers model process steps that denote either an operation or an inspection activity. A process step can include (i) an input product, that can be e.g. raw material or component, and that can be picked from a storage or is a result of the previous process step, (ii) a capability, i.e. skill required to execute the step and (iii) an output product, which is a result of executed capability on the input product and is either placed in a storage or transferred to the next process step. Every product and capability can have constraints, e.g. width, height, color, which are considered by Orchestrator when it decides which resources are able to perform a process step. Some capabilities require parameters to be specified e.g. position must be specified in order to place a brick on a brick pedestal. Also, a material flow can be specified by defining if a product needs to be picked from a storage, placed to a storage,

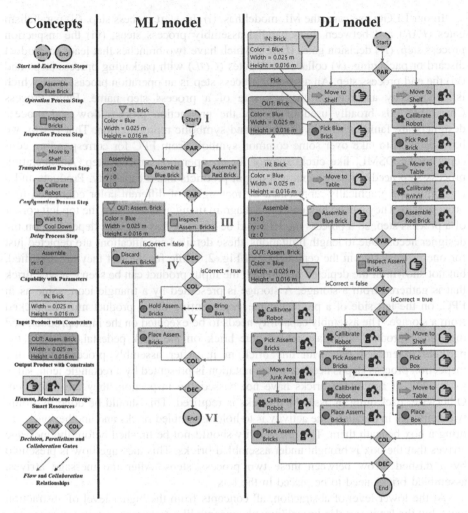

Fig. 2. A production process model example

or it is a result of the previous process step. As specified process steps need to be connected using relationships – links between process steps, the language has a concept to model a workflow. Process steps can be connected so as to form a sequence or a set of parallel workflow branches. Additionally, selection and iteration patterns can be also added to the workflow. For this purpose, we are using a gate concept – a modeling concept that is used to connect multiple workflow branches. The language also supports a message flow, i.e. collaboration of resources. This concept is used if two or more process steps need to be executed in parallel, but one process step must not finish its activity or start the next one before it gets a message that another process step finished its activity. Using described concepts, a process designer can be focused only on process steps that must be executed and need not to worry about production logistic and resources that will execute the process steps.

In our LEGO use case, the ML model has: (i) the start process step, (ii) parallelism gates (*PAR*) and between them parallel assembly process steps, (iii) the inspection process step, (iv) decision gates (*DEC*), which have two branches that leads to product discard or packaging, (v) collaboration gates (*COL*) with packaging process steps and (vi) the end process step. An assembly process step is an operation process step, which is denoted by a circle on the left side of a process step name. Flow Process Chart (FPC) is broadly used to specify the production process flow and process designers are familiar with its graphical and symbolic representation. That is why we have decided to take over some common symbols from FPC for corresponding concepts in the DSML, like circle symbol for an operation process step. An operation process step needs to have input and output products and a capability. Products and a capability are graphically represented by rectangles of different color connected to a process step. They can be hidden from a diagram using a ± button at the top left corner of a process step, so a process model could be more or less complex depending on the designer needs. Due to length limitations, these detailed specifications are depicted just for one process step in the central part of Fig. 2, while for the rest they are specified, but not shown. In the depicted ML model, the input product can be seen – a blue brick that is gathered from a storage. A storage is presented by a triangle icon, same as in FPC, on the left side of a product name, representing that a product must be picked from a storage. The assembly capability needs to be executed on the input product, and the output product is the assembled blue brick on the brick pedestal, basically the partially assembled flag with this brick in it. After assembly process steps, the inspection process step is needed, which notation is presented by a rectangle icon, same as in FPC. If assembled bricks have not passed the inspection, they are discarded. Otherwise, packaging of assembled bricks is required. This should be done by doing two activities in parallel. One activity is to hold assembled bricks and another one is to bring a box beneath them. The first activity should not be finished before the message arrives that the box is brought under assembled bricks. This message flow is presented by a dashed arrow between these two process steps. After the message arrives, assembled bricks need to be placed in the box.

At the lower level of abstraction, all concepts from the higher level of abstraction exist, but the language also has additional concepts like resources, specific storages and new process step representations. Orchestrator uses these concepts to fill existing ML models with production logistics and smart resources. At this level, process steps can also represent activities like transportation, configuration, i.e. calibration of machines, or delay, i.e. necessary waiting. A specific storage must be defined for every input product that must be gathered from a storage and for every output product that must be placed in a storage. Process steps additionally have a resource that will execute a capability on input products. A resource can be a human worker or a machine. This is important information especially for code generation. For every process step human-readable or machine-readable instructions will be generated, depending on the provided information. Using all presented concepts, production process models are ready for code generation and consequently for an execution.

In the LEGO use case, we present in detail only one "pick" and one "assemble" process step of the DL model. Other process steps are expanded in a similar way. One assembly process step is assigned to a human worker, and another is assigned to a mobile robot. Both human worker and mobile robot must execute additional transportation process steps in order to pick a brick from the smart shelf and place it on the assembly table. In contrast to the human worker, the mobile robot in this use case needs to execute additional configuration process steps after transportation. The mobile robot is not equipped with the machine vision modules and therefore it must be calibrated after each movement to determine its position. Transportation and configuration process step notations are presented by an arrow, same as in FPC, and a gear wheel icon respectively. These process steps only include a capability, without products. The input product of the "pick" process step has the specific storage, i.e. the smart shelf, added by Orchestrator. Its output product is the same picked product. The input product of the "assemble" process step is the output product from the "pick" process step, which means it does not have to be gathered from a storage. Its output product is the brick, which will be assembled at the specific storage, i.e. the assembly table.

Using the DL model, it is possible to generate instructions to both mobile robot and human worker. The executor sends instructions to the mobile robot or the human worker and waits for their response. Once a resource completes an activity, the next one is sent. The process is finished after the execution reaches the end process step.

4 Conclusions and Future Work

In this paper we presented an application of the developed DSML for modeling production processes in an assembly use case and described its basic concepts. This language is used as one of the main elements of the MDSD approach that aims to improve the flexibility and the automation level of production. The DSML can be used to (i) make faster and more precise process designs, (ii) make less faults during process design, (iii) enable faster changes of production process models in the era of Industry 4.0 and (iv) model a human-machine interaction. Also, the DSML models are used by Orchestrator to manage the production, as it is important to plan process activities and integrate processes within the industrial system [14].

The language has been evaluated by process designers on the shop floor within a small-scale industrial production setup. We plan to further evaluate the language in additional industrial use cases and also by independent researches and process designers in order to improve the domain concept coverage and the tooling stability. Also, we plan to further investigate related research and provide a systematic literature review on production process modeling and execution.

Although a lot of concepts identified in [5] were already implemented in the presented DSML, there are additional concepts that can be added in order to improve the language domain coverage, like: (i) unordered sets of process steps, (ii) quality assurance with completion and acceptance criteria, (iii) error handling flows, (iv) process variations and (v) sub-processes. Also, we plan to implement a new modeling tool feature to monitor execution of every process step and thus enable detection of delays or badly modeled process steps. Finally, ML and DL models could be generated from existing product specification formats, like Computer Aided Design (CAD) models.

Acknowledgment. The research in this paper is supported by KEBA AG Linz.

References

1. Lu, Y.: Industry 4.0: a survey on technologies, applications and open research issues. J. Ind. Inf. Integr. **6**, 1–10 (2017). https://doi.org/10.1016/j.jii.2017.04.005
2. Crnjac, M., Veža, I., Banduka, N.: From concept to the introduction of Industry 4.0. Int. J. Ind. Eng. Manag. **8**, 21–30 (2017)
3. Dorofeev, K., Profanter, S., Cabral, J., Ferreira, P., Zoitl, A.: Agile operational behavior for the control-level devices in plug & produce production environments. In: Proceedings of 24th IEEE International Conference on Emerging Technologies and Factory Automation (ETFA), pp. 49–56. IEEE, Zaragoza (2019)
4. Zhao, H., McLoughlin, L., Adzhiev, V., Pasko, A.: "Why do we not buy mass customised products?" – An investigation of consumer purchase intention of mass customised products. Int. J. Ind. Eng. Manag. **10**, 181–190 (2019). https://doi.org/10.24867/IJIEM-2019-2-238
5. Vještica, M., Dimitrieski, V., Pisarić, M., Kordić, S., Ristić, S., Luković, I.: Towards a formal description and automatic execution of production processes. In: Proceedings of 2019 IEEE 15th International Scientific Conference on Informatics, pp. 463–468. IEEE, Poprad (2019). https://doi.org/10.1109/Informatics47936.2019.9119314
6. Keddis, N.: Capability-based system-aware planning and scheduling of workflows for adaptable manufacturing systems (2016)
7. Pisarić, M., Dimitrieski, V., Babić, M., Veselinović, S., Dušić, F.: Towards a plug-and-play architecture in Industry 4.0. In: Proceedings of 17th International Scientific Conference on Industrial Systems (IS'17), Novi Sad, Serbia, pp. 136–141 (2017)
8. Xu, L.D.: Enterprise systems: state-of-the-art and future trends. IEEE Trans. Ind. Inform. **7**, 630–640 (2011). https://doi.org/10.1109/TII.2011.2167156
9. Xu, L.D., Xu, E.L., Li, L.: Industry 4.0: state of the art and future trends. Int. J. Prod. Res. **56**, 2941–2962 (2018). https://doi.org/10.1080/00207543.2018.1444806
10. Korean Standards Service Network (KSSN): KS A 3002 Standard. https://www.kssn.net/en/. Accessed 05 Apr 2020
11. Ahn, H., Chang, T.-W.: Measuring similarity for manufacturing process models. In: Moon, I., Lee, G.M., Park, J., Kiritsis, D., von Cieminski, G. (eds.) APMS 2018. IAICT, vol. 536, pp. 223–231. Springer, Cham (2018). https://doi.org/10.1007/978-3-319-99707-0_28
12. Zor, S., Schumm, D., Leymann, F.: A proposal of BPMN extensions for the manufacturing domain. In: Proceedings of the 44th CIRP International Conference on Manufacturing Systems, Madison, Wisconsin, USA, pp. 1–7 (2011)
13. Lütjen, M., Rippel, D.: GRAMOSA framework for graphical modelling and simulation-based analysis of complex production processes. Int. J. Adv. Manuf. Technol. **81**, 171–181 (2015). https://doi.org/10.1007/s00170-015-7037-y
14. Stevanov, B., Gračanin, D., Kesić, I., Ristić, S.: An application of period batch control principles and computational independent models for supporting the overhaul process of the railway braking devices. Int. J. Ind. Eng. Manag. **4**, 95–101 (2013)

Towards an Industry-Applicable Design Methodology for Developing Reconfigurable Manufacturing

Alessia Napoleone[1][(✉)] ⓘ, Ann-Louise Andersen[1] ⓘ,
Thomas Ditlev Brunoe[1] ⓘ, Kjeld Nielsen[1] ⓘ, Simon Boldt[2] ⓘ,
Carin Rösiö[2] ⓘ, and David Grube Hansen[3] ⓘ

[1] Department of Materials and Production,
Aalborg University, Aalborg, Denmark
alna@mp.aau.dk
[2] Department of Industrial Product Development, Production and Design,
Jönköping University, Jönköping, Sweden
[3] Department of Technology, Entrepreneurship and Innovation,
University of Southern Denmark, Sonderborg, Denmark

Abstract. The concept of the Reconfigurable Manufacturing System (RMS) was introduced for the first time almost 20 years ago as a new manufacturing system concept with functionality and capacity being dynamically changeable through modularity, integrability, diagnosability, and customization. Since its introduction, the RMS concept has been extensively researched from various perspectives and new trends are today increasing its relevance. This research revisits the current status of both RMS research - in terms of research domains and trends - and RMS practice - in terms of potentialities and limitations towards broad industry application. Based on this, a design methodology in four steps is proposed and, to ensure its industry-applicability, the existence or lack of tools for each step is summarized as a basis for future research developments.

Keywords: Reconfigurable Manufacturing System · Changeable manufacturing · Reconfigurability · Design methodology

1 Introduction

The concept of the Reconfigurable Manufacturing System (RMS) was initially introduced by Koren in the late 1990's with the aim of providing capacity and functionality on demand and as an intermediate paradigm between the Dedicated Manufacturing System (DMS) with rigid structures and high efficiency and the Flexible Manufacturing System (FMS) with high in-built a-priori flexibility [1]. Today, the concept both maintains and increases its relevance in education, research and practice [2–4]. Furthermore, new and additional competitive factors going beyond rapid responsiveness and lower cost motivates RMS in today's manufacturing environment [5], e.g. in relation to environmental performance aspects such as recycling, de-manufacturing and

© IFIP International Federation for Information Processing 2020
Published by Springer Nature Switzerland AG 2020
B. Lalic et al. (Eds.): APMS 2020, IFIP AICT 591, pp. 449–456, 2020.
https://doi.org/10.1007/978-3-030-57993-7_51

re-manufacturing [6, 7] and in regard to implementation of smart manufacturing and industry 4.0 related technologies [3, 8]. Therefore, this research revisits the RMS paradigm from both academic and practice perspectives. In particular, the contribution focuses on: (i) outlining dominant research domains and trends in relation to reconfigurability, (ii) evaluating current relevance and limitations of industry application, and based on this (iii) proposing a four-step RMS design methodology to aid the wider industry transition and provide a basis for future research developments.

2 RMS in Research: Dominant Research Domains and Trends

Since the RMS concept was coined, RMS and "reconfigurability" – or equivalently "changeability" at factory and firm levels - have received broad attention in research.

2.1 The Two Domains of Research on RMS

Overall, there are two domains covered by literature; these are: (i) the design and (ii) the operations (and management) of such systems. Examples of research on RMS design include design methodologies [9, 10], economic evaluation of reconfigurability [11, 12], design of reconfigurable machines [13], reconfigurability characteristics and their implementation [14], and identification and modelling of platforms as a foundation for reconfigurability [15, 16]. Operational issues include process plan generation for reconfigurable systems [17, 18], configuration selection problems [19, 20], reconfiguration management [21] and scalability planning [22, 23].

In their traditional interpretation, RMSs are highly automated systems composed of CNC machines and/or Reconfigurable Machine Tools. More recently, RMSs have been more extensively interpreted as systems enabled by a multitude of aspects that can be designed and operationalized in a vast array of company and context specific forms [4, 24].

Literature reviews have also been conducted (e.g. [3, 25]) remarking that both the design and operation domains need further research. The main conclusion similar in all reviews is the need for practical guidelines driving industrial companies in the transition toward the RMS paradigm. Indeed, the implementation of RMS is still an open issue to the manufacturing professionals [25]. Case studies and best practices efficiently driving the transition of modern industrial companies toward RMS are needed [3].

2.2 Reasons for the Increase of Interest in RMS

There are two additional reasons for RMS to keep and increase its theoretical importance around 20 years since the introduction: (i) its relevance to deal with the paramount need for manufacturing companies to consider sustainability issues [7, 26] and (ii) the potentialities represented by the inclusion of more recent digital technologies into the RMS paradigm [27, 28]. Regarding sustainability, higher reconfigurability of manufacturing systems leads to better environmental and economic performance, as well as to reduce the energy consumption [3]. RMSs are emerging as one of the most popular manufacturing strategies to achieve sustainable manufacturing [7]. Indeed, RMSs can achieve high system sustainability thanks to their capability of producing multiple generations of products [5].

Regarding digital technologies, recent development of advanced diagnostics and cyber physical manufacturing systems can facilitate the design and operations of RMS [5]; Cyber-Physical Systems have been proposed in the manufacturing area as suitable technologies for supporting rapid reconfiguration and system evolution at shop floor level [27]. Despite the interesting insights, there is still a lack of literature focusing on the synergic relationship between RMS and Cyber-Physical Systems [3].

3 RMS in Practice: Potentials and Limitations

The authors of this paper have previously conducted a survey [29] of manufacturing companies, analyzing the potential of implementing RMS, as well as the barriers towards this. The general conclusion of this study was that few of the companies had skills and competences in place for developing RMS. Some differences were identified in terms of the readiness for developing reconfigurability in the different cases, which seemed to relate to which industry they were operating within, where electronics manufacturing seemed to have the highest degree of coordination between product design and manufacturing system design, which is essential when developing RMS. Furthermore, applying a long-term view when planning manufacturing system development and economically justifying them was observed in some companies but not others. The presence of enablers of reconfigurability was also analyzed. Generally, most companies had only few or none enablers present. Also, the companies generally recognized that their current level of the enablers was lower than what was actually needed to achieve the desired level of reconfigurability. The presence of specific enablers depended somewhat on different characteristics of the companies.

In another more recent study from the same authors, eight different cases were analyzed, addressing companies that were currently doing development or implementation of reconfigurability [30]. This study analyzed the potentials in doing reconfigurability across the cases. In all cases it was found that reconfigurability did in fact hold a potential, however, on different levels and time frames. For example, low volume, high variety tended to have more potential in operational reconfigurations on short term, whereas higher volumes tended to have more potential on tactical and strategic level for reconfigurability. Due to these differences, the enablers that would enable reconfigurability in the different cases were also widely different. This clearly influences how reconfigurability should be developed in these companies, and contributes to the point that not one generic set of enablers can be applied to all companies, and thus not one single RMS development methodology can be applied to all companies, and therefore a context dependent method should be introduced.

4 Towards a Design Methodology

As both research and practice suggest the need for practical and context dependent guidelines driving industrial companies in the transition toward the RMS paradigm, a RMS design methodology is proposed in this section.

The suggested methodology is based on a generic design methodology provided by Andersen et al. [2], which has been chosen for two reasons: (i) it is academically relevant, as it is built based on literature and (ii) also it attempts to support practitioners, providing a mapping of the different design challenges, suggested procedures, and applicable tools. The suggested RMS design methodology involves four steps consisting in several activities as shown in the figure below (Fig. 1); to ensure its applicability in industry, in each step, specific tools should be provided. In this section, some representative tools available in literature have been associated to individual steps and those not covered by specific tools have been identified as needing further research. The methodology is described in the remainder.

Step 1. Classification of Potential and Goals. This step covers planning and making strategic decisions about the development project. A major challenge in this step is the life-cycle perspective and the uncertain nature of predictions [2]. Scenario analysis should allow for getting insight into the real-market uncertainties, by considering market demand stochastically and not deterministically [25]. The definition and monitoring of KPIs based on measures of characteristics of reconfigurability could support the evaluation of system structural performance [31, 32]. To quantify the potential in RMS compared to conventional manufacturing systems, scenario analysis and participatory approaches should aim at involving firms in the definition of future production requirements and the corresponding most suitable manufacturing paradigms [9, 14]. For each consistent scenario of the future, the projected factory should be analysed to draw conclusions about the evolution of the objects in the factory and their cost-effectiveness [33]. Requirements should be well analysed and described, also recurring to conventional planning tools (e.g. requirements list) [34]. Finally, to prioritize objectives and requirements, the Analytical Hierarchy Processing method could be used [10, 35].

Step 2. Development of Concept for Reconfigurable Production. At this stage, decisions should ensure that both product and manufacturing processes are designed for reconfigurability and that the two designs are adequately related with each other. In recent years, digitalization throughout the entire Product Lifecycle has allowed manufacturing companies for significant coordination gains between product and production system design, holding the potential of elevating companies to reach new levels of reconfigurability. One of the main challenges related to that is the effort in promptly updating the information when the system needs to be reconfigured. To ensure the adequate design of products, products should be classified based on either their morphological or technological features, clustering techniques or visual inspection can be used to this end [36]. Bill-of-Materials trees and a tree dissimilarity measure can be used to allow matching integer programming model to address commonality of products and form product families [37]. To ensure reconfigurability, products should then be grouped based on production flow features. Techniques such as the Rank Order Clustering algorithm or the use of similarity coefficients [38, 39] are the most widespread to this end. Based on company-specific data and following an iterative (and collaborative) approach, the relationship between the manufacturing system and its respective products can be studied and integrated product-process (object-oriented/functional) modelling can be achieved [40, 41]. The use of tools such as axiomatic design techniques and function-means formalism allow for achieving maximum possible decoupling of functional requirements based on existing functional requirements and the future functional requirements in order to enable a minimum of functional change when changes occur [36]. In this step, the definition of production platforms, i.e. sets of manufacturing subsystems developed to form a common structure from which a stream of products can be efficiently produced [40], is an important enabler of reconfigurability [41]. To define such platforms, a classification scheme of manufacturing systems [42] and functional modeling [40] are appropriate tools. Decisions on manufacturing modules and granularity level can be made using tools such as Design Structuring Matrix and Cladistics [36, 43]. Finally, the definition of KPIs and the use of visualization tools allow for evaluating different design concepts [35].

Step 3. System Design. This step is industry-specific and may need the definition of general tools. The implementation of a function-driven object-oriented methodology [44] supports the following activities. First, the reconfigurability needs should be defined. Second, an evaluation of the existing manufacturing setup to identify primary functions, terminal functions and possible suited modules should be performed. The identified modules are to be included in the system design and should be modelled and simulated, to evaluate the design solution candidates through a trade-off analysis between reusing existing modules and designing new modules [45]. Third, existing modules - either internally developed at the company and/or commercially available - should be classified through a module tree analysis [46]. A structural tree of the modules evaluates the constraints in reconfiguring the modules. The function tree, the module tree and the structural tree yield a module library from which industry specific RMS design prototyping is enabled. Finally, in this step, the right technology should be selected and the degree of automation for each operation should be defined.

Step 4. Anchoring/Realisation. This step consists in the detailed design of the RMS. As the previous one, this step may need the definition of general tools. Moreover, issues such as the integration design of systems can be very case-specific, making the generalization of tools even more challenging. Overall, this step needs detailed specifications and documentation from the previous step, especially if the actual development of new modules is outsourced to technology suppliers. Furthermore, tools to optimize ramp-up procedures and quickly operationalise implemented changes are paramount to ensure cost-effective reconfigurations over time.

Overall, the first two steps of the RMS design methodology proposed are well represented by tools already available in literature, the remaining two steps deserve further investigation to enable companies to use the proposed methodology.

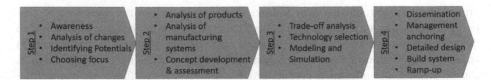

Fig. 1. Four-step methodology to design RMS

5 Conclusions and Future Work

This research proposes a methodology in four steps to design RMS. The methodology is based on available literature and considers the need of practitioners for context dependent guidelines. To ensure its applicability in industry, further research is needed. Indeed, the suggested methodology needs to be consolidated through the identification of relevant and industry-applicable tools for each individual activity (see Fig. 1) of the four steps and how they affect the characteristics of reconfigurability, as well as effect on sustainability and digitalization. Furthermore, many activities might require an adaptation of the already available tools or even the creation of new adequate and hopefully generalizable tools.

To pursue this objective, further research is needed. Above all, collaborative projects with companies might provide valuable insights to ensure the applicability of the method in industry.

Acknowledgements. This research was supported by the REKON project whose partners are Aalborg University, Jönköping University, the University of Southern Denmark, and The Danish Technological Institute. REKON is funded by The Danish Industry Foundation.

References

1. Koren, Y., Heisel, U., Jovane, F., et al.: Reconfigurable Manufacturing Systems. CIRP Ann. Manuf. Technol. **48**(2), 527–540 (1999)
2. Andersen, A., Brunoe, T.D., Nielsen, K., et al.: Towards a generic design method for reconfigurable manufacturing systems - analysis and synthesis of current design methods and evaluation of supportive tools. J. Manuf. Syst. **42**, 179–195 (2017)
3. Bortolini, M., Galizia, F.G., Mora, C.: Reconfigurable manufacturing systems: literature review and research trend. J. Manuf. Syst. **49**, 93–106 (2018)
4. Russo Spena, P., Holzner, P., Rauch, E., et al.: Requirements for the design of flexible and changeable manufacturing and assembly systems: a SME-survey. Procedia CIRP **41**, 207–212 (2016)
5. Koren, Y., Gu, X., Guo, W.: Reconfigurable manufacturing systems: principles, design, and future trends. Front. Mech. Eng. **13**(2), 121–136 (2017). https://doi.org/10.1007/s11465-018-0483-0
6. Tolio, T., Bernard, A., Colledani, M., et al.: Design, management and control of demanufacturing and remanufacturing systems. CIRP Ann. **66**(2), 585–609 (2017)
7. Dubey, R., Gunasekaran, A., Helo, P., et al.: Explaining the impact of reconfigurable manufacturing systems on environmental performance: the role of top management and organizational culture. J. Clean. Prod. **141**, 56–66 (2017)

8. Napoleone, A., Pozzetti, A., Macchi, M.: Core characteristics of reconfigurability and their influencing elements. IFAC-PapersOnLine **51**(11), 116–121 (2018)
9. Andersen, A., ElMaraghy, H., ElMaraghy, W., et al.: A participatory systems design methodology for changeable manufacturing systems. Int. J. Prod. Res. **56**(8), 1–19 (2018)
10. Abdi, M.R., Labib, A.W.: A design strategy for reconfigurable manufacturing systems (RMSs) using analytical hierarchical process (AHP): a case study. Int. J. Prod. Res. **41**(10), 2273–2299 (2003)
11. Andersen, A., Brunø, T.D., Nielsen, K., et al.: Evaluating the investment feasibility and industrial implementation of changeable and reconfigurable manufacturing systems. Flex. Serv. Manuf. J. **29**, 449–477 (2017)
12. Kuzgunkaya, O., ElMaraghy, H.A.: Economic and strategic perspectives on investing in RMS and FMS. Int. J. Flex. Manuf. Syst. **19**(3), 217–246 (2007)
13. Bi, Z.M., Lang, S.Y., Verner, M., et al.: Development of reconfigurable machines. Int. J. Adv. Manuf. Technol. **39**(11–12), 1227–1251 (2008)
14. Rösiö, C.: Supporting the Design of Reconfigurable Production Systems (2012)
15. Brunoe, T.D., Sørensen, D.G., Andersen, A., et al.: Framework for integrating production system models and product family models. In: Procedia CIRP, Proceedings of CIRP Conference on Manufacturing Systems, pp. NA. (2018)
16. Gedell, S., Michaelis, M.T., Johannesson, H.: Integrated model for co-development of products and production systems-a systems theory approach. Concurrent Eng. **19**(2), 139–156 (2011)
17. Touzout, F.A., Benyoucef, L.: Multi-objective sustainable process plan generation in a reconfigurable manufacturing environment: exact and adapted evolutionary approaches. Int. J. Prod. Res. 1–17 (2018)
18. Chaube, A., Benyoucef, L., Tiwari, M.K.: An adapted NSGA-2 algorithm based dynamic process plan generation for a reconfigurable manufacturing system. J. Intell. Manuf. **23**(4), 1141–1155 (2012)
19. Koren, Y., Gu, X., Guo, W.: Choosing the system configuration for high-volume manufacturing. Int. J. Prod. Res. **56**(1–2), 476–490 (2018)
20. Xiaobo, Z., Wang, J., Luo, Z.: A stochastic model of a reconfigurable manufacturing system part 2: optimal configurations. Int. J. Prod. Res. **38**(12), 2829–2842 (2000)
21. Kurniadi, K.A., Lee, S., Ryu, K.: Digital twin approach for solving reconfiguration planning problems in RMS. In: Moon, I., Lee, G.M., Park, J., Kiritsis, D., von Cieminski, G. (eds.) APMS 2018. IAICT, vol. 536, pp. 327–334. Springer, Cham (2018). https://doi.org/10.1007/978-3-319-99707-0_41
22. Deif, A.M., ElMaraghy, W.: Investigating optimal capacity scalability scheduling in a reconfigurable manufacturing system. Int. J. Adv. Manuf. Technol. **32**(5–6), 557–562 (2007)
23. Wang, W., Koren, Y.: Scalability planning for reconfigurable manufacturing systems. J. Manuf. Syst. **31**(2), 83–91 (2012)
24. Napoleone, A., Andersen, A.-L., Pozzetti, A., Macchi, M.: Reconfigurable manufacturing: a classification of elements enabling convertibility and scalability. In: Ameri, F., Stecke, K.E., von Cieminski, G., Kiritsis, D. (eds.) APMS 2019. IAICT, vol. 566, pp. 349–356. Springer, Cham (2019). https://doi.org/10.1007/978-3-030-30000-5_44
25. Khanna, K., Kumar, R.: Reconfigurable manufacturing system: a state-of-the-art review. Benchmarking Int. J. **26**(8), 2608–2635 (2019)
26. Khezri, A., Benderbal, H.H., Benyoucef, L.: A sustainable reconfigurable manufacturing system designing with focus on environmental hazardous wastes, pp. 317–324. IEEE (2019)
27. Ribeiro, L., Bjorkman, M.: Transitioning from standard automation solutions to cyber-physical production systems: an assessment of critical conceptual and technical challenges. JSYST **12**(4), 3816–3827 (2018)

28. Lanza, G., Stricker, N., Peters, S.: Ad-Hoc rescheduling and innovative business models for shock- robust production systems. Procedia CIRP **7**, 121–126 (2013)
29. Andersen, A., Nielsen, K., Brunoe, T.D.: Prerequisites and barriers for the development of reconfigurable manufacturing systems for high speed ramp-up. In: Anonymous Proceedings of the 3rd International Conference on Ramp-up management. Elsevier (2016)
30. Andersen, A.-L., Brunoe, T.D., Christensen, B., Bejlegaard, M., Sorensen, D.G.H., Nielsen, K.: Tailored reconfigurability: a comparative study of eight industrial cases with reconfigurability as a key to manufacturing competitiveness. In: Benyoucef, L. (ed.) Reconfigurable Manufacturing Systems: From Design to Implementation. SSAM, pp. 209–245. Springer, Cham (2020). https://doi.org/10.1007/978-3-030-28782-5_11
31. Rösiö, C., Aslam, T., Srikanth, K.B., et al.: Towards an assessment criterion of reconfigurable manufacturing systems within the automotive industry. Procedia Manuf. **28**, 76–82 (2019)
32. Maganha, I., Silva, C., Ferreira, L.M.D.: Understanding reconfigurability of manufacturing systems: an empirical analysis. J. Manuf. Syst. **48**, 120–130 (2018)
33. Wiendahl, H., Heger, C.L.: Justifying changeability. A methodical approach to achieving cost effectiveness. J. Manuf. Sci. Prod. **6**(1–2), 33–40 (2004)
34. Tracht, K., Hogreve, S.: Decision making during design and reconfiguration of modular assembly lines. In: ElMaraghy, H. (eds.) Enabling Manufacturing Competitiveness and Economic Sustainability. Springer, Heidelberg. https://doi.org/10.1007/978-3-642-23860-4_17
35. Park, J.: Improved methodology for RMS adaptability evaluation. Int. J. Precis. Eng. Manuf **18**(11), 1537–1546 (2017)
36. Bejlegaard, M., ElMaraghy, W., Brunoe, T.D., et al.: Methodology for reconfigurable fixture architecture design. CIRP J. Manuf. Sci. Technol. **23**, 172–186 (2018)
37. Kashkoush, M., ElMaraghy, H.: Product family formation for reconfigurable assembly systems. Procedia CIRP **17**, 302–307 (2014)
38. Prasad, D., Jayswal, S.C.: Assessment of a reconfigurable manufacturing system. Int. J., Benchmarking (2019)
39. Goyal, K.K., Jain, P.K., Jain, M.: A comprehensive approach to operation sequence similarity based part family formation in the reconfigurable manufacturing system. Int. J. Prod. Res. **51**(6), 1762–1776 (2013)
40. Michaelis, M.T., Johannesson, H., ElMaraghy, H.A.: Function and process modeling for integrated product and manufacturing system platforms. J. Manuf. Syst. **36**, 203–215 (2014)
41. Brunoe, T.D., Andersen, A., Sorensen, D.G., et al.: Integrated product-process modelling for platform-based co-development. Int. J. Prod. Res. 1–17 (2019)
42. Sorensen, D.G.H., ElMaraghy, H., Brunoe, T.D., et al.: Classification coding of production systems for identification of platform candidates. CIRP J. Manuf. Sci. Technol. **28**, 144–156 (2020)
43. Lameche, K., Najid, N., Castagna, P., et al.: Modularity in the design of reconfigurable manufacturing systems. IFAC-PapersOnLine **50**, 3511–3516 (2017)
44. Gwangwava, N., Mpofu, K., Tlale, N., et al.: A methodology for design and reconfiguration of reconfigurable bending press machines (RBPMs). Int. J. Prod. Res. **52**(20), 6019–6032 (2014)
45. Gadalla, M., Xue, D.: An approach to identify the optimal configurations and reconfiguration processes for design of reconfigurable machine tools. Int. J. Prod. Res. **56**(11), 3880–3900 (2018)
46. Mpofu, K., Tlale, N.: A morphology proposal in commercial-off-the-shelf reconfigurable machine tools. Int. J. Prod. Res. **52**(15), 4440–4455 (2014)

Reconfigurable Manufacturing: Lesson Learnt from the COVID-19 Outbreak

Alessia Napoleone[1]([✉]) [iD] and Lorenzo Bruno Prataviera[2] [iD]

[1] Department of Materials and Production, Aalborg University, Aalborg, Denmark
alna@mp.aau.dk
[2] Department of Management, Economics and Industrial Engineering, Politecnico di Milano, Milan, Italy

Abstract. To compete in the current volatile and unpredictable context, manufacturing firms increasingly need reconfigurability, i.e. the capability to adapt the production capacities and functionalities of their manufacturing systems according to evolving product families. To be attractive for practitioners, reconfigurability should require a reasonably low effort. In 2020, the COVID-19 outbreak has quickly twisted market requirements: in an unexpected market context, many firms have been reconfiguring their plants and networks to satisfy, with low efforts, the surge in the demand for very specific products. This paper analyses the reaction upheld by specific Italian manufacturing firms to the outbreak, to derive practical insights on possible ways to achieve reconfigurability in manufacturing. As for results, four insights are provided, regarding: the pre-existing know how held by firms; their network configuration; the modularity of products; and the use of smart and digital technologies. Additionally, remarking the relevance of collaboration between different firms, this paper sows the seeds for linking the reconfigurability theory with the dynamic capabilities theory.

Keywords: Reconfigurable manufacturing · Scalability · Convertibility · COVID-19

1 Introduction

Manufacturing companies are nowadays dealing with volatile and unpredictable market requirements and, to keep their competitiveness over time, they need to develop the reconfigurability capability [1, 2]. Reconfigurability - referred to as changeability at plant and firm levels in several papers - is the capability of a manufacturing firm to repeatedly change or rearrange its manufacturing systems with a reasonable effort in order to produce evolving product families [3, 4]. Indeed, reconfigurability allows to provide the exact production capacities and functionalities needed, when needed [5]. To make reconfigurability attractive for practitioners, reconfigurations should require reasonably low efforts, in terms of reconfiguration time, cost and ramp-up time [6, 7].

The year 2020 will be certainly remembered for the COVID-19 pandemic. This virus affects the respiratory system and, in the frequent event of complications of the

© IFIP International Federation for Information Processing 2020
Published by Springer Nature Switzerland AG 2020
B. Lalic et al. (Eds.): APMS 2020, IFIP AICT 591, pp. 457–465, 2020.
https://doi.org/10.1007/978-3-030-57993-7_52

infection, people need support of breathing and intensive care. The virus has spread rapidly from China to all over the world, putting health systems of many countries into a crisis: the rapid contagion of many people determines the overcrowding of hospitals. For this reason, many governments have been imposing partial or total lockdowns. As an added precaution, people have been required to wear masks when leaving their homes and to sanitize frequently their hands. In this landscape, a huge demand for masks and sanitizing gels from common people and ventilators from hospitals has been rising and has been replacing the demand for manufacturing items such as clothing and vehicles.

In this new and unexpected scenario, some firms have been reconfiguring their plants and networks to satisfy, in a very short time period and at affordable costs, the high request for masks, sanitizing gels and ventilators. Indeed, given the emergency situation, these firms have kept the reconfiguration effort as low as possible. For this reason, such crisis can add interesting insights on how to achieve reconfigurability in manufacturing. Thus, the research question addressed in this paper is: "What reconfigurability-related insights are manufacturing firms reacting to the COVID-19 outbreak providing to the academic and business communities?" Specifically, this research captures concrete insights from the reactions - during the period from February to April 2020 - to the outbreak of a group of Italian manufacturing firms serving the Italian market. To this end, Sect. 2 provides a theoretical frame to the research, Sect. 3 describes the adopted methodology, Sect. 4 carries out the analysis and outlines the results of the investigation and Sect. 5 provides the conclusions and feedback for further research.

2   Theoretical Frame

According to literature, the characteristics of reconfigurability are: modularity, integrability, diagnosability, scalability, convertibility and customization. Modularity and integrability mean the functionalities of the system and its components being separated into units with standard interfaces that can be easily combined and changed [8]. Modularity and integrability are closely related [1, 9]. Diagnosability allows quick identification of the sources of quality and reliability problems [10] and quick correction of operational problems [11] within the manufacturing system. Scalability allows incremental changes of capacity, rapidly and economically [12]. Convertibility 'allows quick changeover between existing products and quick system adaptability for future products' [10]. Customization allows adaptation of system configuration for producing the required product families [4, 10]. These characteristics allow for reducing the reconfiguration effort, thus making reconfigurability attractive for practitioners.

Among the 6 characteristics, scalability and convertibility are those directly related to manufacturing systems' responsiveness to sudden changes: scalability to changes in demand and convertibility to changes in product mix [13]. Indeed, scalability and convertibility directly contribute to the goal of the reconfigurable systems, which is providing exactly the capacity and functionality needed when needed [5, 14].

Several authors have worked at the identification of enablers of scalability and convertibility (see for example [6, 14–16]. Specifically, this paper relies on the observation that, being "reconfiguration" characteristics (i.e. directly related to systems responsiveness to changes), scalability and convertibility are supported by "configuration" enablers such as the modularity and integrability characteristics [17, 18].

3 Research Design

This study examined implemented actions in terms of changes in the production capacity and/or functionality of production systems and identified the enablers of such actions; thus, providing insights on enablers of scalability and convertibility. Multiple cases were analyzed to increase external validity and to reduce risks to misjudge singular events [19]. As units of analysis, Italian manufacturing firms of different sizes, serving the Italian market and reacting to the COVID-19 outbreak from February to April 2020 were considered, as Italy emerged as one of the countries that was hardest hit by the epidemic. Given the dramatic situation, it was not possible to directly interview firms' representatives. Consequently, the main sources of information for the analysis were firms' websites and national business magazines. To corroborate the evidences and to strengthen a formal chain of evidence, a formal database was established [20]. To support study's construct validity, multiple data sources were triangulated and additional materials available online, such as industry reports or public documents, were included in the database [19]. To increase study's internal validity the collected information was contextualized into the available theory on reconfigurability.

Sample selection was based on a theoretical sampling, driven by the opportunity to gain accessibility to the type of phenomenon of interests [20]. The sample of investigation is represented in the following table (Table 1). Overall, 21 cases were selected. Although this convenience sample may have determined a possible bias [20], this was considered coherent with the aim of this investigation, i.e. to observe general trends in the existing scenario and to provide prompt insights for further research.

Table 1 provides general information about the cases, including the industry in which they operate. Firms' names are not provided for confidentiality reasons. In the last two columns, Table 1 specifies the outcome of the production process (i.e. the final product) and the production stage in which each firm contributed. Indeed, some firms were involved in all production stages, while some others contributed in specific stages of the manufacturing process of the final product. As shown in Table 1, cases were divided into 5 groups according to the presence of sectorial commonalities or due to the collaboration among firms with respect to the final product. This classification supported the interpretation of the results of the analysis as clarified in the following section.

Table 1. Sample of investigation

Firm (id)	Sector	Size[a]	Product	Production stages
F.1.1	Rubber and plastics	L	Ventilators	All stages
F.1.2	Weapons	L	Ventilators	Manufacturing of a component
F.1.3	Manufacturing consultancy	S	Ventilators	Manufacturing of a component
F.2.1	Textile and clothing (luxury)	L	Masks	All stages
F.2.2	Textile and clothing (luxury)	M	Masks	All stages
F.2.3	Textile and clothing (luxury)	L	Masks and medical scrubs	All stages
F.2.4	Textile and clothing	L	Masks and medical scrubs	All stages
F.2.5	Textile and clothing (luxury)	L	Masks and medical scrubs	All stages
F.2.6	Textile and clothing	S	Masks	All stages
F.2.7	Textile	S	Masks	Manufacturing of fabrics
F.2.8	Textile	S	Masks	All stages
F.2.9	Textile and clothing	S	Masks	All stages
F.2.10	Textile	L	Masks	All stages
F.2.11	Luxury packaging	S	Masks	All stages
F.3.1	Pharmaceutical	L	Sanitizing gel	All stages
F.3.2	Chemicals (hair products)	L	Sanitizing gel	All stages
F.3.3	Chemicals (cosmetics)	M	Sanitizing gel	All stages
F.4	Medical devices	M	Membrane oxygenator	All stages
F.5.1	Medical devices	S	Ventilators	All stages
F.5.2	Automotive	L	ventilators	Some stages
F.5.3	Automotive	L	Ventilators	Some stages

[a]According to the European Commission, classification in Large (L), Medium (M) and Small (S) firms (based on number of employees).

4   Analysis of the Cases and Results

The great majority of the analyzed firms (except F.3.1, operating in the pharmaceutical industry, and F.4 and F.5.1, producing medical devices) would have had their plants closed down. This was due to both (i) the absence of demand for their products (e.g. the luxury clothing, the cosmetics and the cars) and (ii) the fact that the Italian Government ordered the temporary suspension of non-critical production.

4.1 Analysis of the Cases

To support the analysis and the interpretation of results, the 21 cases have been sorted into five groups (see Table 1).

The first group includes two firms from different sectors, which both cooperated with F.1.3 - a consulting company operating in the field of the industrial and mechanical engineering - in order to provide ventilators to Italian hospitals. Specifically, F.1.3 patented a 3D printed valve to turn snorkeling masks into ventilators. Thanks to F.1.3's idea, low cost ventilators could be manufactured and made available in a very short time period. Consequently, F.1.1, manufacturer of snorkeling masks, started collaborating with F.1.3 and realized a mold that allowed the industrialization of the valve, thus furtherly increasing the production of ventilators. In addition, F.1.2, a producer of weapons, also cooperated with F.1.3 by using its 3D prototyping printers for the production of the valve. To quickly identify suppliers for the required raw materials, F.1.2's Chief Executive Officer exploited social media virtual networks. In this way, the firm found suppliers of raw materials from both Italy and Germany.

The second group includes 11 firms from the textile and clothing industry (except F.2.11, which produces customized luxury packaging). They all supplied masks to hospitals and pharmacies. F.2.1 quickly introduced a new treatment at one of its printing plants to make water-repellent fabric (involving around 50 people). Moreover, it involved its distribution partners all over the Italian territory (around 500 people) for the packaging and distribution of masks. Overall, it already had the required know-how and technology, but needed to widely increase the production capacity at the fabric printing plant. F.2.2 completely revolutionized its operations, with tailors working from home to produce and pack masks. Every day, staff people brought the non-woven fabrics, rubber bands and underwire to the tailors, while collecting ready-for-distribution masks. F.2.4 acquired special machines to realize a semi-automatic line to produce masks and medical scrubs, and exploited digital technologies to train tailors. F.2.8 and F.2.10 reconverted their production plants in record time to provide masks. Finally, F.2.11 exploited its operations and expertise to use the material normally used to pack jewelry items to produce masks.

The third group includes three firms operating in the chemicals industry, including the pharmaceutical and the cosmetics ones, which produced sanitizing gel. For example, F.3.1 dedicated one of its plants (already dedicated to the production of medication in gel) to the sole production of the sanitizing gel.

F.4 is the smallest (and the only Italian) firm in the world producing extracorporeal membrane oxygenators. These devices are used in hospitals for patients in extreme situations, where also ventilators are not enough to support the breathing activity of people. It quadrupled its production capacity in a few weeks by moving 130 people out of 220 total employees on the production systems.

The last group of firms includes F.5.1, a firm producing medical devices, and 2 firms within the automotive industry, which have been grouped due to their collaboration to produce ventilators. F.5.1 is the only Italian firm producing ventilators and experienced a sudden increase in the demand for such devices. Thus, it collaborated with F.5.2 and F.5.3, who manufactured some components and supported some assembly phases for the ventilators production.

The automotive industry deserves further exploration and international firms operating out of Italy can add relevant insights to the results of this research. Being characterized by high technology investments, this industry can provide a variety of different product families, such as masks, protective visors, and even ventilators. In Brazil, a firm used 3D printing to produce masks; in Spain, another firm used 3D printers to manufacture visors; in Germany, two others used 3D printers to manufacture ventilators; finally, two further firms in China assembled protective suits and masks.

4.2   Results of the Investigation

Overall, the results of this analysis in terms of reconfigurability can be synthesized in four main points, which have been also represented in Fig. 1:

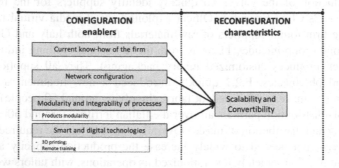

Fig. 1. Results of the investigation (adaptation of part of the framework provided by [17])

1. Current know how held by firms. As stated in Sect. 2, reconfigurability should allow a firm to change or rearrange its manufacturing systems so to be able to produce any kind of product family. The epidemic has shown that to ensure reasonable efforts, firms rearranging their operations should be already provided with the required know how. For example, firms in the textile and clothing industry supplied masks, while firms in the chemical sector supplied sanitizing gel. Conversely, the automotive appears as the most reconfigurable industry, as these firms were capable to provide a variety of different product families thanks to the exploitation of up to date technologies.
2. Configuration of the network of firms involved in the value chain of the end products. The many examples of successful collaboration not only confirmed the importance of inter-firm linkages to create value, but also demonstrated that capabilities can be synergistically combined or exploited by supply chain partners [21].
3. Modularity of products. According to literature, it enables the modularity and integrability characteristics of manufacturing processes [22–24]. To this end, the modularity of the product given by the combination of the snorkeling mask with the recently patented valve is very representative. On the one hand, it allowed F.1.1 to clearly identify the specific processes needing reconfiguration, i.e. manufacturing a

mold to produce the new valve instead of the traditional valve needed by conventional snorkeling masks. Moreover, regarding F.1.2, the modularity of the end product allowed the firm to clearly identify its role in the overall value chain, i.e. converting its prototyping department to produce the valves and supply them to F.1.1.

4. Smart and digital technologies. The possibility to remotely train employees (in this specific situation, to avoid the spread of the virus) is an interesting enabler of reconfigurability. Combined with augmented reality technologies, remote training is a powerful tool to support the "conversion" of operators' skills within plants. Also, the use of social media to share information and potentially build new network collaborations (as per F1.2) provides some food for thoughts. Finally, 3D printing is a very powerful technology to achieve conversion of specific functionalities, as brightly shown in the many examples in the automotive industry.

Lastly, collaboration between firms along products' value chains supported the reduction of the reconfiguration effort, as it allowed to distribute roles along the value chain based on the available plants and know-how of each entity. For this reason, further research could broaden the perspective from a firm-level to a supply chain-level, by exploring the link between the reconfigurability theory and other well-established theories, e.g. the dynamic capabilities theory. Dynamic capabilities are defined as the firm's abilities "to integrate, build, and reconfigure internal and external competences to address rapidly changing environments" [25], and have been progressively expanded from a resource-based view approach (i.e. how firms create competitive advantage and value) to address the relationships a firm has with other firms, as managing interorganizational relationships is a key to success [26]. Some researchers argued that the dynamic capabilities theory helps address how to respond to the business changing environment, but may fail to describe exactly the capabilities to be operationalized [26]. By linking the dynamic capabilities theory with the reconfigurability theory, it might be possible to bridge the organization's capacity to efficiently and responsively change operations and develop its resources [25], with the actions and efforts required at different manufacturing levels, from the workstation to the plant [4, 17].

5 Conclusions

In order to face the COVID-19 outbreak, many firms have been reconfiguring their plants and networks to satisfy, with low reconfiguration efforts, the surge in the demand for specific products such as masks, sanitizing gels and ventilators. Based on the analysis of reactions of selected manufacturing firms to this crisis, this paper provides some practical insights on enablers of the scalability and convertibility characteristics, thus on possible ways to achieve reconfigurability in manufacturing.

The main limitation of this work is that, given the dramatic situation, it was not possible to conduct in-depth analysis of the cases. Indeed, in future research, the authors aim at focusing on a subset of the cases analyzed in this work in order to provide a detailed analysis of the specific manufacturing systems and subsystems that were the subject of the changes, the related enablers and the managerial challenges rising from the reconfiguration process. On the other hand, focusing on multiple cases, this investigation aimed at providing prompt and as broad as possible food for thought for both practitioners and academics. Indeed, production managers interested in reconfigurability can acquire insights about the benefits of investing in - among the others - product modularity and 3D printing. Moreover, the analysis has brought into light two aspects offering high potentialities to the reconfigurability theory and thus deserving further research. These are: (i) smart and digital technologies, which support the characteristics of scalability and convertibility and (ii) collaboration along value chains, which promises to reduce reconfiguration efforts. Regarding the latter, this paper sows the seeds for linking the reconfigurability theory with the dynamic capabilities theory.

References

1. Shaik, A.M., Rao, V.V.S.K., Rao, C.S.: Development of modular manufacturing systems - a review. Int. J. Adv. Manuf. Technol. **76**, 789–802 (2015)
2. Setchi, R.M., Lagos, N.: Reconfigurability and reconfigurable manufacturing systems - state-of-the-art review. In: 2nd IEEE International Conference on Industrial Informatics, pp 529–535 (2004)
3. Azab, A., ElMaraghy, H.A.: Mathematical modeling for reconfigurable process planning. CIRP Ann. – Manuf. Technol. **56**, 467–472 (2007)
4. Rösiö C (2012) Supporting the design of reconfigurable production systems
5. Koren, Y.: General RMS characteristics. comparison with dedicated and flexible systems. In: Chapter 3 in Reconfigurable Manufacturing Systems and Transformable Factories, pp 27–45 (2006)
6. Andersen, A.-L., Larsen, J.K., Brunoe, T.D., Nielsen, K., Ketelsen, C.: Critical enablers of changeable and reconfigurable manufacturing and their industrial implementation. J. Manuf. Technol. Manag. **29**, 983–1002 (2018)
7. Goyal, K.K., Jain, P.K.K., Jain, M.: Optimal configuration selection for reconfigurable manufacturing system using NSGA II and TOPSIS. Int. J. Prod. Res. **50**, 4175–4191 (2012)
8. Andersen, A.-L., Brunoe, T.D., Christensen, B., Bejlegaard, M., Sorensen, D.G.H., Nielsen, K.: Tailored reconfigurability: a comparative study of eight industrial cases with reconfigurability as a key to manufacturing competitiveness. In: Benyoucef, L. (ed.) Reconfigurable Manufacturing Systems: From Design to Implementation. SSAM, pp. 209–245. Springer, Cham (2020). https://doi.org/10.1007/978-3-030-28782-5_11
9. Mehrabi, M.G., Ulsoy, A.G., Koren, Y., Heytler, P.: Trends and perspectives in flexible and reconfigurable manufacturing systems. J. Intell. Manuf. **13**, 135–146 (2002)
10. Mehrabi, M.G., Ulsoy, A.G., Koren, Y.: Reconfigurable manufacturing systems and their enabling technologies. Int. J. Manuf. Technol. Manag. **1**, 1–21 (2000)
11. Gumasta, K., Kumar Gupta, S., Benyoucef, L., Tiwari, M.K.: Developing a reconfigurability index using multi-attribute utility theory. Int. J. Prod. Res. **49**, 1669–1683 (2011)
12. Elmaraghy, H.A.: Flexible and reconfigurable manufacturing systems paradigms. Int. J. Flex. Manuf. Syst. **17**, 261–276 (2006)
13. Maganha, I., Silva, C., Ferreira, L.M.D.F.: Understanding reconfigurability of manufacturing systems: an empirical analysis. J. Manuf. Syst. **48**, 120–130 (2018)

14. Napoleone, A., Andersen, A.-L., Pozzetti, A., Macchi, M.: Reconfigurable manufacturing: a classification of elements enabling convertibility and scalability. In: Ameri, F., Stecke, Kathryn E., von Cieminski, G., Kiritsis, D. (eds.) APMS 2019. IAICT, vol. 566, pp. 349–356. Springer, Cham (2019). https://doi.org/10.1007/978-3-030-30000-5_44

15. Beauville, A., Klement, N., Gibaru, O., Roucoules, L., Durville, L.: Identification of reconfigurability enablers and weighting of reconfigurability characteristics based on a case study. Procedia Manuf. 96–101 (2019)

16. Rösiö, C., Aslam, T., Banavara, K., Shetty, S.: Towards an assessment criterion of reconfigurable manufacturing systems within the automotive industry. Procedia Manuf. **28**, 76–82 (2019)

17. Napoleone, A., Pozzetti, A., Macchi, M.: A framework to manage reconfigurability in manufacturing. Int. J. Prod. Res. **56**, 3815–3837 (2018)

18. Singh, A., Gupta, S., Asjad, M., Gupta, P.: Reconfigurable manufacturing systems: journey and the road ahead. Int. J. Syst. Assur. Eng. Manag. **8**, 1849–1857 (2017)

19. Voss, C., Tsikriktsis, N., Frohlich, M.: Case research in operations management. Int. J. Oper. Prod. Manag. **22**, 195–219 (2002)

20. Yin, R.K.: Case Study Research, 4th edn. (2009)

21. Zacharia, Z.G., Sanders, N.R., Nix, N.W.: The emerging role of the third-party logistics provider (3PL) as an orchestrator. J. Bus. Logist. **32**, 40–54 (2011)

22. Brunoe, T.D., Andersen, A.L., Sorensen, D.G.H., Nielsen, K., Bejlegaard, M.: Integrated product-process modelling for platform-based co-development. Int. J. Prod. Res. 1–17 (2019)

23. Sorensen, D.G.H., Elmaraghy, H., Ditlev, T., Nielsen, K.: Classification coding of production systems for identification of platform candidates. CIRP J. Manuf. Sci. Technol. **28**, 144–156 (2020)

24. Joergensen, S.N., Hvilshøj, M., Madsen, O.: Designing modular manufacturing systems using mass customisation theories and methods. Int. J. Mass Cust. **4**, 171 (2012)

25. Teece, D.J., Pisano, G., Shuen, A.M.Y.: Dynamic capabilities and strategic management authors. Strateg. Manag. J. **18**, 509–533 (1997)

26. Wang, C.L., Ahmed, P.: Dynamic capabilities: a review and research agenda. Int. J. Manag. Rev. **9**, 31–51 (1895)

Digital Assistance Systems: Augmented Reality and Virtual Reality

Virtual and Augmented Reality as a Digital Support to HR Systems in Production Management

Danijela Lalić, Dunja Bošković, Bojana Milić, Sara Havzi, and Jelena Spajić

Faculty of Technical Sciences, Department of Industrial Engineering and Management, University of Novi Sad, TrgDositejaObradovića 6, Novi Sad, Serbia
{danijelalalic, stankovicj}@uns.ac.rs

Abstract. Digital transformation has disrupted every domain of production management, as well as the human resource management as one of the production manager's most important responsibilities. Besides of product and process design and issues involving planning and control of quality and capacity, production management also includes responsibility for organization and supervision of the workforce. In new industry operations, it is important to anticipate human resource requirements, as well as to translate them into recruiting and training programs in order to develop a base of highly skilled and qualified workers capacitated for installed machinery and equipment.

According to the relevant literature review, integration of virtual and augmented reality technology in any business process has a proven potential for employee engagement improvement and memory retention capacity.

The aim of this research is to provide a comprehensive summary of using VR and AR technologies as a digital support for managing human elements in operating systems. This study found that VR and AR can be successfully used in improving workers' productivity, enhancing employee training, reducing costs, making worksites safer and closing the skills gap more effectively and efficiently. This study could encourage both academics and practitioners to seek innovative use of VR and AR technologies in a particular industry as digital tools that saves time and costs in human resource management.

Keywords: VR and AR technologies · Human resource management · Production management

1 Introduction

Combining different digital technologies with production and business processes represent one of the pillars of industry 4.0. In order to support digital transformation initiatives, many industries adapt a technology-driven approach in their function and activities, by creating "smart" working environment within production system [1].

In order to overcome the shortage of fit workforce, long-time adaptation and defective work, production systems are taking advantages of technologies to better

© IFIP International Federation for Information Processing 2020
Published by Springer Nature Switzerland AG 2020
B. Lalic et al. (Eds.): APMS 2020, IFIP AICT 591, pp. 469–478, 2020.
https://doi.org/10.1007/978-3-030-57993-7_53

recruit and preserve new employees. Engineers and technicians of the 21st century must be equipped with highly advanced skills in their function area and they must be sharp in process fault diagnosis and decision making. Human resource systems are responsible for recruiting, developing and managing of skillful labor force, and those systems need a digital support in order to keep production and other operational activities running with minimal disruption. Each year, *Gartner* identifies the *"Top 10 Strategic Technology Trends"* and some of the key trends published for 2019 are related to autonomous things, augmented analytics, immersive experience etc. This research [2], for example highlights the fact that AR technologies will be embedded in enterprise application (e.g. HR, sales, marketing function etc.) in order to optimize the decisions and actions of all employees within their context. In addition, *Gartner* has presented the latest technological innovations that are transforming HRM: VR and AR application in corporate learning, learning experience platforms, VR assistants in human capital management, AI in talent acquisition, employee experience tech, VR recruiting assistants and so forth [3].

The purpose of this paper is to analyze the current state of implementation of virtual and augmented reality in a field of human resource management in production systems. The research focus is to review the literature in Directory of Open Access Journals (DOAJ) and provide a comprehensive summary of potential opportunities of VR and AR technologies as a digital support for managing human elements in operating systems.

2   Theoretical and Conceptual Perspectives

Digital technologies have transformed every domain of production management: planning and production approaches, business development models, use of technologies, shifts in traditional operational tools and processes etc. As one of the strategic fields in production management, human resource management (HRM) is also experiencing a digital transformation in its working approach.

This section highlights the importance of human resource in production management as well as the importance of virtual and augmented reality in modern industry.

2.1   The Importance of Human Resource in Production Management

The multidimensional and fundamentally disruptive character of change causes problems in maintaining the characteristics of workflows and structures in production systems [4]. The increasing intensity of technological shifts necessitates finding a solution that will provide the ability to adapt the structures of the company and thus mitigate the effects of change.The production manager must plan and control the process of production so that it moves smoothly at the required level of output while meeting cost and quality objectives [5].

A more than century-old theory of work measurement and time study introduced by Taylor and the Gilbreth's, still have an application in today's fast-paced, technology-driven world. In his publications on production management, Taylor set the scene for developments in many business functions and disciplines including *human resources* [6].

One of the Taylor's most important contributions are incentive systems for motivation and rewarding high levels of worker output, as well as the identification of new functions for managers relating to the selection and training of new employees [7, 8]. These HRM tendencies are still relevant and ongoing. According to Beatty and Schneier [9], the main areas of strategic choices in HRM are: *work design, performance measures, selection, development, rewards and communication*. Therefore, HRM is linked to strategic choices of quality, flexibility, investment and cost reduction by the use of a functional and performance approach [10, 11], which means that manufacturing strategy and production management are usually related to performance appraisal, work design, career management, training and development etc. Today's biggest challenge to HR profession is to learn more about the effective application and appropriate use of new technologies in order to improve their working processes [12].

2.2   The Usage of Virtual and Augmented Reality

There are many scenarios of industrial application of VR and AR solutions, from visualization of prototype technology components to the complex development of interactive workshops for personnel at hazardous industries [13].

Virtual reality (VR) represents a three-dimensional computer simulation of real world environments that can be explored and interacted through a person [14]. These simulations are interactive and are capable of responding to user inputs making it interactive in real time [15]. The VR is the computer-generated simulation of a three-dimensional image or environment that may be interacted within an apparently real or physical manner by a person with the use of a special digital system, which includes a helmet with a display screen inside or gloves outfitted with sensors [16].

Unlike virtual reality, augmented reality (AR) implements fragments of virtual reality and incorporates them into real world. Using technology it aligns real and virtual objects while running interactively in real-time [17]. Augmented reality (AR) stocks the same concept, but in place of interacting in a nonexistent surrounding (digital fact), AR makes use of the existing environment at the same time as implementing virtual elements to appear as if both are together at the same time [18]. AR is a kind of interactive, reality-based display environment that takes the capabilities of computer-generated display, sound, textual content and effects to enhance the user's real-world experience [19]. AR combines real and computer-based scenes and images to deliver a unified but enhanced view of the world.

In terms of the comparison of virtual reality and augmented reality, VR is a fully immersive and closed experience with no sense of the real world, while in AR user can see a real world with digital information overlay, which implies that a real world remains central to the experience, enhanced by virtual details.

3 Potentials of VR and AR Implementation for HR Systems in Production Management

Access to the internet and other digital technologies can further enhance the sense of human connection, especially for people facing physical and social barriers [20]. In this respect, VR and AR becomes a transcendent experience, almost mystical in its ability to permit humans to go beyond their known realities [21]. Thus, it is of great significance to examine how new trends in technology, especially VR and AR, are being used for HRM activities in production systems.

3.1 Identification of VR/AR-Human Resource-Production Management Relations in Journals with Open Access

In order to analyze the available researches about application of VR and AR in human resource management in a field of production management (PM), the journals available through the Consortium of Libraries of Serbia for Unified Procurement (KoBSON) were analyzed. The journals were divided into three groups according to the three analyzed areas: HR, VR/AR and PM. Based on the availability of the journal through the repository of KoBSON, which are also members of the Directory of Open Access Journals (DOAJ), a listing of the frequency of articles dealing with this interdisciplinary topic found in each journal are presented in the Tables 1, 2 3. For each group of journals, the keywords of the other two research areas were used to identify the number of articles that covers all three analyzed areas.

Based on this review, it can be concluded that there is a lack of research that analyzes the use of new VR/AR technologies in human resource management in the field of production management. This topic and trends require a multidisciplinary approach in research and represent an unexplored, but challenging and current field for research.

Exploring this topic, we found some articles dealing with the application of VR/AR technologies in HRM in specific industries, whose key conclusions are presented in the next part of the paper.

3.2 A Literature Summary of Using VR/AR Technologies for HR Systems in Production Management

In recent years there has been an active development and growth of investments in VR and AR business, and the number of VR users is growing around the world [13]. Transformation of the role of VR and AR is evident as well: from gaming technologies, used mainly for entertainment purposes, to modern and effective tool applicable in the business environment (both for managing employee training, recruiting purposes, marketing, branding, and for main operational business processes, for example, measurement, 3D visualization, and modeling) [22]. Zhao et al. [13] indicate that VR and AR allow managers to improve their current technologies, identify weak points, reduce risks and time for testing, rather than using real objects and processes.

Table 1. The frequency of HR and VR/AR articles in top listed PM journals by KoBSON

Journals	IF 2018	Launched (year)	Human resourcei dentified	Virtual reality identified	Augmented reality identified	HR and VR and AR identified	Field of research
International journal of operations and production management	4.111	1980	775	9	2	9	Performance management; smart manufacturing; work organization
Production and operations management	2.171	1992	1	1	–	1	Manufacturing; individualization
Advances in production engineering and management	2.047	2006	–	1	–	–	Product customization
Anbar management services. Production abstracts	–	–	–	–	–	–	–
Baking management; the production magazine for volume Bakers	–	1996	–	–	–	–	–
Brazilian journal of operations and production Management	–	2004	12	–	–	–	Process management; training; work performance
Independent journal of management and Production	–	2010	48	4	1	6	Organizational performance; training
International journal of production Management and Engineering	–	2013	1	–	–	–	Evaluation; modeling; human capital
Journal of engineering, project, and Production Management	–	2011	40	2	2	3	Project management
Journal of production and operations Management	–	2011	5	–	–	–	Work performance; human capital

(*continued*)

Table 1. (*continued*)

Journals	IF 2018	Launched (year)	Human resourcei dentified	Virtual reality identified	Augmented reality identified	HR and VR and AR identified	Field of research
Management and production engineering Review	–	2010	1	–	–	–	Motivation; knowledge management
Production and inventory management Journal	–	1959	–	–	–	–	–

VR offers HR employees a new way to provide an interesting experience for candidates and employees through basic HR processes – hiring, adapting, training and organizing work [23]. Its interactivity allows not only assessing the competences and skills of a candidate or employee, but also identifying his strengths and weaknesses.

Analyzing the modern possibilities of VR and AR tools, it is clear that these technologies can become an indispensable assistant and support in HR management.

By using VR and AR technology, companies can develop simulations, a type of game for *attracting and hiring talent*, or an *interactive course* for an employee and in general everything that a given workplace can offer. This can be a *great way to attract people* and a useful working approach in *teaching* them some of the skills they may need to succeed [24]. Also, through these technologies many companies could *collaborate with remote employees*. With VR and AR technologies, companies can *conduct recruiting and staff selection* more efficiently, by presenting their employer brand to potential employees through an immersive experience.

In new operations particularly, it is important to anticipate human resource requirements and to translate them into recruiting and training programs so that a nucleus of appropriately skilled operators is available as production machinery and equipment are installed [5]. Integrating VR and AR technologies in this type of HR planning *reduces the chance that expensive capital equipment will stand idle* and that effort, time, and materials will be lost during startup and regular operations.

In addition, VR and AR can *contribute to team building activities*, significantly *reduce the economic and time costs of staff training* (especially travel cost and hotel accommodation) and improve staff adaptation in general. It allows *distance meetings* with remote employees or business partners located anywhere in the world. It is possible to *demonstrate in detail and visualize* the innovations, projects and its advantages, to attract the attention of the colleagues and audience etc. In production systems, the special value of VR and AR application in HRM can be a *vivid insight in the flow of the main operational processes in production, visualization of potential weaknesses, operations that can and should be automated*, etc.

Many studies show that through immersion in VR and AR, individuals can get "a contextual visualization of the environment to assist with an event or task while

Table 2. The frequency of HR and PM articles in top listed VR/AR journals by KoBSON

Journal	IF 2018	Launched	Human resource identified	Production system	HR and PM identified	Field of research
Virtual reality	2.906	1995	3	5	1	Learning technology
Journal of virtual reality and broadcasting	–	2004	5	12	–	Tracking; performance analysis

Table 3. The frequency of VR/AR and PM articles in top listed HR journals by KoBSON

Journal	IF 2018	Launched (year)	Virtual reality identified	Augmented reality identified	Production management identified	VR/AR and PM identified	Field of research
Journal of human resources	3.857	1966	–	–	–	–	–
Human resource management review	3.625	1991	–	–	10	–	Knowledge management
International journal of human resource management	3.150	1990	6	1	37	1	Manufacturing; knowledge management
Human resource development quarterly	3.000	1990	9	–	7	–	Training; job education
Human resource management	2.934	1961	4	–	16	–	Learning; work performance
Human resource management journal	2.843	1990	2	–	9	–	Training; work performance
Human resources for health	2.547	2003	2	14	212	–	Education; work performance
Human resource development review	2.487	2002	4	1		–	Training; HR development
Asia Pacific journal of human resources	0.891	1962	–	–	13	–	Work Performance

(*continued*)

Table 3. (*continued*)

Journal	IF 2018	Launched (year)	Virtual reality identified	Augmented reality identified	Production management identified	VR/AR and PM identified	Field of research
German journal of human resource management - Zeitschrift fur Personal forschung	0.759	1987	1	–	2	–	Organizational development

remaining within the bounds of the system" [25]. Contextual learning and interactivity based on engagement has a much higher contribution for learning [26], which is approved by an experiment of comparison of traditional training methods (TTM) and virtual reality-based training systems (VRTS). This experiment compared attributes between TTM and VRTS, such as comfort, ease of learning, ease of use, interactivity and engagement, and the results showed that VRTS are *easier for learning and use and more engaged* [27].

4 Conclusion

As a new technology trend that marked a last decade, virtual and augmented reality is increasingly being used for work simulation, but still it is not widely used in all functions and all areas of production management. This is evidenced by the very small number of articles published in journals on the SCI list (*Science Citation Index list*) that deals with this interdisciplinary topic. A literature review indicates that introduction of modern technologies, such as VR and AR, can support the design, engineering, management, and delivery of services, as well as employee engagement and memory retention capacity for working processes. In that manner, represented technologies meet the needs of the workforce as a significant stakeholder category in a business system, in a new, intelligent and innovative way.

Summarizing the results of the research analysis, we can draw a conclusion that VR and AR technologies are not used only in entertainment sector. Moreover, these are proved to be effective and useful tools in managing corporate business processes, in our case, primarily observed in HRM activities. Empirical studies suggest that companies are starting to realize that VR and AR can be used in simultaneously training, recruitment, employee engagement and knowledge retention, in increasing productivity, reducing costs and time and in ensuring safe and secure working conditions. Also, numerous studies show that VR and AR will reduce costs, improve the performance indicators of the company as a whole, and take a strong competitive advantage. It is clear that VR and AR can become HR digital support in main operational activities in production management. The coherence among production management and HR strategy systems is substantial for the attainment of business success.

However, despite the existing successful examples and results of using VR and AR in the labor market, as well as their benefits in the work of HR specialists, if we consider the cost and complexity of technology implementation, this trend still poses challenges and questions. Therefore, this study could stimulate further research of new potential fields of VR and AR application in particular companies, sectors, industries, or even countries.

References

1. Crnjac, M., Veža, I., Banduka, N.: From concept to the introduction of industry 4.0. Int. J. Ind. Eng. Manag. **8**(1), 21–30 (2017)
2. Gartner: Gartner Identifies the Top 10 Strategic Technology Trends for (2019). https://www.gartner.com/en/newsroom/press-releases/2018-10-15-gartner-identifies-the-top-10-strategic-technology-trends-for-2019. Accessed 30 Jan 2020
3. Gartner: Hype Cycle for Human Capital Management Technology. ID: G00371398 (2019)
4. Ćosić, I.P., Maksimović, R.M.: Proizvodni menadžment. Fakultet tehničkih nauka, Univerzitet u Novom Sadu, Novi Sad (2014)
5. Britannica: Production management: industrial engineering (2008), https://www.britannica.com/technology/production-management. Accessed 20 Feb 2020
6. Taylor, F.W.: The Principles of Scientific Management. Harper & Row, New York (1911)
7. Tracey, W.R.: Human Resources Management & Development Handbook, 2nd edn. American Management Association, New York (1994)
8. Myers, L.A.: One hundred years later: what would Frederick W. Taylor say? Int. J. Bus. Soc. Sci. **2**(20), 8–11 (2011)
9. Beatty, R.W., Schneier, C.E.: New HR roles to impact organizational performance: from "partners" to "players". Hum. Resour. Manag. **36**(1), 29–37 (1997)
10. Pasupa, T., Suzuki, S.: Impact of work-sharing on the performance of production line with heterogeneous workers. Int. J. Ind. Eng. Manag. (IJIEM) **10**(4), 284–302 (2019)
11. Korobaničová, I., Kováčová, N.: Human capital investment: practices and measurement in Slovak enterprises. Int. J. Ind. Eng. Manag. (IJIEM) **9**(3), 139–146 (2018)
12. Swanson, R.A., Holton, E.F.: Foundations of Human Resouce Development. Berrett-Koehler Publishers, Inc., San Francisco (2001)
13. Zhao, H., Zhao, Q.H., Slusarczyk, B.: Sustainability and digitalization of corporate management based on augmented/virtual reality tools usage: China and other world IT companies' experience. Sustainability **11**, 4717 (2019). https://doi.org/10.3390/su11174717
14. Ahmed, S.: A review on using opportunities of augmented reality and virtual reality in construction project maagement. Organ. Technol. Manag. Constr. **10**, 1839–1852 (2018)
15. Burdea, G., Coiffet, P.: Virtual Reality Technology. Wiley, Hoboken (2003)
16. Whyte, J.: Industrial applications of virtual reality in architecture and construction. J. Inf. Technol. Constr. (ITCon) **8**(4), 43–50 (2003)
17. Van Krevelen, D., Poelman, R.: A survey of augmented reality technologies, applications and limitations. Int. J. Virtual Reality **9**(2), 1 (2010)
18. Dunleavy, M., Dede, C.: Augmented reality teaching and learning. In: Spector, J.M., Merrill, M.D., Elen, J., Bishop, M.J. (eds.) Handbook of Research on Educational Communications and Technology, pp. 735–745. Springer, New York (2014). https://doi.org/10.1007/978-1-4614-3185-5_59

19. Loijens, L.W., Brohm, D., Domurath, N.: What is augmented reality? In: Loijens, L.W. (ed.) Augmented Reality for Food Marketers and Consumers, p. 356, Wageningen Academic Publishers, Wageningen (2017)
20. Guo, B., Bricout, J.C., Huang, J.: A common open space or a digital divide? A social model perspective on the online disability community in China. Disabil. Soc. **20**(1), 49–66 (2005)
21. Hinchcliffe, T.: Virtual reality takes consciousness research into mystic realms of the divine play. The Sociable (2017)
22. eMarketer: Augmented Reality Marketing and Advertising (2018). https://www.emarketer.com/content/augmented-reality-marketing-and-advertising-2018. Accessed 29 Jan 2020
23. Korenková, V., Závadský, J., Lis, M.: Linking a performance management system and competencies: qualitative research. Eng. Manag. Prod. Serv. **11**, 51–67 (2019)
24. Ideal: 4 Innovative Ways Companies Are Using AR in Recruiting (2019). https://ideal.com/ar-recruiting/. Accessed 18 Feb 2020
25. Randeniya, N., Ranjha, S., Kulkarni, A., Lu, G.: Virtual reality based maintenance training effectiveness measures – a novel approach for rail industry. In: IEEE 28th International Symposium on Industrial Electronics (ISIE), pp. 1605–1610 (2019). https://doi.org/10.1109/isie.2019.8781351
26. Gutiérrez, M.: Augmented reality environments in learning, communicational and professional contexts in higher education. Digit. Educ. Rev. **26**, 22–35 (2014)
27. Xu, J., Tang, Z., Yuan, X., Nie, Y., Ma, Z., Wei, X., et al.: A VR-based the emergency rescue training system of railway accident. Entertain. Comput. **27**, 23–31 (2018)

Application of Virtual Reality Technologies for Achieving Energy Efficient Manufacturing: Literature Analysis and Findings

E. G. Nabati[1]([✉]) [ID], M. T. Alvela Nieto[1] [ID], A. Decker[2] [ID],
and K.-D. Thoben[1] [ID]

[1] Faculty of Production Engineering, BIK-Institute for Integrated Product
Development, University of Bremen, 28359 Bremen, Germany
{nabati,malvela,thoben}@uni-bremen.de
[2] BIBA - Bremer Institut für Produktion und Logistik GmbH at the University of
Bremen, 28359 Bremen, Germany
dec@biba.uni-bremen.de

Abstract. Improvement in current manufacturing settings for enabling energy efficiency is a challenge for many manufacturers. Although virtual reality has been so far applied in manufacturing for training, visualization and product development, the use of this technology in manufacturing for increasing energy efficiency has been less addressed. This paper investigates the potential of virtual reality for a better analysis of energy demands in manufacturing. By envisioning and illustrating energy flows and consumption, virtual reality can support energy efficiency. The paper provides a systematic review of the literature. The findings are analysed from the perspective of research gaps in making virtual-based technologies to enable energy-efficient manufacturing. Particularly, the elements and factors (opportunities) and methods that can be transmitted from current research to energy-efficient manufacturing, are identified and discussed.

Keywords: Manufacturing · Energy efficiency · Virtual reality

1 Introduction

Today's manufacturing is one of the world's biggest consumer of energy. By 2030 a target of 32.5% energy savings has been endorsed through negotiations between the European Commission and Parliament [6]. Consequently, European manufacturers face today the challenge of reducing energy consumption while maintaining quality and productivity. Besides, advances of Industry 4.0 provide new opportunities to better measure energy, understand its patterns or mechanisms and improve manufacturing operations concerning energy. Determining and understanding energy consumption at each stage of manufacturing is crucial for enabling energy efficiency. Though improvements in energy efficiency (EE) have been made across all branches of manufacturing, significant potential still exists [5].

© IFIP International Federation for Information Processing 2020
Published by Springer Nature Switzerland AG 2020
B. Lalic et al. (Eds.): APMS 2020, IFIP AICT 591, pp. 479–486, 2020.
https://doi.org/10.1007/978-3-030-57993-7_54

One technology of Industry 4.0 that can further contribute to the efficient consumption of energy is virtual reality (VR). In general, VR makes it possible for users to step into a three-dimensional (3D) illustration of a real-world environment, through a computer interface [13]. VR-solutions pose good potential for saving energy in manufacturing industries. Since they can add a layer of energy information to the machinery and equipment. Areas of research, such as smart buildings and facility management, have managed earlier than manufacturers to adapt VR to the energy analysis. For example, authors including [9] provided a VR-tool for the modeling and analysis of energy as well as its 3D-visualization within buildings.

The findings on VR-solutions from the area of smart buildings can be transferred into the manufacturing industries, i.e., analyzing the higher energy consumers on the shop floor of a manufacturing plant. Inspired by this possibility, this research seeks to identify the components (elements) of manufacturing, such as machinery and processes, other than buildings, which affect the energy consumption in manufacturing. In addition, factors and opportunities to include in the energy modeling with VR are noted. Knowing the available methods is also important for developing VR-solutions about energy. To the best authors' knowledge, engineering tools for the design and development of VR-applications in energy-efficient manufacturing (EEM) are not published or reported yet. Further, results of surveys as [2, 4] suggest that only a few studies have tackled VR-technologies for achieving efficiency in terms of energy consumption. Consequently, practical studies related to EE on VR from the current research need to be identified; so that meaningful insight can be leveraged.

This paper provides an overall analysis of the potential of VR into EEM, whereby it answers the following research questions (RQ) through a review of state-of-the-art:

RQ1. Which factors and elements should be considered for the transmission of currently available research to apply VR for increasing EE in manufacturing?

RQ2. What are the methods available in the literature to apply VR in EEM?

The paper is structured as follows: Sect. 2 presents the literature search methodology. Section 3 reveals and discusses the results of the literature review. Section 4 reports the findings in terms of research gaps as well as the knowledge acquired after the analysis of studies. Here limitations of VR are also presented. In Sect. 5, conclusions are drawn.

2 Methodology Based on Systematic Review of Literature

For the literature review, a methodology called PRISMA [16] is adopted. Two leading online databases, Scopus and Google Scholar, are selected. While Scopus provided papers with a good scientific contribution, Google Scholar is used as a complementary search tool to find articles from a more practical point of view. As Fig. 1 shows, three sets of keywords are searched. The period considered is 2004–2020. The first search criteria lead to around 928 articles. The identified papers were screened through reading the title and 106 papers are selected. The excluded papers primarily addressed VR in, i.e., reconfigurable manufacturing systems and sustainable engineering education. These trends within manufacturing are not the focus of this paper. Afterward, abstracts

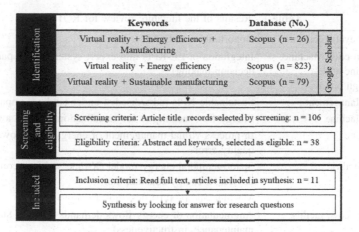

Fig. 1. Methodology for literature review

and keywords of 106 papers were assessed. The result was a selection of 38 eligible papers for this study. These papers were read in full-text and later, 11 papers were selected for answering the above research questions.

3 Results and Discussion

The results of the literature review are recapitulated in Table 1 and Table 2. The answers to RQ1 are provided in the Table 1. In order to understand the elements and factors, column "(Level) Elements" investigates to what extent state-of-art of VR is linked to which elements of the manufacturing level(s). The considered manufacturing levels in this paper are operational and tactical. Therefore, the first column of Table 1 assesses the area of application within manufacturing. Next, the column "Opportunities to EEM" shows the results of identified factors related to energy efficiency. This column also assesses the focus of the studies on different aspects of EEM.

In contrast, Table 2 assesses, which environment(s) the research has been validated on (case studies). The review of case studies reveals manufacturers the feasibility and potential of VR-applications in particular environments and it indicates similarities (or not) for possible transfers into new practical studies. For the RQ2, the last column of Table 2 presents methods and tools for implementing VR. Furthermore, the next two sub-sections analyse the contents of Table 1 and Table 2 concerning VR for EEM. In Sect. 3.1, the analysis of Table 1 respecting to RQ1 is presented. Section 3.2 provides a discussion about Table 2 for RQ2.

3.1 Elements and Factors in Current Research to Apply VR for Increasing EE in Manufacturing

Table 1 shows that the gathered studies of VR mainly focus on the operational level. Among the results of Table 1, 8 of 10 selected papers address VR in EEM for the operational layer of manufacturing. The elements of the operational level are process,

Table 1. Results of the literature review for RQ1

Ref.	(Level) Elements	Opportunities to EEM
[1]	Process, Machine, Line at design phase	Integration of EE-KPIs into expert systems (transparency, decision-making)
[3]	Management	Sustainable KPIs (adv./disadv., understanding, impacts)
[15]	Machine	Energy-flow techniques for visualization (causes, awareness)
[11]	Line	In-process virtual management of energy, workflow, and quality error
[8]	Facility	Spatio-temporal energy model (X-time series, y-consumption devices, z-energy consumption)
[12]	Process, machine	Machine and product design to EE (awareness, transparency)
[10]	Process, facility	Augmentation of energy flows demands (process states, maintenance, instructiveness)
[17]	Management	KPIs as integrative energy management
[18]	Line	Visual interface for asset information
[14]	Facility	Immersive thermal simulation in virtual environment

machine, line and facility. The classification of these elements can be considered valid, as many approaches within EEM, such as the study of [7], divide the analysis of energy into the same set of elements. Also, the analysis of Table 1 shows that the current research has addressed these elements individually. That is, there is still no research, which examines the flows of energy between the elements of manufacturing, especially during operation. Therefore, developing a model of processes-machines-lines and their interdependencies in a manufacturing facility can better evaluate energy demands.

Other findings from the Table 1 shows that the majority of the research concentrates on the transparency of energy performances. As energy is not visible to the human eye, which complicates the impairment of energy efficiency. Therefore, the availability and visualization of energy data and information of energy assets, for example, in the form of sustainable key performance indicators (KPIs) or flows increase awareness about demands and support its efficiency [1, 10, 12, 15, 17, 18]. Nevertheless, energy demands in real applications are influenced by complex settings, such as the effects of different process parameters, workflows and quality requirements. But energy flows and energy consumers considering multiple configurations of parameters are almost absent in the literature (Table 1).

In [8, 10, 12, 14, 15], computer-aided design (CAD) models are used for the interactive examination and manipulation of VR-applications. However, most geometries on VR are not reflecting the real dimensions of, i.e., a certain machine. So, it makes the energy model inaccurate. Moreover, visualizations of many energy flows in one component or many components in one visualization such as [8, 14, 15] in Table 1 can become unclear to the observer.

Besides, energy demands in [15] were assumed to be constant, whereas the energy losses of, i.e., a cooling system, were neglected. Furthermore, the EE-KPIs defined in

[1, 3] do not account for the fluctuation of the process times and/or cycle times. Both process time and cycle time influence the energy consumption of a particular line at the production phase. Thus, energy performances can become misleading when time-series factors are not taken into account.

Lastly, from Table 1, an estimation about the potential of the energy savings through VR-solutions is neither visualized nor (at least) quantified. Despite the fact that evaluative information about the savings (actual and ideal energy demand) may raise awareness among manufacturing practitioners. In this context, a VR-based solution can assist in determining the energy costs of a process or machine with a particular set of parameters and predefined quality.

3.2   Methods of VR for Enhancing EEM

Firstly, simulation and CAD modeling are the most common methods listed in Table 2. The VR-tools in Table 2 were mainly selected concerning to the case studies. As an example, VueOne is an engineering software environment, which supports the assembly. It is selected by [1], respecting the case study of the battery assembly.

About the methods that are specifically designed for the analysis of EE in manufacturing, there are only a few works available (Table 2). For machines, the technique of particle system on VR allowed the visualization of dynamic changes in energy flows over time [8]. In the particle system, the direction of energy flows is also highlighted. In [11], a 3D-regression method evaluated the correlations of workflow, consumption of energy and quality error. However, evaluation of other potential factors affecting energy demands as settings of process variables were not included.

Secondly, a tendency in Table 2 exists to base VR on point-cloud models and particle systems when it comes to virtual buildings [8, 18]. These methods can be combined with the use of drones and photogrammetry for quicker creation of 3D-models on VR. This approach from smart buildings is also applicable and rentable in manufacturing when it comes to elements such as lines and building of a factory.

Thirdly, the literature analysis showed that the majority of the VR-methods in Table 2 are developed from a theoretical point of view. Then, their performances are validated in specific case studies and experiments [1, 3, 18]. Hence, there is a need for contributions from a more practical point of view, which addresses the real-world application of VR in EEM.

Lastly, in the context of manufacturing, VR-technologies constitute augmented reality (AR), mixed reality (MR or XR) and virtual manufacturing (VM) [12, 13]. According to [12], AR is VR placed over the real world, but with the provision of additional information. Thus, the authors of [12] infer that AR can be seen as a subset of VR. MR encompasses both virtual and AR technologies.

Moreover, VM is a term represented as a virtual world for manufacturing. This paper addressed all these mentioned VR-technologies.

Table 2. Results of the literature review for RQ2

Ref.	Case Study	Method(s): Tool(s) of VR
[1]	Battery module assembly	Discrete event simulation tools: VueOne, Witness DES
[3]	Serious-games learning env.	Virtual twins
[15]	Turning, milling	3D-Sankey, Billboad and 3D-Particle methods: CAD
[11]	Shop-floor	3D-Virtual simulation
[8]	None	VR with immersive visual data mining: 3D-CAVE, CAD
[12]	None	Discrete event simulation and 3D-particle methods:CAD
[10]	Galvanic and oven process modules	Holographic augmentation, interactive visualization: CAD
[18]	Railway maintenance	4D reality, point-cloud methods
[2]	Human operators, packaging, interior tractor	3D-Visualisation suite: RTT DEltaGen, Siemens Jack, Autodesk VRED, ESI ICIDO

4 Findings

From the previous section, it can be drawn that VR in EEM has been mostly used to reduce the time required to collate and understand energy information. An energy model for the context of manufacturing should consist of many elements such as machinery, production line, facility, processes and interdependence of energy demand from them. More detail about the essential factors in the application of VR for EEM, namely, transparency of energy flows, assessing energy demands and energy losses, process parameters affecting energy demands are discussed in Sect. 3.1. The highlighted opportunities to EEM on VR have a high degree of flexibility. They are quickly adaptable, as they are not bounded by physical hardware. This allows to experience different settings and/or scenarios of higher energy consumers that are, in reality, too costly or not available in hardware.

Further, our observations show that a tendency exists in the literature to research VR-technologies related to time and costs, quality and reduction of design errors. However, the different settings of parameters influence the results in the form of energy but also in the form of emissions and wastes of processes, e.g., in a milling process. Wastes and emissions are difficult to integrate on VR and hence their embodied energy can not be quantified. To our understanding, it is also a matter of what designers (users) can do from a VR-technology standpoint but also how human actions in the virtual environment influence decision making.

Additionally, best practices and benchmarks of energy efficiency in manufacturing on VR-solutions are still not published. Probably, as a consequence of the ambiguity of the cause-effect relationships in the manufacturing processes.

Limitations of VR in EEM. Although the VR's advantage in reproducing a controllable environment is desirable for application in EEM, there are some limitations too. (1) Costs of establishing a VR-based system is rather high.

Before designing a VR-based system for EEM, the long-term benefits of this technology, in terms of savings, should be calculated against its costs. (2) Multi-sensor illustration of energy flows. It is challenging to split several energy flows and illustrate them in a virtual environment. There can be overlaps between the illustrations of energy. This point can confuse the observers or bring errors in energy analysis. (3) The danger of continual use for the health of employees. On the one hand, the currently available head mount glasses for VR and MR are heavy. The weight is because of battery or processing appliances. Therefore, they might cause problems such as neck pain for the employee if they are used for a long time. On the other hand, they are placed over the eyes. Too much use can cause eye-sight problems.

5 Conclusions

Our research provides a literature review on 11 papers about VR-technologies for enhancing energy efficiency in the manufacturing domain. Opportunities and tools of VR for the context of EEM were presented and discussed extensively in Sects. 3 and 4. The results of the analysis admit that using VR on EEM can improve knowledge about energy consumption in manufacturing environments. Future studies may transfer, combine and adjust the analysed methods (Sect. 3.2) of VR for further exploring its opportunities in EEM (Sect. 3.1 and 4). As the deployment of VR-technologies and its usability demands considerable energy at a cost to manufacturing too.

Beyond the scope of this paper, several types of research tackle the connection of digital twins to VR for establishing digital factories of the future. However, they do not discuss VR in energy analysis about efficiency, considering a whole factory. Therefore, there is a need for future research of EEM on VR, not only as a stand-alone solution but also as a multi-level holistic approach.

It should be noted that in this paper, because of limitation in space, only the results of the analysis for 11 selected papers that has the most relevancy to the research questions, have been published. Analysis of all 38 eligible papers from the perspective of EEM will later be provided in the special issue.

References

1. Assad, F., Alkan, B., Chinnathai, M.K., Ahmad, M.H., Rushforth, E.J., Harrison, R.: A framework to predict energy related key performance indicators of manufacturing systems at early design phase. Procedia CIRP **81**, 145–150 (2019). https://doi.org/10.1016/j.procir.2019.03.026
2. Berg, L.P., Vance, J.M.: Industry use of virtual reality in product design and manufacturing: a survey. Vir. Real. **21**(1), 1–17 (2016). https://doi.org/10.1007/s10055-016-0293-9

3. Chaim, O., Muschard, B., Cazarini, E., Rozenfeld, H.: Insertion of sustainability performance indicators in an industry 4.0 virtual learning environment. Procedia Manuf. **21**, 446–453 (2018). https://doi.org/10.1016/j.promfg.2018.02.143
4. Choi, S., Jung, K., Noh, S.D.: Virtual reality applications in manufacturing industries: past research, present findings, and future directions. Concurrent Eng. **23**(1), 40–63 (2015). https://doi.org/10.1177/1063293X14568814
5. EIA: Digitalisation and Energy (2017). https://www.iea.org/reports/digitalisation-and-energy
6. European-Commission: Report from the commission to the European parliament and the council (2017). https://publications.europa.eu/en/publication-detail/-/publication/a554e5f0-d4f5-11e7-a5b9-01aa75ed71a1/language-en
7. Fysikopoulos, A., Pastras, G., Alexopoulos, T., Chryssolouris, G.: On a generalized approach to manufacturing energy efficiency. Int. J. Adv. Manuf. Technol. **73**(9–12), 1437–1452 (2014). https://doi.org/10.1007/s00170-014-5818-3
8. Haefner, P., Seessle, J., Duecker, J., Zienthek, M., Szeliga, F.: Interactive visualization of energy efficiency concepts using virtual reality. Eurographics Assoc. (2014). https://doi.org/10.2312/EUROVR.20141346
9. Ham, Y., Golparvar-Fard, M.: 3D visualization of thermal resistance and condensation problems using infrared thermography for building energy diagnostics. Vis. Eng. **2**(1), 1–15 (2014). https://doi.org/10.1186/s40327-014-0012-0
10. Juraschek, M., Büth, L., Posselt, G., Herrmann, C.: Mixed reality in learning factories. Procedia Manuf. **23**, 153–158 (2018). https://doi.org/10.1016/j.promfg.2018.04.009
11. Katchasuwanmanee, K., Cheng, K., Bateman, R.: Simulation based energy-resource efficient manufacturing integrated with in-process virtual management. Chinese J. Mech. Eng. **29**(6), 1083–1089 (2016). https://doi.org/10.3901/CJME.2016.0714.080
12. Mawson, V.J., Hughes, B.R.: The development of modelling tools to improve energy efficiency in manufacturing processes and systems. J. Manuf. Syst. **51**, 95–105 (2019). https://doi.org/10.1016/j.jmsy.2019.04.008
13. Mujber, T.S., Szecsi, T., Hashmi, M.: Virtual reality applications in manufacturing process simulation. J. Mater. Process. Technol. **155–156**, 1834–1838 (2004). https://doi.org/10.1016/j.jmatprotec.2004.04.401
14. Nugraha Bahar, Y., Landrieu, J., Pére, C., Nicolle, C.: CAD data workflow toward the thermal simulation and visualization in virtual reality. Int. J. Interact. Des. Manuf. (IJIDeM) **8**(4), 283–292 (2013). https://doi.org/10.1007/s12008-013-0200-5
15. Pelliccia, L., Klimant, P., Schumann, M., Pürzel, F., Wittstock, V., Putz, M.: Energy visualization techniques for machine tools in virtual reality. Procedia CIRP **41**, 329–333 (2016). https://doi.org/10.1016/j.procir.2015.10.013
16. PRISMA: Transparent Reporting of Systematic Reviews and Meta-Analysis. http://www.prisma-statement.org. Accessed 22 Mar 2020
17. Schulze, M., Nehler, H., Ottosson, M., Thollander, P.: Energy management in industry – a systematic review of previous findings and an integrative conceptual framework. J. Cleaner Prod. **112**, 3692–3708 (2016). https://doi.org/10.1016/j.jclepro.2015.06.060
18. Whyte, J., Broyd, T.: Viewing asset information: future impact of augmented reality. In: Proceedings of 32nd CIB W78 Conference, pp. 754–761 (2015)

Smart Products in Smart Manufacturing Systems: An Opportunity to Utilize AR?

Joshua Gross and Thorsten Wuest[✉]

West Virginia University, Morgantown, WV 26505, USA
jjg0016@mix.wvu.edu, thwuest@mail.wvu.edu

Abstract. The evolution of manufacturing throughout time has allowed our industrial world to develop and ever faster create various products in large numbers using a myriad of industrial manufacturing processes. However, like everything in the world, time moves forward and the evolution does not stop but accelerate. Therefore, the implementation of Augmented Reality (AR) through the use of the internet of things, low cost sensors, and free programming languages, are all contributing factors to further advanced the industry. These implementations will allow for faster data processing, quicker error recovery time, loss and error prevention, a wider range of employees at different skill levels to be productive in a manufacturing environment. The implementation of an Arduino based sensor system into the manufacturing process enables data streaming to an AR device. This system allows for instant data streaming and visualization to the user/operator with information pertaining to the status of the product ('state'), key developments, and changes in the product/or system, any associated errors, and the best way to proceed with resolving them. The AR enabled system with its capability to streaming relevant information prevents losses associated with product quality issues and/or process down-time among a myriad of other applications. Preliminary research shows the ability to collect data from the product in addition to data processing on an external device to later be used on an augmented reality device.

Keywords: AR · Augmented reality · Smart glasses · Smart manufacturing · Smart product · Industry 4.0

1 Introduction

The ongoing fourth industrial revolution is enabled by data, data processing, and connectivity mainly through the internet of things [1]. Digitalization of data and processes aims to decrease production time, prevent errors and mistakes, and facilitates rapid designing and prototyping of one-of-a-kind products [2]. The emergence of smart manufacturing will allow for all of these to occur while enabling individuals and companies to oversee their entire manufacturing process. This monitoring of the process enables this to be done in high detail, remotely, and with minimal effort. Real-time in-situ data collection and analysis is key to the future of manufacturing and this project aims to contribute to the progress in this field through an example of a novel in-situ data collection application using smart products during the production process itself.

© IFIP International Federation for Information Processing 2020
Published by Springer Nature Switzerland AG 2020
B. Lalic et al. (Eds.): APMS 2020, IFIP AICT 591, pp. 487–494, 2020.
https://doi.org/10.1007/978-3-030-57993-7_55

As technology further develops, systems such as the one explained in this paper can collect data in real-time and then be used in a visualization method, such as AR. [3]. The majority of smart manufacturing systems collect data of the to-be-manufactured part via sensor systems integrated in the machine tool and/or assembly line [11]. In this case, the to-be-manufactured smart product collects the manufacturing process data via a system integrated sensor system. The idea is that the smart product collects data of the manufacturing process in real-time, and the insights from the analyzed data is provided to the operator as decision support via an Augmented Reality (AR) application.

The integrated sensor system allows for rapid and specific data analysis pertaining to individual to-be-manufactured products by shop floor employees. In large scale manufacturing processes, product errors and production line down time can cost companies large amounts of money [4]. Having manufacturing floor employees overseeing the manufacturing process and products with AR is expected to contribute to the prevention and resolution of product associated errors [5, 13]. The aim of this research is to demonstrate the application of AR in combination with a smart-connected product within the manufacturing process and show that the AR integration allows for rapid product data observance in addition to error resolution via a test-bed cyber-physical production system.

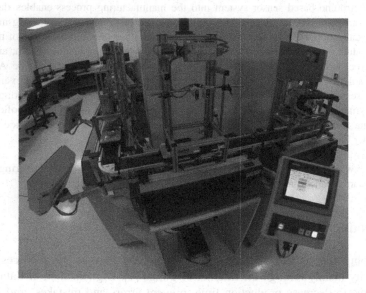

Fig. 1. Testbed setup – CPlab smart manufacturing system

Our experimental setup and development of the Arduino based sensor system is detailed in the following, touching upon how it is utilized in order to achieve data collection, analysis, and user feedback. The research is conducted in a test-bed comprised of a FESTO Didactics cyber-physical laboratory (CP-lab) (see Fig. 1). The eight-stage smart manufacturing system manufactures a simulated cell phone case that consists of two separate plastic parts that are manipulated and assembled in a fully automated manufacturing process. This data and analysis allows us to instantly track the progress and working state of a single product in order to give the operator instant feedback. However, this test-bed application can be theoretically applied to a much larger scale in many different scenarios such as automotive part monitoring, machine and part maintenance, and quality control of products. The data processing combined with the AR applications allows the operator to instantly and easily read out all of the pertinent information regarding the part that they are inquiring into.

The paper is structured as follows: in Sect. 2, a brief overview of the background and state of the art in smart product based process monitoring and AR applications in manufacturing is provided. Following, the research methodology is depicted in Sect. 3 before initial results are presented in Sect. 4. Section 5 concludes the paper and provides a short outlook on future research and potential future applications of the CPlab/AR setup.

2 Background and State of the Art

AR offers significant potential with regard to improving the overall manufacturing system and its processes [12]. Currently, AR is being utilized in the manufacturing process to improve quality control, maintenance, and assembly. Within the last three years, AR has been directly applied to the following industries: medical, military, robotics, and manufacturing [2]. Porsche, for example, is actively using AR to ensure that manufactured parts meet the design expectations and dimensions. By simply looking at a part, the AR glasses will "instantly gauge the dimensional accuracy, surface finish, tolerances and interference and other potential issues" [6]. Continually, Boeing uses AR to assist manufacturing floor employees with the electrical components installation to ensure accuracy and decrease installation time. Furthermore, the use of AR in this application also ensures the employee are not missing any components [7].

Another identified current AR application in manufacturing is utilized by ThyssenKrupp, a large industrial company among others in the elevator industry. AR is used to scan a staircase to measure all dimensions which are instantly sent to the manufacturing department. Furthermore, the AR allows the customer to see what the stair lift will look like after installation [6]. In the healthcare industry, GE Healthcare is using AR for "projecting the work instructions onto the parts and use sensors to monitor the assembly and give feedback to the operator" which inherently increases accuracy and efficiency [8]. With the implementation of AR, "activities, such as design, planning, machining, etc., are done right the first time without the need for subsequent re-works and modifications" and therefore enables error prevention [2]. Cyber-Physical systems such as the laboratory set-up used in this study enable a more accurate manufacturing process through the internet of things as well as AR. While a one-of-a-kind part is being produced, "the part is checked and verified against product design data in particular its dimensions and tolerances" which ensures that the part is being created to the proper specifications [9]. Furthermore, Anderl states, "as products or components of products are based on cyber-physical systems their smart sensors are able to deliver data about the products' or the components' condition". If this data is sent to an AR system for analysis, the worker can utilize the information in real-time and "predictive maintenance can be taken" [9]. AR would allow any worker to observe the part during the manufacturing process while being shown how the part being produced compares to the design and specifications. Continually, the construction industry is currently utilizing AR "to address defects that might be overlooked in the inspection process" [10]. This same technology can be applied to the manufacturing industry as a way to constantly monitor the part being produced. This constant observance in addition to the data display through AR will therefore prevent errors as well as help correct any existing ones. These examples of current AR applications demonstrate its potential when being fully implemented into the manufacturing process at all stages to improve efficiency, accuracy, and safety.

The current laboratory set up used for this study includes an Arduino Nano based sensor system which allows for high customization to collect data on various attributes of the product during production. As of now, the sensor system is capable of tracking acceleration and magnetic field, has a toggle switch for tracking mode, and a SD card reading to store all of the collected data. Figure 2 shows a CAD rendition of the mock cell phone with the Arduino Nano and associated sensors used to collect said data.

Fig. 2. Arduino nano sensor system CAD layout

Due to limitations within the Arduino Nano and space constraints within the product's volume, the data is currently not processed in real-time. Off-the-shelf sensors are easier to use and deploy but have high physical and programmatic complications when it comes to customization of the solution. A custom-made Arduino based sensor system allows for high customizability at a low cost.

The implementation of the sensor system into the CP-lab system allows for customized data tracking throughout the entire manufacturing process whereas most current industries have the ability to strictly track physical location or status. For example, our sensor system in the CP-lab system will allow the user to see how the part is oriented, which station it is at, the temperature, and current progress through the manufacturing process whereas current tracking methods would simply read out how far along the part is in the manufacturing process. Table 1 shows a comparison of different sensor systems used for tracking in industry. This table compares barcodes/data matrices, radio frequency identification (RFID), off-the-shelf sensors (OTS), and our Arduino sensor system. Barcodes or data matrices are patterns that encode data that can be read by a scanner therefore showing the user the encoded data. RFID tags send data regarding a product through the use of radio waves and an antenna. If these tags have their own power source, they are categorized as being 'active', otherwise they are 'passive'. The OTS sensor is available to anyone and can be purchased online and comes with capabilities determined by the manufacturer. Based on this table it is clear that the Arduino system has the most potential and capability. The boxes that are marked with a '(x)' indicates a sort of caveat. Regarding the passive RFID, this has the ability to locate if and only if it is connected to the machine itself. In its own, the passive RFID does not have the ability to locate items. The OTS sensor is customizable to a certain degree. The OTS can be customized within the spectrum that the manufacturer allows. Outside of the guidelines set by the manufacturer, the OTS cannot be customized.

3 Case Study of Smart Manufacturing Testbed

The Arduino Nano based sensor system is directly placed inside the beginning half of the product. As the product goes through the different stages of placement, drilling, laser measuring, turning, heating, compression, and sorting, data is collected and placed onto the SD card. The data is in the form of an Excel file which is then imported into Python. In Python, the data can be processed in practically any fashion before continuing. Once the raw data has been processed and analyzed, it is then embedded into an Android compatible graphic user interface (GUI) such as Kivy, where is it made tangible and can be interacted with. This GUI is what presents the data in a user-friendly fashion to the user and data can be sorted and organized. Due to the Android compatibility, the GUI can be compressed into an installer executable and placed onto the Android based AR glasses where the user will directly and most practically be interacting with the processed data. Figure 3 illustrates the principle structure of the project and how all of the steps lead to enabling better decision making for the user, the manufacturing engineer, on whether or not to take action.

Due to the nature of Arduino single board computer systems, the sensor system is highly customizable and can be changed easily to collect different data types. Furthermore, Arduinos allow for the pre-processing of data such as ignoring certain factors, actively looking for outliers or false data, or searching for anticipated data. Having 'clean' data coming out of the sensor system enables faster, easier, and more accurate results and feedback to come out of the Python data processing code.

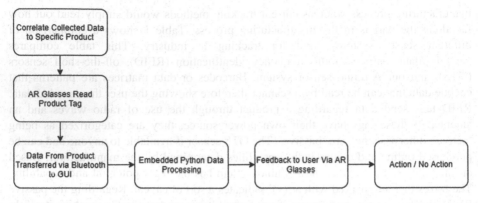

Fig. 3. Theoretical project work flow

4 Results

The results so far reflect the current stage of development of the ongoing research project. At this point, the smart-connected product is capable of actively and reliably collecting data during the manufacturing process. The acquired sensor data contains multiple sensor measurements and visualization of the data enables an analysis of the smart-connected products progress and changing state through the multi-stage mart manufacturing system. However, the wireless connectivity to the AR glasses and/or network is still development. While the Arduino system provides several advantages (see Table 1), it is bulkier and difficult to fully integrate in the product itself. Therefore, certain adjustments to the manufacturing process itself were necessary.

Some findings at this stage include: struggles in data transfer between devices, inability to access certain features on the AR glasses, and the inability to extract useful data off of the CP-lab system. However, the sensors system has been able to collect

Table 1. Comparing popular tracking technologies with regard to data processing capabilities

	Barcode/data matrix	RFID (Passive)	RFID (Active)	OTS	Arduino sensor system
Identify	x	x	x	x	x
Identify + Locate	x	(x)	x	x	x
Identify + Locate + Sense	–	–	x	x	x
Identify + Locate + Sense + Communicate	–	–	–	x	x
Identify + Locate + Sense + Communicate + Process Data	–	–	–	–	x
Customizable	–	–	–	(x)	x

data containing elapsed time, 3-axis acceleration, orientation, and the magnetic field. This data is compiled into an MS Excel sheet on an SD card to be used for data processing. Note that this data flow is not wireless due to limitations with the Arduino Nano which is not Bluetooth capable at the moment. Furthermore, using the current sensor system makes it difficult to collect data while in the CP-lab system as the wiring interferes with the laser sensors thus sending a false signal to the system and therefore making a faulty part.

Due to challenges faced in multiple stages of our ongoing research project, there is limited tangible data available as of this point in time. Other limitations include unexpected barriers, such as ability to gain developer access on the AR glasses thus limiting testing ability with the connection between the data and the glasses. Continually, this prevents the installation of any custom made software to be placed onto the glasses and therefore the data processing code cannot be directly utilized on the glasses. Another limitation includes the lack of available space inside of the manufactured part which limits the number and size of sensors to be used.

5 Conclusions and Future Work

The initial results of this project show promise with regard to providing a richer data picture seamlessly to the operator via AR. However, there are several challenges that need to be addressed to further the research. Certain obstacles can be overcome relatively quickly whereas others will take a lot more time and resources. For example, redesigning and developing the sensors system will prevent the interference with the laser measuring system and therefore prevent false signals to be sent to the CP-lab system, a relatively easy solution. However, other issues such as the lack of access to the AR glasses and lack of functionality in the glasses cannot simply be solved and require more resources and collaboration with the manufacturer of the AR equipment.

Continuing research regarding the implementation of AR into the manufacturing process offers high potential for a case study in addition to real-world applications. Actively contributing to Industry 4.0 and Smart Manufacturing will continue to grow the field in addition to further advance and optimize the manufacturing process thus increasing productivity, efficiency, safety, and saving money. Refinement of the sensor array enables the opportunity for highly customized data tracking and therefore detailed feedback to the user. RFID tags are currently used in many industries but are limited in their tracking capability. The use of AR will allow for tracking throughout the entire manufacturing process and therefore potentially prevent recalls, prevent full process shut downs, and potentially save parts that have encountered manufacturing errors. Regarding industries that do not have any sort of tracking, a system like this could revolutionize their company. Being able to track the parts your company is producing offers many benefits and allows a company to utilize the collected data and become more efficient and productive in their manufacturing.

The utilization of the Arduino based sensor system allows for high customization. Many off-the-shelf sensors are non-customizable and therefore you either collect all of the data that they're capable of collecting or you don't use the sensor at all. Our system allows for the user or company to decide which data they want to collect and which data is negligible to them. This reduces the data processing time and therefore gives the user more in-depth feedback in less time.

Acknowledgements. This work was supported by the J. Wayne & Kathy Richards Faculty Fellowship in Engineering at West Virginia University and the Research Apprenticeship Program (RAP) at the WVU Office of Undergraduate Research.

References

1. Schlick, J.: Cyber-physical systems in factory automation-towards the 4th industrial revolution. In: 2012 9th IEEE International Workshop on Factory Communication Systems, p. 55. IEEE, May 2012
2. Ong, S.K., Yuan, M.L., Nee, A.Y.C.: Augmented reality applications in manufacturing: a survey. Int. J. Prod. Res. **46**(10), 2707–2742 (2008)
3. Zheng, P., et al.: Smart manufacturing systems for Industry 4.0: conceptual framework, scenarios, and future perspectives. Front. Mech. Eng. **13**(2), 137–150 (2018)
4. Salonen, A., Tabikh, M.: Downtime costing—attitudes in Swedish manufacturing industry. In: Koskinen, K., et al. (eds.) Proceedings of the 10th World Congress on Engineering Asset Management (WCEAM 2015), pp. 539–544. Springer, Cham (2016). https://doi.org/10.1007/978-3-319-27064-7_53
5. Qeshmy, D.E., Makdisi, J., da Silva, E.H.D.R., Angelis, J.: Managing human errors: augmented reality systems as a tool in the quality journey. Procedia Manuf. **28**, 24–30 (2019)
6. Vyas, K.: 5 Cool Augmented Reality Applications in the Manufacturing Sector, 12 March 2018. https://interestingengineering.com/augmented-reality-applications-manufacturing-sector
7. Rathbone, E.: Real world applications of Augmented Reality (AR) in manufacturing, 18 August 2018. http://www.manufacturinglounge.com/real-world-applications-of-augmented-reality-ar-in-manufacturing/
8. Kellner, T.: How Augmented Reality Improves Manufacturing Productivity, 20 April 2018. https://www.ge.com/reports/game-augmented-reality-helping-factory-workers-become-productive/
9. Anderl, R.: Industrie 4.0-advanced engineering of smart products and smart production. In: Proceedings of International Seminar on High Technology, vol. 19 (2014)
10. Behzadi, A.: Using Augmented and Virtual Reality Technology in the Construction Industry, pp. 350–351 (2016)
11. Mittal, S., Khan, M.A., Romero, D., Wuest, T.: Smart manufacturing: characteristics, technologies and enabling factors. Proc. Inst. Mech. Eng. Part B: J. Eng. Manuf. **233**(5), 1342–1361 (2019)
12. Nee, A.Y., Ong, S.K., Chryssolouris, G., Mourtzis, D.: Augmented reality applications in design and manufacturing. CIRP Ann. **61**(2), 657–679 (2012)
13. Uva, A.E., Gattullo, M., Manghisi, V.M., Spagnulo, D., Cascella, G.L., Fiorentino, M.: Evaluating the effectiveness of spatial augmented reality in smart manufacturing: a solution for manual working stations. Int. J. Adv. Manuf. Technol. **94**(1-4), 509–521 (2017). https://doi.org/10.1007/s00170-017-0846-4

Evaluation of Augmented Reality in Industry

Tone Lise Dahl^(✉) , Manuel Oliveira , and Emrah Arica

SINTEF, Trondheim, Norway
{tone.lise.dahl,manuel.oliveira,
emrah.arica}@sintef.no

Abstract. Augmented Reality (AR) is seen as a key technology for the development of smart manufacturing. Despite the many possibilities and affordances of this emerging technology, it is a fairly new technology in industry without widespread adoption. Research indicates that there are many affordances of using this technology in industry as well as some challenges. However, there seems to be a lack of research on how to evaluate AR in industry. Based on literature and a case study, we propose guidelines for evaluating AR based on identified dimensions.

Keywords: Industrial augmented reality · Evaluation · Guidelines

1 Introduction

Augmented Reality (AR) refers to a real-world environment enhanced with computer-generated information such as sound, video or graphics. AR can be delivered by using smartphones, tablets, head-mounted-displays (HMDs) and projectors [12, 14]. The last few years, augmented reality technology (AR) has arisen in manufacturing [9] and is considered one of the nine enabling technologies that will power the transformation supported by Industry 4.0 initiative [4, 10, 13]. Although industrial augmented reality (IAR) is one of the key pillars of the industry 4.0 enablers, adoption levels remain low in industry [8]. There also seems to be a lack of research about how to assess IAR in real industrial environments, namely the manufacturing shop floor. The lack of literature on the subject is the genesis for the creation of practical guidelines to evaluate IAR by distilling the lessons learnt from the evaluation studies conducted in the HUMAN research project over a period of two years.

This paper is structured with a theoretical background about AR and evaluation of IAR, followed by a description of the HUMAN project and lessons learnt from the evaluation activities focused on the use of an IAR solution to cognitively augment the worker on the shop floor. The paper then distils the lessons into a set of guidelines to assist in the evaluation of IAR in real manufacturing work environments.

B. Lalic et al. (Eds.): APMS 2020, IFIP AICT 591, pp. 495–502, 2020.
https://doi.org/10.1007/978-3-030-57993-7_56

2 Theoretical Background

In this section, we present three categories based on literature to consider when evaluating industrial augmented reality: lab or industrial environment, safety and operability challenges and usability and interface.

2.1 Evaluating AR in Industry

Lab or Industrial Environment
Evaluating AR in industry can be conducted in a lab or in a real industrial environment. When searching for literature, most of the studies we found was conducted in a lab and there seems to be few studies conducted on the shop floor. A survey shows that most of the technical studies have been carried out only in laboratory settings, without implementing the AR system in a real context [2]. Most implementations of AR for assembly seems to be carried out in laboratory settings, and AR studies targeting ergonomics issues have previously been entirely carried out in laboratory settings, with real case applications still lacking in the literature. Laboratory studies typically represent a proof-of-concept of the AR applicability and should be seen as the first step for the development of a scalable solution [2]. While evaluations conducted outside the lab considers the state in which the current system is, evaluations in real environments is important because the system should ultimately be used in the real industrial context [5].

Safety and Operability Challenges
When evaluating AR in a real industrial context, there seems to be some safety and operability challenges that might present a major obstacle, such as working in construction sites [3]. Changes in worker's workload, time of the day, and location of the room are examples of unquantifiable factors that might skew the findings in the process. In addition, gathering data on an active job site for a pilot study presents potential safety and financial risks for the contractor when using unproven and untested technologies. Also, tracking the environment and accurately displaying the content requires well-lit areas and is very sensitive to heavy shadows [3].

Usability and Interface
Usability is an essential variable of all Machine-Interface (HMI) when complexity and number of functions increase. If a technology is not regarded as easy to use and easy to understand, it will not enhance the user's performances and process at hand and will not be accepted by the users [6]. User interface is described as "does not require special knowledge to use, user friendly and easy to use, with minimum interactions required", and has been identified as one important feature for the future adoption of AR [11]. A consequence of evaluating AR with operators is that they might spend more time to complete the task in total, especially in the first steps, because they don't have previous experience with the technology and therefore might need time to understand instructions given in the AR-system [9]. When assessing usability, it is important that usability is measured relative to the chosen group of users within the specified scope of tasks [6]. The System Usability Scale (SUS) has been used to measure usability [6], others have

added questions to a questionnaire based on NASATLX [9] and formulated a hypothesis and conducted a post-experiment questionnaire to evaluate ease of use, satisfaction level, and intuitiveness for each instruction mode [12]. The ultimate desired state of an IAR system that prove its usability, is if the system was deployed to the end-users and is being used without requiring constant presence of the developers. It is also important evaluate if the AR system is developed with input of industrial partners. This is an important factor as it usually introduces a level of reality to a prototype [5].

3   HUMAN Project

The HUman MANufacturing (HUMAN) project was an European H2020 project aimed to develop a platform that is contextually aware of the factory and the human operator to support the operator in performing their tasks with the desired quality, whilst ensuring their well-being. The development of the solutions was permeated with co-creation principles, engaging with different stakeholders in manufacturing companies from inception to deployment, where evaluation played a crucial role in collating feedback and validation. An outcome of the HUMAN project was a fully integrated industrial AR system that aims to increase manufacturing productivity whilst providing support for quality assurance (KIT-AR).

3.1   KIT-AR

Three distinct end-user organizations contributed to the co-creation process that led to the development of KIT-AR: Airbus, Comau and Royo Group. As shown in Fig. 1, KIT-AR technology consists of four interactive system modules.

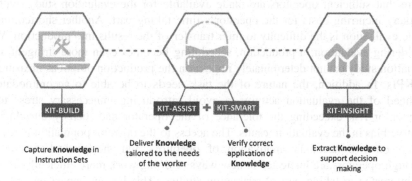

Fig. 1. KIT-AR system

3.2   The Evaluation Studies

The evaluation studies conducted at the three end-users, had the following lifecycle stages: data collection, technical testing, UX testing formative evaluation study and a final study. For the purpose of training the reasoning of the KIT-SMART modules, data was gathered from multiple sensors and the KIT-AR solution. This data gathering happened at shop floor level with the operators. It usually came together with the technical testing. The particular instance of the KIT-AR solution was tested with operators performing their everyday tasks. Preliminary tuning of KIT-AR occurred during all interactions with initial feedback being obtained from operators. Normally, technical testing went together with data collection in the same visit. A particular session to assess the UX of the KIT-AR solution, used a mix of quantitative and qualitative methods and tools. The aim was to improve iteratively the user interface until one can focus on the utility of the solution. With a formative evaluation study, the KIT-AR service was evaluated from all aspects, including the perception of utility. In-depth discussion to expand the initial responses was carried out to understand the underlying motivation and explore potential alternatives to inform the subsequent development cycle. At this stage, the key assumptions of the final study were validated, namely the KPIs. The final stage of evaluation corresponded to the assessment of utility of the KIT-AR solution. The chosen KPIs were measured to determine the impact assessment.

3.3 Lessons Learnt

As a result of the evaluation process in each of the three end-user organizations, several lessons were distilled and are succinctly summarized in this section.

Operators Availability and Scheduling

A fundamental reality of conducting evaluation studies in an industrial environment is that production will not change due to evaluation. The traditional approach is to reduce the impact in production and setup an offline area to setup the experiment for evaluation. However, the human resources are limited, and adequate planning is necessary to ensure that sufficient operators are made available for the evaluation study, with the company incurring costs for the operator's time taking part. Another shortcoming of offline evaluation is the difficulty to infer transfer of the results into production. When considering evaluation in production, scheduling becomes even more stringent as the evaluation study cannot determinately impact on the production output as measured by the KPIs. In addition, the nature of the task needs to be able to accommodate the overhead of the evaluation activity to avoid introducing unnecessary stress to the operator or risk exceeding the tolerance of the operator and thereby introducing a negative bias in the evaluation results. The access to the operator population is severely limited on two accounts: motivation of operators and the production planning. Although operators are interested in new ways of doing work more efficiently, they are less interested in taking part of evaluation studies. This has an impact on operators' approach of using novel tools that are not easily integrated into existing work practices without an adequate change management process. The production planning imposes constraints on the availability of operators, thus making quantitative studies extremely difficult to carry out. Consequently, one approach used in HUMAN was to conduct qualitative studies with real operators and complement the population of potential participants with students or workers with different roles. This approach requires an experimental design that attempts to characterize the differences between the different subject populations, thus increasing the credibility of combining the evaluation results from both populations. Ultimately, one must plan for small number participants and consider the fusion of evaluation results from operators and additional participants of different type. It is clear that the company cost of the operator's time, and the impact of using the AR solution, needs to be considered in the evaluation study.

Utility

Traditionally, evaluation studies are conducted in a session-based manner in well-controlled conditions and with hands-on support from researchers. The real assessment of the utility of an AR solution is when the corresponding AR device is left over a period of time within easy access of the operators, who then have the option to either use the solution or not. Consequently, the operator will only use the solution if it deemed of value, with clear benefits in terms of productivity and/or quality by means of doing less mistakes. In addition to monitoring of the usage of an AR solution, one can complement with relevant tools such as diaries [1].

Lack of Control

A key distinguishing aspect of field evaluation versus a laboratory setting is the almost excruciating lack of control on the work environment. A manufacturing company will not modify the work environment for the benefit of the study, in particular when considering the study in production and not an offline setting. As part of the evaluation methodology adopted in HUMAN, extensive technical testing was carried out to validate the usage of technology considering the constraints of the work environment, such as:

- the production environment had significant impact on the use of wireless connectivity, which enforced edge computing;
- the HoloLens device (version 1) is highly susceptible to the amount of luminosity that had an impact on the rendering of holograms and consequently requiring redesign of the instruction sets in some cases;
- The seasonal ambient temperature of the work environment may have an impact on the correct functioning of the IAR device.

In any case, the potential acceptance of any deviations to the work environment requires careful negotiation with different stakeholders in the manufacturing company beyond the expected operator and managers, extending to include social actors such as trade unions. Under no conditions should an evaluation study compromise the health and safety regulation of the work environment.

Quality of User Interface and Content

The quality of the user interface has significant impact on the evaluation results and consequently, it is highly relevant to have appropriate tools to assess the usability with the purpose of ensuring the focus is on the utility of the solution. The expectations of operators in a production environment are high and there is less tolerance for poor usability, thus the recommendation is to iteratively improve the solution until a usability tool such as SUS [7] indicate that acceptable UX has been achieved. However, even then, one should design the effectiveness of the interface design, possibly experimenting different variants of the user interface. In addition to the quality of the user interface, one needs to consider the quality of the content of the AR solution being used. Consequently, it is recommended that the instructions are created by a product engineer or individual with appropriate expertise and experience. An alternative is to involve experienced operators to co-create the instruction sets. However, irrespective of how content is created, it is recommended to conduct heuristic evaluation on the quality of the content.

Onboarding
The introduction of a new technology, such as AR, requires learning of the solution to enable operators to build the appropriate mental model. This onboarding must be considered when conducting the evaluation to eliminate the learning effect as it will distort the results otherwise and possibly introduce bias in the analysis and interpretation of the collated data.

4 Evaluation Guidelines

Based on the lessons learnt in the HUMAN project, combined with the limited knowledge reported in literature concerning IAR evaluation in real work environments, a set of four guidelines for evaluating IAR is proposed in the following subsections:

Experimental Design
A fundamental premise of evaluation of IAR in real manufacturing work environments is the fact that the experimental design must accommodate the constraints of the industrial environment in terms of:

- **Technical.** The characteristics of the work environment may negatively impact the correct operation of the IAR solution. *Consequently, it is necessary to accommodate adequate testing and piloting of the experimental design.*
- **Cost.** There is always a cost to the company to run the evaluation with potential risk to loss of productivity, exacerbating the cost further. *It is necessary to negotiate with the company the financial implications and possibly modify the experimental design to accommodate the cost impact.*
- **Participant population.** The workers are an extremely scarce resource that impose constraints on number of participants affecting the experimental design. *Start the discussion with production managers early to identify the actual number of participants available. Consider the fusion of qualitative results of studies involving workers with quantitative results from studies involving non-workers.*
- **Production.** The production planning dictates when evaluation activities can take place and the health/safety regulations cannot be compromised. *Consider the need to conduct the evaluation study over a long enough period to accommodate the production schedule.*
- **Return on Investment (ROI).** There is a cost of conducting evaluation on the shop floor. *Understand the needs of the company and manage their expectations concerning the outcome of the evaluation. Strive to associate evaluation goals to the business as it contributes to an understanding of potential ROI.*

Consequently, it is necessary to plan in advance for the evaluation and negotiate with the relevant stakeholders, from management to team leaders.

Content Quality
An IAR solution provides digital overlay of knowledge to workers and traditionally assessing the impact of the quality of the content is disregarded when conducting evaluation studies. *Consider the following two measures:*

- *Co-design the instructions with the workers and relevant stakeholders. This reduces the impact of poorly designed content;*
- *Conduct heuristic evaluation of the content quality with trainers/experienced worker. This measure may contribute to the improvement of the quality of the content or to understand the limitations of the final instance of the content.*

Interface and Usability
It is fundamental to ensure that the User eXperience (UX) is well designed so usability is not a barrier to utility. *Consequently, one should consider the following measures:*

- *Strive to improve the UX until the law of diminishing returns applies. This may involve changes to the development of the solution or content workarounds;*
- *Assess the impact of the different devices on the UX, both from the constraints on the interface and the ergonomics;*
- *Understand the impact of the UX on the outcome of the evaluation results by doing a small pilot and combining it with an heuristic evaluation by UX experts;*
- *It is fundamental to have onboarding of the operators in the use of IAR as they require a learning period to acquire the mental model of the system.*

Execution
The most well-planned evaluations are subject to the uncertainties of production realities and as such may disrupt the evaluation activities. *As such, it is necessary to be able to adapt, but most importantly use every opportunity to gather data and conduct analysis incrementally to best understand how to make necessary changes to the evaluation activities to mitigate the negative impact of disruption.*

5 Conclusion

The presented guidelines are not exhaustive, neither comprehensive, but are an initial approach that builds upon the experience of two years in conducting iterative evaluation studies using IAR. The aim is to provide insights on how to improve evaluation activities in real industrial work environments towards establishing a good practice of research on the shop floor.

Acknowledgements. The authors would like to thank the operators that took part of the evaluation activities using the KIT-AR solution. This work was partially funded by the Norwegian Research Council (#28026) and the H2020 HUMAN project (Grant Agreement no: 723737).

References

1. Bolger, N., Davis, A., Rafaeli, E.: Diary methods: capturing life as it is lived. Annu. Rev. Psychol. **54**, 579–616 (2003). https://doi.org/10.1146/annurev.psych.54.101601.145030
2. Bottani, E., Vignali, G.: Augmented reality technology in the manufacturing industry: a review of the last decade. IIE Trans. **51**, 284–310 (2019)
3. Chalhoub, J., Ayer, S.K.: Exploring the performance of an augmented reality application for construction layout tasks. Multimed. Tools Appl. **78**, 35075–35098 (2019)
4. Davies, R.: Industry 4.0: digitalization for productivity and growth. Eur. Parliamentary Res. Serv. **1** (2015)
5. Fite-Georgel, P.: Is there a reality in Industrial Augmented Reality? In: 2011 10th IEEE International Symposium on Mixed and Augmented Reality, Basel, pp. 201–210 (2011)
6. Holm, M., Danielsson, O., Syberfeldt, A., Moore, P., Wang, L.: Adaptive instructions to novice shop-floor operators using augmented reality. J. Ind. Prod. Eng. **34**(5), 362–374 (2017). https://doi.org/10.1080/21681015.2017.1320592
7. Lewis, J.R., Sauro, J.: The factor structure of the system usability scale. In: Kurosu, M. (ed.) HCD 2009. LNCS, vol. 5619, pp. 94–103. Springer, Heidelberg (2009). https://doi.org/10.1007/978-3-642-02806-9_12
8. Masood, T., Egger, J.: Adopting augmented reality in the age of industrial digitalisation. Comput. Ind. **115**, 103112 (2020). https://doi.org/10.1016/j.compind.2019.07.002. ISSN 0166–3615
9. Mourtzis, D., Zogopoulos, V., Xanthi, F.: Augmented reality application to support the assembly of highly customized products and to adapt to production re-scheduling. Int. J. Adv. Manuf. Technol. **105**, 3899–3910 (2019). https://doi.org/10.1007/s00170-019-03941-6
10. Romero, D., Stahre, J., Taisch, M.: The operator 4.0: towards socially sustainable factories of the future. Comput. Ind. Eng. **139**, 106128 (2020). https://doi.org/10.1016/j.cie.2019.106128. ISSN 0360-8352
11. Stoltz, H., Giannikas, V., McFarlane, D., Strachan, J., Um, J., Srinivasan, R.: Augmented reality in warehouse operations: opportunities and barriers. IFAC-PapersOnLine **50**(1), 12979–12984 (2017). ISSN 2405-8963
12. Uva, A.E., Gattullo, M., Manghisi, V.M.: Evaluating the effectiveness of spatial augmented reality in smart manufacturing: a solution for manual working stations. Int. J. Adv. Manuf. Technol. **94**, 509–521 (2018). https://doi.org/10.1007/s00170-017-0846-4
13. Zolotová, I., Papcun, P., Kajáti, E., Miškuf, M., Mocnej, J.: Smart and cognitive solutions for operator 4.0: laboratory H-CPPS case studies. Comput. Ind. Eng. **139**, 105471 (2020). https://doi.org/10.1016/j.cie.2018.10.032. ISSN 0360-8352
14. XR association: XR Primer 2.0: A Starter Guide For Developers (n.y)

Circular Products Design
and Engineering

Finding and Capturing Value in e-Waste for Refrigerators Manufacturers and Recyclers

Clarissa A. González Chávez[1]([⊠]), Mélanie Despeisse[1],
Björn Johansson[1], and David Romero[2]

[1] Chalmers University of Technology, Gothenburg, Sweden
{clarissa.gonzalez,melanie.despeisse,
bjorn.johansson}@chalmers.se
[2] Tecnológico de Monterrey, Monterrey, Mexico
david.romero.diaz@gmail.com

Abstract. In today's highly competitive world, companies need to rethink how they create and capture value at all stages of their offering's lifecycle. A major challenge is to integrate sustainability as a core source of value creation in their business model rather than as an add-on. E-Waste is one of the fastest-growing waste streams globally, and its value is still largely uncaptured. Urban communities generate high environmental and health impacts due to the e-waste produced by households. This paper aims to evaluate the value retained in refrigerators' components at their end-of-life. This research work presents findings on how recyclers identify, categorise, and capture value from e-waste. Although we focus on refrigerators recyclers, the results could motivate refrigerators manufacturers to collaborate with recyclers for a more circular economy.

Keywords: Refrigerators · Circular Economy · Sustainable business models · Materials recycling · Waste Electrical and Electronic Equipment · WEEE · e-Waste

1 Introduction

Sustainable business model innovation, in the context of the circular economy, looks at how organisations create and capture value at every stage of their offerings' journey to and back from the market [1]. The low-level of integration that organisations have achieved so far between their business models with sustainability is mainly due to treating sustainability as an add-on or a barrier rather than as a new source of value [2], currently being missed, destroyed, or wasted [3]. Many manufacturers miss opportunities to create and capture value while products are in use or even at their end-of-their-life (EOL) when they are recycled or discarded [2, 3]. One reason for it is the vision of recycling as the go-to-option and a lack of exploration of value uncaptured from used products [4–6] through other circularity strategies such as remanufacturing [7, 8]. A significant example of a case in which value is not always retained is electronic waste (e-waste); one of the fastest-growing streams of global waste. The last decades have shown a worrying increase in the amount of e-waste generated by urban communities;

B. Lalic et al. (Eds.): APMS 2020, IFIP AICT 591, pp. 505–512, 2020.
https://doi.org/10.1007/978-3-030-57993-7_57

the potential environmental impacts are associated with the toxic chemicals found in most electronic devices. This situation calls for different circularity strategies to collect, sort, and process disposed *materials and parts/components* for their resale, reuse, repair, refurbish, remanufacture, repurpose, and recycling [7, 8].

Environmental Regulation Agencies have insisted that attention must be paid when dealing with Waste Electrical and Electronic Equipment (WEEE) because they contain toxic materials (e.g., heavy metals, polybrominated diphenyl ethers, phthalates, and polyvinyl chloride). If managed improperly, the disposal of WEEE can adversely affect the environment and human health [9]. Some examples of large household products that are categorised as e-waste are refrigerators, freezers, electric stoves, microwaves, washing machines, dryers, air conditioners, to mention a few.

The production of large quantities of e-waste is a consequence of increased global consumption of electronic products and an outcome to technological products obsolescence caused by fast-paced new technology developments [10]. Refrigerators are one of the products that fall under the definition of e-waste, meaning that their treatment must follow the WEEE regulations from the European Union [11]. Some companies have found and created a business case out of the management of the EOL of these electrical and electronic products. However, current documented solutions are limited to the recycling of refrigerator components, disregarding other possible circular solutions. Part of this challenge relates to the founding of business cases, which has been limited because the economic viability of material recycling requires high volumes that are not be always reachable at trial-stages of a business case. Additionally, there is a high level of complexity caused by uncertainty and lack of data within supply chains, which relates to the quantity, quality, and timing of inputs for circular processes [12]. Particularly in e-waste treatment, recyclers have very limited visibility of the amount and state of the EOL products that they will receive in their facilities, which limits their planning capabilities and the possibility of innovative thinking.

The purpose of this research work is to identify and understand which are the disposed materials and parts/components of refrigerators that retain the most value at the EOL. This could provide recycling companies with a better understanding of how they could prioritise material handling, which leads to innovations in their production line. Although these efforts have an impact mainly in the part of the supply chain that handles EOL products, it is expected that the understanding of value both in material and data could help close-the-loop back to refrigerator manufacturers in a circular supply chain [13].

2 Research Question and Method

The research question is *how to identify and understand which are the disposed materials and parts/components of refrigerators that retain the most value at the EOL?* The research method followed is a *state-of-the-art literature review* [14] about e-waste, business models, and Circular Economy. The purpose of this literature review is to identify (new) sources of value at EOL of refrigerators, and other home appliances, which allow the authors to extend their search opportunities while creating generalisation statements on how to prioritise material handling to maximise value capture.

To begin the literature review, the authors explored the following search string in Scopus: *(TITLE-ABS-KEY ("refrigerator" OR "home appliances") AND TITLE-ABS-KEY ("recycling" OR "end-of-life") AND TITLE-ABS-KEY ("spare parts" OR "materials"))*.

The search in Scopus gave place to 163 documents. After screening the abstracts, the authors selected 85 papers that showed a contribution to answering the stated research question, meaning that they referred to material value at the EOL of electronic appliances or explicitly techniques and technologies for recycling. However, from this selection, only 68 records where found online, mainly because the other 17 belonged to conference proceedings that were not public, or with the full text translated to English (Fig. 1).

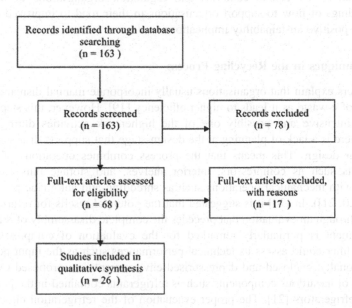

Fig. 1. PRISMA diagram of literature review process

3   Literature Review

The process of categorizing the literature review findings started with two main categories, which were previously specified in the research question, valuable materials and recycling techniques. However, the articles included an extensive amount of methods used for assessment of the process and innovative proposals for value generation, which led the authors to create two additional categories that reflected the value of previous contributions. Finally, the findings from the literature review are grouped into four categories for further scrutinization: (i) methods for the analysis of recycling process, (ii) techniques in the recycling process, (iii) materials categorised as valuable, and (iv) innovative proposals for value generation.

3.1   Methods for Analysis of the Recycling Process

The use of *dynamic flow analysis,* which can estimate a product lifecycle length, can help to calculate the state of metals and plastics contained in obsolete refrigerators [15].

Also, the application of IoT has been explored in refrigerators, where through sensors, Bluetooth, and RFID technology there is the potential to provide visibility of maintenance requirements and make life-length estimations [16].

This proposition can be useful to face one of the main challenges identified in EOL management organisations such as remanufacturers and recyclers; the high levels of uncertainty on the input of circular process, given that the demand or input of the circular process/system is difficult to predict.

Also, authors in [17] and [18] make use of material flow analysis and Life Cycle Assessment (LCA) in China to compare different EOL strategies for e-waste. This type of information can enable countries and regulation organisations to have better understandings of how to support organisations in their road to improved operations that allow positive sustainability implications.

3.2   Techniques in the Recycling Process

Some papers explain that organisations usually incorporate manual dismantling in the treatment of e-waste as it leads to higher efficiency [19]. However, this step is usually manually intensive and possibly one of the higher-risk activities during recycling because there is a lack of planning at the design-stage that supports disassembly, such as modular design. This means that the process combines operations where major components such as compressors, interior shelves, and storage bins are removed manually with mechanical operations such as shredding and automatic physic sorting (see [17, 20, 21]). In [20] it is suggested that the potential resells for refurbishment is analysed through an evaluation that precedes the complete disassembly of refrigerators. This statement is particularly remarked for the evaluation of compressors, which through a filter could assess its technical performances such as the input power [22].

Additionally, enclosed and depressurised environments are proposed to avoid the dispersion of hazardous components such as refrigerants contained in the polyurethane foam of refrigerators [21]. The proper evacuation of the refrigeration circuit shall be ensured by monitoring devices that adapted to the extraction system; appliance volume appliance shall be integrated into the extraction system [23].

3.3   Materials Categorised as Valuable

In [15, 17, 24], the materials highlighted are precious metals (Au, Ag), common Metals (i.e., Fe, Al, Cu, Sn), and toxic metals (i.e., Pb, Sb, Cd, Hg). However, the main environmental benefits are due to the recycling of steel, aluminium and copper [17].

After resource recovery, valuable resources such as copper, scrap, metal, and plastics are sold or exported to recycling companies, and low-value residues such as oils, waste refrigerant, and urethane are disposed to landfills or incinerated. The authors state that with a more active recycling of urethane, it will be possible to recycle most of the resources from waste refrigerators collected by both the formal and informal sectors [25].

To avoid the degradation of the quality of copper produced, all materials are processed to make copper cathode because no brass or wire will be produced in this recycling process. Magnetic separation is proposed to remove steel from scrap. Then non-ferrous metals and plastics shall be treated by air separation. Finally, light metals such as Aluminum and heavy metals such as copper are separated by density separation [26].

Regarding plastics, the material used is mainly polystyrene, which represents a high value in terms of the market prices for this secondary raw material. The techniques for separation are usual ones like swim sink separation and hydro cyclone classifier [23] (Fig. 2).

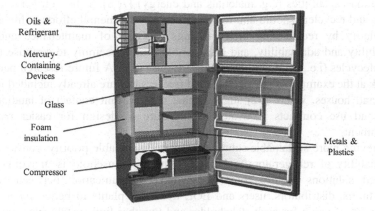

Oils &
Refrigerant

Mercury-
Containing
Devices

Glass

Foam
insulation

Compressor

Metals &
Plastics

Fig. 2. Recyclable materials and parts of a refrigerator

3.4 Innovative Proposals for Value Generation

The recycling of materials could be critical for countries with high metal demand, such as China and Japan. In China, only 40% is met by domestic deposits, and in Japan [26] new strategies are being developed to look ad deep ocean mining to avoid importing metals. Therefore, the efficient recycling of refrigerators and other types of e-waste could be highly beneficial to help cover this demand [27].

An innovative strategy is proposed in [28], where the use of fibber extracted from refrigerator door panels (FERD) and waste plastic in bituminous mixes for road construction. Also, [29] suggests diverse applications that generate insulation materials of EOL refrigerators. For example, due to their versatility, polyurethane (PU) foams have many different applications, such as sponges, filling materials in furniture, automotive seats and clothes, among others.

For strategies that include upcycling or finding higher value in an EOL product than just the recycling of the material components, this process would require examination of the end-of-life product to try and choose an activity that goes higher in the waste pyramid, through reuse or refurbishment [24]. However, a rigorous and fair comparison of EOL handling options for domestic refrigerators is much more complicated than simple policy perspectives such as the waste hierarchy might suggest [17, 30].

4   Conclusions and Outlook

This paper focused on contributing to a better understanding of the emerging circular business opportunities for the refrigerators manufacturers and recyclers, particularly those circularity opportunities at the middle-of-life (MOL) and EOL of refrigerators.

Circularity strategies present a wide range of strategies ordered from high-level strategies like resale, reuse, repair, refurbish, and remanufacture to low-level strategies such as repurpose (e.g., parts cannibalization) and recycling based on their resource-conservation capabilities (e.g. materials and energy) [7, 8]. Thus, refrigerators manufacturers and recyclers should aim to move their environmental efforts to higher levels of circularity by redesigning their offerings for ease of maintenance and repair, upgradability and adaptability, and disassembly and reassembly to servitise them for longer lifecycles (i.e., product lifecycle extensions) [31]. A future research perspective is to look at the example of refrigerators and freezers that are already included in rentals of flats and houses, where [32] suggests that the constant contact of landlords with service and use contracts motivates manufacture to design for easier repair and refurbishment.

Achieving more sustainable solutions is an undiscussable priority, considering that the availability of refrigerators and freezers in any household is unavoidable. The mentioned solutions require compromise and communication between suppliers, manufacturers, distributors, users and EOL treatment plants to better understand the prioritisation of value for each stakeholder and together find sustainable value.

Through strengthened supply chains that have visibility along the entire lifecycle of a product, we could foresee in a future scenario where recycling is not the first choice for e-waste treatment. Recycling could one of the last options to recover the value of materials, parts and components so that virgin material extraction is reduced and therefore the environmental impact of resources extraction can be decreased.

Future research in terms of material value requires more exploration of how to create business cases out of small material fractions to make use of the polymers retrieved in refrigerators. Also, the use of alternative materials which lead to components that can be designed for more circular strategies could support a more sustainable future.

Finally, higher-level circularity strategies will offer not only a better environmental performance to the refrigerator manufacturers and recyclers, but also new revenue streams based on MOL and EOL services as they start exploring the vision of circular refrigerators.

References

1. Geissdoerfer, M., Vladimirova, D., Evans, S.: Sustainable business model innovation: a review. J. Clean. Prod. **198**, 401–416 (2018)

2. Yang, M., Vladimirova, D., Evans, S.: Creating and capturing value through sustainability. Res.-Technol. Manag. **60**(3), 30–39 (2017)
3. Bocken, N., Short, S., Rana, P., Evans, S.: A value mapping tool for sustainable business modelling. Corp. Gov. **13**(5), 482–497 (2013)
4. Yoon, H., Jang, Y.C.: The practice and challenges of electronic waste recycling in Korea with emphasis on Extended Producer Responsibility (EPR). In: IEEE International Symposium on Electronics and the Environment, pp. 326–330 (2006)
5. Lee, S.J., Cooper, J., Hicks, G.: Characterization of monitor recycling in Seattle, Washington. Reg. Environ. Change **10**(4), 349–369 (2010)
6. Tong, X., Tao, D., Lifset, R.: Varieties of business models for post-consumer recycling in China. J. Clean. Prod. **170**, 665–673 (2018)
7. Thierry, M., Salomon, M., Numen, J.V., Van Cazenove, L.: Strategic issues in product recovery management. California Manag. Rev. **37**(2), 114–135 (1995)
8. Potting, J., Hekkert, M., Worrell, E., Hanemaaijer, A.: circular economy: measuring innovation in the product chain. Policy report. PBL Netherlands Environmental Assessment Agency, The Hague (2017)
9. Jang, Y.C.: Waste Electrical and Electronic Equipment (WEEE) management in Korea: generation, collection, and recycling systems. J. Mater. Cycles Waste Manag. **12**(4), 283–294 (2010)
10. Widmer, R., Oswald-Krapf, H., Sinha-Khetriwal, D., Schnellmann, M., Böni, H.: Global perspectives on e-waste. Environ. Impact Assess. Rev. **25**(5), 436–458 (2005)
11. European Parliament: L197/38 – WEEE Directive (Recast) 2012/19/EU. Official Journal, European Union, June, pp. 38–71 (2012)
12. Bressanelli, G., Perona, M., Saccani, N.: Challenges in supply chain redesign for the circular economy: a literature review and a multiple case study. Int. J. Prod. Res. **57**(23), 7395–7422 (2019)
13. Romero, D., Molina, A.: Reverse - green virtual enterprises and their breeding environments: closed-loop networks. IFIP, AICT **408**, 589–598 (2013)
14. Grant, M.J., Booth, A.: A typology of reviews: an analysis of 14 review types and associated methodologies. Health Inf. Libraries J. **26**, 91–108 (2009)
15. Li, X., Ren, Q., You, X., Yang, Y., Shan, M., Wang, M.: Material flow analysis of discarded refrigerators from households in urban and rural areas of China. Resour. Conserv. Recycl. **149**, 577–585 (2019)
16. Fiore, S., Ibanescu, D., Teodosiu, C., Ronco, A.: Improving waste electric and electronic equipment management at full-scale by using material flow analysis and life cycle assessment. Sci. Total Environ. **659**, 928–939 (2019)
17. Osisanwo, F., Kuyoro, S., Awolede, O.: Internet refrigerator – a typical Internet of Things (IoT). In: 3rd International Conference on Advances in Engineering Sciences & Applied Mathematics, pp. 59–63 (2015)
18. Lu, B., Song, X., Yang, J., Yang, D.: Comparison on end-of-life strategies of WEEE in China based on LCA. Front. Environ. Sci. Eng. **11**(5), 7 (2017)
19. Umeda, Y., Miyaji, N., Shiraishi, Y., Fukushige, S.: Proposal of a design method for semidestructive disassembly with split lines. CIRP Ann. – Manuf. Technol. **64**(1), 29–32 (2015)
20. Kim, K., Cho, H., Jeong, J., Kim, S.: Size, shape, composition and separation analysis of products from waste refrigerator recycling plants in South Korea. Mater. Trans. **55**(1), 198–206 (2014)
21. Ruan, J., Qian, Y., Xu, Z.: Environment-friendly technology for recovering nonferrous metals from e-waste: eddy current separation. Resour. Conserv. Recycl. **87**, 109–116 (2014)

22. Ng, Y.T., Lu, W.F., Song, B.: Improving green product design with closed-loop product recovery information. Key Eng. Mater. **572**(1), 12–15 (2014)
23. Keri, C.: Recycling Cooling and Freezing Appliances. In: Waste Electrical and Electronic Equipment Handbook, pp. 339–351 (2012)
24. Nguyen, D.Q., Ha, V.H., Eiji, Y., Huynh, T.H.: Material flows from electronic waste: understanding the shortages for extended producer responsibility implementation in Vietnam. Procedia CIRP **61**, 651–656 (2017)
25. Yi, S., Lee, H., Lee, J., Kim, W.: Upcycling strategies for waste electronic and electrical equipment based on material flow analysis. Environ. Eng. Res. **24**(1), 74–81 (2019)
26. Motoori, R., McLellan, B.C., Tezuka, T.: Environmental implications of resource security strategies for critical minerals: a case study of copper in Japan. Minerals **8**(12), 558 (2018)
27. Wang, J., Ju, Y., Wang, M., Li, X.: Scenario analysis of the recycled copper supply in china considering the recycling efficiency rate and waste import regulations. Resour. Conserv. Recycl. **146**, 580–589 (2019)
28. Baxter, J.: Systematic environmental assessment of end-of-life pathways for domestic refrigerators. J. Clean. Prod. **208**, 612–620 (2019)
29. Dos Santos, L.M., Carone, C.L.P., Dullius, J., Ligabue, R., Einloft, S.: Using different catalysts in the chemical recycling of waste from flexible polyurethane foams. Polimeros **23**(5), 608–613 (2013)
30. Ranadive, M.S., Hadole, H.P., Padamwar, S.V.: Performance of stone matrix asphalt and asphaltic concrete using modifiers. J. Mater. Civil Eng. **30**(1), 1–9 (2018)
31. Bakker, C., Wang, F., Huisman, J., den Hollander, M.: Products that go round: exploring product life extension through design. J. Clean. Prod. **69**, 10–16 (2014)
32. Fiore, E.: New strategies for the refrigerator in the transition towards a circular economy. In: Proceedings of Relating Systems Thinking and Design 7 (RSD7), pp. 134–148 (2018)

Circular, Green, Sustainable Manufacturing

Sustainable Business Model Innovation in the Furniture Supply Chain: A Case Study

Mikhail Shlopak[✉], Bella B. Nujen, and Jon Halfdanarson

Møreforsking Molde AS, Molde, Norway
{mikhail.shlopak,bella.b.nujen,
jon.halfdanarson}@himolde.no

Abstract. The growing insight among firms to transit towards a more sustainable society requires new or modified ways of doing business. However, there are few tools developed to help firms incorporate sustainability aspects when endeavoring to design new sustainable business model innovations. In this paper, we explore how the application of TLBMC and the concept of VU can lead to the discovery of uncaptured opportunities and trigger potential changes to the role of retailers along the furniture supply chain.

Keywords: Sustainable business model innovation · Triple layered business model canvas · Value uncaptured · Supply chain management

1 Background

The European furniture industry is currently facing a number of economic, environmental and regulatory challenges, which seem to affect almost every tier in its supply chain – from raw materials and parts-suppliers, to producers and retailers. Simultaneously, the competition is getting tougher, as demand for low-cost furniture is increasing worldwide. This, in combination with high labor, raw materials and energy costs, makes it difficult for companies focusing on high-quality products to compete globally [1]. Further, the technological developments in manufacturing, logistics and information systems have enabled new types of distribution channels. Particularly, the ever-growing volumes of direct sales from producers to end-users via internet have disrupted the traditional supply chain structure. However, the effects are not restricted to changes in the buying behavior of end-users. On the contrary, digital transformations are contributing to lowering entry barriers in most industries, as the need for capital is considerably decreased (c.f. no need for physical stores and/or expensive marketing strategies) which can have significant consequences also for large actors in established sectors. Recently, one of Europe's largest furniture manufacturers aired concerns about miscalculations regarding their product-line due to decreased knowledge in end-customer preferences, which had a negative impact on their market shares. Their assumption was that this knowledge now is communicated through diverse retailers, which decreased the supply chain transparency, hampering forecasting efforts [2]. Thus, among all the actors in the furniture supply chain, retailers are probably in the most vulnerable situation since they act as intermediates who intervene between the

B. Lalic et al. (Eds.): APMS 2020, IFIP AICT 591, pp. 515–523, 2020.
https://doi.org/10.1007/978-3-030-57993-7_58

original source of supply and the ultimate consumer [3]. This enforces changes on both micro (cf. single firm) and meso (cf. industrial network) levels, which requires stakeholders along the supply chain to conduct strategical decisions regarding their Business Models (BMs).

While technological innovations have become a key ingredient for business success, it is accompanied by an ever stronger focus on sustainability [4]. As a response to such conditions, researchers argue that firms need to be creative in terms of integrating innovation that help conserve and improve, social, environmental and financial resources into their strategies [5] by the help of sustainable and innovative BMs.

With this backdrop, the conditions motivate for a study dealing with the changing roles of retailers in the furniture supply chain when embracing a more sustainable strategy. To accommodate such motivation, this paper explores potentialities and implications for designing Sustainable Business Model Innovation(s) (SBMI) by combining the Triple Layered Business Model Canvas (TLBMC) methodology and the concept of Value Uncaptured (VU).

2 Transition Towards Sustainable Business Model Innovation

Despite growing attention to BM innovation in academia and business practice, it is a nascent research area, nonetheless not a new phenomenon. The discussion regarding how to define what a BM is, and what can be considered a BM innovation, is ongoing. In spite of not having managed to reach a clear consensus for the terms, there are some common properties covering theoretical and practical assumptions when addressing the first term, namely, as the logic of how firms do business, create, deliver and capture value [6]. Others, highlight that designing a BM can be considered as a firm's dynamic capability, as it exemplifies some sort of reconfiguration and adaptation to changing environments [7]. When combining [6] and [7] explanations of what a BM is – value and transformation become the central elements of the framework(s). The same authors advocate the use of BMs as a means for commercialization of new ideas. As such, they broaden the BM definition by including innovation as a natural element and therefore seem to incline to the phenomenon as a *BM innovation*, which this paper adheres to.

As mentioned in the previous section, sustainability is one of the key ingredients for business success [4]. This mirrors the research focus in the field of BMs, which now includes new subdomains derived from the need to incorporate eco-efficiency and social responsibility practices of firms, referred to as SBMI. In addition to the original BMs, SBMIs focus on a wider range of stakeholder interests, including environment and society. Circular BMs (CBMs) is another subcategory, which is closely related to SBMI [8] with a specific focus on how to utilize the economic value retained in products after consumption while emphasizing environmental elements [9]. In this research we explore potential synergy effects of two frameworks: the TLBMC [5] and the concept of VU [4], however, chose to mention CBMs as it includes a sustainability foci. TLBMC extends [6]'s original BM canvas, by adding two additional layers: an environmental layer based on lifecycle perspective and a social layer based on a stakeholder perspective. Thus, TLBMC enhances the visual understanding of how firms generate economic, environmental and social value(s). Regarding VU, [4] distinguish between four forms of VU: value surplus, value absence, value missed and value destroyed, which they apply throughout the product life cycle (PLC).

Hence, by combining TLBMC and VU, we encounter more contemporary issues. This can trigger the discovery of new business opportunities and shed light on potential changes to the role of retailers along the furniture supply chain.

3 Research Methodology and Findings

This study employs a single case design with an explorative approach where the TLBMC is applied and conducted through a business process mapping method. The majority of papers targeting SBMI in most scientific fields are primarily developing new methodologies, frameworks and tools [10], while this study contribute with a real-world application case. The study was conducted through semi-structured interviews, workshops, and site-visits during a period of six months. This approach allowed both researchers and the case representatives to actively take part in the research activities which increased the understanding of the phenomenon under investigation. The rich insights received were discussed within the research team until a consensus of the analysis was reached. This was then triangulated with SCM and SBMI literature, and with internal and external document analysis, in order to increase the validity in accordance with [11]'s recommendations. As such, the paper respond to the call of [10] who highlight the scarce number of case studies in SBMI research. Hence, the major benefit of the qualitative approach is that it provides a depth and richness of data which is difficult to attain in quantitative research, especially when addressing issues not yet adequately researched [11, 12]. The rest of this section provides the findings, starting with a short introduction of the case company, depicts the applied TLBMC methodology and sources of VU.

3.1 From AS-IS to TO-BE

The case company is a Norwegian SME office-furniture retailer, which is locally owned and mainly serves customers operating within its own region. (Henceforth, from now on referred to as retailX). Recently, retailX investigated various strategies to enhance possibilities for growth and its viability along the supply chain, which resulted in a goal of becoming *the sustainable choice* in their market. To achieve this, they needed to establish the current state of affairs (state of AS-IS). This was accomplished by applying the original canvas of [6], which mapped the existing BM of retailX, including the economic situation which also represents the first layer of the TLBMC, while designing the future SBMI situation, i.e. the TO-BE state, was accomplished by additional two layers.

In the AS-IS state, the main customer segment is represented by private companies (70–80%), followed by the public sector and end-consumers. retailX's core value proposition (VP) is *quality, flexibility and quick response time*. The revenue is mainly generated through sales of new products and solutions (90-95% of total revenue), while additional services such as guidance and product maintenance constitute a very small fraction of total revenue. Purchased products from furniture producers constitute the largest part (60%) of the total costs. Social media, e.g., Facebook and the company's website are rarely used as a channel for marketing and sales.

Next, an analysis of the social layer of the TLBMC of the firm was conducted. This step substitutes the nine original elements of [6] with a stakeholder management approach to assess the social benefits and impacts of a firm (see [4] for a thorough examination). This layer suggests choosing local and regional producers in terms of quality and reputation, as this could provide support for businesses around them. When not applicable, retailX should focus on Scandinavian producers, to limit the risk of alienating themselves from their desired image. Similarly, their employment strategy should promote local recruitment apprentices' programs. This stimulates long-term collaboration with education institutes, and commitment with potential employees. As for governance, it is a locally owned company setting long-term decisions, which now includes an explicit sustainability strategy. As such, retailX can operate as a sustainability-enabling actor towards their public-sector customers who must follow strict sustainability regulations. Other customer segments are to be served through a higher degree of involvement, e.g. by customized solutions. Hence, the mapping of the layers indicated that social implications are limited. Thus, retailX could contribute with social value and benefits by combining a so-called 'made in X' strategy with their sustainability ambitions. If pursued, the VP (i.e. social value-element) would be *contributing with regional prosperity and a local sustainability culture.*

Subsequently, environmental elements –the third and last layer of the TLBMC which is the proposed TO-BE scenario, suggests that the VP (i.e. functional value-element) is *to provide a tailor-made and healthy work environment through long lasting products.* Thus, production and the use-phase are strongly intertwined. Depending on the type of customization, the furniture would be contingent of the level of reusability concerning material utilization and functionality, which again, determines the possibilities for PLC extension. Accordingly, production should target low environmental impact through restoring, remanufacturing, and repurpose. Eco-labelled materials should be used whenever possible. To increase material requirements, only producers adhering to strict ecolabels (e.g. the Nordic Swan Ecolabel) are chosen. Serving the market with resource-efficient products with longer lifespan, meaning less environmental impact, enhances opportunities for innovation.

Hence, despite investigating each layer sequentially, it is not three isolated stages that are mapped and examined. Instead, the three-layer analysis contributes with vertical coherence [5] as it helps to identify and visualize untapped business opportunities more holistically.

3.2   Applying the Concept of VU

To enhance the transition towards SBMI further, a modified list by [4] was used as benchmarking. It summarizes 26 main sources of VU elements identified across different phases of a PLC. By combining this benchmark with the TLBMC methodology, retailX representatives identified 34 sustainable value capture possibilities, as well as suggested ways to transform them into value opportunities, as illustrated in Table 1.

Table 1. Sources of VU and countermeasures/value opportunities identified in the PLC phases of the case company

Sources of VU	Details	Countermeasure/value opportunity
Beginning of life (BOL)		
Customer needs	Unknown potential customers	Increased marketing efforts, better use of social media. More frequent visits of cold customers
	Potential customer needs	Better communication with active customers, more frequent follow-up
	Overpromising	Clarity in communication with suppliers and partners to ensure correct information is communicated
Contract	Low-profit contracts	Avoid tenders and large agreements where margins are small and opportunities for additional sales are absent. Find what is unique for each contract
	Unclear service contracts	Full review of all agreements – spend time on wordings and clarifications
Finance	Low profits	Create package-solutions that hit the market and hence, that customers are willing to pay extra for
Planning	Unclear strategic plan	Set aside time to work strategically
Middle of life (MOL)		
Customers' VU	Customers' unprofessional use of products	Customer follow-up; offer courses in the use of products to create/secure customer loyalty
Service	Excess service	Get paid when conducting extra customer service
	Missed service opportunities	Improve customer follow-up
	Lack of service experience	Better training of employees
	No calculation and/or control of service cost	Use project accounting
	Low service charges	Develop after-service packages (today: competence for which the company is not paid)
Customer needs	Unknown needs – real needs, potential needs, hidden needs, future needs	This can be picked up in status meetings or general follow-up if the questions are correct.
	Changes in customer needs	Follow customer, media and competitors closer than today
Delivery	Delays in delivery	Impose requirements on suppliers regarding information, and ensure that the customer is kept updated

(*continued*)

Table 1. (*continued*)

Sources of VU	Details	Countermeasure/value opportunity
	Sending wrong products or components	Read order confirmations carefully. Close cooperation with suppliers
	Delays in deliveries	Consider having local suppliers/producers
Risks	Market risks	Create a diversified portfolio of customers
	Policy risks	Close dialogue with suppliers
Waste of resources	Waste of energy	Consider moving to another facility that is more energy efficient
	Underutilized resources	Focus on better utilizing of employees; transportation/vehicles that are not fully utilized
Competition	Lost customer loyalty	Competition from online retailers. Make sure to highlight the benefits of using the company (cf. proximity aspects e.g. if problems would occur)
	Pressure from producers	Ensure good dealer agreements, close relationships, and being ahead of changes
End of life (EOL)		
Recycle	No or little recycling	Provide a return program
	Lack of awareness/knowledge of recycling	Promote the company as a sustainable retailer
	Valuable materials in discarded products	Find actors/customers who can use materials in production
	No customer demand for recycling	Enhance public perception of recycling/reuse products. Play on emotions; campaigns, marketing
	Lack of recycling methods	Create simple guidelines
Reuse	Idle, usable, re-purchased old products	Effective handling of used furniture that can be sold as-is and promoted "as good as"
	Insufficient use of usable old products	Use materials and parts in new products and in after-service work
	Usable products discarded by customers	Centralize the reuse, collection, repair facility
Remanufacture	No or little remanufacturing	Reclaim embedded value (used furniture, underutilized by-products in combination with repaired and new parts)
	Lack of capacity to undertake remanufacturing	Find partners and/or upskill existing workforce

From Table 1, it is apparent that VU elements in the BOL, all target important areas within customer relations management, contracting and planning. Thus, all seven countermeasures illustrate the existence of value missed (VM), i.e., value which exists and is required but is not exploited [4]. However, with regards to redesigning the current BM, it is unclear if suggested measures would result in a more sustainable and innovative strategy, albeit they are still important to capture, if not it is inefficient use of internal resources.

Along the MOL phase, as many as 17 countermeasures are suggested to accommodate different dimensions of VU. Again, all (except from one), contribute with limited sustainability business opportunities, however, manage to capture some untapped economic opportunities, through production service system activities [10]. For instance, providing follow-up courses and after-service programs, increase customer loyalty and inward cashflow. The one left is what [4] refer to as value destroyed (VD), i.e., value with negative consequences. Hence, from a sustainability perspective, VD refers to environmental and societal damage. In this case, it concerns waste of energy, where the suggestion was to consider changing location to facilities, which were more energy efficient. However, the countermeasure could also be perceived as value absent (VA), i.e., value which is required but does not exist [4]. As such, the new facilities can be considered as a required asset that could be achieved but have not yet been met.

It is in the EOL phase most sustainable opportunities seem to be found, where six of ten countermeasures target specific SBMI elements. For instance, a wide range of reuse options based on recycling programs, second-hand retailing, and remanufacturing are suggested. Hence, a higher degree of reuse and remanufacturing will result in lower environmental footprint than manufacturing of new products. This is in line with the proposed TO-BE state. Despite their potential however, most of these are VA, as retailX lacks appropriate equipment and adequate knowledge and therefore strongly depends on supporting infrastructure.

4 Discussion and Closing Remarks

This study has explored how TLBMC in combination with the VU concept can affect strategic decisions targeting SBMI, and its potential implications for retailers operating in the furniture supply chain. As the study illustrates, the combined method is useful when designing the vision and key elements of a more sustainable strategy, which simultaneously aims to balance financial, environmental and social perspectives. However, to operationalize the proposed SBMI (cf. TO-BE) and its VP, it is crucial to systematically analyze opportunities that lie in each element of the new model, and hence the potential to enter new markets. This is quite interesting, since often it is the end-product and the calculated economic gains of a firm that are being evaluated when searching for new business opportunities and markets, and not necessarily potentialities that lie in e.g. environmental benefits. This finding is in line with recent studies and reinforces the notion that existing BMs fail to consider sustainability as a source to innovation [1]. Furthermore, the study indicates that the role played by the retailer during the transition of 'becoming sustainable' imposes a clear change, especially if they choose to focus on the redesigned suggestions proposed along the TLBMC stages and later by the concept of VU – through recycling, reuse and remanufacturing operations, i.e., towards the EOL. This corresponds with the findings and recommendations of [4], while the element of the changing role of the stakeholder(s) within the supply chain is added to the theoretical body of knowledge.

Thus, for furniture retailers to embark on the proposed TO-BE situation (which mirrored the VU sources in EOL) successfully, they need to develop new skills to safeguard against power dependence issues in the supply chain. For instance, producers might have an advantage with regards to remanufacturing as they often invest in advanced equipment in their manufacturing operations and possess adequate know-how, which is difficult for retailers to achieve as they traditionally are not involved with development nor manufacturing. This notion highlights potentialities and/or implications for the role of retailers. Thus, it enforces retailer-firms which are about to redesign their BMs in order to maintain or strengthen their viability in the furniture supply chain to broaden their strategies from a micro- to a meso-level perspective. This is particularly important to consider, as embarking on a SBMI strategy not only concerns internal changes but also impose new conditions for inter-organizational strategies.

Although our case provides some interesting findings, it should be interpreted in the context of the limits inherent in qualitative research, such as the lack of generalizability due to the application of a single case company, which sets the direction for future studies. Thus, we encourage others to continue investigating the application of SBMI frameworks to enhance the extant however limited literature on BMs. Here a special attention should be given to what the consequences of SBMIs' may have for the interaction and existing relationships between stakeholders in the furniture supply chain by including a production network perspective and thus a larger sample of firms should be included.

Funding and Acknowledgments. The authors express their appreciation to the case company and to The Norwegian Research Council for their financial support.

References

1. Forrest, A., Hilton, M., Ballinger, A., Whittaker, D.: Circular Economy Opportunities in the Furniture Sector. European Environmental BureauBelgium, Brussels (2017)
2. Loutfi, A.A.: Blockchain and Incumbent Manufacturing Value Chains Applicability and Adoption Use case. Ekornes, NTNU (2018)
3. Olsson, R., Gadde, L.-E., Hulthén, K.: The changing role of middlemen—strategic responses to distribution dynamics. Ind. Mark. Manag. **42**(7), 1131–1140 (2013)
4. Yang, M., Evans, S., Vladimirova, D., Rana, P.: Value uncaptured perspective for sustainable business model innovation. J. Clean. Prod. **140**, 1794–1804 (2017)
5. Joyce, A., Paquin, R.L.: The triple layered business model canvas: a tool to design more sustainable business models. J. Clean. Prod. **135**, 1474–1486 (2016)
6. Osterwalder, A., Pigneur, Y.: Business Model Generation: A Handbook for Visionaries, Game Changers, and Challengers. Wiley, Hoboken (2010)
7. Teece, D.J.: Business models, business strategy and innovation. Long Range Plan. **43**(2–3), 172–194 (2010)

8. Antikainen, M., Valkokari, K.: A framework for sustainable circular business model innovation. Technol. Innov. Manag. Rev. **6**(7), 5–12 (2016)
9. Linder, M., Williander, M.: Circular business model innovation: inherent uncertainties. Bus. Strategy Environ. **26**(2), 182–196 (2017)
10. Evans, S., et al.: Business model innovation for sustainability: towards a unified perspective for creation of sustainable business models. Bus. Strategy Environ. **26**(5), 597–608 (2017)
11. Eisenhardt, K.M.: Building theories from case study research. Acad. Manag. Rev. **14**(4), 532–550 (1989)
12. Voss, C.: Case research in operations management. In: Researching Operations Management, pp. 176–209. Routledge (2010)

A Basic Study on Scheduling Method for Electric Power Saving of Production Machine

Masayuki Yabuuchi[1]([✉]), Toshiya Kaihara[1], Nobutada Fujii[1], Daisuke Kokuryo[1], Satoko Sakajo[2], and Yoshito Nishita[2]

[1] Graduate School of System Informatics, Kobe University,
1-1 Rokkodai-cho, Nada, Kobe, Hyogo 657-8501, Japan
yabuuchi@kaede.cs.kobe-u.ac.jp, kaihara@kobe-u.ac.jp,
nfujii@phoenix.kobe-u.ac.jp, kokuryo@port.kobe-u.ac.jp
[2] Mitsubishi Electric Corporation,
8-1-1 Tsukaguchi honmachi, Amagasaki, Hyogo, Japan
Sakajo.Satoko@ds.MitsubishiElectric.co.jp,
Nishita.Yoshito@cb.MitsubishiElectric.co.jp

Abstract. At present, energy consumption all over the world is increasing, and various approaches to energy issues such as the Sustainable Development Goals (SDGs) are in progress. In Japanese manufacturing industry, the introduction of factory Energy Management System (EMS) and the improvement of production equipment are being carried out in order to reduce energy consumption. Accordingly similar considerations are also important issues for production scheduling. In this paper, based on the assumption that renewable energy and EMS will eventually be introduced in the future, we focus on factories and utility companies, and at the same time, try to realize a scheduling method that improves energy efficiency with keeping production performance, and evaluate it by computational experiments.

Keywords: Flexible flow shop scheduling · Power saving · Optimization · Production machine

1 Introduction

As energy demand in the world increases with the development of the economy, problems such as the depletion of fossil fuels due to the increase of energy consumption and increase of CO_2 emissions causing global warming becomes more serious. Therefore, various countries around the world collaborate altogether for Sustainable Development Goals (SDGs), and work on energy issues with the aim of realizing a sustainable society [1]. The industrial sector, including the manufacturing sector, accounts for more than 50% of the total energy consumption, and in today's era of rapid electrification, power saving in the

© IFIP International Federation for Information Processing 2020
Published by Springer Nature Switzerland AG 2020
B. Lalic et al. (Eds.): APMS 2020, IFIP AICT 591, pp. 524–530, 2020.
https://doi.org/10.1007/978-3-030-57993-7_59

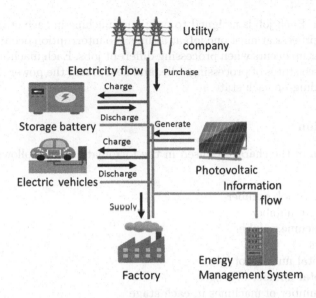

Fig. 1. Target model

industrial sector is considered an important initiative [2]. In the manufacturing industry, energy saving is promoted by introducing an Energy Management System (EMS) with energy-efficient equipment, and by scheduling in consideration of power consumption. Among them, research on scheduling aimed at improving production efficiency and energy efficiency has attracted attention because it could be realized at a lower investment cost than such as purchasing a new system or equipment [3].

In the target model (Fig. 1), electricity used in the factory is supplied by purchasing from a utility company or by generating electricity from renewable energy such as PhotoVoltaic(PV). A storage battery stores electricity from a utility company during the time when the electricity charge is low, and discharges the electricity to factory during the time when the electricity charge is high. In addition, efficient use of renewable energy is realized by positioning multiple Electric Vehicles (EVs) as moving batteries. Furthermore EMS predicts power demand and PV power generation, and determines the operation plan of each power generation facility and the EV charging and discharging schedule.

In this paper, we first focus on two models, utility company and factory, and perform scheduling for power saving and production efficiency.

2 Problem Statement

In this paper, the problem is formulated based on the reference [4]. A Flexible Flow Shop (FFS) covered in this paper (Fig. 2) is described as follows: J jobs must be processed in the I stages, and all jobs are processed in the same order. There are L machines in each stage, and each machine has difference in ability. No machine failure occurs. All jobs and machines are available from the start of production. Each job is assigned to only one machine in each stage, and each machine can process at most one job at a time. No interruption occurs during job processing. Setup occurs when processing different jobs. Each machine belongs to one of the three states of processing, idle, and setup, and the power consumption differs depending on each state.

2.1 Notation

The definition of the characters used in the formulation is as follows:

- Index
    - j, k, h: job number
    - i: stage number
    - l: machine number
- Parameters
    - J: total number of jobs
    - I: total number of stages
    - L: number of machines in each stage
    - P_{ilj}: processing time of job j at machine l on stage i
    - ST_{iljk}: setup time from job j to job k at machine l on stage i
    - PE_{il}: energy consumption per Time Slot (TS) at machine l on stage i during processing
    - IE_{il}: energy consumption per TS at machine l on stage i during idle
    - SE_{il}: energy consumption per TS at machine l on stage i during setup
    - $SOTEC$: total energy consumption value when solving the total energy consumption minimization scheduling problem
    - SOC_{max}: makespan value when solving the makespan minimization scheduling problem
    - α: weighting parameter of the objective function
- Variables
    - TEC: total energy consumption
    - C_{max}: makespan (the completion time of the last job on the last machine)
    - pe_{il}: total energy consumption during processing at machine l on stage i
    - ie_{il}: total energy consumption during idle at machine l on stage i
    - se_{il}: total energy consumption during setup at machine l on stage i
    - pt_{il}: total processing time at machine l on stage i
    - it_{il}: total idle time at machine l on stage i
    - st_{il}: total setup time at machine l on stage i
    - $t1_{il}$: work start time at machine l on stage i
    - $t2_{il}$: work end time at machine l on stage i
    - c_{ij}: completion time of job j in stage i
    - $x_{iljk} = \begin{cases} 1 \text{ if job } j \text{ precedes job } k \text{ at machine } l \text{ on stage } i \\ 0 \text{ otherwise} \end{cases}$

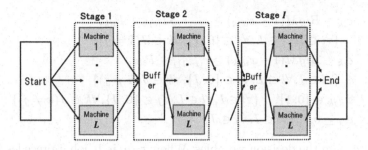

Fig. 2. An example of flexible flow shop

2.2 Formulation

The formulation of this paper is shown below.

$$\text{Min. } \alpha * \frac{TEC}{SOTEC} + (1 - \alpha) * \frac{C_{max}}{SOC_{max}} \tag{1}$$

$$\text{where } TEC = \sum_{i \in I} \sum_{l \in L} (pe_{il} + se_{il} + ie_{il}) \tag{2}$$

$$C_{max} = \max\{c_{ij}\}, \quad \{\forall i \in I, \forall j \in J\} \tag{3}$$

$$pe_{il} = pt_{il} * PE_{il}, \quad \{\forall i \in I, \forall l \in L\} \tag{4}$$

$$se_{il} = st_{il} * SE_{il}, \quad \{\forall i \in I, \forall l \in L\} \tag{5}$$

$$ie_{il} = it_{il} * IE_{il}, \quad \{\forall i \in I, \forall l \in L\} \tag{6}$$

$$pt_{il} = \sum_{j \in \{0,J\}} \sum_{k \in J, k \neq j} x_{iljk} * P_{ilk}, \quad \{\forall i \in I, \forall l \in L\} \tag{7}$$

$$st_{il} = \sum_{j \in J} \sum_{k \in J, k \neq j} x_{iljk} * ST_{iljk}, \quad \{\forall i \in I, \forall l \in L\} \tag{8}$$

$$it_{il} = t2_{il} - t1_{il} - pt_{il} - st_{il}, \quad \{\forall i \in I, \forall l \in L\} \tag{9}$$

$$t1_{il} = 0, \quad \{\forall i \in I, \forall l \in L\} \tag{10}$$

$$t2_{il} = C_{max}, \quad \{\forall i \in I, \forall l \in L\} \tag{11}$$

$$\text{sub.to } \sum_{j \in \{0,J\}, j \neq k} \sum_{l \in L} x_{iljk} = 1, \quad \{\forall i \in I, \forall k \in J\} \tag{12}$$

$$\sum_{j \in J, j \neq k} \sum_{l \in L} x_{ilkj} \leq 1, \quad \{\forall i \in I, \forall k \in J\} \tag{13}$$

$$\sum_{h \in \{0,J\}, h \neq j, h \neq k} x_{ilhj} \geq x_{iljk}, \quad \{\forall i \in I, \forall l \in L, \forall j, k \in J, j \neq k\} \tag{14}$$

$$\sum_{l \in L} (x_{iljk} + x_{ilkj}) \leq 1, \quad \{\forall i \in I, \forall j \in J, k = j+1, ..., Job, j \neq k\} \tag{15}$$

$$\sum_{k \in J} x_{il0k} \leq 1, \quad \{\forall i \in I, \forall l \in L\} \tag{16}$$

$$c_{i0} = 0, \quad \{\forall i \in I\} \tag{17}$$

$$c_{ik} + BigM(1 - x_{iljk}) \geq c_{ij} + ST_{iljk} + P_{ilk},$$
$$\{\forall i \in I, \forall l \in L, \forall j \in \{0, J\}, \forall k \in J(k \neq j)\} \qquad (18)$$
$$c_{ik} + BigM(1 - x_{iljk}) \geq c_{(i-1)j} + P_{ilk},$$
$$\{\forall i \in I, \forall l \in L, \forall j \in \{0, J\}, \forall k \in J(k \neq j)\} \qquad (19)$$
$$x_{iljk} \in \{0, 1\}, \quad \{\forall i \in I, \forall l \in L, \forall j \in \{0, J\}, \forall k \in J(k \neq j)\} \qquad (20)$$
$$c_{ij} \geq 0, \quad \{\forall i \in I, \forall j \in J\} \qquad (21)$$

x_{iljk} and c_{ij} are the decision variables. When x_{iljk} is 1, job j precedes job k at machine l on stage i, otherwise, x_{iljk} is 0. c_{ij} is integer decision variable that indicates completion time of job j on stage i.

Objective function (1) is intended for minimizing the weighted sum of the total energy consumption of Eq. (2) and the makespan of Eq. (3). The reason for using these two as an evaluation index is that to change the degree of consideration of total energy consumption and makespan in scheduling by changing the value of a weight parameter α. $SOTEC$ and SOC_{max} are obtained by setting the objective function to TEC or C_{max} for the same formulation. Equation (2) is sum of the total energy consumption in each state (processing, idle, setup). Equation (3) is the completion time of the last job on the last machine. Equations (4)–(6) calculate the power consumption in each state(processing, idle and setup) of machine l on stage i. Equations (7)–(9) calculate the time in each state (processing, idle and setup) of machine l on stage i. Equations (10) and (11) set the work start time and work end time of machine l on stage i. Equations (12)–(19) are constraint equations and have the same meanings as the constraint equations (2) to (9) in the formulation in Chapter 5 in reference [4]. In this paper, constraint (18) considers only setup time between different jobs. Constraint (19) considers only the completion time of the previous stage of the job.

3   Computational Experiment

In order to evaluate the influence of the weight parameter α of the objective function, the computational experiments are performed. In the experiments, we perform the sensitivity analysis for α which is the weighting factor of the total energy consumption and makespan. CPLEX12.9 [5] is used to solve the scheduling problem. The evaluation criteria are as follows:

- TEC: total energy consumption
- C_{max}: makespan

3.1   Experimental Condition

The initial setup conditions are hypothetically determined. In general higher speed machine with powerful actuators requires more electric energy. We consider this assumption is commonly observed in real shop floor. Therefore, this experiment assumes that each stage has two type machines: Machine 1 in each stage has a high job processing speed but high power consumption. Machine 2 in each stage has a slower job processing speed than Machine 1, but consumes less power than Machine 1. The experimental conditions are as follows. [ ] indicates a uniform random number.

- I: total number of stages = 2
- L: number of machines in each stage = 2
- J: total number of jobs = 8
- P_{i1j}: processing time of job j at machine 1 on stage i = [10, 20]
- PE_{i1}: power consumption per TS at machine 1 on stage i during processing = 80
- IE_{i1}: power consumption per TS at machine 1 on stage i during idle − 8
- P_{i2j}: processing time of job j at machine 2 on stage i = [30, 40]
- PE_{i2}: power consumption per TS at machine 2 on stage i during processing = 10
- IE_{i2}: power consumption per TS at machine 2 on stage i during idle = 1
- ST_{iljk}: setup time from job j to job k at machine l on stage i l = 5
- SE_{il}: power consumption per TS at machine l on stage i during setup = 5

3.2   Experimental Result

In the experiment, the parameter α used for the weighted sum of the objective function is changed between 0 and 1. When α is increased, the weight for minimizing the total energy comsumption in the objective function increases. Whereas if it is decreased, the weight of the minimization of the makespan increases. Table 1 shows the results of total energy consumption and makespan when α is changed. Considering the results in Table 1, when the weight of the total energy consumption increased, total energy consumption is reduced and makespan is increased. And when we increased the weight of makespan, total energy consumption is increased and makespan is reduced. So, there is a trade-off relationship between total energy consumption and makespan under this experimental conditions, and a decision maker can decide the priority degree of total energy consumption and makespan in a scheduling by deciding α. However, when α exceeds 0.7, the values of total energy consumption and makespan change significantly, so it is difficult to finely adjust the α value close to the total energy consumption and makespan schedule assumed by decision makers.

Table 1. Results of experiment

α		0.0	0.1	0.2	0.3	0.4	0.5	0.6	0.7	0.8	0.9	1.0
TEC	Avg.	14790.7	14357.4	14155.5	14084.3	13974.4	13923.9	13730.2	13681.5	13126.0	11725.2	11364.6
	S.D.	337.22	482.01	550.60	552.73	531.65	505.70	552.07	556.72	473.18	398.17	182.71
C_{max}	Avg.	119.9	119.9	120.2	120.5	121.1	121.5	123.8	124.9	145.7	233.6	290.0
	S.D.	4.18	4.18	4.13	3.81	4.23	4.14	4.66	4.38	25.87	41.96	18.38

4   Conclusion

In this paper, we proposed a scheduling method aiming at productivity improvement and power saving for a flexible flow shop type production line. In this method, it is assumed that more detailed and specific energy management can be provided by dividing the state of the machine into three states: processing, idle, and setup. And we solved the optimization problem related to both productivity and energy efficiency in our hypothetical target production line as basic research. In the computer experiment, scheduling that saves total energy was possible by deciding the value of α, and changing the degree of consideration of makespan and total energy consumption. However, it is not clear how to set the value of α so that the decision maker can create a schedule of total energy consumption in this experiment. Therefore, as the next step, it is necessary to clearify the relationship between the degree of consideration of makespan and the degree of consideration of total energy consumption, for each value of α, by scheduling with experimental conditions set according to a more realistic factory model.

In addition, it is also important to reduce the cost in the manufacturing industry, so we aim to reduce not only the power consumption but also the power cost in this research. Therefore, we assume that the long-term goal is to propose not only factory scheduling but also an energy allocation plan that reduces the power cost according to the power demand of the factory resulting from the scheduling. The installation of renewable energy system, batteries, or EVs, is now spreading into factory operation. Therefore, in factories including those systems, the analysis between production performance and energy saving with sophisticated scheduling methodology becomes more important issues, and it is our obvious next step.

References

1. Nilsson, M., et al.: Towards an integrated framework for SDGs: ultimate and enabling goals for the case of energy. Sustainability 5(10), 4124–4151 (2013)
2. International Energy Outlook (2019). https://www.eia.gov/outlooks/ieo/. Accessed 21 Mar 2020
3. Gahm, C., et al.: Energy-efficient scheduling in manufacturing companies: a review and research framework. Eur. J. Oper. Res. 248(3), 744–757 (2016)
4. Ruiz, R., et al.: Modeling realistic hybrid flexible flowshop scheduling problems. Comput. Oper. Res. 35(4), 1151–1175 (2008)
5. ILOG CPLEX-IBM. https://www.ibm.com/jp-ja/products/ilog-cplex-optimizati on-studio. Accessed 3 Feb 2020

Sustainability in Fabric Chains and Garments for a Circular Economy

Solimar Garcia[1]([✉]) [iD], Irenilza de Alencar Nääs[1] [iD],
Pedro Luiz de Oliveira Costa Neto[1] [iD],
João Gilberto Mendes dos Reis[1] [iD], Valdice Neves Pólvora[1] [iD],
Luiz Antonio de Lima[1] [iD], Angel Antonio Gonzalez Martinez[1] [iD],
and Vanessa Santos Lessa[2] [iD]

[1] Paulista University, São Paulo, Brazil
solimar.garcia@docente.unip.br
[2] Mackenzie Universitie, São Paulo, Brazil

Abstract. The society has been driven to create parameters for sustainable development and to transposition into the circular economy. Sustainability strategies were assessed in fabric value chain and clothing. To discuss this subject, we analyzed the results found using the information published in the current literature about sustainability in the textile chain. The results indicate that the fabric and clothing production chain needs to expand sustainable practices, such as selective collection, reuse, recycling, and proper disposal of textile waste, and to improve the population's awareness of the theme, one of the obstacles to sustainability. The adoption of recycling will be a qualitative leap for the circular economy in the studied business chains and will just happen when education becomes a priority. The results show it is urgent to change the paradigm in society in order to enter a circular and sustainable economy.

Keywords: Textile residue · Waste textile · Reverse logistics

1 Introduction

Society, in general, seeks new forms of development, which contributes to reducing and limiting the use of natural resources, contemplating three pillars of sustainability, or the triple bottom line (TBL): profit, environment, and society, proposed by Elkington in 1997 [17], with the maintaining of the natural resources, and seek activities that can lead to a circular economy in advances of industry 4.0.

In Brazil, the National Solid Waste Policy (PNRS), introduced by Law No. 12.305/2010, led to responsibility for the proper disposal of waste to companies [11] and implemented reverse logistics for some segments, including agrochemicals, tires, and batteries. The daily production of garbage is estimated at 10 million tons, two billion tons per year [32]. Brazilians produced 215,000 t/day of waste [5]. Data from 2018 show that the damage reaches US$ 40 billion per year, with recycling reaching only 3% of the 80 million tons of annual wastes [9].

B. Lalic et al. (Eds.): APMS 2020, IFIP AICT 591, pp. 531–537, 2020.
https://doi.org/10.1007/978-3-030-57993-7_60

On the other hand, one of the largest generators of waste and environmental pollution is the textile and garment chain. In the world, textile production, cotton or synthetic, moves US $ 797 billion [4]. The fabrics and apparel textile industry as an essential segment in the Brazilian economy, which is amongst the five most significant in the world, and produced US$ 48 billion in 2019, representing 8% of the Brazilian GDP [2].

The destination of waste from the textile and clothing industry is part of the complexity and difficulty of bringing sustainability to the supply chain. In Brazil, these numbers are diffuse, and no agency has specific information on reuse and recycling of textiles [36]. This waste is considered with the total number of urban waste in Brazilian standard NBR 10.004 [6].

In addition to the chemicals used in textile production, there is also the aggravating factor of fast fashion, these low prices products, which generate excessive consumption and waste. The reuse of textile waste and discarded clothing can reduce the negative impact on the textile chain; however, reverse logistics is still insipient in the segment. It is also necessary to recycle and reuse fabrics in the production phase or collection of clothes discarded by the consumer, since the disposal is done incorrectly and without care for the environment.

There is no information about the waste generated by the disposal of clothes done by the final consumer, and that can be recycled. The recycling and reuse industry, part of reverse logistics and the circular economy, can generate 1.8 trillion euros by 2030 [29].

There are still few companies that work with the recycling of fabrics, reuse of production residues, and discarded clothes. These activities are carried out by handicraft and charity initiatives, which involve an inexpressive result. Indeed, Brazil imports fabric waste, because the recycling does not have the quality to be used for the companies of that segment.

Therefore, the research question is: how to bring sustainability to the textile chain and put it on the path of the circular economy, being the objective of this article to discuss recycling and reverse logistics as a driving to circular economy.

2 Background

Reverse logistics is one of the most critical factors for economic and social growth and can be supported for innovation and sustainability [14]. The knowledge of consumer behavior it is a be there are as a path in the search for textile sustainability [21]. Consumers, on the other hand, demand the sustainability of the companies and their products [34].

The Brazilian Association of Technical Standards defines the rejects of domestic and commercial activity in urban centers, which including clothes in brazilian standard NBR 10.004 [6]. The textile waste and the used clothing are discarged with other types recycled waste.

In Brazil and all countries, there is the same difficulty in treating waste textiles. France has a national tissue recovery program whose policy has held the waste producer for fabric, clothing, and footwear producers since 2017 [12, 30]. In Brazil, this prerogative is still under discussion, as an addendum to Law No. 12.305/2010 [11].

The use of second-hand clothing can reduce greenhouse gas emissions by 53%, pollution, and chemical production processes by 45% [16]. Recycling and reuse contribute to reducing the exploitation of natural resources to produce new products [1, 15].

Despite this, the country cannot properly recycle and reuse its waste and needs to import textile waste [4]. In 2013, Brazilian recyclers imported nearly 10,000 tons of textile waste, more than $ 11 million, and attributed this to people's lack of information and unorganized waste collection [3]. [22] show that these imports between 2013 and 2018 were 74,000 tonnes and a loss of US $ 42 million.

[24] attributed to Brazil a loss of US$ 600 million for not recycling and improving the working conditions of the cooperatives of waste pickers, the main responsible for this work in the country, and running without any governmental support.

The increase in waste use rates positively affects the performance of sustainability indicators but depends on awareness, as observed by [25]. A lack of recycling culture and higher costs of removal, transportation, and logistics has been found by [36]. This behavior associated with a lack of tax incentives is an aggravating factor for the implementation of reverse logistics.

3 Methods

To discuss this subject, we analyzed the results found in Garcia [21–23], also using the information published in the current literature about sustainability in the textile chain.

These previous studies were based on data mining and government data related to the output of the fabric and clothes processing supply chain, as well as the way consumers face recycling old garments.

4 Results and Discussion

Brazilian consumers' awareness of sustainability about cotton clothing was identified by [21] using data mining. The dissemination of a more sustainable lifestyle, with healthier habits, can contribute to the reduction of the carbon footprint, ecological footprint, and sustainability of the planet [21, 31].

When dealing with solutions that affect not only the citizen but big companies, and the whole of society, change of paradigm is challenging to implement [10]. It is likely that at some point, it will be necessary that both companies and consumers, be forced to change their choices and use. The influence of policies applied to sustainability on political and citizen attitudes was assessed by [35], and the authors noted that such changes might not be suitable to organize this sector

Garcia [21] show that the reduction in the use of vehicles, changes in diet, and in the way of buying clothes can impact sustainability. These habits can make people more aware to avoid excessive purchasing of unnecessary clothes and other items produced by fast fashion. It was also evidenced that the income and the value consumed in clothes interfere in the sustainable behavior of the surveyed Brazilians, although the results is suitable for the textile chain, the result cannot be expanded to other segments of the population, as the sample of respondents was restricted and limited to high income and education levels.

Garcia [22] provide an overview of the reverse logistics and disposal of the fabrics in the production chain of clothes in Brazil, country that only 3% of the waste generated is recycled. According to calculations by Brazilian Association of Public Cleaning and Special Waste Companies (Abrelpe), about 45 million tons of waste that could be recycled, and be not, could yield about US$ 750 million a year to the country [5].

Fabric companies must import waste from other countries [22], disregarding the potential for generating income and sustainable businesses that result in this investment because the population does not know about recycling of this waste. Brazilians are not trained about the selective collection (66%), and 39% do not separate organic waste from recyclable waste [20].

The recycling and reverse logistics performed by the textile and clothing industry in Brazil, based on the National Solid Waste Policy (PNRS) and Brazilian legislation, has been studied by [23]. It was found that companies are not responsible for the final destination of their products, which occurs only in some industrial sectors such as tires, lubricating oils, and pesticide packaging [11].

The Brazilian Association of Public Cleaning and Special Waste Companies [5] attributed a possible loss to the country of approximately US$ 30 billion per year for not recycling products that could be recycled, but are otherwise wasted.

The country is the largest in the European Union with 67 million inhabitants, France and it aims to recover 50% of the production of annual solid waste. Such anti-action represents a recovery of 300,000 tonnes, or 4.6 kg per person, over the total sold in clothing, bedding and sneakers [18].

Zonatti [37] reports that of the 175 thousand tons of solid textile waste generated in Brazil, about 90% were incorrectly discarded. A clothing cluster in the outskirts of São Paulo houses around 1200 companies that produce 12 tons of textile waste per day, about 2% of the country's total, estimated at 175,000 tons/year. Of these, 36,000 are reused in the production of blankets, twine, new clothes, and yarns [19]. According to [28], this number considers the loss of 10% of the cutting process, of which recyclers reprocess 70,000 tons (40%), and 60% go to landfills and dumps. [13] estimate approximately 10% of the textile production in waste with an inadequate final destination.

The actions carried out for the recycling and reuse of textiles, all over the world, point to charitable activities [27]. [8] show that the clothing banks of charities provide directly to the recycling companies. In the United Kingdom, the collection of textile waste is done by charitable organizations that resell in their stores, and surplus stocks are sold to recycling companies [26].

In Brazil, collectors of recyclable material, live in poverty and are integrated into cooperatives or associations with the support of local governments [7, 27]. The waste collection of fabrics and clothing is just a charity activity in Brazil and has no government support [23].

Currently, 60% more clothes are consumed than 15 years ago. These clothes are kept in the consumer closet for half of their useful life, and a third of them are discarded in after a year. Responsible for 8% to 10% of global greenhouse gas emissions, the fashion industry pollutes more than combined air and sea transport [33].

5   Final Remarks

The discussion in search of appropriate governmental policy is an emergency. The scenario is even worse in developing countries due to the lack of structure for recycling and reuse, and the absence of environmental awareness of the general public. When studying the implications of investment in innovation for a textile and clothing chain and its relationship to the circular economy, legislation, and practices, we confirm that are small-scale and handicraft activities that require government support for advances. The National Solid Waste Policy, with action plans for the implementation of reverse logistics in various industrial sectors, has been under discussion at the Brazilian Congress since 2011, without any concrete results.

The support of the responsible authorities must also reach the collectors, with adequate legislation to regulate people's working conditions and quality of life. Such activities are highly harmful and challenging for waste workers.

Acknowledgment. The authors wish to thank the Paulista University, CAPES, and CNPQ.

References

1. Abramovay, R.: An agreement for the circular economy. Análise. vol. 83, p. 21, FGV, Rio de Janeiro (2014)
2. Abit. Associação Brasileira da Indústria Têxtil e de Confecção: Brazilian Association of the Textile and Clothing Industry. Profile of the textile and clothing sector (2020). http://www. abit.org.br/cont/perfil-do-setor. Accessed May 2020
3. Amaral, M.C., Baruque, R.J., Ferreira, A.C.: A national solid waste policy and reverse logistics in the national textile and clothing sector. In: 2nd Textile and Fashion Scientific Congress, Contexmod (2014). http://www.contexmod.net.br/index.php/segundo/article/view/67. Accessed Feb 2020
4. do Amaral, M.C., Zonatti, W.F., da Silva, K.L., Karam Junior, D., Amato Neto, J., Baruque-Ramos, J.: Industrial textile recycling and reuse in Brazil: case study and considerations concerning the circular economy. Gest. Prod. **25**(3), 431–443 (2018). http://dx.doi.org/10. 1590/0104-530X3305
5. Associação Brasileira de Empresas de Limpeza Pública e Resíduos Especiais. Abrelpe. Brazilian Association of Public Cleaning and Special Waste Companies. Overview of solid waste in Brazil 2017 (2018). http://abrelpe.org.br/panorama/. Accessed Mar 2020
6. ABNT. Associação Brasileira de Normas Técnicas, Brazilian Association of Technical Standards NBR 10004 (2004). Accessed 30 Nov 2004
7. Baruque-Ramos, J., Amaral, M.C., Laktim, M.C., Santos, H.N., Araujo, F.B., Zonatti, W.F.: Social and economic importance of textile reuse and recycling in Brazil. In: IOP Conference Series: Materials Science and Engineering, Presented at the 17thWorld Textile Conference AUTEX 2017 (2017). https://doi.org/10.1088/1757-899X/254/19/192003

8. Bianchi, C., Birtwistle, G.: Sell, give away, or donate: an exploratory study of fashion clothing disposal behaviour in two countries. Int. Rev. Retail Distrib. Consum. Res. **20**, 353–368 (2010). https://doi.org/10.1080/09593969.2010.491213

9. Boehm, C. (2018). Brasil perde R$5,7 bilhões por ano ao não reciclar resíduos plásticos. Brazil loses R $ 5.7 billion a year by not recycling plastic waste, Agência, Brasil, 7 June 2018.   http://agenciabrasil.ebc.com.br/geral/noticia/2018-06/brasil-perde-r-57-bilhoes-por-ano-ao-nao-reciclar-residuos-plasticos. Accessed Feb 2019

10. Boström, M., Micheletti, M.: Introducing the sustainability challenge of textiles and clothing. J. Consum. Policy **39**(4), 367–375 (2016). https://doi.org/10.1007/s10603-016-9336-6

11. Brasil. Low n.º 12.305, 2 August 2010. http://www.planalto.gov.br/ccivil_03/_ato2007-2010/2010/lei/l12305.htm. Accessed May 2020

12. Bukhari, M.A., Carrasco-Gallego, R., Ponce-Cueto, E.: Developing a national programme for textiles and clothing recovery. Waste Manag. Res. **36**(4), 321e331 (2018). https://doi.org/10.1177/0734242X18759190

13. Campos, T.T.S.C., Mendes, F.D., Costa, S.M.: Textile waste, raw material that generates income. In: International Fashion Business Congress 2017, São Paulo, Brazil (2017). http://cinm.org.br/cinm/anais/2017/03_03_06_Res%C3%ADduos%20T%C3%AAxteis.pdf. Accessed Feb 2020

14. Castaño, M.S., Méndez, M.T., Galindo, M.Á.: Innovation, internalization and business-growth expectations among entrepreneurs in the services sector. J. Bus. Res. **69**(5), 1690–1695 (2016). https://doi.org/10.1016/j.jbusres.2015.10.039

15. Castro, A.B.C., Amato Neto, J.: Innovation in the fashion industry: the contributions of Marxist theory to the fashion universe. In: Production Engineering Symposium (Simpep), Anais, Bauru, 19 2012. Global supply networks: challenges and trends in the globalized world. Bauru, Unesp, 2012 (2012). http://sistemasproducao.net/redecoop/images/pdf/congressos/xix-simpep-2012-amato3.pdf. Accessed Feb 2020

16. Ecosign: Textile recycling as a contribution to circular economy and production waste enhancement   (2017).   http://www.ecosign-project.eu/news/textile-recycling-as-a-contri bution-to-circular-economy-and-productionwaste-enhancement/. Accessed Mar 2020

17. Elkington, J.: Enter the triple bottom line. In: 1997 Cannibals with Forks: The Triple Bottom Line of 21st Century Business, Capstone, Oxford (1997)

18. European Commission: Circular economy in practice - reducing textile waste (2017). https://ec.europa.eu/easme/en/news/circular-economypractice-reducing-textile-waste. Accessed Jan 2020

19. Freire, E., Lopes, G.B.: Implications of the National Solid Waste Policy for waste management practices in the clothing industry. Redige: revista de design, inovação e gestão estratégica, vol. 4, 1 April 2013

20. Gama, M.: Research shows that Brazilians know little about collection and recycling. Pesquisa mostra que brasileiro sabe pouco sobre coleta e reciclagem. Folha de S. Paulo, 25 June 2018 (2018). https://www1.folha.uol.com.br/mercado/2018/06/pesquisa-mostra-que-brasileiro-sabe-pouco-sobre-coleta-e-reciclagem.shtml. Accessed Feb 2020

21. Garcia, S., Cordeiro, A., de Nääs, I.A., de Costa Neto, P. L.O.: The sustainability awareness of Brazilian consumers of cotton clothing. Journal of Cleaner Production. V. 215, 1 April 2019, p. 1490–1502 (2019A). https://doi.org/10.1016/j.jclepro.2019.01.069

22. Garcia, S., Nääs, I.A., Costa Neto, P.L.O., dos Reis, J.G.M.: Reverse logistics and waste in the textile and clothing production chain in Brazil. In: Ameri, F., Stecke, K., von Cieminski, G., Kiritsis, D. (eds.) Advances in Production Management Systems. Production Management for the Factory of the Future. APMS 2019. IFIP Advances in Information and Communication Technology, vol 566. Springer, Cham (2019). https://doi.org/10.1007/978-3-030-30000-5_23

23. Garcia, S., de Nääs, I.A., de Costa Neto, P.L.O., dos Reis, J.G.M.: Disorganization of the reverse logistics and recycling of textile waste delay advances in the Brazilian circular economy. In: Abstract in Proceedings 8th International Workshop on Advances in Cleaner Production (2019C). http://www.advancesincleanerproduction.net/8th/files/proceedings_8th. pdf. Accessed May 2020

24. Geraque, E.: Brazil loses R $ 3 billion a year for not recycling waste. Brasil perde R$ 3 bilhões ao ano por não reciclar resíduos. Estadao.com. 23 out. 2019 (2019). https:// sustentabilidade.estadao.com.br/noticias/geral,brasil-perde-r-3-bilhoes-ao-ano-por-nao-reciclar-residuos,70002559053. Accessed Mar 2020

25. Heidari, R., Yazdanparast, R., Jabbarzadeh, A.: Sustainable design of a municipal solid waste management system considering waste separators: a real-world application. Sustain. Cities Soc. **47**(2019), 101457 (2019). https://doi.org/10.1016/j.scs.2019.101457

26. Kim, C.S., Kim, K.R.: A case study comparing textile recycling systems of Korea and the UK to promote sustainability. J. Text. Apparel Technol. Manag. **10**, 1e11 (2016)

27. Leal Filho, W., et al.: An overview of the problems posed by plastic products and the role of extended producer responsibility in Europe. J. Clean. Prod. **214**, 550e558 (2019). https://doi. org/10.1016/j.jclepro.2018.12.256

28. Lorenzetti, L.(s/d).: The Importance of reusing textile waste in São Paulo. A Importância do Reaproveitamento de Resíduos Têxteis em São Paulo. https://www.tratamentodeagua.com. br/artigo/reaproveitamento-residuos-texteis-sp/. Accessed Mar 2020

29. Mckinsey: Europe's circular economy opportunity (2015). https://www.mckinsey.com/ business-functions/sustainability-and-resource-productivity/our-insights/europes-circular-economy-opportunity. Accessed Mar 2019

30. OECD. Organization for Economic Co-operation and Development: Resource Productivity in the G8 and the OECD. A Report in the Framework of the Kobe 3R Action Plan. Paris (2011). https://www.oecd.org/env/waste/47944428.pdf

31. Ecological Footprint. (s/d). Questionaire to calculate the index in Brazil. http://www. pegadaecologica.org.br/2015/pegada.php. Accessed Feb 2020

32. United Nations (2018). https://nacoesunidas.org/humanidade-produz-mais-de-2-bilhoes-de-toneladas-de-lixo-por-ano-diz-onu-em-dia-mundial/. Accessed May 2020

33. United Nations (2019). https://nacoesunidas.org/agencias/onumeioambiente/. Accessed May 2020

34. Valenzuela-Venegas, G., Salgado, J.C., Díaz-Alvarado, F.A.: Sustainability indicators for the assessment of eco-industrial parks: classification and criteria for selection. J. Clean. Prod. **133**, 99–116 (2016). https://doi.org/10.1016/j.jclepro.2016.05.113

35. Xu, C.-K., Cheng, H., Liao, Z., Hu, H.: An account of the textile waste policy in China (1991–2017). J. Clean. Prod. **234**, 1459–1470 (2019). https://doi.org/10.1016/j.jclepro.2019. 06.283

36. Zonatti, W.F., Amaral, M.C., Gasi, F., Baruque-Ramos, J., Duleba, W.: Recycling of waste from the textile and clothing sector in Brazil: overview and related actions. Sustentabilidade em Debate, **6**(3), 50–69 (2015). http://dx.doi.org/10.18472/SustDeb.v6n3.2015.15892

37. Zonatti, W.F.: Generation of solid waste from the Brazilian textile and clothing industry: materials and processes for reuse and recycling. Doctoral Thesis in Sustainability - School of Arts, Sciences and Humanities at the University of São Paulo, São Paulo, Brazil (2016)

Planning Environments of Hospital Laboratories: An Exploratory Study

Aili Biriita Bertnum$^{(\boxtimes)}$ ⓘ, Marco Semini, and Jan Ola Strandhagen ⓘ

Department of Mechanical and Industrial Engineering,
Norwegian University of Science and Technology, 7491 Trondheim, Norway
{aili.b.bertnum, marco.semini, ola.strandhagen}@ntnu.no

Abstract. Hospital laboratories are facing challenges of increasing demand and limited budgets. Planning and control can improve resource utilization, reduce work-in-progress and shorten throughput times, but to achieve such benefits, there is a need for a strategic fit between the planning and control system and the unique planning environment of the hospital laboratory. Existing research on planning environments focuses mainly on manufacturing companies, whereas hospital laboratory planning environment research is scarce. The aim of the study is to characterize a hospital laboratory's planning environment based on an exploratory case study. The findings indicate an overall strategic fit of the case laboratory's planning environment, but a lack of strategic fit between large batch sizes and low set-up times. Hospital laboratory planning environment research must be further developed through multiple case studies, as hospital laboratories are different in service provision and organizational structure. This study increases knowledge on planning environments in hospital laboratories, and suggests topics for future research.

Keywords: Planning environment · Service operations · Hospital laboratories

1 Introduction

Test results from hospital laboratories are a vital support for physicians in decision making regarding a patient's health. Thus, hospital laboratory throughput time, also called turnaround time, is crucial to prevent delays in patient treatment [1]. With continuously increasing demand and limited budgets, hospital laboratories are facing a challenging future. They need to improve utilization of existing resources, while at the same time reduce work-in-progress and shorten throughput times. An appropriate planning and control system can support these objectives, but it requires the planning and control system to be aligned with the characteristics of the planning environment [2]. A lack of such a strategic fit will negatively affect performance [2].

Planning environments are company-specific, and its characterizing variables are typically related to the product, market and manufacturing of the specific company [3–5]. Most research related to planning environment and strategic fit takes a manufacturing point-of-view. Planning environment research in hospital laboratories, however, is scarce. The aim of the study is, therefore, to characterize the planning environment of a hospital laboratory, which provides a starting point for the generation of knowledge on how to plan and control hospital laboratories.

© IFIP International Federation for Information Processing 2020
Published by Springer Nature Switzerland AG 2020
B. Lalic et al. (Eds.): APMS 2020, IFIP AICT 591, pp. 538–545, 2020.
https://doi.org/10.1007/978-3-030-57993-7_61

A single and exploratory case study of a hospital laboratory department at a Scandinavian hospital was performed to achieve an in-depth understanding of its planning environment. The control model methodology has been used as a systematic approach to visualize and analyze the hospital laboratory's current production and logistics system [6]. Furthermore, Buer et al. [5] compiled existing manufacturing planning environment research into a framework for mapping planning environments, which has been used in this study to map the planning environment of the hospital laboratory.

The paper has the following structure. In Sect. 2, relevant literature on planning environments is reviewed and common hospital laboratory planning and control challenges are introduced. In Sect. 3, the hospital laboratory is described by the control model methodology and Buer et al. [5]'s planning environment mapping framework. The planning environment's strategic fit and its planning and control challenges is discussed in Sect. 4. The paper ends with suggestions for future research in Sect. 5.

2 Planning Environments

Numerous authors have investigated manufacturing planning environment variables and categorizations. Hayes and Wheelwright [3] developed the product-process matrix, which is probably one of the most recognized frameworks for choosing manufacturing processes based on product and market characteristics. Manufacturing planning environment research is often based on the customer order decoupling point (CODP). E.g., Jonsson and Mattsson [4]'s four generic planning environments categorizations and Stavrulaki and Davis [7]'s further development of the product-process matrix, were based on the well-known CODPs: engineer to order (ETO), make to order (MTO), assemble to order (ATO) and make to stock (MTS).

Buer et al. [5] identified 30 planning environment variables from relevant literature and developed a framework for mapping planning environments in manufacturing companies. In the framework, the variables are grouped into three categories: product, market and manufacturing. Ranges of values are defined to each variable, which are sorted based on the CODPs. The framework reveals the company profiling, which can be used to assess the strategic fit of the product, market and manufacturing variables, where a lack of strategic fit provides the basis to evaluate planning and control related changes.

The different functions in healthcare systems, such as hospital laboratories, provide various healthcare services. To the best of our knowledge, there exists no planning environment framework from a service operations-perspective, such as Buer et al. [5]. However, Wikner et al. [8] introduced two additional service operations decoupling points. The customer adaptation decoupling point (CADP) marks where the service is adapted to a specific customer. The customer contact decoupling point (CCDP) refers to the type of customer contact, either front-office, back-office or a combination.

Nguyen et al. [9] mapped the planning environment of three outpatient departments in Danish hospitals, revealing large differences in patient requirements, patient flow and resource availability. While hospital laboratories have no patient contact, they are, like outpatient departments, highly different in service provision and organizational structure. Laboratories can be centralized with the ability to analyze all incoming samples, or decentralized where each unit is responsible for a specific analysis field [1]. E.g., microbiological laboratories identify microscopic organisms in biological samples, whereas pharmacological laboratories detect the share of drugs and medicine.

Several planning and control challenges are present in hospital laboratories. An unbalanced workload is common due to the unpredictable nature of accidents and illnesses, which makes it challenging to balance demand and supply [10]. Batch-based processing is also common in hospital laboratories, due to large material costs, among other. Large batches often cause prolonged processing times, and may lead to a specific operation only being performed once a day. Thus, samples coming in after the operation has been run, would have to wait until the next day to be processed [11]. In addition, machine-based operations with long durations are often being run during the night, which causes a one-day delay for all test results [12].

3   Case Study

The case study involves a pharmacological laboratory department at a large Scandinavian hospital, offering analyses of the share of drugs, medicine and other substances in biological samples, such as blood and urine. Emergency preparedness around the clock for samples requiring immediate analysis is also offered, but is usually a negligible disruption due to its low occurrence. The product, market and customers of the case laboratory are described in Sect. 3.1. The production processes and logistics are described in Sect. 3.2, and visualized as an AS-IS control model in Fig. 1.

3.1   Product, Markets and Customers

The case laboratory delivers test results, which contains verified and interpreted information from the analysis of the biological sample. Test results are often used to detect drug and alcohol misuse, or to assess the effect of a medicine in patient treatment. The laboratory is able to analyze almost 300 substances. Several substances can be analyzed by one analysis method, and will be further described in Sect. 3.2.

Approximately 200 000 biological samples are delivered to the case laboratory on a yearly basis. More than 40% of the demand concerns drug analysis, which is usually performed in urine samples because of its longer drug tracking time, compared to blood samples. Analysis of Vitamin D and medicine make up approximately 25% and 20% of the demand, respectively. These analyses are usually done in blood and serum samples for higher accuracies of substance share. The remaining 15% of demand concern many specialized and low demand substances, including forensic examinations with higher requirements to quality and traceability.

Seasonal variations are observed, such as an increase in demand in advance of public holidays. In addition, weekly variations in incoming samples are common due to the postal service operating from Monday to Friday. This results in least incoming samples on Monday and most incoming samples on Tuesday. However, the seasonal and weekly variations do not impose a need for extra capacity.

The customers are the health professionals requesting the analysis of one or several substances, and supplying the biological sample. The patient, on the other hand, is both the end customer and the provider of this raw material. There are three main customer types: health professionals from the hospital itself, local healthcare institutions and regional healthcare institutions. They are differentiated by geographical distance, sample transportation mean and ordering system, and will be further described in Sect. 3.2.

3.2   Production and Logistics

The production and logistics activities are visualized in Fig. 1, and are further described. Hospital orderlies collect and deliver samples from the hospital and local healthcare institutions twice a day. Samples from regional healthcare institutions are delivered daily by mail due to the geographical distance, which prolongs delivery time with 1–3 days. In the receive process, samples are coupled with the corresponding order. It defines the case laboratory's CODP, best characterized as ATO as chemicals are ready-mixed, but the analysis is postponed until a sample with an order is in place. Paper-based orders from local and regional healthcare institutions are delivered with the samples, and are manually registered into the laboratory information system (LIS). Electronic orders from the hospital and a few local healthcare institutions are collected from the shared information system (XIS). Samples coming from the hospital are ready-registered, while other samples are manually registered into LIS. Adaptations to customer orders happen already in the registration process and presents the CADP.

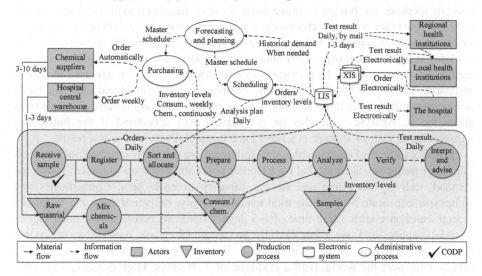

Fig. 1. AS-IS control model of the hospital laboratory department

Both new arrivals and stored samples are sorted and allocated into racks specifying the analysis method, which is decided by the analysis plan. Samples not being processed on the day of arrival are placed in inventory. There are strict storage requirements due to the limited sample shelf life. E.g., some samples need to be frozen to prevent the substance from evaporating. Thereafter, the samples are prepared, entailing small operations, such as moving the biological material into the correct tube when delivered in the wrong tube, dividing the biological material into several tubes when several analysis methods are required, and centrifuging blood into serum. The samples are then processed into analyzable tests, entailing pipetting, evaporation, dissolving, adding chemicals, heat-treating, or a combination, specified by the analysis method. Processing takes place in various manual-labored workstations, and semi-automated machines and robots, which require manual sample transportation as well as manual machine refill.

The analyzable tests are pipetted onto plates and placed into the analysis machines. The samples are stored for a given period in case there is a need to redo the analysis. The analysis machines are programmed based on the analysis plan at the end of the workday. It takes 5 min to analyze a single sample, and the analysis time increases correspondingly with the batch size. The next morning, the analysis machines are emptied and cleaned. Bioengineers verify the analysis by checking if the test results are within the reference values. A doctor is responsible for interpreting the results, and can also give advices regarding adjustments to or change of medicine. Then, the test result is sent to the customer, either electronically through XIS, or paper-based by mail. The CCDP constitute a mix of front-office activities, e.g., test result reporting and consultation, and back-office activities, e.g. procuring materials and preparing for analysis.

The customers place call-off orders based on the cyclic master schedule, which states the analysis methods to be run on a given day. This schedule is based on factors such as historical demand, test result urgency and samples' shelf lives. Around 60 analysis methods are run on a regular basis. Low demand and medium demand analyses are run twice a month and twice a week, respectively, in batches of 10 to 20 samples, and high demand analyses are run daily in 2–3 batches of 100 samples. The workday starts with making a daily analysis plan stating the final schedule of analysis methods. Analyses should be performed to schedule, as test results are used in patient treatment. Yet, for cost reduction reasons, postponement is considered when the batch size requirement for running the analysis is not met, given that the samples' shelf lives allow for it. Analyses can also be run earlier than scheduled if the batch size requirement is met, or if there is a need for a faster delivery of the test result.

Inventory levels of consumables and equipment are manually checked once a week. The order frequency is controlled by a reorder point and order-up-to system, given the demand, delivery lead-time and storage capacity of each item. Consumables and equipment constitute 50% of the total material supply, delivered from the hospital's central warehouse with a lead-time of 1–3 days. Chemicals constitute the other half of material supply, and are controlled by an automatic stock replenishment system tracking the actual usage of each chemical. Chemicals are delivered from chemical suppliers all over the world, with a lead-time of 3–10 days. High consumption materials have deliveries weekly, e.g. disposable gloves, pipettes and certain gas types. Materials with a very low consumption, such as machine parts can be ordered as seldom as every second year.

The summary of the product, market and manufacturing variables of the case laboratory's planning environment is provided in Table 1. The planning environment is characterized based on Buer et al. [5]'s mapping framework for manufacturing companies.

Table 1. The planning environment of the pharmacological laboratory department

	Variables	Values			
	CODP	ETO	MTO	**ATO**	MTS
Product	Level of customization	Fully customer specific	**Allows some specifications**		None
	Product variety	High	**Medium**		Low
	BOM complexity	<5 levels	3-5 levels	1-2 levels, several items	**1-2 levels, few items**
	Data accuracy	Low	Medium		**High**
	Level of process planning	None		Partial process planning	**Fully designed process**
Market	P/D ratio	<1		1	**>1**
	Demand type	Customer order allocation		Calculated requirements	**Forecast**
	Demand source	Customer order		**Stock replenishment order**	
	Volume/frequency (per year)	Few large customer orders	Several customer orders with large quantities	Large number of customer orders with medium quantities	**Frequent call-offs based on delivery schedules**
	Customer demand frequency	Unique	Block-wise or sporadic	**Regular**	Steady (continuous)
	Time distributed demand	**Annual figure**		Time distributed	
	Demand characteristics	Dependent		**Independent**	
	Type of procurement ordering	Order by order procurement		**Order releases from a delivery agreement**	
	Inventory accur.	Low	Medium		**High**
Manufacturing	Mfg. mix	Mixed products		**Homogenous products**	
	Shop floor layout	Fixed-position	**Functional**	**Cell**	Product
	Production type	Single unit production	**Small series**	**Serial production**	Mass production
	Throughput time	Years	Months	**Weeks** | **Days**	Hours
	Major operations	High	Medium		**Low**
	Batch size	Equal to customer order quantities	**Small, equal to one week of demand**	**Medium, equal to a few weeks of demand**	Large, equal to a month's demand or more
	Production order repetition freq.	Non-repetitive production	Production with infrequent repetition		**Production with frequent repetition**
	Fluctuations of capacity req.	High	Medium		**Low**
	Planning points	High	**Medium**		Low
	Set-up times	**Low**	Medium		High
	Sequencing dependency	None	**Low**	Medium	High
	Part flow	One-piece flow	Overlapped	Lot-wise	**Bulk (batch)**
	Material flow complexity	High	**Medium**		Low
	Capacity flex.	**High**	Medium		Low
	Load flexibility	High	**Medium**		Low

4 Discussion

The planning environment of companies often falls rather homogeneously within one of the four CODPs, which indicates a strategic fit between product, market, and manufacturing variables [5]. The case laboratory resembles manufacturing companies, with functional entities performing specific tasks that combined make up the final product. Its planning environment has many values within ATO, the case laboratory's CODP, and MTS (see Table 1), indicating an overall strategic fit. However, some variables deviate as well, which can have a negative effect on performance [1]. E.g., low set-up times and high capacity flexibility are usually associated with ETO or MTO companies.

The case study is in agreement with the literature inasmuch as unpredictable demand and unbalanced workload present hospital laboratory-related planning and control challenges. The case study further points out large varieties of both incoming raw materials and analysis methods, as well as limited sample shelf lives. However, a mismatch is identified between the case study's batch sizes and batch-based part flow on one hand, and low set-up times and high capacity flexibility on the other hand (see Table 1). Large batch sizes give longer processing times, which is especially true for the analysis process in the case study. A single sample takes 5 min to analyze, whereas a batch of 100 samples will correspondingly take more than 8 h to analyze. Nighttime analysis itself delays the test result delivery with one day [12].

According to a recent study of a hospital laboratory, reducing nighttime analysis, balancing the workload, and increasing the number of batches can result in a 20% reduction of throughput time [12]. It is also found that increasing the frequency of operations, even from once to twice a day, can largely reduce throughput times [11]. The case laboratory runs large batch sizes due to high fixed batch-related costs, such as expensive materials. However, the low set-up times should make it possible to reduce the batch sizes, as well as increase the number of batches and analysis frequency. It will result in a more balanced workload, and have a large impact on the case laboratory's throughput time and performance.

5 Conclusion

Planning and control can improve resource utilization, reduce work-in-progress and shorten throughput times in hospital laboratories, but it is important to have a strategic fit with the planning environment. Existing research on hospital laboratory planning environment is scarce, and there exists no known service operations framework for mapping planning environments. Therefore, this study characterized a hospital laboratory's planning environment with a mapping framework for manufacturing companies. The findings indicate an overall strategic fit of the case laboratory's planning environment, but a lack of strategic fit between large batch sizes and low set-up times. The low set-up times present an improvement possibility inasmuch as they allow processing in small batches.

A limitation of this study is the use of a single case, which makes it difficult to generalize the findings to other hospital laboratory types. We suggest executing multiple case studies to compare planning environments of different hospital laboratory types. This study also revealed a lack of a framework for mapping planning environments in service operations, which also presents a future research topic.

Acknowledgements. This research received funding from the strategic research area NTNU Health in 2020 at NTNU, Norwegian University of Science and Technology. We also want to acknowledge the case hospital laboratory taking part in this study.

References

1. Dolci, A., Giavarina, D., Pasqualetti, S., Szóke, D., Panteghini, M.: Total laboratory automation: do stat tests still matter? Clin. Biochem. **50**, 605–611 (2017)
2. Berry, W.L., Hill, T.: Linking systems to strategy. Int. J. Oper. Prod. Manag. **12**(10), 3–15 (1992)
3. Hayes, R.H., Wheelwright, S.C.: Restoring our Competitive Edge: Competing Through Manufacturing. Wiley, New York (1984)
4. Jonsson, P., Mattsson, S.-A.: The implications of fit between planning environments and manufacturing planning and control methods. Int. J. Oper. Prod. Manag. **23**(8), 872–900 (2003)
5. Buer, S.-V., Strandhagen, J.W., Strandhagen, J.O., Alfnes, E.: Strategic fit of planning environments: towards an integrated framework. In: Temponi, C., Vandaele, N. (eds.) ILS 2016. LNBIP, vol. 262, pp. 77–92. Springer, Cham (2018). https://doi.org/10.1007/978-3-319-73758-4_6
6. Strandhagen, J.O., Skarlo, T.: A manufacturing business process reengineering method: design and redesign of a production control model. In: Browne, J., O'Sullivan, D. (eds.) Re-engineering the Enterprise. ITIFIP, pp. 187–198. Springer, Boston, MA (1995). https://doi.org/10.1007/978-0-387-34876-6_18
7. Stavrulaki, E., Davis, M.: Aligning products with supply chain processes and strategy. Int. J. Logist. Manag. (2010)
8. Wikner, J., Yang, B., Yang, Y., Williams, S.J.: Decoupling thinking in service operations: a case in healthcare delivery system design. Prod. Plan. Control **28**(5), 387–397 (2017)
9. Nguyen, V.T., Sommer, A.F., Steger-Jensen, K., Hvolby, H.H.: Hospital planning environment variables applied in practice: a multiple danish case study. In: Grabot, B., Vallespir, B., Gomes, S., Bouras, A., Kiritsis, D. (eds.) APMS 2014. IAICT, vol. 439, pp. 667–674. Springer, Heidelberg (2014). https://doi.org/10.1007/978-3-662-44736-9_81
10. Leeftink, A.G., Boucherie, R.J., Hans, E.W., Verdaasdonk, M.A.M., Vliegen, I.M.H., Van Diest, P.J.: Predicting turnaround time reductions of the diagnostic track in the histopathology laboratory using mathematical modelling. J. Clin. Pathol. **69**(9), 793–800 (2016)
11. Hewer, E., Hammer, C., Fricke-Vetsch, D., Baumann, C., Perren, A., Schmitt, A.M.: Implementation of a 'lean'cytopathology service: towards routine same-day reporting. J. Clin. Pathol. **71**(5), 395–401 (2018)
12. Leeftink, A.G., Boucherie, R.J., Hans, E.W., Verdaasdonk, M.A.M., Vliegen, I.M.H., van Diest, P.J.: Batch scheduling in the histopathology laboratory. Flexible Serv. Manuf. J. **30**, 171–197 (2016). https://doi.org/10.1007/s10696-016-9257-3

Knowledge and Practices Towards Sustainability and Circular Economy Transitions: A Norwegian Manufacturing Perspective

Jon Halfdanarson[1(✉)] and Nina Pereira Kvadsheim[1,2]

[1] Møreforsking Molde, Britvegen 4, Molde, Norway
{Jon.Halfdanarson,Nina.p.kvadsheim}@himolde.no
[2] Faculty of Logistics, Molde University College, Britvegen 2, Molde, Norway

Abstract. The extant literature shows that companies are willing to transition into sustainability and the circular economy (CE) yet lack the knowledge and skills to transform their actions to meet sustainability challenges in a meaningful way. Indeed, for companies to act in an environmentally responsible way, they must know enough about environmental issues, yet literature on this knowledge standpoint is missing. This paper assesses the knowledge and practices among manufacturing companies working towards sustainability and CE transitions. The study employs a survey design and in-depth interviews with 20 firms from the manufacturing industry in Norway. This study contributes to the theoretical understanding of sustainability and CE transitions by providing insight into the knowledge and practices of manufacturing firms, which may at the same time facilitate decision-makers in planning for the development of a CE and promote the sustainable development of the manufacturing industry in Norway.

Keywords: Sustainability · Circular economy · Sustainability knowledge and practices · Manufacturing industry

1 Introduction

Competitive pressures, innovation and market potentials, regulatory concerns, and a sense of corporate social and environmental responsibility have prompted many companies to engage in sustainability issues in recent years [1]. Sustainability is used here as a common notion referring to "development that meets the needs of the present without compromising the ability of future generations to meet their own needs" [2, p. 3]. From the business perspective, the circular economy (CE) is understood as a model that is "restorative and regenerative by design, and aims to keep products, components, and materials at their highest utility and value at all times" [3, p. 1]. In this study, CE is viewed as an approach to implement the much-discussed concept of sustainable development [4]. The sustainability and CE transitions are due to the many environmental problems (e.g. climate change, resource depletion), which are brought about by unsustainable consumption and production patterns [5]. In fact, to develop society and the corporate world towards a more sustainable state, an incremental

© IFIP International Federation for Information Processing 2020
Published by Springer Nature Switzerland AG 2020
B. Lalic et al. (Eds.): APMS 2020, IFIP AICT 591, pp. 546–553, 2020.
https://doi.org/10.1007/978-3-030-57993-7_62

continuous transition is needed, which according to [6] is the response to a number of persistent problems confronting today's modern societies. To be able to respond to these challenges, [7] advocates that we need the will to do it - a sense of urgency, a will that follows from an attitude of concern and we need to develop knowledge of sustainability/CE, which will then be transformed into sustainable patterns of human activities. Succinctly put, if companies have knowledge of sustainability and CE, then they should be able to understand what drives and blocks sustainability/CE transitions, and how such transitions can be accelerated [6]. This is consistent with Velenturf and Jopson [8], who argue that companies are willing to transition into sustainability and CE yet lack the knowledge and skills to transform their actions to meet sustainability challenges in a meaningful way. Indeed, for companies to act in an environmentally responsible way, they must know enough about environmental issues [9]. However, numerous theoretical frameworks have been developed to explain this gap between the possession of knowledge and awareness related to sustainability and displaying behavior that consciously seeks to minimize the negative impact on the environment (e.g. minimize resource and energy consumption, use of non-toxic substances, reduce waste production). Although various studies have been undertaken, no definitive explanation has yet been found [10].

Against this backdrop, this study aims to assess the knowledge and practices among manufacturing companies working towards transitioning into sustainability and the CE. This focus on manufacturing companies can be justified on the following grounds: Firstly, companies are endowed with resources and capabilities, as such they have the potential to drive the change towards a more sustainable economy [1]. Secondly, they are the most influential institutions within the market, which is the most dominant coordinating institution in the world [11] and thus any strategy aiming at increasing sustainability cannot be pursued without their involvement. Thirdly, those companies that dominate economic activity are increasingly viewed as a major cause of the current ecological crisis [12, 13] and hence it is essential that they commit to being proactive in the transition towards a more sustainable economy [13, 14]. This study therefore contributes to burgeoning research on sustainability and CE in the manufacturing industry. By contextualizing it to the Norwegian manufacturing industry, it provides a novel counter-point company perspective on knowledge and practices towards sustainability/CE.

The paper proceeds as follows. Section 2 reviews literature related to knowledge and practices towards sustainability and the CE. Section 3 describes the method employed by the study, followed by analysis and discussion in Sect. 4. Finally, Sect. 5 presents the closure and limitation of the study.

2 Knowledge and Practices in Sustainability and CE Transitions

Sustainability transitions are long-term, multi-dimensional, and fundamental transformation processes through which established socio-technical systems shift to more sustainable modes of production and consumption [15]. However, there is little research on knowledge and practices related to sustainability and CE transitions. Extant literature focused on the gap between awareness and behavior; for instance, Blake [16] looked into the value-action gap in environmental policy, and on the external environmental pressure on firms and their behavior [17]. While Kollmuss and Agyeman [10] found that increases in environmental knowledge and awareness generally did not lead to pro-environmental behavior. Regarding studies that focused on the awareness and behavior of firms toward developing a CE, Lin [18] found increasing CE knowledge levels among industrial firms. However, as can be seen from the review of literature, despite the wealth of evidence concerning environmental awareness and the behavior of firms, there is little research on the knowledge and practices of firms in transitioning into sustainability and CE. Thus, this study seeks to contribute to knowledge for sustainability and CE transformation and should therefore be deemed essential.

In the subsequent section, the method employed in this study is presented.

3 Method

Considering the study's objective, a multiple-case-study approach was deemed appropriate since it is suitable for replication purposes [19]. In contrast to a single case study, a multiple-case-study approach increases external validity and reduces observer bias [20]. The case companies for this study were selected from an industrial cluster that comprises 50 companies from different industries (e.g. heavy machinery, IT, plastic, lighting system). Since it is typical in case study research to select cases by applying specific criteria, instead of selecting a random or stratified sample [21], the following main selection criteria were applied in this study: (1) if the company was a manufacturing company with either in-house or outsourced production, and (2) if the company was interested in exploring business opportunities under the sustainability logic, where the business model(s) is aligned with the triple bottom line.

Data were collected through a survey, where 20 manufacturing companies with different market segments (e.g. advanced equipment to maritime/casting industry) responded to the self-administered questionnaires via Quest Back. The survey design was chosen as it is often the most direct and cost-effective way of soliciting the respondents' opinions about the subject of interest [22]. In order to gain an in-depth understanding of the companies' perspectives on sustainability/CE, semi-structured interviews were conducted with the CEO and departmental managers of eight of the 20 companies. To allow for data triangulation [19], these data sources were supplemented with document analysis of official documents such as sustainability/CE articles and company websites.

The next section presents the analysis and discussion of the study.

4 Knowledge and Practices Towards Sustainability and CE

The study's results indicate that the companies have a relatively good general understanding about sustainability, have a positive view of it and a relatively strong willingness to act toward its development. Figure 1 shows different viewpoints of how companies understand sustainability. These definitions are categorized according to the similar elements identified in all the given definitions (20 in total). Here we can see that there is a strong focus on the long-term perspective and a strong awareness of the three dimensions of sustainability. For example, 30% of the companies report that sustainability is concerned with assuming that nature and the environment are not an inexhaustible resource and so, it is essential to protect them and use them rationally, by making sure that their businesses do not harm the environment. While 60% of the companies defined sustainability through the following interconnected pillars: environment, economic and social and the future generation. This definition corresponds to the one provided by the widely acknowledged Brundtland Report 'Our Common Future' describing it as "development which meets the needs of the present without compromising the ability of future generations to meet their own needs" [10, p. 43].

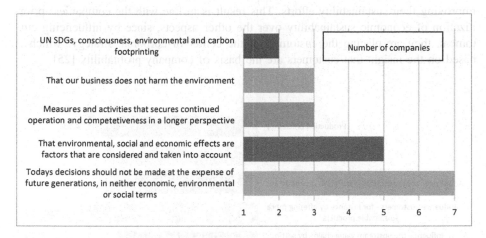

Fig. 1. Different aggregations of interpretations of "Sustainability" and what that means to the companies

Considering the CE, the results indicate that most of the firms had heard of the CE (95%) and most of them could identify CE with regeneration and recycling of waste, minimization of resource consumption and waste production. This result corresponds to Lin et al's [18] finding that most industrial firms have increasing CE knowledge levels.

Further, the survey reveals how the companies ranked how important different dimensions of sustainability are for them. Unsurprisingly, the economic aspect of sustainability is identified as the most important for all the studied companies. This is also evident in Gusmerotti et al's [23] study, where the findings suggest that the economic drivers are the only effective lever for the transition towards more sustainability. On the other hand, social sustainability is ranked as more important than environmental sustainability. This result is somehow unexpected, especially bearing in mind that social sustainability is often overlooked relative to the other two aspects. What is more, from the in-depth interviews it shows that most of these companies under study are regarded as "cornerstone companies" and as such, they view the social aspect of their role in the region as very important. Consequently, these companies recognize the significance of their relationships with people, communities and society, and thus social responsibility becomes part of their core business strategy and they consider how their activities affect people. Ultimately, this might lead to unlocking new markets, becoming the source of innovation for new product lines, raising internal morale and employee engagement as well as helping retain and attract business partners, all of which are of vital importance for business competitiveness, survival and local community development [24].

Additionally, the survey identifies the measures that the companies perceive as their best possibility to improve their work with environmental sustainability. As illustrated in Fig. 2, influencing the upstream value chain by setting environmental requirements to purchased goods, is seen as the least promising area for action. While influencing customers by offering more sustainable products, is identified as the best measure of improving their sustainability efforts. This result is in line with the companies' prioritization of economic sustainability over the other aspects, since by influencing customers, they are placing the customers at the center of corporate strategy, which is based on the insight that customers are the basis of company profitability [25].

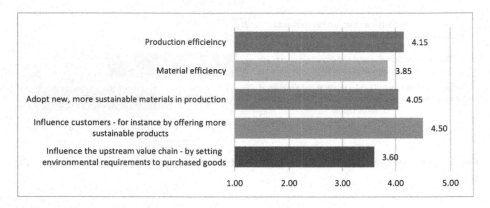

Fig. 2. Best chances of improving the sustainability efforts of the company

Besides, interview data reveal the barriers that are most relevant for the companies under study when it comes to implementing sustainable business models (SBMs). These barriers are structured following three categories: 1) regulatory, 2) market and financial and 3) behavioral and social. The most frequently mentioned barrier is lack of economic incentive, followed by financial risk. This is due to the complex nature of SBMs and the typically higher initial cost and investment required for implementation [26]. This implies that a great deal of advances in economic model innovation will need to be made if these companies are to effectively become sustainable.

The results also describe the actions currently being taken by the companies in how they work with sustainability. Figure 3 shows a range of different approaches among the companies, from having a central role in the company's strategy to having no particular focus on sustainability at all.

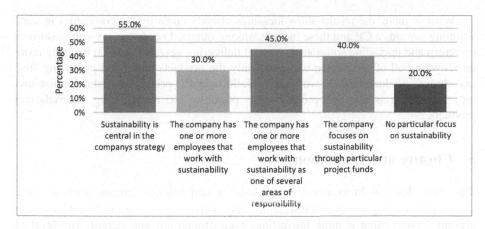

Fig. 3. How does the company engage in sustainability?

In addition, the results indicate that approximately 60% of the companies already have plans of transitioning into a CE, 20% do not have any plans, whereas about 20% report that CE is irrelevant for them due to the complexity of their products (their products have a lifespan of 50 years and due to their material mix, it is impossible to reuse them after end of life). Moreover, the results show different ways on how the companies can approach CE (see Fig. 4). Most of the companies (80%) report developing new markets and innovative business models, as one way of making a shift to a CE. This is in consonance with EMF [27], who assert that the shift to a CE requires innovative business models that either replace existing ones or seize new opportunities.

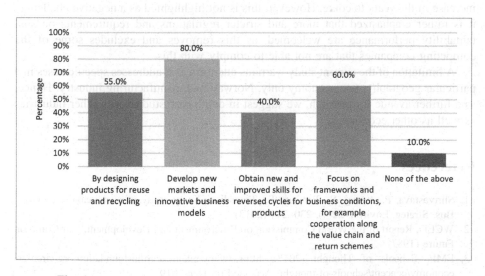

Fig. 4. How the companies identify ways to approach the circular economy

What is more, the results show measures already taken by the companies in transitioning towards a CE and these include, among others, 1) cooperation with customers on return and upgrading solutions instead of delivering new products; 2) focusing more on recycling all of production waste not only the products and avoid producing "use and throw" products and 3) working by following CE principles (reduce, reuse and recycle) – with as effective production as possible, and recirculating materials and products.

5 Closure and Limitation

This study has sought to assess the knowledge and practices among manufacturing companies working towards transitioning into sustainability and the CE. The results present a picture that is quite interesting, even though not unexpected. The level of knowledge and practices regarding sustainability is generally high among the companies under study. This can partly be explained by the high level of requirement and regulation Norwegian industry is faced with, both domestic and internationally. The Norwegian business culture, where taking extended responsibility for social and environmental conditions, also play an important role. Thus, although the level of knowledge and practices seem fairly high, we see a difference in their perception of "sense of urgency". Some companies are focusing on only meeting minimum requirements, while others are inspired in doing more – although not all know how to proceed to increase their effort. One important aspect concerning this industry's sustainability efforts is the ability to adapt to new regulations and requirements. From this study, it is clearly stated that the industry has an increased focus on sustainability from company ownership and management perspective, and that this focus is expected to increase in the years to come. However, this is not highlighted as a negative challenge, it is rather emphasized that more and stricter regulations and requirements on sustainability performance are welcomed, as this removes and excludes some of the competing companies that are not able to comply with this.

A limitation of the current study warrants attention as it addresses specific cases in a particular geography, one economy only, Norway and manufacturing industry. Hence, as a further avenue for research, we suggest in-depth case studies with other industries as well as other economies.

References

1. Shrivastava, P., Ivanaj, S., Persson, S.: Transdisciplinary study of sustainable enterprise. Bus. Strateg. Environ. **22**(4), 230–244 (2013)
2. WCED, Report of the World Commission on Environment and Development: Our Common Future (1987)
3. EMF, Schools of Thought (2017). https://www.ellenmacarthurfoundation.org/circular-economy/concept/schools-of-thought. Accessed 05 Dec 2019
4. Kirchherr, J., Reike, D., Hekkert, M.: Conceptualizing the circular economy: An analysis of 114 definitions (2017)

5. Köhler, J., et al.: An agenda for sustainability transitions research: State of the art and future directions. Environ. Innov. Soc. Transitions **31**, 1–32 (2019)
6. Grin, J., Rotmans, J., Schot, J.: Transitions to Sustainable Development: New Directions in the Study of Long Trem Transformative Change, 4. Routledge, New York (2010)
7. Grelland, H.H.: Sustainability and care: on a philosophical contribution to the project of sustainability. In: Johnsen, H.Chr.G., et al. (eds.) Higher Education in a Sustainable Society, A Case for Mutual Competence Building. Springer, Heidelberg (2015)
8. Velenturf, A.P.M., Jopson, J.S.: Making the business case for resource recovery. Sci. Total Environ. **648**, 1031–1041 (2019)
9. Kempton, W., Boster, J., Hartley, J.: Environmental Values in American Culture. MIT Press, Cambridge (1995)
10. Kollmuss, A., Agyeman, J.: Mind the gap: why do people act environmentally and what are the barriers to pro-environmental behavior? Environ. Educ. Res. **8**(3), 239–260 (2002)
11. De Angelis, R.: Business Models in the Circular Economy: Concepts, Examples and Theory. Springer, Cham (2019). https://doi.org/10.1007/978-3-319-75127-6
12. Porter, M.E., Kramer, M.R.: Creating shared value: how to reinvent capitalism and unleash a wave of innovation and growth. Harv. Bus. Rev. **89**(1/2), 62–77 (2011)
13. Schaltegger, S., Lüdeke-Freund, F., Hansen, E.G.: Business models for sustainability: a co-evolutionary analysis of sustainable entrepreneurship, innovation, and transformation. Organ. Environ. **29**(3), 264–289 (2016)
14. Hahn, T., Figge, F.: Beyond the bounded instrumentality in current corporate sustainability research: toward an inclusive notion of profitability. J. Bus. Ethics **104**, 325–345 (2011)
15. Markard, J., Raven, R., Truffer, B.: Sustainability transitions: an emerging field of research and its prospects. Res. Policy **41**(6), 955–967 (2012)
16. Blake, J.: Overcoming the 'value-action gap' in environmental policy: tensions between national policy and local experience. Local Environ. **4**(3), 257–278 (1999)
17. Liu, Y.: Investigating external environmental pressure on firms and their behavior in Yangtze River Delta of China. J. Clean. Prod. **17**(16), 1480–1486 (2009)
18. Lin, H., Zhang, B., Tao, H.: The conditions and institution innovation of manufacturefirms' development circular economy. Bus Times **17**, 93–94 (2009)
19. Yin, R.K.: Case Study Research and Applications : Design and Methods, 6th edn. SAGE Publications, Inc., London (2018)
20. Voss, C., Tsikriktsis, N., Frohlich, M.: Case research in operations management. Int. J. Oper. Prod. Manag. **22**(2), 195–219 (2002)
21. Eisenhardt, K.: Making fast strategic decisions in high velocity environments. Acad. Manag. J. **32**(3), 543–576 (1989)
22. Hui, W., Lui, S.M., Lau, W.K.: A reporting guideline for IS survey research. Decis. Support Syst. **126** (2019)
23. Gusmerotti, N.M., Testa, F., Corsini, F., Pretner, G., Iraldo, F.: Drivers and approaches to the CE in manufacturing firms. J. Clean. Prod. **230**, 314–327 (2019)
24. Sundström, A., Ahmadi, Z., Mickelsson, K.: Implementing social sustainability for innovative industrial work environments. Sustainability **11**(12), 1–16 (2019)
25. Gupta, S., Lehmann, D., Ames, S.: Valuing customers. J. Mark. Res. **XLI**, 7–18 (2004)
26. Oghazi, P., Mostaghel, R.: Circular business model challenges and lessons learned-an industrial perspective. Sustainability **10**(3), 1–19 (2018)
27. EMF, Towards a CE: Business Rationale for an Accelerated Transition. Greener Manag. Int. 20 (2015)

A Methodology to Integrate Sustainability Evaluations into Vendor Rating

Alessandro Fontana, Silvia Menato, and Andrea Barni[✉]

University of Applied Sciences and Arts of Southern Switzerland, ISTePS,
Manno, Switzerland
{alessandro.fontana, silvia.menato,
andrea.barni}@supsi.ch

Abstract. This paper is meant to presents a concrete methodology to integrate the vendor rating into a Request for Quotation process carried out in a sharing economy context where MaaS digital platforms are exploited. After an analysis of the current state of the art of sustainable decision making into vendors' selection and simplified LCA techniques, the different steps of the methodology are in depth illustrated: the Resource instantiation, the Sustainability Suppliers Ranking and the Quotation-specific impacts calculation. The methodology deployment in the manufacturing context is then described, focusing on the resource instantiation phase that allows a rapid, but rigorous environmental characterization of suppliers offer. The described path, developed and tested in the MANUSQUARE EU project, could be easily adapted to other digital platforms and further extended to different industrial sectors.

Keywords: Simplified LCA · Vendor rating · Digital platforms

1 Introduction

The sharing economy, that is, digitized platforms for peer-to-peer exchanges, has gained momentum in several sectors of the economy [1]. The value delivered through this kind of platforms can derive from a simplification of transactions between stakeholders, or by providing services or products on the top of technological building blocks used as a foundation. According with Evans & Gawer [2], in certain cases Multi Sided Platforms can play both roles, facilitating exchanges or transactions between different users, buyers, or suppliers relying on a product or technology provided as foundation [3]. In the context of Manufacturing as a Service, companies are more and more willing to sell (and buy) manufacturing capacity instead of new equipment. The success of this market largely depends on the ability of easily connecting B2B customers minimizing efforts, reducing costs and shortening times in the interaction and provision of services, being able to create the desired level of trust among parties, allowing transactions to take place. The integration of sustainability oriented concerns, first in the creation of trust among parties, and then in the selection of the most interesting vendor has recently gained consensus as a critical decisional factor [4, 5]. Rarely, sustainability is however taken into consideration with digital platform ecosystems.

© IFIP International Federation for Information Processing 2020
Published by Springer Nature Switzerland AG 2020
B. Lalic et al. (Eds.): APMS 2020, IFIP AICT 591, pp. 554–562, 2020.
https://doi.org/10.1007/978-3-030-57993-7_63

In this work we propose a methodology to integrate sustainable decision making into vendors' selection within the boundaries of MaaS digital platforms. The methodology has been designed in order to ease the environmental sustainability evaluation of the manufacturing processes offered by adopting a simplified LCA approach. This decision, in line with the context of a digital platform, limits time and resources needed to provide the assessment, still maintaining the scientific approach provided by LCA in impacts calculation.

2 Relation to Existing Theories and Works

2.1 Simplified LCA for Decision Making

In the last decades, LCA has evolved as mainstream tool for guiding more sustainable decisions at industrial level and by policy makers, encouraged by the increased research in the field and the increased number of LCA-based EPDs in industry [6]. Since the early 2000s, LCA has been promoted as an instrument for green decision-making in EU policy [7]. Indeed, LCA allows to measure the cumulative impacts associated with the flow of energy and material in production systems, according to ISO 14044:2006, thus providing solid information on upstream and downstream activities useful for decision making both at company and supply chain level [8]. Yet real application cases of LCA in decision support activities related to the supply chain management are remarkably sparse in literature [9, 10]. Applying LCA in practice still results to be a convoluted process [11], that requires high level of knowledge on different methodological choices and high availability of data to perform data inventory. This has led to investigations on how to simplify LCA, though retaining the comprehensive nature of life cycle approach: according to the ISO standard, "the level of detail of an LCA study depends on the subject and the intended use of the study", thus simplifications need to be in line with this definition and the intended application of the study. From a recent literature review [12], in most cases simplifications are motivated by time constraints, limited resources and scarce data availability, resulting in different adopted approaches: partial neglect of upstream/downstream processes, reduction of the evaluated environmental impacts, use of a threshold to determine which components are studied, combination of qualitative and quantitative data, use of secondary data [13]. Screening LCA and streamlined LCA are the two most addressed strategies in literature for life cycle simplification, differing mainly in the scope and the impact categories. In [14], the authors provide a further classification of the simplified approaches based on literature studies and applied case studies, recognizing 10 approaches, differing in the goal, the accuracy of the inventory and the comprehensiveness of the impact assessment.

Among these, two approaches are used in combination in this study: the screening approach combined with the use of tool/database approach has been applied to simplified LCA for supporting vendor rating based decisions, reducing the effort in the inventory phase, thanks to the acceptance of lower data quality. The combination of these approaches, that will be presented in the following chapter, fits with the goal of the study to assess several impact categories and to make results readable to practitioners in order to take decisions.

2.2 Vendor Rating Systems

Violation of corporate ethics and national laws caused by a lack of environmental and social responsibility in supply chain operations, together with a growing concern for the lifecycle impact of supplied products and services [15, 16], have drawn the attention of companies towards sustainable supplier selection (SSS). These approaches are meant to support supplier selection in the constitution of consolidated, sustainable supply chains [17]. In the last years, among the three types of indicators constituting an SSS cockpit (Economic, Environmental, Social) the environmental ones gained particular momentum. According to a recent literature review [4], the most cited indicators exploited to integrate environmental conscious supplier selection can be considered as follows: green image, environmental management system, environmental competencies, pollution control, green product, resource consumption, ECO-design and green technology innovation. While these indicators are largely adopted and suitable to assess and rank suppliers with the objective of setting up stable relationships in a B to B environment, these are not applied in a digital platform ecosystem where fast and dynamic transactions, subject to network effects, take place. In a digital platform, the rating system is strictly connected with the concept of vendor/supplier trust: all transactions require a minimum level of trust between participants in order to occur. This is because any exchange requires a credible commitment that no parties will renege on their side of the agreement after the fact. Without this, transactions may not occur even if they would benefit both parties [18]. To achieve this level of trust, indicators are adopted to rate customer or suppliers behaviors and are generally quantified in terms of stars or points on a 1 to 5 scale [19]. These indicators can be objective, i.e. deriving from the type, number, quality of the transaction, and subjective, usually related with users' reviews. The integration of these two types of rating systems is able to strongly influence consumer purchase decisions and buying behavior [20]. Rating and review systems, especially in a business environment, are meant to complement certification and warranty instruments and tend to become relatively more effective than them, the larger the number of transactions that the platforms facilitate [21]. However, none of the previous described schemes addressed the need of calculating and providing evidence of the supplier environmental performances in the context of a digital platform.

3   Methodology Design and Description

This section is meant to present in detail the methodology designed and deployed to integrate the assessment of the sustainability performances of suppliers into vendor selection process in the context of a digital platform. The platform, being developed within the MANUSQUARE project[1], supports the matchmaking of manufacturing resources by not limiting its capabilities to the sole manufacturing equipment sharing, but extending the potential to the resources of the whole manufacturing ecosystem value network [22]. By starting a Request for Quotation (RFQ), a customer can identify, in the platform ecosystem, the suppliers that best match its request in terms of resource offered, cost of transaction and environmental impact of the supplied resource.

Through the calculation of the appropriate environmental indicators, the MANUSQUARE Sustainability Assessment (MSA) aims therefore at supporting customers in introducing into the decision-making process the evaluation of the environmental performances, as a choice parameter. On the other side it provides suppliers in the evaluation of the environmental impacts of their process, making them aware of the current level of performance and allowing to determine possible improvement interventions. This is to be performed into three moments of the RFQ process, in order to (automatically) rank and pre-select the suppliers and then to ponder each quotation from the sustainability point of view: i. the Resource instantiation, ii. the Sustainability Suppliers Ranking and the iii. Quotation-specific impacts calculation.

3.1 Resource Instantiation

Along the RFQ process, the Resource instantiation is a propaedeutic step since allows that each supplier belonging to the digital platform environment can characterize their manufacturing processes form the environmental point of view, formalizing a simplified, guided, but effective, LCI data gathering and LCIA data generation.

In order to guarantee the sustainability assessment comparability of the manufacturing capabilities, Process Templates (PT) are created. PT have indeed a twofold scope: (i) to allow to describe the LCI data of similar processes in a coherent way, thus enabling their LCA comparability; (ii) to guide and support suppliers in process modeling by ensuring a simplified but reliable and representative description of their manufacturing operations from a sustainability perspective. PT are meant to formalize the LCI description of the processes, where for each specific process, inputs (e.g. electricity, steel) and outputs (e.g. steel scrap, wasted oil) are identified and quantified. In this context, all similar processes are characterized by the same list of inputs and outputs, while it is possible to change their quantities that are distinctive, passing from a supplier to another one or, within the same supplier, from an equipment to a different one.

For each PT, default LCI data and the related environmental impacts (LCIA data) are obtained exploiting the Ecoinvent database. Each PT is related to a specific Functional Unit, that is meant to quantify the function of the process in analysis, e.g. 1 kg of removed steel for milling.

---

[1] MANUSQUARE (H2020 GA 761145) project aims to create a European manufacturing platform for the exchange of the unused resources and production capacity.

Starting form Ecoinvent background data, the percentage contribution of inputs and outputs to the selected environmental indicators is evaluated in order to identify process parameters critical from the LCA point of view. For instance, concerning the Climate Change indicator of the milling operation, it has been calculated that the inputs "Electricity" and the "Factory operation (heat)" represent above 80% of the indicator value.

Through this Pareto analysis, performed by MANUSQUARE LCA experts, whenever a new operation type is introduced into the ecosystem, it is determined which are LCI data that are actually affecting most of the process environmental impacts. The identified crucial parameters are thus considered as "free" parameters that, starting from the default value proposed by the MANUSQUARE platform, can be customized by the supplier in order to better represent its manufacturing operation, thus determining more specific indicators values.

3.2   Sustainability Suppliers Ranking

After resource instantiation, the MSA is meant to support the first step of the RFQ process, where the customer is inserting its request and the MANUSQUARE platform is to pre-select the potential suppliers of the manufacturing processes identified by the request in order to provide the customer with a restricted and ordered list of suppliers that is automatically prepared by the MANUSQUARE platform considering, amongst the other parameters, their environmental performances calculated by the MSA. Since in this RFQ phase most of the technical information concerning the manufacturing operations required are not yet detailed by the customer or are described in way that is impossible to be automatically retrieved by the MANUSQUARE Platform, the calculation of sustainability indexes related to the request of the customer is based on an "average" impacts evaluation, but maintaining at the same time a connection with the specific RFQ. For each process contained in RFQ and for each supplier that is able to provide the list of operation identified in the RFQ, the MSA is meant to exploit the PT that have been already generated by the suppliers during their environmental characterization. Specifically, the Functional Unit of each PT included in the request is fixed to the unitary value. Then, a total impact related to the RFQ in analysis, is calculated by the MSA for each supplier by summing the impacts of the unitary PT involved in the request. After this calculation, it is possible to define a sustainability ranking of the suppliers made considering that the higher are the index values calculated, the lower is their position in the classification. The ranking is carried out considering the Average Sustainability Impacts (ASI) for each process performed by each supplier. After that, the ASI of each process are summed for each supplier in order to obtain the Environmental Imapcts (EI) of each Supplier. Thanks to different EI_{Sn} calculated, the MANUSQUARE Platform is able to rank suppliers considering the impacts generated during the realization of the processes included in the RFQ, advantaging the lower EI.

3.3 Quotation-Specific Impacts Calculation

After suppliers ranking and a possible further selection of suppliers directly performed by the customer, the suppliers interact with the customer in order to detail the RFQ, gathering all the information that are missing from the first request.

By receiving process details of each quotation, the supplier performs a feasibility and financial evaluation (STEP 1) and can calculate the specific impact value related to the offered processes (STEP 2) and provide customer with the real expected manufacturing impacts. In STEP 2, the calculation of the environmental indicators is performed exploiting the PT of the operation involved by the RFQ and using specific quantifications of the functional unit. The supplier retrieves the PT, instantiates them with the specific RFQ data and calculates the related environmental impacts that then are provided to the customer with the other information that characterize the offer (price, expected time to delivery...).

4 Methodology Deployment in Resource Instantiation

The crucial point for the deployment of the methodology here presented is the Resource instantiation: the possibility to characterize the vendor offer from the sustainability point of view in a rapid, uniform, standardized and scientifically sound way. For this reason, this section is specifically focalized on the description of the Resource instantiation process supported by the MSA.

Resource instantiation is meant to prepare and characterize the supplier offer thanks to the PT definition. A preliminary set of manufacturing processes have been analyzed in order to select a baseline list of processes and populate a database to be offered to vendors and customers. The identification of the production processes has been carried out by mapping the most adopted processes in existent MaaS ecosystems. The following classes are the ones considered: Type (e.g. CNC, 3D printing), Sub-Type (e.g. for CNC: milling, turning), worked material (e.g. for milling: metal or plastic); specific worked material (e.g. for milling, metal: steel, brass...). Considering the possible combinations, a total of 62 manufacturing processes have been identified.

In order to characterize the supplier operation, the list of the classified processes has been matched with the available dataset into the Ecoinvent database[2]. In addition to the class above mentioned, Ecoinvent is also considering the degree of finishing for chipping metal working processes and the geographical location (e.g. impacts data on milling performed in EU). The main result of the matching with Ecoinvent is that most of the operation identified can be characterized considering both the LCI and LCIA point of view, with the exclusion of 3D printing that is not available in the v3.3 Ecoinvent version analyzed. The next step in resource instantiation is the preparation of the PT. The identified dataset from Ecoinvent is downloaded and then imported into the MSA that, exploiting the Unit Process (UPR) data (the inputs and outputs expressed in terms of other Ecoinvent dataset) and the related environmental impacts, is able to perform a pareto-like analysis that is meant to highlight the most impactful LCI data.

---

[2] https://www.ecoinvent.org/.

The MANUSQUARE LCIA experts mode allows to determine a threshold percentage as a parameter that can be chosen by the expert. For a selected manufacturing process, this evaluation is performed on the complete set of the IMPACT2002 + indicators methodology that is offering both a midpoint and endpoint vision. For a specific process, the LCI parameters identified through the pareto analysis are the relevant ones from the environmental point of view. After that, the PT is ready and available to be exploited by the supplier that can thus modify this limited set of parameters using primary data gathered from a specific process, assuring at the same time a better representation of the specific process impacts compared to the one obtained via default values (taken from Ecoinvent). The vendor can decide to customize only a part of the set, considering the trade-off between the input relevance its measurement capability, data availability and measurement costs.

5 Conclusion

In this paper, a methodology to integrate sustainability oriented decision making into vendor rating selection, in the context of MaaS digital platforms, has been presented. The defined methodology and the related software provide suppliers with the possibility to rapidly obtain an LCA of their manufacturing processes, allowing them to give a quantitative analysis in terms of environmental impacts of the manufactured products. To provide an instrument suitable to a digital platform environment, the Life Cycle Inventory phase, the more expensive in LCA, has been extremely eased, exploiting the use of well-founded background data, but, at the same time, giving to suppliers the possibility to personalize suppliers' operation information in order to obtain the calculation of environmental indicators that are actually able to represent the impacts related to the specific process. The adoption of Process Templates, standardizing the way LCIA is applied across the different suppliers, allows the comparability of the provided data, making them suitable for the creation of suppliers ranking. The methodology has been deployed on a set of manufacturing processes and is now ready to be tested in the industrial scenario. As a next step, the methodology will be extensively validated implementing it in the operational environment of the MANU-SQUARE platform. A subset of users will be taken as reference to assess to which extent this methodology enables to reduce the effort required to implement LCIA analysis.

Acknowledgment. The work presented here was part of the project "MANU-SQUARE - MANUfacturing ecoSystem of QUAlified Resources Exchange" and received funding from the European Union's Horizon 2020 research and innovation programme under grant agreements No 761145.

References

1. Geissinger, A., Laurell, C., Öberg, C., Sandström, C.: How sustainable is the sharing economy? On the sustainability connotations of sharing economy platforms. J. Clean. Prod. **206**, 419–429 (2019)
2. Evans, P.C., Gawer, A.: The Rise of the Platform Enterprise-A Global Survey (2016)
3. Landolfi, G., Barni, A., Menato, S., Cavadini, F.A., Rovere, D., Dal Maso, G.: Design of a multi-sided platform supporting CPS deployment in the automation market. In: 2018 IEEE Industrial Cyber-Physical Systems (ICPS), pp. 684–689 (2018)
4. Zhou, X., Xu, Z.: An integrated sustainable supplier selection approach based on hybrid information aggregation. Sustainability **10**(7), 2543 (2018)
5. Barni, A., Fontana, A., Menato, S., Sorlini, M., Canetta, L.: Exploiting the digital twin in the assessment and optimization of sustainability performances. In: 2018 International Conference on Intelligent Systems (IS), 2018, no. i, pp. 706–713 (2018)
6. Toniolo, S., Mazzi, A., Simonetto, M., Zuliani, F., Scipioni, A.: Mapping diffusion of environmental product declarations released by European program operators. Sustain. Prod. Consum. **17**, 85–94 (2019)
7. European Commission: Integrated Product Policy Building on Environmental Life-Cycle Thinking (2003)
8. Finnveden, G., et al.: Recent developments in life cycle assessment. J. Environ. Manag. **91**(1), 1–21 (2009)
9. van der Giesen, C., Cucurachi, S., Guinée, J., Kramer, G.J., Tukker, A.: A critical view on the current application of LCA for new technologies and recommendations for improved practice. J. Clean. Prod. **259**, 120904 (2020)
10. Cheng, W., Appolloni, A., D'Amato, A., Zhu, Q.: Green public procurement, missing concepts and future trends – a critical review. J. Clean. Prod. **176**, 770–784 (2018)
11. Magelli, F., Boucher, K., Bi, H.T., Melin, S., Bonoli, A.: An environmental impact assessment of exported wood pellets from Canada to Europe. Biomass Bioenergy **33**(3), 434–441 (2009)
12. Jenssen, M., de Boer, L.: Implementing life cycle assessment in green supplier selection: a systematic review and conceptual model. J. Clean. Prod. **229**, 1198–1210 (2019)
13. Hung, C.R., Ellingsen, L.A., Majeau-Bettez, G.: LiSET: a framework for early-stage life cycle screening of emerging technologies. J. Ind. Ecol. **24**(1), 26–37 (2020)
14. Gradin, K.T., Björklund, A.: The Common Understanding of Simplification Approaches in Published LCA Studies – A review and mapping (2015)
15. Seuring, S., Müller, M.: From a literature review to a conceptual framework for sustainable supply chain management. J. Clean. Prod. **16**(15), 1699–1710 (2008)
16. Hashemi, S.H., Karimi, A., Tavana, M.: An integrated green supplier selection approach with analytic network process and improved grey relational analysis. Int. J. Prod. Econ. **159**, 178–191 (2015)
17. Jafarzadeh Ghoushchi, S., Dodkanloi Milan, M., Jahangoshai Rezaee, M.: Evaluation and selection of sustainable suppliers in supply chain using new GP-DEA model with imprecise data. J. Ind. Eng. Int. **14**(3), 613–625 (2017). https://doi.org/10.1007/s40092-017-0246-2
18. Watt, M., Wu, H.: Trust mechanisms and online platforms: a regulatory response (2018)
19. Zloteanu, M., Harvey, N., Tuckett, D., Livan, G.: Digital identity: the effect of trust and reputation information on user judgement in the sharing economy. PLoS ONE **13**(12), e0209071 (2018)
20. Pettersen, L.: Rating mechanisms among participants in sharing economy platforms, First Monday, vol. 22, no. 12 (2017)

21. Belleflamme, P., Peitz, M.: Inside the Engine Room of Digital Platforms: Reviews, Ratings, and Recommendations (2018)
22. Bettoni, A., Barni, A., Sorlini, M., Menato, S., Giorgetti, P., Landolfi, G.: Multi-sided digital manufacturing platform supporting exchange of unused company potential. In: 2018 IEEE International Conference on Engineering, Technology and Innovation (ICE/ITMC), pp. 1–9 (2018)

Environmental and Social Lifecycle Assessments

Travel-Times Analysis and Passenger Transport Disutilities in Congested American Cities: Los Angeles, New York, Atlanta, Austin, and Chicago

Helcio Raymundo and João Gilberto M. dos Reis[✉]

RESUP/Postgraduate Programme in Production Engineering,
Universidade Paulista, Dr. Bacelar, 1212,
04026-002 São Paulo, São Paulo, Brazil
helcioru@uol.com.br, betomendesreis@msn.com

Abstract. Travel-Times Analysis can produce biases in Urban Mobility assessments. Conversely, Disutilities Analysis fulfills the requirement to assess Urban Mobility by travel-time, monetary costs, and environmental performance. Thus, an experiment regarding Los Angeles, New York, Atlanta, Austin, and Chicago compares Automobile and Public Transportation Travel-Times with Total Disutilities Cost per Mile. Public Transportation, even with limitations, can be competitive, at least in two cities: Atlanta and New York. The results confirm the broader scope of the Disutilities Analysis in Urban Mobility appraisals.

Keywords: Disutilities · Passenger transport · Urban mobility · Travel-time · American cities

1 Introduction

People usually consider traffic jams and variations in journey time as the cost to 'acquire' displacements or a kind of price for sharing progress, independently if they use Automobile or Public Transportation [1–4]. However, this issue has been comprehensively studied as a consequence of determining occurrences, by Traffic Engineering, because of vehicle excess [5], Economics, due to loss of production derived from the lost time in congestions [6], and Urban Planning, as the result of poor distribution of activities in urbanized areas [7].

On the other hand, more recently, the authors of this paper have been conducted several studies and researches regarding Passenger Transport Disutilities as a manner to evaluate mobility performance. As a matter of principle, it is supported that, despite supplying the means for people's displacements, Passenger Transport causes losses, inconveniences, and disadvantages that can be understood as disutilities. Passenger Transport Disutilities imposed on Passengers are Time and money spending (Cost), Insecurity (unsafe conditions as to traffic accidents), and Discomfort, and, on Society, Negative Impacts on Communities. In all these studies and researches, Time appears to be one of the most critical disutilities components, as it somehow influences all the other components [8–13].

© IFIP International Federation for Information Processing 2020
Published by Springer Nature Switzerland AG 2020
B. Lalic et al. (Eds.): APMS 2020, IFIP AICT 591, pp. 565–572, 2020.
https://doi.org/10.1007/978-3-030-57993-7_64

Under these conditions, the research question is, how can we assess urban mobility more comprehensively besides analyzing only travel-times? This issue allows us to state the purpose of our article, showing why the analysis of passenger transport disutilities is more comprehensive than travel-time analysis in urban mobility assessments.

Thus, a study of travel-times behavior from its standard practices [5], to a more accurate analysis of the mobility of congested American cities can be useful to more in-depth the understanding of Time and its role and influence in disutilities assessments.

In this sense, we pick among the ten top worse Corridors in the 20 most congested American cities [14], five cities (and their correspondent Corridors) to compare Automobile and Public Transportation travel-time behavior in a random weekday with a Disutilities Analysis.

There are typical differences in travel-times, particularly for Automobile, consistent with the literature [5]. This means pronounced rush-hours in the afternoon in all cities. Diversely, Public Transportation is less susceptible to variations the more protected from the general traffic it is, mainly in case of buses, but with some influence of the overcrowding along the day even in closed systems, like subways, for example [15].

On the other side, Disutilities Analysis shows less influence of travel-times variations, bringing about not so intuitive outcomes, because it considers the state of the art of Urban Mobility evaluation, by including not only travel-time, but monetary costs, and environmental performance [15]. Thus, the Automobile keeps out of rush-hours Total Disutilities Cost per Mile practically constant. Similarly, Public Transportation, even sometimes more expensive due to (the Cost of) Time, show stable values in most cities all day long and, consequently, its competitiveness.

2 Materials and Methods

The scientific method is a process for conducting an investigation or study [16]. Our investigation, to answer the research question, comply with five steps:

- Stating the problem- Travel-Times Analysis produces biases in urban mobility assessments?
- Making observations - Disutilities analyses consider, in addition to travel times, travel costs, and environmental performance of transportation modes.
- Forming a hypothesis - Disutilities analysis fulfills the requirements to reduce travel-time analysis biases.
- Testing the hypothesis by conducting an experiment or a case study - Five corridors from the 20 most congested in five U.S. cities were selected, and travel-times and disutilities for Automobiles and Public Transportation were compared.
- Drawing a conclusion based on results and its discussions – In urban mobility performance evaluation, disutility analysis is more comprehensive and produces more enlightening results than a simple time-based analysis.

Thus, the collection of 24 h per day of travel-time of five Corridors/cities [14] for Automobile and Public Transportation, building up 240 numbers. The cities are Los Angeles, New York City, Atlanta, Austin, and Chicago.

2.1   Data and Information in the INRIX Global Traffic Scorecard [14]

Table 1 shows the five worst Corridors in the U.S. and Table 2 the 20 most congested cities in the country [14].

Table 1. Top 10 Worst Corridors in the U.S. (Source: Adapt [14]

Rank	City	Road Name	From	To	Distance (Miles)	Daily delay (minute)/ Yearly Delay (hour)
1	Los Angeles	I-5	I-10	I-605	12.7	20/80
2	New York	I-95	Bruckner Expressway	George Washington Bridge	8.3	16/64
3	Atlanta	I-85/ I-75	T. Mathis Parkway	College Park	24.1	16/64
4	Austin	I-35	West Slaughter Lane	East Dean Keaton Street	13.9	16/64
5	Chicago	I-290	I-294	I-90	13.6	14/56

Table 2. Top 20 most congested cities in the U.S. (Source: Adapt [14])

2019 congestion rank	Urban area	Hour lost in congestion per year
1	Boston, MA	149
2	Chicago, IL	145
3	Philadelphia.PA	142
4	New York, NY	140
5	Washington, DC	124
6	Los Angeles, CA	103
7	San Francisco, CA CA	97
8	Portland, OR	89
9	Baltimore, MD	84
10	Atlanta, GA	2
11	Houston, TX M	81
12	Miami, FL	81
13	New Orleans, LA	79
14	Seattle, WA	74
15	Stamford, CT	74
16	Providence, RI	70
17	San Diego, CA	70
18	Austin, TX	69
19	Sacramento, CA	64
20	Dallas, TX	63

2.2   Data and Information Organization

March 12th, 2020 (before Coronavirus effects), is the weekday adopted. Google Maps® provides, for Automobile and Public Transportation (bus lines in all cities, except in Atlanta - combination fifty-fifty of bus and train), the hourly travel-time of each Corridor. Corridors are a given element of reality. They differ as they are, e.g., Automobiles (typically) can run all the time, and Public Transportation mainly buses run on average 18 to 20 h per day. The results are shown in Table 3, extreme values highlighted.

Table 3. Travel-Time in the Selected Cities – Automobile (Auto) and Public Transportation (PT) (Minutes) (Source: authors)

Hour	Los Angeles		New York		Atlanta		Austin		Chicago	
	Auto	PT	Auto	PT	Auto	PT	Auto	PT	Auto	PT
12 AM	16	105	20	50	30	74	24	71	24	118
1	16	105	20	50	30	80	22	71	22	137
2	16	105	20	50	30	80	22	71	20	99
3	16	105	18	50	30	80	22	71	24	104
4	16	80	20	49	30	68	24	71	20	109
5	16	83	20	59	30	68	22	71	28	105
6	22	58	35	55	35	73	24	75	20	109
7	28	82	40	54	45	72	55	81	30	113
8	16	81	50	52	55	63	60	81	22	91
9	24	87	50	52	50	71	40	81	24	109
10	26	91	45	52	45	71	30	81	20	97
11	28	97	45	53	40	71	30	83	24	125
12 PM	30	106	50	53	45	71	30	83	20	103
1	35	71	45	55	50	71	30	82	22	125
2	55	73	60	57	55	70	30	94	20	100
3	70	65	60	58	75	79	40	91	24	114
4	80	73	65	48	100	80	65	88	22	102
5	85	73	65	55	100	78	65	85	28	119
6	70	68	50	52	80	75	45	86	22	139
7	45	74	35	50	55	68	30	83	24	93
8	26	90	26	47	40	68	28	90	20	99
9	20	109	22	45	35	83	26	80	24	94
10	18	108	28	45	35	83	26	87	20	99
11	18	115	28	55	35	83	26	71	24	104

Time, Cost, Insecurity, and Discomfort, as disutilities imposed on Passengers, and Infrastructure, Noise, Local Gases, and GHG (greenhouse gases), imposed on Society, are calculated in line with [10], updated some sources [17–20]. By adding Time (as a function of income), to Cost (proportional to expenses and fares), and pollution (related to the distance of displacement), and dividing by the correspondent distances of displacement in each Corridor, one obtains Total Disutilities Cost per Mile. Insecurity, Discomfort, and Infrastructure as non-monetary values are, therefore, disregarded in the calculations. Table 4 displays the results, extremes values underlined.

3   Results and Discussions

Automobile travel-time behaves as usual in American cities, with the 'traditional' afternoon peak from 03:00 to 08:00 PM. New York is crowded all day, from 06:00 AM, and Austin also has a morning rush-hour, as well as Atlanta, albeit more discreetly. The differences between the highest and lowest values are in Los Angeles (5.31), New York (3.61), Atlanta (3.33), Austin (2.95), and Chicago (1.50).

Public Transportation rush-hours can hardly be characterized, and travel-times usually oscillate less with Automobile. Here we have in Los Angeles (1.98), Chicago (1.53), Atlanta and Austin (1.32), and New York (1.31). Public Transportation is faster than Automobile in the afternoon rush hour in Los Angeles, New York, and Atlanta (slower in Austin and Chicago). The relations are in Los Angeles (6.56), Chicago (6.32), Austin (3.35), New York (2.95), and Atlanta (2.67).

Table 4. Total Disututilies per Mile (US Dollars/Mile) – Auto and PT (Source: authors)

Hour	Los Angeles		New York		Atlanta		Austin		Chicago	
	Auto	PT	Auto	PT	Auto	PT	Auto	PT	Auto	PT
12 AM	1.10	2.91	1.59	2.66	1.07	1.15	1.43	2.44	1.44	3.94
1	1.10	2.91	1.59	2.66	1.07	1.22	1.37	2.44	1.38	4.55
2	1.10	2.91	1.59	2.66	1.07	1.22	1.37	2.44	1.32	3.34
3	1.10	2.91	1.50	2.66	1.07	1.22	1.37	2.44	1.44	3.50
4	1.10	2.26	1.59	2.61	1.07	1.07	1.43	2.44	1.32	3.66
5	_1.06_	2.32	_1.57_	_3.05_	_1.06_	1.04	_1.34_	_2.42_	1.55	3.51
6	1.24	_1.67_	2.25	2.87	1.12	1.10	1.40	2.54	_1.30_	3.64
7	1.39	2.29	2.47	2.82	1.25	1.09	2.36	2.73	1.62	3.77
8	1.08	2.27	2.93	2.73	1.38	_0.97_	2.52	2.73	1.36	3.07
9	1.29	2.42	2.93	2.73	1.32	1.07	_1.90_	2.73	1.43	3.64
10	1.34	2.53	2.70	2.73	1.25	1.07	1.59	2.73	1.30	3.26
11	1.39	2.68	2.70	2.78	1.19	1.07	1.60	2.79	1.43	4.15
12 PM	1.44	2.91	2.93	2.78	1.25	1.07	1.60	2.79	1.30	3.45
1	1.57	2.01	2.70	2.87	1.32	1.07	1.60	2.76	1.36	4.15
2	2.08	2.06	3.38	2.96	1.38	1.06	1.60	_3.13_	1.30	3.35
3	2.48	1.85	3.38	3.00	1.63	1.18	1.91	3.04	1.43	3.80
4	2.73	2.06	_3.61_	2.55	_1.96_	1.19	_2.67_	2.95	1.36	3.42
5	_2.88_	2.06	_3.61_	2.87	_1.96_	1.17	_2.67_	2.85	_1.55_	3.96
6	2.47	1.93	2.93	2.73	1.70	1.13	2.05	2.88	1.36	_4.59_
7	1.85	2.11	2.28	2.66	1.40	1.07	1.61	2.81	1.44	3.15
8	1.36	2.52	1.87	2.52	1.20	1.07	1.55	3.03	1.32	3.34
9	1.20	3.01	1.68	_2.43_	1.14	_1.26_	1.49	2.72	1.44	_3.18_
10	1.15	2.99	1.96	_2.43_	1.14	_1.26_	1.49	2.93	1.32	3.34
11	1.15	_3.17_	1.96	2.89	1.14	_1.26_	1.49	2.44	1.44	3.50

Regarding Total Disutilities per Mile, the relations remain when compared to travel-times, but with lower values: Los Angeles (2.71), New York (2.25), Austin (1.96), Atlanta (1.85), and Chicago (1.24). The same happens with Public Transportation, as we have: Los Angeles (1,89), Chicago (1,50), Atlanta (1.30), Austin (1.29), and New York (1.25). The relation between Public Transportation with Automobile is 3.37 in Chicago, 2.65 in Los Angeles, 1.96 in Austin, 1.77 in New York, and 1.14 in Atlanta.

Table 5 shows the relation between extreme values.

Table 5. Rates of extreme values (Source: authors)

Mode of transportation	Method of analysis	Los Angeles	New York	Atlanta	Austin	Chicago
Auto	Travel-Time	5.31	3.61	3,33	2,95	1.50
	Disutilities	2.71	2.25	1.85	1.96	1.24
	Dis/Travel	**0.51**	**0.62**	**0.56**	**0.66**	**0.83**
PT	Travel-Time	1.98	1.31	1.32	1.32	1.53
	Disutilities	1.89	1.25	1.30	1.29	1.50
	Dis/Travel	**0.95**	**0.95**	**0.98**	**0.98**	**0.98**
PT × Auto	Travel-Time	6.56	2.95	2.67	3.35	6.32
	Disutilities	2.65	1.77	1.14	1.96	3.37
	Dis/Travel	**0.40**	**0.60**	**0.43**	**0.59**	**0.53**

Here there are appealing findings. Total Disutilities Cost per Mile consistently represents by 51 to 83% of Automobile travel-time and 40 to 59% in the comparison of Public Transportation versus Automobile. The same does not happen in the case of Public Transportation, for which the influence, even consistent, is a small one.

4 Conclusions and Outlook

From the Travel-Time Analysis, we could (wrongly) understand that if Automobile 'suffered' less in traffic jams, everything would be settled, and Public Transportation would remain in a secondary plan. Conversely, Disutilities Analysis strengthens the idea that there is only one way to improve Passenger Transport, both Automobile and Public Transportation: by the reduction of their disutilities.

Atlanta, followed by New York, has currently in their Corridors, Public Transportation, even with limitations, competitive concerning Automobile. Automobile remains convenient only in the late hours of the night, and the dawn, when Public Transportation does not work or works bad or little, once Automobile follows the money (demand), and Public Transportation is a 'supply's slave.'

If we established conclusions only based on the analysis of travel times, we could propose as public policy the eradication of Public Transportation by bus in all cities, because, except at peak-hours, Automobiles are usually faster than buses and trains.

Disutility Analysis, however, shows that Public Transportation is competitive concerning the Automobile in Atlanta, and New York, and needs to improve more in Los Angeles, Austin, and Chicago.

This paper points out that Urban Mobility evaluation, only from Travel-Time Analysis, can produce biases as an inherent risk of any societal or economic approach. Diversely, Disutilities Analysis, besides travel-time, introduces monetary costs and environmental performance. Although there are vast (and expected) differences in Automobile travel-times, it is understandable that a more comprehensive method (focused on Passengers and Society), such as Disutilities Analysis, can and should be strengthened and refined. Further studies are needed to confirm the main findings of this paper. In the meantime, it is hoped that Disutilities Analysis can drive the use of Passenger Transport with fewer disutilities in the next future.

References

1. Chang, J.S.: Assessing travel time reliability in transport appraisal. J. Transp. Geogr. **18**(3), 419–425 (2010)
2. Manley, E.D., Cheng, T.: Understanding road congestion as an emergent property of traffic networks. In: 14th WMSCI (2010)
3. Falcocchio, J.C., Levinson, H.S. (eds.): Road Traffic Congestion: A Concise Guide. STTT, vol. 7. Springer, Cham (2015). https://doi.org/10.1007/978-3-319-15165-6
4. Downs, A.: Why traffic congestion is here to stay….and will get worse. ACCESS Mag. **1**(25), 19–25 (2004). https://escholarship.org/uc/item/3sh9003x
5. Wolshon, B., Anurag, P.: Traffic Engineering Handbook. Wiley, Hoboken (2016)
6. Weisbrod, G., Don, V., George, T.: Measuring the economic costs of urban traffic congestion to business. Transp. Res. Rec. **1839**(1), 98–106 (2003)
7. Levy, J.M.: Contemporary Urban Planning. Taylor & Francis (2016)
8. Raymundo, H.: Minimizing passenger transport disutilities: a methodology to measure quality and performance. (Doctoral Dissertation). Paulista University, Brazil (2018)
9. Raymundo, H., dos Reis, J.G.M.: Passenger transport disutilities in the US: an analysis since 1990s. In: Ameri, F., Stecke, K.E., von Cieminski, G., Kiritsis, D. (eds.) APMS 2019. IAICT, vol. 567, pp. 118–124. Springer, Cham (2019). https://doi.org/10.1007/978-3-030-29996-5_14
10. Raymundo, H., dos Reis, J.G.M.: Measures for passenger transport performance evaluation in urban areas. J. Urban Plan. Dev. **144**(3) (2018)
11. Raymundo, H., dos Reis, J.G.M.: Urban mobility at risk in Brazil: passenger transport disutilities increase from 2003 to 2014. In: International Conference on Network Enterprise & Logistic Management. Paulista University, Brazil (2018)
12. Raymundo, H., dos Reis, J.G.M.: Measuring passenger transport quality by disutilities. In: 6th International Conference in Information, Systems, Logistics and Supply Chain Conference, Kedge University, France (2016)
13. Raymundo, H., Reis, J.G.M.: Passenger transport drawbacks: an analysis of its "disutilities" applying the AHP approach in a case study in Tokyo, Japan. In: Lödding, H., Riedel, R., Thoben, K.-D., von Cieminski, G., Kiritsis, D. (eds.) APMS 2017. IAICT, vol. 513, pp. 545–552. Springer, Cham (2017). https://doi.org/10.1007/978-3-319-66923-6_64
14. Reed, T. INRIX Global Traffic Scorecard (2020). https://inrix.com/scorecard/

15. van Wee, B., Annema, J.A., Banister, D. (eds.) The Transport System and Transport Policy: An Introduction. Edward Elgar Publishing (2013)
16. Trefil, J., Hazen, R.M.: The Sciences: An Integrated Approach. Wiley, Hoboken (2016)
17. Zheng, L., Hensher, D.A.: Crowding in public transport: a review of objective and subjective measures. J. Public Transp. **16**(2), 6 (2013)
18. Bureau of Labor Statistics - BLS. Occupational Employment Statistics/May 2018 Metropolitan and Nonmetropolitan Area Occupational Employment and Wage Estimates, November 2019 (2019). https://www.bls.gov/oes/current/oessrcma.htm
19. American Automobile Association - AAA. Your driving costs: how much are you really paying to drive. Heathrow, FL, September 2019 (2012). https://www.aaa.com/AAA/common/AAR/files/AAA-Your-Driving-Costs.pdf
20. van Essen, H., et al.: Handbook on the External Costs of Transport, Version 2019 (No. 18.4 K83. 131). European Commission – EC, February 2020 (2019). https://ec.europa.eu/transport/sites/transport/files/studies/internalisation-handbook-isbn-978-92-79-96917-1.pdf

Socio-Cultural Aspects in Production Systems

The Interdependencies of Quality Management, Knowledge Management and Innovation Performance. A Literature Review

Marina Zizakov[ID], Stana Vasic[✉][ID], Milan Delic[ID],
Marko Orosnjak[ID], and Srdjan Vulanovic[ID]

Faculty of Technical Sciences, University of Novi Sad, 21 000 Novi Sad, Serbia
vasic.stana@uns.ac.rs

Abstract. Quality management should represent one of the most common approaches to improving quality and innovation performance. Still, it is shown that this is not always the case. To find the real cause of the contradictory results, a literature review was conducted. Some authors propose that knowledge management might present the missing link between quality management and innovation performance. Therefore, in this research, the importance of knowledge management will be considered, as a key mediator between quality management on innovation performance. Thus, this paper aims to provide answers to: "What does quality management need to provide, to support innovation performance?", "How does knowledge management contribute to innovation performance?" and "How does knowledge management mediate the relationship between quality management and innovation performance?". Knowledge management provides benefits for innovation performance, under certain organizational conditions and mechanisms. The lack of proper knowledge management among employees can be the cause of shortcomings in the relation between quality management and innovation performance.

Keywords: Quality management · Knowledge management · Innovation performance

1 Introduction and Theoretical Background

In the last two decades, quality management has been one of the most common approaches for improving quality and innovation performance [1]. Further, quality management is perceived as a philosophy that strives for continuous organizational improvement. Quality management can include establishing quality policies and quality objectives, and processes, to achieve these quality objectives through quality planning, quality assurance, quality control, and quality improvement [2]. Accordingly, organizations with a higher level of quality management maturity may benefit from: higher product/service quality, increased customer and employee satisfaction, lowered costs, as well as improved financial and innovation performance. This implies that a high level of maturity in quality culture may foster positive effects on the organizational

© IFIP International Federation for Information Processing 2020
Published by Springer Nature Switzerland AG 2020
B. Lalic et al. (Eds.): APMS 2020, IFIP AICT 591, pp. 575–582, 2020.
https://doi.org/10.1007/978-3-030-57993-7_65

competitive advantage and innovational capabilities [3]. Moreover, it encourages the conquest of new and existing markets [4].

However, some studies claim the opposite. Namely, quality management does not always produce the expected results. Such findings contradict previously mentioned theoretical bases [5–10]. Hence, it could be argued that power of quality management, in creating an adequate environment and culture of supporting innovations, is still a subject of debate by many authors [7, 9, 11, 12].

Subsequently, it is necessary to find a real cause of such contradictions, and, accordingly, to explore certain fostering organizational aspects, which should contribute to the positive impact of quality management on the innovation performance. Some authors propose that knowledge management might present the missing link between these two [1, 3, 13–15].

The ISO 9001: 2015 puts a great emphasis on learning. Consequently, the organization should identify needs and trends and accordingly constantly improve the competence of employees [16]. By involving employees in the improvement of the work process, assigning responsibilities and providing opportunities for training, positive effect on motivation, awareness and attitudes towards changes is created [14, 17–19]. Therefore, in this research, the importance of knowledge management will be considered, as a key mediator of a positive influence between quality management and innovation performance.

Knowledge management is the systematic management of an organization's knowledge assets to create value and meet tactical and strategic requirements [1, 14, 15, 20, 21]. Knowledge management could influence the adequate application of knowledge in processes, development of employee awareness, and quality culture [1, 15, 20, 22]. Accordingly, many researchers have concluded that knowledge management should encourage the maintenance of existing and new knowledge, and, thus, contribute to the innovation performance, overall [1, 14, 15, 19, 20]. Innovation performance could be defined by new ideas or creativity to improve the products, processes, procedures that increase the significance, usefulness and performance of the products, services and process [14, 15, 23].

The question is, "What does quality management need to provide, to support innovation performance?" Further, it is also necessary to determine "How does knowledge management contribute to innovation performance?" and "How does knowledge management mediate the relationship between quality management and innovation performance?".

2   Methodology

The research methodology in this paper builds upon a Systematic literature review (SLR).

Firstly, the research questions were defined, according to the previously mentioned theoretical assumptions. These are:

- RQ1: "What does quality management need to provide, to support innovation performance?"

- RQ2: "How does knowledge management contribute to innovation performance?"
- RQ3: "How does knowledge management mediate the relationship between quality management and innovation performance?"

After that, we need to define research keywords in accordance with research questions. The keywords are defined as follows:

"QUALITY MANAGEMENT" OR "QUALITY MANAGEMENT SYSTEM" OR "*QM" OR "TOTAL QUALITY MANAGEMENT" OR "ISO 9001" AND "KNOWLEDGE MANAGEMENT" AND "INNOVATION" OR "INNOVATION PERFORMANCE"

These keywords were used to define search queries, within SCOPUS indexed database. The query has returned 108 papers.

To get more accurate results, the search query was refined. The first phase of the search was performed on titles, abstracts and keywords, to above-mentioned "inclusion criteria" (Table 1). The re-definition of search results has returned 42 papers, in total.

Then, papers were assessed by their title, abstract and their content. Some papers were found to be non-related to our scope of review. Thus, they were removed from further analysis. (i.e. "Non-related criteria" - Table 1.) Finally, based on NR exclusion criteria (Table 1), out of 42, 20 papers were retained.

In the second phase, the authors removed seven more papers. The reason that papers were excluded from the further analysis is that they were not technically available through portals and index databases, as well as accessible for downloads. In overall, 13 papers were subdued for detail analysis.

Further, considering the forward and backward citation criteria, a total sum of 17 articles were added, increasing our final list of papers to 30.

Table 1. Inclusion and exclusion criteria

I/E criteria	Sub-criteria	Criteria explanation
Inclusion criteria	Full-text papers (FTP)	Selected studies that are only abstracts, presentations or posters will not be included in the study
	Language (LAN)	Full text of the article must be written in English
	Time frame (TF)	Selected studies must be published between 2010-2020 to be included in the SLR
	Selected studies (SS)	Studies included journal articles, conference papers
	Subject area (SA)	"Engineering", "Business, Management and Accounting", "Decision Sciences", "Social Sciences"
Exclusion criteria	Non-related (NR)	NR1: Paper is not related to manufacturing organizations
		NR2: Paper relates to health care organizations, biotechnology, pharmacy, hospital industry or aerospace industry
		NR3: Paper relates to university and government

3 Results and Discussion

The results of the literature review are presented in this section. Regarding the type of analyzed papers, there are 25 academic journals (83%) and only 5 conference papers (17%), of which 23 are based on empirical research (questionnaire/interview/survey) (72%), and 9 on literature review and research framework (28%). The papers are mostly from 2010 (20%), 2017 (23%) and 2019 (23%), and slightly less from 2011 (7%), 2012 (10%), 2015 (4%), 2016 (9%) and 2018 (4%). The research originates mainly from Asia (52%), Europe (24%), Africa (10%), America (9%) and Australia (5%) and was conducted in the manufacturing industry. Only two papers come from Serbia and the wider region in a transitional economy.

The greatest focus of the literature review was on the identification of constructs, by which the examined factors were operationalized, and on the nature of the relationship between these factors (Table 2). Summarizing the results, we conclude that the factors of QM with the highest frequency are: customer focus (16), leadership (14), employee management (12), and process approach (10). Factors with slightly lower frequency are: continuous improvement (8), supplier management (7), learning (7), strategic and systematic approach (5), teamwork and quality chain (4), effective communications (and culture) (4), information (measurement) and analysis (4). In the case of knowledge management, factors that stand out the most are: knowledge application (6), knowledge dissemination (6), and knowledge acquisition (5), whereas knowledge transfer/sharing (4), knowledge creation (3), and knowledge storage (2) are factors with slightly lower frequency. While, for innovation performance, the factors are product and service innovation (6), and process innovation (6).

Based on this, the proposed research framework is presented in Fig. 1.

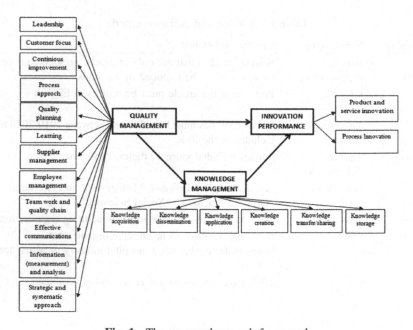

Fig. 1. The proposed research framework

When it comes to the relationship between factors, the vast majority of studies examine relationships between quality management and innovation performance. This is shown in Table 2. The nature of relationships between used constructs in these studies is also given (i.e. positive (+)/negative (−)/both (±)). The table includes papers in which knowledge management represents a mediating connection between quality management and innovation performance and five of these mediating effects are positive.

Table 2. The nature of relationships between quality management, knowledge management, innovation performance (+ positive, −negative, +− both)

	(Total) quality management	Knowledge management	Innovation performance
(Total) quality management		14(+)	22(+), 1(−), 5(±)
Knowledge management	8(+)		18(+)
Innovation performance	2(+)		

Based on the literature review, it could be argued that, in most cases, quality management produces positive results on innovation performance, with the strong positive mediator influence of knowledge management. Also, the majority of short-comings in a strong positive mediator relationship between quality management and innovation performance are related to the lack of human awareness and knowledge in quality culture (i.e. 5(±)) [1, 8, 10, 12–15, 18, 20, 23, 24].

3.1 Answer to RQ1: "What Does Quality Management Need to Provide, to Support Innovation Performance?"

Quality management should create a work environment that fosters creativity, motivates employees to be innovative thinkers and take risks, thus, enhancing innovation performance [14, 18]. Leadership has primary responsibility for developing adequate climate, by setting innovational goals, on all organizational levels. Leadership must provide the necessary resources and establish an atmosphere of trust, teamwork, empowerment and people management. The autonomy of decisions and the idea of sharing knowledge among employees should lead to innovation [1, 7, 13, 14, 18, 25]. For achieving this, a higher level of employee awareness is necessary, where knowledge management plays a predominant role. This brings to the forefront the importance of learning climate among employees. Learning is a key factor in creating innovations and developing awareness [26]. Thus, employees must continually acquire new knowledge and share it among themselves. Subsequently, the acquisition of knowledge may lead to the development of an adequate quality culture [1].

3.2 Answer to RQ2: "How Does Knowledge Management Contribute to Innovation Performance?"

Through the papers of the literature review, results show a positive relationship between knowledge management and innovation performance (Table 2) Knowledge management can significantly contribute to the development of innovation performance, if organizations have the capacity to acquire, develop and share knowledge [14]. Acquiring knowledge from inside and outside of the organization leads to knowledge modification of employees, and increasing creating values, including new product development and innovation performance enhancement [12, 15, 20, 27].

3.3 Answer to RQ3: "How Does Knowledge Management Mediate the Relationship Between Quality Management and Innovation Performance?"

Some authors recognize quality management to be a precursor of knowledge management, while others claim the opposite [15, 27]. Nevertheless, in both cases, they should have a positive impact on innovation performance [1, 3, 15, 20, 22, 27]. By implementing quality management, besides internal organizational benefits, organizations are also encouraged to improve relationships with suppliers and customers, which, eventually, leads to the development of organizational innovations [28]. To achieve the expected results, they must acquire as much knowledge as possible about the needs and expectations of stakeholders, and, also, develop strong ties with them. This is where knowledge management has a predominant role. Also, to respond to users' needs and expectations on time, they need to expand their existing knowledge [29]. This underlines the purpose of knowledge management as well, and, at the same time, a contribution to innovations are, clearly evident. Moreover, many authors found that quality management practices facilitate the creation and expansion of knowledge within an organization [15, 17–19, 30].

One of the basic principles of quality management is learning, employee involvement and teamwork. It is believed that through the application of knowledge management and quality management, simultaneously, companies can improve both innovation and efficiency. Consequently, the implementation of quality management should increase organizational efficiency and reduce costs [31–33]. In conclusion, organizations aiming to improve innovation performance should work on achieving the synergistic effect between knowledge and quality management.

4 Conclusion

We conclude the following, if the leadership is fully committed to quality management, involves employees and encourages them to acquire and create knowledge, transfer/share and storage knowledge through various trainings and motivations, in this case, quality management benefits innovation performance through knowledge management. Also, the shortcomings of the relationship between quality management and innovation performance are mostly caused by the lack of proper knowledge management among employees.

The main limitation of this study is the use of one database – Scopus. This leaves space for further research in other literature sources. More to say, there are only two studies on this subject, that were carried out in a transitional economy of Serbia and the wider region. Thus, future empirical research is planned to be conducted in this region. The lack of research data implies the need for further work, in resolving shortcomings of quality management, especially in relation to innovation performance.

References

1. Honarpour, A., Jusoh, A., Nor, K.: Knowledge management, total quality management and innovation: a new look. J. Technol. Manag. Innov. **7**(3), 22–31 (2012)
2. ISO Online Browsing Platform. https://www.iso.org/obp/ui/#iso:std:iso:9000:ed-4:v1:en. Accessed 12 May 2020
3. Prajogo, D.I., Sohal, A.S.: TQM and Innovation: A literature review and research framework. Technovation **21**(9), 539–558 (2001)
4. Leker, J., Herzog, P.: Open and closed Innovation - different innovation cultures for different strategies. Int. J. Technol. Manag. **52**(3–4), 322–343 (2012)
5. Abrunhosa, A., Moura E Sá, P.: Are TQM principles supporting Innovation in the Portuguese footwear industry? Technovation **28**(4), 208–221 (2008)
6. Hoang, D.T., Igel, B., Laosiri Hongthong, T.: The impact of total quality management on innovation: findings from a developing country. Int. J. Qual. Reliab. Manag. **23**(9), 1092–1117 (2006)
7. Perdomo-Ortiz, J., Gonza'lez-Benito, J., Galende, J.: Total quality management as a forerunner of business innovation capability. Technovation **26**(10), 1170–1185 (2006)
8. Singh, P., Smith, A.: Relationship between TQM and innovation: an empirical study. J. Manuf. Technol. Manag. **15**(5), 394–401 (2004)
9. Manders, B., De Vries, H.J., Blind, K.: ISO 9001 and product innovation: A literature review and research framework. Technovation **48–49**, 41–55 (2015)
10. Shan, A.W., Ahmad, M.F., Nor, N.H.M.: The mediating effect of Innovation between total quality management (TQM) and business performance. In: IOP Conference Series: Materials Science and Engineering, Vol. 160, International Engineering Research and Innovation Symposium (IRIS), Malaysia (2016)
11. Rafailidis, A., Trivellas, P., Polychroniou, P.: The mediating role of quality on the relationship between cultural ambidexterity and innovation performance. Total Qual. Manag. Bus. Excellence **28**(9–10), 1134–1148 (2017)
12. Moreno-Luzon, M., Gil-Marques, M., Valls-Pasola, J.: TQM, innovation and the role of cultural change. Ind. Manag. Data Syst. **113**(8), 1149–1168 (2013)
13. Zeng, J., Anh Phan, C., Matsui, Y.: The impact of hard and soft quality management on quality and innovation performance: an empirical study. Int. J. Prod. Econ. **162**, 216–226 (2015)
14. Hamdoun, M., Chiappetta Jabbour, C.J., Ben Othman, H.: Knowledge transfer and organizational innovation: impacts of quality and environmental management. J. Cleaner Prod. **193**, 759–770 (2018)
15. Hung, Y.R., Lien, Y.B., Fang, S.C., McLean, G.N.: Knowledge as a facilitator for enhancing innovation performance through total quality management. Total Qual. Manag. Bus. Excellence **21**(4), 425–438 (2010)

16. ISO Online Browsing Platform. https://www.iso.org/obp/ui/#iso:std:iso:9001:ed-5:v1:en. Accessed 12 May 2020
17. Asif, M., Vries, H.J., Ahmad, N.: Knowledge creation through quality management. Total Qual. Manag. Bus. Excellence 24(5–6), 664–677 (2013)
18. Mokhlis, C.E., Elmortada, A., Sbihi, M., Mokhlis, K.: The impact of ISO 9001 quality management on organizational learning and innovation: proposal for a conceptual framework. Periodicals Eng. Nat. Sci. 7(2), 944–951 (2019)
19. Ooi, K., Teh, P., Chong, Y.L.A.: Developing an integrated model of TQM and HRM on KM activities. Manag. Res. News 32(5), 477–490 (2009)
20. Yusr, M.M., Mokhtar, S.S.M., Othman, A.R., Sulaiman, Y.: Does interaction between TQM practices and knowledge management. Int. J. Qual. Reliab. Manag. 34(2), 955–974 (2017)
21. Drucker, P.F.: Knowledge-worker productivity: the biggest challenge. California Manag. Rev. 41(2), 79–94 (1999)
22. Jiménez-Jiménez, D., Martínez-Costa, M., Para-Gonzalez, L.: Implications of TQM in firm's innovation capability. Int. J. Qual. Reliab. Manag. 37(2), 279–304 (2019)
23. Dedy, A.N., et al.: An analysis of the impact of total quality management on employee performance with mediating role of process innovation. In: IOP Conference Series: Materials Science and Engineering 131(1), 012–017 (2016)
24. Abu Salim, T., Sundarakani, B., Lasrado, F.: The relationship between TQM practices and organisational innovation outcomes: moderating and mediating the role of slack. TQM J. 31(6), 874–907 (2019)
25. Ershadi, M.J., Najafi, N., Soleimani, P.: Measuring the impact of soft and hard total quality management factors on customer behavior based on the role of innovation and continuous improvement. TQM J. 31(6), 1093–1115 (2019)
26. Kovacevic, D., Djurickovic, T.: Knowledge management as critical issue for successful performance in digital environment. Econ. Organ. 10(2), 89–99 (2013)
27. Honarpour, A., Jusoh, A., Nor, K: Total quality management, knowledge management, and innovation: an empirical study in R & D units. Total Qual. Manag. Bus. Excellence 29(1), 1–19 (2017)
28. Lalic, B., Medic, N., Delic, M., Tasic, N., Marjanovic, U.: Open Innovation in developing regions: an empirical analysis across manufacturing companies. Int. J. Ind. Eng. Manag. 8(3), 111–120 (2017)
29. Brunswicker, S., Ehrenmann, F.: Managing open innovation in SMEs: a good practice example of a german software firm. Int. J. Ind. Eng. Manag. 4(1), 33–41 (2013)
30. Colurcio, M.: TQM: a knowledge enabler? TQM J. 21(3), 236–248 (2009)
31. Modarres, M., Pezeshk, J.: Impact of total quality management on organisational performance. Int. J. Bus. Environ. 9(4), 356–389 (2017)
32. Donate, M.J., Sánchez de Pablo, J.D.: The role of knowledge-oriented leadership in knowledge management practices and Innovation. J. Bus. Res. 68(2), 360–370 (2015)
33. Martínez-Costa, M., Martínez-Lorente, A.R.: Does quality management foster or hinder Innovation? An empirical study of Spanish companies. Total Qual. Manag. Bus. Excellence 19(3), 209–221 (2008)

Insights from a Top-Down Lean Subprogram Deployment in a Production Group: A Tactical Perspective

Sara Linderson[✉], Monica Bellgran, and Seyoum Eshetu Birkie

KTH Royal Institute of Technology, Södertälje 151 81, Sweden
linderso@kth.se

Abstract. Global production companies spend a noticeable amount of resources on developing lean subprograms deployed within the corporate group. Despite the objective of achieving overall improvements, the expected performance might default due to inefficient deployment processes. Unforeseen lag or resistance to centralized programs has in previous studies shown to be influenced by contextual characteristics of the recipient, such as absorptive capacity, national culture, and factory size. How should deployment plans be designed while considering the characteristics within the corporate group? The research purpose here, is to explore the intentions and reasoning behind the designed deployment plan within a corporate group. Based on insights from a real case, this paper presents three various tactical deployment approaches of possible eight theoretical configurations, here called 'horizontal,' 'parallel,' and 'delegated' deployment. They differ principally by cascading approach, degree of freedom, and centralization of targets. The concept of 'deployment tactics' is introduced as a way to understand how the deployment plans are arranged given the contextual characteristics, and shows that the context dependency in lean subprogram deployment can be managed in various ways within a company.

Keywords: Sustainable implementation · Global operations management · Strategy management

1 Introduction

Many corporate production groups develop a tailored lean program as a way to coordinate and reach consensus about the company's dialect on lean [1]. Ideally, the benefits from a shared program come with making an impact and improving business performance in all sites within the corporate group. However, developing and deploying such a corporate lean program is a challenging task when it comes to creating a balance between global conformity and local adaptation [2]. Can we assure that centralized attempts to implement lean in corporate groups do not become a waste in itself?

The existing lean transfer literature emphasizes mainly major lean implementation programs [3–5]. The research presented in this is paper investigates implementation on the next level, i.e. how strategic *lean subprograms* are deployed within a corporate group *as part of* their overall lean program. This view is somewhat highlighted in Danese *et al.* (2017), who recognize different types of transfer approaches in a global

© IFIP International Federation for Information Processing 2020
Published by Springer Nature Switzerland AG 2020
B. Lalic et al. (Eds.): APMS 2020, IFIP AICT 591, pp. 583–590, 2020.
https://doi.org/10.1007/978-3-030-57993-7_66

lean setting [6]. Lean subprograms support the lean journey in different ways, e.g. by campaigns to reinforce a shared mindset, or by deploying assessment frameworks to track and steer the development progress. It also implies that the corporate production group could have several lean subprograms deployed at the same time, all to achieve overall business improvements. The number of failed lean subprogram cascading in the organization is somewhat unknown, but the success rate of lean subprograms that can be inferred from previous research is not higher than 30% [7]. With the widespread impact lean has on global production companies, it is necessary to gain further understanding and knowledge to improve the efficiency of the deployment programs. The exploratory research presented here aims to attain further insight on intentions and reasoning behind top-down lean deployment approaches by investigating different deployment arrangements within a corporate production group. We suggest that the managerial perspective of sustainable production in corporate groups includes how to utilize deployment tactics to improve the efficiency of such top-down deployments.

2   Theoretical Framework

2.1   Lean Management in Global Corporations

As already mentioned, many global corporations develop a company-specific production system (XPS) conceptualized in structures considerably inspired by the Toyota Production System [1]. Despite the plethora of definitions, this study views lean production as a holistic system combining tools, methods, principles, and strategies [8]. In contrast to the well-known challenges of lean implementation [9], the management of lean in global settings derives additional challenges. A network composed of multiple production sites allocated worldwide leads to rather complex structures to manage since the sites are not isolated from each other [10]. Previous research often investigates the challenges with integration and organization among the production sites, as well as the balance in decision-making between headquarters and sites, thus, takes primarily a coordination perspective [2, 10]. Balancing the decision-making vertically is dominantly deciding the degree of autonomy of the site in either centralized, integrated, or decentralized structures [10]. However, inspired by Danese *et al.* (2017), this study takes primarily a configurational view to learn about the joint influence of contextual characteristics in lean deployment [6].

Structured processes for implementing or reinforcing lean through corporate programs can achieve positive global outcomes [11]. Such tailored XPS programs aims for a reduced heterogeneity in mindset and increased global conformity of the corporation's lean journey [2]. However, a single program is seldom sufficient [5], and a lean journey builds on the implementation of several subprograms to continuously improve the business in a strategic way [12]. Since a deployment process of subprograms relies on its recipients, a business' competitive advantage relies on how well institutionalized they are by the production sites within the corporate group [2]. Thus, the deployment process becomes crucial to realize the strategic purpose of the program.

A lean subprogram is for this paper defined as a multi-site improvement program to improve the business performance by reinforcing the global structure for XPS or harmonization of lean mindset within the network. Examples of lean subprograms are maturity assessments, capability assessments, and innovative implementation processes.

The stream of lean transfer literature has presented several variables influencing the transfer of lean practices within a corporate group [6, 12]. Coordination aspects are dominantly in focus by investigating the challenges with a resource-based view [9, 13]. In contrast, this study focusses on joint effects of the absorptive capacity of the recipient [13], factory size [8, 14], and national culture [6, 14]. For instance, a collectivistic culture (e.g., in China) is characterized by precedence to follow orders that could somewhat facilitate the deployment of a program initially [6, 14, 15]. Similarly, previous studies showed initial resistance to deployed programs in individualistic cultures (e.g., in the US) [ibid.].

3   Methodology

A single case study, aligned with views of Yin (2009), has been followed approximately for one year [16]. The case was bounded to the deployment of a centralized lean subprogram within the production branch of the corporate group. The globally initiated lean subprogram had the purpose of assessing and improving a particular set of lean capabilities in the entire organization, which implies both operational and service functions. The lean capability assessment framework (LCF) was cascaded from the global lean office via lean managers at a division's level to a large number of sites in 17 countries. Delimitations of the scope resulted in inclusion of the three divisions clustered geographically by the market (Asia, America, and Europe).

The collection of data was gathered with a mixed-method approach. Five semi-structured interviews with global decision-makers in lean promoting functions were conducted. Interviews were executed face-to-face or virtually (approx. 1–1.5 h). Intentions behind the decisions of the designed deployment plan, and the expected outcomes of the arrangement was the main focus during interviews. Furthermore, questions gathering insight regarding any issues or ad-hoc solutions was asked. The data collection consisted of a transcript of the recorded interviews, documents, and communication material used internally. Triangulation of data assured verification of contradictory statements and was after that, deductively analysed with a focus on the decisions and intentions behind the plan for deploying the LCF.

4   Results

4.1   Global Deployment of a Lean Subprogram

The case company had more than a decade of lean experience, although a more centralized corporate lean program was initiated about 2016. The lean journey consisted of several deployed lean subprograms before the LCF studied here, such as lean maturity assessments and campaigns. A shift from a rather tool-based framework resulted in the categorization of lean practices into bundles called basic requirements, business process management, Six Sigma, and additional elements. Inadequate lean capabilities, recognized as a general point to improve in the corporate group, triggered the strategic decision to develop a lean capability framework (LCF). The LCF had the purpose of assessing and elevating lean knowledge based on a certification system where the employees' theoretical knowledge, and for some, a demonstration in practice, was tested.

The assessment framework was highly standardized, with no room for local adaptation. The framework included sets of criteria clustered in 10 different categories, which together constituted the bundle of 'basic requirements.' Depending on a set of intra-organizational roles, various assessment requirements were formulated in the criteria.

Together with the launch in early 2019, the decision that 80% of all targeted employees should complete the basic requirements until the end of 2020 got communicated. A global directive was that leaders should go first to acquire the sufficient prerequisites needed to coach the employees in their teams. However, the execution details for the deployment of the LCF to a local level (i.e., the sites) was delegated to the division's lean managers to decide. The assessment progress was regularly followed-up globally. Further description of the deployment plans is found in the following section.

4.2   Deployment Plans

The reasoning behind the plan for the deployment is described for the three divisions Asia, America, and Europe separately. Some of the contextual characteristics are similar between the division, such as the dominant individualistic culture in America and Europe (see Table 1). Table 1 also presents the decided deployment variables, which includes cascading approach, degree of freedom, and centralization of target.

Table 1. Contextual characteristics and deployment variables at the various divisions.

Context characteristics	ASIA	AMERICA	EUROPE
National Culture*	Majority collectivistic	Majority individualistic	Majority individualistic
Factory Size**	Small/Medium/Large	Small/Medium/Large	Small/Medium/Huge
Deployment Variables			
Cascading Approach	Top-down cascading with a focus on the deployment sequence among hierarchical levels	Cascading with a focus on the timing for initiation of the program among different roles	Delegation of the responsibility to the sites, to plan the deployment. A focus on enhancing integration
Degree of freedom	*Low* Steering on the division level. Common categories on site level. Recommendation provided. Lower levels could not choose	*High* Steering on the division level. Option to choose on individual level. Recommendations provided	*High* No steering on the division level. Option to choose on site level. No recommendations provided
Centralization of Target (amount of completed categories)	1st year: 3 2nd year: 7	1st year: 5 2nd year: 5	2nd year: 10 (same as global target)

* Based on the same categorization as Netland (2016) [14].
**Small (<49), Medium (<249), Large (<1000), and Huge (>1000).

Asia: The deployment plan was to rigorously cascade the LCF, starting with the management team at the division level, which included all factory managers. The management team on site level was then responsible for choosing three categories that the whole site should mutually focus on for the first year. The option to choose was to enable adjustments for lean maturity at the site level, local site needs, and ensure engagement by enhancing the ownership of the program. The intention was not to deploy the LCF further vertically in the organization until a completed horizontal deployment. The horizontal deployment was a deliberate approach and explained to be essential to ensure sufficient capability among the leaders. Two of the most lean mature sites were located within the Asian division and there where pilots prior to the deployment.

America: The deployment plan focused mainly on the time when the LCF should be introduced to the various roles. Factory managers were prioritized to start ahead by getting introduced to the LCF first. After some months, the LCF was introduced to support functions in parallel, and at the same time, individuals on the shop floor in parallel. The freedom to choose among the categories was deliberately to adapt to 'the entrepreneurial spirit of the population.' The population within the production network in the American region was generally lean immature due to many new acquisitions (60% of the people within the last three years), meaning that many sites were entirely new to the corporate production program. The segregated population was considered as a significant factor in the planning of the deployment approach within the region. The plan to deploy the LCF to various roles in parallel to each other was believed to avoid slowing down the sites that were further in their lean transformation, and therefore, would want to progress quicker in the LCF deployment. Insights from pilots within the division were expressed to be important and had influenced the deployment plan.

Europe: The deployment plan of deliberately letting the sites be responsible for their own deployment plan meant that no steering took place at the division level. The idea of deliberately delegating the responsibility for the deployment to the sites was decided with consensus among the sites in the European division. The reasoning behind the decision was to integrate the deployment of the LCF to existing plans at the site level. An rigorous work with local plans for elevating lean maturity were developed prior the LCF without the steering of the regional lean team, and thus, the reasoning was not to interfere with those plans through top-level steering. Also, another underlying purpose of not steering the deployment from division level, was to prevent 'deployment-inertia,' meaning that the sites had experienced several previous deployments of centralized programs and experienced frustration of performing additional activities that interfered with existing plans. The lean maturity within the region is roughly classified as medium. There were no pilots prior the deployment of LCF, unlike the other division.

5 Analysis and Discussion

Despite a centralized global deployment, a partially delegated decision-making for the cascading approach at a divisional level yielded in three various deployment plans. These plans differed prominently in the cascading approach, degree of freedom, and centralization of targets. Interestingly, the deployment plans were arranged to fulfill the strategic purpose of the centralized lean subprogram with the intention to prevent predicted deployment inefficiencies caused by the contextual characteristics within the division. For instance, the American division predicted that 'a very heavy-handed centralized approach' would not work for their employees. Therefore they had a higher degree of freedom when choosing among the various categories (classified as *low* in Fig. 1.). This reasoning aligns with the findings by Danese *et al.* (2017) regarding the dominance of the individualistic culture within the division [6].

Taking contextual variables into account when planning the arrangement of the deployment could be described as a tactical deployment approach (see Fig. 1). To exemplify this further, the Asian division planned a rigorous top-down cascading deployment with a tactical stage-gate principle. With a focus on the sequence when deploying top-down along the organization hierarchy, the stage-gate principle promoted a completed horizontal deployment before the program was cascaded vertically (classified as a *strong* cascade approach in Fig. 1). The importance of leaders' capability to support employees were highly motivated and aligned with Liker's principle 'grow leaders that thoroughly understand the work, live the philosophy, and teach it to others' [17]. However, the top-down cascading was presumably enabled by the significant large proportion of the collectivistic culture within the Asia division, perhaps avoiding issues with stickiness in the initiation phase [6]. Also, the 'horizontal' deployment tactic could work oppositely, to hold back, as a tactic to prevent workers to routinely implement practices without involvement by managers. Another enabler that supported the 'horizontal' tactical approach was the initial focus on a rather low amount of categories, considering the time needed to adjust for the impact of the change that a new program made. The freedom of choice regarding the option to choose categories was rather narrow, however, not absent.

The American and European tactical approach differed from the Asian by having a weaker cascading approach. The similarity could be related to the similar dominance of individualistic national culture since both the American and European predicted a possible resistance to a centralized global subprogram. However, the European 'delegated' tactical approach could probably be related to the large/huge factory sizes in this division. The American 'parallel' tactical approach differs in that sense with a high degree of centralized common targets in the division. Moreover, since large production sites have a more complicated structure with administrative tasks, it may affect the implementation of lean practices negatively [8]. It could, therefore, imply requirements of a higher degree of coordination to deploy a lean subprogram to large or huge production sites successfully. Thus, the reasoning behind the delegated deployment tactic in Europe could be valid, considering the risk of superficial implementation, and thus, the absence of expected performance improvement, as discussed in [2].

	Cascading Approach (Strong/Weak)	Degree of Freedom (High/Low)	Centralization of Targets (High/Low)
Horizontal	Strong	Low	High
Parallel	Weak	High	High
Delegated	Weak	High	Low

Fig. 1. Framework for the arrangement of deployment plans for three tactical deployment approaches.

6 Conclusion

Many corporations that aim for centralized efforts to deploy lean within the production group, experience challenges with resistance and unexpected inefficiencies while doing so [15]. Sustainable implementation implies that centralized lean subprograms cascaded within the corporate group should not result in superficial implementations, nor cause inertia for global initiatives [2]. The tactical view presented here helps to cope with the challenges of polishing deployment plans to fulfill the strategic purpose of the program by minimizing deployment inefficiencies. The three various tactical deployment approaches, of eight theoretically possible configurations, highlights variables seen as important in the planning phase of the deployment. However, further research would provide more comprehensive generalizations and validate the relevance of the remaining five theoretical configurations. Beyond the need to strengthen the external validity, investigating which of the various deployment tactics are most successful and under what circumstances, deeper discussions are required.

Although some early findings indicate following recommendations to managers; (1) It could be valuable for the corporate management to closely consider the vitality of a global completion target, since undesirable effects, such as 'certification-hunting', might counteract the strategic purpose and lead to superficial implementation, (2) Site level management could benefit from being aware of the global approach to understand local requirements, for instance, decentralized goal setting, and (3) The global lean office could consider how to mitigate possible risks with resistance to programs with a tailored deployment approach, i.e. allow different intra-organizational arrangements. However, at the same time consider support for various requirements of particular cascading approaches, for example, with deployment principles (e.g. stage-gate principle) to enable flexibility in the arrangements, rather than 'one size fits all'. In other words, one approach is not necessarily the most suitable for all. The tactical perspective allows for more thoughtful arrangements where the influential contextual characteristics of each site within a corporate group could be taken into consideration. One must remember, the ultimate purpose of excelling in efficient and sustainable deployment is to avoid the paradoxical situation of lean deployment become a waste in itself.

References

1. Netland, T.: Exploring the phenomenon of company-specific production systems: one-best-way or own-best-way? Int. J. Prod. Res. **51**, 1084–1097 (2013). https://doi.org/10.1080/00207543.2012.676686
2. Netland, T.H., Aspelund, A.: Multi-plant improvement programmes: a literature review and research agenda. Int. J. Oper. Prod. Manag. **34**, 390–418 (2014). https://doi.org/10.1108/IJOPM-02-2012-0087
3. Bellgran, M.: A corporate perspective on global management and development of lean production systems: a case study. In: Handbook of Research on Design and Management of Lean Production Systems, pp. 270–289. IGI Global (2014)
4. Netland, T.H., Aspelund, A.: Company-specific production systems and competitive advantage a resource-based view on the Volvo production system. Int. J. Oper. Prod. Manag. **33**, 1511–1531 (2013). https://doi.org/10.1108/IJOPM-07-2010-0171
5. Scherrer-Rathje, M., Boyle, T.A., Deflorin, P.: Lean, take two! Reflections from the second attempt at lean implementation. Bus. Horiz. **52**, 79–88 (2009). https://doi.org/10.1016/j.bushor.2008.08.004
6. Danese, P., Romano, P., Boscari, S.: The transfer process of lean practices in multi-plant companies. Int. J. Oper. Prod. Manag. **37**, 468–488 (2017). https://doi.org/10.1108/ijopm-12-2014-0571
7. Jadhav, J.R., Mantha, S.S., Rane, S.B.: Exploring barriers in lean implementation. Int. J. Lean. Six Sigma **5**, 122–148 (2014). https://doi.org/10.1108/IJLSS-12-2012-0014
8. Shah, R., Ward, P.T.: Lean manufacturing: context, practice bundles, and performance. J. Oper. Manag. **21**, 129–149 (2003). https://doi.org/10.1016/S0272-6963(02)00108-0
9. Netland, T.H.: Coordinating production improvement in international production networks: what's new. In: Johansen, J., Farooq, S., Cheng, Y. (eds.) International Operations Networks, pp. 119–132. Springer, London (2014). https://doi.org/10.1007/978-1-4471-5646-8_8
10. Scherrer, M., Deflorin, P.: Linking QFD and the manufacturing network strategy: integrating the site and network perspectives. Int. J. Oper. Prod. Manag. **37**, 226–255 (2017). https://doi.org/10.1108/IJOPM-07-2014-0350
11. Netland, T.H., Sanchez, E.: Effects of a production improvement programme on global quality performance: the case of the Volvo Production System. TQM J. **26**, 188–201 (2014)
12. Demeter, K., Losonci, D.: Transferring lean knowledge within multinational networks. Prod. Plan Control **30**, 211–224 (2019). https://doi.org/10.1080/09537287.2018.1534272
13. Maritan, C.A., Brush, T.H.: Heterogeneity and transferring practices: implementing flow manufacturing in multiple plants. Strateg. Manag. J. **24**, 945–959 (2003). https://doi.org/10.1002/smj.311
14. Netland, T.H.: Critical success factors for implementing lean production: the effect of contingencies. Int. J. Prod. Res. **54**, 2433–2448 (2016). https://doi.org/10.1080/00207543.2015.1096976
15. Boscari, S., Danese, P., Romano, P.: Implementation of lean production in multinational corporations: a case study of the transfer process from headquarters to subsidiaries. Int. J. Prod. Econ. **176**, 53–68 (2016). https://doi.org/10.1016/j.ijpe.2016.03.013
16. Yin, R.K.: Case Study Research: Design and Methods, 4th edn. SAGE, London (2009)
17. Liker, J.K.: The Toyota Way 14 Management Principles from the World's Greatest Manufacturer. McGraw-Hill Education, New York (2004)

Tools for Evaluating Human Factor Aspects in Production and Logistics System

Vivek Vijayakumar[✉] and Fabio Sgarbossa

Norwegian University of Science and Technology, Trondheim, Norway
vivek.vijayakumar@ntnu.no

Abstract. Even though the advancement of technology has a great influence on the production and logistics system (PLS), companies are more dependent on manual human work because of their cognitive ability and flexibility. Inversely, many decision support models in PLS have neglected the characteristics of human workers which could degrade their working conditions. Therefore, this paper would assist the managers in a production and logistics system to evaluate the current workload on their workers. This study would suggest different tools for evaluating the human factor aspects of operations management. Initially, the paper introduces the three aspects of human factors such as physical, mental and psychosocial. Thereafter, tools for evaluating these aspects are presented. The tools are NMQ, NASA TLX, SWAT, and JCQ. Then, this paper summarizes the contribution of tools towards the production and logistics system by classifying it into three segments such as process, system settings, and technology.

Keywords: Human factors · Production and logistics system · System settings · Process · Technology

1 Introduction

Production and logistics systems are in a thrust to sustain their operations process with globalization and the challenging market. Thus, researchers are active in developing decision support system that improves the production and logistics system (PLS). Also, operations processes necessitate a huge volume of manual work, such as material handling and assembly even though automation provides a great opportunity. This is because humans are more flexible with their blend of motor and cognitive skills. However, decision support models for production and logistics have neglect the characteristics of human workers, which resulted in unrealistic planning outcomes that could harm the workers employed in the system [1]. Thus, it is important to understand the human worker characteristics when planning and designing a system, the worker's characteristics could be classified under three aspects such as mental, physical, and psychosocial [2]. Analyzing the characteristics of human workers would help operations managers to properly plan and take decisions at the strategic level to improve the design of products, processes, and workstations. Also in recent research papers, they explain the importance of considering human factors in production and logistics system [3]. However, there still exist a gap in literature that shows how to evaluate HF in production and logistics system. Therefore, purpose of this paper is to address different

© IFIP International Federation for Information Processing 2020
Published by Springer Nature Switzerland AG 2020
B. Lalic et al. (Eds.): APMS 2020, IFIP AICT 591, pp. 591–598, 2020.
https://doi.org/10.1007/978-3-030-57993-7_67

tools that would assist the managers to evaluate HF aspects in production and logistics system. The paper is being built on integrative review methodology [4], by examining the literature and thereby synthesizing the results into a model elaborating the relationship between the tools and PLS.

The rest of the paper is structured as follows. The next section introduces the three aspects of HF. Section 3 describes the tools for evaluating the workload on operators. Section 4 explains the contribution of tools towards PLS. Finally, the paper winds up with a conclusion.

2 Three Aspects of HF

According to IEA council(2000), human factors are defined as "*Ergonomics (or human factors) is the scientific discipline concerned with the understanding of interactions among humans and other elements of a system, and the profession that applies theory, principles, data, and methods to design in order to optimize human well-being and overall system performance*". Therefore, HF could be explained as the relationship between humans and the system. Therefore, there is a great need to understand different aspects of humans, thus they are classified into three aspects, which are explained below,

Mental Aspect: or the Cognitive Aspect is defined as the cognitive ability of humans to make decisions and solve problems based on their attention, learning and forgetting capabilities. For example, assembly workers require excessive cognitive demand due to the high amount of information, system complexities and variants of components required in assembling [5]. It is seen that with the increase in product variation could increase the mental load to the assembly operators [6].

Physical Aspect: The physical wellbeing of humans to perform a task. The increased level of physical fatigue is studied under the physical aspect. Fatigue could be general body fatigue or fatigue to a particular muscle of a worker engaged in manual work. For instance, workers who are engaged in manual material handling experience physical fatigue and discomfort which account for a high risk of developing musculoskeletal disorders (MSDs). Thus, operators are encouraged to take a break in between to reduce the fatigue accumulation on them [7].

Psychosocial Aspect: is defined as the individual's demand at work concerned with his or her ability to control the activities and utilize their skills. It is seen that when workers demand high psychological factor with low control on their work would lead the workers to high stress and ill health [8]. Factors like high autonomy, high control and a high degree of variety could improve employee's motivation [9]. In today's working life these factors contribute to encourage better health at work.

Therefore, to develop a better healthy and working environment, there is a need to consider these aspects of human factors from management point of view when designing and planning new processes in a production and logistics system.

3   Tools for Evaluating Workload on Operators

For evaluating the workload on the operators engaged in manual workload from a system level, questionnaires had proved to be one of the best methods to collect the necessary data from workers [10]. The questionnaire could be self-administered by the worker, which eliminates the chances of observer bias. Also, Questionnaires would reduce the cost of collecting data, by avoiding the practicality of scheduling and follow up of scrutiny [11]. Moreover, questionnaires are the finest subjective assessment technique that could assist managers to evaluate the workload and its effects on labors with long term perspective.

Thus, the questionnaires were selected based on literature search. Initially, the keywords and syntax for the search of tools were defined based on the three HF aspects. Thereafter, the paper with the most potential and relevant questionnaires under each human factor aspects are extracted out. Finally it showed up to be, NMQ [12] under physical aspect; SWAT and NASA TLX [13] under mental aspect and JCQ [14] under psychosocial aspect were selected. When NMQ, NASA TLX and SWAT evaluates the workload, JCQ is the tools which evaluates the outcomes from the workload.

Nordic Musculoskeletal Questionnaire (NMQ)

NMQ is a standardized questionnaire for the analysis of musculoskeletal symptoms in a worker. They focus mainly on the symptoms that are associated with the work settings [15]. Also, the NMQ serves in decision making in occupational health practices [12]. NMQ consists of 28 questions which could be classified into two types of question-naires, the general questionnaire and specific questions dealing on the low back, neck, and shoulder. General questions are structured based on "Do musculoskeletal troubles occur in a given population and if so, in what parts of the body are they localized?". The questions are structured based on 9 anatomical regions. The respondent has to reflect on the trouble caused in each anatomical region during the preceding 12 months. Thereafter, a special questionnaire focuses on the regions which are most common to musculoskeletal symptoms. Questions are based on the symptoms and the duration of the past time such as the previous 7 days, the last 12 months and entire life. An analysis is done based on the severity of the symptoms in terms of their effect on the work and during their leisure time and also in terms of duration of the symptoms during the past 1 year [12].

NASA TLX- Task Load Index

NASA TLX is a multidimensional rating procedure that provides an overall workload score based on the weight-average rating on six subscales. They are mental demands, physical demands, temporal demands, own performance, and frustration. In which the first three describe the demand based on the worker such as mental, physical and temporal and the rest three-dimension explains the interaction of the worker with the task such as effort frustration and performance [16]. NASA TLX is a two-step eval-uation procedure consisting of weights and ratings. Initially, the weight of each dimension provides data on the diagnostic information about the nature of the workload imposed by the task and each subscale is tallied in a range from 0 to 5. Where 5 corresponds to the most important factor. Thereafter, numerical ratings for each scale reflects on the magnitude of each dimension for a given task. Each scale is presented as a 12 cm line divided into 20 intervals. The overall workload score for each subject is computed by multiplying each rate by its weight given to that dimension by the subject [17].

SWAT- Subjective Workload Assessment Technique
SWAT is a subjective rating technique that uses three levels such as low, high and medium for each of three dimensions of time load, mental effort load and psychological stress load to assess workload [18]. The sensitivity of the tool has been shown in a variety of task: Memory task, manual control tasks, display monitoring [13]. SWAT uses three distinct steps i.e. scale development, event scoring and calculating. Under the scale development, each operator sort 27 cards in a combination of three levels of each of three dimensions. Thereafter event scoring, in which actual rating of workload for each given task. Finally calculating, the three-dimensional rating is converted into numeric scores between 0 and 100 using the interval scale developed in the first step [18].

Job Content Questionnaire (JCQ)
JCQ is a tool which has been developed to assess the psychosocial characteristic of jobs. JCQ is associated with the domains of demand control, thereby classifying the worker under the following realms, such as active (high demand and high control), passive (low demand and high control), high strain (high demand and low control) and low strain (low demand and high control) [19]. JCQ could be used by the management to analyze the work quality of its workers. It allows the testing of new technologies, worker motivation and job satisfaction [14]. JCQ contains 5 subscales. They are decision latitude, psychological demand, social support, physical demand, and job insecurity. These subscales all together have a length of 49 questions. Decision latitude describes skill discretion, decision authority, skill underutilization, workgroup decision authority, formal authority, and union influence. Psychological demands define psychological demands, role ambiguity, concentration, and mental work disruption. Social support describes socioemotional, instrumental and hostility support from supervisors as well as coworkers. Physical demands define general physical loading, isometric load, and aerobic load. Job insecurity describes general job insecurity and skill obsolescence.

4   Contribution of Tools Towards PLS

To analyze the involvement and usage of tools in production and logistics system from a managerial perspective, PLS at the system level is classified into three segments such as process, system settings, and technology. The process is determined as the combination of different tasks to achieve a goal. For example, the assembly process, order picking process, etc. The system refers to where and how the process should be performed. For instance, workstation layout and configuration in an assembly system; in order picking process, rack layout, order picking system such as parts to picker and picker to parts are the system settings. Technology provides a mainstay for the entire system and also responsible for proper communication between each task under the system. For example, the level of automation in an assembly process and the assistive technologies in an order picking process. Finally, the contribution of different tools in each segment are discussed below (Fig. 1).

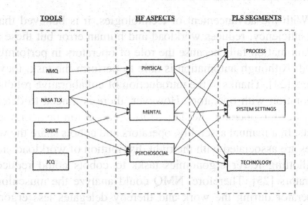

Fig. 1. Contribution of tools towards PLS

Process: HF aspects should be considered as a crucial integral part of the process mapping. While mapping a process, information regarding check points, critical decisions and feedback loop are only considered. However, integrating HF could improve an existing process to attain an enhanced workplace. Thus, there exists a necessity to have a generic view on HF aspects while mapping a process [20]. NASA TLX is the most appropriate tool while mapping a process for improvements concerned with workers. NASA TLX can measure the mental, physical and psychosocial demand. Besides, it is capable of measuring the effort, performance, and frustration, operators could face in a new process.

System Settings: Evaluating HF aspects in System settings could improve the configuration of the system, by improving workplace for operators. Therefore, it is necessary to evaluate the workload of each HF aspect. In an assembly system, configuring the workstation based on the operators could maximize the productivity of workers by reducing their physical fatigue [21]. In an order picking warehouse, there exists different storage assignment methods that could minimize the total travel distance and time [22]. Thus, NMQ could address the physical fatigue in anatomical areas were the musculoskeletal symptoms are common. Also, in an assembly process, the workers have a great need for cognitive demand due to the physical layout of the workstation and also due to the high level of complexities associated with assembling the products. However, these issues could be met with when there exists a low time pressure. On the other side, high time pressure can increase the workload on operators [5]. In this scenario, SWAT and NASA TLX are the most appropriate tool to measure the mental workload on operators. SWAT could evaluate mental effort load, psychosocial stress load and time load, but TLX measures additional dimension i.e. physical demand. Finally, worker's satisfaction is an important factor as it could impact workers' productivity, quality, and health [23]. Thus, it is important to analyze the work quality in a system setting. JCQ is the most optimum tool to analyze the work quality. JCQ mainly measures the ability of workers to take decisions in their settings, the emotional difficulties the workers face in their work and also evaluate the support operators receive from their superiors and coworkers.

Technology: With the advancement of technologies, it is believed that technologies could improve efficiency, reduces workload and human error but these aptitudes were not satisfied. Automation fails because the role of operators in performing the work is often misjudged. Although automation is able to perform the task, they lack the flexibility of workers [24]. Thanks to the introduction of collaborative robots, which works in close collaboration with operators. However, there is a need to determine the proportion of activities the operator should perform. This could be achieved by analyzing the 3 HF aspects. In a manual assembly, operators and cobots share the work tasks. The main challenges are associated with the right distribution of workload among operators and cobots. Allotting fewer ergonomics tasks to cobots could reduce the physical fatigue of operators [25]. Therefore, NMQ could analyze the musculoskeletal symptoms of an operator during the work and thereby delegates less ergonomic tasks to cobots. Automation could also influence the cognitive demand of operators; automation could change the task from direct involvement to monitoring. However, all operators are not passive with monitoring the task, further reducing their feedback from the system [24]. To analyze the cognitive demand of the operator, tools like SWAT and NASA TLX could be used. Where SWAT could be more adaptable in this situation because of its three-dimensional scale provides a psychological model of workload judgment. Also, Automation creates a work environment in which demand for work is high but the decision latitudes decline, this could affect the physical aspects of the operator ranging from heart disease to depression [24]. JCQ could predict the psychosocial characteristics of the work. JCQ's scale measures the demand for work and the decision latitudes from an operator's perspective.

5 Conclusion

Which is the best tool? The answer to this question is neither one tool could be placed in the first position. Each tool is assessing different aspects of HF. Hence, this paper introduced three aspects of humans such as mental, physical and psychosocial. Thus, NMQ was introduced to assess the physical aspects, NASA TLX and SWAT were introduced to assess the mental aspects and JCQ was introduced to analyze the psychosocial aspects. Thereafter, the contribution of the tools toward the PLS is studied, by classifying PLS into three segments such as Process, System Settings, and Technologies. Finally, this paper would assist the managers to choose the appropriate tool in evaluating PLS. The extension of this paper would suggest conducting an empirical study on evaluating the PLS segments by choosing an appropriate tool.

References

1. Grosse, E.H., Calzavara, M., Glock, C.H., Sgarbossa, F.: Incorporating human factors into decision support models for production and logistics: current state of research. IFAC PapersOnLine 50(1), 6900–6905 (2017)
2. Neumann, W.P., Dul, J.: Human factors: spanning the gap between OM and HRM. Int. J. Oper. Prod. Manag. 30(9), 923–950 (2010)
3. Sgarbossa, F., Grosse, E.H., Neumann, W.P., Battini, D.: Human factors in production and logistics systems of the future. Annu. Rev. Control 49, 295–305 (2020)
4. Snyder, H.: Literature review as a research methodology: an overview and guidelines. J. Bus. Res. 104, 333–339 (2019)
5. Brolin, A., Thorvald, P., Case, K.: Experimental study of cognitive aspects affecting human performance in manual assembly. Prod. Manuf. Res. 5(1), 141–163 (2017)
6. Lim, J.T., Hoffmann, E.R.: Strategies in performing a manual assembly task. Int. J. Ind. Ergon. 50, 121–129 (2015)
7. Rose, L.M., Neumann, W.P., Hägg, G.M., Kenttä, G.: Fatigue and recovery during and after static loading. Ergonomics 57(11), 1696–1710 (2014)
8. de Jonge, J., Bosma, H., Peter, R., Siegrist, J.: Job strain, effortreward imbalance and employee well-being: a large-scale cross-sectional sudy. Soc. Sci. Med. 50, 1317–1327 (2000)
9. Demerouti, E.: Job characteristics, flow, and performance: the moderating role of conscientiousness. J. Occup. Health Psychol. 11, 266–280 (2006)
10. Malchaire, J., Roquelaure, Y., Cock, N., Piette, A., Vergracht, S., Chiron, H.: Musculoskeletal complaints, functional capacity, personality and psychosocial factors. Int. Arch. Occup. Environ. Health 74(8), 549–557 (2001). https://doi.org/10.1007/s004200100264
11. Offenbächer, M., Ewert, T., Sangha, O., Stucki, G.: Validation of a German version of the'Disabilities of Arm, Shoulder and Hand 'questionnaire (DASH-G). Zeitschrift für Rheumatologie 62(2), 168–177 (2003)
12. Kuorinka, I., et al.: Standardised Nordic questionnaires for the analysis of musculoskeletal symptoms. Appl. Ergon. 18, 233–237 (1987)
13. Rubio, S., Diaz, E., Martin, J., Puente, J.M.: Evaluation of subjective mental workload: a comparison of SWAT, NASA-TLX, and workload profile methods. Int. Assoc. Appl. Psychol. 53, 61–86 (2004)
14. Karasek, R.A.: The new work organization, conductive production and work quality policy. In: Labor Market Changes and Job Insecurity: A Challenge for Social Welfare and Health Promotion, pp. 78–105 (1998)
15. Dickinson, C.E., Foster, A.F., Newman, S.J., O'rourke, A.M., Thomas, P.G.: Questionnaire development: an examination of the nordic musculoskeletal questionnaire. Appl. Ergon. 23 (3), 197–201 (1992)
16. Hart, S., Staveland, L.: Development of NASA-TLX (Task LoadIndex): results of empirical and theoretical research. In: Hancock, P.A., Meshkati, N. (eds.) Human Mental Workload, pp. 139–183 (1988)
17. Hart, S.G.: NASA Task load Index (TLX). Volume 1.0; Paper and pencil package (1986)
18. Reid, G., Nygren, T.: The subjective workload assessment technique: a scaling procedure for measuring mental workload. In: Hancock, P.A., Meshkati, N. (eds.) Human Mental Workload, pp. 185–218 (1988)
19. Karasek, R., Brisson, C., Kawakami, N., Houtman, I., Bongers, P., Amick, B.: The job content questionnaire (JCQ): an instrument for internationally comparative assessments of psychosocial job characteristics. J. Occup. Health Psychol. 3, 322 (1998)

20. Neumann, W.P., Village, J.: Ergonomics action research II: a framework supporting the integration of HF into work system design. Ergonomics **55**, 1140–1156 (2012)
21. Battini, D., Faccio, M., Persona, A., Sgarbossa, F.: New methodological framework to improve productivity and ergonomics in assembly system design. Int. J. Ind. Ergon. **41**, 30–42 (2011)
22. Calzavara, M., Glock, C.H., Grosse, E.H., Persona, A., Sgarbossa, F.: Analysis of economic and ergonomic performance measures of different rack. Comput. Ind. Eng. **111**, 527–536 (2017)
23. Grosse, E.H., Glock, C.H., Jaber, M.Y., Neumann, W.P.: Incorporating human factors in order picking planning models: framework and research opportunities. Int. J. Prod. Res. **53**, 695–717 (2015)
24. Lee, J.D., Seppelt, B.D.: Human factors in automoation design. In: Springer Handbook of Automation, pp. 417–436 (2009)
25. Malik, A.A., Bilberg, A.: Complexity-based task allocation in human-robot collaborative assembly. Ind. Robot Int. J. Robot. Res. Appl. **46**(4), 471–480 (2019)
26. Khodakarami, M., Shabani, A., Saen, R.F., Azadi, M.: Developing distinctive two-stage data envelopment analysis models: an application in evaluating the sustainability of supply chain management. Measurement **70**, 62–74 (2015)
27. Seuring, S., Müller, M.: From a literature review to a conceptual framework for sustainable supply chain management. J. Cleaner Prod. **16**(15), 1699–1710 (2008)
28. Leseure, M.: A critical review of the social dimension of sustainability in operations management. In: Proceedings of the fifth International EUROMA Sustainable Operations and Supply Chain Forum, Kassel, Germany (2018)

Economy and Its Symbiosis with Circularity

Abelino Reis Guimarães Neto[✉]⬤, Rodrigo Rodrigues⬤,
Jacqueline Zonichenn Reis⬤, Julio Cesar Raymundo⬤,
and Rodrigo Franco Gonçalves⬤

Universidade Paulista (UNIP), São Paulo, SP, Brazil
reisabelino@gmail.com,
rodrigo.rodrigues01@hotmail.com,
zonichenn@hotmail.com, juliocesar@fatecpg.com.br,
rofranco212@gmail.com

Abstract. The risks of harming the future of humanity through the several negative impacts on the environment generated by the linear economy are already been verified, both academically and professionally. It is essential to convert the linear production into circular, providing the possibility of achieving net sustainability. The state of the art of Economy has been modeling itself into a sustainable *umbrella concept*, which must be used to generate wealth and protect the environment. Economy and Circularity are aspects of social relationship that have been together since the beginning on macro, meso and micro-levels. This study has created an analysis tool for the Circular Economy based on the economic analysis tool of the IS-LM curves. This tool makes it possible to identify the Sustainability Margin Point, from the intersection between the curves of Governmental Protective Measures and Protective Postures of Citizens and Governments. Such analysis allows a better understanding and planning of the actions of each of the economic agents: citizens, companies, and governments.

Keywords: Circular economy · Sustainability · Umbrella concept

1 Introduction

The relationship between Economic Science and Circularity goes deeper than a synergistic connection. It is a relationship where the vitality of the economy in a society invariably generates circularity in the coexistence between its individuals, as the simple fact that there is no purchase without selling, or selling without purchase. Such circularity between people inevitably causes several economic impacts, making the vitality such of the economy as of the circularity a symbiotic relationship.

The Circularity subject is presented by Leontief [1] as a grounding for the economic process, where the use of resources is reproduced endlessness times to reach the consumption arising for human demands. To Parkin [2], the economic cycles show themselves to the economy in the connection between GDP and aggregate demand, where the variation of these macro agents is influenced. Both perspectives are connected to the economy definition by Robbins [3], which exalts the relationship between unlimited needs and limited resources. Both the subject of reproduction as the

B. Lalic et al. (Eds.): APMS 2020, IFIP AICT 591, pp. 599–606, 2020.
https://doi.org/10.1007/978-3-030-57993-7_68

relationship of economic cycles occur in a continuous process to reach human demands. As pointed by Georgescu-Roegen [4], nature imposes limits on economic growth.

This article aims to present a logical structure for the scope of the Circular Economy (CE), using the analogy between its premises as an *umbrella concept* of sustainability, divided into macro, meso, and micro levels, through an economical tool called IS-LM. Based on articles of high academic and professional value, and books that are extremely relevant to the current days, this study is structured with the first section introducing what leads to the perception of the symbiosis between economy and circularity. The second section presents a previous analysis of the state of the art of the Circular Economy and it is subdivided into 3 more parts. The first one will present the importance of the macro-level and governments actions; the second one will regard the transformation of supply chains into eco-industrial parks (EIP), and the synergistic activities between industries; the third subsection presents the micro-level and the purchase and sales relationship between companies and customers. In the third section, the logic of the symbiotic structure between economy and circularity is presented graphically, and finally, in the fourth section, the conclusion and discussion are exposed.

2   The Circular Economy

The state of the art of the Circular Economy portrays a huge concern, both from the academic and professionals, in delimiting the parameters that guide such science, but also to outline its definition with maximum clarity.

The importance of decreasing the impacts of human production is an aspect that recurs frequently in the CE, whether through the elimination of waste materials or reduction in the emission of pollutants, it is essential to confirm the net sustainability achieved [5], making it possible to confirm the environmental benefits from businesses with a perspective on the CE [6–8]. To reach this result, the participation of the whole society in its various spheres is fundamental, mainly understanding that the consumption, be of energy, primary resources, finished products or services, needs to be aligned with the premises of sustainability [5, 9]. This context is connected with the three dimensions presented by WCED [10]: economic, environmental, and social. These dimensions represent individuals and institutions, which are responsible for preserving nature, guaranteeing a healthy future for the environment. Individually these actors (citizens, governments, and companies) are unable to fully organize the transformation from the linear model to a new circular model. It is necessary to divide the activities by levels of macro, meso, and micro [11–13].

The combination of the actions of each one will stimulate sustainable results. This study proposes that the division of these levels in the CE can be compared to the active participation of these players in the Economy. In this similar organization, governments operate on macro issues, the supply chains operate at the meso level, and companies with consumers, operate at the microeconomic level [14], as we will propose in this study.

2.1 Macro-Level and Government's Activities

Among these players, the only ones that can impose rules and acts as mediators are governments. Regardless of the political characteristics of countries, the role of mediator and promoter of policies is an essential characteristic of governments. To reach the implementation of the CE, governments must realize their important role in informing and disseminating what is not allowed, and never imposing what to do [15]. Impositions on ventures and businesses discourage and reduce the expectations of the enterprising class, which must decide where to invest its resources in [11].

The role of governments at the macro-level for the promotion of CE is characterized reactively, with fines and fees, limiting what is not acceptable and harmful to the environment, and proactively with public policies for financing projects, culture, information and education [16], created from the concepts in the CE, which in turn, should be seen as an *umbrella concept* of sustainable strategies [7]. Governments see the economic system from a macroeconomic perspective, with capable tools to conduct a global analysis. For the perception of symbiosis in the CE, it will be essential to create analogies between the analytical tools of macroeconomics and sustainability [6]. An important tool for macro analysis is the IS-LM curves, which list fundamental economic agents, such as interest rates, demand for money, fiscal and monetary policies with the evolution of income [2], where the intersection of the curves informs the possible result to be reached, given the margin of adhesion of the actions taken.

By definition IS - investment saving, and LM - liquidity preference money supply. The choice for this tool is justified because its structure requires an analysis of the actions of the three agents. Therefore, it will be presented in this subsection, but it represents the actions of all the agents.

The proposed analogy is expressed in Fig. 1, where the "y" axis represents human production, the "x" axis represents the negative impacts of human production on the environment, the negative slope curve represents the government's protective measures (GPM) where assertive measures (consistent penalties and eco-business's financing) increase production and reduce impacts. The positive slope curve is divided between what is in line with government policies (below the protective measures curve) and actions that are irregular to public guidelines, that is, it is divided between a protective stance and a negligent attitude, of citizens and organizations.

The intersection between the curves is the possible result of production and its impact on the environment, or the point referring to the Sustainability Margin (SM), which is a reference to how much the impact on the environment has been increased or decreased due to the sum of government measures with the adjustments absorbed by society. The displacements of the curves must also be observed, with the displacement of both the Government Protective Measures curve as the Posture curve of Citizens and Organizations must always move upwards, raising sustainability in line with increased productivity.

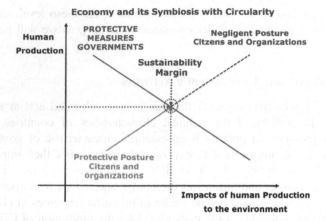

Fig. 1. Analogy between the macro tool IS-LM, which analyzes the possible results of government measures with income, with the CE. Source: the authors.

For the displacement to occur in this direction, it is necessary that government tools, fines, and fees, investment and financing, culture and education, are working harmoniously, and companies and citizens absorb these changes completely.

Figure 2 shows a real gain in combating the negative impacts caused by human production, where the SM point rises to its previous condition and decreases both the percentage of impact per unit and the impact on its global relationship. This scenery can occur both by maximizing the efficiency of all public policies, which lead to the readjustment of institutions and people, cause we live the future today when we guarantee the means for life tomorrow [10].

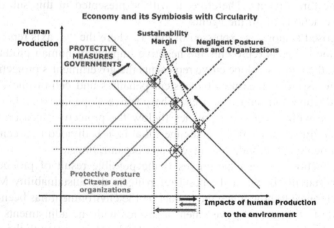

Fig. 2. Displacement of curves, both for Protective Measures and for Posture upwards, generating a context of increasing the sustainability margin. Source: the authors.

This figure shows that the SM point moves three times, once for each displacement of the curves. First, it moves down and to the right, with the elevation of the Measures curve, then it moves for its maintenance returning to the initial point of Impact, with the shift of the Posture curve upwards, and finally, it moves to the left and upwards with another readjustment of the Posture curve, and at this point, we have a gain at the Sustainability Margin.

2.2 Meso-Level and the Formation of Supply Chains in the CE

The executing actors of this operation, in the productive activities, are citizens and companies, these, in turn, should foster partnerships that guarantee current business and enable new business. Currently, competition between companies has taken on a much greater proportion, making the competition not just between them, but between supply chains [17].

At the meso level, it can be found the largest individual industries producers of impacts on the environment and transforming these negative impacts into new businesses causes the creation of new added and financial values, uniting the common interests of organizations [11, 18]. It is based on new product engineering, new modeling, and new designs, where companies can redesign their businesses, linking a consumer network to a large part of the surplus from their production process [12, 19]. By consuming these surpluses, the companies′ networks foster their interests while reducing the impact of their activities. This corroborates the construction of EIPs, which, when they become closed circuits, fail to expose a large part of their resources to the environment, which in another business structure would reach the end of their useful life, not returned to the production process [20]. EIPs arise to close the surplus production circuits, extend the useful life of the residues of the production processes in new productions in a closed supply chain. It creating a park where industries generate environmental and financial values by consuming surplus from other [11, 21].

The actions of companies at the meso level must be connected with regional public policies, but mainly meet the perception of revenues of private entrepreneurs, because this factor is decisive to keep private investments directed to eco-business. It is, in this context, that productive companies redesign their processes and products, create businesses and partners [22]. Consequently, meso level activities contribute socially, so that all the Supply Chain may achieve sustainability.

2.3 Micro-level and Relationship Between Companies, Consumers and the Environment

At the micro-level, we can see the relationship between companies and consumers. A society without rules in defense of the environment, without policies to promote culture and education on sustainability, creates a shallow understanding of this obligation with nature [23].

It is essential that the activities generated by the CE businesses produce results in favor of net sustainability [5]. It is also crucial that profit is not considered the only purpose. One way to guarantee these results is to think about new product designs and projects, planning the extraction and disposal of the resources that will be used and disposed of [24]. For that, we can use eco-efficiency strategies, like the cradle-to-cradle concept [20], as well as planning to replace natural products with synthetic resources. Promoted by governments, these actions must be absorbed by consumers, who must rethink their consumption posture [25]. This synergistic strength between governments and consumers should lead companies to promote new sustainable businesses in their supply chains [26, 27], as the creation of eco-industrial-parks, where productivity is connected to environmental protection [11]. This umbrella concept will form a structure that will help to reduce the extraction of scarce natural resources [8], giving time for the rehabilitation of the environment, ensuring conditions for a sustainable future.

In this context, the micro-level is directly related to what companies produce and is accepted by consumers, as well as the destination of their packaging and products at end of service life [18]. A change of posture in the structure of governments and institutions influences their citizens to be informed and to become more critical, reducing the trade of products with unknown origin and destination. Until the culture and critical position reach most people, the global transformation to a fully sustainable economy will be largely in the hands of governments and institutions.

3   Link Between the Three Players in the CE

The link between citizens, companies, and governments in the symbiosis between economy and circularity is an infinite spiral link, where the actions of its agents are exponential capacity tools for the transformation of the reality in which they live.

Figure 3 demonstrates how the macro-level involves the whole society, the meso-level involves the entire supply chain and its evolution in EIP's, and the micro-level involves the relationship between company and customers.

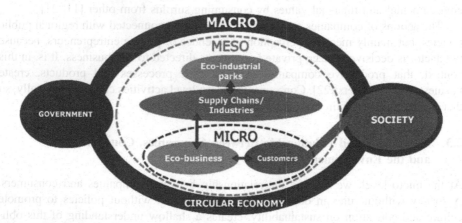

Fig. 3. Connection between agents in the symbiotics of the Circular Economy and the performance of the macro, meso and micro levels. Source: the authors.

This relationship among the actors makes it possible to see graphically how each one relates and is positioned in the symbiotic environment of the Circular Economy, and emphasizes that the economic life of agents is made up of well-defined links, and mainly bilateral, with no purchase without selling, or selling without purchase. There is no economy without circularity or society without the environment.

4 Conclusion and Discussions

The Circular Economy can be observed as the *umbrella concept* of sustainability, which uses the organization of macro, meso, and micro-levels to direct its path towards net sustainability. In this organization, the macro-level is composed of reactive public policies (taxes and fines), and proactive through financing and investment in ecological industrial parks, culture and education. The meso-level encourages the wealth production and the reduction of negative impacts on the environment, from the reengineering of its products, which enables new partnerships and businesses. At the micro-level, companies and customers exchange with each other products with origin and destination linked to net sustainability. This structure can be analyzed by analogy, using already consolidated tools, such as the IS-LM curve.

Despite strongly presenting its proposals, the present study leaves open empirical data that can corroborate its valuation with the academic and professional environment, as well as it lacks the fundamental depth at each level (macro, meso, and micro). It is also welcome more concrete discussion on solutions for the needed reforms to achieve sustainability, emphasizing the desire to deepen this theme in future studies.

We can't repeat the mistakes made by Linear Economy, where the world economy generates wealth and wonders, together with hunger, social exclusion and aggression to the environment. We can no longer claim ignorance of this path that went wrong.

References

1. Leontief, W.: Die Wirtschaft als Kreislauf. Laupp, Tübingen (1928)
2. Parkin, M.: Economy. 8th edn. Translation: Cristina Yamagami. Pearson, São Paulo (2009)
3. Robbins, L.: An Essay on the Nature and Importance of Economic Science. Editora Saraiva, São Paulo (2007)
4. Georgescu-Roegen, N.: The Entropy Law and the Economic Process. Harvard University Press, Cambridge (1971)
5. Korhonen, J., Honkasalo, A., Seppälä, J.: Circular economy: the concept and its limitations. Ecol. Econ. **143**, 37–46 (2018)
6. George, D.A.R., Lin, B.C.-A., Chen, Y.: A circular economy model of economic growth. Environ. Modell. Softw. **73**, 60–63 (2015)
7. Blomsma, F., Brennan, G.: The emergence of circular economy: a new framing around prolonging resource productivity. J. Ind. Ecol. **21**(3), 603–614 (2017)
8. Murray, A., Skene, K., Haynes, K.: The circular economy: an interdisciplinary exploration of the concept and application in a global context. J. Bus. Ethics **140**(3), 369–380 (2017)
9. Frosch, R.A., Gallopoulos, N.E.: Strategies for manufacturing. Sci. Am. **261**(3), 144–153 (1989)

10. WCED, Special Working Session: World commission on environment and development. Our Common Future **17**, 1–91 (1987)
11. Sakr, D., et al.: Critical success and limiting factors for eco-industrial parks: global trends and Egyptian context. J. Clean. Prod. **19**(11), 1158–1169 (2011)
12. Jackson, M., Lederwasch, A., Giurco, D.: Transitions in theory and practice: managing metals in the circular economy. Resources **3**(3), 516–543 (2014)
13. Kirchherr, J., Reike, D., Hekkert, M.: Conceptualizing the circular economy: An analysis of 114 definitions. Resour. Conserv. Recycl. **127**, 221–232 (2017)
14. Ghisellini, P., Cialani, C., Ulgiati, S.: A review on circular economy: the expected transition to a balanced interplay of environmental and economic systems. J. Clean. Prod. **114**, 11–32 (2016)
15. Schulze, G.. Growth Within: A Circular Economy Vision for a Competitive Europe, pp. 1–22. Ellen MacArthur Foundation and the McKinsey Center for Business and Environment (2016)
16. Geels, F.W.: Ontologies, socio-technical transitions (to sustainability), and the multi-level perspective. Res. Pol. **39**(4), 495–510 (2010)
17. Corrêa, H.L.: Supply Chain Management: Integrating Supply Chains in the Globalized World. 1st edn. Editora Atlas SA, São Paulo (2000)
18. Zhu, Q., Geng, Y., Lai, K.-h.: Circular economy practices among Chinese manufacturers varying in environmental-oriented supply chain cooperation and the performance implications. J. Environ. Manag. **91**(6), 1324–1331 (2010)
19. Lacy, P., et al.: Circular Advantage: Innovative Business Models and Technologies to Create Value in a World Without Limits to Growth. Accenture, Chicago (2014)
20. Braungart, M., Mcdonough, W., Bollinger, A.: Cradle-to-cradle design: creating healthy emissions–a strategy for eco-effective product and system design. J. Clean. Prod. **15**(13–14), 1337–1348 (2007)
21. Fang, Y., Cote, R.P., Qin, R.: Industrial sustainability in China: practice and prospects for eco-industrial development. J. Environ. Manag. **83**(3), 315–328 (2007)
22. Gibbs, D., Deutz, P.: Reflections on implementing industrial ecology through eco-industrial park development. J. Clean. Prod. **15**(17), 1683–1695 (2007)
23. Melosi, M.: Garbage in the Cities: Refuse, Reform and the Environment. Revised edn. University of Pittsburgh Press, Pittsburgh (2005)
24. Reh, L.: Process engineering in circular economy. Particuology **11**(2), 119–133 (2013)
25. Zhijun, F., Nailing, Y.: Putting a circular economy into practice in China. Sustain. Sci. **2**(1), 95–101 (2007)
26. Macarthur, E., et al.: Towards the circular economy. J. Ind. Ecol. **2**, 23–44 (2013)
27. Zeng, H., et al.: Institutional pressures, sustainable supply chain management, and circular economy capability: empirical evidence from Chinese eco-industrial park firms. J. Clean. Prod. **155**, 54–65 (2017)

Data-Driven Manufacturing
and Services Operations Management

First Steps to the Digital Shadow of Maintenance Services' Value Contribution

Frederick Birtel[1]([⊠]), Achim Kampker[2], and Volker Stich[1]

[1] Research Institute for Industrial Management (FIR) at RWTH Aachen University, Campus-Boulevard 55, 52074 Aachen, Germany
Frederick.Birtel@fir.rwth-aachen.de
[2] Chair Production Engineering of E-Mobility Components at RWTH Aachen University, Bohr 12, 52072 Aachen, Germany

Abstract. Industrie 4.0 is said to have major positive effects on productivity in manufacturing companies. However, these effects are not visible yet. One reason for this is the lack of understanding of maintenance services as a crucial value contributing partner in production processes, although scientific literature already highlighted the importance of indirect maintenance costs. In order to retrieve the unused potential of maintenance services, a digital shadow in form of a sufficiently precise digital representation is required, providing a data model for the value of maintenance actions so that asset and maintenance strategies can be optimized later on. Using case study research for process manufacturers, the first research contribution of this paper consists of 21 value contributing elements being identified. The second contribution is a reference processes model, showing seven major process steps as well as the required intra-organization interaction on an information technology system level. Therefore, it provides the base for the missing data model shaping the targeted digital shadow of maintenance services' value contribution.

Keywords: Industrie 4.0 · Digital shadow · Maintenance services · Maintenance value contribution · Intelligent maintenance systems

1 Introduction

The advance of the digital interconnectedness in industrial companies during the past years, also referred to as *smart factories* or *Industrie 4.0*, has increased the awareness of manufacturing companies for their own digital transformation in order to keep up with the global competition. However, that interconnection between cyber-physical systems and people, combined with an unlimited access to real-time data [1, 2] that could drastically accelerate critical entrepreneurial decision making [3], has not led to an increase in productivity across those companies so far [4], as often Industrie 4.0 use cases do not become successful business cases especially in maintenance departments. One reason for that are still dominating isolated information technology (IT) systems within the companies, which prevent information getting from the information source to a decision-making stage, so that also intelligent maintenance applications or assistance systems [1] cannot fulfill the promised potential [5]. Another reason is the lack of

© IFIP International Federation for Information Processing 2020
Published by Springer Nature Switzerland AG 2020
B. Lalic et al. (Eds.): APMS 2020, IFIP AICT 591, pp. 609–616, 2020.
https://doi.org/10.1007/978-3-030-57993-7_69

understanding of maintenance services as a crucial value contributing partner in manufacturing companies' production processes. Value thereby represents the positive change of a manufacturing company's balance sheet in general or even the increase in profit (EBIT) or return rates (e.g. ROCE). This results in investments for maintaining the assets, e.g. maintenance personnel and equipment, being held back. Additionally, a regular adjustment of the cost-optimal mix of maintenance strategies consisting of reactive, preventive and even predictive measures according to the asset condition and risk assessment are not executed effectively [6]. Both factors may not result in an increase of *direct maintenance costs* from spare parts, labor and external service providers in the short term, but they lead to a significant increase of *indirect maintenance costs*. These are the result of, for instance, lost contribution margins due to unplanned downtimes [7], subsequent contractual penalties or even loss of customer orders [8]. Thus, entrepreneurial decisions, e.g. choosing the right maintenance strategy mix and making sustainable asset investments, are made on an incomplete information basis [9].

The main reason for that lack of information or visibility is not technological but organizationally driven [10]. Currently, there is no approach available to identify that information for costs or effects in manufacturing companies on an information system level, which is required to determine the value maintenance services can add to the company's balance sheet. So, in terms of the concept of Industrie 4.0, a *digital shadow* is required in order to retrieve the full potential of a company's digital transformation [11].

2   Theoretical Background

2.1   The Digital Shadow as Part of the Internet of Production

The digital shadow represents "an integrated database that generates a sufficiently precise digital representation of the whole enterprise in real-time", primarily on a process level [12] and therefore must be differentiated from the *digital twin* as a simulation-capable digital representation of a physical asset [13]. In that context, the digital shadow serves as a transition layer within the 'Internet of Production' providing a domain-specific data model connecting different IT systems [14]. Thus, the digital shadow does not represent an optimizing application in the first place but forms the required basis for a variety of analytical applications (e.g. maintenance/asset investment strategy) improving the management's data based decision making [15].

The concept of the digital shadow was applied to production environments in the first place in order to increase the visibility in factory and production planning [16]. It was then adopted to industrial services and provided a reference process model as initial point for a sufficient data model which focused on the service execution level only [11]. However, a comparable approach defining value contributing elements, a reference process model as well as a data model for the value of maintenance services is still unavailable.

2.2   Requirements for a Digital Shadow for Maintenance Services

The digital shadow itself does not optimize decision making for maintenance services, but it serves as a tool to provide the required visibility. In order to develop it, three major steps are required [14]. First, it is required to identify and clarify elements representing the value contribution of maintenance services and to link them to specific information [11]. Second, the elements and referred information have to be linked to a reference process, fulfilling the purpose of reutilization [17]. Based on the reference process and its steps, a data model can be derived completing the definition of the digital shadow [12]. This paper contributes to the identification of the value contribution elements/information and the resulting reference process model while the development of the data model for the required time series observation of the value elements as well optimized decision making based on that digital shadow are explicitly *not* subject of this paper (see level three and four in Fig. 1).

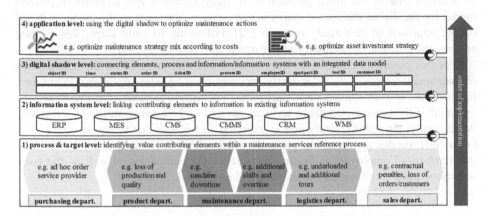

Fig. 1. Concept of the digital shadow of the value contribution of maintenance services

In scientific literature, value contributing elements of maintenance services have already been subject of discussions [18], though that previous work is generally incomplete in two specific areas. First, the value contributing elements are considered from a direct and indirect cost perspective, respectively, while positive effects of maintenance actions on the company value are not included [19]. Second, the determined elements are incomplete as they are restricted to a close maintenance perspective only and do not take into account effects appearing in other organizational units of the company (e.g. loss of customer orders monitored in the sales department). This is enhanced by the effect that value contributing elements additional to known maintenance-related downtime costs become visible with a time delay (e.g. shortened asset lifetime). Therefore this paper points out the value contributing elements particularly considering intra-organizational boundaries as well as time delays.

In order to form the targeted data model for the digital shadow of maintenance services' value contribution, a reference process model is required containing core functions (process steps), cross-section functions (e.g. reports, contracts) and a data management (e.g. resources, employees) [20]. Regarding the reference process and the related process steps, a variety of models is already described. Most of them refer to or are similar to the previous work of German standardization initiatives (e.g. DIN31051) [21]. However, those process models do not consider the existing intra-organizational exchange of data and information required to determine the value contribution of maintenance services leading to an insufficient data management. Thus, this paper introduces a reference process model focusing on the core process steps which provide interfaces to the value contributing elements and referring information across the organization and information systems. Therefore, this paper contributes the first two levels of the concept of the digital shadow as summarized in Fig. 1.

3 Methodology

In order to address the given problem of defining elements and a reference process model for the digital shadow of maintenance services, the work in this paper is based on the approach of case study research [22]. Following its eight steps, this method ensures the practical applicability of the qualitative results later on.

For this paper, we chose cases from process manufacturers. Here, the added value of maintenance services in that industry becomes clear because unplanned downtimes, for instance, have an immediate impact on the production process, thus increasing the potential of the value maintenance services can add to the balance sheet of a company. Additionally, the value contribution is expected to be high due to the loss of contribution margins due to production and quality losses [23]. Other structuring factors were the numbers of employees indicating the size of the companies as well as the complexity of assets used within the manufacturing process.

Table 1. Overview of selected cases

No.	Industry	Employees	Asset complexity
1	Steel	>10,000	High
2	Textile	ca. 500	Medium
3	Pharmaceutical	>0,000	High
4	Automotive supplier	ca. 2,000	Medium
5	Food	ca. 1,800	Low
6	Food	ca. 1,200	Low
7	Paper	ca. 300	Medium

The cases and qualitative results were recorded in form of triangulation [22]. The identification and assessment of the value-adding elements, referred information and the reference process model were jointly modeled by experts from the selected companies, following a semi-structured interview. Moreover, the data was supplemented by internal company data, e.g. operating instructions, balance sheets and a comprehensive literature analysis. Seven case studies, as shown in Table 1, were analyzed, but no significant addition was made to the examined contributing elements, information and process steps after the fifth case study, because the findings were repetitive. Thus, the termination criteria (eighth step of the case study research approach) were met.

4 Modeling and Results

4.1 Identifying and Evaluating Value Contributing Elements

Following the methodology of case study research for process manufacturers, 21 elements were identified to have an impact on the value contribution of maintenance services. Those elements were then classified into two groups. The first group comprises all the elements which contribute a positive value to the company and should therefore be maximized, such as output and product quality increase. The other group contains elements causing additional costs that consequently influence the companies' value negatively (e.g. loss of contribution margins or contractual penalties due to missed delivery dates). In order to identify the most relevant elements out of the two groups, the elements were evaluated qualitatively according to their effect size regarding the value of the company and their significance, meaning the extent to which they can be influenced by maintenance measures directly or indirectly as shown by the framework downtime consequential costs [6].

Those elements with a great effect size and high significance to maintenance actions were identified as most relevant while other elements were excluded from further modeling (e.g. commissioning costs and image loss). The results of all identified and evaluated elements are shown in Fig. 2 were the subject of the subsequent design of the reference process model.

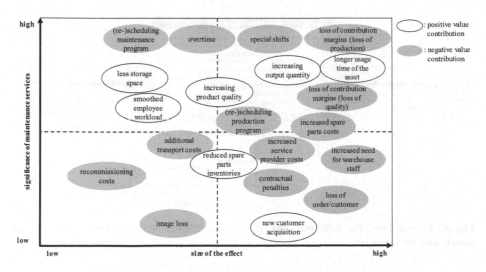

Fig. 2. Case study results for value contributing elements

4.2   Modelling of a Reference Process

In the next step, the selected elements were first broken down to their information level required to retrieve them on IT system level (s. example information in Fig. 3), also following the approach of case study research and literature review. Then, the elements and referred information were transferred into a reference process model. Figure 3 shows the seven process steps as well as the involved departments of a company in which the relevant value contributing elements and related information are monitored (e.g. sales, purchasing and logistics). The reference process model considers them as an information source that provides the basis used to assign the elements to maintenance action as part of the shown process steps (s. examples in Fig. 3), although many value contributing elements do not occur within the maintenance departments directly but delayed.

Furthermore, the process model's data management identifies all involved information technology (IT) systems, such as the computerized maintenance management system (CMMS), the enterprise resource planning (ERP), the customer relationship management (CRM), the warehouse management (WMS) or the manufacturing execution system (MES) (s. Fig. 1). Consequently, the process model allows the distinct assignment of a value contributing element and their related information (s. Fig. 2) to maintenance actions within a specified period of time. Therefore, it provides a useful basis for the central data model shaping the targeted digital shadow of maintenance services' value contribution.

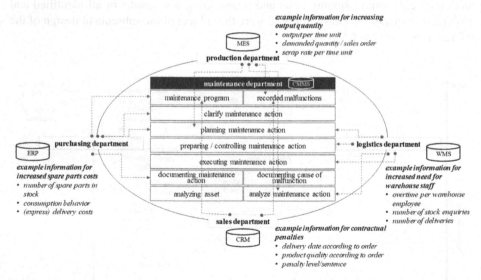

Fig. 3. Extract from the reference process for maintenance services within the relevant stakeholder environment

5 Conclusion and Outlook

This paper demonstrates that intra-organizational visibility is required to uncover time-delayed value contributing effects of maintenance actions in form of a digital shadow of maintenance services' value contribution. Using the research approach of case study research 21, elements are shown and organized by the size of their effect (impact) and the significance of maintenance services for their appearance (s. Fig. 2). Besides the dominating elements of contribution losses due to loss of production or quality, further elements (e.g. efforts for re-planning maintenance, contractual penalties) have been identified, representing an extended scientific understanding of maintenance services' value contribution. Moreover, the paper demonstrates that the information referring to the qualitative evaluated elements are monitored in different departments as well as different IT systems within a company. The presented core function of the reference process model with its seven process steps allows to connect maintenance actions with the value contributing elements and information. It sets up the basis for the data model as last key element of the digital shadow.

Hence, future research can build on the contributed model in order to describe how different IT systems on a database level can interact so that domain-specific requests can be answered with real-time data and information using entity relationship models, for instance. Furthermore, design recommendations are needed for the implementation of a digital shadow in practice. In this context, future work may also specify the identified value contributing elements on an existing KPI (key performance indicators) level so that current IT systems and management models can be adapted to the presented concept more easily. Thus, finally utilizing the digital shadow (s. Fig. 1), e.g. to choose the correct maintenance strategy mix as well as asset management strategy in respect of the whole asset life cycle, could become the key to retrieving the full potential of existing and future Industrie 4.0 solutions for maintenance services in manufacturing companies.

References

1. Lee, J.: Industrial AI. Applications with Sustainable Performance, 1st edn. Springer Singapore, Singapore (2020)
2. Schuh, G., Anderl, R., Gausemeier, J., ten Hompel, M., Wahlster, W. (eds.): Industrie 4.0 Maturity Index. Die Digitale Transformation von Unternehmen gestalten. Acatech Studie. Herbert Utz, München (2017)
3. Porter, M.E., Heppelmann, J.E.: How smart connected products are transforming competition. Harvard Bus. Rev. **92**, 64–88 (2014)
4. Rammer, C., et al.: Produktivitätsparadoxon im Maschinenbau. Zentrum für Europäische Wirtschaftsforschung (ZEW); Fraunhofer-Institut für System- und Innovationsforschung (ISI), Mannheim/Karlsruhe (2018). http://www.impuls-stiftung.de/studien. Accessed 5 Mar 2020
5. Bienzeisler, B., Schletz, A.: Industrie 4.0 Ready Services. Technologietrends 2020, Stuttgart (2014)
6. Pawellek, G.: Integrierte Instandhaltung und Ersatzteillogistik. Vorgehensweisen, Methoden, Tools, 2nd edn. VDI-Buch. Springer Vieweg, Berlin (2016)

7. Milojevic, M., Nassah, F.: Digital Industrial Revolution with Predictive Maintenance. Are European businesses ready to streamline their operations and reach higher levels of efficiency? CXP Group (2018). https://www.sitsi.com/pacs-european-trend-study-digital-industrial-revolution-predictive-maintenance. Accessed 5 Mar 2020

8. Kuhn, A., Schuh, G., Stahl, B.: Nachhaltige Instandhaltung. Trends, Potenziale und Handlungsfelder nachhaltiger Instandhaltung; [Ergebnisbericht der vom BMBF geförderten Untersuchung "Nachhaltige Instandhaltung"]. VDMA, Frankfurt am Main (2006)

9. Lundgren, C., Skoogh, A., Bokrantz, J.: Quantifying the effects of maintenance – a literature review of maintenance models. Procedia CIRP 72, 1305–1310 (2018)

10. Roy, R., Stark, R., Tracht, K., Takata, S., Mori, M.: Continuous maintenance and the future – foundations and technological challenges. CIRP Ann. 65(2), 667–688 (2016)

11. Harland, T.: Gestaltung des Digitalen Schattens für Instandhaltungsdienstleistungen im Maschinen- und Anlagenbau, vol. 160, 1st edn. Schriftenreihe Rationalisierung. Apprimus, Aachen (2019)

12. Schuh, G., Jussen, P., Harland, T.: The digital shadow of services: a reference model for comprehensive data collection in MRO services of machine manufacturers. Procedia CIRP 73, 271–277 (2018)

13. Uhlemann, T.H.-J., Lehmann, C., Steinhilper, R.: The digital twin: realizing the cyber-physical production system for industry 4.0. Procedia CIRP 61, 335–340 (2017)

14. Schuh, G., et al.: Change request im produktionsbetrieb. In: Brecher, C., Klocke, F., Schmitt, R., Schuh, G. (eds.) Internet of Production für Agile Unternehmen. AWK Aachener Werkzeugmaschinen-Kolloquium 2017, 1st edn., pp. 109–131. Apprimus, Aachen (2017)

15. Bauernhansl, T., Krüger, J., Reinhart, G., Schuh, G.: WGP-Standpunkt Industrie 4.0 (2016). https://www.ipa.fraunhofer.de/content/dam/ipa/de/documents/Presse/Presseinformationen/2016/Juni/WGP_Standpunkt_Industrie_40.pdf. Accessed 4 Mar 2020

16. Bauernhansl, T., Hartleif, S., Felix, T.: The digital shadow of production – a concept for the effective and efficient information supply in dynamic industrial environments. Procedia CIRP 72, 69–74 (2018)

17. Schütte, R.: Grundsätze Ordnungsmäßiger Referenzmodellierung. Konstruktion Konfigurations- und Anpassungsorientierter Modelle. Neue Betriebswirtschaftliche Forschung, vol. 233. Gabler, Wiesbaden, s.l. (1998)

18. Lorenz, B.: Wertorientierte Gestaltung der Betrieblichen Instandhaltung, 1st edn. Schriftenreihe Rationalisierung, Bd. 109. Apprimus, Aachen (2011)

19. Biedermann, H. (ed.): Wertschöpfendes Instandhaltungs- und Produktionsmanagement. Erfolgreich durch Innovationen in Management und Technologie. Praxiswissen für Ingenieure: Instandhaltung. TÜV Media, Köln (2007)

20. Kallenberg, R.: Ein Referenzmodell für den Service in Unternehmen des Maschinenbaus. Schriftenreihe Rationalisierung und Humanisierung, Bd. 44. Shaker, Aachen (2002)

21. DIN Deutsches Institut für Normung e.V.: DIN 31051: Grundlagen der Instandhaltung. Beuth, Berlin (2019)

22. Eisenhardt, K.M.: Building Theories from Case Study Research. The Academy of Management Review 14(4), 532–550 (1989)

23. Parida, A., Kumar, U.: Maintenance productivity and performance measurement. In: Ait-Kadi, D., Ben-Daya, M., Duffuaa, S.O., Raouf, A., Knezevic, J. (eds.) Handbook of Maintenance Management and Engineering, 1st edn., pp. 17–41. Springer, London (2009)

Reshoring of Service Operations: Evidence from a Delphi Study

Paolo Gaiardelli[✉] , Albachiara Boffelli ,
Matteo Kalchschmidt , Daniel Bellazzi,
and Simone Orom Samorani

University of Bergamo, Viale Marconi, 5, 24044 Dalmine, BG, Italy
{paolo.gaiardelli,albachiara.boffelli,
matteo.kalchschmidt}@unibg.it, {d.bellazzi,
s.samorani}@studenti.unibg.it

Abstract. The reshoring phenomenon has been explored mainly in the context of manufacturing, while research on business service still appears lacking behind. To address this gap, the article explores the reshoring phenomenon relevance in the context of business services. The research applies a Delphi method developed along three rounds involving a panel of 18 experts. The results show that, although still being in its infancy, the reshoring phenomenon will impact significantly business services in the next future, but with its own specificity, thus deserving dedicated future research streams. Particularly the experts highlight that the main drivers leading to business service reshoring are quite different with respect to ones identified in manufacturing reshoring literature. Moreover, this study indicates that service reshoring will be fundamental in all the business services in which the technology cannot be considered as the main driver for service delivery and that requires a strong human relationship.

Keywords: Service operations · Reshoring · Delphi-study

1 Introduction

Attracted by internalisation and location advantages, many companies over the years have offshored their activities to low-wage countries [1], affecting not only manufacturing operations [2] but also business services [3]. The latter refers to all the activities supporting business through the delivery of intangible outcomes, such as maintenance, IT, R&D, marketing, customer service, finance and so forth. Recently many companies have started to bring back their activities to their home countries. This phenomenon, called reshoring, can be defined "as the voluntary partial or total relocation of business activities previously offshored, whether back home or to another location" to serve the local, regional or global demands [3]. While many studies have been developed to analyse the main characteristics of production reshoring, exploring its main factors [4, 5], the research on business service reshoring still appears lacking behind. This shortcoming may be due to the lack of systematic data available on the phenomenon, and its relatively small scale. To fill this gap, this paper provides an exploration of main drivers and companies' characteristics shaping this phenomenon in the business service

B. Lalic et al. (Eds.): APMS 2020, IFIP AICT 591, pp. 617–624, 2020.
https://doi.org/10.1007/978-3-030-57993-7_70

context, as a first step of a wider study on business service reshoring relevant factors, including barriers, enablers, and outcomes. The following research questions are addressed in this article: *What drivers are the most impacting on service reshoring? What are the company characteristics that influence the service reshoring phenomenon?*

To do so, a pool of academic and business experts in service management is involved in a three-round Delphi study to redirect existing theories in reshoring of production operations into the business service context. The achieved results allow to identify the main drivers and companies' characteristics affecting the phenomenon, as well as to trace its potential future scenarios and developments.

2 Literature Review and Conceptual Model

Literature has mostly focused on identification of the drivers for reshoring [5]. Until now, the majority of the identified drivers have concerned the reshoring of manufacturing activities [5, 6]. While many of these drivers can apply also to service reshoring, some others can be attributed only to the manufacturing context, because they do not consider the specificity of services - namely, intangibility, inseparability, heterogeneity and perishability [7, 8]. Therefore, the full list of drivers' categories and their elements identified in manufacturing reshoring literature need to be further explored to test its significance into the service context. Table 1 reports the list of categories and the corresponding references.

Table 1. Drivers' categories from reshoring literature.

Category	Examples	References
Managerial mistakes	Offshoring implementation mistake, overhasty offshoring effect	[3, 5]
Cost	Labour costs' gap reduction, sourcing and administrative costs	[5, 9]
Market characteristics	Host market size reduction, new market penetration opportunity, capacity availability	[5]
Service level	Higher service level, reduced responsiveness	[5, 9]
Innovation-related	Innovation potentiality loss, open innovation	[5, 6]
Risk-related	Exchange rate, political and social risks	[5, 6]
Supply chain-related	Higher delivery time, synergies across the value chain	[5, 10]
Entrepreneurial-related	Emotional elements, focus on core activities, pursue of the initial offshoring strategy	[3, 11]

In recent contributions, scholars claimed that contingency theory is a relevant theoretical lens when considering location decisions [12]. This theory assumes that organizations adapt their structures to maintain fit with changing contextual factors, so as to attain high performance [13]. Then, identifying important contingency variables that distinguish between contexts emerges as fundamental to explain a phenomenon in light of the contingency theory [14]. In line with [3], five factors can be considered as relevant in defining the context of reshoring, namely company's sector, company's size, the offshoring duration (i.e. the length of stay in the offshore country), the previous experience in moving services across national borders, and the type of service. All of them will be considered as characteristics possibly affecting the service reshoring phenomenon, as reported in the conceptual model (Fig. 1).

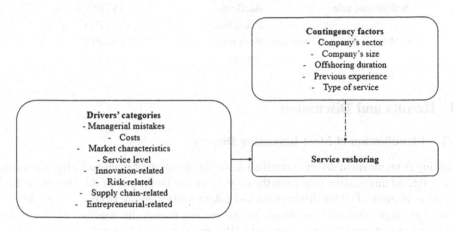

Fig. 1. Conceptual model

3 Research Methodology

The main goal of this research is to reach a consensus on a complex, interdisciplinary problem that, due to the lack of systematic data available and its relatively small scale, cannot be answered through empirical evidence. Therefore, a Delphi study was identified as the most suitable approach to develop the exploration. A Delphi study can be described as a qualitative forecasting technique based upon a systematic, anonymous and iterative communication process among a representative group of experts [15]. According to the goal of this research, a modified e-Delphi method was adopted. Characterised by a mix of pre-selected items and open qualitative questions derived from a literature analysis and structured according to the research model, the e-Delphi study was carried out in three rounds and involved a panel list of 18 experts coming from industry and academia. Selection of each members was carried out in order to consider different viewpoints of the topic under investigation, thus reducing "certain polarization of preferences and responses" [16]. Moreover, the total number of participants was identified in order to reduce potential individual biases that can distort the aggregate responses [17, 18]. The panel of experts includes both practitioners with an academic background and strong involvement in research, and scholars with a background in service or in reshoring and ongoing collaborations within industry. Table 2 reports the descriptive characteristics of the panel of experts.

Table 2. Experts' characteristics.

Characteristic	Categories	# of experts (%)
Nationality	Italian	10 (56%)
	European (excluding Italy)	4 (22%)
	Extra-European	4 (22%)
Years of experience	Less than 5	6 (33%)
	Between 5 and 10	5 (28%)
	More than 10	7 (39%)
Professional role	Academic	15 (83%)
	Practitioner	3 (17%)
Background/field of expertise	Reshoring	6 (33%)
	Service	12 (67%)

4 Results and Discussion

4.1 Identification of Most Impacting Drivers

Starting from the main drivers identified from the literature of manufacturing reshoring, we collected quantitative data from the experts. In the first round of the Delphi method, a first evaluation of all the drivers on a 1–5 Likert scale (ranging from 1 = 'very low' to 5 = 'very high' impact) was asked. In the second round, the medians of the whole panel were transparently communicated [19]; on average, 11 experts over 18 did not change their answers and the standard deviation of the answers decreased by 9%. In the third round, the drivers were divided into most impacting (the ones with median higher than 3) and least impacting (the ones with mean lower than 3). All the experts were asked to indicate whether they agreed to include the first group as impacting drivers and exclude the second one [19], and eventually to revise their evaluation on the single drivers. On average, 15 experts over 18 did not change their evaluation and the standard deviation of the answers furtherly decreased by 4%. The drivers that resulted to be critical for the business service reshoring phenomenon, with a mean above 3.5 and a median of 4.0, are the reduction in the labour costs' gap (mean 3.82, median 4), the higher service level and responsiveness that can be reached in the home country (both mean 3.76, median 4), the increased possibility to innovate and differentiate from competitors at the home country (mean 3.53, median 4), the risks connected with the cultural differences (mean 3.76, median 4), the higher delivery time for the provision of the service from the host country (mean 3.76, median 4) and the change in the business strategy (mean 3.94, median 4). The only excluded category was the market characteristics, but it is important to specify that the experts gave for granted the fact that the main market was in the home country.

4.2 Assessment of the Effect of Companies' Characteristics

Concerning the contingency factors considered, the same procedure adopted for the drivers' analysis was followed: first evaluation in the first round, feedback and possibility to revise the answer in the second round (on average 11 out of 18 experts did not change their answers), and confirmation of inclusions and exclusions in the third round. Along the process the average standard deviation reduced from 1.38 to 1.14. In the end, company's sector and the offshoring duration resulted to be highly relevant in influencing the service reshoring decision. Concerning the type of service instead, we were interested to know what type of business services were the most likely to be reshored. As a consequence, in the first round an open question was asked and the replies were collected and categorized. In the second and third rounds the experts were asked to order the type of services according to their likelihood of being reshored. Without any doubt the types of business services most likely to be reshored are the customer service and the maintenance, where the contact with customer is fundamental to enhance service quality.

4.3 Analysis of Future Scenarios

In order to reach the maximum exploitation of the experts' opinions, we also asked experts to provide a qualitative assessment of future scenarios concerning the phenomenon of business service reshoring. The answers collected in the first round, were then categorized and proposed again for a quantitative assessment in the following rounds. In this case, the future scenarios were rated on a Likert scale from 1 ("Completely disagree") to 5 ("Completely agree"). Table 3 reports the descriptive statistics of the categories of topics and some among the most relevant examples of future scenarios provided by the experts.

Table 3. Descriptive statistics of the future scenarios' categories.

Categories	Examples	A	M	SD
Alternatives to reshoring	"Other types of location decisions are more likely to happen (nearshoring, offshoring to another country, etc.)"	3.44	4	0.95
Economics	"Offshoring is not economically convenient anymore"	2.38	2	0.63
Enablers	"Digital technologies (e.g. AI systems, digital presence) may reduce the need for reshoring"	3.56	4	0.94
Governance	"Relational issues with offshored suppliers and the willingness to decrease the supply chain complexity are important for service reshoring"	3.16	3	0.84
Service as the core business	"As more and more firms 'servitize', there will be a change in the level of reshoring as firms realize the amount of 'local' support that needs to be provided"	3.25	3	0.88
Triggers	"Service reshoring as a result of higher labour costs, more responsiveness to the local market, need of better interaction between customer care and R&D"	3.39	3	0.86
Type of activities	"Highly strategic services should be moved closer to customers in order to increase their value and time performance"	3.67	4	0.93

Note: A = Average; M = Median; SD = Standard Deviation

In the end, we were able to develop a unique future scenario by summarizing the most relevant settings put forward by the experts: "Service reshoring will be fundamental in all those business services in which the technology cannot be the main driver and that requires a strong human relationship. This type of business services corresponds, usually, to the highly strategic and most customized ones which should be moved closer to customers in order to increase their value and time performance. Meanwhile, ancillary and routinary service works may follow a cost-based approach and can remain offshored or automated. An enabler of this scenario is, of course, the late trends in digital technologies which help in automatizing the service. Moreover, the scenario is incentivized by the recent trends in which service activities have been becoming the core activities of a company and this emphasizes more their reshoring".

4.4 Discussion

Our research pointed out that there are no driver's categories characterizing reshoring of business services other than those already identified in the manufacturing sector. However, not all driver's categories emerged as relevant. In particular, experts acknowledged that market characteristics are not so important for business services reshoring. Therefore, it can be stated that this phenomenon does not depend on market pressures, but rather derives from choices made directly by the companies to increase their competitiveness. In particular, the relocation of the service business activities to the place of origin, are related to the necessity to have a higher level of service, in terms of quality, speed and responsiveness. Indeed, by creating greater proximity between the service provider and the customer, their relationship is facilitated and communication between the two parties is made more effective, thus stimulating mutual involvement and more valuable processes. This result is in accordance also with service inseparability, a characteristic that presupposes services are place-dependent, i.e. they can only be used where they have been created. Therefore, this consideration adds an important contribution to previous literature on business services reshoring. In fact, as explained by [3], reshoring phenomenon of business services was previously generally interpreted as a reaction to failure or as a persistent strategy, namely keeping on pursuing the same objectives that led the offshoring decision. Instead, the results hereby provided prove the specificity of the business service reshoring phenomenon, being the main drivers substantially different from the motivations leading the manufacturing reshoring, namely quality and lead time issues [5, 12].

The higher importance that experts attributed to drivers related to the operational perspectives for service business reshoring is also consistent with service perishability. Indeed, this characteristic, implies the need for instant use of services and therefore a higher difficulty in planning resources to manage demand. Therefore, shortening of the service chain through reshoring makes it possible to centralize both front-office and back-office activities, making it easier to coordinate and plan service delivery, thus improving service speed and responsiveness. This result is also supported by the type of services that experts believe will be more easily transferred to the country of origin. These are solutions that require the direct presence of the service provider during delivery, such as customer service and maintenance management.

Finally, in line with the characteristic of service inconsistency, the centralization of activities, resulting from reshoring, on the one hand favors the standardization of back-office activities and on the other hand supports the mass customization as requested by the market. This aspect emerges as fundamental especially when considering business services that experts believe will be more likely to undergo a reshoring phenomenon. Nevertheless, the study suggests that all the considerations can be considered applicable, only in circumstances where technology does not intervene directly in service delivery, as the introduction of technological innovation in service delivery changes the intrinsic characteristics of the service itself [20].

5 Conclusions, Limitations and Further Developments

5.1 Theoretical and Practical Contribution

The theoretical contribution of the study lies in the provision of a preliminary knowledge about the service reshoring, by leveraging on what has already been found and tested in the manufacturing context. The application of the Delphi method allowed to overcome the limitations surrounding the studied phenomenon (e.g., lack of secondary information, primary cases inaccessibility, dynamicity features). Furthermore, by relying on a panel of trustable experts, we were able to derive insights about the relevance and characteristics of the reshoring phenomenon in the service context. For managers, the study provides valuable insights about what elements to consider when assessing a reshoring decision (i.e. the drivers) and the characteristics of the context that they need to take care of.

5.2 Limitations and Further Developments

Even if this research provides different insights for advancement of knowledge of service business reshoring, it presents some limitations that need further improvements. Although we carefully selected experts ensuring a mix of theoretical and practical expertise within the panel, the study involved mainly academics. Therefore, future works could address a more practical point of view, involving mainly managers and practitioners. Moreover, as this study lies on specific components of reshoring (drivers and contingency factors), future studies will explore other dimensions of the phenomenon including but not limited to barriers and outcomes. Finally, future research will have the opportunity to analyse how the pandemic will change companies' propensity to reshore their business services.

References

1. Kinkel, S., Maloca, S.: Drivers and antecedents of manufacturing offshoring and backshoring-a German perspective. J. Purch. Supply Manag. 15, 154–165 (2009)
2. Fratocchi, L., Di Mauro, C., Barbieri, P., et al.: When manufacturing moves back: concepts and questions. J. Purch. Supply Manag. 20, 54–59 (2014)

3. Albertoni, F., Elia, S., Massini, S., Piscitello, L.: The reshoring of business services: reaction to failure or persistent strategy? J. World Bus. **52**, 417–430 (2017)
4. Eisenhardt, K.M., Nujen, B.B., Halse, L.L., et al.: A new paradigm for systematic literature reviews in supply chain management. J. Oper. Manag. **9**, 37–46 (2018)
5. Barbieri, P., Ciabuschi, F., Fratocchi, L., Vignoli, M.: What do we know about manufacturing reshoring? J. Glob. Oper. Strateg. Sourc. **11**, 79–122 (2018)
6. Wiesmann, B., Snoei, J.R., Hilletofth, P., Eriksson, D.: Drivers and barriers to reshoring: a literature review on offshoring in reverse. Eur. Bus. Rev. **29**, 15–42 (2017)
7. Kotler, P.: Marketing Management, Analysis, Planning, Implementation, and Control, Philip Kotler. Prentice-Hall International, London (1994)
8. Grönroos, C.: Service Management and Marketing: Managing the Moments of Truth in Service Competition. Jossey-Bass, San Francisco (1990)
9. Stentoft, J., Olhager, J., Heikkilä, J., Thoms, L.: Manufacturing backshoring: a systematic literature review. Oper. Manag. Res. **9**(3–4), 53–61 (2016). https://doi.org/10.1007/s12063-016-0111-2
10. Gray, J.V., Skowronski, K., Esenduran, G., Rungtusanatham, M.J.: The reshoring phenomenon: what supply chain academics ought to know and should do. J. Supply Chain Manag. **49**, 27–33 (2013)
11. Kinkel, S.: Future and impact of backshoring-Some conclusions from 15 years of research on German practices. J. Purch. Supply Manag. **20**, 63–65 (2014)
12. Johansson, M., Boffelli, A., Olhager, J., Kalchschmidt, M.: A meta-analysis of reshoring case studies: the influence of contingency factors on the relocation decision, New Orleans (2019)
13. Donaldson, L.: The Contingency Theory of Organizations (2014)
14. Sousa, R., Voss, C.A.: Contingency research in operations management practices. J. Oper. Manag. **26**, 697–713 (2008)
15. Kembro, J., Näslund, D., Olhager, J.: Information sharing across multiple supply chain tiers: a Delphi study on antecedents. Int. J. Prod. Econ. **193**, 77–86 (2017)
16. Yaniv, I.: Group diversity and decision quality: amplification and attenuation of the framing effect. Int. J. Forecast. **27**, 41–49 (2011)
17. Ogden, J.A., Petersen, K.J., Carter, J.R., Monczka, R.M.: Supply management strategies for the future: a Delphi study. J. Supply Chain Manag. **41**, 29–48 (2005)
18. Huscroft, J.R., Hazen, B.T., Hall, D.J., et al.: Reverse logistics: past research, current management issues, and future directions. Int. J. Logist. Manag. **24**, 304–327 (2013)
19. Gordijn, S.J., Beune, I.M., Thilaganathan, B., et al.: Consensus definition of fetal growth restriction: a Delphi procedure. Ultrasound Obstet. Gynecol. **48**, 333–339 (2016)
20. Romero, D., Gaiardelli, P., Pezzotta, G., Cavalieri, S.: The impact of digital technologies on services characteristics: towards digital servitization. In: Ameri, F., Stecke, K.E., von Cieminski, G., Kiritsis, D. (eds.) APMS 2019. IFIP AICT, vol. 566, pp. 493–501. Springer, Cham (2019). https://doi.org/10.1007/978-3-030-30000-5_61

Digital and Physical Testbed for Production Logistics Operations

Jannicke Baalsrud Hauge[1,2(✉)], Masoud Zafarzadeh[1],
Yongkuk Jeong[1], Yi Li[3], Wajid Ali Khilji[1], and Magnus Wiktorsson[1]

[1] KTH Royal Institute of Technology, Södertälje, Sweden
jmbh@kth.se
[2] Bremer Insitut fur Produktion und Logistik GmbH (BIBA), Bremen, Germany
[3] Fraunhofer-Chalmers Centre for Industrial Mathematics, Gothenburg, Sweden

Abstract. Digitalisation and automation of existing processes are key factors for competitive industry, but still logistics operations are often dominated by manual work. A shift towards higher degree of automation within existing infrastructure is often challenged by high cost and complex processes, thus a return-on-investment is hardly achievable within decent time. The experience has shown that it is hard to assess all restrictions and interactions between new and old components before any new equipment or infrastructure is implemented and put into operation. This paper presents and discusses if the usage of digital twins representing and simulating a physical part can support the related assessing and decision-making processes. In this context, this paper presents a production logistics test-bed includes physical devices, an IoT-infrastructure and simulation software for innovation as well as operational management purposes.

Keywords: Technology assessment · Cyber-physical system · Production logistics

1 Technology Assessment Challenge

The cost of logistics is often high, but with minimal value-added contribution [1, 2]. Consequently, stakeholders are looking into how to use technology to offer the same or better services at a lower cost [3–5].

This trend encounter several challenges, which concerns more the implementation of different components in an existing operative environment than the technical development [6, 7]. A key challenges is related to assessing how different new components will interact with the existing systems - i.e. a typically challenge when dealing with technology introduction in complex system [5]. The usage of test-beds can contribute to overcoming these challenges [8]. However, it will not sufficiently contribute to understand the interactions of new components in an industrial operative environment, since there are several context related challenges such as physical limitations. For example, a challenge is related to the decentralised decision-making process carried out by the autonomous robots (like automated guided vehicles, or smart cargo) [1, 3, 9]. The usage of digital twins can help in overcoming this challenge, since it can visualise

© IFIP International Federation for Information Processing 2020
Published by Springer Nature Switzerland AG 2020
B. Lalic et al. (Eds.): APMS 2020, IFIP AICT 591, pp. 625–633, 2020.
https://doi.org/10.1007/978-3-030-57993-7_71

the differences between the optimal path based on algorithms and the optimal path based on the inbuilt decision-system in the AGV.

The focus of this article is to discuss how digital twins can contribute to support the decision-making process of selecting the right components for a specific task both related to the degree of automation and the digitalisation of the operations. The rest of the article first describes the requirements on a digital twin used for decision-making; secondly how the manipulation of the digital twin can be used for a better understanding of the system and components interactions, before the test-bed we are using is described in more detailed. Finally, we describe how the different components are integrated and interacting and as well as the first results. The last section discusses the main challenges and the next steps.

2 Digital Twin Preconditions for Production Logistics' Activities Planning

Technology introduction has a large impact on the organisation of operational processes both at managerial and operative level [9]. Therefore, it is not sufficient to only pay attention to the technical aspects, but also required to predict their outcomes and based on that, make right decisions. According to [10] digital twins can support planning as well as prediction of the working processes. Regarding the definition of digital twin, we build it upon the definition by Tao et al. [9] p. 3566 as well as the characteristics of digital twin as described in [9] in respect to (a) real-time reflection (b) interaction and convergence and (c) self-evolution. As described in the introduction, a main challenge of introducing concepts like IoT, CPS, and Industrie 4.0 etc. in existing environments is the assessment of how the technology will affect the whole organisation and interact with existing solutions. According to [11–13] digital twins that can be manipulated can support the decision-making process. Regarding the assessment of autonomous and decentralized decision-making, which is required in cyber-physical systems [14, 15] it is hard to model these with the right interactions with other system components and with the right routing (decided upon by the autonomous object) [3, 10]. However based on experiences on importing sensor data from a lab-environment into the virtual environment, comparing the routes and interaction with the first simulations, and then modify and manipulate these data in the digital twin (by using game mechanics), a better system understanding can be achieved [16].

Digital twin can mirror or simulate complex scenarios very close to the reality [9, 15–17]. Besides providing an opportunity to be used as a learning and awareness-increasing tool in which operators, or management can use virtual reality (VR) tools to experience the real working conditions with high precision [18], the digital twin can support the introduction of new technologies and installations within the existing physical environment [18, 19]. In this case, we simulate the working processes and observe the material movements, machines, robots etc. and their interactions [20]. One of the Swedish test-beds focuses on production logistics, i.e. it focuses on the material and information handling within the production system, with strong and integrated interfaces to supply chain management. This physical test-bed should allow testing of a) man to material technologies b) robot to material c) material to man and d) material to robot. Furthermore, in order to realise the latter, it should explore the usage of Real time locating system (RTLS) and the interaction and operation of different AGVs. It should be set up to meet the industrial need for improved demand assessment, dynamic and more efficient milk-runs, shortened cycle times, reduced bullwhip effects, highly transparent and integrated supply chains as well as improvements in production planning, real-time information flows, end-to-end supply chain transparency and general improvements in flexibility [21]. By the four pillars of technology support, real-time information, interoperability and decentralized decisions core technology areas needed should include real-time data acquisition, organization, and management; digital twin representation; data analytics for logistics applications; and digital twin-based shop-floor management and control [17].

3   The Physical and Digital Test-Bed

3.1   Physical Environment

The focus of the first set-up is on connecting equipment and RTLS, since these are a prerequisite for being able to realise a transparent and efficient material flow from one warehouse to a production site as visualised in Fig. 1. The initial demonstration scenario is to kit three different parts in two different kits by introducing a UR (collaborative robot), an AGV, a Kinect vision system, and a RTLS. The AGV transport the parts from storage position to the UR robot station, which performs the kiting with the help of the vision system. The kitted parts will be transported by the AGV to the assembly station at the end.

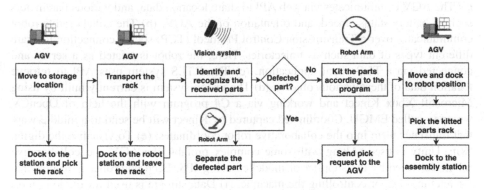

Fig. 1. Material flow process within the testbed

In order to investigate the problems mentioned in Sect. 2, the physical objects and the digital twin are integrated in a single system, which components communicate via a data streaming bus. This system interconnects all components to make use of digital twin of the real-world scenario. As a first step, communication between each component was realised. A data streaming bus, which will hold and serve messages wherever needed was chosen for this purpose. Secondly, there is an application layer, which is required in order to write business logic or calculations. In addition, data storage and digital twin ought to be connected through the application layer. Figure 2 represents the system architecture for the production logistics digital twin.

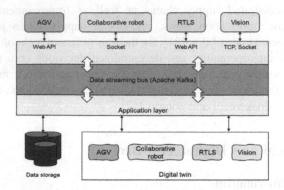

Fig. 2. Production logistics digital twin system architecture

3.2 Digital Environment Building the IoT Solution

In the digital environment, replica components of the physical environment are defined. Each replicated component has to go through the data streaming bus and application layer to send and receive information from the physical environment since the operating systems, data formats, and communication methods are different by each component. Next describes communication between the components in more details: (a) The AGV communicates via web API to share location data, and various parameters such as battery status, speed, and orientation of the AGV. (b) The collaborative robot communicates over a Transmission Control Protocol (TCP) socket connection to share different types of data such as trajectories. Here, the robot is treated as a server and connected via a TCP client application. (c) The RTLS system uses API to retrieve location data of these various objects. (d) The vision system is currently built by using Microsoft Xbox Kinect and working via a C# program with the help of OpenCV wrapper, called EMGU. Coordinated captured by Kinect will be send to a middle-ware that translates them into the collaborative robot coordinates. (e) To visualise the digital twin, Unity is used. Along with some complex prefabs like AGV and collaborative robot, delivered by the supplier or modelled using IPS. Each controller is responsible for fetching data or controlling the machine. (f) Data storage is used for the long-term data solution for data analytics, or data mining aiming to replay a particular scenario. The next section describes the different possibilities we have for the models in the digital twin, as well as outlines what we currently mainly look at.

The digital environment does not only mirror the physical environment in the testbed, but also allow 'manipulation' to allow experimentation with different technologies and equipment prior to the decision in a virtual world.

3.3   Applications for Workstation Design

As described above, it is needed to know what granularity our models should have, depends on what we intend to use them for. For the purpose of the test-bed and the given requirements, we need different granularities for different manipulations. Therefore, three examples in this spectrum of applications are presented. (a) engineering of workstations, (b) layout planning and (c) collaborative robotics. This will cover all the levels we need in the test-bed on long term and gives an overview of the different levels of required granularities. In order to realise the three different cases, specific modelling tool is used: a detailed analysis of robotic workstation design and AGV route planning has been carried out through IPS simulation tool shown in Fig. 3. The UR robot trajectories during the kitting process is simulated to calculate the required space to place kitting boxes, loading rack, and AGV docking position. Besides, the required distances for safe operation is calculated here. The AGV movement within the testbed area is simulated based on IPS route planning algorithm, which is the optimal path. The simulated path can be compared with actual path taken by the AGV to compare the deviations and root cause analysis.

Fig. 3. Using IPS simulation tool to engineer workstation design and AGV route planning within the testbed environment

3.4   Applications for Logistics Operations Analysis

The digital twin is used both with pure simulation data as well as with data from what we already have in operation to figure out the integration and interaction of AGV and picking robot investigating how the AGV is doing its mission scheduling and how this can be improved. Interaction and interference with existing systems as well as to decide upon the right new object (like the type of AGV) is a challenge as described earlier. Secondly, another challenge is that there is limited information about the algorithm the AGVs are using for calculating their path. In this case, we have however full control over the algorithm the digital twin of the AGV (modelled using IPS), which is the optimised algorithm. Comparing the results of the digital twin optimised algorithm and the physical movements of the AGV can give valuable information on the behaviour and thus help in the assessment of the suitability for implementation in different environments. Furthermore, the integration of the physical data in the digital twin allows a better visualisation that can be used for: (a) Detailed investigation of the exact movements of the AGV or collaborative robot (as shown in Fig. 4). (b) Using a re-play function as well as combining different experiments in one single digital twin scenario helps to understand the variation in movements as well as to recognise patterns (i.e. continuously occurring deviations between real movements and optimised calculated paths). (c) To explore an environment, which might have no or limited access (either using VR, AR or a 3D computer model on the PC). This can be used for teaching purposes to explain the interaction of the different components as well as for letting the students try out simple actions in a safe environment. Figure 4 illustrates this possibility. The picture to the left shows the digital model of the lab environment. The viewer can use a camera to move around and experience the room. Besides the detail of the models- here the path of the AGV- is visualised. The image to the right shows the movement of the physical AGV (data imported in the Unity model via the communication bus).

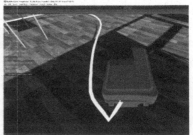

Fig. 4. Tracking AGV in real time within the digital twin

The digital twin has the capability to start the different physical operations via the digital twin interface. This opens up the possibility for carrying out experiments in risk areas. In this case, except few individuals, most of the personnel do not have the right access to operate the physical equipment on site, can perform experiments through digital twin. This increases the possibilities to utilise expensive lab equipment to a higher degree.

The mixed-reality environment, which we have described here, is in its prototypical implementation phase and the results are preliminary, but promising. During the last semester, the lab used as part of a master course for production logistics. Here a group of students carried out experiments studying the exact movements of the AGV in the physical lab. At that time, it was not possible to import and store the data in the digital twin for visualisation, but the collected data will now be imported and compared with the ideal (optimised) movements. Secondly, the first tests of using the digital twin for educational purposes have been successfully tried out in different labs. We have therefore now integrated our digital–physical twin environment for educational purposes in a digitalisation course. The remote control scenario is so far working well as long as it is operated within the network.

In the next step, it will also be possible to run and manipulate the model from outside. This will allow us to connect different test-beds to one single digital test-bed in order to look at larger challenges. The simulated optimized route in the digital twin will be compared to the actual chosen route by AGV in the physical environment. Besides, quality control checkpoints needs to be located as well as to investigate how to embed this into the material flow process.

4 Discussion and Conclusion

The focus of this article is to discuss how digital twins can be used for technology assessment. The digital twin has been used to analyse workstation design and AGV route planning with a focus on understanding how the granularity in the modelling used in the digital twin affect the transferability of the results achieved with the digital twin technology assessment to a physical world. By using a testbed environment, it has been possible to compare the technology assessment in the digital twin with a technology assessment of the physical environment and based on this draw conclusion about the need of granularity differences in the modelling. Main conclusion is that the granularity of the model is one of the key limiting factors for using a digital twin for technology assessment of real-world/physical logistical operations.. In this case, picking operation is simulated to analyse required space, cycle time, and safety. Compare to a manual system, a fully automated system is less flexible as human has much higher level of intelligence, but it has drawbacks such as mistakes, fatigue and less availability, however looking into the degree of granularity for the models, the experiments shows that this can be fairly low as long as we are only interested in cycle time and costs, but needs to be high for safety and medium for space usage For AGV route planning, the results showed how the AGV might behave in the physical environment compare to IPS simulated model. For these first experiments, a low granularity was needed, the required space, routes, possible hinders and safety concerns could be sufficiently well analysed. The collaboration with UR robot is another issue, which we could analyse by using digital twin and where we have to conclude that a high granularity is required.

In general, the primary results of how digital twin can be used for technology assessment in production logistics are promising. However, more tests and investigations are required to be able to be more explicit.

Acknowledgment. The present work was carried out partly within the project DIGILOG (Produktion 2030, Vinnova) and UniLog (Central Baltic program, grant no. CB743). This presentation does not represent the opinion of the European Community or Vinnova, and the European Community and Vinnova are not responsible for any use that might be made of its content.

References

1. Veres, P., Bányai, T., Illés, B.: Intelligent transportation systems to support production logistics. In: Jármai, K., Bolló, B. (eds.) Vehicle and Automotive Engineering. LNME, pp. 245–256. Springer, Cham (2017). https://doi.org/10.1007/978-3-319-51189-4_24
2. Christopher, M.: Logistics and Supply Chain Management, 5th edn. Prentice Hall (2016)
3. Forcolin, M., et al.: EURIDICE - IoT applied to logistics using the intelligent cargo concept. In: Thoben, K.-D., Stich, V., Imtiaz, A. (eds.) ICE Proceedings (2011)
4. Zunder, T., et al.: Is it possible to manage and plan co-modal freight transport without a centralised system? Int. J. Appl. Logist. (IJAL) 3(2), 15 (2012)
5. Strandhagen, J.O., et al.: Logistics 4.0 and emerging sustainable business models. Adv. Manuf. 5, 359 (2017). https://doi.org/10.1007/s40436-017-0198-1
6. Patil, Y.: 6 key IoT implementation challenges for enterprises to consider (2018). https://www.saviantconsulting.com/blog/iot-implementation-challenges-enterprises.aspx
7. Ek, I., Wiggberg, M., Frykblom, P.: Hur kan staten främja användandet av digitaliseringens möjligheter i näringslivet?, vol. 2. Östersund (2018)
8. Bosson, H., Ingmarsson, J.: Digitalisering av svensk industri-kartläggning av svenska styrkor och utmaninger. Roland Berger AB (2016)
9. Tao, F., et al.: Digital twin driven product design, manufacturing and service with big data. Int. J. Adv. Manuf. Techn. 94, 3563–3576X (2018)
10. Yao, F., Keller, A., Ahmad, M., Ahmad, B., Harrison, R., Colombo, A.W.: Optimizing the scheduling of autonomous guided vehicle in a manufacturing process. In: 2018 IEEE 16th International Conference on Industrial Informatics (INDIN), Porto, pp. 264–269 (2018)
11. Brenner, B., Hummel, V.: Digital twin as enabler for an innovative digital shopfloor management system" in the ESB logistics Learning Factory at Reutlingen University. Procedia Manuf. 9, 198–205 (2017)
12. Ştefan, A., et al.: Approaches to reengineering digital games. In: ASME International Design Engineering Technical Conferences and Computers and Information in Engineering Conference, vol. 1B: 36th Computers and Information in Engineering Conference (2016). V01BT02A051. https://doi.org/10.1115/detc2016-60061
13. Baalsrud Hauge, J.: An educational framework for supporting the implementation of the intelligent cargo concept. Int. J. Adv. Logist. 5(2), 86–100 (2016). https://doi.org/10.1080/2287108x.2016.1185317
14. VDI-Richtlinie, VDI 3633 Simulation von Logistik-, Materialfluss- und Produktionssystemen – Begriffe
15. Nokelainen, P., Nevalainen, T., Niemi, K.: Mind or machine? Opportunities and limits of automation. In: Harteis, C. (ed.) The Impact of Digitalization in the Workplace. PPL, vol. 21, pp. 13–24. Springer, Cham (2018). https://doi.org/10.1007/978-3-319-63257-5_2
16. David, J., Lobov, A., Lanz, M.: Leveraging digital twins for assisted learning of flexible manufacturing systems. In: 2018 IEEE 16th International Conference on Industrial Informatics (INDIN), Porto, pp. 529–535 (2018)
17. Zhuang, C., et al.: Digital twin-based smart production management and control framework for the complex product assembly shop-floor. Int. J. Adv. Manuf. Technol. 96(1–4), 1149–1163 (2018)
18. Pfohl, H.C.: Produktionslogistik. In: Logistiksysteme. Springer, Heidelberg (2018)
19. Baalsrud Hauge, J.M., Engström, A., Stefan, I.A., Strömgren, J.: Bridging educational and working environments through pervasive approaches. In: Alcañiz, M., Göbel, S., Ma, M., Fradinho Oliveira, M., Baalsrud Hauge, J., Marsh, T. (eds.) JCSG 2017. LNCS, vol. 10622, pp. 296–307. Springer, Cham (2017). https://doi.org/10.1007/978-3-319-70111-0_27

20. Toivonen, V., et al.: The FMS Training Center - a versatile learning environment for engineering education. Procedia Manuf **23**, 135–140 (2018)
21. Hofmann, E., Rüsch, M.: Industry 4.0 and the current status as well as future prospects on logistics. Comput. Ind. **89**, 23–34 (2017)

Principles and Research Agenda for Sustainable, Data-Driven Food Production Planning and Control

Maggie Bresler[✉], Anita Romsdal, Jan Ola Strandhagen,
and Olumide E. Oluyisola

Norwegian University of Science and Technology, 7491 Trondheim, Norway
maggie.bresler@ntnu.no

Abstract. This paper investigates the topics of data, sustainability, and production planning and control in food supply chains from the perspective of industrial food producers. To stay competitive in an industry with low profit margins, strong competition, and sustainability concerns, food producers need new solutions. The capture, digitization, and use of producer and downstream supply chain data enable opportunities for using data in new ways to address the existing challenges. This study proposes some principles for sustainable, data-driven production planning and control (PPC) such as capturing real-time data and tacit knowledge for use in PPC. It then investigates how these principles can impact the sustainability for food producers and the overall supply chain, by giving benefits such as reduced food waste, lower inventory levels, and reduced planning time and effort. Future research topics should address topics such as data availability, use of data in PPC, potential value of data, sustainability trade-offs, and the applications of digital technology in PPC.

Keywords: Food industry · Production planning and control · Sustainability

1 Introduction

Previous studies have highlighted a need to increase sustainability and reduce food waste in food supply chains [1, 2], and companies need to investigate novel ways of increasing sustainability. A major contributor to food waste is an imbalance in supply and demand [3, 4], where for instance unsold inventories of perishable products produced in advance of customer orders are scrapped in large amounts in all stages of the supply chain [5]. Data and information sharing in supply chains has long been widely heralded for the potential to better match supply and demand [6–8]– leading many companies to invest heavily in information technologies to manage data and information [9, 10]. Further, advanced concepts and models for supply chain collaboration and information sharing have been developed, such as efficient consumer response, and collaborative planning, forecasting and replenishment [11, 12]. Yet, after over 30 years of research and development, few companies actually share information and proliferation of both technologies and models for supply chain information sharing remains limited [13, 14]. Simultaneously, the rise of digital technologies has a potential to

© IFIP International Federation for Information Processing 2020
Published by Springer Nature Switzerland AG 2020
B. Lalic et al. (Eds.): APMS 2020, IFIP AICT 591, pp. 634–641, 2020.
https://doi.org/10.1007/978-3-030-57993-7_72

transform the way data is used, both to improve current operations and innovate how processes in supply chains are carried out [15, 16].

This paper investigates data sharing in food supply chains from the perspective of industrial food producers. Based on the assumption that data from downstream actors is available, the purpose of the paper is to propose a set of principles for how such external data can be used and combined with internal data to change the way food production is planned and controlled with an ultimate aim of reducing food waste and increasing sustainability. The result is a research agenda that outlines issues and ideas for how to achieve sustainable, data-driven food production planning and control.

2 Theoretical Background

2.1 Sustainability and Food Supply Chains

In addition to the overriding necessity to be economically viable, society now expect firms to balance their financial, environmental, and social goals [17]. For environmental aspects, since planning and control includes managing resources, the consumption of resources such as water, energy, and materials are relevant. Also, along with food waste, other wastes and pollution can be created during manufacturing such as greenhouse gas emissions, waste-water, or other non-food production waste including hazardous waste, food losses, and packaging material waste [18]. Social metrics that relate directly to PPC are more difficult to identify, but PPC utilizes human personnel, so job satisfaction is as an important aspect to consider [19]. Furthermore, the food industry has distinguishing characteristics that set it apart from other industrial sectors. Food is perishable, so there are product-dependent constraints on inventory holding time as well as handling and storage environment requirements. Industrial food production seeks maximize efficiency and minimize long change-over and set-up times. Production is sequence dependent, with certain colors, flavors, and allergens produced after others to shorten the changeovers as well. Demand of some food products is dependent on seasons, holidays, and promotions. Food supply chains consist of many actors, including raw material suppliers, producers, wholesalers, retailers, and consumers [20].

2.2 Planning and Control of Production and Supply Chains

PPC can follow a variety of strategies, from engineer-to-order to make-to-stock (MTS) strategies; the difference is how much planning and production is based on customer orders or forecasts. For MTS, production is based on forecasts which are made using methods that include moving average, exponential smoothing, and algorithms accounting for trend and seasonality. After forecasting, production planning is done periodically at different aggregation levels (by time or groups of products) and must also be integrated with the inventory distribution needs at various stages of the supply chain. Plans are typically created using enterprise resource planning (ERP) and advanced planning and scheduling (APS) software systems, but these plans are not integrated and optimized across supply chain actors [21].

However, it is becoming increasing necessary for manufacturing firms compete not just individually with other firms, but as a supply chains since a lot of the profitability is derived through proper planning and control of the activities of the extended supply chain [22]. Supply chain planning and control takes into account the needs of multiple supply chain actors together. This is important as many benefits, such as reduced bullwhip, can be gained by thinking about how to optimize the whole system and not just the processes of one actor. Strandhagen, Dreyer and Romsdal [23] presented the Principles for Intelligent, Demand-Driven Control as a step towards realizing more demand-driven supply chain relationships. These principles include capturing and using real-time data for decision-making and performance measurement, sharing data across the supply chain, and moving the customer-order decoupling-point (CODP) toward less-forecast based and more order-based approaches such as make-to-order (MTO).

2.3   Digital Technology

Traditionally, planning and control was carried out through the use of ERP and APS systems for planning, using input static and historical data and optimization parameters to plan production. However, these systems still heavily rely on human input for updating parameters and providing accurate and complete data. To make production "smarter", there is a growing trend to use Industry 4.0 methods such as artificial intelligence (AI) to address a wide variety of industrial challenges. AI is a broad category of learning-based algorithms that have the potential to find patterns in data that humans cannot and use these underlying patterns to make suggestions in, for example, the planning and control of food production. There is research being done to apply AI to PPC, with application areas such as product family and layout optimization, identifying the right control strategy, and predicting supply chain disruptions [24, 25]. In order to use digital technology, the data must be collected and digitized. RFID and networked sensors can collect and transmit data in real-time to give a picture of the current state various points in the supply chain, from production to inventory [26]. While there is not yet a consensus among practitioners about how or whether all data has value and what specific data has value, it is believed that real-time process-monitoring data is useful in forecasting and production situations [16], and data such as remaining shelf life has been shown to improve alignment of supply and demand [27].

3   Method

This is a conceptual paper that explores the use of data to improve PPC. In the theoretical background, we outlined key concepts and trends that are expected to have an impact on PPC in the food sector. Through the illustrative example of a food producer, we highlight current practices and challenges to show the industry need and desire for data-driven PPC. These are then used in the following chapter to develop a set of principles for sustainable, data-driven PPC by considering the challenges of current food PPC, what different types of data are useful to PPC, what new data and technology are now available, and how the data should be used within existing or new processes. We then discuss their potential impact on sustainability because, while the principles do have specific elements of sustainable practice, the sustainability implications of all the principles are not immediately obvious. Finally, the literature, principles and discussions are synthesized into an agenda for further research.

4 Brynild – An Illustration of Food PPC Challenges

Brynild Gruppen is a medium-sized Norwegian food producer with nearly 200 employees and an annual revenue of EUR 70 mill. The company's factory produces 46 variants of sugar confectionery products, 44 chocolate variants and 50 nut variants. The Norwegian market for confectionery and snack products is dominated by large international actors and Brynild Gruppen has a market share of approx. 14%. Their main customers are the four Norwegian wholesaler – retailer dyads that control 100% of the retail market, with wholesalers requiring a 98% service level. Consumer demand for snacks and confectionery products is highly seasonal and affected by promotional activities and product introductions, making demand forecasting difficult.

Brynild Gruppen's production strategy is mainly MTS for standard products, with build-up of inventory of seasonal products months in advance. The products typically have a shelf-life of 6–18 months, and products that approach or pass their industry-standard sell-by date are sold at reduced prices through alternative sales channels or scrapped. Brynild Gruppen has limited access to data from the supply chain beyond orders from wholesalers, an annual joint planning with retailers regarding timing and product variants for promotional activities and product launches, and the opportunity to buy aggregated sales data from a national grocery database. The company's seasonal products are sold on buy-back agreements, where customers in some cases have been credited up to 35% for unsold goods at season end. Thus, Brynild Gruppen carries a large portion of the risk associated with seasonal products, while having little or no insight into actual consumer demand or influence over inventory levels in retail stores. This complicates demand forecasting and production planning and limits the company's ability to quickly respond to changes in demand. The consequences include both lost income and scrapping of unsold products in several supply chain stages. To improve sustainability and supply chain performance, Brynild Gruppen has initiated an innovation research project together with their largest customer, one other food producer, two ICT system providers and three research institutions. One of the purposes is to explore how data from downstream actors in the supply chain can be used in PPC – and thereby create a smart, transparent, sustainable food supply chain.

5 Principles for Sustainable, Data-Driven PPC

In this section, we firstly adapt the existing principles for intelligent, demand-driven supply chains [23] to the PPC context (see Table 1). Secondly, we discuss how the application of the proposed principles can impact on sustainability in a food context, outlining effects for both food producers and for downstream supply chain actors.

Table 1. Principles for sustainable, data-driven PPC

P1	Promotional plans from producer/brand owner and downstream actors should be transformed into data to be used for PPC
P2	Historic demand data on seasonal products from the producer/brand owner and downstream actors should be transformed into data to be used for PPC
P3	Real-time data on demand and inventory levels from retailers and wholesalers should be transformed into data to be used for PPC
P4	Real-time data on finished goods and WIP inventory levels should be captured at the producer and used for PPC
P5	Tacit planning knowledge and experience on production planning should be captured and transformed into data to be used for PPC
P6	Tacit knowledge of production processes and machines/production lines should be captured and used for PPC
P7	Real-time performance data (including sustainability performance) should be captured, measured, and used for performance visualization and PPC
P8	Plans should be adjusted based on updated data from the producer and downstream supply chain
P9	AI and learning-based analytics should be applied to gain new PPC insights
P10	The proportion of automated PPC processes should be increased to minimize planning time and reduce repetitive tasks for human planners, freeing up human planners for more complex PPC tasks
P11	The CODP should be continuously evaluated, exploring potential for more order-based or hybrid production strategies (both across product range and over time/seasons)
P12	Sustainability trade-offs should be considered in PPC and visualized to support human decision-making

The principles presented above are aimed at improving PPC and subsequently sustainability. In the following paragraphs, we discuss the potential impacts the principles can have in a food supply chain context, both for producers and downstream stages. The use of data on promotional plans (P1) and seasonal demand (P2) in PPC will enable better alignment of supply and demand in the supply chain – subsequently decreasing food waste from overproduction and reducing lost sales due to stockouts. Any reduction of food waste will also reduce the expenditure of raw materials and other resources. Using real-time data in PPC (P3, P4, P7, P8) will also better align supply and demand, as well as increase food producers' responsiveness and flexibility to changes in the supply chain. This can allow for lower inventory levels, which in turn can increase inventory turnover and increase the days of remaining shelf life available in the downstream stages of the supply chain. This again reduces the risk of food waste of expired products in wholesale, retail and consumer households.

In particular, real-time data on demand and inventory levels (P3) of new products would allow a producer to adjust production volumes to early sales data, giving them time to ramp up production to avoid lost sales of a popular item or halt production to avoid food waste of a failed launch. Additionally, more real-time monitoring of performance (P7) on parameters such as inventory levels and product quality (e.g. temperature, humidity and remaining shelf life) through RFID and networked sensors can reduce food waste from quality degradation. However, while adjusting plans based on real-time data (P8) will improve the quality of the plans, it also requires an increase of planning cost through the increase of time and resources needed for the adjustments. Applying AI and learning-based analytics (P9) on PPC-relevant data can provide new and valuable insights, thereby reducing planning effort, time and cost. Automation of planning processes (P10) will also reduce the amount of repetitive planning tasks, thus leading to higher levels of job satisfaction for planners. The transformation of tacit knowledge to digital data (P5, P6) has the potential to improve PPC. Standardized knowledge can be used to improve production and planning processes – increasing speed, quality, efficiency, flexibility, etc. However, it is unclear how these principles could affect social sustainability. Digitizing tacit knowledge may make training easier but could also make planners feel less valuable and contribute to loss of deep experiential knowledge once algorithms replace human decision making. Any reconsideration of CODP towards more order-based production (P11) could reduce the risk of food waste due to overproduction. However, more order-based strategies such as MTO could be applicable for non-standard products (such as planned promotions) as the customer lead time expectations for standard products is typically considerably shorter than production lead time. Thus, hybrid approaches could be considered to ensure the high service level requirements are still met.

Considering all the above principles are expected to have impacts on sustainability, some indicators should be used to measure positive and negative effects (P12). Although food waste is an important indicator, it can be hard to measure and therefore other indicators should be included, such as inventory levels and remaining shelf life. It is not clear how different types of data can be used in PPC to achieve the potential benefits, nor is it clear if there are trade-offs, e.g. between financial and environmental sustainability, that should be considered in the application of the principles.

6   Towards a Research Agenda

In order to achieve the principles for sustainable, data-driven PPC discussed in the previous chapter in the food supply chain context, research is needed in some key areas. The topic of data availability is an underlying premise. Studies are needed to investigate which data would be useful for PPC, which data is currently available, which data is not captured, and how to capture and share data. In addition, how to use such data in PCC, including the development of logic and algorithms. Further, investigating how data can be utilized to improve existing processes and also how processes should be changed to better align supply and demand and thereby realize potential benefits. The full potential value of data also warrants further investigation. While food supply chain actors are interested in implementing new methods and technologies, wholesalers and retailers are likely to be hesitant to share data if all the benefits go to the producer. Therefore, studies into how the shared data can improve performance and identifying the possible benefits for producers and their downstream supply chain partners is needed. Key data mentioned in the principles also includes real-time data and tacit knowledge. Neither of these data types has been extensively studied in relation to PPC, so the capture and use of these data types in PPC should be investigated, both conceptually and empirically. In addition, while potential sustainability implications of the principles were outlined in chapter 5, several key questions remain. One relevant topic is how sustainability trade-offs can be accounted for in PPC, both in automated and human decision-making. Finally, in order to utilize new methods and technology to exploit the data, there is need for further study in how digital technology can be used in PPC.

7 Conclusion

This paper has illustrated how food producers can increase supply chain sustainability through data-driven PPC. Our proposed set of principles can be used by actors in the food supply chain to guide future collaboration and information sharing initiatives. However, the research agenda shows that more studies are needed before the principles can be implemented and the sustainability effects achieved. We believe there are great possibilities for increasing the application of data and technology in PPC to increase sustainability. While this study has limitations including the lack of validation of the principles and generalizability (which could be remedied through more rigorous methodology such as a structured literature review, multiple case studies, or a survey), this research has shown that there are great possibilities for increasing the application of data and technology in PPC to increase sustainability.

Acknowledgement. The research presented in this paper was conducted in collaboration with the DigiMat project, with financial support from NTNU, the participating companies and the Research Council of Norway.

References

1. Papargyropoulou, E., Lozano, R., Steinberger, J.K., Wright, N., Ujang, Z.B.: The food waste hierarchy as a framework for the management of food surplus and food waste. J. Clean. Prod. **76**(C), 106–115 (2014)
2. Gustavsson, J., Cederberg, C., Sonesson, U., Van Otterdijk, R., Meybeck, A.: Global Food Losses and Food Waste (2011)
3. Mena, C., Adenso-Diaz, B., Yurt, O.: The causes of food waste in the supplier–retailer interface: evidences from the UK and Spain. Res. Conserv. Recycl. **55**(6), 648–658 (2011)
4. Parfitt, J., Barthel, M., Macnaughton, S.: Food waste within food supply chains: quantification and potential for change to 2050. Philos. Trans. R. Soc. B **365**(1554), 3065–3081 (2010)
5. Priefer, C., Jörissen, J., Bräutigam, K.-R.: Food waste prevention in Europe – a cause-driven approach to identify the most relevant leverage points for action. Res. Conserv. Recycl. **109**, 155–165 (2016)
6. Lee, H.L., So, K.C., Tang, C.S.: The value of information sharing in a two-level supply chain. Manage. Sci. **46**(5), 626–643 (2000)
7. Zhou, H., Benton, W.C.: Supply chain practice and information sharing. J. Oper. Manage. **25** (6), 1348–1365 (2007)

8. Wang, X., Disney, S.M.: The bullwhip effect: progress, trends and directions. Eur. J. Oper. Res. **250**(3), 691–701 (2016)

9. Fawcett, S.E., Osterhaus, P., Magnan, G.M., Brau, J.C., McCarter, M.W.: Information sharing and supply chain performance: the role of connectivity and willingness. Supply Chain Manage. **12**(5), 358–368 (2007)

10. de Freitas, D.C., de Oliveira, L.G., Alcântara, R.L.C.: A theoretical framework to adopt collaborative initiatives in supply chains. Gest. Prod. **26**(3), e4194 (2019)

11. Fliedner, G.: CPFR: an emerging supply chain tool. Ind. Manage. Data Syst. **103**(1), 14–21 (2003)

12. Wood, A.: Efficient consumer response. Logist. Inf. Manage. **6**(4), 38–40 (1993)

13. Panahifar, F., Heavey, C., Byrne, P.J., Fazlollahtabar, H.: A framework for collaborative planning, forecasting and replenishment (CPFR): state of the art. J. Enterp. Inf. Manage. **28** (6), 838–871 (2015)

14. Kembro, J., Näslund, D.: Information sharing in supply chains, myth or reality? A critical analysis of empirical literature. Int. J. Phys. Distrib. Logist. Manage. **44**(3), 179–200 (2014)

15. Ustundag, A., Cevikcan, E.: Industry 4.0: Managing The Digital Transformation. SSAM. Springer, Cham (2018). https://doi.org/10.1007/978-3-319-57870-5

16. Oluyisola, O., Sgarbossa, F., Strandhagen, J.O.: Smart production planning and control: concept, use-cases and sustainability implications. Sustainability **12**(9), 3791 (2020)

17. Purvis, B., Mao, Y., Robinson, D.: Three pillars of sustainability: in search of conceptual origins. Sustain. Sci. **14**(3), 681–695 (2019)

18. Zarte, M., Pechmann, A., Nunes, I.L.: Indicator framework for sustainable production planning and controlling. Int. J. Sustain. Eng. **12**(3), 149–158 (2019)

19. Fernández-Macías, E.: Automation, Digitalisation and Platforms: Implications for Work and Employment (2018)

20. Romsdal, A.: Differentiated production planning and control in food supply chains. Doctoral thesis at Norwegian University of Technology and Science (NTNU), 2012:16 (2014)

21. Chopra, S.: Supply Chain Management: Strategy, Planning, and Operation. Pearson, Harlow (2016)

22. Vollmann, T.E.: Manufacturing Planning and Control for Supply Chain Management (2005)

23. Strandhagen, J., Dreyer, H.C., Romsdal, A.: Control model for intelligent and demand-driven supply chains. In: Managing Global Supply Chain Relationships: Operations, Strategies and Practices, pp. 49–70. IGI Global (2011)

24. Garetti, M., Taisch, M.: Neural networks in production planning and control. Prod. Plan. Control **10**(4), 324–339 (1999)

25. Brintrup, A., Pak, J., Ratiney, D., Pearce, T., Wichmann, P., Woodall, P., McFarlane, D.: Supply chain data analytics for predicting supplier disruptions: a case study in complex asset manufacturing. Int. J. Prod. Res. **58**(11), 3330–3341 (2019)

26. Strandhagen, J.O., Vallandingham, L.R., Fragapane, G., Strandhagen, J.W., Stangeland, A. B.H., Sharma, N.: Logistics 4.0 and emerging sustainable business models. Adv. Manuf. **5** (4), 359–369 (2017)

27. Kiil, K.: Aligning Supply and Demand in Grocery Retailing. Norwegian University of Science and Technology, Trondheim (2017)

Product-Service Systems in DSN

Agile Guideline for Development of Smart Services in Manufacturing Enterprises with Support of Artificial Intelligence

Mike Freitag[1](✉) and Oliver Hämmerle[2]

[1] Fraunhofer IAO, Nobelstraße 12, 70569 Stuttgart, Germany
mike.freitag@iao.fraunhofer.de
[2] Institut für Arbeitswirtschaft und Technologiemanagement IAT,
Universität Stuttgart, Nobelstraße 12, 70569 Stuttgart, Germany

Abstract. The shift from product-oriented to service-oriented business requires a rethink, especially in traditional companies in the mechanical and plant engineering industry. This guideline for the development of Smart Services is intended to illustrate the complexity and thus improve their handling, supporting the planning and modelling of a Smart Service. The Design Thinking Process is the first step in understanding the challenges associated with the reorientation of the business and in designing appropriate solutions. In the second step, an important part of the rethinking process of companies is the proactive development, revision or complete redesign of their business models. The third part of this guideline is the concept of agile service engineering with support of artificial intelligence, which can be understood as a link between the design thinking process and business model development and can be used as a management tool.

Keywords: Smart Service · Design thinking · Business model · Agile service engineering · Artificial intelligence

1 Introduction

This guideline describes the step-by-step development of Smart Services, especially in manufacturing sector. The term "Smart Services" refers to data-based, individually configurable service offerings consisting of services, digital services and products that are organized and provided via integrated platforms [1].

It is becoming increasingly important to offer suitable Smart Services to complement the products of manufacturing enterprises. Therefor an integrated development and subsequent management of these Smart Services is of central importance. Figure 1 illustrates the essential elements of this guideline for the development of Smart Services on the basis of the 3 phases:

- Design Thinking [2–4],
- Business model [5] and
- Agile Service Engineering [6].

B. Lalic et al. (Eds.): APMS 2020, IFIP AICT 591, pp. 645–652, 2020.
https://doi.org/10.1007/978-3-030-57993-7_73

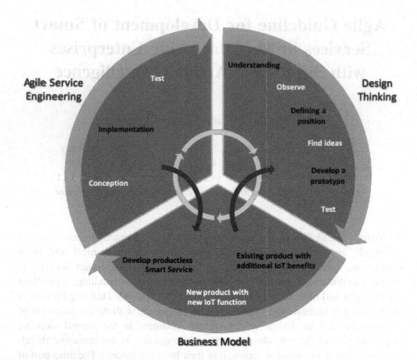

Fig. 1. The 3 essential components in the development of Smart Services with their respective phases

When a Smart Service is developed, both the three phases and the sub-processes in these phases can be repeated iteratively. Each of these three phases is already iteratively in progress. Especially in Design Thinking and agile Service Engineering, the iterative approach is a core element of the process model. The development of alternatives also plays an important role in business model modeling. In the approach presented in this paper, the possibilities of iteration are limited (dark grey arrows) due to small and medium-sized companies.

The individual phases are described below and are illustrated with examples.

2 Design Thinking

Plattner et al. [2] propose the 6 phases understanding, observing, defining a position, finding ideas, developing a prototype and testing, which are assigned to Design Thinking and shown in Fig. 1. These 6 phases are described below.

- Understanding
  - One possibility for this phase are expert interviews. Iterations are desired here.
- Observe
  - One possible tool is to use unknown test customers who document the user experience.

- Defining a position
  - The Institute of Design at Stanford provides a good overview of possible methods [3] like Customer Journey Map.
- Find ideas
  - The classical tool for this is brainstorming [4].
- Develop a prototype
  - Prototypes are to be used to create solutions that are comprehensible to the user in order to receive feedback from customers [4]. Prototypes are something haptic, such as Lego.
- Test
  - What do the testers particularly like? What wishes do they express? Which questions are asked? Do the testers have new or additional ideas?

3 Develop New Business Models

The development of new business models is based on innovative, smart products and services, which will increase added value and thus significant growth for companies in the future. The creation of data-driven business models is the core of the development of strategies for IoT.

"Business model" should be understood as the mapping of the performance system of a company or part of a company. In a simplified form, it describes how the company creates customer value through saleable products and services, what resources it needs to do so and how the service is provided [6]. If the products are "smart" and can collect data, this also means that companies can offer their customers added value beyond the actual product benefits: Smart services can be created in this way. As a result, business models are no longer limited to a pure product orientation, but are also data and service driven [1, 7–9].

When developing new business models in IoT, there are various options for companies, especially in the relationship between existing or newly developed products and the associated Smart Services, which are briefly described below. For introduction, three possible options of business models are presented here, which are particularly suitable for SMEs and are easy to implement.

Existing Product with Additional IoT Benefits

Here, products that are already established on the market and have possibly been used in the same way for some time are supplemented with IoT features, thus creating additional benefits. This variant represents the lowest level of IoT business models. This model uses the data generated by the purchase and use of a product to offer a new product or an addition to the original product. This allows completely new products to be developed or existing products to be improved. Therefor an innovative value proposition can be created, whereby previously unfamiliar customer groups can also be tapped, for example, by IoT services with agreed savings targets, Services to prevent machine/system failures, analysis and optimization solution for reducing consumption, data as a separate business, etc.

"Heidelberg Prinect" is a suitable case study and is briefly described below.

Case Study »Heidelberg Prinect«

"Heidelberg Prinect" offers intelligent machines that autonomously organize and run standardized print processes. This requires the harmonious interaction of six key factors: involving customers, reduce touchpoints, increase productivity and runtime, reduce waste and inventory, optimize consistency and repeatability and business intelligence. Figure 2 illustrates the concept of Heidelberg Prinect.

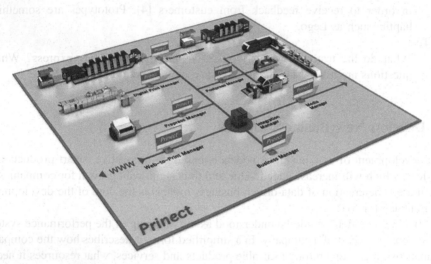

Fig. 2. Concept of Smart Service "Heidelberg Prinect" [10]

New Product with New IoT Function

Here, new products are developed that would not exist without the possibilities of IoT. In other words, a company uses the technologies of IoT to generate an innovative product that is fully equipped with new IoT functions. Companies previously unfamiliar with the industry can thereby establish disruptive innovations in markets previously unknown to them. Example: sale of new products with IoT function, sale of sensors for data acquisition, purchase of IoT applications in the "App Store" of an ecosystem.

The "Trumpf Axoom Eco-System" represents a suitable case study [11].

Develop Productless Smart Services

Many enterprises use agile methods in development of productless Smart Services. There are a number of different methods that can be used. They have some elements in common: they develop a service in small steps that are not planned in advance. To develop a new Smart Service it is necessary to use iterative cycles, this means that the results are tested and evaluated and the results of the tests are incorporated into the next interactive cycle. Furthermore, they are strongly user-centric, so the wishes and reactions of the users are considered at every stage of development.

Considerations of customer processes, the design of a digital ecosystem and the optimization of usability and user experience are also of great importance in the development of a Smart Service. Companies can use data to supplement completely productless Smart Services. Sensor data-based optimization of services, subscription for data analysis software solutions (SaaS models) and revenue share of the platform operator for applications on the platform are just some examples of productless Smart Services.

In order to develop a sustainable business model it is necessary to define a marketing strategy from a business management perspective. The determination of the clientele should be separated from the consideration of the users. Not every user group is automatically a customer group and willing to pay for the Smart Service - and even if the willingness to pay is positive, pricing is not always optimal, since in addition to relative willingness to pay indirect network effects must also be considered. This can be observed especially in Smart Services.

The market launch strategy starts with the definition of a problem or a user or customer group. Through agile development, in which the hypotheses are gradually captured and tested, a service can be developed with very high accuracy, which is also demanded by users and paid for by the clientele. At the same time, in order to prepare the actual market launch, the marketing and sales concept must be developed and implemented on the basis of the value proposition. This should be as iterative as product development. However, other factors are also decisive. Thus, it must be examined which (potential) competitors offer or will offer similar services in the future and whether they offer advantages from the point of view of the target person (price, use, access, range of functions, image, etc.).

This knowledge can be used to further develop and adapt the service or value proposition. The "DigitalClone" from Sentient Science is a suitable example for productless Smart Service [12].

4 Agile Service Engineering

One possible approach to manage the Smart Service is agile service engineering. This can be described by the three phases of conception, implementation and test, which in turn can be assigned to the three levels of business model management, smart service management and network management. These three levels contain a total of 12 development modules for the three phases of conception, implementation and test [13–16].

Figure 3 shows the three phases of agile service engineering with their respective 4 development modules.

The entire process is therefore not only focused on the Smart Service alone, but aims at the Smart Service as a holistic solution. As a result, the levels of business model management and network management are also considered. Each of the three phases contains four development modules.

Artificial Intelligence is part of the Smart Service Management. In a study by Fraunhofer IAO [18], companies that already have experience in using AI-applications were interviewed. The vast majority of the AI-applications were assigned to the provision of services (59%). Customer support (39%) and manufacturing (18%) follow at a considerable distance. If marketing and sales are added to the first two areas, an astonishingly high number of applications in which a high level of customer reference

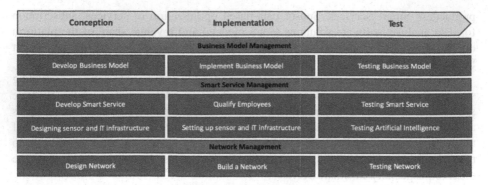

Fig. 3. 3 Phases of agile service engineering [17]

and possibly even direct customer integration can be assumed. From this it can be concluded that the use of artificial intelligence in companies does not only affect their own managers and employees, but to a large extent also the customers of the companies.

The study revealed basic AI-functionalities used by the respective applications. Data and information extraction are used most frequently (78%), followed by data-based forecasting (59%) and decision support and automation (51%).

Case Study »Heidelberg Prinect Production Manager«

To take the example of the Heidelberg Prinect from Sect. 3, the "Prinect Production Manager" - a new usage concept in the form of a rental model of the Prinect business intelligence platform - can be used as an example of agile service engineering. The Production Manager enables print shops of all sizes to use all the integration functions of the Prinect production workflow exactly as they need it. Customers can use all the Smart Service functions at any time. However, they do not pay for the licenses for the individual components but only for the actual monthly data consumption, which is calculated in m^2. The user fee also includes all automatic software updates so that the workflow is always up to date. While the necessary hardware is installed on the customer's premises, parts of the selected Prinect components are cloud-based.

"The digitalization of all processes is not a question of company size. If a print shop wants to remain competitive, it needs to address the issue," says Anthony Thirlby, Head of Prinect at Heidelberg. "It's about developing a digital business model that focuses on end customer requirements in terms of quality, flexibility, productivity, availability and delivery reliability. This can only be achieved with digitized, largely autonomous processes that enable print shop operators to focus on their customers.

5 Summary

The shift from product-oriented to service-oriented business requires a rethink, especially in traditional companies in the manufacturing industry. This guide for the development of Smart Services supported by Artificial Intelligence is intended to illustrate the complexity and thus improve their handling, supporting the planning and modelling of a Smart Service.

The Design Thinking process is important for understanding the challenges associated with the reorientation of the business and in designing appropriate solutions. Building on the Design Thinking process the proactive development, revision or complete redesign of their business models is an important part of the rethinking process of companies, that want to remain competitive and take advantage of the opportunities offered by IoT. The concept of agile service engineering as a management tool to manage the Smart Service can be understood as a link between the design thinking process and business model development.

Acknowledgements. This work has been partly funded by the German Federal Ministry of Education and Research (BMBF) through the Project "SmARtPlaS (No. 02K18D112), the project "DigiLab NPO – Digitallabor für Non-Profit-Organisationen 4.0" (No. 02L18A230) and the project "VARIETY", founded by the French Goverment. The authors wish to acknowledge the Commission, the Ministry and all the project partners for their contribution.

References

1. Arbeitskreis Smart Service Welt: Smart Service Welt – Umsetzungsempfehlungen für das Zukunftsprojekt Internet-basierte Dienste für die Wirtschaft. Abschlussbericht, acatech, Berlin (2015)
2. Plattner, H., Meinel, C., Weinberg, U.: Design-thinking - Understand-Improve-Apply. Landsberg am Lech: Mi-Fachverlag. Springer, Heidelberg (2009)
3. Brenner, W., Uebernickel, F., Abrell, T.: Design thinking as mindset, process, and toolbox. In: Brenner, W., Uebernickel, F. (eds.) Design Thinking for Innovation, pp. 3–21. Springer, Cham (2016). https://doi.org/10.1007/978-3-319-26100-3_1
4. Schallmo, D.R.A.: Design Thinking erfolgreich anwenden. So entwickeln Sie in 7 Phasen kundenorientierte Produkte und Dienstleistungen, Springer Gabler, Wiesbaden (2017)
5. Wirtz, B.W., Schilke, O., Ullrich, S.: Strategic development of business models implications of the Web 2.0 for creating value on the internet. Long Range Plan. **43**(2–3), 272–290 (2010)
6. Stich, V., Schumann, J.H., Beverungen, D., Gudergan, G., Jussen, P.: Digitale Dienstleistungsinnovationen Smart Services agil und kundenorientiert entwickeln. Springer Vieweg Berlin (2019)
7. Bundesministerium für Wirtschaft und Energie: Existenzgründungsportal des BMWi (2017). http://www.existenzgruender.de/DE/Unternehmen-fuehren/Erfolgsfaktoren/Kooperationen/Kooperationsformen/inhalt.html. Accessed 4 Nov 2019
8. Dhar, V., Agarwal, R.: Big data, data science, and analytics: the opportunity and challenge for IS research. Inf. Syst. Res. **25**(3), 443–448 (2014)
9. Emmrich, V., Döbele, M., Bauernhansl, T., Paulus-Rohmer, D., Schatz, A., Weskamp, M.: Geschäftsmodell-Innovation durch Industrie 4.0: chancen und Risiken für den Maschinen- und Anlagenbau. München, Stuttgart: Dr. Wieselhuber & Partner, Fraunhofer IPA (2015)
10. Heidelberger Druckmaschinen AG: Hompage der Heidelberg Prinect (2019). https://www.heidelberg.com/global/de/lifecycle/workflow/prinect_overview.jsp. Accessed 4 Nov 2019
11. Trumpf: Homepage von Trumpf (2019). https://www.trumpf.com/de_AT/unternehmen/presse/pressemitteilungen-global/pressemitteilung-detailseite-global/press/release/maschinen-sprechen-axoom-uebersetzt/. Accessed 4 Nov 2019

12. Sentient Science: Homepage der Sentient Science (2019). https://sentientscience.com/platform/. Accessed 4 Nov 201
13. Freitag M., Kremer D., Hirsch M., Zelm M.: An approach to standardise a service life cycle management. In: Zelm, M., Sinderen, M., Pires, L.F., Doumeingts, G. (eds.) Enterprise Interoperability, pp. 115–126. Wiley, Chichester (2013)
14. Freitag, M.: Ein konfigurierbares Vorgehensmodell für die exportorientierte Entwicklung von technischen Dienstleistungen. Dissertation, Universität Stuttgart, Fraunhofer Verlag, Stuttgart (2014)
15. Freitag, M., Hämmerle, O.: Smart Service Lifecycle Management. Wt werkstattstechnik online 106, H 7/8, S. 477–482 (2016)
16. Wiesner, S., Thoben, K.-D.: Cyber-physical product-service systems. In: Biffl, S., Lüder, A., Gerhard, D. (eds.) Multi-Disciplinary Engineering for Cyber-Physical Production Systems, pp. 63–88. Springer, Cham (2017). https://doi.org/10.1007/978-3-319-56345-9_3
17. Freitag, M., Wiesner, S.: Smart service lifecycle management: a framework and use case. In: Moon, I., Lee, Gyu M., Park, J., Kiritsis, D., von Cieminski, G. (eds.) APMS 2018. IAICT, vol. 536, pp. 97–104. Springer, Cham (2018). https://doi.org/10.1007/978-3-319-99707-0_13
18. Bauer, W., Ganz, W., Hämmerle, M., Renner, T.: Künstliche Intelligenz in der Unternehmenspraxis – Studie zu Auswirkungen auf Dienstleistung und Produktion. Fraunhofer Verlag, Stuttgart (2019)

Collaborative Design and Engineering

Framework for Identifying Gripper Requirements for Collaborative Robot Applications in Manufacturing

Omkar Salunkhe[✉] [iD], Patrik Fager, and Åsa Fast-Berglund [iD]

Department of Industrial and Material Sciences,
Chalmers University of Technology, Gothenburg, Sweden
omkar.salunkhe@chalmers.se

Abstract. Robots designed for collaborative applications based on the inter-action between human operators are on the rise in the industry. With the involvement of humans, special consideration should be given to select the end effector of cobot generally referred to as grippers. This paper presents a framework for the identification of gripper requirements in a systematic way. The paper first provides general information on DFAA analysis and task allocation methods used in the framework. Different levels of interaction and gripper principles are also presented. Scenarios for varying levels of interaction are presented, followed by the framework to identify gripper requirements with an explanation for each step in the framework. The advantages of using the proposed framework are shown in the discussion, followed by concluding remarks.

Keywords: Collaborative application · Gripper · Framework · SII-Lab

1 Introduction

Robots designed for collaborative applications, as a stand-alone entity, is a manipulator with advanced sensors that enhance its capabilities to work alongside a human [1]. Cobots need to work together with humans to achieve an actual collaboration. The complete setup of cobot, gripper, and workspace arrangement to perform a specific task along with a human is called a collaborative application. There is a growing interest in collaborative applications in industry. With cobot applications, the interplay between the human operator, the manipulator, i.e., the robot arm and the gripper, are central for performance. While the manipulator controls the movement of components, the gripping tool is responsible for grasping and holding onto the component, thereby playing a pivotal role in realizing the cobots activities.

This paper aims to improve the understanding of how to identify gripper requirements for different levels of cooperation in collaborative applications within manufacturing settings.

The paper takes on a conceptual approach to address its' aim, considering the gripper requirements for different levels of cooperation in kitting and assembly processes. For each process type, gripper requirements for four different levels of

© IFIP International Federation for Information Processing 2020
Published by Springer Nature Switzerland AG 2020
B. Lalic et al. (Eds.): APMS 2020, IFIP AICT 591, pp. 655–662, 2020.
https://doi.org/10.1007/978-3-030-57993-7_74

interaction are discussed based on the available literature about the topic and based on the previous case research that has involved the different process types. This is followed by a method to identify gripper requirements for collaborative applications. The scope of the Gripper selection processes is limited to operational requirements. Strategic requirements are not considered in this paper.

The structure of the paper is as follows. The theoretical framework is presented in Sects. 2, reviewing previous research. Additionally, the four levels of cooperation are described in the context of an assembly and kitting process in Sect. 3, followed by a framework outlined in Sect. 4. The paper ends with a discussion and conclusion with future research presented.

2   Design for Automated Assembly (DFAA)

Design for Assembly (DFA) is an integral part of any product and process development. The aim of this process, as stated by Boothroyd in [2], is to achieve efficient assembly by reducing complexity in product design and assembling the product in the form of manual or automated assembly with the lowest possible cost. The ease of assembly is not just dependent on DFA but also in the way the part or component is fed, handled and assembled and involves issues such as placing and handling problems and feeding difficulties [2]. This method is further developed to increase automation. Design for Automated Assembly (DFAA) is presented in [3] where the need for addressing part presentation in the form of shapes and sizes, alignment, and complexity in assembly operations is highlighted. A further step towards automatic assembly is to understand the assembly sequence of components. step towards automatic assembly is to understand the assembly sequence of components. This is done in the DFAA analysis on a component level to determine if the component is a candidate for integration with another component. The analysis is based on the properties of the component such as shape, weight length, graspability, orientation, error rate, degree of roughness and ability to hooking and the components in relation to the component it will be assembled with, which includes the assembly motions, access for assembly, fitting, tolerances, risk to loose orientation after assembly, method of attachment, control/adjustment.

Further development of this relationship is to use a Hierarchical Task Analysis (HTA), a precedence graph [4], or an ABC-analysis (Assembly By Constrains) [5]. All three methods give relation to how and when the different components need to be assembled. It could differ depending on if the assembly is manual or automatic.

2.1   Task Allocation and Levels of Interaction

For any type of collaborative work, it is essential to learn and understand the skills and capabilities of the operators and machines before designing the process. This can be done in the skill-based task allocation process [6]. Weichhart [7] has extensively presented agent (represented as humans operator) based task allocation process. Operators 4.0 typology is based on using industry 4.0 technology along with human operators to carrying out manufacturing tasks [8]. Task allocation is done using operator 4.0 focusing on operator skill matching and using industry 4.0 technology which can be useful in the collaborative application if the workspace requires extra support tools for the operator such as exoskeleton or AR/VR glasses.

While considering task allocation, it is essential to consider the different levels of interactions a collaborative application can achieve. As defined by Bauer et al. [9] following are the different levels of interactions in the context of collaborative applications.

1. Cell: Traditional cage scenario where the robot is isolated in a cage.
2. Coexistence: Human and robots work alongside each other without the presence of any cage though workspace is not shared
3. Synchronized: Human and robot shared workspace. Only one interaction partner (i.e., either human or robot) is actively working in the workspace.
4. Cooperation: Shared workspace where both humans and robots have tasks to perform. This task is not simultaneously performed at the same location of a product or component.
5. Collaboration: Humans and robots work simultaneously on the same product or component.

2.2 Gripper Principles, Selection Criteria's and Frameworks

Grippers are highly influenced by the geometry of the part, and it's graspability [6]. Guidelines for designing grippers are presented in [10] from two different perspectives, one to increase throughput and others to increase reliability. These guidelines include different kinds of advice, for example, to avoid the unnecessary weight of gripper, include functionality on gripper fingers, design gripper to grasp parts securely, having sufficient approach clearance while picking and placing a part which can be applied even while selection a gripper for collaborative application. Traditional frameworks for gripper selection focus on parameters such as part geometry, handling process, and process environment. For example, the methodology developed by [11] focuses on grasping principles for parts defined by DFA methods. The grasping principle generates minimum requirements for grippers along with environmental requirements, advice, and warning. Though the method is extensive and well developed with feedback for redesigning parts for assembly, a limitation for its use in a collaborative application is the lack of specification on human involvement in an assembly task. Pham [12] defines five primary factors in a gripper selection process, namely, component, task, environment, robot, and gripper. Each factor has its sub-criteria, which helps in finding vital requirements for gripper selection. The method developed by Schmaltz [13] uses the factors presented by Pham [12], such as part data in the form of its geometry, environmental factors along with the assembly information, and the device used. The method generates a set of grippers based on the input parameters. The methods consider environmental and task parameters but lack human factors, thus unsuitable for collaborative application. Thereby, the current paper, which takes human factors into account in the context of gripper selection, make up an important extension of the available literature.

3 Collaborative Robot Applications in Manufacturing

Pick-and-place tasks the most common tasks for collaborative robot applications [14] these pick-and-place tasks can be performed in assembly, kitting, and load-unload operations. Different levels of interactions between the robot and the human demands different requirements on the gripper. Below are examples from assembly and kitting.

Coexistence Assembly: A coexisting assembly is where the cobot and operator work in series in a shared workspace. An example of coexistence assembly is present here [15] where cobot used for assembling nut on wheel hub while operators' tasks include replenishing the material rack and check the assembly if the robot reports so.

Coexistent Kitting: Boudella [16] considered a coexistent kitting process. In the process, the operator and the robot prepared kits in series, working at different workspaces. In addition to picking components, the robot was also responsible for removing empty bins and discarding internal packaging.

Synchronized Assembly: Operators and cobot perform work in a synchronized manner in the same workspace with only one entity working at a time in a simultaneously performed in a synchronized manner. As shown in Fig. 1, the operator waits with a nut in had while the cobot puts fuse in the box. Only after the cobot finishes placing the fuse and leaving the fuse box area, the operators start assembling the nut.

Synchronized Kitting: Based on the setup presented in [16], it is easy to imagine a process where an operator and a cobot take turns at kitting components at the same workspace. This shared workspace would take up more space than the individual workspaces in [16], as all components would have to be stored at the same workspace

Cooperative Assembly: Operator and cobot share the workspace and work alongside each other. Similar to synchronized work, the but operator and cobot are working on the same part parallelly. As shown in Fig. 2, the operator is assembling nuts while the cobots in placing fuses on the same battery box.

Cooperative Kitting: Fager in [17] considered a cooperative kitting process. The process involved a cobot mounted on an AGV that helped the operator sort components into a batch of kits. The operator and cobot worked on different order lines, cooperatively.

Collaborative Assembly: A fully collaborative assembly is where the operator and cobot work together on the same part at the same time. As shown in Fig. 3, the cobot pick's and places the nut at the designated location with the use of its gripper while the operator tightens it.

Collaborative Kitting: While it is not apparent how a collaborative kitting process could be set up, tasks such as removing packaging where the robot holds a component for the operator or a quality inspection where the operator could display a component to the cobot, which then, by utilizing, e.g., object recognition, checks that the component is free from damage.

Fig. 1. Synchronized work   **Fig. 2.** Cooperation work   **Fig. 3.** Collaboration work

4   Analysis

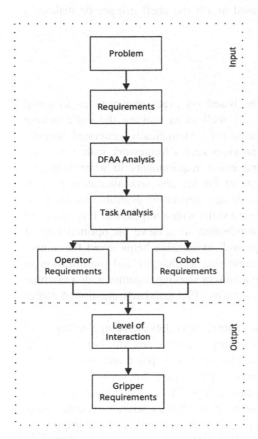

Fig. 4. Framework for identifying gripper requirements

Problem

A clear problem description should be formulated about the proposed operation. Problem description can include, for example, why and how the task can be solved.

Requirements

All the requirements to solve the problem presented in step 1 should be gathered. These requirements can include, for example, the number of components, part geometry, cycle time.

DFAA Analysis

DFAA analysis is explained in Sect. 2.1. Tools such as DYNAMOO++ are helpful in DFAA analysis.

Task Analysis

Task analysis present in Sect. 2.2 should be used to identify the potential of task allocation between human operator and machine, i.e., cobot.

Operator Requirements

Operator requirements are, for example, ergonomic requirements that should be considered. Furthermore, the skill and comfortability of the operator to work together with a cobot should be analyzed.

Cobot Requirements
Cobot requirements include the payload capacity, TCP reach, degrees of freedom, speed and acceleration should be considered.

Level of Interaction
As a result of previous steps, a few options of the level of interaction are generated based on the DFAA and Task analysis. All levels obtained should fulfill the requirements of safety and security standards for industrial robots listed in ISO 10218-1:2011, ISO 10218-2:2011 and for collaborative robots in ISO/TS 15066:2016.

Gripper Requirements
Specifications for gripper required to solve the problem are generated form the input process. The requirement specification should include gripper types such as two or three-finger gripper, power types such as pneumatic or electric, and other similar specifications that can be either be purchased as off the shelf gripper or making a customized gripper.

5 Discussion and Conclusions

Identifying and choosing gripper should be based on exact requirements to avoid unnecessary cost and compatibility issues, as well as in making the collaborative application safe. This choice should be based on systematically generated requirements. The method presented in this paper provides such a framework with a focus on the combined requirements of humans and cobot requirements in a collaborative application. Furthermore, the proposed steps of DFAA and task allocation provide feedback on changing and improving product design, generating assembly instructions, and methodically distributing tasks by matching skills with competence. It is crucial to find the right balance between the task distribution to achieve an optimal rate of productivity and quality. Having these steps well in advance helps avoid the unnecessary cost in money and time that may cause due to changes and modification to product and operation in later stages. Having a human working together with a machine such as a cobot requires a lot of safety and security. ISO standards mentioned earlier presents many of such requirements.

Assembly and kitting operations in the context of collaborative applications are explained in Sect. 3. Different levels of interaction present many similarities in their operating procedure. For example, the principles of pick-n'-place and grasp- ability apply to both assembly and kitting operations. An advantage for such similarities is useful when finding requirements for selecting a gripper. Thus, the framework can be applied for selecting gripper for assembly operation or kitting operation or collectively for both. The advantage of the collective approach is the reusability of the gripper for other operations in either kitting or assembly. Reusability also increases the flexibility of the collaborative application with the possibility to apply at various workstations with similar requirements.

To conclude, this paper presents a framework for identifying gripper requirements for collaborative application. The steps presented in this framework, such as DFFA and task allocation, not only help in identifying gripper requirements but also in detecting potential improvement in design, as well as workstations. Additionally, the steps in the proposed framework involve human consideration at every stage, thus making this paper an essential contribution to the available literature, where consideration to humans and collaborative tasks, for the most part, have been neglected in frameworks for gripper selection.

The proposed framework also helps in identifying potential safety threats in the context of developing a collaborative application. Future work will focus on build collaborative robot application demonstrators with different levels of interaction using the proposed framework.

Acknowledgment. The authors would like to thank The Swedish National Agency for Research and Innovation "VINNOVA" and Produktion2030 for funding the research project "Demonstrating and Testing smart digitalization for sustainable human-centered automation in production" and providing the opportunity to conduct this research.

References

1. Campbell, K., Weihl, C.: Cobots: man and machine team up for workplace productivity. Weld. J. **97**, 34–39 (2018)
2. Boothroyd, G., Alting, L.: Design for assembly and disassembly. CIRP Ann. Manuf. Technol. **41**, 625–636 (1992). https://doi.org/10.1016/S0007-8506(07)63249-1
3. Kashyap, S.: A feature-based framework for attachment level snap-fastener design in product design for automated assembly. In: Proceedings of the 1999 IEEE International Symposium on Assembly and Task Planning, ISATP'99 (Cat. No.99TH8470), pp. 51–56. IEEE (1999)
4. Roy, U., Banerjee, P., Liu, C.R.: Design of an automated assembly environment. Comput. Des. **21**, 561–569 (1989). https://doi.org/10.1016/0010-4485(89)90017-1
5. Morris, G., Haynes, L.: Robotic assembly by constraints. In: 1987 Proceedings of the IEEE International Conference on Robotics and Automation, pp. 1507–1515. Institute of Electrical and Electronics Engineers (1987)
6. Malik, A.A., Bilberg, A.: Complexity-based task allocation in human-robot collaborative assembly. Ind. Rob. **46**, 471–480 (2019). https://doi.org/10.1108/IR-11-2018-0231
7. Weichhart, G., Fast-Berglund, A., Romero, D., Pichler, A.: An agent- and role-based planning approach for flexible automation of advanced production systems. In: 2018 International Conference on Intelligent Systems (IS), pp. 391–399. IEEE (2018)
8. Romero, D.: Towards an operator 4.0 typology: a human-centric perspective on the fourth industrial revolution technologies. In: 46th International Conferences on Computers and Industrial Engineering, CIE 2016, pp. 0–11 (2017)
9. Bauer, W., Bender, M., Braun, M., Rally, P., Scholtz, O.: Lightweight Robots in Manual Assembly – Best to Start Simply. Examining Companies' Initial Experiences with Lightweight Robots, p. 63. Frauenhofer-Institut für Arbeitswirtschaft und Organ, IAO, Stuttgart (2016)
10. Causey, G.C., Quinn, R.D.: Gripper design guidelines for modular manufacturing. In: Proceedings of the IEEE International Conference on Robotics and Automation, vol. 2, pp. 1453–1458 (1998). https://doi.org/10.1109/ROBOT.1998.677309

11. Fantoni, G., Capiferri, S., Tilli, J.: Method for supporting the selection of robot grippers. Procedia CIRP **21**, 330–335 (2014). https://doi.org/10.1016/j.procir.2014.03.152

12. Pham, D.T., Yeo, S.H.: Strategies for gripper design and selection in robotic assembly. Int. J. Prod. Res. **29**, 303–316 (1991). https://doi.org/10.1080/00207549108930072

13. Schmalz, J., Reinhart, G.: Automated selection and dimensioning of gripper systems. Procedia CIRP **23**, 212–216 (2014). https://doi.org/10.1016/j.procir.2014.10.080

14. Fast-Berglund, Å., Romero, D.: Strategies for implementing collaborative robot applications for the operator 4.0. In: Ameri, F., Stecke, Kathryn E., von Cieminski, G., Kiritsis, D. (eds.) APMS 2019. IAICT, vol. 566, pp. 682–689. Springer, Cham (2019). https://doi.org/10.1007/978-3-030-30000-5_83

15. Salunkhe, O., Stensöta, O., Åkerman, M., Berglund, Å.F., Alveflo, P.A.: Assembly 4.0: wheel hub nut assembly using a cobot. IFAC-PapersOnLine **52**, 1632–1637 (2019). https://doi.org/10.1016/j.ifacol.2019.11.434

16. Boudella, M.E.A., Sahin, E., Dallery, Y.: Kitting optimisation in Just-in-Time mixed-model assembly lines: assigning parts to pickers in a hybrid robot–operator kitting system. Int. J. Prod. Res. **56**, 5475–5494 (2018). https://doi.org/10.1080/00207543.2017.1418988

17. Fager, P., Calzavara, M., Sgarbossa, F.: Modelling time efficiency of cobot-supported kit preparation. Int. J. Adv. Manuf. Technol. **106**, 2227–2241 (2020). https://doi.org/10.1007/s00170-019-04679-x

A Novel Value Driven Co-creation Framework

Geir Ringen[✉], Halvor Holtskog, and Torgeir Welo

Norwegian University of Science and Technology, 7034 Trondheim, Norway
geir.ringen@ntnu.no

Abstract. The Environmental awareness is growing throughout the society and the pressure on manufacturing companies, and their extended value chain, to operate in a more sustainable way. Designing products that can be controlled throughout their value chain and life cycle is one option to secure reuse of the material stream. We hypothesize that increased collaboration and common understanding among industrial stakeholders will promote improved products with regards to sustainability criteria. To test our hypothesizes a model for cross-industry and cross industry and academia collaboration is outlined. This model emphasizes three distinct levels of collaboration, team, company and cluster, and the life cycle stages of a product. Understanding these levels and stages are important not only for assuring correct and rational behavior among actors but also for facilitating a long-term sustainable business model development. This article presents the theories and arguments behind the model and initial results from an aluminum product case. Further verification and calibration of the model will be done by adding case studies as input to the collaboration model.

Keywords: Innovation model · Co-creation · Aluminium product case study

1 Introduction

Increasing pressure to develop products of higher quality, with added functionality, at a lower cost, and in shorter time frames unquestionably brings about some dichotomies. The examples of high quality vs. low cost, less resources and time vs. higher performance, and increased robustness vs. lower weight all illustrate well known contradictions which become more and more important to optimize. Only companies that can manage such conflicting objectives and in an adaptive manner consistently and timely bring new and innovative products to market will be regarded as long-term partners. In this regard, Utterback [1] claimed that the main challenge is to develop the ability to innovate products, processes, and the organization, seeing them dependent of each other as a whole. To this overall picture, companies must comply to requirements and expectations regarding sustainability criteria as well as increase their understanding and ability to utilize enabling technologies for improving product lifecycle performance.

Product development capability [2], the ability to use and integrate existing organizational and inter-organizational competences, is seen as fundamental to introducing a successful new product. It is argued that success is especially challenged by technology changes and global competition, meaning that product development capability must contain features beyond competence utilization. For instance, Barney [3]

© IFIP International Federation for Information Processing 2020
Published by Springer Nature Switzerland AG 2020
B. Lalic et al. (Eds.): APMS 2020, IFIP AICT 591, pp. 663–671, 2020.
https://doi.org/10.1007/978-3-030-57993-7_75

emphasized that such capability must be valuable, rare, and imperfectly imitable. Others start from the firm level [4] and see resource utilization as a driving force behind successful product development and competitive advantage. A third stream of litera- ture, with contributors like Nelson and Winter [5], concluded that technological and organizational progress is driven by mechanisms of variation, selection, and retention. Hence, this evolutionary perspective focuses heavily on continuous innovation and mastering of change.

The coming decade is expected to become a crucial period for industrial companies as they more frequently have to respond to global challenges. Environmental awareness is growing throughout the society and the pressure on manufacturing companies to operate in a more sustainable way is increasing. Having control of, and insight into, the entire value chain is becoming a significant part of running a business [6]. However, for many manufacturing companies, that are not distributing their products themselves, knowledge of the complete life cycle of the products is limited. Furthermore, insights into users and end of life stages are particularly restricted. Understanding these stages are important not only for assuring correct behavior but also for facilitating a long-term sustainable business development. On the other side, the amount of available tech- nologies for enabling information tracking throughout the product life cycle is increasing.

Many manufacturing companies do not have control over the distribution chain, and find it difficult to obtain complete information on use and reuse [7]. In many value chains, information exchange is very limited due to lack of interest of sharing knowledge or understanding of what information that is important. The point of departure for industrial design is the end user, on a general level or through deep insights. Insights can be achieved through interviews, observations, experiences or co- design where design for sustainable behaviour aims at supporting greener choices by buyers and users of products.

This paper seeks to initiate a framework for cross-collaboration co-creation strategies towards improved product development processes for a more circular economy.

2 Theory

Innovation today is about bringing together different actors at different levels, ranging from the individual, to the group, organization and inter-organizational levels. The concept of organizational learning is therefore dependent on those groups and teams that are able to learn; if they cannot, the organization cannot learn [8]. This view is supported by Senge [9], who stated, *"team learning is vital because teams, not indi- viduals, are the fundamental learning units in modern organizations."* Groups are social systems in which sharing, learning, and organizational behavior take place, and they can play a central role in both supporting individual learning and opening new opportunities for interventions. Individual, group and departmental learning are thor- oughly discussed in the previous chapters, so the main body of this chapter is con- cerned with the organizational and the inter-organizational level.

In a complex world system are developed to reduce complexity, and trust may serve as a building block in creating these systems. Luhmann [10] regarded trust as reduction of complexity; he saw trust as a function for establishing and maintaining a complex world. He also argued for trust as an input condition to abstract systems, stating that *"without trust it cannot stimulate supportive activities in situations of uncertainty or risk."* Giddens [11] defined trust as *"confidence in the reliability of a person or system, regarding a given set of outcomes or events, where that confidence expresses a faith in the probity or love of another, or in the correctness of abstract principles and technical knowledge."* This means he believed that the result of actions is not random, but is directly linked to the characteristics of the system. As discussed above, the automotive industry has clear characteristics described in the transaction cost economic. By showing trust Giddens [11] argued for a mild form of hostage taking or being called upon. The trusted party will then feel an obligation to act in a certain way, and the actions will be revised during the time of the relationship. In such relations based on trust lies an idea that humans create risk and that this risk cannot be eliminated, only reduced. This is done in a rational and conscious way when the risk can be calculated.

Bowersox et al. [12] defined supply chains as value-adding relations of partially discrete yet interdependent units that cooperatively transform raw materials into finished products through sequential, parallel, and/or network structures. The supply chain management (SCM) literature analyses how firms are affected by their participation in global production networks [13], and it views supply chains as networks of organisations that are involved in different ways to produce value in the form of products and services in the hands of the ultimate consumer [14].

The key technologies developed in the early and mid-20th century were developed primarily by large diversified enterprises. This diversification, along with vertical integration, provided these firms with a competitive advantage over smaller competitors. Realizing the increased knowledge mobility and availability of venture capital to capitalize on knowledge, Chesbrough and Vanhaverbeke concluded that the traditional model had reached its limits [15], and suggested open innovation means a break with the traditional paradigm.

From this Chesbrough and Vanhaverbeke [15] derived the following definition of open innovation: *"Open innovation is the use of purposive inflows and outflows of knowledge to accelerate internal innovation, and expand the markets for external use of innovation."* The increased global flow of goods, services, knowledge and capital implies that firms increasingly obtain ideas and knowledge from distributed knowledge networks and open innovation [16] in addition to their internal knowledge base. This transition from stable conditions, often in local and national markets, to global competition and more tailor made products has also increased the interest in innovation and organizational learning [17]. Tidd et al. [18] asserted that innovation networks have become popular as a means of innovation across organizations. Such networks may be viewed as a new hybrid form of organization that has the potential to replace both firms and markets and create a kind of a *"virtual corporation"*. The model of open innovation by Chesbrough [16] is based on the same idea: to have an open flow of ideas and technology between the firm and its environment. He focused on the notion that good ideas are worthless without capital and a superior business model, saying that firms can and should use both external and internal ideas to create value and internal and external paths to market [15]. This concept draws on for instance the theories of absorptive capacity and spillovers of industrial R&D.

Network ties often reflect formal collaboration, but the knowledge flow, which is the main focus, may be separated into formal and informal ties. The former reflects planned channels for knowledge exchange, whereas the informal ties are viewed as more interesting and valuable due to unforeseen knowledge opportunities [15]. In this perspective the open innovation theory turns into more of a networking perspective, where the competitive advantage can be found in the community of companies rather than in the individual company. On the other hand Lorenz and Valeyre [19] asserted that innovation activities still critically depend on factors internal to the firm, in particular on the job training related to solving technical and production related problems. Another perspective of network innovation models is co-opetition, where collaboration and competition are not mutually exclusive, but can actually coexist and create benefits from joint dynamics among competitors [20]. Evans et al. discuss the advances of sustainable business models, which take into account the extended responsibility companies has for their products and services in value chain and life cycle perspective [21].

3   Method

This study is part of the Norwegian Research Council funded project VALUE, reporting upon 6 in-depth interviews done in one of the application cases. The interviews were recorded and transcribed, and the informants read and approved the transcriptions. This formed the backbone of the case study.

The innovation model, hypothesized to support rapid innovation in the context of developing more complex products with

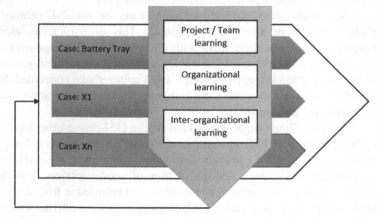

Fig. 1. Innovation model.

increasing number of interfaces both physically and virtual, is illustrated in Fig. 1. There are identified three important, and connected, intra- and inter-organizational levels where learning takes place [22]. The first one is at the team level where a group of individuals are dedicated towards closing knowledge gaps related to product features. The next level emphasizes how knowledge at group level relates to the whole organization. This can be horizontally and vertically integrated knowledge, where the particular product innovation is put into a business context and where knowledge accumulates through tacit and explicit channels. The third level involves inter-organizational learning, and how the network of the firm can be involved to speed up open innovation processes. We will in the following project this model through a real innovation case, and discuss how feedback-loops from the different learning levels can improve the next innovation process according to product lifecycle performance.

4 Results of Application Case

The case company develops and manufactures critical light-weight safety parts for the automotive industry and has been doing that for more than 50 years. More than 10 million components are supplied to demanding customers annually. However, the electrification trend in the transport sector spurs the need for increasing light-weight solutions to compensate for added total vehicle weight due to batteries. They see that the automotive industry is changing. As a result of the United Nations goal of stopping global warming to a maximum of 2 °C increase, heavy regulations have been, and will continue to be implemented to reduce emissions in the transportation industry. This has led to a dramatic and rapid change in the automotive industry towards low and zero emission vehicles.

The electrification of passenger vehicles is arguably the biggest shift in the automotive industry since Henry Ford introduced the assembly line in the early 20th century. The push from the governments are coupled with a few pioneering manufacturers which has demonstrated that the technology is ready to be used and it is possible to produce desirable vehicles which is in demand from customers. Over the past years, especially over the last year, there has been a continuous spate of announcements from car-manufacturers declaring their intensions and plans to electrify their product portfolio. Some have even pledged to only produce electric vehicles, whether they are pure electric or electrified, within the next decade. The change to electric drivetrains comprises new vehicle architecture as traditional requirements for engine, gearbox, driveshafts and fuel tanks are redundant in electric vehicles. These would be replaced by smaller, more compact electric motors coupled with a large battery. As these types of vehicles are weight-critical, the current and future market pull creates new opportunities for suppliers of light-weight materials such as aluminium to be put to use in new areas and products. In this connection, one of the product categories with the larger potential is aluminium battery trays. For the case company battery trays are seen as an interesting and complementary product to the existing product portfolio, where deep knowledge about utilizing and forming aluminium may be a steppingstone towards further growth. However, the case company realises that material and process knowledge derived from the existing markets and product portfolios are not sufficient to take on the assumed complexity of making battery trays. Some of the identified requirements affecting the battery tray are given below:

- The primary task of the battery housing is to protect and enclose the energy required to propel the car.
- The battery cells are temperature sensitive, meaning the efficiency of the battery cells are dependent on operating in a temperature range. If the temperature is too high, the capacity will decrease along aging of the battery. If the temperature is too low, the internal resistance in the cells increase and performance decrease.
- Protection from moisture, rain, dust and particles is important for the operation and lifetime for the batteries. Therefore, all battery housings are enclosed in one way or another using sealants, high internal air pressure or membranes.
- Safety requirements: As most battery packs are substantial in size and weight, they have significant effects on the crash structure of the car. There are also official requirements for transporting lithium-ion batteries.
- It is desirable to have a lightweight battery housing, as extra weight decreases the efficiency of the car and shortens the driving range.
- The battery housing is not to be a source of vibration, which will affect the safety of the batteries and the comfort of the passengers.
- The battery housing is a highly customized component since it has to incorporate and satisfy designs that comply with the defined size and shape of space in the vehicle, as well as the mounting points to the vehicle, and it must incorporate all the internal components to fit inside the housing.

At the project team level the new product concept, battery tray, was seen as innovative and interesting, although the potential manufacturing processes to be selected for realizing the product were known from before. The potential risks and rewards were more related to the system complexity, where number of sub-components must be assembled in a cost-effective way. Historically the company was used to do welding, a process now done in other parts of the global production network. The team was also discussing the possibility of just developing a product to be produced elsewhere due to assumed high value chain costs of transporting systems to the customer from remote production sites, and the proposed process of do a lot of welding for final assembly. An interesting finding was that this realization of just being part of the initial development phase, spur some ideation among the local team. A novel tooling approach for extruding aluminium profiles was developed to make innovative profile designs, aiming at reducing volume to be transported (50%), reduce welding (50–60%), and increase the panel width (250%). This is one of many initiatives taken at team level, impacting the maturity of a future product concept.

At the level of organizational learning the company has a long history of producing high volume components to demanding customers, controlling the aluminium value chain from casting, extrusion, forming and to final assembly. The combination of long history, value chain control, and a stable workforce at local and regional level over time, lays a good foundation for identifying, transferring, and utilizing knowledge. However, some dynamics in ownership since mid-1990s have influenced this stock of knowledge, especially in terms of customer proximity and how the is organized towards customer satisfaction. Currently, the company is part of large multinational company with a strong foothold in global value chains – such also for the automotive segment. This new way of organizing the local manufacturer gives better access, and a stronger tie, to key customers, but also a potential longer way for information and knowledge to travel from the source to those who are in charge of developing new solutions. However, the accumulated knowledge in terms of an innovative battery tray was presented at the Shanghai Motor Show in 2017.

At the inter-organizational learning added complexity in the product interfaces required a more open innovation process, including a network of academia and industrial partners to create feasible solutions. From a business perspective the case company early identified sets of risk related to be in the value chain of supplying battery trays. First, immature industry standards and fast developing technology are key factors to be carefully evaluated before going into a new product/system segment. Second, technology risk was noted as high due to consequences of not being able to safely protect the batteries under all possible conditions. Third; competence capability is seen as crucial to develop a sustainable solution for an emerging and demanding market. Actions taken to reduce risk were comprehensive. But, being in the business of development and manufacturing of critical aluminium safety parts for decades, one of the most trusted customers was accompanied to form a joint development project. Here risks and opportunities were identified and broken down to small tasks, where also external potential knowledge actors were mapped according to capability and capacity. Examples of sub-tasks are; selection of semi-finished goods, welding techniques, calibration for dimensional accuracy, crash impact, weight optimization etc. Academic partners were selected as contributors to these sub-tasks, but the co-creation intensity and level differentiates depending on actor strength within the field of expertise. On the business side, a broad network of strategic partners was selected to develop a modular and scalable solution for light-weight e-mobility. This solution was ready for launch in 2019.

5 Conclusion

This paper seeks to illustrate the complexity of bringing new innovations to the market, where all levels of the organization, and it's extended network, have to be mobilized in order to close the knowledge gaps. Innovation theory has in recent years developed towards emphasizing cross-boundary and inter-organizational innovation, seeing the value of bringing a broad array of views into consideration when the landscape of developing new products and services become more complex. However, this paper supports the importance of being open, but without forgetting the core of the company. The latter is exemplified by the innovation capability of local engineering teams, combining extrusion and forming skills to prototype entire new solutions. At the organizational level, stating time dependent objectives for closing critical knowledge gaps turned important for urging the organization. Involving academic and strategic business partners is also viewed as important when newness is defined along all the dimensions: market, process and product. We propose an innovation model that integrates this local team innovation capability with the organizational learning and inter-organizational dimensions. Playing out these three capabilities simultaneously when heading for step-change innovation in in-mature markets is valuable when doing it carefully and with awareness. This is the key finding from this paper. We will continuously develop this innovation model based on additional cases.

References

1. Utterback, J.: Mastering the Dynamics of Innovation. Harvard Business School Press, Cambridge (1994)
2. Stalk, G., Evans, P., Shulman, L.E.: Competing on capabilities: the new rules of corporate strategy. Harv. Bus. Rev. **70**(2), 57–69 (1992)
3. Barney, J.: Firm resources and sustained competitive advantage. J. Manage. **17**(1), 99–120 (1991)
4. Prahalad, C.K., Hamel, G.: The core competence of the corporation. Harv. Bus. Rev. **68**(3), 79–91 (1990)
5. Nelson, R.R., Winter, S.G.: An Evolutionary Theory of Economic Change. Harvard University Press, Cambridge (1982)
6. den Hollander, M.C., Bakker, C.A., Hultink, E.J.: Product design in a circular economy: development of a typology of key concepts and terms. J. Ind. Ecol. **21**(3), 517–525 (2016)
7. Gmelin, H., Seuring, S.: Determinants of a sustainable new product development. J. Clean. Prod. **69**, 1–9 (2014)
8. Pawlowsky, P.: The treatment of organizational learning in management science. In: Dierkes, M., et al. (eds.) Handbook of Organizational Learning & Knowledge. Oxford University Press, New York (2001)
9. Senge, P.M.: The Fifth Discipline: The Art & Practice of The Learning Organization. Currency Doubleday, New York (1990)
10. Luhman, N.: Trust and Power: Two Works by Niklas Luhmann. Wiley, New York (1979)
11. Giddens, A.: The Consequences of Modernity. Polity Press, Cambridge (1990)
12. Bowersox, D.J., Closs, D.J., Stank, T.P.: 21st Century Logistics: Making Supply Chain Integration a Reality. Council of Supply Chain Management Professionals, Oak Brook (1999)
13. Dicken, P.: Global Shift. Mapping the Changing Contours of the World Economy, 5th edn. Sage, London (2007)
14. Christopher, M.: Logistics and Supply Chain Management. Creating Value-Adding Networks. Prentice Hall, Harlow (2005)
15. Chesbrough, H., Vanhaverbeke, W.: Open Innovation: Researching a New Paradigm. Oxford University Press, Oxford (2006)
16. Chesbrough, H.: Open Innovation: The New Imperative for Creating and Profiting from Technology. Harvard Business School Publishing Corporation, Boston (2003)
17. Jacobsen, D.I., Thorsvik, J. (eds.): Hvordan Organisasjonen Fungerer, 3rd edn. Fagbokforlaget, Bergen (2007)
18. Tidd, J., Bessant, J., Pavitt, K.: Managing Innovation: Integrating Technological, Market and Organizational Change, 3rd edn. Wiley, New York (2005)
19. Lorenz, E., Valeyre, A.: Organizational forms and innovative performance: a comparison of the EU-15. In: Lorenz, E., Lundvall, B.Å. (eds.) How Europe's Economies Learn. Coordinating Competing Models. Oxford University Press, Oxford (2006)
20. Ritala, P., Kraus, S., Bouncken, R.B.: Introduction to coopetition and innovation: contemporary topics and future research opportunities. Int. J. Technol. Manage. **71**(1–2), 1–9 (2016)

21. Evans, S., et al.: Business model innovation for sustainability: towards a unified perspective for creation of sustainable business models. Bus. Strategy Environ. **26**(5), 597–608 (2017)
22. Rothaermel, F.T., Hess, A.M.: Building dynamic capabilities: innovation driven by individual-, firm-, and network-level effects. Organ. Sci. **18**(6), 898–921 (2007)

Autonomous Mobile Robots in Hospital Logistics

Giuseppe Fragapane[1](✉) ⓘ, Hans-Henrik Hvolby[1,2] ⓘ,
Fabio Sgarbossa[1] ⓘ, and Jan Ola Strandhagen[1] ⓘ

[1] Department of Mechanical and Industrial Engineering, Norwegian University
of Science and Technology, Trondheim, Norway
giuseppe.fragapane@ntnu.no
[2] Centre for Logistics, Department of Materials and Manufacturing Engineering,
Aalborg University, Aalborg, Denmark

Abstract. The recent advances in technology have increased flexibility in
indoor mobility and human-robot collaboration, opening up new opportunities
to perform material handling tasks, especially in narrow, dynamic environments,
such as hospitals. Sensing devices, powerful on-board computers, artificial
intelligence, and collaborative equipment allow autonomous mobile robots
(AMRs) to drive and fulfill material handling activities autonomously. In hospitals, material handling activities are widely performed manually. This study
investigates five innovative applications of AMRs, highlighting their benefits
compared with other material handling systems applied in hospitals, and presenting research needs. The study concludes that AMRs can support and collaborate closely with hospital personnel to increase value-added time for patient
care.

Keywords: Autonomous mobile robots · Material handling · Hospital ·
Logistics

1 Introduction

Automating material handling activities can significantly improve efficiency and productivity in the healthcare sector, since hospitals, compared to other industries, still,
often perform these activities manually. A large survey conducted in the US, Canada,
and Germany exposed that nursing's none–value-adding and non-nursing activities
(e.g., delivery and retrieval of food trays, ancillary, or housekeeping services) consume
around 40% of nurses' time [1]. Many of these activities could have been accomplished
by other hospital personnel or advanced material handling systems [2–4]. However,
finding the appropriate material handling system and level of automation for addressing
hospitals' and patients' requirements is quite challenging [5]. The common material
handling systems applied in hospitals allow low flexibility in mobility. Automated
guided vehicles (AGV) cannot bypass obstacles and enter wards or departments due to
safety and space concerns. Automated vacuum collection systems, pneumatic tube
systems, and overhead transportation systems often have only fixed pick and/or
delivery stations in departments. The low flexibility in mobility makes it difficult to

© IFIP International Federation for Information Processing 2020
Published by Springer Nature Switzerland AG 2020
B. Lalic et al. (Eds.): APMS 2020, IFIP AICT 591, pp. 672–679, 2020.
https://doi.org/10.1007/978-3-030-57993-7_76

automate material handling in the so-called last 50 m, referring to the distance in the department to the patient, as well as in other departments.

The need for more flexibility has pushed the development of autonomous mobile robots (AMRs). Thanks to ubiquitous sensors, powerful on-board computers, artificial intelligence (AI), and simultaneous location and mapping (SLAM) technology, AMRs can understand their operating environments and navigate in facilities without the need to define and implement reference points in advance. AMRs are often small and agile, and they show their strength in high-traffic environments and low-volume transportation. Due to AMRs' characteristics, they can access narrower areas, interact with healthcare personnel and patients, and provide more services, such as assistive activities. AMRs have shown great potential in automotive, warehousing and process industry, in which they have supported increased production flexibility and productivity [6]. The potential of AMRs' high accessibility and flexibility in providing services has not been exploited and investigated in hospital environments.

Therefore, the aim of this paper is (I) to describe innovative material handling services and applications of AMRs in hospitals, (II) to compare them with other material handling systems in hospitals, and (III) to highlight future research needs for AMRs in hospital logistics. Two case studies have been conducted and three examples from the literature are presented to achieve these objectives.

The rest of the paper is organized as follows. The next section provides background information on traditional material handling systems in hospitals. Section three introduces and explains the cases and examples in which AMR has been applied in hospitals. The fourth section compares AMRs with other material handling systems in hospitals. The study ends with recommendations for future research areas for hospital logistics and AMRs.

2 Theoretical Background

2.1 Material Handling Systems in Hospitals

Logistics and material handling are crucial parts of the healthcare industry. Depending on the characteristics of the goods and the delivery requirements, a material handling system can be assigned to these tasks. Small objects, e.g., samples being delivered to laboratories, are mainly sent via pneumatic tube systems in hospitals due to time constraints. While automated vacuum collection systems are only used for return transportation of waste or linen, overhead transportation systems are used for both incoming and return transportation of loads of up to 15 kg to different departments. For transportation of heavier and bigger goods, AGVs have demonstrated good results in distributing high-volume goods to many pick-and-place positions and traveling long distances within hospitals without disturbing the hospital traffic [7]. The current material handling systems in hospitals are still largely dependent on human interaction for preparing, loading/unloading, and sending the items.

In contrast, AMRs have been recently introduced to hospitals, and their applicability in hospital logistics has not been exploited. AMRs possess a wide array of small and power-efficient sensing technologies, such as integrated laser scanners, 3D cameras, accelerometers, gyroscopes, etc., which allow them to digitalize an environment. Processing the sensing data with simultaneous location and mapping technology enables an AMR to create a map of its environment and calculate its position [8]. Unlike AGV systems, in which the central unit makes all routing and thus navigation decisions for all AGVs, AMRs can plan collision-free paths, make real-time decisions to avoid collisions, and so navigate in dynamic and unpredictable environments. AI techniques such as vision systems and machine learning enable the identification and classification of obstacles. These learning techniques enable AMRs to solve complex control problems in unfamiliar, real-world environments.

The main characteristics of the aforementioned material handling systems are shown in Table 1. A recent literature review in material logistics pointed out that standards and best practices for how to transport goods in hospitals barely exist [9]. To the best of the authors' knowledge, the applicability and research needs of AMRs in hospital logistics have not been addressed.

Table 1. Characteristics of automated material handling systems in hospitals

	Automated guided vehicle	Autonomous mobile robot	Automated vacuum collection system	Overhead transportation system	Pneumatic tube system
Capacity load	1–500 kg	1–100 kg	1–50 kg	1–15 kg	up to 2 kg
Transportation speed	1–2 km/h	3–4 km/h	20–70 km/h	2–3 km/h	10–25 km/h
Services provided	Transportation	Transportation, collaboration, assistance, etc.	Only return transportation	Transportation	Transportation
Service points	Fixed pick and delivery points	Flexible pick and delivery points	Fixed pick and delivery points	Fixed pick and delivery points	Fixed pick and delivery points
Navigation	Fixed guided path	Autonomous in predefined zones	Fixed tube path	Fixed guided path	Fixed tube path

3   Cases and Examples

3.1   Case 1: Sterile Instrument Transportation

Sterile instruments are transported in wagons from and to departments in a closed-loop logistics system by an AMR. The sterile processing department is responsible for picking and sending the sterile instruments required for medical treatment from the storage area to the departments. After usage at the department level (e.g., operating room), the goods are sent back to the central sterile processing department for cleaning, inspection, and sterilization. Hospital personnel can request, send, and track transportation via a tablet. Due to the logistics setup and the reliable transportation offered by the AMR, sterile goods can be sent Just-in-Time and demand-based on demand (Fig. 1).

There are 10 pick and delivery stations located among five different levels in the case hospital. The AMR can open doors, use elevators, enter departments, bypass obstacles, handle dynamic environments, and reach the destination pickup-and-delivery station to deliver the sterile instruments. The AMR delivers approximately 60 wagons daily and substitutes one full-time employee.

Fig. 1. AMR in sterile instrument logistics [10]

3.2   Case 2: Personalized Cancer Medicine Transportation

In chemotherapy treatments, patients receive personalized cancer medicine that has a short lifetime and can cost several thousand euros. The medicine is produced in the pharmaceutical department in the basement of the case hospital, while the actual treatment takes place several floors above it. Therefore, high-precision delivery, reliability, safety, and security are required for the transportation of medicine between the two departments.

The case hospital uses an AMR to transport the medicine in a locked drawer from the basement through the hospital to the final destination in the department [10]. After delivery, the AMR returns to the pharmaceutical department and waits to receive the next order (Fig. 2). The AMR reduces the healthcare personnel's responsibility and the amount of time involved in the transportation of medicine. This helps healthcare personnel increase patient care and value-added time and thus has enabled the return of the initial investment within one year.

Fig. 2. Sending and delivery of cancer medicine with secured transportation [10]

3.3 Example 1: AMR Providing Telemedicine

AMRs with teleoperating and medical equipment can be controlled by a human from a long distance and perform tasks in dynamic environments [11]. Tele-operation enables a new method of using this valuable resource and eases the high risk of infectious disease transfer. Physicians and specialists can communicate with patients and perform some of their duties at a safe distance from infected patients. A telemedicine robot with autonomous navigation technology has been introduced in hospitals in the US [12]. While the AMR moves from room to room, the physician can easily connect for patient consults and access clinical documentation, patient data, and medical imaging (Fig. 3). Digitizing and robotizing the material handling activities will provide data for and insights into new options for process improvement.

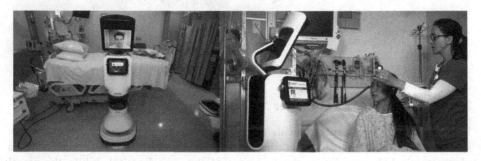

Fig. 3. AMR providing telemedicine [12]

3.4 Example 2: Assistive, Collaborative AMR in the Hospital Laboratory

AMRs with manipulators can assist workers by interacting with humans as robotic coworkers. In other industries, AMRs are used as assistive systems and can mount several heavy parts of a car body together at different stages along the car assembly line [13], thus increasing both productivity and quality while simultaneously reducing fatigue levels among workers. A dual-arm mobile robot has been introduced to a US hospital laboratory [14]. The AMR was designed to work alongside medical staff and help complete lab workers' repetitive tasks (Fig. 4).

Fig. 4. Assistive, collaborative AMR in a hospital laboratory [14]

It can sense and navigate its way around its human coworkers autonomously and simultaneously learn to find optimized routes from one location to another. The vision for using AMRs in laboratories is that they will take over a wide range of repetitive and time-consuming activities, such as preparation of medicines, loading and unloading centrifuges, pipetting and handling liquids, and picking up and sorting test tubes.

3.5   Example 3: AMR Disinfecting Rooms

Hospitals must clean and disinfect rooms after usage to reduce the spread of hazardous bacteria. Hospitals are strategizing to reduce the risk of such spread and simultaneously increase awareness [15]. The development of UV-C light systems significantly supports the destruction of bacteria. UV-C light systems need 10 min of exposure time to kill 99.99% of bacteria [16]. While the equipment can often be found on wheels and is moved manually from room to room, AMRs provide a platform for autonomously transporting the equipment into and within rooms (Fig. 5a). Therefore, an AMR can cover more surfaces compared to a fixed UV-C system and reduce the exposure of hospital personnel to bacteria (Fig. 5b). Further, it can collect relevant data during the disinfection process and communicate when the room is ready for usage.

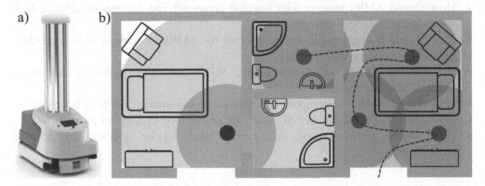

a)   b)

Fig. 5. a: AMR with disinfection equipment [16]. **b**: Left room disinfected with stationary equipment; right room disinfected by AMR (green/blue areas symbolizes disinfection range)

4   Discussion and Conclusion

Unlike other material handling systems applied in hospitals, AMRs utilize AI for decision making, which significantly increases their flexibility in performing material handling activities in hospitals. AI especially supports AMRs' decision making in path and motion planning. While typically, an A* algorithm is applied in path planning to find the shortest path, AI allows analysis of the dynamic environment and reacts appropriately to congestions. Machine learning techniques can suggest optimized paths based on previous deliveries. These processes increase the reliability of precision delivery, which is crucial in hospitals since small delivery deviations can have large impacts on patient treatment. For instance, missing instruments or medicine will postpone treatments or negatively impact the health of the patient. Robust and reliable material handling systems like AMRs are crucial for transferring material flows that can highly impact patient health from manual to automated.

AI can further support interaction between humans and machines, enabling assistive or collaborative tasks. Vision-based sensing, manipulators for grabbing and handling probes, and the use of machine learning allow AMRs to learn to perform a wide variety of repetitive activities. AMRs can function as robotic coworkers in laboratories, autonomously improving both specific processes and overall performance. This allows for the reduction of workload for highly trained laboratory workers.

AMRs can deliver to the point-of-use, the patient, and so cover a wide service area. For many years, mobile robots were a virtually unimaginable and practically unacceptable solution in healthcare support. People could not associate hospitals with a production environment. The increased social acceptance of AMRs allows integration into departments and wards. AMRs can deliver to the point of use, the patient, and so cover a wide service area. The integration of AMRs as transporting, collaborating, or assisting robots allows a rethinking of logistics and material handling activities in hospitals. Therefore, future research should focus on:

- What manual material handling activities should AMRs assist with or take over, and when?
- How should AMRs interact with hospital personnel and patients to achieve high social acceptance and safety?
- How should hospital goods be transported by AMRs to achieve high reliability, productivity, safety, and quality?
- How should AMRs be integrated with AGVs and other stationary automated material handling systems?
- How should AMRs be designed and planned at the strategic level in hospitals?
- How can the optimal number of AMRs be determined in hospital logistics?
- How should path planning and motion planning be adapted for hospital environments?

Acknowledgment. This research received funding from the strategic research area of NTNU Health in 2020 at NTNU. The authors would also like to express their gratitude to the Regional Development Fund in Denmark for supporting the project "Reference architecture and open standards". Finally, the authors gratefully acknowledge the case hospitals that made it possible to carry out this study.

References

1. Yen, P.Y., et al.: Nurses' time allocation and multitasking of nursing activities: a time motion study. In: AMIA Annual Symposium Proceedings, vol. 2018, p. 1137. American Medical Informatics Association (2018)
2. Aiken, L.H., et al.: Nurses' reports on hospital care in five countries. Health Aff. **20**(3), 43–53 (2001)

3. Kudo, Y., Yoshimura, E., Shahzad, M.T., Shibuya, A., Aizawa, Y.: Japanese professional nurses spend unnecessarily long time doing nursing assistants' tasks. Tohoku J. Exp. Med. **228**(1), 59–67 (2012)

4. Wong, D., Bonnici, T., Knight, J., Gerry, S., Turton, J., Watkinson, P.: A ward-based time study of paper and electronic documentation for recording vital sign observa-tions. J. Am. Med. Inform. Assoc. **24**(4), 717–721 (2017)

5. Granlund, A., Wiktorsson, M.: Automation in internal logistics: strategic and operational challenges. Int. J. Logist. Syst. Manage. **18**(4), 538–558 (2014)

6. Fragapane, G., Ivanov, D., Peron, M., Sgarbossa, F., Strandhagen, J.O.: Increasing flexibility and productivity in Industry 4.0 production networks with autonomous mobile robots and smart intralogistics. Ann. Oper. Res., 1–19 (2020). https://doi.org/10.1007/s10479-020-03526-7

7. Fragapane, G.I., Bertnum, A.B., Hvolby, H.H., Strandhagen, J.O.: Material distribution and transportation in a norwegian hospital: a case study. IFAC-papersonline **51**(11), 352–357 (2018)

8. Bloss, R.: Simultaneous sensing of location and mapping for autonomous robots. Sens. Rev. **28**(2), 102–107 (2008)

9. Volland, J., Fügener, A., Schoenfelder, J., Brunner, J.O.: Material logistics in hospitals: a literature review. Omega **69**, 82–101 (2017)

10. MIR Homepage. https://www.mobile-industrial-robots.com/en/insights/case-studies/. Accessed 4 Apr 2020

11. Papadopoulos, I., Koulouglioti, C., Lazzarino, R., Ali, S.: A systematic review of enablers and barriers to the implementation of socially assistive humanoid robots in health and social care. BMJ Open **10**(1), 1–13 (2019)

12. Intouch Homepage. https://www.businesswire.com/news/home/20130506005495/en/InTouch-Health-iRobot-Announce-Customers-Install-RP-VITATM. Accessed 4 Apr 2020

13. Angerer, S., Strassmair, C., Staehr, M., Roettenbacher, M., Robertson, N.M.: Give me a hand—the potential of mobile assistive robots in automotive logistics and assembly applications. In: 2012 IEEE International Conference on Technologies for Practical Robot Applications (TePRA), pp. 111–116. IEEE (2012)

14. Yumi Homepage. https://new.abb.com/news/detail/37301/abb-demonstrates-concept-of-mobile-laboratory-robot-for-hospital-of-the-future. Accessed 4 Apr 2020

15. Goldmann, D.A., et al.: Strategies to prevent and control the emergence and spread of antimicrobial-resistant microorganisms in hospitals: a challenge to hospital leader-ship. JAMA **275**(3), 234–240 (1996)

16. UVD Robots Homepage. http://www.uvd-robots.com/. Accessed 4 Apr 2020

Interorganizational Learning in Manufacturing Networks

Geir Ringen[1]([⊠]), Frode Paalsrud[1], and Eirin Lodgaard[2]

[1] Norwegian University of Science and Technology, 7491 Trondheim, Norway
geir.ringen@ntnu.no
[2] SINTEF Manufacturing, Enggata 40, 2830 Raufoss, Norway

Abstract. The ability to acquire and utilize new knowledge within an inter-organizational context is considered a key factor for gaining competitive advantage. This study aims at investigating how organizations do cross-border collaboration in the context of realizing Industry 4.0 principles at the operational level. The ever demand for advances in products, processes and systems, in a symbioses of product- and service performance, require new skills and knowledge at both organizational and inter-organizational level. This study investigates three case companies, and their maintenance departments, in order to understand if and how their role has changed in parallel with the adaption and implementation of Industry 4.0.

Keywords: Interorganizational learning · Case study · Industry 4.0

1 Introduction

Industry 4.0 is an area that has received great interest in the last decade, especially among scholars and scientists. The opportunities that industry 4.0 can bring for industries are seemed to be of great value in terms of efficiency based on improved decision support systems at the machine-human interface, HES, connectivity throughout the value chain, and maintenance operations [1]. Industry 4.0 is predicted to significant impact product life cycles and product value chains, where increased digitization, automation and connectivity among companies in complex and comprehensive value chains will change the existing industrial collaboration platforms and how they operate and function. Additionally, it is anticipated that industries will become more flexible and effective in resource allocation. Traditionally, clusters are considered as a number of firms that share some key characteristics, and they may compete with each other where rivalry and competitiveness can be an important driver for innovation. Because of somewhat similarities in production capabilities performance benchmarking can enhance increased efficiency and competitiveness across the cluster as a whole [2]. However, globalization, product diversity, shorter product life cycles, and sustainable measures increase complexity beyond traditional geographical and/or complementary clusters [3].

The nature of networks and value chains is contextual according to type of market and industry. There can be dispersed and complex value chains, requiring many actors and processing steps, to manufacture the final product to global markets, and smaller

© IFIP International Federation for Information Processing 2020
Published by Springer Nature Switzerland AG 2020
B. Lalic et al. (Eds.): APMS 2020, IFIP AICT 591, pp. 680–686, 2020.
https://doi.org/10.1007/978-3-030-57993-7_77

and more local entities to serve market areas. Number of organizational interactions in combination with level of innovation according to product, process and system accumulates uncertainty. Thus, complexity in terms of unknowns and interdependent, non-linear factors that cannot be solved by existing methods, rules, systems and processes has to be managed [4].

In organizational learning, the word inter is adding a new dimension to learning. Interorganizational relations are "relatively enduring transactions, flows, and linkages that occur among or between an organization and one or more organizations in its environment" [5]. This concept sheds new light on how knowledge and learning are located not only inside organizations, but also outside, where organizations are being part of a larger network of both social and material relationship. This sort of relations are set to cross organizational boundaries [6]. Despite different designation on the term interorganizational learning and its meaning, such as joint learning, horizontal learning, shared learning, relationship learning, network learning, they are applicable to project how learning and knowledge creation may form in value chains and networks. Selnes and Sallis [7] defines relationship learning as: "*a joint activity between a supplier and a customer in which the two parties share information, which is then jointly interpreted and integrated into shared relationship-domain specific memory that changes the range or likelihood of potential relationship-domain-specific behavior*". Another view of interorganizational network is that these networks are created in order to share some sort of knowledge, and that an alliance of learning for developing dynamic capabilities is formed in which some will be learners and some will be teachers [8].

Developing abilities to adapt methods and operations according to the changes that happens in company surroundings is considered an important asset for companies [9]. In relationship learning, there are three sub-processes included; Information sharing, joint sense-making, and knowledge integration. Information sharing may act as the fundament for relationship learning [7]. It is discovered that information sharing is central for work-relationships to function, and that information must be exchanged to make coordination and planning possible. This is believed to ultimately make operational efficiency possible. Secondly, it is believed that dialogue and communication is a key factor for common interpretation and sense-making among the participants in the relationship. This is especially important when considering how different organizations can be, and that there exist clear differences on how new information are being interpreted and made sense of.

This paper addresses the following research question: How can interorganizational learning enhance Industry 4.0 realization and operational effectiveness?

2 Method

A qualitative research approach is typically used to discover new insights on a topic or area where there is little information available. Some possible advantages of conducting a qualitative research is that one can reveal new insights in areas that have received relatively little research, and it can help understand complexities, situations, processes, relationships, systems or people. In qualitative research it is easier to test the validity of certain assumptions, claims, theories, or generalizations in a real-world context, and it can help bring forward new information to verify, develop and improve concepts or theories on a phenomenon. For instance the theory of informal collaboration in geographical clusters [10] is an assumption to be tested by the proposed method. Within a certain area, qualitative research can help reveal obstacles and problems that may exist, as well as giving the opportunity to evaluate the effectivity of certain practices [11]. To help answer the research question in this study, there have been conducted semi-structured interviews of operators and managers in three different case companies within a defined industrial cluster. The organizational level of interest is the maintenance department. This selection is made by hypothesizing that maintenance departments are central in the transition towards an Industry 4.0 state. All three organizations are well established manufacturing companies in the medium size segment, mainly exporting goods and product out of Norway.

The data gathering aimed at receiving insight and information within the defined topic and scope of this study from a practical real-world perspective. The interview guide was constructed in way that it should be executed in the same fashion for all respondents, letting the interviewee describe, explain and share their thoughts, knowledge and understanding, based on their own interpretations and views on the field of study was an important part of the research. By asking open questions and allow for individual interpretation and understanding to be highly evident, there was believed that new, interesting and objective data could be revealed. Despite having a structured, or semi-structured interview guide prepared, the interviews tended to be conversation about their practices, understanding and insight on the topic, which is often desired in such scenarios. The companies, respondents and their answers will be kept anonymous and neutral in this article.

The interview guide consists of the three parts: introduction, key-questions and additional questions. The main part, key questions, is supported by 15 questions, where the objective is asked about frequency of interaction, type of interaction, importance of interaction, relevance of interaction, roles (and equality) in interaction, content and scope for interaction, barriers/enablers in interaction, how knowledge is developed, shared and integrated, evolution of interaction and your role in influencing knowledge networks.

Critics to this method and approach is that the sample size is small and not necessarily representative of the broader population. Thus, generalization is difficult – and it is difficult to tell how far the findings are biased by the researcher's own opinions and the way the interviews where conducted.

3   Results

3.1   Case A

Results from the interviews at case company A demonstrates low degree of interorganizational learning, at least in an organized and formal manner. In the maintenance and manufacturing departments, there are considered to be a low degree of interaction with other maintenance departments across the industrial cluster. But there exists informal interaction in terms of informal meetings between workers that have some sort of personal relations with other workers in the cluster. These connections stem from the fact that people in the past has been colleagues in the same company or that they are sharing hobbies and/or neighborhood. There are considered to exist some sort of exchange in experience and knowledge at this level, but because of the degree of informality it is categorized as transfer of tacit knowledge. The workers confirm that they do seek other industries to gain new insight and to understand how other practices unfold due to change in technology. Their supplier base is also reported as a valuable source of information, where frequent, planned or un-planned meetings with suppliers due to particular issues or fixed service schedules increase the bandwidth to externals. The interviewee points out that being a part of regional industrial cluster has been a decisive factor for their ability to develop and grow the business in recent years. Access to local competence, personnel, personnel rotation, and equipment are just a few decisive contributions for this development. The department also reports that they in the future will work more pro-actively towards the outside world, particularly in making spare parts available for others through open digital systems.

3.2 Case B

The same tendency seems to apply to case company B, where little organized inter-action with other companies and maintenance departments, inside and outside the industrial cluster, is reported. The limited number of relations that exist between the companies is said to be an important factor for the limitations in communication. They claim that relationships were stronger before, but now diluted because of the changed nature of the cluster in terms of number of companies, core products and changes in the resource pool of the different companies. The cluster has evolved from one relatively big cornerstone company towards more than 40 separate companies targeting different segments and markets. This journey has taken 20–30 years, so ties and bonds exist between those employees that has been part of the described transition. There is reported no formal structure for interacting with other firms, and the perceived busy work mode leaves little room for interacting with others. The highest ranked type of outside interaction is with their suppliers. High degree of learning and knowledge-creation is reported to happen at the intersections with their existing suppliers of core technology for manufacturing of their products. Case company B asserts that they are continuously leveraging their technology, and they make regular investments and replacements to improve their maintenance performance. Investments in robots, control systems, machinery and equipment are about many technological investments that are made recently. Frequent interaction and communication with suppliers are central in this technological evolution. This source of information guides decisions with regards to Industry 4.0 based on insights and common understanding on how new technology can improve manufacturing capability. Supplier meetings are regarded as learning sessions, where as many as possible of the maintenance workers are involved to create a common understanding and baseline for further learning.

3.3   Case C

Case company C reports in general that learning processes are internally focused due to the long term systematic continuous improvement program going on. Improving existing capacities and capabilities have been the focal point for some time, impacting how internal knowledge creation, sharing and realization is organized through lean-principles. The reasoning by this operational strategy is reported to be rooted in a combined need for cost-cutting as well as producing at high capacity utilization. Perceived daily intensity to maintain and operate critical equipment for producing the demanded quantity is said to limit communication with other organizations. High utilization of human and technological capabilities is argued to reduce their ability to engage in learning activities related to new technologies possible available in the cluster and value chain. This "constant" situation makes interorganizational learning unpractically and difficult. Competing from a defined high-cost country, and numerous lean programs, leaves no free capacity to educational activities or learning from neighboring companies. The growing dynamic of the industrial cluster is also said to be a barrier for inter-organizational level, because it requires a lot of effort to keep updated on what the others do. Some years ago, there were closer bonds between the firms, and the interpersonal connections were more frequent. This led to a situation where the threshold for interacting outside the firm was lower, and it was also in some cases more necessary and practically needed, because the industrial cluster was more homogenous. Despite the lack of organized inter-organizational learning, there are to some extent reported interaction and learning from the supplier base. Especially new investments and implementation of new technologies spur curiosity and knowledge creation and sharing within the company as well as between the company and the particular suppliers. Case C is also part of large international company, getting impulses from sister plants in the global production network.

4   Discussion and Conclusion

Learning and knowledge creation is considered as a difficult and fuzzy domain, hard to express, measure and manage. This is often the situation at organizational level, so how can we approach it from an inter-organizational learning perspective. It is claimed that the latter perspective is becoming more and more important as technology and organizations increase its complexity. Increasing number of materials, product interfaces, ICT implementations, service contents, sustainability criteria, suppliers and collaborators – all adds uncertainties and thus complexity to the manufacturing system. In interorganizational learning, where learning across firms intends to reduce level of uncertainty, there is expected that organizations in value chains adapt and change accordingly. Learning across firms can help organizations increase their capabilities and capacities in order to innovate faster at product, process and system level. A general advice towards establishing inter-organizational learning among organizations is that strengths, weaknesses, challenges and opportunities among the actors should be defined. Defining focus areas and clear goals are recommended to create efficient and trustful interorganizational networks, where rules and practices for all the organizations to follow can help make shared knowledge-creation and sharing less challenging. Creating a high degree of synergy and interdependency should also be sought of, additionally, investigating what kind of knowledge is needed both internally and externally.

Collaboration platforms for interorganizational learning in the maintenance department in the three manufacturing companies can be divided into the regional cluster, supplier base and international production network. For the former, informal and irregular interactions is reported, where tacitness is the common learning mode, and where frequency and number of connections are declining due to cluster evolution. The reasons are plentiful - from scarcity of resources to be allocated to external activity, to limited information about what their neighbors do, and that sufficient information is to be found at other sources as for instance through their supplier base or sister plants. The strongest inter-organizational learning platform is the supplier base. Here, frequency, number of contact points, formality and insights with regards to Industry 4.0 are common parameters among all three case companies. All companies say they want to increase their number of interactions with externals at all collaboration platforms, believing that the way forward is about combining formal vs informal work modes in relations to other companies in clusters and value chains to keep up the technological phase. All three case companies particularly claim to have too little formal interaction with their neighbors in the defined regional industrial cluster, a potential low-hanging fruit to increase their learning component.

The future maintenance departments as an inter-organizational learning node must comply to the criteria; awareness and understanding of system interconnections in their near and distant proximity, cause-and effect understanding upon process and product development internal and external, overview of expanding areas of generic technology developments, improved skills to become better problem-solvers with a more holistic perspective.

Interacting with organizations that are different, or contrasting, can foster new ways of approaching challenges and questions. New insight from heterogeneous organizations can help develop entirely new work modes and practices. Contrasting and diverse knowledge can be also be acquired. This can bring new and unique ideas to the organization, which can be combined with the existing base of experience and knowledge, creating a potential for generating new ways of exploiting learning situations. However, our findings somehow support a study by Holmqvist that interorganizational learning is similar to intraorganizational learning, where differences in learning conditions seem to depend upon degree of collaboration rather than the kind of collaboration [12]. The study gives practical advice to companies about awareness of interorganizational learning on parameters such as sources, frequency, role, value, relevance. This can be viewed in accordance with for instance a study by Gibb et al. claiming a situated learning approach along the dimensions "learning to perform" and "learning to compete" [13]. In such, awareness is stage one towards utilization of the learning in products, processes and systems that increase competitiveness of the firm.

Some general considerations on interorganizational learning is that it can help increase the resource management in the value chain. Thus, interorganizational learning can contribute to release resources, it can help understanding where resources are originated, how they should be utilized, and how practices can be learned, shared and implemented.

References

1. Pereira, A.C., Romero, F.: A review of the meanings and the implications of the Industry 4.0 concept (2017)
2. Bathelt, H., Malmberg, A., Maskell, P.: Clusters and knowledge: local buzz, global pipelines and the process of knowledge creation. Sage **28**(1), 31–56 (2004)
3. Aelker, J., Bauernhansl, T., Ehm, H.: Managing complexity in supply chains: a discussion of current approaches on the example of the semiconductor industry. Procedia CIRP **7**, 79–84 (2013)
4. Nason, R., It's Not Complicated: The Art and Science of Complexity in Business. Rotman-UTP Publishing (2017)
5. Oliver, C.: Determinants of interorganizational relationships: integration and future directions. Acad. Manage. Rev. **15**(2), 241–265 (1990)
6. Mariotti, F.: Exploring interorganizational learning: a review of the literature and future directions. Knowl. Process Manage. **19**(4), 215–221 (2012)
7. Selnes, F., Sallis, J.: Promoting relationship learning. J. Mark. **67**(3), 80–95 (2003)
8. Oliveira, G.M., Silva, A.B.: How can inter-organizational learning and dynamic managerial capability improve cluster performance? In: 3rd International Conference on Clusters and Industrial Districts (2018)
9. Howard, M., Caldwell, N.: Procuring Complex Performance: Studies of Innovation in Product-Service Management. Routledge (2011)
10. Dahl, M.S., Pedersen, C.Ø.R.: Knowledge flows through informal contacts in industrial clusters: myth or reality? Res. Policy **33**(10), 1673–1686 (2004)
11. Leedy, P.D., Ormrod, J.E.: Practical Research: Planning and Design. Pearson Education Limited, Harlow (2015)
12. Holmqvist, M.: Intra- and interorganisational learning processes: an empirical comparison. Scand. J. Manag. **19**(4), 443–466 (2003)
13. Gibb, J., Sun, A., Albers, S.: Network learning: episodes of interorganizational learning towards a collective performance goal. Eur. Manage. J. **35**(1), 15–25 (2017)

Author Index

Abdallah, Ali II-117, II-138
Abe, Jair Minoro I-333
Abner, Brunno II-19
Acerbi, Federica II-695, II-703
Agha, Mujtaba Hassan I-217
Agia, Jorge Luiz Dias II-601
Agrawal, Tarun Kumar I-259
Ahmed, Waqas I-217
Ait Malek, Hasnaa I-408
Åkerman, Magnus II-46
Alfnes, Erlend II-529
Alipour-Vaezi, Mohammad II-197
Allavena, Thierry I-408
Alpan, Gülgün I-250
Alvela Nieto, M. T. I-479
Alves, Anabela C. II-406
Amaro, Paulo II-406
Ameri, Farhad II-263
Andersen, Ann-Louise I-449, II-758
Andersen, Bjørn I-243
Andrlić, Berislav I-325
Angelopoulos, John I-169
Anisic, Zoran I-115
Apostolou, Dimitris II-245
Arica, Emrah I-495
Aschehoug, Silje Helene II-3

Baalsrud Hauge, Jannicke II-108, II-749
Babarogic, Sladjan I-197
Baboli, Armand II-460
Bakalis, Serafim II-649
Balc, Nicolae II-138
Barbieri, Cosimo II-283
Barni, Andrea I-99, I-554
Behrens, Larissa II-749
Bekar, Ebru Turanoglu II-57
Bellazzi, Daniel I-617
Bellgran, Monica I-583, II-108, II-740
Ben-Ammar, Oussama I-275
Benderbal, Hichem Haddou II-501
Benhamou, Latifa I-227
Berrah, Lamia I-123, I-433
Berruet, Pascal I-391
Bertnum, Aili Biriita I-538

Bertoni, Alessandro II-314
Birkie, Seyoum Eshetu I-583, II-740
Birtel, Frederick I-609
Blüher, Till II-338
Bockholt, Markus Thomas II-758
Boffelli, Albachiara I-617
Bøgh, Magnus Abildsten I-427
Bokhorst, J. A. C. I-187
Boldt, Simon I-449
Bonilla, Silvia Helena II-631
Bonollo, Franco II-185
Bošković, Dunja I-469
Boucher, Xavier II-361, II-501
Boujemaoui, Ali II-443
Bousdekis, Alexandros II-245
Bouzekri, Hamza I-250
Bozorgi-Amiri, Ali II-460
Bresler, Maggie I-634
Brünnhäußer, Jörg I-149
Brunoe, Thomas Ditlev I-449, II-758
Buchmeister, Borut I-73
Burchiu, Sorin II-547

Cannas, Violetta G. II-590
Capawa Fotsoh, Erica I-391
Castagna, Pierre I-391
Cavalieri, Sergio I-295
Cerqueus, Audrey II-501, II-518
Chandima Ratnayake, R. M. II-379, II-396
Chapel, Claude I-433
Chaudhuri, Atanu II-723
Chavez, Zuhara II-108, II-740
Choi, Sung Soo II-230
Christensen, Flemming Max Møller II-640
Cimini, Chiara I-295
Ciric, Danijela II-122
Clivillé, Vincent I-433
Colli, Michele II-758
Corcoran, Fintan J. II-275
Cornet, Christian II-731
Corti, Donatella I-28
Cosma, Cosmin II-138
Costa, Luciana Melo II-601
Coulon, Anne II-361

da Cruz Correia, Paula Ferreira　I-307, II-601, II-631
da Silva Lima, Nilsa Duarte　II-616, II-624
da Silva, Marcia Terra　I-131, I-381
Dahl, Tone Lise　I-495
Dakic, Dusanka　I-54
Danielsen, Antoni Vike　II-146
de Alencar Luz, José Alberto　II-609
de Alencar Nääs, Irenilza　I-531, II-616, II-624
de Araújo, Fernanda Alves　I-307, II-631
de Lima, Luiz Antônio　I-333, I-531
de Neufville, Richard　I-418
de Oliveira Costa Neto, Pedro Luiz　I-531
de Souza, Aguinaldo Eduardo　II-601, II-631
de Souza, Jonatas Santos　II-631
Decker, A.　I-479
Defèr, Florian　I-11
Delic, Milan　I-575
Delorme, Xavier　II-518
Despeisse, Mélanie　I-505, II-57
Dietrich, Fabian　II-165
Dimitrieski, Vladimir　I-441, II-469
Do Noh, Sang　II-230, II-238
Dolgui, Alexandre　I-275, II-493, II-509
dos Reis, João Gilberto M.　I-565
dos Reis, João Gilberto Mendes　I-237, I-307, I-531, II-601, II-609, II-631
dos Santos, Nilza Aparecida　I-131, I-381
Dreyer, Heidi　II-425
Duda, Jan　II-91
Dukovska-Popovska, Iskra　II-640

Emmanouilidis, Christos　II-649
Erkoyuncu, John Ahmet　II-731
Essaadi, Imane　I-418
Estender, Antonio Carlos　I-131, I-381, II-601
Etienne, Alain　I-408
Exner, Konrad　II-338

Fager, Patrik　I-267, I-655
Farahani, Saeed D.　II-723
Fast-Berglund, Åsa　I-267, I-655, II-31, II-37, II-46
Feld, Thomas　II-291
Fenies, Pierre　I-315
Fenies, Pierres　I-227
Ficko, Mirko　I-73

Flores-García, Erik　II-238
Fontana, Alessandro　I-554
Forçan, Luiz Roberto　I-333
Formigoni, Alexandre　I-237, II-609, II-631
Fragapane, Giuseppe　I-672
Frank, Jana　II-330
Franke, Felix　II-74
Franke, Susanne　II-74
Freitag, Mike　I-645
Friedewald, Axel　II-538
Fries, Christian　II-581
Fujii, Nobutada　I-399, I-524, II-307, II-679, II-686

G. Nabati, E.　I-479
Gaiardelli, Paolo　I-617, II-275, II-432
Gamboa, Francisco　I-391
Gamme, Inger　I-243
Gandia, Romain　I-433
Gao, Xuehong　I-3
Garcia, Solimar　I-531
Gerdin, Magnus Bjerkne　II-31
Gharaei, Ali　I-82
Ghasemkhani, Ahmad　II-254
Gianessi, Paolo　II-518
Giard, Vincent　I-227, I-250
Gibaru, Olivier　II-477
Giskeødegård, Marte　II-565
Gogineni, Sonika　I-149, II-154
Gonçalves, Rodrigo Franco　I-325, I-599
González Chávez, Clarissa A.　I-505
Gracanin, Danijela　II-122
Gramegna, Nicola　II-185
Gravemeier, Laura Sophie　II-291
Greggio, Fabrizio　II-185
Gregori, Johann　II-573
Gross, Joshua　I-487
Gützlaff, Andreas　I-179

Haddou Benderbal, Hichem　II-493
Halfdanarson, Jon　I-515, I-546
Halse, Lise Lillebrygfjeld　II-174
Hamid, Mahdi　II-254
Hämmerle, Oliver　I-645
Hanayama, Yuta　II-670
Hansen, David Grube　I-449
Hanson, Robin　I-267
Harada, Mizuki　II-307
Harrison, David　II-275

Hashemi-Petroodi, S. Ehsan II-509
Hauge, Jannicke Baalsrud I-107, I-625
Havzi, Sara I-469
Heuer, Tammo I-343
Hodig, Björn II-46
Holst, Lennard II-330
Holtskog, Halvor I-663
Hribernik, Karl II-245
Hrnjica, Bahrudin II-66
Hvolby, Hans-Henrik I-672

Ichikari, Ryosuke II-661
Irie, Kyohei II-679
Islam, Md Hasibul II-740
Ivezic, Nenad I-197

Jæger, Bjørn II-174
Jahn, Niklas II-538
Jelisic, Elena I-197
Jensen, Peter Meulengracht II-758
Jeong, Yongkuk I-625, II-529
Jin, Xuefeng I-3
Johansson, Björn I-505
Johansson, Mats I. I-267
Jung, Bo Ra II-230

Kaihara, Toshiya I-399, I-524, II-307, II-679
Kalaiarasan, Ravi I-259
Kalchschmidt, Matteo I-617
Kampker, Achim I-609
Kang, Jeong Tae II-230
Kang, Yong-Shin II-230
Keepers, Makenzie I-107
Khilji, Wajid Ali I-625
Kim, Goo-Young II-238
Kim, Hyung Sun II-230
Kim, Hyun-Jung II-206
Kiritsis, Dimitris I-82, II-222, II-443
Kjersem, Kristina II-565
Klančnik, Simon I-73
Klement, Nathalie II-477
Klymenko, Olena II-174
Kokuryo, Daisuke I-399, I-524, II-307, II-679
Konstantinidis, Konstantinos Panagiotis I-427
Kordić, Slavica I-441
Kortum, Henrik II-291
Kovalev, Sergey II-509

Krajoski, Goran II-469
Kramer, Kathrin Julia I-363
Kristensen, Jesper Hemdrup II-758
Kulvatunyou, Boonserm I-197
Kvadsheim, Nina Pereira I-546, II-557

Lalić, Bojan I-115, I-139, I-287, II-100, II-122
Lalić, Danijela I-469
Lamy, Damien II-501, II-518
Lee, Dae Yub II-230
Lee, Je-Hun II-206
Lee, Sang Hyun II-230
Lee, Sangho II-230
Leone, Deborah I-99
Lepenioti, Katerina II-245
Lepratti, Raffaello I-91
Lerher, Tone I-73
Lessa, Vanessa Santos I-531
Lewandowski, Marco II-245
Li, Dan II-31
Li, Yi I-625
Liborio Zapata, Melissa I-123
Lied, Lars Harald II-83
Linderson, Sara I-583
Lindow, Kai II-154
Linnartz, Maria I-209
Liu, Sichao II-213
Lödding, Hermann I-351, II-538
Lodgaard, Eirin I-680, II-3, II-425
Lohse, Oliver I-91
Lolic, Teodora I-54, II-122
Lorenz, Rafael II-387
Louw, Louis II-165
Lu, Jinzhi I-82, II-222
Lüftenegger, Egon II-130
Luković, Ivan I-441

Macchi, Marco II-695, II-711
Mahmoodjanloo, Mehdi II-254, II-460
Maibaum, Judith I-179
Maiellaro, João Roberto I-237
Maier, Janine Tatjana I-343
Majstorovic, Vidosav I-139, I-287
Mangini, Clayton Gerber II-616
Marjanović, Uglješa I-139, I-287, II-100, II-299
Marjanovic, Zoran I-197

Martinez, Angel Antonio Gonzalez   I-531
Martins, Geraldo Jose Dolce Uzum   I-325
Masmoudi, Faouzi   I-275
Mebarki, Nasser   I-391
Medbo, Lars   I-267
Medic, Nenad   I-115, II-299
Medini, Khaled   II-731
Melacini, Marco   I-45
Menato, Silvia   I-554
Mentzas, Gregoris   II-245
Meyer-Hentschel, Michael   I-91
Milić, Bojana   I-469
Mizuyama, Hajime   I-37, II-387
Mogos, Maria Flavia   II-83
Mohammad-Nazari, Zahra   II-197
Moia, Roberto Padilha   I-237
Monti, Andrea   I-28
Moretti, Emilio   I-45
Morinaga, Eiji   II-485
Mourtzis, Dimitris   I-169
Mundt, Christopher   I-351
Mwesiumo, Deodat   II-557

Napoleone, Alessia   I-449, I-457
Nascimento, Samira Sestari   I-333
Netland, Torbjørn H.   II-387
Neto, Abelino Reis Guimarães   I-599
Neto, Manoel Eulálio   II-624
Neubert, Gilles   II-361
Nickel, Jonas   I-149, II-154
Nielsen, Christian Møller   I-427
Nielsen, Kjeld   I-449
Nieman, Scott   I-197
Nishita, Yoshito   I-524
Nonaka, Tomomi   II-686
Noran, Ovidiu   II-547
Nujen, Bella Belerivana   I-515, II-557
Nyhuis, Peter   I-343

Oh, Hakju   I-197
Ojsteršek, Robert   I-73
Okuma, Takashi   II-661
Oleszek, Sylwester   II-91
Oliveira, Manuel   I-495
Oluyisola, Olumide E.   I-634
Orellano, Martha   II-361
Orosnjak, Marko   I-575

Paalsrud, Frode   I-680
Palčič, Iztok   I-73
Palm, Daniel   II-165
Palmquist, Adam   II-31
Panayiotou, Nikolaos A.   I-373
Paul, Magdalena   II-501
Pauritsch, Manfred   II-138
Pavlović, Marko   II-100, II-299
Pero, Margherita   II-590
Petroni, Benedito Cristiano A.   I-325
Pezzotta, Giuditta   II-314, II-322, II-338,
     II-347
Pichler, Andreas   II-46
Pierné, Antoine   II-731
Pietraroia, Dario   I-28
Pinto, Roberto   II-338, II-347
Pirola, Fabiana   I-295, II-314, II-322
Pisarić, Milan   I-441, II-469
Polenghi, Adalberto   II-695, II-711
Pólvora, Valdice Neves   I-531
Powell, Daryl   I-243, II-3, II-425, II-432
Powell, Daryl John   II-83, II-417
Pozzetti, Alessandro   II-711
Prataviera, Lorenzo Bruno   I-457
Primas, Matthias   II-117
Psarommatis, Foivos   II-443

Quenehen, Anthony   II-477

Raabe, Håkon   I-243
Rabelo, Ricardo J.   II-19
Rakić, Slavko   II-100, II-299
Rakiz, Asma   I-315
Rao, Subba   I-91
Ratnayake, R. M. Chandima   II-371
Raymundo, Helcio   I-565
Raymundo, Julio Cesar   I-599
Reinhart, Gunther   II-501
Reis, Jacqueline Zonichenn   I-325, I-599
Reljić, Vule   II-11
Riedel, Ralph   II-74, II-573
Ringen, Geir   I-663, I-680
Ristić, Sonja   I-441
Roda, Irene   II-695, II-711
Rodrigues, Rodrigo   I-599
Romero, David   I-107, I-505, II-19, II-37,
     II-46, II-432, II-547
Romsdal, Anita   I-634

Rosenberg, Felix   I-19
Rösiö, Carin   I-449
Rossi, Stefano   I-267
Roucoules, Lionel   II-477
Ruggero, Sergio Miele   I-131, I-381

Sacomano, José Benedito   I-131, I-381
Sakajo, Satoko   I-524
Sala, Roberto   II-314, II-322
Salunkhe, Omkar   I-267, I-655
Samorani, Simone Orom   I-617
Santhiapillai, F. P.   II-371, II-379, II-396
Sarkar, Biswajit   I-217
Sauermann, Frederick   I-179
Scharmer, Valerie M.   I-19
Schmidt, Matthias   I-343, I-363
Schneider, Daniel   II-501
Schuh, Günther   I-11, I-179, II-330
Schulz, Julia   I-19
Semini, Marco   I-538, II-529
Šenk, Ivana   II-11
Sgarbossa, Fabio   I-158, I-591, I-672
Shady, Salama   I-399
Sharifi, Elham   II-723
Shimmura, Takeshi   II-661, II-670, II-686
Shirazian, Shadi   II-451
Shlopak, Mikhail   I-515
Siadat, Ali   I-408
Siatras, Vasileios   I-169
Simeunovic, Nenad   II-299
Simonetto, Marco   I-158
Slama, Ilhem   I-275
Sloth, Simon Hummelshøj   I-427
Softic, Selver   II-66
Solheim, Anja Bottinga   II-417
Sousa, Rui M.   II-406
Spajić, Jelena   I-469
Staal, Lasse G.   II-723
Stark, Rainer   I-149, II-154, II-338
Stavrou, Vasileios P.   I-373
Stefanovic, Darko   I-54, II-122
Steger-Jensen, Kenn   II-640
Stergiou, Konstantinos E.   I-373
Stettiner, Caio Flávio   I-237
Stevanov, Branislav   I-54
Stich, Volker   I-11, I-209, I-609, II-330
Stojadinovic, Slavenko   I-287
Stoll, Oliver   I-82, II-275, II-283

Strandhagen, Jan Ola   I-538, I-634, I-672, II-529
Strandhagen, Jo Wessel   II-529
Sun, Shengjing   II-222
Sung, Inkyung   I-427

Tabourot, Laurent   I-123
Taisch, Marco   II-695, II-703
Tanizaki, Takashi   II-670
Tappia, Elena   I-45
Tarjan, Laslo   II-11
Tarrar, Malin   II-37
Tasić, Nemanja   I-115, I-139, II-100
Tavakkoli-Moghaddam, Reza   II-197, II-254, II-451, II-460
Tegeltija, Srdjan   II-11
Tejić, Branislav   II-11
Thevenin, Simon   II-509
Thiery, Stephane   II-477
Thoben, K.-D.   I-479
Thomas, Oliver   II-291
Thorvald, Peter   II-37
Thürer, Matthias   II-432
Todorovic, Tanja   I-139
Toloi, Rodrigo Carlo   II-631
Traussnigg, Udo   II-117
Turcin, Ioan   II-117, II-138
Turgut, Ali   II-165

Ungern-Sternberg, Roman   II-581

Vahedi-Nouri, Behdin   II-451
Vasic, Stana   I-575
Vendrametto, Oduvaldo   II-601
Verjus, Hervé   I-433
Vijayakumar, Vivek   I-591
Vještica, Marko   I-441, II-469
von Stietencron, Moritz   II-245
Vulanovic, Srdjan   I-575

Wæhrens, Brian Vejrum   II-723, II-758
Wagner, Carsten   I-363
Wakamatsu, Hidefumi   II-485
Wang, Lihui   II-213
Wang, Xi Vincent   II-213
Waschull, S.   I-187
Welo, Torgeir   I-663
West, Shaun   I-82, II-275, II-283

Wiendahl, Hans-Hermann   II-581
Wiesner, Stefan   II-749
Wiktorsson, Magnus   I-259, I-625, II-213,
     II-238, II-529
Wilson, John G.   I-63
Witte, Heiko   I-149
Woo, Jong Hun   II-529
Wortmann, J. C.   I-187
Wuest, Thorsten   I-107, I-487, II-432

Yabuuchi, Masayuki   I-524
Yang, Hyungjoon   II-206
Yang, Jinho   II-230, II-238

Yasuda, Daiki   II-485
Yelles-Chaouche, Abdelkrim R.   II-493
Yoder, Reid   II-263

Zaeh, Michael F.   I-19
Zafarzadeh, Masoud   I-625
Zambetti, Michela   II-338, II-347
Zambiasi, Saulo P.   II-19
Zandbiglari, Kimia   II-263
Zarvic, Novica   II-291
Zheng, Xiaochen   I-82, II-222
Zivlak, Nikola   I-115
Zizakov, Marina   I-575

Printed in the United States
by Baker & Taylor Publisher Services

Printed in the United States
by Baker & Taylor Publisher Services